**KRLA ARCHIVES**

# KRLA
*Chronological Archives
Volume 1
Oct 9 1964 to July 24, 1965*

# KRLA ARCHIVES

Back in the early days of Rock & Roll, radio stations played a huge role in preomoting artists. Now that may sound obvious, but radio is an audio media, so it makes sense that they played music over the airwaves. What may be less obvious is the riole some some radio stations played in other media.

KRLA was one of the leaders on the West Coast in bringing not just music, but the artist persona to their audiences. Radio stations had long since learned that printed "playlists" were one way to expand their reach and influence. But after a while, they realized that playlists weren't the only thing worth printing.

The KRLA newsletter started out as a self-promotional piece, but evolved into what its audienced really cared more about: news on their favorite artists.

Okay, maybe it wasn't hard news and maybe it was barely a step above (if at all above) what the fan magazines like FLIP and 16 were going to start offering. Still, it offered a way for the station to connect to the audience outside the radio waves. It offered a way to engage teen boys better, as well. And that was a powerful thing.

In presenting these original issues, we've moved a few of the pages around to ensure that the spreads still lined up. Not a big deal to most people unless you are severly OCD and have access to the original issues.

these earliest issues, through the middle of summer 1965 heavily feature the Beatles, along with the Beach Boys and other then-current bands. Sit back, relax, and get the feeling of what it was like to be a teenager in 1964 and 1965.

Copyright © 2016 White Lightning Publishing

# KRLA ARCHIVES

# RINGO TO ENTER HOSPITAL; OPERATION

(Story in Col. 1)

# KRLA BEAT

## OPERATION FOR BEATLE.....

NEW YORK—Ringo Starr has announced that he will enter the hospital later this fall for his much talked about throat operation. He made the announcement at a press conference in New York just before the four fabulous Beatles left this country to return to England.

### RUMOR CONFIRMED

For months, there have been rumors that Ringo intended to have the operation, but it was finally confirmed when he made his statement to the press. Ringo does not know at this date just when he is to enter the hospital.

The operation will only take a few hours, but the famous drummer said that he expected to be in the hospital at least three days to catch up on some much needed rest. It is rumored that the three days will be sometime when the group does not have other pressing committments, and will give John, George, and Paul a short vacation.

### CONFIDED IN DAVE

Ringo didn't disclose the name of the hospital he is planning for his operation, however, when the group was in Los Angeles, Ringo confided to Dave Hull that it will be the University College Hospital where he was taken after his collapse last spring. The operation itself is very simple. Since Ringo never had his tonsils or adenoids removed, the main purpose of the operation will be to remove them, along with several small growths which cause our boy to get frequent attacks of tonsillitis, and sometimes cause Ringo to come down with very bad colds.

### ASKS FOR TONSILS

Other than his throat, Ringo is in excellent condition. One fan has already asked for the tonsils to be preserved for her, but Ringo doesn't know yet whether he will answer her request. Everyone in the world joins KRLA in wishing him a speedy recovery.

Production, Design And Content By Bonnie Golden

## KRLA TOP FORTY

| | | | | |
|---|---|---|---|---|
| 1. | PRETTY WOMAN | Roy Orbison | 21. HAUNTED HOUSE | Gene Simmons |
| 2. | BABY BABY ALL THE TIME | The Superbs | 22. TOBACCO ROAD | Nashville Teens |
| 3. | BABY I NEED YOUR LOVIN' | Four Tops | 23. UNDER THE BOARDWALK | The Drifters |
| 4. | A SUMMER SONG | Stuart & Clyde | 24. IT'S ALL OVER NOW | Rolling Stones |
| 5. | BREAD & BUTTER | The Newbeats | 25. MAYBE I KNOW | Lesley Gore |
| 6. | DANCING IN THE STREETS | Martha & Vandellas | 26. FROM A WINDOW | Billy J. Kramer |
| 7. | DO WAH DIDDY | Manfred Mann | 27. WHEN I GROW UP | Beach Boys |
| 8. | WHERE DID OUR LOVE GO | The Supremes | 28. EVERYBODY LOVES SOMEBODY | Dean Martin |
| 9. | REMEMBER | The Shangri-Las | 29. HELP YOURSELF | The Standells |
| 10. | IT HURTS TO BE IN LOVE | Gene Pitney | 30. BECAUSE | Dave Clark Five |
| 11. | G.T.O. | Ronny & Daytonas | 31. DO I LOVE YOU | The Ronettes |
| 12. | SELFISH ONE | Jackie Ross | 32. HOUSE OF THE RISING SUN | The Animals |
| 13. | WE'LL SING IN THE SUNSHINE | Gale Garnett | 33. LITTLE HONDA | The Hondells |
| 14. | YOU REALLY GOT ME | The Kinks | 34. GATOR TAILS & MONKEY RIBS | The Spats |
| 15. | DEATH OF AN ANGEL | The Kingsmen | 35. RINGO FOR PRESIDENT | The Young World Singers |
| 16. | HE'S IN TOWN | The Tokens | 36. YOU'LL NEVER GET TO HEAVEN | Dionne Warwick |
| 17. | LA LA LA LA LA | The Blendells | 37. FUNNY | Joe Hinton |
| 18. | RIDE THE WILD SURF | Jan and Dean | 38. SAY YOU | Ronnie Dove |
| 19. | OUTSIDE LOOKING IN | Anthony & Imperials | 39. LETTER FROM ELAINA | Casey Kasem |
| 20. | HAVE I THE RIGHT | The Honeycombs | 40. BABY DON'T YOU DO IT | Marvin Gaye |

## TOP TEN ALBUMS

| | | |
|---|---|---|
| 1. | HARD DAY'S NIGHT | BEATLES |
| 2. | SOMETHING NEW | BEATLES |
| 3. | ALL SUMMER LONG | BEACH BOYS |
| 4. | RAG DOLL | FOUR SEASONS |
| 5. | AMERICAN TOUR | DAVE CLARK FIVE |
| 6. | KEEP ON PUSHING | IMPRESSIONS |
| 7. | MORE OF ROY ORBISON'S GREATEST HITS | |
| 8. | LOUIE LOUIE | KINGSMEN |
| 9. | THE ROLLING STONES | ROLLING STONES |
| 10. | BEATLES SONG BOOK | HOLLYRIDGE STRINGS |

## TOP TEN OLDIES

| | | |
|---|---|---|
| 1. | In the Still Of The Night | The Satins |
| 2. | Peggy Sue | Buddy Holly |
| 3. | Gee | The Crows |
| 4. | What's Your Name | Don & Juan |
| 5. | Come Go With Me | The Dell-Vikings |
| 6. | Mountain of Love | Harold Dorman |
| 7. | Ya Ya | Lee Dorsey |
| 8. | Big Bad John | Jimmy Dean |
| 9. | Mother-in-law | Ernie K-Doe |
| 10. | Could This Be Magic | The Dubs |

Many of KRLA's listeners have wondered why they can't buy "Thinking of You Baby" by the D.C. Five, and "I'll Be Back Again," by the Beatles. Since KRLA's records are shipped to us directly from England, we get them before any other person in the U.S. of A. even knows they're out! These KRLA exclusives can only be heard on KRLA . . . just another way of saying KRLA listeners are first in EVERYTHING!

## HI, HULLABALOOERS!

This is the scuzzy Hullabalooer himself, believe it or not! The only D.J. in the world who blows his own horn! Welcome to the KRLA Beat. I put it together with my own little hands, and you'd better like it. (Or I'll get YOU!) Seriously, this is KRLA's way of showing you how much we like you... even you, silently snickering to yourself off in a corner there! (I didn't mean YOU, the serious one). You'll find a lot of scoops inside about your four favorites . . . "WHAT FOUR FAVORITES?" . . . SHUT UP! (That was Maud Skidmore. She doesn't really know who the Beatles are. But she does a good job of pretending!) MAUD! GET THAT BEATLE WIG OFF! On second thought, maybe she does know!

Back to the subject . . . the pictures inside were taken by KRLA, and are so exclusive that they are printed in disappearing ink! You won't see them anywhere else. (Everyone else turned them down). Anyhow, what do you think of this newspaper. (newspaper?) (yes, newspaper!) I'd appreciate it if you'd let me know. I'd appreciate it even more if you'll write your answer on any old dirty dollar bills you happen to have lying around. Or even dirty old pennies. I'm not choosy! Now turn the page for the shock of your life!

## D.C. FIVE HERE SOON

LOS ANGELES—KRLA scored again when they snapped up the Dave Clark Five for an exclusive Los Angeles appearance at the Long Beach Auditorium on November 25th. The boys will be met at the airport by KRLA D.J.'s, and plans are being made for

(Cont. on page 4)

# KRLA ARCHIVES

HI, I'M BOB EUBANKS! Here is your own personal minute-by-minute guide of the Beatles' stay in Los Angeles. KRLA newsmen and photographers were there every minute to give all our listeners a guided tour through Beatle-land! (And that's the same as K*R*L*A*N*D) The boys were so much fun to be with that I wish you all could have been with me. But since you weren't, here's the next best thing! Before they left, they asked me to give you their personal thanks for the groovy way they were treated in Los Angeles. So, from the Beatles . . . and from me . . . Thanks!

3:30 PM . . . THE BEATLES ARRIVE! Without telling a soul (except KRLA), the idols of millions land in Los Angeles to be cleared through customs. Derrick Taylor looks around to see if the coast is clear . . .

3:40 PM . . . It is, and so the boys slowly step down the ramp pausing for the KRLA photographer as they come down. The first they said was "Hey, it's sunny . . . we can go swimming!"

4:40 AM The boys are whisked into a security car and driven to the home in Bel Air where they will stay while they are in town. Ringo, in the back seat, is already half asleep. P.S.: He got to sleep later!

6:00 PM Press conference time! Out at Bob Eubanks' Cinnamon Cinder, he and Reb Foster introduce the Beatles and tell members of the press that they can start asking questions . . . and they started asking!

"WHAT ABOUT JANE ASHER, PAUL?" "W and all, but we certainly aren't married. found her yet, but I'm having a blast loo

"YOU WANTED TO SAY SOMETHING, RINGO?" "Uh . . . yes. Can I have a drink of water? Thanks. Now tell me, when do we get to ask all YOU people some questions?" Bob Eubanks handed Ringo the glass, but didn't save it!

8:00 PM 'B DAY' IS HERE! The Bowl started filling at 3:00 in the afternoon! Everyone hoped to catch a glimpse of their beloved Beatles, but the boys were secretly brought in only a few minutes before the show.

9:00 PM The other acts have performe Dave Hull, Reb Foster, Bob Eubanks is a moment of silence . . . and then

Ringo's hair is flying. His hands are going so fast that they're just a blur in the air. Every time he moves his head, the screams grow louder. Will anyone ever be able to forget 'B Day'? We doubt it!

Too soon, the boys take their final bow. By the time the screams have stopped, they are halfway to Bel Air for a three day vacation in Los Angeles before resuming their cross country tour.

2:00 PM It's over. The Beatles are lea the weather knew how sad Los Angel them at the airport to say a last fina

Photography by ROBYN HILL

# KRLA ARCHIVES

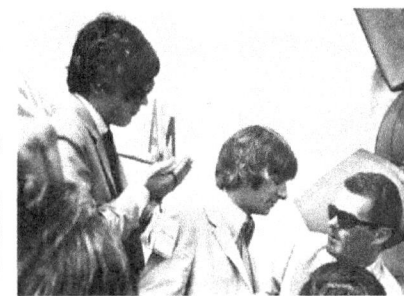  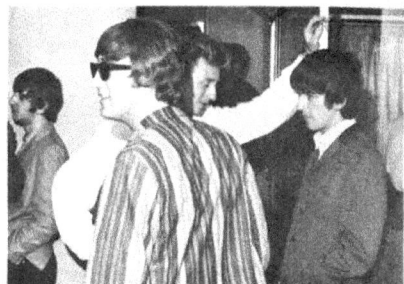

3:42 PM KRLA's newsman, Jim Steck, was right there to tape exclusive interviews with all four Beatles . . . something no one else was able to do. Then the boys took off for San Francisco's Cow Palace.

4:10 PM Finally, the Beatles arrive back in L.A. for their performance. Again, they land secretly so that crowds wouldn't mob them. Again, KRLA is first on the scene! The boys were groggy and half asleep . . .

4:25 PM . . . But they still were able to smile and talk with KRLA newsmen. The only thing they could talk about, though, was getting some sleep before the long, hard day's night ahead of them.

at about her? Oh, we're good friends . . . I'm looking for the perfect girl. Haven't I king!"

"WHAT DO YOU THINK OF AMERICAN GIRLS, GEORGE?" "THEY ARE JUST TOO MUCH! I really dig them! Never saw a country before where EVERY ONE of the girls were truly gear, but I haven't seen one here that missed yet!"

"JOHN, ARE YOU LEAVING THE GROUP?" "Rubbish! Wouldn't have anyone to pick on if I did. Besides, if I left these poor clods, they wouldn't know what to do. I'm the only one they listen to!" (Paul laughed)

d . . . the KRLA D.J.'s walk on stage . . . . . . the audience grows quiet . . . there . . . "HERE THEY ARE . . . THE BEATLES!!!!"

They look at Ringo . . . he adjusts his drums. Paul tunes his guitar. The audience screams louder and louder . . . . finally, Ringo is ready. He gives the signal. The boys turn and face the stage . . . and sing.

"I want to hold your hand . . ." The girls let him know by their screams that they want to hold his, too! The screams go on . . . and the Beatles sing . . . and sing . . . and sing. There's never been anything like it!

ing. The day is cloudy, almost as though as was to see them go. Jim Steck meets goodbye . . .

2:10 PM . . . BUT WAIT! WHAT'S THIS? WHY THE SURPRISED LOOK ON JOHN AND GEORGE'S FACES? COULD IT BE . . . YES, BY GUM, IT IS! THE BEATLES MAY BE LEAVING K*R*L*A*N*D BUT KRLA ISN'T LEAVING THE BEATLES!

2:13 PM With the KRLA 'hookey-players' safely tucked inside, the doors are closed, and the plane takes off . . . Yes, they're gone. But don't cry too hard . . . because they'll soon be back!

KRLA ARCHIVES

*This Saturday, KRLA has a . . . er, treat coming up. It seems that Bobby Pickett has bewitched everyone into thinking that they'd love to have his monsters here at KRLA, and as for the outcome . . . we'll let him tell you about it . . .*

HELLO BOYS AND GOULS . . . HEH, HEH, HEH!

I want to tell you a MONSTROUS secret . . . starting this Saturday, some friends of mine will be with me at KRLA for a monster's holiday . . . sort of a serious party . . . in fact, a GRAVE party . . . heh, heh, heh. You see me here with one of my friends . . . his name is Alvin . . . he's quite harmless, really. The non-emotional type. COLD BLOODED, you might say! Alvin is bringing his zombie friend, Zelda. Zelda is a Beatle fan . . . but she doesn't want their autograph . . . no, she wants to drink their blood!

I'll introduce you to the "people" you will meet on Saturday . . . first, meet Gerrald, the surfin' Goul. Gerrald and I have been quite close ever since we met . . . in a CEMETERY one Halloween. Both of us tried to pull the other's mask off . . . till we found out that neither one was wearing a mask!

Hortense, my favorite vampire, will melt your heart in no time. Then she'll drain it. Hortense always has refreshments for her guests . . . COLD BLOOD ON ICE . . . Heh, Heh, Heh!

Gerrald and Hortense have been going together for three months now. It's quite a sight to see them . . . Gerrald, packed with bandages, paddling out on his surfboard . . . and Hortense right behind him, grabbing any of Gerrald's bandages she can reach. They make such a lovely couple!

Barney, the shapeless blob, is a killer! He tells jokes. He'll SLAY you . . . if you get near enough to let him!

All of you will fall in love with Tubby, the twisting toad. He's been a good friend ever since he fell into some stew I was making. Of course, I fished him right out. I already had a toad in the stew!

You'll also meet my four little friends from England, the Cockroaches. They're a singing group. Their names are Jom, Gerge, Pill, and Rungo. They're very good, actually, and have a new twist to their act. The audience sings, and THEY do the screaming! Their latest record, "I Wanna Hold Your Throat," is a rage. (An outrage!)

You'll meet lots of interesting characters on my show . . . and if you're not careful, you might even become one yourself! In fact, just to show you how good natured I am, the first person who writes in and tells me how many of my friends were on the first show will get a record album and an autographed picture of me . . . signed, of course, in blood! Send your entries to KRLA, 1401 South Oak Knoll, Pasadena, California.

Now for a little information about myself . . . I was born at midnight . . . it was a full moon . . . there was thunder and lightening outside, too. The thunder was from the doctor. He was afraid my parents couldn't pay the bill. The date was October 31. The year was 1664.

I lost most of my family during the Salem witch burnings. My nerves were so shot by this that I had to retire to a nice cool vault and sleep for a few hundred years.

One day a KRLA D.J. accidently kicked open the stone to my tomb. Alas, the poor man was found at daybreak. However, I managed to disguise myself well and took over the poor man's show the next day. Unfortunately, I was discovered by Reb Foster, who kicked me out. When I came to, I found myself outside the station, pounding on the door. But although he wouldn't let me back inside, I got my revenge. I sent him Maud Skidmore!

After months of pounding at the door, KRLA took pity on me and let me inside. After someone brushed the cobwebs off my clothes, and the moss from the north side of my face, they agreed to let me have my own show. It starts this Saturday, and you'd better be listening . . . DO YOU HEAR? YOU'D BETTER LISTEN . . . OR ELSE . . . HEH, HEH, HEH! YOU WILL LISTEN! YOU ARE GETTING SLEEPY . . . YOU WANT TO TURN ON THE RADIO . . . YOU WANT TO LEAVE IT AT KRLA AND NOT SHUT IT OFF TILL I COME ON . . . HEH, HEH, HEH! YOU WILL SIT BY THE RADIO WITHOUT MOVING WHILE I SPEAK . . . YOU WILL! HEH, HEH, HEH, HEH, HEH, HEH . . . . . . .

# DUSTY ILL

WEST INDIES—British star Dusty Springfield was stricken with a virus this week while she was on tour in the West Indies. Doctors suspect that she may also have food poisoning; however, they say that her condition is not serious. She was planning to leave for America just as the illness struck.

WILL REST FOR A WEEK

Although she is in good condition, doctors have ordered her to rest for at least a week before resuming the tour. After her recovery, Dusty will make a stopover in Los Angeles where it is rumored that she will visit the KRLA studios.

. . .

# D.C. 5 ....

KRLA to also host a party in their honor. In keeping with the station's tradition of bringing all of England's top groups to K*R*L*A*N*D*, future visits by the Rolling Stones, Gerry and the Pacemakers, and Dusty Springfield are also being discussed.

KRLA WANTS TO KNOW WHAT YOU THOUGHT OF OUR 'PAPER'! WOULD YOU LIKE TO SEE SOMETHING LIKE IT EVERY WEEK? LET US KNOW!

# Peter Feels Much Better

LONDON — Peter Asher, of Peter and Gordon fame, is reported feeling better today and will be out of the hospital this week. The boys had interrupted their entire schedule in hopes that Peter would get better with some rest, but it was necessary to hospitalize him. His illness was described as a stomach ailment. When Peter was in town several months ago, he told KRLA newsmen that he hadn't been feeling well. It is reported that Jane Asher, Peter's sister, goes to see him every day. As soon as Peter is allowed out of bed, the boys will start on a tour of Scotland. They will return to this country in late spring or early summer of next year.

# FAX ............. ON ......... WAX!

BY REB FOSTER

**Hi, everyone, this is Reb Foster** speaking. I've gone out and gathered some super scoops on all your record favorites, so that you can have all the fax on wax in the record world! KRLA listeners are always in the know, you know! Now, on with the exclusive news, brought to you, of course, by K*R*L*A! (and me).

**DAVE CLARK** denies that he is thinking of marriage. Rumors say that he is getting serious about a girl in London, but KRLA newsmen checked on this, and it is untrue.

The marriage of **ANNETTE** and **JACK GILARDI** will take place early this January. Annette is having her gown designed by a California designer, and **SHELLEY FABARES** will be matron of honor.

**THE HONEYCOMBS**, who's recording of "Have I The Right" is climbing towards the number one position, are making arrangements to tour America early this spring. The boys are quite handsome, and have always wanted to come to America.

**BOBBY PICKETT**, recording star, joins the KRLA staff this Saturday for one of the most unusual shows in the world. You'll meet some very merry monsters, and if you listen to the show alone with the lights off . . . well, that's your fault!

Right now, I'm in Central America with the **STANDELLS**. We're having a great time, but I sure do miss all of you! It's very hot here, but the girls are going crazy over the Standells. In case you didn't know, **LARRY TAMBLYN**, the leader of the group, is **RUSS TAMBLYN'S** brother!

**PAT AND LOLLY VEGAS** are in San Francisco right now, and filling the house every night. They have one of the greatest acts I've ever seen!

I'll be back next week, so all of you hold on tight! See you soon! (And with the most beautiful tan in the world!) (I mean, I won't see you with the tan! It's mine!)

KRLA's ratings are now the highest of any station in Los Angeles, thanks to you, KRLA listeners. All the staff of the station wishes to take this opportunity to thank you, and to tell you that we would like to hear from you with any suggestions you may have to make KRLA even better!

# BEATLE BITS...

**Dick Moreland here,** John Lennon hat and everything! Just thought you might like to know a few of the little unknown facts about the Beatles that no one else has ever printed before . . . so here they are!

Most of you know that they bought their clothes at the Beau Gentry while in Los Angeles. But did you know that many stars buy their clothes there too, and so do most of the KRLA D.J.'s? The boys were told about the shop by the Rolling Stones, who were in K*R*L*A*N*D a few months ago.

Speaking of the Rolling Stones, John Lennon loves them, and George is having them teach him how to play the guitar the way they do. John has every one of their records, and spends hours listening to them.

No one knew that Paul disappeared for a few hours from Bel Air, but now the secret can be told! Paul combed his hair back, disguised himself with sunglasses, and went walking in Hollywood. The reason no one knew about it was because he started sightseeing at 6:00 in the morning!

Here are a few of the different little habits of each Beatle . . . Ringo, when he is nervous, constantly keeps smoothing his hair. When he is excited, he turns the rings on his fingers. If Ringo has a red mark on his finger, you know he's twisted the ring so much that he had to take it off! John, on the other hand, is perfectly deadpan. When he is mad, he doesn't say anything, but his foot starts twitching. Paul pulls at his ear lobe whenever he is thinking about something. George bites his lower lip. All four boys are very polite and seldom lose their temper.

Well, it's time to go riding off into the sunset . . . see you on the radio!

# New Show On KRLA

**Starting this Saturday, KRLA presents something new in the way of radio shows. Bobby Pickett, who has had many hit records, including Monster Mash and Monster Holiday, makes his radio debut at 7:30.**

**Bobby is planning on bringing a carload of 'friends' with him to keep KRLA listeners entertained . . . and they will be, as Zelda Zombie, Hortense Vampire, and the screaming Cockroaches, Jom, Gerge, Pill, and Rungo, cavort over the air. It will be the most unusual show ever heard in the southland, and to sum up the opinions of many noted figures, "Radio may never be the same!"**

# CASEY'S CORNER!

**HI! This is Casey!** So many of you have asked questions about "Letter From Elaina" that I thought I'd take this opportunity to answer a few of them!

Elaina is in her teens. When she wrote me the letter, I had no idea that it would touch all of you the way it did me. When I read it on the air, and got such enthusiastic results from all of you, I thought of making a record of the letter. Since Elaina's mother didn't want the publicity to affect her daughter, she made me promise not to reveal Elaina's last name. Elaina, of course, is thrilled to death with the record. "Not because it's a record," she told me, "But because George might hear it now!" Don't worry, Elaina, he has! (and loved it!)

When I spoke with the Beatles' press agent, I managed to get a list of some of the Liverpool slang they use. You already know what Gear and a few other words mean, but now I'll give you the rest of the list so that you can talk "Beatle Talk."

'You've got cheek' means 'You're pretty nervy!' 'Fooney" means funny, and 'Roobish' is rubbish, which is anything that's silly or untrue. The Beatles never say shut up. What they do say is "Shurrp'! Pulling the lower lip up between the teeth and blowing air through it is a polite way of calling someone a liar! 'Screamies' are fans. No explanation needed there! 'Knock yourself out' means 'Be my guest.' When the Beatles call someone a pip, they mean he is completely unnecessary! 'Wild' means that something has soul.

Well, the boss is calling. Maybe it's because I was so busy writing this that I'm late for my show! See you later!

# Hull Elected

KRLA D.J. Dave Hull was chosen as one of America's eight D.J.'s to be a member of Ringo's Presidential Cabinet by Teen Screen Magazine. Teen Screen conducted a national Ringo for President campaign, with eight D.J.'s selected by popular vote for the cabinet. Dave Hull won by a large margin to represent the West Coast. Publisher Shelley Heiman stated that Hull is represented by the National Teenage Party, and reported to KRLA that the platform of the Teenage Party is "Let's get down off this platform and have a party!"

ACCEPTANCE SPEECH

In his acceptance speech, Hull promised to kill the school bill, and any other kind of bill he can think of. It is a well known fact that he hates bills! Hull also stated that he will perform his duties with complete conviction, steadfast strength, and utter abandon.

. . .

# KRLA ARCHIVES

# NEW EPSTEIN DISCOVERY 'BIG AS THE BEATLES'

(Story in Col. 1)

# KRLA BEAT

Production, Design And Content By Bonnie Golden

## BRIAN HERE WITH SHOW

HOLLYWOOD — Brian Epstein, in town for a two week stay, has confided to KRLA that he has a new dsciovery who will "have as much impact on America as the Beatles did!" Mr. Epstein, the most famous manager in the world, says that Tommy Quickley, new English sensation, will take America by storm.

### HERE FOR TWO WEEKS

When Mr. Epstein came to Los Angeles for two weeks, many people thought that he would be discussing the Beatles' next movie, rumored to be shot in this country. However, this was not the case. Brian stated that he was here with his two other groups, Gerry & the Pacemakers and Billy J. Kramer to take care of arrangements for their shows and to get some rest before arranging for Tommy Quickley's visit to Los Angeles on November 25th.

### "TOP STAR IN WORLD"

When asked if he had as much faith in his new discovery as he had in the Beatles, Brian replied "I have faith in all my artists, but this boy electrified me." KRLA asked if he thought Tommy would be as big as the Beatles.

"Not only that," Brian stated, "But I think this boy will be the biggest star in the world!"

### DISCOVERED AT AUDITION

Tommy was discovered early in 1963 when he auditioned at a ballroom outside Liverpool. Brian happened to be in the manager's office while Tommy was playing, and decided right then and there that he wanted to manage him.

### WAS ON TV SHOW

Although Quickley is unknown in this country, he is the fastest rising star in England. He has appeared with the Beatles many times, and has been taped for a Shindig show shown a few weeks ago. Tommy is 19, lives in Liverpool, has brown eyes and hair, and stands 5'11".

## KRLA TOP THIRTY

1. BABY LOVE .................. The Supremes
2. OPPORTUNITY .................. The Jewels
3. DANCING IN THE STREET .... Martha & Vandellas
4. PRETTY WOMAN .................. Roy Orbison
5. LAST KISS .................. J. Frank Wilson
6. SHE'S NOT THERE .................. The Zombies
7. INTO SOMETHING GOOD .... Herman's Hermits
8. YOU REALLY GOT ME .................. The Kinks
9. THE JERK .................. The Larks
10. TOBACCO ROAD .......... The Nashville Teens
11. I'M ON THE OUTSIDE .......... Little Anthony
12. RIDE THE WILD SURF ............ Jan & Dean
13. BABY I NEED YOUR LOVING ...... The 4 Tops
14. DEATH OF AN ANGEL ........ The Kingsmen
15. HURTS TO BE IN LOVE ........ Gene Pitney
16. DOOR IS STILL OPEN .......... Dean Martin
17. BABY ALL THE TIME .......... The Superbs
18. BABY DON'T YOU DO IT .......... Marvin Gaye
19. LITTLE HONDA .................. The Hondells
20. TIME IS ON MY SIDE ........ The Rolling Stones
21. IF YOU WANT THIS LOVE ...... Sonny Knight
22. HAVE I THE RIGHT? .............. Honeycombs
23. DO WAH DIDDY .............. Manfred Mann
24. GAITOR TAILS, MONKEY RIBS ...... The Spots
25. BREAD AND BUTTER ............ The Newbeats
26. WHAT LOVE IS MADE OF ........ The Miracles
27. I LIKE IT ............ Gerry & The Pacemakers
28. GIRL (WHY YOU WANNA) ...... The Temptations
29. A SUMMERSONG .............. Stuart & Clyde
30. DON'T WANT TO SEE YOU AGAIN .. Peter & Gordon

### TOP TEN ALBUMS

1. A HARD'S DAY'S WORK — BEATLES
2. EVERYBODY LOVES SOMEBODY — DEAN MARTIN
3. SOMETHING NEW — BEATLES
4. THE ANIMALS
5. MORE OF ROY ORBISON'S GREATEST HITS
6. ALL SUMMER LONG — BEACH BOYS
7. TRINI LOPEZ AT PJ's
8. RAG DOLL — 4 SEASONS
9. JOHNNY RIVERS AT WHISKEY A GO GO
10. KINGSMEN, VOL. 2

### TOP TEN OLDIES

1. Susie Q — Dale Hawkins
2. Twilight Time — Platters
3. I Walk The Line — Johnny Cash
4. I'll Never Dance Again — Bobby Rydell
5. Then He Kissed Me — Ronnettes
6. Tower Of Strength — Gene McDaniels
7. Hurt — Timi Yuro
8. Get A Job — Miracles
9. Latin Lupe Lu — Righteous Brothres
10. Roses Are Red — Bobby Vinton

### TOP TEN UP AND COMERS

1. When You Walk in the Room — The Searchers
2. Is It True? — Brenda Lee
3. Everything's Alright — The Newbeats
4. So Fine / Lind-Lu — The Standells
5. Walking in the Rain — The Ronettes
6. Gone, Gone, Gone — The Everly Brothers
7. B-By Don't Go — Sonny & Cher
8. Ringo — Lorne Green
9. Shaggie Dog — Mickey Lee Lane
10. Thou Shalt Not Steal — Dick & Deedee

## HI, HULLABALOOERS!

Bet you just couldn't wait till Wednesday this week, could you? After all, that's when my wonderful column comes out! And without my wonderful column, where would you be? All right, forget I ever asked! Geesh! What kind of friends are you anyhow? As honorary editor, I deserve a little respect! But I did get one compliment this week... I was told that my column is the best one in the paper, and that I'm the greatest d.j. in the world. Of course, my mother better say that. I'm bigger than her! "YOU SURE ARE, FATSO!" Oh, no! It's Maud Skidmore again! Maud, Reb's right inside ... go breathe on his neck, please! "WOULDN'T THINK OF IT, LUV...YOU'VE GOT SO MUCH MORE NECK!" Are you calling me fat? "WELL, I HEARD THAT THE LAST TIME YOU WENT THROUGH A REVOLVING DOOR, YOU HAD TO GO THROUGH IN FOUR SECTIONS!" Maud, you and I are through! Reb, get this pest out of here! "IT'S NO USE ... REB LOCKED ME OUT. WHY, HE WOULDN'T EVEN LET ME KISS BILLY J. KRAMER!" What do you mean he wouldn't let you, Maud? "WELL, I ASKED HIM TO HOLD BILLY J. DOWN FOR ME SO THAT I COULD KISS HIM, AND HE WOULDN'T DO IT. BUT I FIXED HIS WAGON!" How? "I GOT BILLY J. TO PROMISE THAT IF I WOULDN'T KISS HIM, HE'D HELP ME HOLD YOU DOWN SO I COULD KISS YOU! AND HERE HE COMES NOW!" Oh, no! I'm leaving! See you next weeeeeeeeek!

**TWO PAGES OF PICS INSIDE!**

## KRLA ARCHIVES

# BACK STAGE WITH REB AT THE BIGGES[T]

THE EVENING STARTS! Reb meets the winner of the "Win A Date With Reb Foster" contest held in the KRLA BEAT. Glynnis Thomas, 15, of Pasadena never had as much fun in her life as she did with Reb.

Reb talks to Billy J. Kramer about his future plans before the show starts. Billy said that Reb was "a gas!" He tried to teach Reb to talk with an English accent, but it didn't work!

Gerry and the Pacemakers rehearse before they go on. From left to right: Les Chadwick, Les Maguire, and of course, Gerry. Gerry was the most popular with all the performers . . . he's too much!

Dick & DeeDee meet Glynnis backstage. After the show, Dick & DeeDee flew to Canada with Gerry Marsden and Billy J. Kramer, plus the Dakotas and Pacemakers. They had a blast with all the groups!

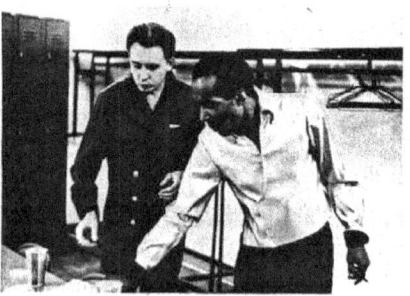

Time for a quick bite between acts! Reb chomped down his food so fast that he didn't even have time to swallow his food before he had to run on stage to introduce the next act . . .

. . . who were Sonny and Cher. Everyone was surprised to see that Cher was a girl, since her voice is so deep. But after their groovy act, there was no doubt in anyone's mind that she is a girl!

Although Glynnis was Reb's date for the evening, he didn't mind letting Gerry kiss her! (guess what . . . Glynnis didn't mind either!) Reb introduced her to everyone in the show.

Guess who showed up to blow his own horn! The scuzzy one, surrounded by the two top boy-girl groups, Dick and DeeDee and Sonny and Cher. Come on, Dave, smile! (He always has a smile!)

Billy J. Kramer liked this picture of him and the Dakotas so much that he asked KRLA to give him copies of it! He also liked reading the KRLA BEAT, and wants lots of copies of this issue!

Billy J. said that this was one of the best pictures of him that he has ever seen. KRLA is the only radio station in the world that has it's own newspaper, and Billy loved the idea!

Robin MacDonald of the Dakotas keeps his eye on Glynnis while Billy J. seems lost in thought. Billy, by the way, is best friends with Gerry of the Pacemakers, and loves America.

Billy J. breaks 'em up! From left to right, Mick Green, Maxfield, Robin MacDonald, and Billy J. The group previewed their next record for the audience. Opinion? It'll be a smash hit!

# KRLA ARCHIVES

## ST SHOW OF THE YEAR

THE SHOW STARTS! Reb and Rosko, another d.j. announce the opening act. The screams were so loud when Reb got on stage that you couldn't hear a word he said. Maybe Reb should be a singer!

The Standells (who were discovered by Reb), open the show with their latest, "Linda Lu." It brought the house down! Left to right: Tony Valentino, Gary Laine, Dick Dodd, Larry Tamblyn.

Reb, Rosko, Glynnis, and the groovy Standells smile for the KRLA camera. The Standells and Reb shared the same dressing room, and every girl in the audience wished they could share it with them!

Round Robin shows everyone how he does the slauson. Round is a local boy, by the way, and is very friendly with Charlie O'Donnell, KRLA's mid morning d.j. Rip it up, Round!

The Superbs sing their hit of "Baby, Baby All The Time" while everyone cheers. Those suits are real leather! Reb has had this group at many of his dances, and they have always been great!

Reb introduces Glynnis to his good friend, Mike Clifford. Mike would have tried to kiss Glynnis too, only Reb's bigger than he is! Mike and Reb spent an hour talking about old times.

Now it's Gerry's turn! When he opened his mouth to sing, the girls nearly fainted. Left to right: Freddie Marsden, Gerry's brother, Gerry, and Les Chadwick. Les Maguire isn't in the picture.

Freddie looks at the belated Pacemaker, Les, while Gerry and the other Les wail away. It was really a night to remember! Those dots on the floor are jelly beans, thrown by screaming fans!

# KRLA ARCHIVES

## EMPEROR "KING" IN MORNING

So many readers have written in asking what Emperor Hudson is really like that you deserve an answer . . . so here it is!

The Emperor has the most popular morning show in Los Angeles, and no one has to ask why! With his thousands of Commandos storming . . . well, storming anything they can think of, anyone who isn't a commando is a . . . FINK! You can be one just by sending in a self addressed, stamped envelope to the Emperor at KRLA.

Hudson, who describes himself as "fair, fat, and none of your business," (he really isn't fat . . . just seductively buxom) (with honest-to-Petey beautiful blue eyes) (real ones!) has decided to take control of Los Angeles with his Commandos. He is busy working on a special duplicating and eliminating machine which will make this possible. The machine will eliminate all teachers, governors, and surf haters. He then plans to duplicate the Beatles and give every girl at least two of them to take home with her! His secret ambition is to duplicate about five Ann-Margrets, which he plans to keep all for himself. Unfortunately, the other d.j.s at KRLA found out about this, and Hudson was last seen running down the hall, with five d.j.s running after him crying "selfish, come back here with those plans for the duplicating machine!" Hudson is thinking of naming his machine "duplapeople," and says that another thing he is going to do is to multiply himself. Why? So he can receive two salaries, of course!

## RECORD BIZ ON THE MOVE

HOLLYWOOD—Our town is fast becoming famous for something else than movie making! In the past two years, the record industry, formerly New York's property, has been moving out to California. Since most of the American artists prefer the warm weather and sunny skies of California to the snow of the biggest city in America, record companies have found it easier to make their headquarters here. Capitol, one of the biggest labels in the entire business (wonder why?) helped the trend by building their fantastic "tower of records," and Liberty has always been here in Hollywood. VeeJay and Philles have recently moved out here also, and many record stars are buying homes in the desert so that they have a place to relax during the times they aren't on tour. Of course, most of the large companies have offices in every major city, but the trend definitely seems to be heading for the stars . . . Hollywood style!

## DAVE HULL FOR SHOW

HOLLYWOOD — The Dick Clark Caravan of Stars, a twice yearly traveling show of top talent, stars on November 13th this year. On tour with the show is Sonny Knight, Lou Christie, the Hondells, Dee Dee Sharp, Brian Hyland, Bobby Freeman, Joey Paige, the Drifters, Johnny Tillotson, the Supremes, the Crystals, and Mike Clifford. The show will hit over 25 cities. Dick Clark has been thinking seriously of sponsoring Dave Hull, if he can make the tour, so that the popular d.j. can do some of the m.c. work in some of the cities where he is so popular. Charlie O'Donnell, however, will stay home to 'keep an eye on the store'!

DUE TO THE MANY PICTURES ON THE GERRY AND THE PACEMAKERS, BILLY J. KRAMER SHOW, REB FOSTER'S "FAX ON WAX" AND BOB EUBANKS' "RECORD REVIEW" WILL NOT APPEAR THIS WEEK. WATCH FOR THEM IN THE NEXT ISSUE OF "KRLA BEAT," OUT NOVEMBER 11th.

KRLA BEAT'S WEEKLY FEATURE, "CONTEST CORNER" WILL NOT APPEAR THIS WEEK DUE TO LACK OF SPACE. NEXT WEEK, "CONTEST CORNER" WILL BE BACK . . . WITH ONE OF THE GREATEST CONTESTS YOU'VE EVER SEEN!

## Zombies Here

NEW YORK—It has now definitely been confirmed that the Zombies, who's record of "She's Not There" just won't quit climbing, will be in this country during Christmas week. They will appear at the giant rock and roll show held every year at the Brooklyn Fox. A tentative tour is being planned for the group, but this has not been set for certain at this time. The boys have stated that they don't want to miss seeing "where the movies are made," which means that if they have any time, they will spend a few days in Hollywood.

## THE STONES: "WE'RE QUIET"

HOLLYWOOD — The Rolling Stones, now in town for personal appearances, will record their next record in this town! Date and place for the recording session is, of course, top secret, but the KRLA BEAT photographer will be there to take pictures for you!

Everyone who has met the group has been amazed at how down to earth and humble the boys really are. "We make a lot of noise," stated one Rolling Stone, "But inside, we're quiet!"

The boys want to see Disneyland, and hope to make the rounds of all the famous night clubs in Hollywood before they leave.

"We love the beach, too," said Mick Jaegar, "and even if it's freezing, we're going swimming, goose bumps and all. We don't have beaches like yours in England."

The boys wish they could spend more time in this country, but pressing committments will limit their stay.

## 'TEENS' RELEASE

LONDON—The next release by the Nashville Teens, currently riding high on the charts with "Tobacco Road" will be titled "Google Eye." The Nashville Teens live up to their name, too! "Tobacco Road" was written by John D. Loudermilk, a well known country and western singer who lives in . . . of course, Nashville! John also wrote "Google Eyes," and just to show that he has nothing against American groups, dashed off "Thou Shalt Not Steal" for Dick and DeeDee, which looks as though it will be a big hit.

The Nashville Teens will make their first appearance in this country on December 19th, where they will appear in a show in New York. They will then start a three week tour of America's major cities, leaving for England and home from Los Angeles.

## CHAD AND JEREMY

HOLLYWOOD — Dean Martin's daughter, Claudia, and movie star George Hamilton held a big party for English stars Chad and Jeremy when they were in town. The star studded party was attended by such guests as Doug McClure, Eddie Fisher, Jackie DeShannon, and many other stars. Although the party was more or less formal, there was such a casual atmosphere that everyone was relaxed and had a very good time. Chad and Jeremy both said that "if this was a sample of Hollywood hospitality, they both liked it." The two stars are unusual in the record business . . . they are both members of the "high society set" in Britain, related to dukes, earls, and other titled people.

## GROUP FOR BBC

LONDON—The Ronettes, always a top group in this country, took England by storm last week when they headlined a show at the London Palladium. The show, which is presented weekly, is called "Sunday Night At The Palladium," and is televised over the BBC. Britain's only tv station. It features all the top groups from England and other countries, and is one of the most popular shows in that country. The Beatles made one of their first big appearances on the show, and it has seen the start of the careers of stars like Gerry & The Pacemakers, The Honeycombs, The D.C. Five, and many other groups.

## WIN BEATLE ALBUM!

Hey, have you heard the news? You can win a free FRLA Album of all the Beatle interviews with Dave Hull and Jim Steck! Yes, and that's not all! Not only will you hear the Beatles answer top secret questions on this groovy album, but EACH ALBUM WILL BE PERSONALLY AUTOGRAPHED BY EVERY KRLA D.J. JUST FOR YOU!

All you have to do to win this gear prize is find a record store that doesn't order the weekly KRLA BEAT. Tell them to order it! If they do, and mention your name, KRLA will send you this great album with all the autographs. Make sure that the store gets your name and address, or else we can't send it to you! And here's the best part! If you get more than one store to order the KRLA BEAT, we won't just give you another album . . . after all, what can you do with two albums? YOU'LL ACTUALLY GET A PHONE CALL FROM THE D.J. OF YOUR CHOICE! Not only that, but the d.j. will answer any questions you ask about the Beatles or any other stars! Just tell the record stores to call Bonnie Golden at KRLA, MU 1-6991, and tell us that you sent 'em . . . and we'll do the rest!

## AMERICA TOP SONGWRITER

NEW YORK—English groups may be hot right now, but American songwriting is still tops! Proof of this is the songwriting team of Gerry Goffin and Carole King, who are on the charts now with Manfred Mann's "Do Wah Diddy," and Herman's Hermits recording of "I'm Onto Something Good." Herman's Hermits have decided to record another Goffin-King number for their next release, too. Title of the new disc is "Show Me Girl," and it will be released in two weeks. KRLA, of course, will get the record before then, and you will hear it first on L.A.'s number one station.

NEXT ISSUE OUT NOV. 11TH

## PERSONALS

Do you want your personals printed? Each week, we'll print any messages you want to send through the KRLA BEAT! Just mail your message in on a post card to: PERSONALS, KRLA BEAT, 1401 South Oak Knoll Rd., Pasadena, California. Keep messages about three lines. You can say anything you want (almost) . . . and it will be printed right here in the KRLA BEAT!

RINGO FOR PRESIDENT!
    "Ringlett" Devoss

Silly Sally, W.H.: The reason they're laughing is because you don't know who your friends really are!
    Waker Upper

John R., C.C.: If you know how much I cared you would come right back where you belong!
    Dolly

To KRLA, Pasadena: You're gear, great and gear again for putting out the greatest newspaper in the world!
    Sharo Mateese

To all the kids at the corner, I didn't mean what I said.
    The Blonde

Rick, Pacoima: Forget it!
    Deadre

Vonnie of Los Angeles is a rat for not calling when he says he will! So there!
    "Stood Up"

Jill, Hollywood: J.L.Y.T.E., because M.L.F.Y.W.N.D.I
    Buggy

Ronnie 4-ever: 2-b-with-u-is-my-d-sire!
    Frannie

Rodger: 'Lil Abner just about describes you! Fink!
    Hurt

Hanna: What's the matter with you? All I said was IF!
    S.A.

George in 4th period math: Hi!
    Girl in 4th row

Allie, I will always care. Please come back!
    Margie

To Dave Hull: Thank you, thank you, thank you!
    All of us

Mike Hill, San Francisco: I haven't heard from you! Why?
    Candy

## HIT SCORED BY CASEY ON TV SHOW

KRLA d.j. Casey Kasem made his first tv appearance as a record star on the Lloyd Thaxton show last week. He did his hit single, "Letter From Elaina" while dancers on the show screamed just as hard for Casey as they do for established record stars.

Casey at this time has no definite plans for a follow up record. His fan mail averages over a sack a day, yet the young d.j. somehow manages to find the time to read each letter. Many of the letters ask Casey for a solution to a personal problem, and he tries to answer all these letters, in addition to sending out as many as 50 autographs each day!

Casey's weekly record hops draw capacity crowds each week, and he always has the top recording talent at every dance.

# KRLA BEAT

## GIANT KRLA GIVEAWAY NOW IN SECOND WEEK
(Story in Col. 1)

Production, Design And Content By Bonnie Golden

## RECORDS GIVEN TO LISTENERS

HOLLYWOOD — The giant KRLA givaway, now in its second week, has had fantastic results! KRLA has given away over 6,000 records to listeners who sent in a post card to Musical Jackpot, KRLA, Pasadena. (P.S.: If you haven't sent your card in, hurry up . . . there's only two weeks left!)

### SACKS OF MAIL

The post office has had to get men with strong backs to bring all the mail to KRLA! The contest averages over two full sacks a day, and thousands of cards are stacked up waiting for each drawing. Before each d.j. goes on the air, he reaches into the huge box where all the cards are stacked and pulls out several handfuls of post cards. After he draws the cards, the box is rearranged to make sure everyone gets a chance. In this way, every record played on KRLA is given to some lucky listener.

### SLEEP NO WORRY

This is one contest that you don't have to worry about missing if you're asleep. Benevolent Bobby Dale, KRLA's gear night time d.j. keeps close track of all the cards he draws. Your records will be sent to you within a few days after the drawing, so there is no need fret missing your name.

### LISTENERS GET TWO GIFTS

One of the cards KRLA got gave the station a really great compliment. It said "The record, if I win it, isn't the only gift I get from KRLA. Just listening to your station is such a treat that I like to think of it as a present too!"

KRLA was really happy to hear that, and we hope you all feel that way. We plan on doing everything we can to help you continue to keep KRLA on top!

## KRLA TOP THIRTY

1. BABY LOVE .................................. The Supremes
2. OPPORTUNITY ............................... The Jewels
3. DANCING IN THE STREET ...... Martha & Vandellas
4. THE JERK ..................................... The Larks
5. I'M INTO SOMETHING GOOD ..... Herman's Hermits
6. SHE'S NOT THERE ........................ The Zombies
7. LAST KISS ............................. J. Frank Wilson
8. PRETTY WOMAN .......................... Roy Orbison
9. IF YOU WANT THIS LOVE ............. Sonny Knight
10. YOU REALLY GOT ME ..................... The Kinks
11. TIME IS ON MY SIDE ................. Rolling Stones
12. TOBACCO ROAD ..................... Nashville Teens
13. ON OUTSIDE LOOKING IN ... Anthony & Imperials
14. RIDE THE WILD SURF ................... Jan & Dean
15. DOOR IS OPEN TO MY HEART ...... Dean Martin
16. THAT'S WHAT LOVE IS MADE OF ... The Miracles
17. LEADER OF THE PACK ............. The Shangri-Las
18. EVERYTHING IS ALRIGHT ............ The Newbeats
19. IT HURTS TO BE IN LOVE .............. Gene Pitney
20. BABY I NEED YOUR LOVING .......... Four Tops
21. HAVE I THE RIGHT ................... Honeycombs
22. BABY BABY ALL THE TIME ........... The Superbs
23. DON'T YOU DO IT ..................... Marvin Gaye
24. T BABY .............................. The Butterflys
25. DA .................................. The Hondells
26. SIDEWA...NG .......................... Jan & Dean
27. WALKING ... RAIN .................... The Ronettes
28. GIRL WHY M ... UE ................ The Temptations
29. I'M GONNA' ............................ Gene Pitney
30. I LIKE IT ...................... Gerry & Pacemakers

## TOP TEN ALBUMS

1. HARD DAY'S NIGHT .......................... BEATLES
2. SOMETHING NEW ............................ BEATLES
3. ALL SUMMER LONG ..................... BEACH BOYS
4. MORE OF ROY ORBISON'S HITS
5. THE KINGSMEN, VOL. 2
6. WHERE DID OUR LOVE GO ........... SUPREMES
7. THE ANIMALS
8. WALK DON'T RUN, VOL. 2 ................ VENTURES
9. VINTON'S GREATEST HITS ......... BOBBY VINTON
10. RAG DOLL ............................. FOUR SEASONS

## TOP TEN OLDIES

1. I've Had It ........................... The Bell Notes
2. I'm Sorry ............................. Brenda Lee
3. Walking The Dog ................... Rufus Thomas
4. Stand By Me ........................ Ben E. King
5. Uptown ............................. The Crystals
6. Only You ........................... The Platters
7. Johnny Angel ................... Shelley Fabares
8. Glad All Over ................... Dave Clark Five
9. At My Front Door ............... The Eldorados
10. The Big Hurt ....................... Toni Fisher

## TOP TEN UP AND COMERS

1. Mountain of Love .................... Johnny Rivers
2. So Fine/Linda Lou ................. The Standells
3. Baby Don't Go ...................... Sonny & Cher
4. Is It True? ............................. Brenda Lee
5. Mr. Lonely ......................... Bobby Vinton
6. Ringo ............................... Lorne Greene
7. Little Marie ......................... Chuck Berry
8. Gone, Gone, Gone .......... The Everly Bros.
9. Unless You Care ................... Terry Black
10. Big Man In Town .................. The 4 Seasons

## HI, HULLABALOOERS!

Geesh, what a week! Half the population of England was right here in jolly old K*R*L*A*N*D! Yes, I've really been the busy boy this week. Gathering moss with the Rolling Stones, convincing the Dakotas that there were 48 other states in the union, making paces with Gerry . . . it's been a wild scene! Actually, they all came over here to see me, you know, since I'm the best honorary editor in the world. At least, I think so. (YOU MEAN YOU REALLY THINK, BIG BOY?) Not again! Maud, can't you leave me alone for just one week? Listen, Maud, I heard that Brian Epstein was thinking of signing you up . . . to be a stand in for his dog! (OH, YEAH? I HEARD HE WANTED TO USE YOU INSTEAD OF A PUMPKIN FOR HALLOWEEN!) Maud, did anyone ever tell you you're like an ancient city . . . Babble-on? (YOU'VE GOT A LOT OF FUNNY MATERIAL. . . . BUT IT'S ALL IN YOUR CLOTHES) And you've got a lot of funny lines, Maud, but they're all in your face! Anyhow, before she starts coming after me again, I just want to tell you that next week I'm going to have a scoop about the Beatles' next movie. It's unbelievable, so watch for it! This is the only place you'll see this information, and you'll never guess who told me! So since you won't guess, I'll tell you! I spoke to George Harrison's mother, and you'll get the scoop right here next week!

## REB ON WAX!

HOLLYWOOD — Reb Foster, one of the most popular d.j.s in California, will make his recording debut this week for the Reprise label. Reb will cut four sides at his session and will release the

(CONT. ON PAGE 4)

# KRLA ARCHIVES

Well, KRLA did it again! We snapped up all the English groups just for you! All of you heard the exclusive interviews Gary Mack got from Gerry, Billy J. and of course, the Rolling Stones. And naturally, the KRLA BEAT photographer was there to get pictures of every minute all three groups spent in K*R*L*A*N*D! In fact, the pictures of the Rolling Stones show were so groovy that we're saving them for a whole section alone in an upcoming issue. KRLA was the only radio station lucky enough to get such exclusive interviews . . . which goes to show that KRLA listeners are always first in EVERYTHING!

When Gary Mack walked into the special section at the airport reserved for KRLA, he was greeted by screaming fans, all waving copies of the KRLA BEAT.

Before he had time to think, Gary for his autograph. These fans were al they wanted Gary, too!

Gary grabbed a snack with the boys, and then showed them a copy of the KRLA BEAT. They loved it and took copies back to England to show to other British stars!

Finally, the Stones arrived! They asked us to come to their hotel room at the Roosevelt. Here, Gary introduces himself to Mick and Keith and starts the first interview.

Gary asks Mick if he has a girl here looking!" Mick plans to come back h his favorite state.

Mick, Keith, and Bill relax for a few minutes before Gary tapes another interview. Brian was unpacking, and Charlie was still in San Francisco getting some confederate money for his Civil War collection.

Mick said that he liked this picture. "I usually don't like my photos," he added, "but this one is pretty good . . . it has something!" Don't you agree with him? Bill and Keith liked it too.

Mick and Keith discuss the songs th which was recorded here in town. K come here again soon.

Joey plays his new record for Mick. He will tour England with the boys this spring. That's Keith's guitar, by the way, and he takes it everywhere he goes. His hobby is playing flamenco songs.

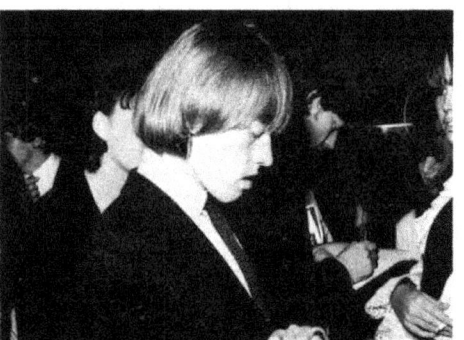

Backstage at the filming of the TAMI show! Here, Brian looks at his watch while Mick signs autographs in the background. Reb Foster and Dick Moreland were there too, and both of them had a blast!

Terry Brown, Bob Eubanks' secretary the show. In the background is Jane M There were over 15 acts on the show.

Photography by ROBIN HILL

# KRLA ARCHIVES

was plunked into a chair and asked there to meet the Rolling Stones, but

Gary decided to take a walk before the Rolling Stones got there . . . imagine his surprise when he ran into Billy J. Kramer and Gerry Marsden, who made a secret stopover in L.A.

None of the fans knew about the surprise arrival either . . . it was a big surprise! But the girls told Gary's tape recorder what a gear surprise it was!

in California. "Not yet, luv, but I'm ere alone when he can, since this is

Mick poses for the KRLA camera. When he saw this picture, he said, "No no one will ever believe that I comb my hair . . . but I do! (He does, Gary saw him!)

Bill Wyman talks about old times with his friend, Joey Paige. Joey met the boys in England and was at the airport to greet them when they landed here in K*R*L*A*N*D.

y are writing for their new album, ith liked Hollywood, and hopes they

"Watch the Birdie, boys!" After this shot, they showed Gary Brian's new guitar. "It's the only one like it in this country," Mick said. You'll see it in pics of the show KRLA had in Long Beach.

Gary asked Keith what his favorite food was. Keith said, "Spaghetti with bacon and butterscotch sauce." Now you know why Gary has that look on his face! Even Mick turned green!

and a good friend of Mick's, discuss lstead, editor of Teen Screen Magazine.

Guess who else was at the show? No, they aren't twins! Dick Moreland and Gerry Marsden do look alike, though! More pics of this show in a future issue. Be sure you don't miss it!

Bill, Charlie (the one who is so interested in the Civil War), Mick, and Keith wait to go on. Brian was still getting dressed.. The boys really tore everyone up!

# KRLA ARCHIVES

DUE TO THE LACK OF SPACE BECAUSE OF THE PICTURE SPREAD IN THIS ISSUE, THE PERSONAL COLUMN WILL NOT APPEAR THIS WEEK. IT WILL RESUME NEXT WEEK AS USUAL. SO SEND 'EM IN!

## RECORD REVIEW

It's Bob Eubanks here, to give you the latest news on record reviews!

Brian Epstein informed me that Tommy Quickley, his new artist, will have his new record released on November 25th. I've heard it, and it's terrific.

The new Beach Boys record, "Dance, Dance, Dance" will probably be their biggest yet. It's a gas.

Watch Little Anthony get another hit with "Goin' Out of My Head." This was written by Teddy Randazzo, and is a really wild song!

The one record that tears me completely up is the new Four Seasons sound of "Big Man In Town." Wow!

One record that has got to make it is "I Had A Talk With My Man," by Mitty Collier. She's an English gal, and the record was number one for a good long while over there. If you've heard it, you know why. Hitsville for this!

Well, that's all the room this week. See you soon, and if you aren't good, I'll get you!

## REB...

two that he thinks are the best. Reb, originally from Texas, was a good friend of the late Buddy Holly, and their voices are remarkably alike.

Although the young d.j. has been at KRLA little more than a year, his show is the most popular late afternoon show in Los Angeles. Reb lives in a rambling bachelor house high in the Hollywood Hills. His good looks and handsome personality have made his dances and personal appearances complete sell outs, while many of the top stars in the recording business are his close friends. Billy J. Kramer and Gerry and the Pacemakers especially requested that Reb be present at their Electronovision filming.

The record will be released sometime next month, and you'll hear it first, of course, on KRLA.

## STAR IN CRASH

OHIO—J. Frank Wilson, who's song, "One Last Kiss" is tops on the KRLA top thirty, was seriously hurt two weeks ago in an auto crash as he was on his way to a performance. His manager, Sonley Roush, was killed. Roush was driving, and apparently fell asleep at the wheel.

J. Frank Wilson said that he will be better soon and will resume the cross country tour he was making at the time of the accident. He suffered chest injuries. Also in the crash was Bobby Wood, a country singer.

### STARS IN OTHER CAR

Following in another car behind Wilson's were other acts in the show. They were Jumpin' Gene Simmons, Murray Kellum, and Travis Wammack. None of the other stars were injured.

---

Would you like to deliver a personal message to the Dave Clark Five? You Would? Groovy! Because all you have to do is send your letter to the boys to the KRLA BEAT, and we will personally deliver the letters to the D.C. 5 as soon as they come into town. Don't send any packages or big envelopes, because we can't deliver anything but letters. Make sure your letter gets here before November 25th, so that you'll be sure they get it. All of you know that most stars try to read their fan mail, but many times you can never be sure if it really gets to the star you have written to. Now not only can you be sure, but positive, because the KRLA BEAT will make sure that they are delivered right into the D.C. 5's hands!

## FAX... ON... WAX!

Hi, this is the Rebel himself to clue you in on the latest happenings! Let's go!

Bill Wyman of the Stones has a nearly two year old son named Stephen. He's pretty cute, too!

Speaking of the Stones, Mick and Keith told me before they left that they plan a secret visit to this country around Christmas. They were to come here and relax for a while. I'll let you know more later!

The new Beatles record will be out November 27th in England and will get here a few days later. It's called "I Feel Fine," and the other side is "She's a Woman." They also have a new album which will be released here December 4th. The album will have 9 songs, all new, written by John and Paul. It's title will be "Beatles For Sale." Don't we wish they were!

If you think you saw Stones rolling along outside the RCA studios on Sunset, you were right! The boys recorded six tracks for their new album there. They asked me not to give the names of the songs, so I can't, but they were written by the boys and are a gas!

Scoop! The Beatles will be returning to this country before August! In fact, they may be here sooner than you think!

Well, that closes it for another week. See you in two weeks with more fax on wax!

---

# CONTEST CORNER!

Hey, do you like The Dave Clark Five? And did you want to go to the show that Bob Eubanks is putting on on November 21? And did you discover that all the tickets were sold out and you couldn't get any? Gee, that's too bad! Were you very disappointed? Did you start muttering un-nice things under your breath and resolve never to buy another Dave Clark record? Well, cheer up! Smile! Why? Well, don't ask us why you should smile ... we have other things to do than sit around thinking about why you should smile. Like, for example, giving the Dave Clark Five away for an hour. Or giving actual press tickets to the show to some lucky reader. Or giving away autographed records, or ... well, you get the idea. So stop bugging us about why you should smile and start entering this contest!

### HERE'S WHAT YOU WIN!

*FIRST PRIZE!*

WIN THE DAVE CLARK FIVE FOR AN HOUR! Yes, you'll not only get to see this groovy show, but you'll be taken backstage, introduced to Dave and his fab group, and actually get to keep them for one whole hour! You can ask questions, take pictures, get autographs, do whatever you want. They belong to you for one hour!

*SECOND PRIZE!*

TWO PRESS TICKETS TO THE SHOW! You'll sit way up front, right with reporters for newspapers and fan magazines. You'll hear all the "in" talk as these people discuss all the groups, and you'll actually see Dave Clark as he is interviewed by the press! Not only that, but you can take along a friend! After all, there are two tickets!

*THIRD PRIZE!*

A PERSONALLY AUTOGRAPHED DAVE CLARK FIVE ALBUM, AUTOGRAPHED BY THE WHOLE GROUP AND BOB EUBANKS! This album will be autographed with your name and a special message from Dave!

HERE'S ALL YOU HAVE TO DO:

Are you good with a dictionary? You'd better be! Start looking through it and find out how many words you can make from "KRLA, RADIO ELEVEN TEN." That's all! We've even been nice enough to make a set of rules for you, and here they are:

1. Make as many words as you can by using the letters in "KRLA, RADIO ELEVEN TEN." No letter can be used more than once in any one word. If there are two A's in a word, you can use it because there are two A's in the sentence. All words must be listed in the dictionary.

2. Entries will be judged by the greatest number of words. In case of a tie, the earliest postmark will be the winner. Entries will be judged by Bob Eubanks and the KRLA BEAT staff.

3. Contest closes November 20th. Winners will be notified by phone. Entries should try to attach an entry blank to their entry.

**ENTRY BLANK**

NAME: ............................................................ AGE: ..............

ADDRESS: .........................................................................

SCHOOL: .................................................... GRADE: ..............

## KRLA ARCHIVES

# WELCOME TO KRLA, DAVE CLARK FIVE
(Story in Col. 1)

# KRLA BEAT

Production, Design And Content By Bonnie Golden

## MIGHT MAKE MOVIE HERE

HOLLYWOOD — The Dave Clark Five, now in Los Angeles for their Long Beach performance, also have another reason for being in Los Angeles Bob Eubanks disclosed today. Dave is to meet with representatives of Warner Brothers Pictures to discuss his next movie.

### SINATRA PARTY

The meeting will take place at a private party, hosted by none other than Frank Sinatra! If all goes well, Dave will be back to this country in January to begin shooting his first full length film for Warner Brothers. He will be the first Englsh siniger to star in a full length movie shot in Hollywood. Although few people know it, Sinatra and some of his friends will also be at the Long Beach performance. It is reported that the D.C. 5 is very excited about meeting Sinatra, and are anxious to be able to make their film in Hollywood.

### SHOW SOLD OUT

The show in Long Beach has been sold out for months! Bob Eubanks signed the boys up as soon as plans were made for the American tour (doesn't he get all the groups first!). They loved this country when they were here last time, and this time they are traveling in their own private plane, containing a living room, bedrooms, a kitchen, and stereo tape recorder!

### NEW RECORD

The latest sound from the group is called "Anyway You Want It" and it looks like the most exciting record since "Glad All Over." The driving beat and wild guitar has that groovy D.C. 5 sound that has made them the second most popular group in the world.

### 55 DAY TOUR

The group consists, beside Dave, of Lenny Davison, Mike Smith, Rick Huxley, and Dennis Payton. They will be in this country for 55 days before returning to England for a rest.

## KRLA TOP THIRTY

1. BABY LOVE .................... The Supremes
2. I'M INTO SOMETHING GOOD .... Herman's Hermits
3. SHE'S NOT THERE ................ The Zombies
4. OPPORTUNITY ..................... The Jewels
5. THE JERK ........................... The Larks
6. LAST KISS ..................... J. Frank Wilson
7. IF YOU WANT THIS LOVE ........ Sonny Knight
8. DANCING IN THE STREET .. Martha & Vandellas
9. TIME IS ON MY SIDE ....... The Rolling Stones
10. OH, PRETTY WOMAN ............ Roy Orbison
11. LEADER OF THE PACK ....... The Shangri-Las
12. YOU REALLY GOT ME ............. The Kinks
13. THAT'S WHAT LOVE IS MADE OF .. The Miracles
14. RIDE THE WILD SURF ............ Jan & Dean
15. SIDEWALK SURFIN' ............... Jan & Dean
16. I'M ON THE OUTSIDE (Looking In) .. Little Anthony
17. EVERYTHING'S ALRIGHT ......... The Newbeats
18. THE DOOR IS STILL OPEN ........ Dean Martin
19. MR. LONELY .................... Bobby Vinton
20. TOBACCO ROAD ........... The Nashville Teens
21. MOUNTAIN OF LOVE ........... Johnny Rivers
22. HAVE I THE RIGHT? .......... The Honeycombs
23. GOOD NIGHT BABY ............. The Butterflies
24. RINGO ......................... Lorne Greene
25. BABY BABY ALL THE TIME ........ The Superbs
26. IT HURTS TO BE IN LOVE ......... Gene Pitney
27. BABY DON'T GO ............... Sonny & Cher
28. I LIKE IT ............ Gerry & The Pacemakers
29. I'M GONNA BE A MAN .......... Gene Pitney
30. DON'T WANT TO SEE YOU AGAIN Peter & Gordon

### TOP TEN ALBUMS

1. A HARD DAY'S NIGHT ................ BEATLES
2. SOMETHING NEW .................... BEATLES
3. MORE OF ROY ORBISON'S GREATEST HITS
4. THE KINGSMEN, VOL. 2
5. THE ANIMALS
6. ALL SUMMER LONG ............... BEACH BOYS
7. WHERE DID OUR LOVE GO ......... SUPREMES
8. THE AMERICAN TOUR ...... DAVE CLARK FIVE
9. THE ROLLING STONES
10. BREAD AND BUTTER .............. NEWBEATS

### TOP TEN OLDIES

1. Sugar Shack ................. Jimmy Gilmer
2. Really Got A Hold On Me ........ Miracles
3. Tragedy ................... Thomas Wayne
4. Love Letters ............... Ketty Lester
5. Then He Kissed Me ............. Crystals
6. Happy Birthday Baby ....... Tune Weavers
7. This I Swear ................. Skyliners
8. Grass Is Greener ........... Brenda Lee
9. She's Not You ............ Elvis Presley
10. Candy Man ................ Roy Orbison

### TOP TEN UP AND COMERS

1. Come See About Me ....... The Supremes
2. Dance, Dance, Dance ..... The Beach Boys
3. Big Man In Town ........... The 4 Seasons
4. Willow Weep For Me ..... Chad & Jeremy
5. Any Way You Want It ...... Dave Clark 5
6. Reach Out For Me ....... Dionne Warwick
7. Love Potion Number 9 ..... The Searchers
8. Run Run Run ............... The Gestures
9. A Happy Guy ............... Rick Nelson
10. Ain't Doin' Bad (part 1) ..... Bobby Bland

## HI, HULLABALOOERS!

I'm sitting here thinking of the delicious turkey I'll be chomping on next week! Boy, the holidays roll around so fast. It hardly seemed like the 4th of July was over before National Dave Hull day was upon us, and now . . . what? You never heard of National Dave Hull Day? Why it's the biggest holiday of the year! You mean they don't even let you off school for it? Well, I like that! "SO DO I!" Oh, no! It's Maud Skidmore, back again to put her feet in her mouth . . . with both hands! "OH, YOU THINK YOU'RE SMART JUST BECAUSE YOU HAVE HORNS, BUT IF YOU DON'T BE GOOD, I'LL TELL EVERYONE ABOUT YOUR TAIL!" Maud, how could you saythat! I thought we agreed to be friends! "NOT UNLESS YOU INTRODUCE ME TO THE DAVE CLARK FIVE!" Sorry, Maud, they'd never forgive me. But back to National Dave Hull Day. "WAIT A MINUTE, BIG BOY, IF YOU CAN'T INTRODUCE ME TO THEM, AT LEAST I CAN HAVE YOU!" Who said? I mean, uh, no you can't! Maud stay away from me! Oh, no! Well, see you next week everyone!Byyyyyyeeee!

## KRLA "SCOOP"— BEATLE FIRST!

HOLLYWOOD—KRLA scored another scoop over everyone when they became the first station in the WORLD to play the Beatles' new record of "I Feel Fine." KRLA listeners heard the record even before it was played in England!

The record was played first by Dave (Scuzzy one) Hull, who proved that he was far from scuzzy when he became the only person in the world to get a copy of the

(CONT. ON PAGE 4)

# KRLA ARCHIVES

It's awful how KRLA keeps, er . . . blowing its own horn, but honestly, have you ever seen such groovy pictures? Yep, we scored again. (It's even getting tiring to say that . . . without being conceited, we keep on scoring). And do you know why? Because of YOU, the greatest listeners in the world! Every English star who has ever been here has said that the KRLA kids (that's you) are great! So actually, it's YOUR fault we keep coming out first with the most! And here's just more proof of it . . . all the groovy scenes backstage at the big Rolling Stones Show, and even groovier scenes of the show itself for those of you who missed it. Next week, KRLA brings you the Dave Clark Five, and if you can't make the show . . . stick right here, same station, and we'll cover it for you in the KRLA BEAT! And one message from the Rolling Stones to All of YOU: You're a gas! And y'know something? We at KRLA second the motion!

Bob Eubanks spends a few minutes before the show with his new Cinnamon Cinder group, Don and the Deacons. The boys are really tearing them up at the C.C., and they were the group that backed the show.

Oops! Looks like the scuzzy one's in trouble again! Actually, Bob wouldn't push our lovable Hullabalooer out the window . . . at least, not while Dave is wearing his tie! But then why is Bob smiling?

Don and the Deacons do one number to start the show off. They're really a great group! Although the boys are young, they have been around for quite a while . . . and they have many fans who know it!

Charlie 'O' announced the Scuzzy Hullabalooer . . . then ran for his life! The screams were so loud that you couldn't even hear Dave's famous horn . . . the one he carries everywhere he goes. He loved the applause!

Finally, the Rolling Stones, stars of the show arrived. They were very tired, and left as soon as the show was over. Here Keith and Charlie Watts make their entrance . . . Charlie loves clothes and always dresses well.

Meanwhile, back in the closed dressing room . . . Bob Eubanks and Keith laugh at a joke Bill is telling . . . he's sitting next to Keith, but you can't see him. You can, though, see Brian's new white guitar!

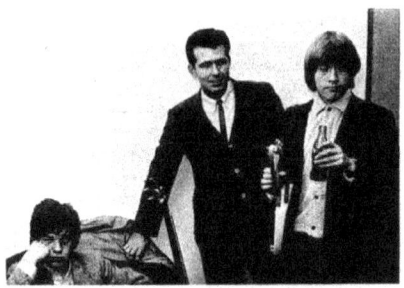
Mick really wasn't sulking in this picture . . . he was just tired. The boys told Bob that they liked him because "you don't wear us out like everyone else does . . . you're good people." Which is a high compliment!

Dave, spending a few minutes with Jimmy, suddenly realizes that the Soul Brothers are nearly through, and Jimmy hasn't even begun to get ready! Panicsville! He had to help Jimmy get ready!

Next, it was Dick and DeeDee's turn. These two stole the show with their groovy act, and DeeDee looked so nice that even the Rolling Stones came to the side of the stage to watch! They were terrific!
Photography by ROBIN HILL

At last, the moment everyone's been waiting for! The three KRLA d.j.'s walk on stage . . . they don't have to say a word . . . the audience knows . . . it's the ROLLING STONES! The screaming starts . . . louder and louder!

With Charlie Watts in the background, Brian and Mick go into action. Brian is one of the most versatile of the Stones . . . he plays guitar, harmonica, piano, and can "fool around on the drums a little."

# KRLA ARCHIVES

Smiles again . . . this time for real! Jimmy Clanton poses with KRLA's two handsome d.j.'s . . . and it's hard to tell just which one's the star, they all look so good! (When Dave pulled his head back, he bumped it!)

The Spats have a quick rehearsal before the show starts. These boys are truly great talents, and will go far. Like to England next year . . . or at least, that's what they hope to do!

The boys wouldn't let anyone in their dressing room except . . . you know who! Here, Bill Wyman talks to Bob about hair . . . while Charlie looks on with . . . well, what is that expression? What's Charlie thinking of?

And now, the most famous d.j. in the world (that's what his mother says, anyhow) comes back to announce the next act . . . carrying, of course, his horn! One thing to notice . . . the stage is clean at this moment.

But it was worth the panic! Jimmy was great, and we all know he'll soon be heading the charts again! He's the only singer who REALLY sings in a Southern accent! (and Very Well, too!)

The Soul Brothers rip it up! Now everyone knows how they got their name! The lead singer reminded everyone of James Brown in looks, and when he opened his mouth . . . the resemblance was even more startling!

Mick wails! Of all the Stones, he has the most fun on stage. By the way, if you'll notice, the stage isn't so clean anymore! And to all of you who threw stuffed animals . . . the boys kept them!

Bill, the quiet one, hardly moves at all when he's singing . . . but who was the girl he kept smiling at in the balcony? It was really a great show, and everyone had a good time . . . and next come the D.C. 5!

# KRLA ARCHIVES

## PERSONALS

Do you want your personals printed? Each week, we'll print any messages you want to send through the KRLA BEAT! Just mail your message in on a post card to: PERSONALS, KRLA BEAT, 1401 South Oak Knoll Rd., Pasadena, California. Keep messages about three lines. You can say anything you want (almost) ... and it will be printed right here in the KRLA BEAT!

Ken & Dan: You like camping just outside Las Vegas and I'd like you to call me.
Cut-off
AT 0-8079

To Melvin: Come see about me because I love you.
From Annette of S.U.

Sir: Thanks for all the pidgers and writty of our favorit groups.
An admirer,
Afan

To Rudy Valona, E. LA.: No matter what everyone else says, I think your singing is fub!
An admirer

To Dave Hull: We'd do anything to meet you. We love you.
Carmen & Delores

AJ T. of J.T.: If you put that tooth under your pillow, you'll have a hard time sleeping.
"Fang"

Janey: Charlie has an autograph for you ... if you can bear it.
Yuk, yuk!

To KRLA: The Garfield gang love you and the Beatles too!
Alice Carlon
BIO

To Robert Battle: You'll never get to heaven if you break my heart.
Gloria Kato

Shelley, my love: You came to me like a voice out of the night ...
Guess who?

John Lennon, Liverpool: WOW!
All of us

Jody of Pacoima: Grow up, he'll never be yours! (I hope)
(that make we)
He's she

Dave and Robin: We still love you. Your cousins, Jan & Mary from El Segundo.

Mick Jagger: You're quite yums, you know. Call me!
JayJay

Please let me win the Dave Clark Five!
Hopeful

I don't know what to say, so I won't say anything.
Wordless

Sandy: Tell your mother to let you stay out later next time.
Joe

## D. J. FAN CLUBS READY

Hey, how would you like to join a really swinging fan club for the d.j. you like best on KRLA? Or even better, how would you like to start a club all your very own, be a chapter president, get to know your favorite d.j., or do all kinds of fun type fan club things? Well, you can! Yep, we've had so many requests for d.j. fan clubs that all kinds of clubs are forming ... and you can even start your own!

Here's a list of the ones already started: DAVE HULL: Write to Colleen Ludwick, 5231 Ivar, Temple City. Dues are $1.00 per year, and you get a monthly newsletter containing all the news about the scuzzy one, plus a membership card. GARY MACK: Write to Gary Mack fan club, KRLA, Pasadena, California. Dues are 25c, and you get a membership card and a picture of Gary. BOB EUBANKS: Write to Janet Wolfe, 7839 Beckett St., Sunland, California. Dues are 50c, and you get a monthly newsletter.

If you want to start your own fan club for Reb Foster, Casey Kasem, Bobby Pickett, Bobby Dale, Emperor Hudson, Dick Moreland, or Charlie O'Donnell, just write a letter to Fan Clubs, KRLA, Pasadena, California. We'll give the letter to the d.j. of your choice!

## C. & J. HERE FOR A WEEK

HOLLYWOOD—English stars Chad and Jeremy are making a surprise stay in K*R*L*A*N*D this week. The boys flew in with Johnny Rivers, the Ventures and a few other stars for a show in San Bernardino, then drove back for a week's rest here in Hollywood. After their short stay, they will return to England.

The boys confided to KRLA that they expect to see the Beatles when they return home, and that George and John are still keen on the idea of returning here without anyone knowing so that they can see the country without the country seeing them! Of course, the minute they set foot here in America, KRLA will be right on the scene with all the news first!

## KRLA SCOOP...

new release. (This is why other d.j.'s go bald early ... from tearing out their hair in frustration because KRLA gets all the hits first!)

## MORELAND TO NASHVILLE

HOLLYWOOD — If you're wondering why Dick Moreland seems to be speaking with a hillbilly accent lately, the answer is simple! Dick spent part of his vacation at the annual country and western music convention in Nashville. The convention was a blast, says Dick. He was able to meet many of the great country singers and see them perform, and "since Nashville is so friendly, I felt just like I was at home," Dick added. Although he would like to return to the home of Elvis Presley, Brenda Lee, and the Nashville sound, Dick won't be able to for a while. But he states that he had so much fun during the short time he was there that "I'll go back someday ... even if I have to walk"!

## NEXT ISSUE OUT NOV. 25

## CONTEST CORNER!!!

It's giveaway time again! And do we have something to give away this time! See, it all started a few weeks ago when WE started thinking. We thought, 'hmmmm, look at all the dates with stars we've been giving away! Really gassy dates, too ... trips to Disneyland, hours back stage with the star of your choice, groovy dates with a d.j., all kinds of goodies.' It made us feel pretty proud of ourselves, we can tell you that! But then we started thinking ... during all these dates, none of the winners got a chance to sit down and have dinner. And YOU know how important it is never to miss dinner, don't you? And you also know that it's important to eat dinner in pleasant surroundings, don't you? And what more pleasant surroundings could you ask for than Fabian? Soooo ... just to show you how much we worry about you being healthy and never missing dinner and all that jazz, we wanted to make sure you were well fed, and ... okay, we'll stop chattering and get on with the contest, since you insist!

* * * * * * * * * * * * * *
### YOU CAN WIN A DINNER DATE WITH FABIAN!
* * * * * * * * * * * * * *

Yes, you heard us right! You can actually win a fab date with this gear guy! And not only that, but you'll have the most fabulous dinner of your life at one of Hollywood's famous restaurants ... just you and Fabe! PLUS ... our KRLA photographer will be there to take pictures of every wonderful moment ... and they'll appear right here in the KRLA BEAT, so that you'll never forget the most wonderful date of your life!

### HERE'S ALL YOU HAVE TO DO:

What do you think KRLA stands for? Now don't go getting all noble on us ... we mean the letters KRLA. Does it stand for "Kool Radio, Los Angeles?" Or maybe "Kute Rita Loves Albert?" Well, don't ask us! If we tell you, WE'LL win the contest! Start thinking of the answer ... and maybe you'll be the winner!

### HOW TO ENTER

1. Write down what you think the letters KRLA stand for, and enclose this with an entry blank to Contest Corner, KRLA, Pasadena, California.
2. YOU MUST ENCLOSE A PICTURE OF YOURSELF WITH YOUR ENTRY!
3. You can make any meaning from the four letters KRLA, but it must be an understandable sentence.
4. All entries must be postmarked by December 1st, 1964. Deadline is midnight, December 1st. Entries will be judged on originality and suitability (whatever that is). Judges will be KRLA and Fabian.

**ENTRY BLANK**

NAME:............................................. AGE:..........

ADDRESS:......................................................

SCHOOL:........................................ GRADE:........

PHONE NUMBER:.............................................

# KRLA ARCHIVES

# PAUL AND RINGO —
# "GIVE US THE FACTS"

(Story in Col. 1)

# KRLA BEAT

Production, Design And Content By Bonnie Golden

*Right after KRLA made the announcement that the Beatles were rumored to be married, we got this letter from a KRLA fan who asked us to print it because she thought it summed up the feelings of all of you . . .*

### AN OPEN LETTER TO PAUL AND RINGO

Dear Paul and Ringo,

A lot of tears were shed in Los Angeles this past week. You see, KRLA received word from a friend of yours that you are both married. We haven't heard from you, so we're writing this letter . . . from Beatle fans everywhere to let you know how WE feel.

You know, when you give someone something that's very precious to you, and they throw it at your feet, it hurts. That's what you've done to us. We've given you our hearts. We buy your records, we watch you on tv, we dream about you at night. And what do you do in return? You show that you don't think enough of us, or have enough faith in us to give even a small part of yourself. Do you think we're so fickle that we would turn against you if you're married? No, we didn't cry because of the news. We cried because it came from someone else, because you didn't trust us enough to tell us yourself.

If you think we're being corny, look at it from our side. We love you. Not because you live in Liverpool or because you sing songs we like, but because of YOU . . . the way you are, the things you do, the happiness you make us feel inside every time we think of you. You're our leaders . . . just like teens before us had James Dean and before that, Rudolph Valentino. But there's never been a leader like you. You've given us something no leader has ever been able to give . . . the ability to make us laugh at ourselves. You aren't rebelling or fighting any cause. You don't tell us where to go or how to get there. You let us be ourselves . . . and maybe that's why we love you so much. You're part of us, not because we made you, but because you made us see so much more than we could ever see before. Do you honestly think that our hearts are so small, or our love so limited that we would shut you out if you admitted you were married? It hurts us to think that you feel we don't care enough to accept you on YOUR terms . . . regardless of what they are. Don't you think we deserve the respect you would show to any of your other friends? Don't you think we deserve the truth?

Okay. That's our side. Now let's look at yours.

First point . . . the news of your marriage might ruin your career. To quote Ringo's famous words, "Rubbish." First of all, you always say you couldn't
*Continued on page 3*

## KRLA TOP THIRTY

| | | |
|---|---|---|
| 1. I'M INTO SOMETHING GOOD | Herman's Hermits |
| 2. THE JERK | The Larks |
| 3. BABY LOVE | The Supremes |
| 4. OPPORTUNITY | The Jewels |
| 5. SHE'S NOT THERE | The Zombies |
| 6. LAST KISS | J. Frank Wilson |
| 7. IF YOU WANT THIS LOVE | Sonny Knight |
| 8. TIME IS ON MY SIDE | The Rolling Stones |
| 9. PRETTY WOMAN | Roy Orbison |
| 10. MOUNTAIN OF LOVE | Johnny Rivers |
| 11. EVERYTHING IS ALL RIGHT | The Newbeats |
| 12. MR. LONELY | Bobby Vinton |
| 13. SIDEWALK SURFING | Jan & Dean |
| 14. LEADER OF THE PACK | The Shangri-Las |
| 15. YOU REALLY GOT ME | The Kinks |
| 16. THAT'S WHAT LOVE IS MADE | The Miracles |
| 17. DOOR IS OPEN TO MY HEART | Dean Martin |
| 18. TOBACCO ROAD | Nashville Teens |
| 19. DANCING IN THE STREET | Martha & Vandellas |
| 20. WALKING IN THE RAIN | The Ronettes |
| 21. COME SEE ABOUT ME | The Supremes |
| 22. GOING OUT OF MY HEAD | Anthony & Imperials |
| 23. RIDE THE WILD SURF | Jan & Dean |
| 24. RINGO | Lorne Green |
| 25. I'M GONNA' BE STRONG | Gene Pitney |
| 26. BABY DON'T GO | Sonny & Cher |
| 27. OUTSIDE LOOKING IN | Anthony & Imperials |
| 28. THOU SHALL NOT STEAL | Dick & Dee Dee |
| 29. HAVE I THE RIGHT | The Honeycombs |
| 30. I DON'T WANT TO SEE YOU | Peter & Gordon |

### TOP TEN ALBUMS

1. HARD DAY'S NIGHT — BEATLES
2. MORE OF ROY ORBISON'S HITS
3. WHERE DID OUR LOVE GO — SUPREMES
4. THE ANIMALS
5. LAST KISS — J. FRANK WILSON
6. GERRY & THE PACEMAKERS/SECOND ALBUM
7. OUTSIDE LOOKING IN — ANTHONY & IMPERIALS
8. BEACH BOYS CONCERT
9. ROUSTABOUT — ELVIS PRESLEY
10. ROLLING STONES

### TOP TEN OLDIES

1. Roll Over Beethoven — Chuck Berry
2. Sun Arise — Rolph Harris
3. Sherry — The Four Seasons
4. I Walk the Line — Johnny Cash
5. We Belong Together — Robert & Johnny
6. When You Dance — The Turbans
7. Michael — The Highwaymen
8. La Bamba — Ritchie Valens
9. Stranger on the Shore — Mr. Acker Bilk
10. Battle of New Orleans — Johnny Horton

### TOP TEN UP AND COMERS

1. Forbidden — Bob Moline
2. Had Talk With My Man — Mitty Collier
3. Sha-La-La — Manfred Mann
4. Right or Wrong — Ronnie Dove
5. Dance Dance Dance — Beach Boys
6. Ask Me — Elvis Presley
7. Saturday Night at Movies — Drifters
8. Willow Weep for Me — Chad & Jeremy
9. Anyway You Want It — Dave Clark 5
10. The Monster Swim — Bobby Pickett

## HI, HULLABALOOERS!

*After reading the letter in the KRLA BEAT, I was asked for my comment. This rumor has popped up so many times that there is only one thing left for anyone to say, and that is this:*

*You say you are hurt because the boys don't trust you enough to tell you the facts. How do you think THEY feel when you show that YOU don't trust them to tell you if and when they do get married? They have denied being married on KRLA for all of you to hear. Don't you trust them enough to believe them?*

Sincerely,

DAVE HULL.

## BOOK BY EPSTEIN

HOLLYWOOD — Brian Epstein, now in town with his new discovery Tommy Quickly, has not only written his own biography, but is having a movie made about his life!

The book, titled "Cellarful of Noise," comes out November 20 and is published by Doubleday and Co. Rumor says that the reason for the name of the book is the "cellarful of noise" where Brian discovered the Beatles . . . and started his career as the most famous manager in the world.

In his book, Brian retells how he got interested in an unknown group when fans walked into his record store to ask for their record. He went to one of England's crowded cellar clubs to see them . . . they turned out to be the Beatles . . . and that's where it all began.

Although he is only 30, Brian Epstein is truly the "boy genius"
*Continued on page 3*

## KRLA ARCHIVES

# SPEND A DAY AT KRLA

Reb Foster and Gary Mack, KRLA's newest addition, look at a new ear phone together. Gary, as you know, is honorary president of the Tommy Quickly fan club.

Charlie 'O' grabs his mail after coming off the air. Charlie and Reb both just cut records, and you never heard two better sounds! Question: can a d.j. be a record star too?

It's Kaser's turn at the mike! Yes, this is the famous KRLA control room, home of the Beatles and every other top singer! Who's record is that one you're playing Casey?

Remember our straw poll? If some of you heard a funny voice taking your votes, now you know why! After all, who but the Scuzzy one would try to answer five phones at once?

Ah, ha! Who have we here? None other than Daphne of Emperor Hudson fame! (To those in the know, she's also called Sia Holliday.) Sia had her own show on KRLA.

Here we are in the record library. Dick Moreland, our record librarie listens to a new release brought over by Dave Fox. Dick hears abo twenty new releases a day!

The record library was where our straw vote took place. Dick, Reb, and some record promoters watch the girls answer phones. They didn't tell who they voted for!

Tuesday is the day all the d.j.'s meet to discuss the week ahead. Left to right: Gary Mack, Dick Moreland, Dave Hull (standing), Charlie 'O', Bob Eubanks, and Reb Foster.

Fun time! Dave shows Reb a closely guarded secret. "It's a pictu Reb . . . a picture I drew of you! What do you think of it, huh? G me your honest opinion, okay?"

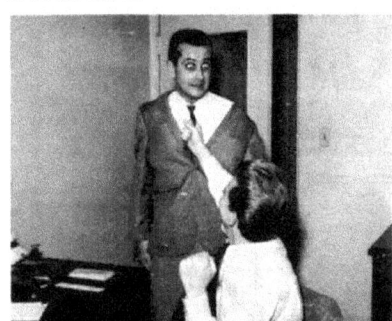

How honest can you get? No, Reb didn't really hit Dave . . . this week, the scuzzy one was wearing REB's tie! Dave and Reb are really very close friends.

In the news room, Bill McMillan and Dick Beebe discuss a KRLA breakthrough that just came over the teletype. How do you like the beard Richard Beebe is wearing?

Surprise time! Reb gets flowers and records from a friend. Being at KRLA is always exciting and fun! There's never a dull moment. (The window behind Reb is the control room.)

# KRLA ARCHIVES

## ALBUM WINNERS

Hey, how are you fixed for Beatle Albums? Not regular ones, but special albums of the Beatles talking and answering all those top secret questions you've always wondered about! Those same groovy interviews that you heard right here on good old KRLA! Not only that, but these albums are autographed by all the KRLA d.j.s and the Dave Clark Five and ... well, any other star you can think of! Personally autographed, especially for you! How can you get one? Simple! If the record store in your neighborhood doesn't carry the KRLA BEAT, just ask them to order it. IF THEY DO ORDER IT, and mention your name and address when they do, YOU'LL GET YOUR OWN AUTO-GRAPHED BEATLE ALBUM OF DAVE HULL AND JIM STECK INTERVIEWING THE BEATLES! The lucky KRLA-ers who have already won Beatle albums are:

Debbie Tearne of Tustin, Jeanette Carmichael of Alhambra, Stephanie Ringstrom and Beth Gould of Temple City, Martha Beddedict of Studio City, Macelle Halajian of Pacoima, Colleen Bliss of Canoga Park, and Simme Bobrosky of L.A. HURRY AND GET YOUR ALBUM NOW!

## Peter And Gordon Tour

NEW YORK—Peter and Gordon are set for another tour of America beginning November 15, (last Sunday), where they will start their tour by appearing on the Ed Sullivan show. No definite date has been set for an appearance in K*R*L*A*N*D, but the boys have said they want to spend a few days here to soak up some sun (?). They landed in New York on the 8th of November and spent a week in New York, where they gave press conferences and did promotion for their new record, "I Don't Want To See You Again." It will be a relaxed tour, since only ten dates are set for personal appearances at this time.

## Casey's Corner

by Casey Kasem

Hi, everyone! It's Kaser time again!

Here's some little known facts about well known people: Starting off with the Newbeats this week, bet you can't guess how they got their start! Dean and Mark, two brothers, were appearing in Louisiana, and were in the middle of a song when Larry Henley, the high voice, jumped up on stage and started singing with them. The three decided to stay together as a group, and everyone has heard the results!

Did you know that when Peter and Gordon were in town in August, Peter had such a bad case of stomach flu that he could hardly get out of bed? Yet he was still nice to everyone!

How about this for a fact! Dick and DeeDee started out being just Dick! He asked DeeDee to fill in on the B side of a record (B side means the other side of the hit side), and when the record was released, d.j.'s liked the side that DeeDee was on and made it a hit! The record of course, was "Mountains High."

That's all for this week! I'll be back in two weeks with more groovy inside facts about your favorites ... see you then!

## TOMMY QUICKLY ARRIVES

HOLLYWOOD — T.Q. Week has finally arrived! Yep, Tommy Quickly is now here in K*R*L*A*N*D! Even Brian Epstein was unprepared for the groovy reception shown by KRLA-ers to his new discovery. Tommy's record hasn't had a chance to hit the charts yet, but already his fan club numbers over 400 members! The club was started by Jeanie Anderson after she read about Tommy here in the KRLA BEAT. Gary Mack, KRLA's newest d.j. is honorary president, and one of the biggest T.Q. fans. The club really swings, and if you want to join, write to Jeanie at 1300 East Broadway, Apt. A, Glendale, California.

### NOT LIKE BEATLES

Unlike other singers who have tried to ride the Beatles' coattails to fame, Tommy is a personality in his own right. His personal appearances are complete sellouts, and when you see him, you'll know why! He is completely unselfconscious on stage, with a certain personality unlike any other star ... and he really wails!

Although Tommy is only 19, he's been singing ever since he was in high school, but he never thought of becoming a "star" until Brian Epstein discovered him at a dance, where he was auditioning. Epstein decided right then and there that he wanted to manage this boy, and it looks like Brian was right! Tommy is "quickly" becoming one of the biggest single singers that England has ever seen! Stay tuned to KRLA for all the latest news about where Tommy is staying and where you can see him.

## REB PULLS A "WIPE OUT"

HOLLYWOOD — Reb Foster, popular KRLA d.j., suffered a "wipe out" on his new motorcycle the first day he got it. Reb was heading to his house in the Hollywood Hills when his cycle skidded and he was thrown to the ground. He suffered a badly lacerated arm and several muscle sprains and bone bruises. Luckily, the bike wasn't going too fast, so Reb wasn't seriously hurt. However, he climbed right back on and drove home, although he says he plans to stay off the cycle "at least until I can move my leg again!" But nothing on earth will make him give it up, he stated, so stay tuned for further ... er, developments!

## BRIAN...

of the record business. In just three short years, he has taken over the management of most of England's top stars, including Billy J. Kramer, Gerry and the Pacemakers, Dusty Springfield, and many others.

Although the book is essentially about Brian's life story, it deals mainly with the story of the Beatles' rise to fame.

All Beatle fans will want to read this groovy book to get the REAL lowdown on their Beatles ... right from the source!

This is Tommy Quickly. Does he have what it takes? Your reaction says YES!

Tommy listens to a playback of his newest record — he's a perfectionist at his recording sessions.

To all Tommy Quickly Fan Club Members from Gary Mack, honorary President:

There will be a special press conference for all Tommy Quickly Fan Club members at the Cinnamon Cinder in North Hollywood on Friday, November 27th at 11:00 A.M. THIS PRESS CONFERENCE IS EXCLUSIVE AND FOR TOMMY QUICKLY FAN CLUB MEMBERS ONLY! If you haven't had a chance to join the club yet, temporary memberships will be given out at the C.C. if you want to get into the press conference. BE THERE ON TIME!

## OPEN LETTER

care less about your career. You say you're just having a good time. If that's true, then why are you shying away from any mention of your "marriage"? Second point, as far as ruining your career ... John is married. We've known he was married ever since that first night on the Sullivan show. You don't see him standing off in a corner all alone, do you?

Now, thinking of you, just you: A secret like marriage, if you're married, is pretty hard to keep secret. With the kind of lives you lead, the strain would probably be unbearable. You'd have to keep worrying about one wrong word, one slip. You'd have to walk on egg shells every minute. Now you've planted a doubt. We don't care what the truth is ... all we want is your answer — are you married or aren't you — yes or no.

Look, we're your friends. It's gone beyond the fan stage ... and we're mature enough to take the news that you're both real live human beings, not beautiful dolls that live in a plastic world. It's you, the real you we want. Married or not. Tell us! We don't want to hear some press agent's releases, we want the facts. We want them from YOU. Please don't let us down again ... this time, we have the right to know!

*

FOR THE KRLA BEAT EDITORIAL ON THIS SUBJECT, TURN TO DAVE HULL'S COLUMN ON PAGE ONE.

*

## KIND OLE' BOBBY D.

HOLLYWOOD — Bobby Dale, otherwise known as Benevolent Bobby, the wonder boy of the airwaves, (no wonder he's a wonder boy ... he keeps everyone wondering!) has proclaimed himself the world's foremost authority on Chuck Berry. B.B. (Benevolent Bobby) has one of the funniest shows on radio, and it's worth staying up until six in the morning just to listen. At least, that's what he says. (Really, the show is so funny that he even cracks up the engineers!)

Bobby has long been a Chuck Berry fan, although he has never met him except for a brief moment. "I touched his guitar string," he brags modestly.

When asked if he would say that Chuck Berry is his idol, Bobby replied, "I have no idols... but I guess you could say that he and Margo Lane are my favorite performers." When asked who Margo Lane is, Bobby said "Margo Lane is anybody you like. Everybody has a Margo Lane."

Bobby is "over 21," describes himself as "six feet of loving kindness, and a really beautiful guy." Although he said it before we did, in this one case, we just have to agree with him!

~~~~~~~~~~

To all of you who have been wondering if you won any of the groovy contests in the KRLA BEAT, don't miss the next issue! We'll be announcing all the winners of the 1110 contest, the Joey Paige contest, and the Dave Clark Five contest!

## BEATLE BITS

by Dick Moreland

Good old D. at the helm here ... (that means Dick Moreland, for those one or two of you out there who don't know!) Anyhow, it's Beatle Bits time again! (Yeah, yeah, yeah!)

Any person who missed the "Beatle weekend" on tv last week was either out of town or dead. Everyone I know had their eyeballs glued tight to the boob tube for the funniest hour on record! That, of course, was the Friday night show of the Beatles' first tour in America. The funny thing is, they really are that groovy and insane in person! Then the Sunday night show where they wailed for an hour ... well, if by that time everyone in California wasn't a confirmed Beatlemaniac, forget it!

Don't know if YOU know, but in case you don't (huh?) the boys' next movie will be in everlovin' color! The plot is a gass, and guess who will be the star Beatle? RINGO! The story has Ringo being followed by a killer ... it's too much!

Hard Day's Night will be released again during the Christmas vacation, so you'll get a chance to see it a few dozen more times (save me a front row seat! Also, plans are being made for an Electronovision show for the four gear guys, but no further word on this is available at this time.

Well, that's about it for this week. I'm off, with my John Lennon hat on my head and my Beatle pillow under my arm. See you in two weeks!

## ENGLISH PEN PALS

Would you like to write to other teens over in England? Would you like to catch up on the Beatles right from the source? The KRLA BEAT is making arrangements with our English contacts to get pen pals all over England for you. We won't finish making the arrangements without the most important thing ... you! We have to know if you want to write to pen pals from Britain ... so let us know! If enough of you say that you want English pen pals, KRLA will set it up and you can mail letters to the KRLA BEAT for us to send to England for you! Sorry, John, George, Paul, and Ringo are too busy to write, but you might even get their next door neighbor! Send those letters in telling us if you like the idea, and we'll do the rest!

# KRLA ARCHIVES

## PERSONALS

Do you want your personals printed? Each week, we'll print any messages you want to send through the KRLA BEAT! Just mail your message in on a post card to: PERSONALS, KRLA BEAT, 1401 South Oak Knoll Rd., Pasadena, California. Keep messages about three lines. You can say anything you want (almost) ... and it will be printed right here in the KRLA BEAT!

Brian and Keith come back! I love you both and I'll be waiting for you.
*Mickey's Pal*

Dave Hull; I love you.
*A Hulabalooer*

To Cret, Andy, Joey, and Cathy: Who likes the Stones?
*Nan*

To K.T.P./T.Q.R.:
H.G.W.A.Y.
*From N.W.V.P./S.Q.R.*

Peter Asher, where ever you are: Doe Doe loves you! But I say up with Rolling Stones and Bobby Dale!
*Musky*

Everybody support the Haunchies, 'cause they're taking over!
*A Haunchie Fan*

Greetings from Florida to all Beatle fans in L.A., especially Dorothy & Criss.
*From Marlene & Debbie*

B.E.:
I'm your bottle of Pepsi forever.
*Miss Physical*

I hugged Keith Richard of the Rolling Stones! Honest!
*Elana 11*

To Robert B. from Gloria K.:
Stop taking me for granted, 'cause you'll never get to heaven if you break my heart.

To Paul McCartney:
I love you, I love you, I love you!
And Dave Hull too!
*With Luv, Donna Dale*

Pearly Babe:
My hair is longer than Brian's, so how about saying hello?
*Tooth*

Janey: Sigh! Somewhere he's breathing! Across the Mersey! (a.M. l.i.f.)
*Eppie*

---

**KRLA BEAT'S WEEKLY FEATURE, "CONTEST CORNER" WILL NOT APPEAR THIS WEEK DUE TO LACK OF SPACE. NEXT WEEK, "CONTEST CORNER" WILL BE BACK**

---

*... This week is Thanksgiving. It's the time of year everyone's supposed to think back and count their blessings. We thought that YOU might be interested in hearing what the KRLA d.j.'s are most thankful for ...*

I'm thankful that I was able to bring the Beatles to the Southland for everyone to see!
*Bob Eubanks*

I'm thankful that I can't begin to count all the things I'm thankful for.
*Casey Kasem*

I'm thankful that I'm here at KRLA and that I'm president of the Tommy Quickly fan club.
*Gary Mack*

I'm thankful to be working at the number one station in the country and that I haven't been sued by Zsa Zsa Gabor!

*E. H.*

I'm thankful that my mother and sister are coming out here to see me.
*Charlie "O"*

I'm thankful for the opportunity to know and work with the Beatles this year.
*Reb Foster*

I'm thankful for the opportunity to know and work with Reb who worked with the Beatles.
*Dick Moreland*

I'm thankful that my hair is growing back!
*Bobby Dale*

I'm thankful that every one of you have been so nice to me this year ... you're the greatest!
*Dave Hull*

AND FROM US AT KRLA...

....HAPPY THANKSGIVING!

# KRLA ARCHIVES

# ROLLING STONES ILL, MUST CANCEL ALL SHOWS

(Story in Col. 1)

# KRLA BEAT

Production, Design And Content By Bonnie Golden

## OVERWORK HITS GROUP

LONDON — The Rolling Stones, second most popular group in the world, have been forced to cancel all personal appearances due to complete exhaustion and illness among all members of the group. Although none of the Stones are now in serious condition, their doctors have confined them to complete bed rest for at least two weeks.

**BRIAN ILL**

Brian Jones was the most seriously ill member of the group. While in New York, he came down with a cold, but refused to cancel out on any of the Stones' personal appearances. By the time the group was ready to leave New York, Brian's cold had turned into pneumonia, and he was rushed to the hospital.

**KEITH COLLAPSES**

The group was scheduled to do a show the next day, even though Brian couldn't make it. While they were rehearsing, though, Keith collapsed from complete physical exhaustion and the show had to be postponed. Keith was put into the hospital for a rest, and will be out in a few days. After Keith's collapse, Andrew Oldham, the group's manager, insisted that Mick, Bill and Charlie each have a complete physical examination. The doctor who examined the boys said that they were all overworked and should have at least two weeks rest before continuing their grueling 3 month personal appearance tour. Although the boys were anxious to get back on the road, their manager insisted the boys relax for the two weeks. "If it were up to them," Oldham said, "They'd keep going till they all dropped. They don't want to disappoint anyone, and they never even think of themselves when there's a show to do. I've seen those boys go on when they haven't slept in days,

*Continued on Page 4*

## KRLA TOP THIRTY

1. THE JERK ................. The Larks
2. TIME IS ON MY SIDE ........ The Rolling Stones
3. I'M INTO SOMETHING GOOD ... Herman's Hermits
4. OPPORTUNITY ............... The Jewels
5. SHE'S NOT THERE ........... The Zombies
6. IF YOU WANT THIS LOVE ..... Sonny Knight
7. BABY LOVE ................. The Supremes
8. MR. LONELY ................ Bobby Vinton
9. OUT OF MY HEAD ............ Little Anthony & Imperials
10. COME SEE ABOUT ME ........ The Supremes
11. WALKING IN THE RAIN ...... The Ronettes
12. OH, PRETTY WOMAN ......... Roy Orbison
13. BABY DON'T GO ............ Sonny & Cher
14. THOU SHALT NOT STEAL ..... Dick & DeeDee
15. LAST KISS ................ J. Frank Wilson
16. LEADER OF THE PACK ....... The Shangri-Las
17. MOUNTAIN OF LOVE ......... Johnny Rivers
18. SIDEWALK SURFIN .......... Jan & Dean
19. COME A LITTLE BIT CLOSER . Jay & Americans
20. EVERYTHING'S ALRIGHT ..... The Newbeats
21. I'M ON THE OUTSIDE ....... Little Anthony/Imperials
22. RINGO .................... Lorne Greene
23. DOOR IS STILL OPEN ....... Dean Martin
24. RIDE THE WILD SURF ....... Jan & Dean
25. DANCE, DANCE, DANCE ...... The Beach Boys
26. UNLESS YOU CARE .......... Terry Black
27. I'M GONNA BE STRONG ...... Gene Pitney
28. THAT'S WHAT LOVE IS MADE OF .. The Miracles
29. NEEDLE IN A HAYSTACK ..... The Velvelettes
30. I DON'T WANT TO SEE YOU .. Peter & Gordon

## TOP TEN ALBUMS

1. HARD DAY'S NIGHT ........ BEATLES
2. SOMETHING NEW ........... BEATLES
3. ALL SUMMER LONG ......... BEACH BOYS
4. BEACH BOYS CONCERT
5. MORE OF ROY ORBISON'S HITS
6. WHERE DID OUR LOVE GO ... SUPREMES
7. TRINI LOPEZ - LIVE AT BASIN STREET EAST
8. THE ANIMALS
9. WALK, DON'T RUN, VOL. 2 . VENTURES
10. BOBBY VINTON'S GREATEST HITS

## TOP TEN OLDIES

1. Devil or Angel ............ Bobby Vee
2. Point of No Return ........ Gene McDaniels
3. Ghost Riders in the Sky ... Ramrods
4. Whole Lotta' Shakin' Goin' On .. Jerry Lee Lewis
5. Heartbreak Hotel .......... Elvis Presley
6. He's Sure the Boy I Love .. The Crystals
7. Tutti-Fruitti ............. Little Richard
8. Kisses Sweeter Than Wine .. Jimmie Rodgers
9. Why Do Fools Fall in Love . Frankie Lymon
10. Rock Around the Clock .... Bill Haley

## TOP TEN UP AND COMERS

1. You've Lost That Lovin' Feelin' ...... Righteous Brothers
2. Right or Wrong ........ Ronnye Dove
3. Ask Me ................ Elvis Presley
4. Forbidden ............. Bob Moline
5. Sha La La ............. Manfred Mann
6. Google Eye ............ Nashville Teens
7. Wild One .............. Martha & The Vandellas
8. Amen .................. The Impressions
9. Talk To Me Baby ....... Barry Mann
10. How Sweet It Is ...... Marvin Gaye

## HI, HULLABALOOERS!

Well, I suppose you've all stuffed yourselves for Thanksgiving last week . . . in fact, to those of you who sent me all your old bones for my junkie float, THANKS A LOT! Geesh! This place smells like an old garbage heap . . . I didn't know there was that much junk in California! "YEAH, BIG BOY . . . THANKS FOR KICKING ME OFF YOUR FLOAT!" Now really, Maud! "I'M INSULTED! GOODBYE FOREVER!" Hey, you mean that? Gee, thanks! Anyhow, now that she's gone, I really want to thank all of you for giving me all your old junk. To the two of you who sent that skunk, I'll deal with you later . . . after I've washed my clothes! Anyhow, I just want to tell you that I'll be looking for you on my float. NO, NO, I don't mean I'll look for YOU on my float, I mean I'll look for you while I'M on the float . . . I mean, oh, forget it!

Anyhow, I'm going home to get a nice long rest before I have to climb up on all that junk . . . but seriously, thanks to all of you for sending it in! See you next week!

## TOMMY QUICKLY

HOLLYWOOD — Tommy Quickly has proved that you don't have to have a hit to be a star! Ever since his arrival in K*R*L*A*N*D, mobs of KRLA-ers have followed him whereever he goes. Tommy's press conference was a huge success . . . it was the first press conference of its kind, exclusive for fans only. No other artist has ever set up a special press conference for fans only, and everyone who went to the bash at the C.C. really appreciated Tommy and Brian Epstein for being so nice.

# KRLA ARCHIVES

## BOB'S BASH — A

The three KRLA d.j.'s check off the acts . . . everyone's here but the D.C. Five, who will arrive later. Bob, Dick, and Dave listen to the screams from the audience . . . and the show hasn't even started!

Bob Eubanks introduces the first act, who are the Vibrants. They appear every night at Bob Eubanks' Cinnamon Cinder in Long Beach and really tear everyone up. They're great!

The Scuzzy one announces Round Robin. Dave always gets a bigger hand than some of the stars of the shows! In fact, when he introduced his mother in the audience, she nearly got mobbed! (So did Dave!)

Round previewed his new song, and everyone liked it. They liked Round, too, and the applause showed it! For all his "roundness" he can really rip it up on stage, and does, time after time! His new one is good!

The Standells and Joey Paige read the latest copy of the KRLA BEAT. Left to right: Larry Tamblyn, Gary Laine, Tony Valentino, Dick Dodd, and Joey. Dick was a Mousekateer!

The Dave Clark Five finally arrived! The first thing they saw was THEIR issue of the BEAT, and they were really excited! Dave sent a copy to his mother, and they asked for more issues for everyone back home!

Wonder why all three d.j.s are out on stage! Could it be . . . yes, it is! It's D.C. Five time! You couldn't even hear the d.j.'s announce the boys, 'cause everyone started screaming! (Wonder why?)

Dave took his place at his drums, gave a smile, and they started singing. The flashing lighting added to the exciting act. Dave started playing drums at 9, and it really paid off in a big way, didn't it!

Photography by ROBIN HILL

## KRLA ARCHIVES

# GREAT SHOW AND THE D.C. 5 TOO!

Next were the O'Jays . . . a really great group! They sang Lonely Drifter and other groovy R 'n' B numbers. The group is made up of all local boys, but chances are they won't stay local long!

Dave Hull shows the Standells his horn . . . are they trying to tell him something? This group stole the show and got more applause than anyone! They were so fab that everyone at the show just flipped!

Dick Moreland shows that Dave isn't the only one who can make a toot in the world! For a surprise, Dick plays a mean sax! And guess who's sax that one is! Uh, huh! Dick tore the D.C. Five up!

Dave announces Joey Paige, the next act. Joey's fan club was there in full force, and the Vibrants, who have worked with him before, did a great job of backing!

Joey's Beatle-type hair won the hearts of everyone! He's one of the fastest rising young stars around! If you were lucky enough to see him, you'll know why! He's very close with the Rolling Stones, too!

Uh, oh, what's this! Believe it or not, it's a policeman putting the "cuffs" on Jim Steck! No, it wasn't because Jim was bad, but because Jim wanted to see how they felt! Now he knows!

The D.C. 5 with Bob, Dick, and Dave read the whole thing through! Doesn't Bob look like he could be one of the group! His suit was exactly like their jackets, and they teased him about it!

Smile pretty, boys! Mike covers Rick so that you can't see his hair . . . "I don't want anyone to know that it's longer than mine," he said! The boys were full of fun and clowned with the d.j.'s.

Dave Clark contest winner Janice Sutliff holds Dave's drumsticks. While Dave didn't have time to teach her how to play, he did show her how to hold them! Rick even gave her a smooch, and Janice didn't complain!

Mike was the one all the girls flipped for. He kept smiling and waving to everyone throughout the act. You can bet that everyone he waved to waved back, too! The boys left right after the show.

When they did "Anyway You Want It," everyone cheered. It was the song that everyone wanted to hear, and is really hitting big on KRLA. Even other stars watched them!

The great variety in their act won many fans for the boys. They did all their hit songs, one after the other. Here you can see Mike waving to one of his fans. They left town the next day.

# KRLA ARCHIVES

DUE TO THE LACK OF SPACE BECAUSE OF THE PICTURE SPREAD IN THIS ISSUE, THE PERSONAL COLUMN WILL NOT APPEAR THIS WEEK. IT WILL RESUME NEXT WEEK AS USUAL. SO SEND 'EM IN!

## FAX... ON... WAX!

### By REB FOSTER

It's time for all the latest happenings in the wax world, so let's get going!

The Beatles will release an album the day after Christmas called "Beatles '65," and it will have seven tunes written by John and Paul.

The Dave Clark Five were scheduled for an appearance in Australia this January, when the news got out that the Rolling Stones and Roy Orbison would be doing a show at the same time. So many tickets were sold for the Stones show that the D.C. 5 had to cancel the whole tour! They really dig the soul sound in Australia! By the way, if you want to write to the Stones, their address is 147 Ivor Court, Gloucester Road, London, England.

The Beatles new album, which won't even be released until December 4th, sold over 550,000 one week after the news about the album was announced!

The Dave Clark Five will be back in Hollywood in January for three months to shoot their movie, "The Dave Clark Story." Sounds as though it'll be a 'Hard Day's Night' for the five!

Did you know that Paul McCartney played piano on Peter & Gordon's record of "I Don't Want To See You Again"? That's one of the grooviest sidemen on record! (Please forgive that pun).

That closes it out for this week! See you in two weeks with more FACTS ON WAX!

## CONTEST WINNERS

*These are the winners of the KRLA BEAT contests! If you haven't won yet, don't worry... there's going to be so many more groovy contests that everyone HAS to win sometime!*

WINNERS OF THE 1110 RECORDS AND AUTOGRAPH CONTEST: Jo Thirloway, Karen Merkler, Karen Terry, Nancy Dickson, Janet Fisher, Lori De Cigaran, Gary Ayres, Laura Carey, Lillian Inorgan, Marilyn Walker, Margret Garcia, Betty Jean Armijo, Rose Frenzel, Judi Fifer, Stephanie Ringstrom, Cathy O'Bryan, Bonnie Russell, Jan Weiss, Mary Porter, Kathy Connell.

WINNERS OF THE JOEY PAGE CONTEST: 1st Prize: Donna Slate; 2nd Prize, Kathy Getty.

WINNER OF THE DAVE CLARK FIVE CONTEST:
1st Prize: Janice Sutliff, 2nd Prize: Sheryl Kunkle, 3rd Prize: Marilyn Walter.

## RECORD REVIEW

### By BOB EUBANKS

There are so many groovy records to talk about this week that I don't know where to get started!

First on the list, and best, if you ask me, is the new one by Gerry & The Pacemakers, "I'll be There." This just has to be the best sound Gerry has ever had, and he'll have to go a long way to beat it. With every record, I like this group more and more!

Even though this one isn't new, (it's been a KRLA exclusive for nearly two weeks), it's still the best sound by any American artist I've ever heard. You all know which one... the Righteous Brothers with "You've Lost That Lovin' Feeling." Wow, that's all I can say! These boys should be dipped in gold for even singing such a gassy record!

The Manfred Mann Group, who are in town this week, are causing lots of action with "Sha La La." It's hard to believe that this English group is English, they have such an American R 'n' B sound!

I'm not even going to say anything about the Beatle newie. The record has already sold a million, and I personally think "She's A Woman," sung by Paul, is the greatest song they've ever done. Leave it to the Beatles!

Well, on that note (hah) I'll close for this week. See you in two weeks!

## STONES...

when they've been so tired that they could hardly stand up, yet they'll go on stage and put on a show that few artists, rested or not, could do."

The Beatles, who have stated many times that the Rolling Stones are not only their favorite group, but their "favorite people," have been spending a lot of time with the Stones since they returned to England. "If they hadn't been forced to stay at home," said John, "We wouldn't have even seen them till Christmas!"

Reb Foster and Burt Jacobs listen to a playback at the Standell's recording session last week. Burt manages the Standells, and is one of Reb's closest friends.

## CONTEST CORNER!

Are you tired of walking home from school all alone? Do people snicker at you as you board that dingy old yellow school bus at three o'clock? Well, now you can end all that! Yep, trust the KRLA BEAT to come up with the answer! No, we aren't going to give you a 1965 convertible! Or a new 1965 skateboard, either! But we ARE going to make sure you don't have to go home alone! How? Well, maybe we'll give you a little puppy dog to trot along beside you. Or maybe we'll send a record star to walk or ride you home. Would you like that? You would? Well, if you'd like that, would you like four record stars? Okay, don't shout at us, we know you would! And because we do know it, we're giving away, not one, not two, but FOUR Record Stars to walk you home from school. Here's how it'll be:

School lets out. You stand on the steps looking all forlorn. Suddenly, you hear a beep! It's coming from a bright red new Mustang convertible with the top down. And inside that new red car is... WOW! Four of the grooviest boys you've ever seen! And they're going to drive you home! Who are they?

### *The Standells!!*

YES, YOU CAN WIN THE STANDELLS TO DRIVE YOU HOME FROM SCHOOL! AND THE SECND PRIZE IS NEARLY AS GREAT!

YOU CAN ALSO WIN THE DAVE CLARK FIVE'S COKE CUPS!

*When the D.C. 5 did their show at Long Beach, they all had a coke before going on. KRLA BEAT gathered up these empty cokes, put 'em in a box, and saved 'em for you! Each one is marked with the name of who drank out of it, and that's second prize! Here's all you have to do:*

*The Standells just recorded a new record about a new dance. And this dance is named after a certain star... we'll give you one hint... it's a boy! (Congratulations) Can you guess who the star is? Okay, stop yelling the answer. We can't hear you out there! Sit down and write it like you're supposed to!*

HERE ARE THE RULES OF THE CONTEST:

1. You must correctly guess what person the new dance is named after.

2. You must mail your answer in on an entry blank to Contest Corner, KRLA BEAT, 1401 South Oak Knoll, Pasadena.

3. Entries must be received no later than December 6th, 1964. See? Isn't that simple?

ENTRY BLANK

NAME: _____ AGE: _____

ADDRESS: _____

SCHOOL: _____ GRADE: _____

PHONE NUMBER: _____

# KRLA ARCHIVES

# DAVE STEALS THE SHOW FROM SANTA
(Story in Col. 1)

# KRLA BEAT

Production, Design And Content By Bonnie Golden

## DAVE IS A BIG HIT

HOLLYWOOD — Santa didn't have a chance when KRLA made the scene at the Santa Clause Lane parade November 25th! Dave Hull's junk float stole the entire show! Dave's float was made up entirely of KRLAers' contributions ... and you can guess how many KRLAers contributed, seeing that Dave Hull is the most popular d.j. in the whole world! Dave started making announcements about his float almost a month before the parade, and junk started pouring in. Doors, tractor tires, street signs, anything you can think of was mailed or brought in to the station by loyal Hullabalooers!

### KITTENS TOO!

While Dave asked for junk, he didn't ask for litter . . . but that's what someone brought him! You guessed it, a litter of . . . kittens! Dave gave the tiny cats away, saying that they might not like it on the float! The float was built the night before the parade by Dave and one of his friends, who also drove the float (dressed in a Mickey Mouse hat). The finished results were surprisingly pretty, proving once again that Hull can always make a nice something out of a worthless nothing! With the green crepe paper background, the float looked like Christmas morning (after everyone's opened their presents!)

### FIRE DEPARTMENT BURNS

The fire department threw a little cold water on the float, though ... literally! Since Dave's float was made up of "combustible materials," the Firemen insisted on hosing down the whole float, just to make sure that it couldn't catch fire! Although the water had a "dampening" effect, it didn't do too much damage to the float. In fact, the crepe paper crinkled up, making the whole thing even prettier. Dave sat on an old chair

*Continued on Page 4*

## KRLA TOP THIRTY

| # | Title | Artist |
|---|---|---|
| 1. | THE JERK | The Larks |
| 2. | OUT OF MY HEAD | Little Anthony & Imperials |
| 3. | OPPORTUNITY | The Jewels |
| 4. | COME SEE ABOUT ME | The Supremes |
| 5. | TIME IS ON MY SIDE | The Rolling Stones |
| 6. | BABY LOVE | The Supremes |
| 7. | IF YOU WANT THIS LOVE | Sonny Knight |
| 8. | SHE'S NOT THERE | The Zombies |
| 9. | I'M INTO SOMETHING GOOD | Herman's Hermits |
| 10. | MR. LONELY | Bobby Vinton |
| 11. | THOU SHALT NOT STEAL | Dick & DeeDee |
| 12. | WALKING IN THE RAIN | The Ronettes |
| 13. | BABY DON'T GO | Sonny & Cher |
| 14. | MOUNTAIN OF LOVE | Johnny Rivers |
| 15. | OH, PRETTY WOMAN | Roy Orbison |
| 16. | THAT'S WHAT LOVE IS MADE OF | The Miracles |
| 17. | LAST KISS | J. Frank Wilson |
| 18. | I'M ON THE OUTSIDE | Anthony & Imperials |
| 19. | SIDEWALK SURFIN' | Jan & Dean |
| 20. | COME A LITTLE CLOSER | Jay & The Americans |
| 21. | I FEEL FINE/SHE'S A WOMAN | The Beatles |
| 22. | RIDE THE WILD SURF | Jan & Dean |
| 23. | LEADER OF THE PACK | The Shangri-Las |
| 24. | EVERYTHING'S ALRIGHT | The Newbeats |
| 25. | RINGO | Lorne Greene |
| 26. | ANY WAY YOU WANT IT | Dave Clark Five |
| 27. | RIGHT OR WRONG | Ronnie Dove |
| 28. | HOW SWEET IT IS | Marvin Gaye |
| 29. | UNLESS YOU CARE | Terry Black |
| 30. | NEEDLE IN A HAYSTACK | The Velvelettes |

## TOP TEN ALBUMS

| # | Title | Artist |
|---|---|---|
| 1. | A HARD DAY'S NIGHT | BEATLES |
| 2. | BEACH BOYS CONCERT | |
| 3. | SOMETHING NEW | BEATLES |
| 4. | THE KINGSMEN, VOL. 2 | |
| 5. | ROUSTABOUT | ELVIS PRESLEY |
| 6. | 12 x 5 | ROLLING STONES |
| 7. | MORE OF ROY ORBISON'S GREATEST HITS | |
| 8. | WHERE DID OUR LOVE GO | SUPREMES |
| 9. | THE DOOR IS STILL OPEN | DEAN MARTIN |
| 10. | WALK DON'T RUN, VOL. 2 | VENTURES |

## TOP TEN OLDIES

| # | Title | Artist |
|---|---|---|
| 1. | Down in Mexico | The Coasters |
| 2. | Annie Had a Baby | The Midnighters |
| 3. | Sweet Nothins' | Brenda Lee |
| 4. | Maybellene | Chuck Berry |
| 5. | Shop Around | The Miracles |
| 6. | Broken Hearted Melody | Sarah Vaughan |
| 7. | Sittin' in the Balcony | Eddie Cochran |
| 8. | Blue Monday | Fats Domino |
| 9. | You Got What It Takes | Marv Johnson |
| 10. | Don't Care If Sun Don't Shine | Elvis Presley |

## TOP TEN UP AND COMERS

| # | Title | Artist |
|---|---|---|
| 1. | As Tears Go By | Marianne Faithful |
| 2. | Ain't Doin' Too Bad | Bobby Bland |
| 3. | Gonna Love You Too | Hullabaloos |
| 4. | Promised Land | Chuck Berry |
| 5. | Wild Side of Life | Tommy Quickly |
| 6. | The Richest Man Alive | Mel Carter |
| 7. | I'll Be There | Gerry & Pacemakers |
| 8. | Call and I'll Be There | P. J. Proby |
| 9. | Little Red Rooster | Rolling Stones |
| 10. | All Day & All of the Night | The Kinks |

## HI, HULLABALOOERS!

Well, this week sure passed "Quickly" (hey, laugh, that was funny!) SO IS YOUR FACE, BIG BOY! Oh no ... Maud can't leave me alone for one minute! Anyhow, I sure showed them all at the Santa Clause Lane parade! Yep, the Hullabalooser did it again! And to those of you who waited until my float was all fixed to grab your junk back, THANKS, Indian givers! By the way, whoever sent me 13 kittens ... come back and get 'em! I don't want them! Well, you may not know it, but Ringo didn't bury his tonsils after all. He gave them to me, and I'm using them for paperweights. Believe it or not, when the doctors finally got the tonsils out, they discovered why the Beatles are such a success ... the tonsils were goldplated! By the way, and this is serious (for a change) Paul's father got married two weeks ago. NO, not to Jane Asher! My goodness! I'm getting out of here ... see you next week!

## RINGO NOW FEELS FINE

LONDON — Ringo Starr, the most popular drummer in the world, is doing fine after his long awaited tonsil operation. News of the operation, which broke here in the KRLA BEAT nearly two months ago, was a great surprise to most Beatle fans. Fears were raised that the operation might make Ringo's voice change drastically, but doctors at the University College Hospital said that the only voice change, if there is any, will be less horseness in Ringo's voice. Derek Taylor, press agent for the Beatles, said that Ringo told him after the operation that now he will be able to face London's cold winters without catching cold!

# KRLA ARCHIVES

*So many letters have come in asking for more backstage scenes of the TAMI show that we couldn't resist any more! So we decided to print the pictures, but that left us with another problem... letters started pouring in asking us to run pictures on Manfred Mann when he came in town last week. Now, Since KRLA always tries to make you happy (you know us!) we decided to run the TAMI show AND Manfred... or Manfreds, if you prefer (there's five of them). When you come right down to it, what more could you want? (Okay, besides the Beatles, that is!)*

Before they leave for the show, Billy J. Kramer, Gerry Marsden, and Bonnie Golden, editor of the KRLA BEAT, looks at pictures of the giant show held by Reb Foster in October. Gerry and Billy J. helped Bonnie pick the pictures for that next issue of the KRLA BEAT!

An English group from America! The Barbarians, who really wail on stage, make their first visit to K*R*L*A*N*D to do the TAMI show. The group is from Rhode Island. Their first record, "You've Got to Understand" comes out this week, and it sounds as though it'll be a hit!

Gerry was the hit backstage! He has one of the wildest senses of humor of any star, and you just can't help but flip for him! Here, he and the Pacemakers wait in their dressing room to go onstage. Gerry said that if he can, he'll be back for a visit in January. All of you out there start crossing fingers!

Dick and Chuck Berry grab a coke. In the background is Charlie Watts... and Chuck Berry is Charlie and the other Rolling Stones' favorite singer. Bobby Dale, well known Berry fan, said later that he grabbed Chuck's old coke cup and took it home and framed it!

Jimmy Clanton was there too, and he looked so good that all the girls flipped! Jimmy and Bob Eubanks are very good friends, and Jimmy has done a lot of shows for Bob. (He said that KRLA was his favorite station, and when someone says that in a soft Southern drawl... well, you would have flipped too!

Here, Gary gets the boys on tape. (Jimmy's on the end). The boys tell Gary all about themselves. Manfred, of course, is the one with the beard, and used to be a music teacher! He has lived in America, so he's no stranger to our shores. Comparing England to America, he said, "you live faster, but we get more done!"

The boys were amazed by the KRLA BEAT. "Why don't they have something like this in England?" they asked. Maybe it's because they don't have a KRLA in England, Manfred! The boys called Dave Hull that night to say hello... they'd heard about him way over in England! They wanted to come out to the station.

# KRLA ARCHIVES

Backstage was a stargazer's heaven! Everywhere you looked you saw some of the greatest stars in the record business! Here, the Rolling Stones sign autographs before they go to their dressing room to get ready. Left to right: Keith Richards, Charlie Watts, Bill Wyman.

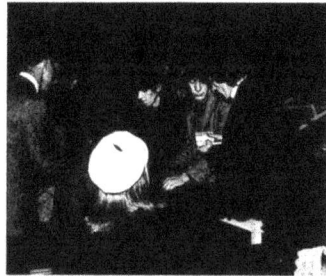

Well, well, look who's here! Dick Moreland and Dick of Dick & DeeDee to one of the Beach Boys. Dick and DeeDee weren't in the show, but D dropped over to say hello to his friends who were in the show. Dick Morel calls the Beach Boys America's answer to the Beatles!

Jan and Dean sit in their dressing room, ready to go on. They were the "master of ceremonies" of the show, and because of the way they clowned around, plans are now being made for a movie starring the two! The movie would have no plot, but would be just an average day in the life of Jan & Dean.

This IS a surprise! B.B. (Benevolent Bobby) (Bobby Dale, that is) showed up to! Actually, Bobby, who never opens his eyes while it's still daylight, was really asleep, but since he's kind of quiet anyway, nobody knew it! Bobby spent most of his time with the Rolling Stones, who are his favorite group.

The Supremes, who just had their hair done, decide to do some work on Without saying how good or bad they were, Dick was called "Old Baldy the next three days! (Just Kidding). Really, the group did a good job of s his hair, but when they started that Beatle bang bit, Dick got up and ran a

Robin MacDonald of the Dakotas looks at a program to see how long it is until the Dakotas and Billy J. go on. Robin was the quiet Dakota and tried to get some sleep between acts, but he couldn't do it! Backstage was like a fantastic party, and no one would leave him alone till he joined the fun, so he did!

The Rolling Stones get ready to go on stage. Charlie laughs at something Bill has said (You can't see Bill, he's off in the corner) while Mick checks out his appearance in the mirror. The Rolling Stones are the only group around who don't wear special outfits on stage.

Dick Moreland talks to Leslie Gore, who added female glamour to the show. Leslie has gotten so pretty lately that it's amazing! She really puts good show, and said that she wants to be a jazz singer . . . she's enough to do it, too! And now . . . on to Manfred and his Mann!!

Gary Mack, KRLA's official "meet 'em at the airport" D.J. shows a copy of the paper to Jimmy O'Neil, host of Shindig. Mike Sheppard of U.A. records holds up a copy of Manfred's new single. The airport was kind enough to allow KRLA in to see the group right after they go through customs.

Gary talks to the manager of the boys, Kenneth Pitts, while Mike Sheppard, who handled arrangements for the group, listens in. Kenneth Pitts was a publicity agent when he heard the boys and thought that they had the quality to be stars. It sure looks like he was right! They plan on staying in town for two weeks.

Now it's fan time! Representatives of the Dave Hull fan club were there to Manfred some stuffed animals and 'trolls' for good luck, and other fans there to give the group kisses . . . also for good luck! Manfred invited the to go to Shindig the next day to see them. Next week, Tommy Quickly pict

Time to relax! The boys sign autographs and chat with Gary. There were so many fans at the airport to see Manfred's Manns (ha, ha) that the boys had to be smuggled out across the field! Manfred, who said that he never takes his hat off, is very intelligent and prefers jazz to rock & roll.

# KRLA ARCHIVES

## PERSONALS

Do you want your personals printed? Each week, we'll print any messages you want to send through the KRLA BEAT! Just mail your message in on a post card to: PERSONALS, KRLA BEAT, 1401 South Oak Knoll Rd., Pasadena, California. Keep messages about three lines. You can say anything you want (almost) ... and it will be printed right here in the KRLA BEAT!

I'm sorry, Sallie, I won't call you "Blimp" again — Please forgive me!
Who - else?

Thanks for trying me again, Luv, I'll be as true as I can!!!
Sis

Bob Eubanks:
Thanks for playing loads of Stone's discs. Tell Mick, Brian, Charlie, Keith, and Bill HI for us. Luv 'em all.
Diane & Carol

Dear Dave Hull:
My sister's boyfriend who is stationed in Hawaii hates the Beatles. So if Clarance can swim, could you please sick 'im on him.
A Beatle Lover & Regular
KRLA Listener

Debbie loves you Dave Clark
A Paul McCartney Fan

Paula Dempsey, I love you and always will. Your mountain of love.
Judy Rodriguez

To Mike of La Puente: What happened between us? I'm doing the chasing this year. "Please come back!"
Desperately Waiting

Miss T. S.: Call me a Gerry if no Stones are rolling around!
J.L.

Emperor Hudson and Davey Hull should rule Calif. We all love you guys!
M.F., Arcadia

REB FOSTER'S "FAX ON WAX" AND BOB EUBANKS' "RECORD REVIEW" WILL NOT APPEAR THIS WEEK. WATCH FOR THEM IN THE NEXT ISSUE OF "KRLA BEAT."

Hey, how would you like to be the proud owner of a piece of the towel used by the Beatles on their last visit to Los Angeles? Well, you can! Jim Steck, who drove the Beatles from their performance at the Bowl, saved the towel they used to mop their faces with ... and you can own a piece of it! Jim cut the towel into pieces and had them mounted in plastic with a special back-card that certifies that it's a real piece of the Beatle's face towel!

If you want to get a piece of towel, send $1.00 and a self addressed, stamped envelope to Jim Steck at Beatle Towel, c/o Jim Steck, 23 Grace Terrace, Pasadena, California. Hurry up while the supply lasts!

## Johnny Ill

LONDON — Brian Epstein, handling star Johnny Rivers in this country before he left for America last week, was forced to cancel all dates and shows for the singer. Johnny became ill and collapsed in his hotel room. He will be out of the hospital this week, but will take it a lot easier than he has been taking it! Johnny has been on the road for three months doing one night stands, and it looks like the pace was too much for him. As soon as he is well enough to go back on tour, he will resume the tour of England. Filling in on some of the shows that Johnny was supposed to do in London is Gene Pitney.

---

IT'S THE FIRST ANNUAL KRLA BEAT AWARD! TIME WHO WILL WIN? VOTE FOR YOUR FAVORITE NOW!

*Who is the most popular record star in America? The Beatles? Or are the Rolling Stones taking over? Are the Beach Boys putting an end to the British sound? Or are the Four Seasons leading the way? Is it true that the D.C. Five are beating the Beatles? Who's REALLY on top? This is your chance to find out ... and your vote will do the choosing!*

The first annual KRLA BEAT award will be presented to the winning group, and results of all the votes received will be published in the KRLA BEAT. Each year, the KRLA d.j.'s will select the five most popular stars in the record business, groups or single artists, and nominate them for the Annual KRLA BEAT Award. Your votes will choose the winner! Now YOU can do something for your favorite star! Send your votes in to KRLA BEAT, KRLA, 1401 South Oak Knoll Rd., Pasadena, California. Results will be published one month from today!

The five stars that the D.J.'s have selected this year are:
- The Beatles
- The Rolling Stones
- The D.C. 5
- The Beach Boys
- The Four Seasons

Vote for the one you think is the top group in K*R*L*A*N*D! Maybe YOUR vote will decide who gets the award! (Use the ballot below)

- - - - - - - - - - - - - - - - -

I think the top group, the group that deserves the KRLA BEAT AWARD, are the_____

My name is_____

and I am_____years old.

## DAVE...

on top of the pile of junk, blowing his own horn, as usual. (Maud Skidmore, who wasn't allowed on the float, reportedly left town in a huff) Halfway through the parade, Dave's fans began "borrowing" souveniers, and Dave finished the parade with only half a float. "Oh, well," he said, "at least now I don't have to worry about getting rid of the darn stuff!"

---

# CONTEST CORNER!

## WIN TOMMY QUICKLY'S SHIRT!

How many times have you noticed the groovy shirt your favorite star was wearing? How many times have you tried to grab said groovy shirt, only to find that (a) The star also thought the shirt was groovy and didn't feel like letting you have it, or (b) 50 big policemen wouldn't let you get close enough to even SEE the shirt, much less make a grab for it! Well, that's all changed! Yep, KRLA BEAT knew that you wouldn't be able to snatch Tommy Quickly's shirt, so we went and snatched it for you! (Mainly because we're bigger than he is!) The shirt was a gift to Tommy from Brian Epstein, has a groovy London label on it, and best of all, has a personal message from Tommy to the winner! Now just in case you don't win first prize, but still want an autographed something, we have another surprise for you! Just as we snatched Tommy's shirt, he was reaching for a handkerchief to put in his jacket pocket. You know us! We grabbed that too! The handkerchief also has a personal message to the winner on it, and both these prizes will be won by a lucky KRLA BEAT reader! (in addition to the five third prizes ... autographed pictures of Tommy!) Here's all you have to do:

*Tommy's favorite food is a dish that was invented over in England and is fairly popular over here. But Tommy doesn't eat his favorite food like most English people ... he likes it served a very different way. Do you know how? If you want to win Tommy's shirt (didn't we tell you he'd give you the shirt right off his back?) than you'd better find out! If your's is the first correct entry we receive, Tommy's shirt will be yours!*

**FIRST PRIZE:** Tommy Quickly's own shirt!

**SECOND PRIZE:** Tommy's hankey!

**THIRD PRIZES:** For five winners, a personally autographed picture of Tommy!

Just fill out the entry blank below, mail it to KRLA BEAT, 1401 South Oak Knoll, Pasadena, California before December 15th. Then sit back and cross your fingers!

**ENTRY BLANK**

NAME:_____ AGE:_____

ADDRESS:_____

SCHOOL:_____ GRADE:_____

PHONE NUMBER:_____

I THINK TOMMY'S FAVORITE FOOD IS_____

_____, SERVED WITH_____

# KRLA ARCHIVES

# MERRY CHRISTMAS AND HAPPY NEW YEAR TO YOU

FIVE CENTS (Story in Col. 1)

## KRLA BEAT

Production, Design And Content By Bonnie Golden

## Our Christmas Card To You...

HOLLYWOOD—The old year is on its way out, and '65 is almost here. We hope its been a good year for you . . . you've sure made it a good year for us! No, we don't mean the fact that you've made us the number one radio station in Los Angeles, or the fact that so many of you became KRLAers during the year. What do we mean? Well, let's take it from the top:

**THE BEATLES**

Last year at this time, only one or two people had hopped on the Beatle bandwagon. Oh, sure, their record had been released, and it looked like "I Want To Hold Your Hand" was going to be a hit. So what? Lots of records had been hits, but no one went ape over the singer. Then, like an avalanche, Beatlemania hit America. And things began to change. Things became fun again! For so long it had been "cool" to be cool . . . to go through life without letting anything affect you. The Beatles changed all that. Suddenly, it was 'cool' to be yourself, to laugh when you wanted to, to enjoy yourself.

**JUST RIGHT FOR KRLA**

The change was perfect for us! Our d.j.s knew how to have fun over the air, and now that they had the chance to do it . . . no holds were barred! (After all, what other station in the world had d.j.s who would stow away on board a plane . . . with the Beatles helping to hide them!) If you have ever been to KRLA, you can see that to our d.j.s, working at KRLA isn't work . . . they have as much fun on the air as you do listening to them! Because of you, we've been able to bring in all the top groups, have them on the air, and start the KRLA BEAT, the first paper of its kind in the world.

That's been your Christmas present to us. It's the best gift

*Continued on Page 4*

## KRLA TOP THIRTY

| # | Title | Artist | # | Title | Artist |
|---|---|---|---|---|---|
| 1. | COME SEE ABOUT ME | The Supremes | 16. | IF YOU WANT THIS LOVE | Sonny Knight |
| 2. | I FEEL FINE/SHE'S A WOMAN | The Beatles | 17. | GOIN' OUT OF MY HEAD | Little Anthony |
| 3. | THE JERK | The Larks | 18. | NEEDLE IN A HAYSTACK | The Velvelettes |
| 4. | MR. LONELY | Bobby Vinton | 19. | RIGHT OR WRONG | Ronnie Dove |
| 5. | LOST THAT LOVIN' FEELIN' | Righteous Bros. | 20. | SHE'S NOT THERE | The Zombies |
| 6. | WALKING IN THE RAIN | The Ronettes | 21. | THAT'S WHAT LOVE IS MADE OF | The Miracles |
| 7. | BABY DON'T GO | Sonny & Cher | 22. | WILLOW WEEP FOR ME | Chad & Jeremy |
| 8. | OPPORTUNITY | The Jewels | 23. | DANCE DANCE DANCE | The Beach Boys |
| 9. | MOUNTAIN OF LOVE | Johnny Rivers | 24. | HOW SWEET IT IS | Marvin Gaye |
| 10. | LEADER OF THE PACK | The Shangri-Las | 25. | UNLESS YOU CARE | Terry Black |
| 11. | TIME IS ON MY SIDE | The Rolling Stones | 26. | AMEN | The Impressions |
| 12. | THOU SHALT NOT STEAL | Dick & DeeDee | 27. | AS TEARS GO BY | Marianne Faithful |
| 13. | I'M INTO SOMETHING GOOD | Herman's Hermits | 28. | COME A LITTLE BIT CLOSER | Jay & Americans |
| 14. | WALK AWAY | Matt Monro | 29. | SCRATCHY | Travis Wammack |
| 15. | BABY LOVE | The Supremes | 30. | REACH OUT FOR ME | Dionne Warwick |

## TOP TEN ALBUMS

| # | Title | Artist |
|---|---|---|
| 1. | 12 x 5 | ROLLING STONES |
| 2. | BEACH BOYS IN CONCERT | |
| 3. | ROUSTABOUT | ELVIS PRESLEY |
| 4. | HARD DAY'S NIGHT | BEATLES |
| 5. | WHERE DID OUR LOVE GO | SUPREMES |
| 6. | ALL SUMMER LONG | BEACH BOYS |
| 7. | BEST OF JIM REEVES | |
| 8. | VINTON'S GREATEST HITS | BOBBY VINTON |
| 9. | MORE OF ROY ORBISON'S GREATEST HITS | |
| 10. | WALK DON'T RUN VOL. 2 | VENTURES |

## TOP TEN OLDIES

| # | Title | Artist |
|---|---|---|
| 1. | Walking to New Orleans | Fats Domino |
| 2. | Let the Good Times Roll | Shirley & Lee |
| 3. | I'm Available | Margie Rayburn |
| 4. | Tragedy | The Fleetwoods |
| 5. | Smokie (pts. 1 & 2) | Bill Black Combo |
| 6. | Butterfly | Charlie Gracie |
| 7. | My True Love | Jack Scott |
| 8. | Stay | Maurice Williams |
| 9. | There's a Moon Out Tonight | The Capris |
| 10. | Guess Things Happen That Way | Johnny Cash |

## TOP TEN UP AND COMERS

| # | Title | Artist |
|---|---|---|
| 1. | I'll Be There | Gerry & Pacemakers |
| 2. | Little Red Rooster | Rolling Stones |
| 3. | All Day & All of Night | The Kinks |
| 4. | Boom Boom | The Animals |
| 5. | Give Him a Big Kiss | Shangri-Las |
| 6. | Promised Land | Chuck Berry |
| 7. | Downtown | Petula Clark |
| 8. | Look of Love | Lesley Gore |
| 9. | Keep Searchin' | Del Shannon |
| 10. | Wild Side of Life | Tommy Quickly |

## HI, HULLABALOOERS!

*This week I'd like to take the time to say something to everyone of you . . . something that comes from my heart. This year has been the most fantastic year of my life. I don't deserve the credit for it, either. YOU are the ones who have made this year so great . . . and I don't know how to thank you enough. It's hard for me to believe that you've done so much for me . . . I only wish there was some way I could tell you how thankful I am. I wish I could thank every one of you personally . . . someday, maybe I'll be able to. Those of you who have come down to the station just to see me, those of you who write so many beautiful letters, those of you who cheer for me at shows . . . you could never know how humble you make me feel. I only hope this year is as great for you as you have made it for me. Thank you . . . for everything.*

## HERMITS IN ACCIDENT

PASADENA — Herman's Hermits, of "I'm Into Something Good" and "Show Me Girl" fame, were involved in a freeway accident while on their way to visit KRLA before they left town.

The accident happened on the exit of the Pasadena freeway. They were in the car with Peter Grant, their agent, and Clive Fox, promotion man from MGM. While they were stopped for their exit, another car, who didn't see that their car was stopped, hit them from behind. The boys were all shaken up, and there was extensive damage done to the car they were riding in.

Fortunately, none of the in-

*Continued on Page 4*

# KRLA ARCHIVES

Herman and the Hermits wait for the elevator to their rooms. Left to right: Barry, Derek, 'Herman' (real name: Peter Noone) Karl, and Derek. They range in ages from 17 to 21.

How's this for a chorus line! Maybe they won't replace the Rocketts, but who cares! Of all the groups KRLA BEAT has worked with, this one was the most down to earth and unaffected. They're a real gas!

Karl and Keith grab a minute's rest while they can. The group left for England last Tuesday, but will be back April 16. (It's unbelievable how good looking they are in person!) They can't wait to be back!

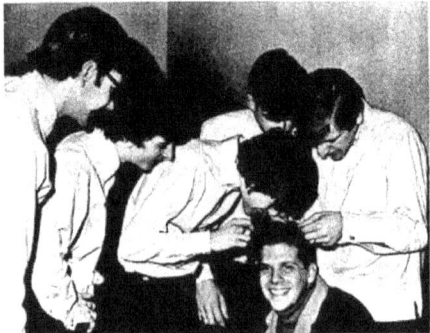
How to change an American into an Englishman in three easy lessons! Here, Herman (with the help of the Hermits) give Clive Fox, their promotion man, an "English" hairstyle. It looked good!

Guess who Herman is talking to? It's the old Scuzzy one himself! Herman had heard of Dave all the way over in England, and Dave was the first person he called when they got in! Dave talked to Herman on the air.

Herman talks to Dave, two of the Hermits read the KRLA BEAT. They were excited to see that their song was number one on KRLA! They wanted to visit KRLA so badly that they came out the next morning.

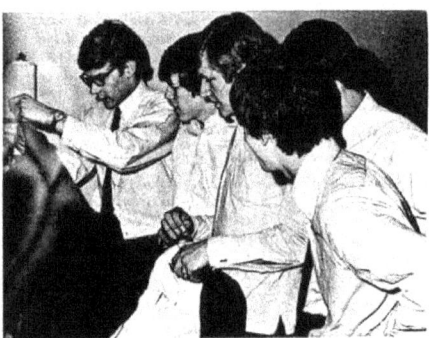
Unpacking time! "Hey, that's my jacket!" "You're out of your gourd! I packed this in New York, it's mine!" Finally, they got everything sorted out and decided to KEEP things separated next time!

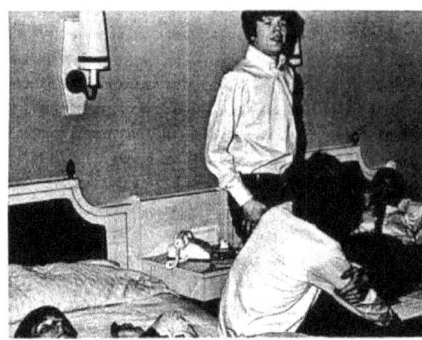
"Come on, don't poop out on me now!" Herman's all ready to go out on the town, but the only response he gets is a fishy look from the Hermits. They had come in from New York without any sleep!

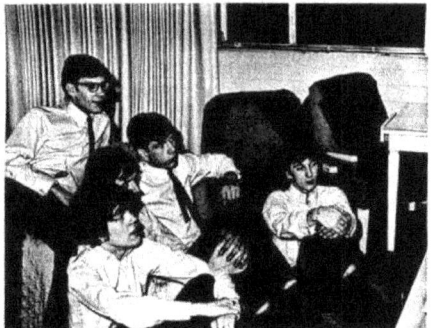
The boys sit back and prepare to spend the evening watching the American "telly" (English for tv). Believe it or not, they like the commercials! They liked Hollywood, but ... "it wasn't like we thought it would be."

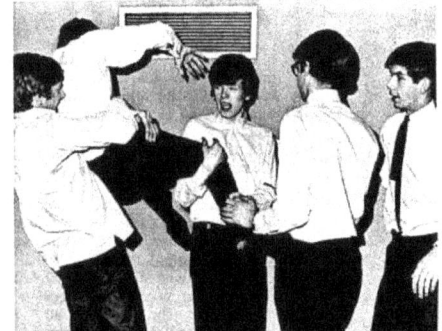
Fun time! Keith punched Herman in the back, Herman thought Karl did it and punched him, so Karl lifted Keith up and wouldn't put him down till he apologized! They're the funniest group in the world!

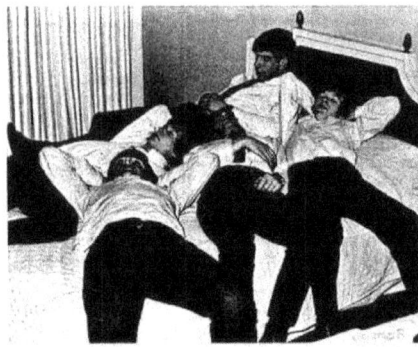
"They're always pickin' on me, just 'cause there's more of them!" The Hermits dragged Herman to the window. "We're going to throw you out, luv!" They didn't, though. "We wouldn't . . . he's nice to have around!"

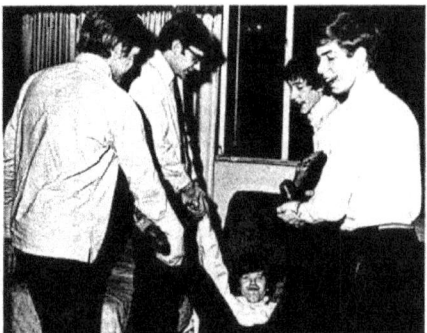
"Hey, you guys, get off my bed!" says Frank Mancini, their manager. The boys were so tired that while waiting for their rooms, they fell asleep! They looked so peaceful that no one had the heart to wake them up.

Photography by ROBIN HILL

# KRLA ARCHIVES

# KRLA ARCHIVES

## PERSONALS

Do you want your personals printed? Each week, we'll print any messages you want to send through the KRLA BEAT! Just mail your message in on a post card to: PERSONALS, KRLA BEAT, 1401 South Oak Knoll Rd., Pasadena, California. Keep messages about three lines. You can say anything you want (almost) . . . and it will be printed right here in the KRLA BEAT!

Linda,
Who wants Mr. D. when you can have A. without bad humor??? (Some finks do.) M.M. (Luv)

Paul McCartney,
I love you! I'm 'so happy you like Dave Hull! Good luck!
Luv from, M.

To T.J.
We love A. but where is T.?
M. & L.

To Jenny McCartney of Chicago:
If our Paul only knew how much we loved him, he'd go steady with both of us!
Linda McCartney of Torrance

Susie Loves Paul, Leslie loves John But I love all of them! Oh Hi! Dave Hull, we love you too!
Rosa

To the Beatles, Clark Five, and The Rolling Stones, YOUR ALL THE GEAR!!
Love, Vickie

Advice to Dave Hull:
STOP saying bad stuff about Dave Clark!!
A Beatlemaniac!

English Penpals:
Yeah
Yeah
Yeah!!!
More info please.
Kris Brown, Reseda

oT Mrs. Waring:
Thanks so much for all you've done for us.
Carole & Lynda

"Stones Forever"
Your Anaheim Fans

Dear Santa,
Please send me one KRLA and a horn just like Dave Hull's for Xmas.
Gina

We luv you Mick and Keith, please come back to L. Ce.
Two "Stone" fans,
Nifty & Carole

I know no one is asking me for my opinion but lets face it the Beatle-records are tough but, the Beatles themselves are "HAS BEENS"
"D.C. 5 RULE"

Reed, eels, and Ericksons! Surprise! Happy December 7th, Beatle Day!
Beatlemaniac, Ricketts!

Warren Pemberton, Keep your mojo working on Denise. Say Hello to Brian Jones too.
Denise

To George Harrison,
I'll always love you! If I don't get you in my Christmas stocking, wait for me. I'll see you in '68.
I love you, LJC.

---

REB FOSTER'S "FAX ON WAX" AND BOB EUBANKS' "RECORD REVIEW" WILL NOT APPEAR THIS WEEK. WATCH FOR THEM IN THE NEXT ISSUE OF "KRLA BEAT."

---

SEND ALL MAIL TO OUR NEW MAILING ADDRESS:
KRLA BEAT
P.O. BOX 702-M
PASADENA, CALIFORNIA

## TO YOU...

anyone could give. We, in return, will give the only thing we can give . . . ourselves. To all of you out there . . . one last thing . . . Merry Christmas . . . and the happiest of New Years!

## HERMITS...

juries required hospitalization. Barry and Derek, of the Hermits, suffered sprained necks, and Herman and Peter Grant, who were in the front seat, both had sprained ankles. Most seriously injured was Clive Fox, who suffered a bad whiplash. The boys were able to make their visit to KRLA a few hours later, and went home to England the next day.

---

And here is our Christmas gift to you! A personal Christmas greeting from the Rolling Stones and Herman's Hermits, autographs that you can cut out and hang on your wall, put in your wallet, or do . . . well, whatever you want to do with them! And below that are some more English Pen Pals, eight groovy Beatle-landers who dig hearing from American pen friends!

Pat
15 Sydney Grove
Gunholme Estate
Walkend on-Tyne
Northumberland, England

Maryilyn Yeoman
The Garage Flat
Abbotsworthy House
Kingsworthy
Winchester, Hants
England

Marilyn Zegar
So. St. Gregory's Crescent
Gravesend, Kent
England

Sheila Ash
23 Waylane Ave.
Datskon Lane
Hackney E. B London
England

Michael P. Bradman
35 Knolton Way
Wescham Court Estate
Slough Bucks, England

Miss J. Tomes
35 Lower Hillmorton Road Rugby
Warwickshire, England

Christoper A. Langley
Desford Boys School
Desford, Nr. Leicester
England

Lynn Mouldie
62 George Rd.
Chingford, London E.H.
England

## KRLA ARCHIVES

# NEW HULLABALOO SHOW WITH BRIAN EPSTEIN

FIVE CENTS  (Story in Col. 1)

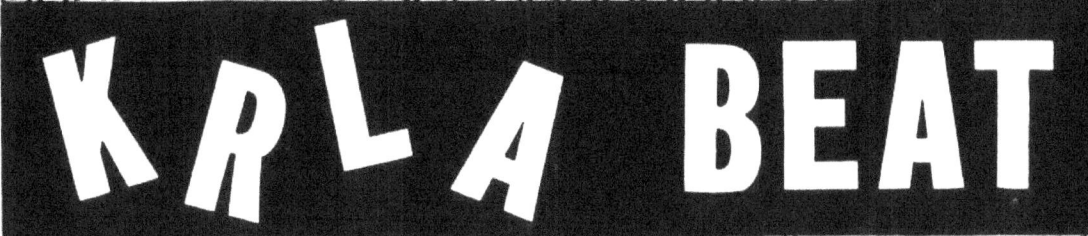

HI, HULLABALOOERS!

## Part Filmed From England

LONDON—A new show called (of all things) "HULLABAL-LOO" will start soon on tv! The new show will be sort of an English version of Shindig, and will be taped partly in England and partly in New York. It will be shown in color, and will be a showcase for some of the English groups who have not yet had a hit in this country, as well as the top hit groups who are chartbusters both in this country and England.

### EPSTEIN TO HOST

MC of the new show will be Beatle manager Brian Epstein, who will host the segment of the show filmed in London. It will have one English act in that country every week, however, Epstein says that as of this date, he has no plans for the Beatles to appear on the show. "One of the first acts will be Gerry and the Pacemakers," Brian told the KRLA BEAT, "and Marianne Faithful will probably be next. I want to have a lot of the 'beat' groups that aren't really big in your country, but are hits in England. Some of these groups are already signed up for the show, for example, Freddie and the Dreamers, The Rebel Rousers, Cliff Bennet, and groups like that. And of course, Tommy Quickly will be there too!"

### MOVIES TOO

Aside from the tv show, Epstein will also produce more movies starring his groups. One movie in particular, "Ferry Across the Mersey," starring Gerry & the Pacemakers and Cilla Black, will be released in this country in another month. "I want to do a few dramatic movies, just to show that some of these groups can do more than sing. I think serious movies, without singing, might go over very well if you had a star with the personality for example, of the Beatles."

## KRLA TOP THIRTY

1. I FEEL FINE/SHE'S A WOMAN .......... The Beatles
2. LOST THAT LOVIN' FEELIN' .......... Righteous Bros.
3. MR. LONELY .......... Bobby Vinton
4. COME SEE ABOUT ME .......... The Supremes
5. I'M INTO SOMETHING GOOD .......... Herman's Hermits
6. WALK AWAY .......... Matt Monro
7. THE JERK .......... The Larks
8. WALKING IN THE RAIN .......... The Ronettes
9. BABY LOVE .......... The Supremes
10. MOUNTAIN OF LOVE .......... Johnny Rivers
11. IF YOU WANT THIS LOVE .......... Sonny Knight
12. GOING OUT OF MY HEAD .......... Anthony & Imperials
13. LEADER OF THE PACK .......... The Shangri-Las
14. BABY DON'T GO .......... Sonny & Cher
15. OPPORTUNITY .......... The Jewels
16. SHE'S NOT THERE .......... The Zombies
17. TIME IS ON MY SIDE .......... Rolling Stones
18. WILLOW WEEP FOR ME .......... Chad & Jeremy
19. DANCE DANCE DANCE .......... Beach Boys
20. SIDEWALK SURFING .......... Jan & Dean
21. UNLESS YOU CARE .......... Terry Black
22. RIGHT OR WRONG .......... Ronnie Dove
23. AS TEARS GO BY .......... Marianne Faithful
24. COME A LITTLE CLOSER .......... Jay & The Americans
25. LEADER OF THE LAUNDROMAT .......... The Detergents
26. THAT'S WHAT LOVE IS MADE OF .......... The Miracles
27. THOU SHALT NOT STEAL .......... Dick & DeeDee
28. NEEDLE IN A HAYSTACK .......... The Velvelettes
29. ANYWAY YOU WANT IT .......... Dave Clark Five
30. LAST KISS .......... J. Frank Wilson

### TOP TEN ALBUMS

1. BEACH BOYS IN CONCERT
2. 12 x 5 .......... ROLLING STONES
3. HARD DAY'S NIGHT .......... BEATLES
4. SOMETHING NEW .......... BEATLES
5. THE BEATLES' STORY
6. WHERE DID OUR LOVE GO .......... SUPREMES
7. A BIT OF LIVERPOOL .......... SUPREMES
8. IT HURTS TO BE IN LOVE .......... GENE PITNEY
9. YOU REALLY GOT ME .......... KINKS
10. LOUIE, LOUIE .......... KINGSMEN

### TOP TEN OLDIES

1. I Want to Hold Your Hand .......... The Beatles
2. My Guy .......... Mary Wells
3. She Loves You .......... The Beatles
4. Louie Louie .......... The Kingsmen
5. Where Did Our Love Go .......... The Supremes
6. Baby Love .......... The Supremes
7. Out of Limits .......... The Marketts
8. I Get Around/Don't Worry Baby .......... Beach Boys
9. Oh, Pretty Woman .......... Roy Orbison
10. Dawn (Go Away) .......... The Four Seasons

### TOP TEN UP AND COMERS

1. I'll Be There .......... Gerry & Pacemakers
2. Promised Land .......... Chuck Berry
3. Makin' Whoopee .......... Ray Charles
4. Downtown .......... Petula Clark
5. Boom Boom .......... The Animals
6. Richest Man Alive .......... Mel Carter
7. Give Him a Big Kiss .......... Shangri-Las
8. Keep Searchin' .......... Del Shannon
9. My Love Forgive Me .......... Robert Goulet
10. Too Many Fish in Sea .......... Marvelettes

*Well, how was your Goo Year? After listening to our exclusive Christmas message from the Beatles, I got sick from laughing so hard. "YOU LOOK SICK, BIG BOY!"* Good grief, Maud, I though you were going to leave me alone for one solid month as a Christmas gift! *"COULDN'T DO THAT, LUV!"* Wow, the things a young, handsome d.j. has to put up with! Anyhow, I hope you all heard my record . . . (how could you miss it!) Yes, five of my loyal Hullabalooers went out and wrote a song for me! Now don't all of you go out and start writing songs just for me! Except, of course, if you're the Beatles! Then you can do anything you want to do! (If I had their money, I'd do anything I wanted to do too!) Anyhow, see you next week!

### NEW COLUMN FOR BEAT

HOLLYWOOD—Starting next month and appearing once a month, DeeDee Sperling, of Dick and DeeDee fame, will write a special column for the KRLA BEAT! Dick and DeeDee just returned from a tour of England, where DeeDee met and became close friends with many English groups such as the Rolling Stones. DeeDee's column will tell KRLA-ers all about the stars she travels with, and will let you in behind the scenes on the gear happenings while Dick & DeeDee are on tour! If you want the inside scoop on any group, or have any questions

# KRLA ARCHIVES

It's Santa Claus time again! And Dave Hull, who decided to get even with the boss for not giving him $5000.00 for a measly old Santa Parade float, built a junk float to get even!

Guess who else was in the parade! The Emperor himself (in his gold Rolls Royce, of course). With him were some very pretty models, who were overawed at being that close to the great emperor!

The floats pull out, and the parade begins. Emperor Hudson waves to all his loyal subjects, who are wishing he would have thrown money instead. The "Emperor" suit is real gold!

Loyal Hullabalooers were there in full force . . . with signs proclaiming how much they loved the Hullabalooer! Dave never has so much fun in his life as he did reading the signs!

"LET'S HEAR IT FOR ME!" Dave and his horn are so well known that the float was the most popular one in the whole parade! Dave was touched by the loyalty you all showed him and "loves you all!"

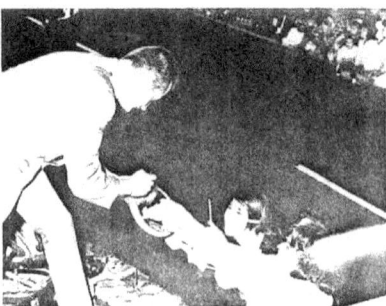
Dave signs autographs for fans who run out to the float. Dave is never too busy to have time for a kind word, and spends more time with his fans than any d.j. in the world!

An overanxious fan jumps up on the float to give Dave a personal Christmas greeting! Dave would have let her ride the rest of the way w htihim, but other girls started jumping on the float, so he couldn't

The Hullabalooer gets mobbed! Everyone wanted a personal souvenir of the Santa Claus Lane Parade, and what better souvenir could they ask for than part of Dave's float?

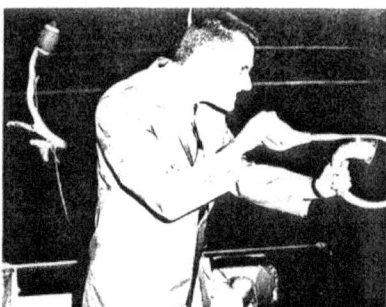
"Back! Back, I say, all you Hullabalooers! You can't have my float!" Dave toots his horn at them, but it didn't work! By the time the parade was over, all he had left was . . .

. . . a pile of . . . JUNK! But instead of getting mad, Dave even helped the Hullabalooers take the junk, and handed them the parts they couldn't reach! He's really great!

In the meantime, the Emperor and his Gold Rolls Royce went riding along, surveying his subjects. The Emperor was cheered along the whole parade route, and can't wait till next year!

Dave is astonished at THIS sign! He wants to give his special thanks to all of you who spent the time making those signs, and also hopes you'll all be there for the parade next year.

# KRLA ARCHIVES

The floats pull out, and the parade begins. Emperor Hudson waves to all his loyal subjects, who are wishing he would have thrown money instead. The "Emperor" suit is real gold!

You didn't know that Reb Foster was a singer too, did you! Well, he is now! Of course, the KRLA BEAT was there to cover Reb's first recording session, and it looks as though we caught him by surprise!

Dave signs autographs for fans who run out to the float. Dave is never too busy to have time for a kind word, and spends more time with his fans than any d.j. in the world!

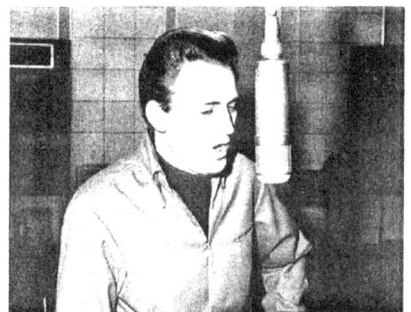

"Something you got . . . makes me spend all my pay . . ." Reb puts a lot of soul into the old blues number. Most singers at their first session have to do take after take, but Reb got done in three!

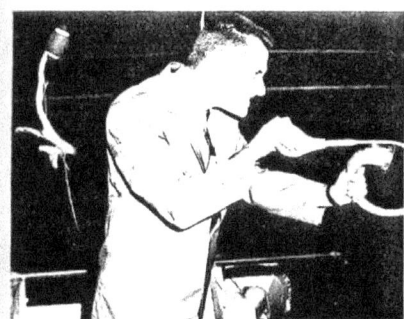

"Back! Back, I say, all you Hullabalooers! You can't have my float!" Dave toots his horn at them, but it didn't work! By the time the parade was over, all he had left was . . .

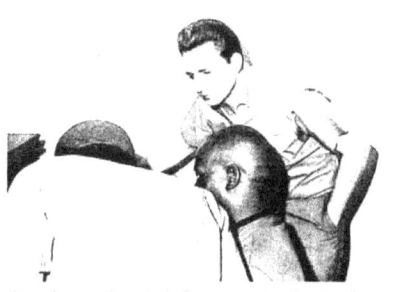

Sonny changes a few notes in the arrangement as the piano player and Reb look on. The record will be out in a few weeks. Wouldn't it be funny if Reb made it his D.J. pick?

Dave is astonished at THIS sign! He wants to give his special thanks to all of you who spent the time making those signs, and also hopes you'll all be there for the parade next year.

Reb finishes the last note . . . and by the happy smile on his face, we know that this one was it! It came out even better than everyone had expected and looks like a hit!

# KRLA ARCHIVES

Sonny Buono, of Sonny & Cher was the a and r man at the session. (An a and r man directs a session like a director directs a play) Here Reb talks to Cher as the musicians warm up.

"Sing into this?" Reb waits for the GO sign. He recorded a song called "Something You Got," and it's a real winner! Reb sounds a lot like Buddy Holly, who was also a friend of Reb's.

"I don't like the way that one sounded . . . let's try it again." This is the most tension filled part of any session . . . getting that one good "take." Reb stayed pretty calm, though!

Sonny Buono and Reb listen anxiously to the playback. In the left corner is the engineer, who handles the controls. Sonny also played the harmonica background on the record.

Eddie Mosely, a good friend of Reb's, gives him his opinion of the session so far. Eddie is a record promoter and knows a lot about records. In the background are some of the controls.

One last take! Things are going fine so far . . . will this one be it? Everyone watching had their fingers crossed, because this one sounded really good! Reb was still relaxed . . . nothing shakes him!

Surprise! Look who showed up to see how things were going! It's Cecil and Gail Tuck! They thought the record sounded great, and Gail even said that as soon as it came out, she would buy it.

Sonny Buono, Reb, and Sonny's partner, Charlie Greene, listen to the final playback. All that remains now is the final "fixing up," called mastering, and the record is ready to be released!

# KRLA ARCHIVES

## PERSONALS

Do you want your personals printed? Each week, we'll print any messages you want to send through the KRLA BEAT! Just mail your message in on a post card to: PERSONALS, KRLA BEAT, 1401 South Oak Knoll Rd., Pasadena, California. Keep messages about three lines. You can say anything you want (almost) . . . and it will be printed right here in the KRLA BEAT!

I'm sorry Rosanna luv, I won't call you "Ringo" anymore.
*Dean F.*

Dave Hull: We luv you, but remember to mention Westchester!!
*Mary*

Mick — Janie thinks of you when she opens her closet, but I think of you when I see cookies! (or half)

To John Stevenson of Alhambra High. I like you a lot!!
*A Alhambra Admirer*

Pat:
J.P. will be as famous as the R.S. and B. Just takes time.
*The girl at the TAMI show*

Mary from Portola:
Quit winning all those contests.
*The loser*

## RECORD REVIEW

**By BOB EUBANKS**

Although it's been on KRLA's play list for a few weeks, the Shangri-Las "GIVE HIM A GREAT BIG KISS" still flips me! I say it's love, I mean L-U-V with that one!

"LITTLE RED ROOSTER," by the Stones, is still KRLA's exclusive, and has some of the greatest guitar work I've ever heard. When asked about the record, Mick Jagger, who does the lead singing, said "We've been talking about doing a rhythm and blues record for so long that it was time we did something about it." Wow, they sure did! Don't fret, though, it may still be released in this country!

The Kinks new one, "ALL DAY AND ALL OF THE NIGHT" is the best effort yet by the boys. Its rough blue sound is going to win a lot more fans for the English group.

Watch for a new country on the Music scene . . . Ireland! No, I'm not kidding! Ireland has long been the home of 'show bands,' rocking groups that are mostly instrumental and don't sing. These groups are catching on like wildflower in England, which means it won't be long until the craze spreads to this country.

That's it for this week! See you in two!

## DEEDEE...

you want DeeDee to answer in her column, write to DeeDee in care of the KRLA BEAT, P. O. Box 702-M, Pasadena, California! DeeDee will read every letter she gets.

Watch for the first column starting in two weeks!

## FAX... ON... WAX!

**By REB FOSTER**

Reb here to give you the lowdown on what's happening in the record business!

Dick and DeeDee, who just returned from a ten day stay in England, report that the Rolling Stones have decided not to come to California for a vacation around Christmastime, as planned. Instead they will go to New York. But don't cry, Stones fans, because here's a hot little scoop! The Stones will pay a secret visit to K*R*L*A* L*A*N*D around January 20th, before they leave for their Australian tour on January 22.

Mick, Keith, and Brian will spend the holidays in New York.

Speaking of the Stones, Mick Jagger was voted the second top male singer in England. First place was awarded to . . . you guessed it, John Lennon! House of the Rising Sun by the Animals was voted best record, and the Rolling Stones were picked as the number one new group!

The Standells, who have been breaking records in Los Angeles, are now setting one in San Francisco! The Hilton Hotel up there is opening a new "Tiger A Go Go" Room, which will cater to the teen and young adult crowd. Headliners at the room's opening will be the Standells!

That's about it for this week. See you in two more with fax on wax!

## IN TOWN!

In case you're interested in the travel plans of your favorite English groups, here's the lowdown on where they'll be when:

ROLLING STONES: Starting a tour of Australia January 22nd, but we have it on good authority that they'll pay a surprise visit to this country before they go on tour.

CILLA BLACK: She'll be over here in April, first to do the Sullivan show and then to make a cross country tour, spending a week in K*R*L*A*N*D.

GERRY & THE PACEMAKERS: You'll see them again either the last week in March or the first week in April. Gerry will probably tape a Shindig show while he is in town.

THE BEATLES: Latest word on their return to this country is that they will be back in late spring. While in town, they will film an hour long tv show and plans are underway also for a bowl concert. Starting in February, they will be over in London working on their new movie. We will print the address of the studio where the film will be shot here in the KRLA BEAT, so watch for it.

HERMAN'S HERMITS: Will be back April 16th to do a tv show

## CONTEST CORNER!!!

How would you like to win a cruddy old piece of paper? What do you mean, you wouldn't? Do you know what cruddy old piece of paper it is? Hey, stop throwing this away in disgust! Wait a minute! This here cruddy piece of paper just happens to be the cruddy piece of paper on which the Rolling Stones and Herman's Hermits wrote their Christmas greetings to the KRLA BEAT! How about them apples! You saw the groovy autographs in the KRLA BEAT last week, didn't you? (What do you mean, you didn't? I'd be ashamed to admit it if I were you!) Anyhow, now those groovy autographs can be yours!

**YOU CAN WIN THE STONES AND HERMAN AND THE HERMITS CHRISTMAS MESSAGE TO THE KRLA BEAT!**

Since there can be only one winner, we also have a second prize. (Don't we always?) Remember a few weeks back, around Thanksgiving, when we had all the D.J.s write what they were most thankful for that Thanksgiving? And remember how each D.J. signed his autograph below his Thanks-thing? You can win those original autogarphs too! Yep, that's the fab second prize in this groovy contest!

### HERE'S ALL YOU HAVE TO DO:

1. We play all kinds of records on KRLA. How many do you think we play every day? Well, guess, why don't you? No, don't guess how many records we played in any one day. Just the average number of records we play every day on KRLA.
2. Send your guess in on an entry blank (it's underneath the rules, silly!) (the entry blank)
3. Entries must be in by January 15th.

**ENTRY BLANK**

NAME:................................................ AGE:............

ADDRESS:..............................................................

PHONE NUMBER:...................................................

HOW MANY RECORDS ARE PLAYED DAILY ON KRLA (about).............

# KRLA ARCHIVES

# MORE ENGLISH GROUPS TO BE HERE THIS MONTH

FIVE CENTS

(Story in Col. 1)

# KRLA BEAT

Production, Design And Content by Bonnie Golden

HI, HULLABALOOERS!

## SIX GROUPS COMING HERE

K•R•L•A•N•D — It looks as though January is going to prove to be just as groovy a month as last November, as far as the group scene goes! The Kinks are scheduled to arrive in town during the first or second week in January, and they'll open the year with a possible appearance on Shindig. These four gear guys are fast becoming one of the top R & B groups in the world, second only to the Rolling Stones. Their latest record, "All Day and All of the Night" is high on KRLA's tune-dex, and going higher, by the looks of things!

### DAVE'S GROUP TOO!

Dave Hull's own English group, the Hullabaloos, will do the Sullivan show in late December, and may also decide to join the crowd and visit K•R•L•A•N•D too! When they first heard about Dave 'adopting' them, they said they didn't want to leave America without at least meeting him! This group went way out for a gimmick . . . they all dyed their hair blonde (?) and let it grow down to their shoulders! But when you see them in person, you'll think it's a gas! They're the only group in the world managed by an honest to goodness titled nobleman!

The Animals will be out here on January 24th for their Shindig show. There's five in this group (as if you didn't know!) and they're the ones who dig blue jeans. In fact, they even had tailored blue jeans made for their performances!

### D.C. FIVE MOVIE

About the biggest news, and the news everyone is waiting for is the scheduled Dave Clarke Five movie, which would keep the group here for at least three months. Look for the story about this elsewhere in this issue. Other

## KRLA TOP THIRTY

| # | Title | Artist | # | Title | Artist |
|---|---|---|---|---|---|
| 1. | I FEEL FINE/SHE'S A WOMAN | The Beatles | 16. | SHE'S NOT THERE | The Zombies |
| 2. | LOST THAT LOVIN' FEELIN' | Righteous Bros. | 17. | TIME IS ON MY SIDE | Rolling Stones |
| 3. | MR. LONELY | Bobby Vinton | 18. | WILLOW WEEP FOR ME | Chad & Jeremy |
| 4. | COME SEE ABOUT ME | The Supremes | 19. | DANCE DANCE DANCE | Beach Boys |
| 5. | I'M INTO SOMETHING GOOD | Herman's Hermits | 20. | SIDEWALK SURFING | Jan & Dean |
| 6. | WALK AWAY | Matt Monro | 21. | UNLESS YOU CARE | Terry Black |
| 7. | THE JERK | The Larks | 22. | RIGHT OR WRONG | Ronnie Dove |
| 8. | WALKING IN THE RAIN | The Ronettes | 23. | AS TEARS GO BY | Marianne Faithful |
| 9. | BABY LOVE | The Supremes | 24. | COME A LITTLE CLOSER | Jay & The Americans |
| 10. | MOUNTAIN OF LOVE | Johnny Rivers | 25. | LEADER OF THE LAUNDROMAT | The Detergents |
| 11. | IF YOU WANT THIS LOVE | Sonny Knight | 26. | THAT'S WHAT LOVE IS MADE OF | The Miracles |
| 12. | GOING OUT OF MY HEAD | Anthony & Imperials | 27. | THOU SHALT NOT STEAL | Dick & DeeDee |
| 13. | LEADER OF THE PACK | The Shangri-Las | 28. | NEEDLE IN A HAYSTACK | The Velvelettes |
| 14. | BABY DON'T GO | Sonny & Cher | 29. | ANYWAY YOU WANT IT | Dave Clark Five |
| 15. | OPPORTUNITY | The Jewels | 30. | LAST KISS | J. Frank Wilson |

## TOP TEN ALBUMS

1. 12 x 5 — ROLLING STONES
2. WALK DON'T RUN VOL. 2 — BEACH BOYS
3. MORE OF ROY ORBISON'S GREATEST HITS
4. SECOND ALBUM — GERRY & PACEMAKERS
5. COAST TO COAST — DAVE CLARK FIVE
6. WHERE DID OUR LOVE GO — SUPREMES
7. HARD DAY'S NIGHT — BEATLES
8. MORE KINGSTON TRIO — KINGSTON TRIO
9. RIDE THE WILD SURF — JAN & DEAN
10. IN CONCERT — PETER PAUL & MARY

## TOP TEN OLDIES

1. Hurt — Timi Yuro
2. Twist and Shout — Beatles
3. Tragedy — The Fleetwoods
4. Hot Pastrami — Dartells
5. Hold Your Hand — Beatles
6. Beep Beep — Playmates
7. April Love — Pat Boone
8. Runin' Scared — Roy Orbison
9. There's A Moon Out Tonight — The Capris
10. Stay — Maurice Williams

## TOP TEN UP AND COMERS

1. Little Rooster — Rolling Stones
2. I'll Be There — Gerry & Pacemakers
3. Boom Boom — The Animals
4. All Day & All Night — The Kinks
5. Wild Side of Life — Tommy Quickly
6. Give Him a Big Kiss — Shangri-Las
7. Downtown — Petula Clark
8. Show Me Girl — Herman's Hermits
9. Look of Love — Lesley Gore
10. Name Game — Shirley Ellis

Hey, did you see those pictures of me on my junky float last week? Guess what! You can have one of them, life size, for only $500.00! Isn't that great! Aren't you excited! Geesh! Forget I ever mentioned it! Anyhow, it's nearly time for the Animals to arrive. "WHEN I LOOK AT YOU, BIG BOY, I THINK THEY'RE ALREADY HERE!" Maud, you don't know what you're saying! If I were an Animal, do you know what I'd do? "NO, WHAT?" I'd take all my money I made from 'House of the Rising Sun,' buy KRLA, and play Beatle records 24 hours a day! Seriously, I like the Animals too. Before I go, let's have a be kind to Animals minute . . . and after that, let's have a be kind to me year! Oh, well, you can't win 'em all! See you next week!

## D.C. FIVE WILL FILM MOVIE HERE

HOLLYWOOD — It has been reported to the KRLA BEAT that the Dave Clark Five will be returning to K•R•L•A•N•D shortly to film their movie, "The Dave Clark Story." When the boys went back to England last month, they said that if everything went well, they would be back January 18th to begin filming. If things have gone well, and they do make the film here, some lucky KRLAers are going to have the time of their lives! Why? Because Dave said before he left that instead of using Hollywood extras to play fans in the film, he would rather use typi-

# KRLA ARCHIVES

# THE B

Ever since the KRLA BEAT started, you have been able to see some of the grooviest pictures in the world of all the top names in the record world, along with real behind the scenes pictures of KRLA's d.j.s These pictures have been taken exclusively for the BEAT, and you will never see them anywhere else. Which leads to a problem! So many of you have requested more pictures of the Beatles, the Dave Clark Five, The Stones, and all the other groups, that we've decided to print highlights from all past issues! So here it is, the best of the BEAT!

Who will ever forget this wonderful day! After days of breathless excitement, the Beatles finally arrived! And of course, all the pictures of their whole stay were in the first issue of the BEAT!

A few issues later, you all got a 'backstage look' at KRLA. Record stars drop in all the time to say hello to their favorite station, and a day at KRLA is enough to make any fan happy!

The d.j. meeting! Our d.j.s meet once a week to discuss the programming policy and make suggestions. Everyone helps to make KRLA number one and keep it there . . . even you!

A few days later, the TAMI Show started filming. 3000 lucky KRLAers got free tickets to the show, courtesy of KRLA. And what a show it was! Every star you can think of was there in person!

With the Rolling Stones, Beach Boys, Billy J., Gerry & the Pacemakers, James Brown, Jan & Dean, Chuck Berry, and even more, it's no wonder that even Benevolent Bobby Dale showed up!

Even the other acts came out to see the boys! Dick & DeeDee, who were in the show, are also good friends with all of them. Jimmy Clanton, The Spats, The Vibrants, and the Soul Brothers were there too!
Photography by ROBIN HILL

Wail, man! This issue seemed to be everyone's all time favorite, (except, of course, for the Beatle one!) The Stones will pay a surprise visit to K*R*L*A*N*D towards the end of January.

# KRLA ARCHIVES

## BEST OF THE BEAT

The press conference at the Cinnamon Cinder gave many of you a chance to see the boys close up. Of all the places they stayed at in this country, they liked K*R*L*A*N*D the best!

How many of you cried at that final bow? All too soon, the gearest group in the world left our town, but we really didn't feel too bad. After all, they said they would be back!

The newest addition to KRLA! Gary Mack, our 'meet 'em at the airport' d.j. talks to Reb. Gary loves meeting the English groups, and they love being greeted at the airport by KRLA!

October and November were the greatest months of the year! First, Reb brought in the Billy J. Kramer, Gerry and the Pacemakers show, and kicked off the start of the group invasion!

This has to be one of the greatest pictures the KRLA BEAT will ever print! Dick and Gerry at the TAMI Show that lots of fun was had backstage. You asked us to run more on the show, so we did!

In the next issue, you were there as Gary Mack made his first trip to the airport to meet the Rolling Stones. It was the first time a lot of you "met" them too, and you all really dug them!

Before you could turn around, it was Dave Clark Five time, and the BEAT was there to cover the show for you (of course!) No wonder they liked that issue! Look at the headline! The show was fab!

A few weeks later, Brian Epstein introduced Tommy Quickly to America! Of course, he picked L.A. for his first stop . . . wonder why? Could KRLA have had anything to do with it? You bet! We're Brian's favorite!

# KRLA ARCHIVES

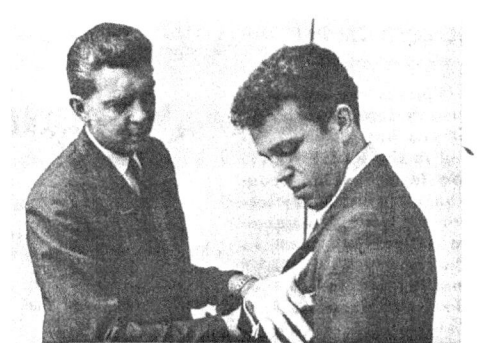

In the second issue, the BEAT took you to Bandstand, with our own Charlie 'O'! Here, Charlie and Bobby Vinton get ready for showtime. Charlie has been with the show for six years!

Who could ever forget Gerry & the Pacemakers? The way he kept winking at everyone in the audience made friends of everyone there! The show was a real gas, and set the 'stage' for other gear shows!

How many of you were lucky enough to see this in person? Remember when Dave, Bob, and Charlie came out to introduce the Stones at their show? Anyone who wasn't a Stone fan then was after the show!

Suddenly, Manfred Mann came in, closely followed by Herman & the Hermits and Peter and Gordon. It's beginning to look as though K*R*L*A*N*D is the headquarters for all the groups!

# KRLA ARCHIVES

THE PERSONAL COLUMN WILL NOT APPEAR THIS WEEK. IT WILL RESUME NEXT WEEK AS USUAL. SO SEND 'EM IN!

Thanks for all those groovy letters so many of you have been writing to the KRLA BEAT. We love hearing from you, and read every letter we get! Remember to address all mail to the new KRLA BEAT mailing address at P.O. Box 702-M, Pasadena, California. And don't forget that you can now order the KRLA BEAT by mail! Just enclose five cents and a self-addressed stamped envelope, and your copy of the BEAT will be sent right out! If you want a back issue, we have those too! Back issues are ten cents, plus a self addressed stamped envelope.

## BEATLE BITS
### by Dick Moreland

It's time for those Beatle bits again!

George has lost so much weight that his doctors are putting him on a special diet! The poor boy only weighs 118 pounds! Don't worry, George, that's the same number of pounds carried by Miss America!

"I Feel Fine / She's A Woman' (you can't say just one title, since both are number one!) sold three quarters of a million records before it was even released! I'll bet it took all of two days to become a million seller!

John and Paul are very serious about writing a Broadway-type musical! The two are even writing plot outlines! They won't quit the Beatles if they become successful playwrites, but as John said, "It's always nice to be well rounded!"

John's new book, tentatively titled "A Spaniard In the Works" will be out in February, or March. They're saying it's even better than John's first one!

Yes, it's true that Ringo was evicted from his apartment! But for a very funny reason! His fans wanted to wish him good luck before he went into the hospital, and they all congregated outside Ringo's apartment to do it! The noise was so great that the apartment manager politely asked the Beatle to move.

That catches you up on the latest... I'll be back in two weeks with more Beatle Bits!

## D.C. Five...

cal teenage fans! This is all the information we were able to get at the time, but KRLA is carefully checking the facts, and you'll get the lowdown next week in the BEAT! Until then, keep your fingers crossed!

## CASEY'S CORNER
### by Casey Kasem

Hi! The Kaser is here to let you in on some more little known facts about well known people!

Did you know that Del Shannon got his start while he was in the Army? He played guitar in an Army production!

The Ronettes were discovered at the famous Peppermint Lounge in New York!

Gene Pitney started in the Music Business as a songwriter! He wrote a song that had too many high notes in it for most singers, recorded it, and was on his way!

The Righteous Brothers started out as two single performers, and one night got up to sing a song together. You know the rest!

Martha and the Vandellas got their start from Marvin Gaye! They did the background music on one of his sessions, and Marvin liked them so much that he helped get them signed to a recording contract!

That's it for this week! I'll be out 'Casing' some facts for you and see you in two weeks!

---

Don't forget to send in your vote for your favorite group! The votes are pouring in, and the top group will get the **KRLA BEAT AWARD!** Our d.j.'s selected the top five groups, but your vote will decide the winner!

The five stars that the D.J.'s have selected this year are:
- The Beatles
- The Rolling Stones
- The D.C. 5
- The Beach Boys
- The Four Seasons

Vote for the one you think is the top group in K*R*L*A*N*D! Maybe YOUR vote will decide who gets the award! (Use the ballot below)

- - - - - - - - - - - - - - - -

I think the top group, the group that deserves the KRLA BEAT AWARD, are the_____

My name is_____

and I am_____years old.

## GROUPS...

groups that may possibly make a short stopover in our town are the Nashville Teens, the Merseybeats, and Peter and Gordon, who were in town last week and hope to return around the middle of January.

---

# CONTEST CORNER!

## WIN A DINNER FROM A D.J.!

*What kind of dates do you like? No, we don't mean those ones you buy in the store all wrapped in yellow cellophane! Dates... like BOYS! Any kind? Well, that settles it then. This contest is just for you! How would you like to have nine groovy boys... er, men waiting for you to choose one of them for your date? How would you like to have that much of a choice! Well, they are and you can! What we mean is, there are nine d.j.s on KRLA, right? So that's nine to choose from! That's right, the choice is yours!*

AND YOU AND YOUR "CHOICE" WILL HAVE AN EVENING YOU'LL NEVER FORGET! FIRST, HE'LL PICK YOU UP AT YOUR HOME, AND THE KRLA BEAT WILL BE RIGHT THERE TO CATCH EVERY WONDERFUL SECOND! THEN YOU'LL BE TAKEN TO A REALLY GROOVY RESTAURANT, AND HAVE THE MOST FABULOUS DINNER YOU'VE EVER HAD WITH THE D.J. THAT YOU HAVE CHOSEN!

**HERE'S HOW THIS DREAM DATE CAN BE YOURS:**

1. There are nine d.j.s on KRLA. (In case you've been sleeping for the past ten years, we'll name them: Bob Hudson, Gary Mack, Charlie 'O', Casey Kasem, Dick Moreland, Reb Foster, Bob Eubanks, Dave Hull, and Bobby Dale). Take your choice!

2. After you've chosen your favorite d.j., tell us why he's your favorite in 25 words or less (use any old piece of paper for this).

3. Fill out the entry blank below, enclose it with your 25 words or less and mail it to us at P.O. Box 702-M, Pasadena, California. (How do you expect to win if you don't mail in the entry!)

4. Each d.j. will read his entries and pick the best one. The final nine entries will be tossed into a box, shaken up, and one will be drawn by one of the newsmen. That one will be the winner!

**START SENDING IN YOUR ENTRIES NOW!**

**ENTRY BLANK**

NAME:............................................................AGE:............

ADDRESS:..................................................................

PHONE NUMBER:........................................................

FAVORITE D.J.:..........................................................

## KRLA ARCHIVES

# "HULLABALOOS" ADOPTED" BY KRLA DISK JOCKEY

FIVE CENTS     JANUARY 14, 1965     (Story in Col. 1)

# KRLA BEAT

Production Design And Content By Bonnie Golden

## MAKES KRLA THEIR HOME

HOLLYWOOD — Dave Hull, second most popular disc jockey in the world, set another first in the record world when he became the only d.j. in America to "adopt" an English group! The group, of course, is the Hullabaloos, hitting this country for the first time with their recording of "I'm Gonna Love You Too." Dave, who is known to his many fans as the Hullabalooer, was the first person in America to play the record. When the group first heard about Dave, their manager contacted him at the station.

### Group From Hull

The similarity of the group's name wasn't the only thing they had in common with Dave. The group, believe it or not, is from HULL, England! The boys called Dave from New York New Year's Eve to wish him a happy New Year, and it was during that conversation that Dave kiddingly suggested he "adopt" them and show them around California when they came to this country. They came down to KRLA as soon as they got into town to meet Dave and the president, vice president, and treasurer of Dave's fan club.

### Marineland

Dave arranged for two of the fan club members to take the group to Marineland and show them various parts of Los Angeles that they had wanted to see. The boys said that they would like to come back to California to spend more time with Dave in the near future.

The group consists of Riky Knight, leader, Harry Dunn, drummer, Andy Woonton, guitar, and Geoff Mortimer, bass. They are four of the nicest, most down to earth boys in the world, and have met (and liked) the Beatles

Continued on Page 4

## KRLA TOP THIRTY

1. LOST THAT LOVIN' FEELIN' ........ Righteous Bros.
2. DOWNTOWN ........................ Petula Clark
3. I FEEL FINE/SHE'S A WOMAN ....... The Beatles
4. COME SEE ABOUT ME ............... The Supremes
5. GOIN' OUT OF MY HEAD ............ Little Anthony
6. MR. LONELY ...................... Bobby Vinton
7. THOU SHALT NOT STEAL ............ Dick & DeeDee
8. NEEDLE IN A HAYSTACK ............ The Velvelettes
9. THE JERK ........................ The Larks
10. WALKING IN THE RAIN ............ The Ronettes
11. WILLOW WEEP FOR ME ............. Chad & Jeremy
12. AS TEARS GO BY ................. Marianne Faithful
13. THE "IN" CROWD ................. Dobie Gray
14. BABY LOVE ...................... The Supremes
15. LOVE POTION NUMBER NINE ........ The Searchers
16. UNLESS YOU CARE ................ Terry Black
17. BABY DON'T GO .................. Sonny & Cher
18. OH NO, NOT MY BABY ............. Maxine Brown
19. ANY WAY YOU WANT IT ............ Dave Clark Five
20. WALK AWAY ...................... Matt Monro
21. ALL DAY & ALL OF THE NIGHT ..... The Kinks
22. I'M INTO SOMETHING GOOD ........ Herman's Hermits
23. KEEP SEARCHIN' ................. Del Shannon
24. THE NAME GAME .................. Shirley Ellis
25. MOUNTAIN OF LOVE ............... Johnny Rivers
26. LOOK OF LOVE ................... Lesley Gore
27. TIME IS ON MY SIDE ............. The Rolling Stones
28. RIGHT OR WRONG ................. Ronnie Dove
29. SHE'S NOT THERE ................ The Zombies
30. OPPORTUNITY .................... The Jewels

## TOP TEN ALBUMS

1. BEACH BOYS CONCERT
2. THE BEATLES' STORY
3. 12 x 5 .................................. Rolling Stones
4. ROUSTABOUT .............................. Elvis Presley
5. THE DOOR IS STILL OPEN .................. Dean Martin
6. WHERE DID OUR LOVE GO ................... Supremes
7. A HARD DAY'S NIGHT ...................... Beatles
8. SOMETHING NEW ........................... Beatles
9. BEATLES '65
10. A BIT OF LIVERPOOL ..................... Supremes

## TOP TEN OLDIES

1. Hurt ............................. Timi Yuro
2. Twist and Shout .................. Beatles
3. Tragedy .......................... The Fleetwoods
4. Hot Pastrami ..................... Dartells
5. Hold Your Hand ................... Beatles
6. Beep Beep ........................ Playmates
7. April Love ....................... Pat Boone
8. Runin' Scared .................... Roy Orbison
9. There's A Moon Out Tonight ....... The Capris
10. Stay ............................ Maurice Williams

## TOP TEN UP AND COMERS

1. Little Red Rooster ...... Rolling Stones
2. Show Me Girl ............ Herman's Hermits
3. Words of Love ........... The Beatles
4. Kansas City ............. The Beatles
5. I'll Be There ........... Gerry & Pacemakers
6. Promised Land ........... Chuck Berry
7. Heart of Stone .......... The Rolling Stones
8. Laugh, Laugh ............ Beau Brummels
9. Tell Her No/Leave Me Be . Zombies
10. The Boy Next Door ...... The Standells

## HI, HULLABALOOERS!

Well, are you all celebrating? Are you all bouncing up and down with joy? Now, don't kas me why, of course you all know! You mean you don't?

Well, sit down! It was exactly one year ago today that "I Want To Hold Your Hand" was released! How about them apples! One year ago today, most of you didn't even know who the Beatles were! And now look. But wait till next year ... you'll be saying the same thing about me! "SING IT, BIG BOY!" Oh, it's you again, Maud. And my day was going so well, too! But that's the kind of thing a rising young star has to put up with. What? Don't think I can't hear what you're muttering out there ... you stop that or I'll say goodbye ... well? Okay, you asked for it. BYE!

## CHANGE IN POP MUSIC

HOLLYWOOD — The big sound isn't the beat sound anymore ... at least, that's the way things are starting to look! "Soul" music ... rhythm and blues, whatever you want to call it, is taking over! Aside from the Beatles, most of the top records today are wailing numbers, with a gutty guitar and heavy drumbeat. The songs that make it today are worlds apart from the type of material that hit "BB" (Before Beatles).

When Manfred Mann was in town, KRLA BEAT asked him what he thought the reason was behind this sudden surge to "down

Continued on Page 4

# KRLA ARCHIVES

Well, you asked for it! Last week when we printed the "best of the BEAT," we never expected to get the reaction we got from you! Letters by the hundred poured in, asking us why we didn't print more of the pics from past issues of the BEAT. Naturally, being the beautiful people we are (and modest, too) we decided to answer your request. Here are the pics you asked for, along with some new ones that you've never seen anywhere before! The KRLA BEAT is the only place in the world where you can see groovy pictures like this every week, taken especially for the KRLA BEAT by our own photographer, Robin Hill! Next week, watch for exclusive pics of the Hullabaloos and the Scuzzy one, Dave Hull!

The second issue of the BEAT showed Charlie 'O' in his true light . . . the light of the camera, that is. Charlie had only been at the station for a few months, and many of you were surprised to discover that he was the same Charlie 'O' who had been on Bandstand for the past six years!

Charlie talks with an old friend of his, Bobby Vinton. Bobby was surprised to discover that Charlie was now a d.j., and asked Charlie if he could come down to the station to see him. Charlie also told Bobby about the record he was going to record later that month. The record will be released soon.

For the first time, many of you were able to see the "behind the scenes" part of KRLA. Here, the BEAT takes you to the weekly d.j. meeting, where our d.j.s meet every Tuesday. Freddy Cannon dropped in and asked what they thought of his new record . . . (Bob was just kidding . . . he really wasn't holding his nose!)

Reb Foster and Dick Beebe talk about a news breakthrough that just came over the air. Dick Beebe is also the voice of Colonel Splendid! And yes, that beard is real! Unfortunately, Maud Skidmore wouldn't hold still for the camera, so we couldn't get a picture of her . . . but one day we'll catch her!

Freddie Cannon steps into the control room where Casey is doing his show to say hello to Casey. And yes, that flag hanging over Freddie's head is a British Union Jack! It's been hanging there ever since the Beatles became popular! Every time one of the groups see it, they crack up!

Then came one of the wildest months KRLA and KRLAers ever saw! Every one of the top English groups came in town . . . and made KRLA their headquarters! And every one of them flipped over the KRLA BEAT! Here, Gerry Marsden and Billy J. Kramer look at a copy. They each took copies home with them.

Here, Gerry with Les of the Pacemakers and Robin of the Dakotas fool around with a few numbers before going onstage at Reb Foster's giant Long Beach show. Gerry is a real gas, and everyone who met him fell in love with him. He'll be back to this country in a few months.

The Standells rip it up on stage. Larry Tamblyn, the leader, is Russ Tamblyn's brother, and Dick Dodd, lead singer and drummer, is a former Mouseketeer . . . and single, too! Reb Foster discovered the group and went to South America with them a few months ago. He had a blast!

Soon after came the Rolling Stones show, brought to you, of course, by Beatle-bringers Bob Eubanks, Dave Hull, and Charlie 'O'. Here, Charlie and Bob talk to Bill Wyman. Bill is the friendliest of the Stones, and had a smile and a nice word for everyone. He's great!
Photography by ROBIN HILL

Dick & DeeDee, two of the greatest people in the world, were on just before the Stones. Watch for DeeDee's new column right here in the BEAT starting next week. If you want to write to her here at the paper, she'll get your letter. She's a good friend of the Rolling Stones.

This is one of the few pictures ever taken of Andrew Oldham, the Stones' manager and producer of all their records. He has also written many of their songs with Keith and Mick, who also wrote "As Tears Go By," Marrianne Faithfull's record. Keith was so tired, he fell asleep!

# KRLA ARCHIVES

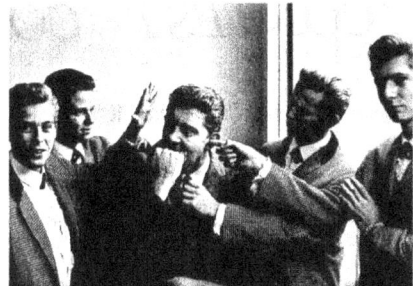

Just to show you that our Charlie isn't as serious as he looks, here's a little clowning around with the Spats! The dressing rooms at the show have a barber chair in one of them . . . and the Spats kidnapped Charlie, plopped him in the chair, and decided to give him a Beatle haircut!

The next issue taught you how to do all the latest dances. Steve and Joy Ciro, two night club dancers who have appeared in many movies and tv shows posed for the KRLA BEAT and demonstrated the Monkey, Swim, and Jerk. Steve and Joy were also in the TAMI show as part of the background dancers.

This is Cecil Tuck, our news director. Here you see him in the middle of a news broadcast. The newsroom is covered with maps of every part of K*R*L*A*N*D so that we can always be first on the spot with every bit of news about YOUR town! KRLA wins awards every year for its news coverage.

Dave Hull goes over a publicity release with Reb Foster. The two d.j.s are very good friends, even though Dave wouldn't allow Maud Skidmore to appear on his junky float! Reb and Dave together are more fun than a barrel of . . . Rolling Stones! (In addition to being wild Beatle fans and friends).

This is the picture that Billy J. just flipped over! He asked the BEAT for copies to take to England with him. Billy wants to come back to this country on a vacation and spend some time just relaxing. He and Gerry are best friends, and both are managed by Brian Epstein.

Gerry has the greatest stage presence of any group we've ever seen . . . except, of course, for the Beatles and Rolling Stones. The audience went wild when he came on stage, and the way he winked at everyone in the audience turned everyone on! He's one act you shouldn't miss.

Backstage at the TAMI show, Bobby Dale talks to one of the Beachboys. The TAMI show pictures are the pics that most of you requested, especially after seeing the groovy show. KRLA made it possible for 3000 of you to not only see the filming of the show, but to actually be in the movie itself!

Brian Epstein brought Tommy Quickly to America and caused all the girls to flip when they got a good look at the groovy Liverpool lad. Arthur, the toy dog given to Tommy by Jack Good, is over in the corner . . . he looks almost lifelike! Tommy had the first fan press conference in the world!

# KRLA ARCHIVES

## PERSONALS

So many of you have sent personals in to the KRLA BEAT that we haven't been able to print all of them, so we're going to omit Reb Foster's FAX ON WAX and Bob Eubanks' RECORD REVIEW this week to catch up on as many personals as possible. Watch for Bob and Reb next week!

**Do you want your personals printed?** Each week, we'll print any messages you want to send through the KRLA BEAT! Just mail your message in on a post card to: PERSONALS, KRLA BEAT, 1401 South Oak Knoll Rd., Pasadena, California. Keep messages about three lines. You can say anything you want (almost) ... and it will be printed right here in the KRLA BEAT!

THREE CHEERS FOR THE MOST WONDERFUL GUYS IN THE WORLD!!! THE KRLA D.J.'S.
  Barbara of Orange High

Anne:
 Four to seven months and it's back to L.V. to see the fab four.
  a fellow clod

M.L. of L.V.N.
 Afraid of showing your face! How about the pix you promised?
  The girl on the phone

Jeff of KENO:
 How about hearing from you!
  girl minus $60.00

Charlie Watts —
 We love you lots!
  Suzanne & Kathie

Pattie:
 Who says I can't???
  Sheri

My Cousin Debbie Loves Paul McCartney but she loves Clarance better (ha ha)! I love John Lennon and Dave Hull!
  Who Else but me?

Hey You Guys: Thanks for the fab phone call, and Bob Eubanks is fab, gear, rave, fave, picky. —Carol, Katy, Barbara, Anne. Miss C. Riley
 43, Springbank, Broadway Chadderton, Lancashire, England

To: Mr. Denis W. Peyton
 I love you, I love you, I love you.
  From: Janice Brown

Derek Taylor,
 Stay in L.A.! Both Jeanie A. & I luv ya! Hurry & give us some stuff on Tommy.
  Ricki W.

Any boy who likes the Stones, and Arl, we'd like to get to know you.
  Anns & Shay
  Call DA 4-2161 or FR 8-6016

Down with the Rolling Boulders. Down with the Dirt Clod Finks. Beatles Forever
  The Rocking Chairs

Beatles:
 You're not the only "Losers." Santa didn't see my KRLA sign either!
  A Loser

Me Darling Dave Clark:
 'ave yer 'eard the way 'at Scuzzy 'ullabalooer talks about yer be 'ind yer back?
  Luv, 'ugs, & xxx, Cathy

Attention all Stone fans:
 To settle it once and for all, MICK IS MINE!!
  Emily

I Love Paul McCartney more than anything! Dave Hull rules!
  Luv from, An Asher

Dave Davies:
 You're all kinky!!! But it's alright cuz you really got me all day and all of the night.
  Ricki W.

John B. & Johnny G.:
 Hope you have fun. If you see Cilla, Liz, or Janet, say hi for me. Us FooHoose Fabbers again!
  Ricki & Cyn

Jennie
 John is mine! Hi to the Scuzzy one.
  Karye

Dave
 You think there is only one Clarence! You should visit our Biology Lab.
  Hullabalooer Beatlemaniac

To Dell Kennedy:
 Hi, fellow Peter Asher-lover! How does it feel to be in the FAB "KRLA BEAT?"
  Luv, Mel

I Love Beatles. I'd rather fight than switch.
  Loyal Fan
  Cindy Lennon

To T.W.
 Keep away from Dave Clark. Go back to the Beatles. The D.C. 5 are contagious anyway the Beatles Rule.
  Me

To the Beatles:
 Debbie Umphenour loves you. I wish you would come see her and sing her a song.
  Luv, a Dave Clark 5 Lover

To The Beatles,
 I love you, I love you, I love you, I love you.
  From a Beatle Lover D.V.S.

"Rocking Chairs Forever"
  Your Westchester Fans

Paul McCartney:
 Can you wash your father's shirt; Oh can you wash it clean?
  Ganks Inc.

Dave Hull:
 Tell Clarance to tell his friends to stop choking me every night.
  All Choked Up

To Dave Hull:
 We love you, but quit choppin the Dave Clark Five!
  Margi & Joy

## HULL...

and Rolling Stones. Their next record, which will be released in two weeks, is called "Beware," backed with "Did You Ever." They flew back to New York last week to tape the new "Hullabaloo" show, and will return to England from there.

## MUSIC...

home" music.

"If you'll listen to the songs that were popular a year ago, you'll see that it hasn't been a sudden thing, but a gradual acceptance, and then liking, of this type of music. I think there are several reasons for it. First of all, today's teenagers are a lot more hip than they were five years ago. They want more to their music than a simple tune and some meaningless words. I'm not saying there weren't good songs before, but quite a bit of them were just insipid recordings that you could forget the minute you heard it. Today's music lovers want depth to their songs. Most of them know enough about the music business to be able to tell when a record is really good or just slickly professional. When you reach 14 or 15 nowadays, you're a lot smarter than someone of the same age five or ten years ago ... you grow up faster. That's why the blues beat is taking over. The words to pop songs today are intelligent ... they mean something. "Time Is On My Side" for example ... it's an old song, but no one was ready for it when it first came out. Now, everyone is. It's not a "slick" song ... the words say something, and the Rolling Stones are saying something when they sing it. Actually, that's the whole thing ... you can't get away with just singing a song anymore. You've got to know what you're singing, and it's got to mean something to you, the singer."

---

## CONTEST CORNER!

### TAKE "POT LUCK" WITH A STAR!

*Welcome to the first "pot luck" contest in the world! Oh, come on now ... don't say that you don't know what a pot luck contest is! You don't? Well, then let's just forget it ... what's that? You don't want to forget it? You want to know what a pot luck contest is? Well, if you insist ... here goes!*

*You all know what pot luck is ... something that you have to take because it's already there ... kind of a last minute thing. That's the way it is sometimes here at the BEAT. Everyone will be calmly sitting around minding their own business (no one ever works ... but they do mind their own business) Anyhow, suddenly, into the midst of all this calm will come Bob Eubanks or Dick Moreland or one of the other d.j.s and calmly say, "Get Gary Mack and go out to the airport ... the whoosis are coming in town in three hours!" What happens? Instant chaos! Everyone starts running around screaming ... grabbing cameras, tape recorders, cars ... and in a few minutes, it's off to the airport to meet one of the English groups. What fun!*

WHAT'S THAT? YOU THINK IT REALLY IS FUN? WELL, HOW WOULD YOU LIKE TO COME WITH US THE VERY NEXT TIME WE GO OUT TO THE AIRPORT TO MEET ONE OF THE GROUPS? NOW, DON'T GO ASKING US WHICH GROUP! WE NEVER KNOW UNTIL WE HEAR THAT THEY'RE COMING IN! THAT'S WHY IT'S A POT LUCK CONTEST!

**HERE'S ALL YOU HAVE TO DO:**

1. Write on a post card addressed to Contest Corner, KRLA BEAT, P.O. Box 702-M, Pasadena, California, exactly why you would like to go out to the airport to meet one of the English groups.

2. The entries will be judged on the basis of neatness, originality, and content. Judges will be the KRLA BEAT editor and Dave Hull.

3. The winner will be notified as early as possible when the next group is coming in town, and taken out to the airport by the KRLA BEAT, introduced to the group, and taken home by the KRLA BEAT.

4. Entries must be in by January 23. Use the entry blank below or a reasonable facsimile. You may enter as many times as you wish.

**ENTRY BLANK**

NAME:_____AGE:_____

ADDRESS:_____

PHONE NUMBER:_____

# KRLA ARCHIVES

# KRLA TO PRESENT GIANT SPECTACULAR

FIVE CENTS     JANUARY 21, 1965     (Story in Col. 1)

HI, HULLABALOOERS!

## 40 STARS TO APPEAR

HOLLYWOOD — KRLA, the station that always scores first, has done it again! This time, KRLA becomes the first station in the world to have its own tv spectacular! Naturally, being KRLA, the spectacular will be about music . . . but not just about Beatle music. The name of the show is "KRLA PRESENTS . . . MILLION DOLLAR MUSIC." It will trace the beginning of rock and roll from the first days of Bill Haley back in 1955 right up to the present Beatle-mad days of today.

### GIANT LINE UP

The show will feature live appearances and film clips of the greatest names in the record business, with a line up never before seen on one show. Among the stars appearing will be the Beatles, Elvis Presley, 4 Preps, Roger Miller, Dick Clark, Jack Good, The Vibrants, Bobby Rydell, The Coasters, Martha & Vandellas, Billy & Lilly, Chuck Berry, Santo & Johnny, Dee Clark, Sam Cooke, Duane Eddy, Danny & the Jrs., Connie Francis, Platters, Bobby Vee, Della Reese, Bobby Darin, Big Bopper, Jan & Dean, Chubby Checker, Skip & Flip, Ray Peterson, Brook Benton, Paul Anka, Diamonds, Fleetwoods, Bill Haley, Jim Reeves, Johnny Horton, and Little Anthony. Also scheduled for the show, but not yet confirmed, are the Rolling Stones, Dion, Shelley Fabares, Isley Brothers, and Jimmy Rogers.

### D.J.S WILL APPEAR

Every one of the KRLA d.j.s will appear for his own segment of the ninety minute show. Opening host will be Hank Mancini, who will introduce the d.j.s.

The spectacular will be shown Thursday, January 28th on Channel 13, KCOP, from 8:30 to 10:00. And we can bet that we don't even have to remind you not to miss it!

## KRLA TOP THIRTY

| # | Song | Artist |
|---|------|--------|
| 1. | LOST THAT LOVIN' FEELIN' | Righteous Bros. |
| 2. | DOWNTOWN | Petula Clark |
| 3. | COME SEE ABOUT ME | The Supremes |
| 4. | GOIN' OUT OF MY HEAD | Little Anthony |
| 5. | I FEEL FINE/SHE'S A WOMAN | The Beatles |
| 6. | THE NAME GAME | Shirley Ellis |
| 7. | LOVE POTION NUMBER NINE | The Searchers |
| 8. | MR. LONELY | Bobby Vinton |
| 9. | THE "IN" CROWD | Dobie Gray |
| 10. | KEEP SEARCHIN' | Del Shannon |
| 11. | THOU SHALT NOT STEAL | Dick & DeeDee |
| 12. | WILLOW WEEP FOR ME | Chad & Jeremy |
| 13. | NEEDLE IN A HAYSTACK | The Velvelettes |
| 14. | AS TEARS GO BY | Marianne Faithful |
| 15. | WALKING IN THE RAIN | The Ronettes |
| 16. | LAUGH, LAUGH | The Beau Brummels |
| 17. | THE JERK | The Larks |
| 18. | ALL DAY AND ALL OF THE NIGHT | The Kinks |
| 19. | OH NO, NOT MY BABY | Maxine Brown |
| 20. | BABY LOVE | The Supremes |
| 21. | LOOK OF LOVE | Lesley Gore |
| 22. | THE RICHEST MAN ALIVE | Mel Carter |
| 23. | ANY WAY YOU WANT IT | Dave Clark Five |
| 24. | WALK AWAY | Matt Monro |
| 25. | HOLD WHAT YOU'VE GOT | Joe Tex |
| 26. | BABY DON'T GO | Sonny & Cher |
| 27. | GIVE HIM A GREAT BIG KISS | The Shangri-Las |
| 28. | DEAR HEART | Andy Williams |
| 29. | UNLESS YOU CARE | Terry Black |
| 30. | THE ADDAMS FAMILY | The Fiends |

## TOP TEN ALBUMS

| # | Album | Artist |
|---|-------|--------|
| 1. | BEATLES '65 | The Beatles |
| 2. | BEACH BOYS IN CONCERT | The Beach Boys |
| 3. | ROUSTABOUT | Elvis Presley |
| 4. | MARY POPPINS | Soundtrack |
| 5. | PEOPLE | Barbara Streisand |
| 6. | MY FAIR LADY | Soundtrack |
| 7. | 12 x 5 | Rolling Stones |
| 8. | THE BEATLES STORY | The Beatles |
| 9. | WHERE DID OUR LOVE GO | The Supremes |
| 10. | EVERYBODY LOVES SOMEBODY | Dean Martin |

## TOP TEN OLDIES

| # | Song | Artist |
|---|------|--------|
| 1. | Sugar Shack | Jimmy Gilmer |
| 2. | Really Got A Hold On Me | Miracles |
| 3. | Tragedy | Thomas Wayne |
| 4. | Love Letters | Ketty Lester |
| 5. | Then He Kissed Me | Crystals |
| 6. | Happy Birthday Baby | Tune Weavers |
| 7. | This I Swear | Skyliners |
| 8. | Grass Is Greener | Brenda Lee |
| 9. | She's Not You | Elvis Presley |
| 10. | Candy Man | Roy Orbison |

## TOP TEN UP AND COMERS

| # | Song | Artist |
|---|------|--------|
| 1. | Words of Love | The Beatles |
| 2. | Kansas City | The Beatles |
| 3. | Heart of Stone | Rolling Stones |
| 4. | Red Rooster/Off Hook | Rolling Stones |
| 5. | The Boy Next Door | Standells |
| 6. | I Can't Stop | The Honeycombs |
| 7. | Tell Her No/Leave Me Be | Zombies |
| 8. | Show Me Girl | Herman's Hermits |
| 9. | Promised Land | Chuck Berry |
| 10. | I'll Be There | Gerry & Pacemakers |

*Well, so you were lucky enough to be able to be here for the latest edition of my wonderful column! I'll bet you couldn't stay away! After all, where else could you find such wit, such intelligence, such charm? "IN THE TELEPHONE DIRECTORY, MAYBE?" Maude, can't you leave me alone for just one week? Honest to Petey (and John, George, Paul, and Ringo too!) Why do you bother me so much? "HOW COULD I LEAVE SOMEONE AS WONDERFUL AS YOU ALONE?" Well, in that case . . . anyhow, next week in the KRLA BEAT, you'll see the results of the first annual KRLA BEAT Awards! And you'll really be surprised by the winners! I mean, you won't be surprised by who won, but you WILL be surprised at how close the voting was between the winning group and the second place group! And so the person who keeps sending in votes for me, thanks, mom! Anyhow, I'll see you next week with the surprising results!*

## YOU GIVE A "HOOT"!

PASADENA—KRLA's annual "hoot" showed that KRLAers everywhere DO give a hoot . . . because they turned out in full force to make the KRLA March of Dimes Hootenanny a 'roaring' success! The Hootenanny featured Joe & Eddie, Jackie De Shannon, The Youngfolk, Hoyt Axton, The Dillards, The Women Folk, and a host of other star attractions. The KRLA d.j.s were there to emcee the show, and wild hand clapping with everyone joining in the singing helped make the lively evening even livelier.

# KRLA ARCHIVES

When Dave Hull became the only disc jockey in the world to have his very own English group, letters started pouring in. You all wanted to see more of the group . . . the Hullabaloos. And so . . . the very minute they came into town, they made their way to KRLA to meet Dave and . . . er, "help" him on the air. If you thought you heard giggles that night, you were right. With the Hullabaloos making a hullabaloo all over the station, it was pretty hard to keep a straight face. The KRLA BEAT was there to catch the fun on camera and share it with you. Here they are . . . the Hullabaloos!

The boys are greeted by Dave at the door. Left to right, they are Goeff (Jeff) Mortimer, Andy Woonton, Riky Knight, and Harry Dunn. Notice those groovy tweed pants!

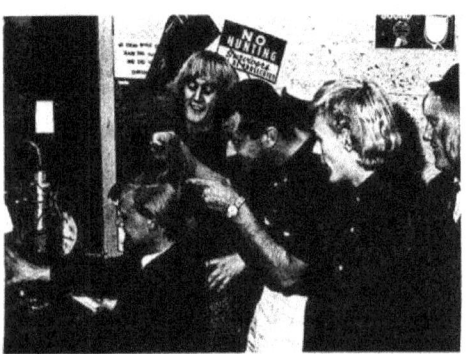
. . . so Dave gives Jeff a short lesson. (No, he wasn't looking for anything . . . he was combing Jeff's hair!) Later on, the boys combed Dave's hair, told him "Let it grow."

They got into Dave's box of horns and said they never had as much fun in their lives! Poor Dave looks like he's ready to shoot himself, but don't worry . . . that horn isn't loaded!

Not only does Dave blow his own horn, but he even has to blow up his own balloons! Yes, these are the famous "Hullabaloons," and the boys took a whole handful back to England!

Nope, it's not Napoleon! The boys form an arch of regimental swords (they look suspiciously like Hullabaloons) while Dave strikes a military pose. He couldn't keep a straight face!

Four members of Dave's fan club beg the boys to join . . . while Dave grins. Left to right, Judy Hamilton, Sec.; Rhio Harper, V.P.; Derra Dawn, Treas.; and Colleen Ludwick, Pres.
Photography by ROBIN HILL

After joining (how could they resist?), the Hullabaloos use Dave's back to sign their autographs on the KRLA BEAT. "Let's see now . . . if I rent my back out at 15c an autograph, I'll be rich!"

# KRLA ARCHIVES

Dave was on the air, so he had to run back into the control room. That's Harry with the umbrella, while Mike Moor, the Hullabaloos' road manager watches from the sidelines.

The boys watch as Dave does his show. They said that American d.j.s have more fun than English d.j.s . . . in fact, Dave looked like he was having so much fun, the boys decided to join him!

Did you ever look up to see a control room full of Hullabaloos? Dave did, and the look of surprise on his face speaks for itself! The boys wanted to know exactly how to be a d.j. . . .

The boys decided to make some "adjustments" to the control board! This group is one of the funniest groups KRLA has ever seen. They thought Dave was the greatest!

Jeff decides to see what Dave looks like as Sherlock Holmes. Dave doesn't look to happy at the thought, and his first words were . . . "You're all under arrest!" They gave Dave the hat.

Now it's Harry's turn . . . Dave tries HIS hat on! But even though Harry gave Dave his umbrella, for some reason, Dave just doesn't look like a Hullabaloo! And speaking of horns . . .!

"HAIL TO THE CHIEF!" This picture is very deceiving, though. While Andy, Jeff, and Harry held Dave's arms, Riky was tying his shoelaces together! They crowned Dave "honorary Englishman"!

Everyone salutes the Union Jack, England's flag, including Dave. After all, with as close as Dave is to the Beatles, he SHOULD be a British citizen! That's Jeff with the flag.

Now it's Dave's turn to be saluted! Dave looks kind of worried . . . but they didn't drop him! They marched around the whole station holding Dave, who was laughing so hard he nearly fell!

Uh, oh! The boys discover the switchboard! "Hello, Liverpool? Ringo Starr, please . . . yes, collect!" The boys are from Hull, and live in a beautiful 80 room castle! And you're all invited!

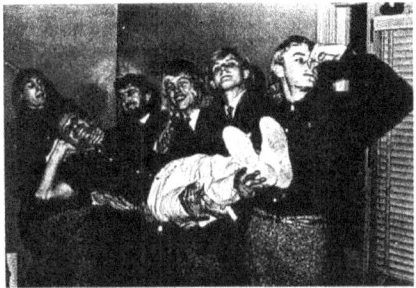

"We're taking you back to England, luv!" Riky seems to be trying to say something . . . but he didn't mean it! They invited Dave to come to England and stay with them when he got there!

Time to go! It was pouring rain, and they only had one umbrella! The boys and Dave said that they'd never laughed so hard in all their lives, and wished they could stay longer.

# KRLA ARCHIVES

## PERSONALS

Do you want your personals printed? Each week, we'll print any messages you want to send through the KRLA BEAT! Just mail your message in on a post card to: PERSONALS, KRLA BEAT, 1401 South Oak Knoll Rd., Pasadena, California. Keep messages about three lines. You can say anything you want (almost) ... and it will be printed right here in the KRLA BEAT!

To All High School Students,
Gardena City Football Champs 1964
Cheryl Kincaide—a Stone Fan of Gardena

Jeanie,
I dreampt about TOMMY last night. He's certainly on the Wild side of life!
Ricki

To the Scuzzy Hullabalooer:
Someone asked you to mention Westchester, which I now hear you do, well, start saying something about WESTWOOD too!
Ricki, Cyn, Sharon & Jeanie

Norman of The Blue Jeans:
Everyone says I look just like you. Especially like on the colour pin-up on a FABulous cover.
A Scuz (Quickly)

Dave Clark,
You are 1,000,000 times better than Ringo-dumb I love you!!! Joy loves Mike S.
Margi N.

Hey Jessie! Bet you never thought you'd see me here, huh? Your Beatle Pal
Judy S.

Dear Paul and Ringo,
See ya' in summer of '65 . . . All our lovin' . . .
F.M. and L.S. luv
P.S.: We love you.

To Linda S. & Patti P.:
For your information, Mick Jagger is MINE! And my girlfriend has dibs on Brian so lay off!!!
Mick's girl (and glad of it too)

To Dave Hull:
Do you still have the yellow feathers? When can we get our banner?
Girls with the hats

To This bee B.:
We miss you, we miss you, we miss you!!
Syl & Peg

Mick J.: Keep on pushing. How's your hand? Been able to use it lately?
An admirer 12 x 5

Thanks for all these groovy letters so many of you have been writing to the KRLA BEAT. We love hearing from you, and read every letter we get! Remember to address all mail to the new KRLA BEAT mailing address at P.O. Box 702-M, Pasadena, California. And don't forget that you can now order the KRLA BEAT by mail! Just enclose five cents and a self-addressed stamped envelope, and your copy of the BEAT will be sent right out! If you want a back issue, we have those too! Back issues are ten cents, plus a self addressed stamped envelope.

## CASEY'S CORNER

by Casey Kasem

So many of you have asked me for more likes and dislikes of your favorite stars that I've spent the last two weeks finding out all the latest facts for you . . . so here goes!

Peter of Peter and Gordon likes girls with long hair who are quiet and intelligent. He's a very serious student of philosophy.

Charlie Watts of the Stones is a jazz fan and will spend hours with anyone who likes jazz! Mick, on the other hand, digs talking about rhythm and blues with someone who knows what they're talking about.

Herman of the Hermits loves to do kooky things, and cracks up over a good practical joke, especially when it's on him.

Gerry Marsden doesn't like the night club scene . . . you'll find him most often just taking a quiet walk with someone he can talk to. Same with Manfred Mann, who digs girls who know how to carry on a good conversation.

I'll be out searching up more little known facts about well known people and bring them here for you in two weeks!

## BEATLE BITS

by Dick Moreland

Hey, all you bittikins out there, it's time for Beatle Bits again!

Did y'know that the Beatles brought more money into England last year than the country's entire export business? And that the Queen of England "adores" the four gear guys and has all their records?

Speaking of money, you all know that the boys made gobs of it last year . . . but do you know how John and Paul made most of their share? Songwriting! Righto, J & P made over four million dollars on songwriting alone!

In fact, the two have become the most sought-after songwriters in the world . . . mainly because every song they've ever written has been a hit!

For those of you who have been worried, George has gained back most of the weight he lost while on tour. And Ringo's voice sounds better than ever now that his tonsils are out.

Anyone who thinks the Beatles have had it better look again. Their album made record history when it became the only album to make the top one spot in two weeks! It went from number 98 on the trade charts to number one . . . and if that means the boys are has beens, pardon me while I laugh . . . or larf!

That's it for this week . . . see you in two!

## CONTEST CORNER!

OKAY, YOU GREEDY THINGS, IT'S GIVEAWAY TIME AGAIN! AND BOYOHBOYOHBOY, WHAT WE'RE GIVING AWAY THIS WEEK! ARE YOU READY? YOU'D BETTER SIT DOWN! OKAY THEN, HERE GOES!

You all read the headline story about the gear show KRLA is putting on in a few more days . . . (if you didn't, forget the whole thing. Any person who'd turn to the back of the paper first to see what the contest is . . . wow, that's all we can say . . .) (But you must be pretty smart to even think of it!) Anyhow, about that show. Pretty fab line up, don't you think? Gee, too bad you'll have to watch it on tv. Don't you wish you could be there? Bet you think that that's what the prize is this week, don't you? Bet you think that we're going to take the winner to the show and let them be with the KRLA BEAT backstage and talk to all the stars and everything. That's what you think, right? Well, you're absolutely right!

**YES, YOU CAN BE THERE IN PERSON AT THE BIGGEST SHOW IN THE WORLD!**

*You'll meet us at the tv station where the show will be filmed . . . and you'll get to meet and talk with every groovy star on the show!*

HERE'S ALL YOU HAVE TO DO:
Tell us, in 50 words or less, exactly why you want to go to the show that KRLA is throwing on the 28th. And hurry up, because you have a very short deadline! Send your entry in to Contest Corner, KRLA BEAT, P.O. Box 702-M, Pasadena, California. Entries must be in by January 24th! Hurry up and send in your entry now!

**ENTRY BLANK**

NAME:........................................................AGE:........

ADDRESS:................................................................

PHONE NUMBER:......................................................

# KRLA ARCHIVES

# ROLLING STONES HERE FOR SURPRISE VACATION

FIVE CENTS     JANUARY 28, 1965     (Story in Col. 1)

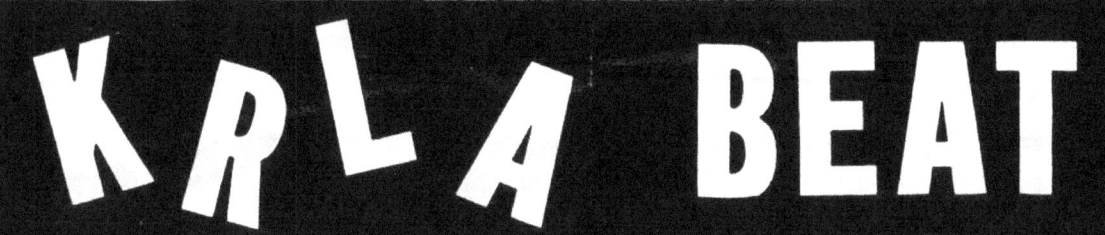

## KRLA BEAT

Production, Design And Content By Bonnie Golden

## WILL RETURN IN 3 WEEKS

Hollywood—The KRLA BEAT prints all the news first! A month ago, the BEAT scooped everyone with the news that the Rolling Stones would fly to this country secretly for a rest before beginning their Australian tour January 22nd. And last week, that's exactly what they did! They arrived from England at 3:30 in the afternoon, Sunday, the 17th, and checked into their favorite hotel, the Beverly Hilton. With them on their three day stay was their producer, Andrew ("Boy Genius") Oldham, who has been responsible for many of their hit records.

**FLEW IN TO SEE FRIENDS**

The Stones flew in especially to be with two of their friends, singer Joey Paige and record producer Marshall Leib. On their first night in town, they visited several famous night clubs, but left early to get some sleep. The next day was a little more hectic. With Joey and Marshall for a guide, the "soul" five went on a buying spree, and spent over $2000.00 on groovy goodies to take back to England. Later, they went to a recording session at RCA, where Bill Wyman made a demonstration tape of a record he had written especially for Joey. After the session, Brian Jones, Keith Richards, Joey Paige, and Andrew Oldham went to a night club to hear Little Anthony & the Imperials, and then went back to the hotel. On their last day in America, Tuesday, they spent the whole day relaxing around the pool and getting a tan.

When interviewed by the KRLA BEAT, they had this to say: Dave Hull and Bobby Dale were their favorite d.j.s in the world, they will be back in three weeks for a longer stay, and the group are on good terms with each other and aren't thinking of breaking up.

## KRLA TOP THIRTY

1. LOST THAT LOVIN' FEELIN' ... Righteous Brothers
2. DOWNTOWN ... Petula Clark
3. THE NAME GAME ... Shirley Ellis
4. LOVE POTION NUMBER NINE ... The Searchers
5. COME SEE ABOUT ME ... The Supremes
6. LAUGH, LAUGH ... The Beau Brummels
7. I FEEL FINE/SHE'S A WOMAN ... The Beatles
8. ALL DAY & ALL OF THE NIGHT ... The Kinks
9. THE "IN" CROWD ... Dobie Gray
10. GOIN' OUT OF MY HEAD ... Anthony/Imperials
11. KEEP SEARCHIN' ... Del Shannon
12. HOLD WHAT YOU'VE GOT ... Joe Texx
13. THE RICHEST MAN ALIVE ... Mel Carter
14. MR. LONELY ... Bobby Vinton
15. OH NO, NOT MY BABY ... Maxine Brown
16. WILLOW WEEP FOR ME ... Chad & Jeremy
17. THE JERK ... The Larks
18. NEEDLE IN A HAYSTACK ... The Velvelettes
19. WALK AWAY ... Matt Monro
20. AS TEARS GO BY ... Marianne Faithful
21. DEAR HEART ... Andy Williams
22. RIGHT OR WRONG ... Ronnie Dove
23. WALKING IN THE RAIN ... The Ronettes
24. TELL HER NO/LEAVE ME BE ... The Zombies
25. BABY DON'T GO ... Sonny & Cher
26. GIVE HIM A GREAT BIG KISS ... The Shangri-Las
27. I'LL BE THERE ... Gerry & The Pacemakers
28. THOU SHALT NOT STEAL ... Dick & DeeDee
29. I GO TO PIECES ... Peter & Gordon
30. HOW SWEET IT IS ... Marvin Gaye

### TOP TEN ALBUMS

1. BEATLES' 65
2. BEACH BOYS IN CONCERT
3. WHERE DID OUR LOVE GO — Supremes
4. ROUSTABOUT — Elvis Presley
5. 12 x 5 — Rolling Stones
6. EVERYBODY LOVES SOMEBODY — Dean Martin
7. A BIT OF LIVERPOOL — Supremes
8. VINTON'S GREATEST HITS — Bobby Vinton
9. THE BEATLES' STORY
10. HARD DAY'S NIGHT — Beatles

### TOP TEN OLDIES

1. Hurt — Timi Yuro
2. Twist and Shout — Beatles
3. Tragedy — The Fleetwoods
4. Hot Pastrami — Dartells
5. Hold Your Hand — Beatles
6. Beep Beep — Playmates
7. April Love — Pat Boone
8. Runin' Scared — Roy Orbison
9. There's A Moon Out Tonight — The Capris
10. Stay — Maurice Williams

### TOP TEN UP AND COMERS

1. Heart of Stone — The Rolling Stones
2. 1000 Dances — Cannable & Headhunt
3. Jolly Green Giant — The Kingsmen
4. Boy Next Door — The Standells
5. I Can't Stop — The Honeycombs
6. Hear My Heartbeat — Herman's Hermit
7. Fannie Mae — Righteous Brothers
8. King of the Road — Roger Miller
9. Twine Time — Alvin Cash & Crawlers
10. Little Red Rooster — Rolling Stones

## HI, HULLABALOOERS!

*Here it is, the issue you've all been waiting for! The results of our first annual KRLA BEAT AWARD. The voting was very close, but of course, no one*

had to tell you who would win first place. But you know, there really isn't any kind of award we can give the Beatles to thank them for all the wonderful things they've given us. Of course, buying their records is one way of saying "thanks," but how can you thank anyone for making the world more fun to live in ... for changing popular music so much that even adults love rock and roll ... for starting a British-American 'exchange' of entertainers that we might never have heard of otherwise ... for uniting teen-agers all over the world in a common bond of excitement and love. Maybe the only way to do it is to come right out and say ... from myself, from all of you, from everyone everywhere; to John, George, Paul, and Ringo ... we're truly grateful!

---

*Because of the Space devoted to the KRLA BEAT Award, all regular features of the KRLA BEAT will not appear this week, but will return in the next issue!*

# KRLA ARCHIVES

When Dave came out to introduce the first act on KRLA's "hoot," the applause was deafening. Every one of the d.j.s and performers gave their time freely to KRLA for the March of Dimes.

One of the newer groups on the folk scene is the Youngfolk, who give a lighthearted, happy glow to any audience. They'll go places! (and not only because they look so good!)

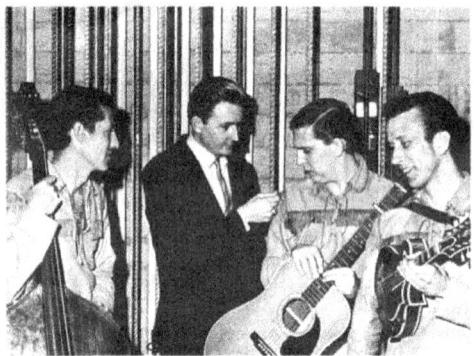

Reb inspects the fringe on one of the Dillards' jackets. This "rural" style group has big city appeal . . . as was seen when they performed. Reb might get a jacket just like that!

Terry Brown, Bob Eubanks' secretary, Charlie 'O', and Dick Moreland go over the lineup. The whole show was perfect, all the way throught. And next year's "hoot" will be great too!

Which way? That-a-way? No, this-a-way! Bob and Dave can even have fun with door signs! They are both very good friends . . . AND very good breaker-uppers if anyone ever needs a laugh!

Onstage, the Womenfolk entrance the audience with their beautiful harmony. Most of the songs the acts did were new to the audience, which added even more to the evening's enjoyment.

Gather 'round, boys! The KRLA d.j.s pose for a group picture . . . while Charlie looks anxiously towards the stage in case anyone misses their cue to go on. (No one did!)

Can you guess who this is with Dave and Bob? Why who else? It's the Little Old Lady From Pasadena! No wonder she looked so familiar! But don't be fooled . . . she still does a mean watusi!

# KRLA ARCHIVES

No, it's not a new folksing duo . . . just a little clowning around from Bob and Dave. But you know something? They sounded pretty good! Wouldn't it be funny if . . . no, that's impossible!

Tim Morgan, who has worked at the Troubador many times, showed what a good voice with lots of feeling can do! Doug Weston, owner of the Troubador, co-produced the show with KRLA.

Bob Eubanks talks to the luckiest girl in America . . . Jackie DeShannon. Why lucky? She was the only girl to go on tour with the Beatles! And she told us that she loved every minute of it!

Framed in backstage sets, Jackie gives her two favorite d.j.s a fan-type squeeze! She says . . . "I don't care if I'm known as a folk or pop singer . . . just so I can sing songs with meaning."

Dick, Charlie, and Dave give the emperor a "royal" inspection! He does cut a rather regal figure in his white spats, gold robe and jeweled crown . . . especially with the gold Rolls!

The Dillards made everyone laugh so hard that the echoes probably still haven't died away! If you ever get a chance to see them, don't miss it. They're really terrific!

And guess who introduced the L.O.L.? None other than our own Emperor! The two had the audience in stitches, and people backstage couldn't stop laughing either! Those two are too much!

Hoyt Axton, well known to all folk fans, gave a performance that made everyone's spine tingle. They loved him! Every act on the show was so good no one could pick a favorite!

# KRLA ARCHIVES

It's go-upstairs-and-get-ready time! Emperor Bob Hudson carries his gold emperor robe, and Casey leads the way. Casey gets better looking every day! All our d.j.s looked terrific that night.

Dave found a set carrier and the fun began! After a wild race backstage, Dave showed that he really does drink TigerShake! Look at those muscles! (Bob has lots of muscles too!)

Backstage, KRLA has a ringside seat. Next to Dick is Penny Dennis, and in the center is John Barrett, our general manager and one of the most wonderful bosses in the world!

Bob Hudson and the Little Old Lady from Pasadena discuss the show. If you weren't lucky enough to be there this year, don't get upset . . . KRLA's "Hoot" will be back next year!

# KRLA ARCHIVES

You voted... and then you waited for the results... and now, here they are... the winners... in the FIRST ANNUAL KRLA BEAT AWARD!

### FIRST PLACE:

the group that contributed the most this year to teenagers and popular music is:

## *The Beatles*

with 657 votes

### SECOND PLACE:

## *The Rolling Stones*

with 656 votes

### THIRD PLACE:

## *The Beach Boys*

with 477 votes

### FOURTH PLACE:

## *The Dave Clark Five*

with 296 votes

### FIFTH PLACE:

## *The Four Seasons*

with 145 votes

AND... IN ADDITION... THE KRLA BEAT HAS SELECTED THE TOP GROUPS IN THESE CATAGORIES:

FOR: *Best Ambassador to this country, best cooperation, and for making the best impression of any group to visit this country:*

**GERRY AND THE PACEMAKERS**

FOR: *Dedication to the type of music they perform, and musical sincerity:*

**THE ROLLING STONES**

FOR: *Best new female group on today's pop scene:*

**THE SUPREMES**

FOR: *Best new male group of 1964:*

**THE RIGHTEOUS BROTHERS**

# KRLA ARCHIVES

# VISA BAN— NO MORE ENGLISH GROUPS HERE

FIVE CENTS     FEBRUARY 5, 1965     (Story in Col. 1)

# KRLA BEAT

Production, Design And Content By Bonnie Golden

## THREE GROUPS CANCELLED

WASHINGTON — The U. S. Labor Department broke the news last week that no more British groups will be granted H-1 visas. This is the visa that permits a group from England to work in this country, and without it, no singer or act from England would be able to perform here. The news means a virtual ban on English groups, since they would not be able to do tours, shows, or anything but promotion while they are in America. Any person who wishes to perform for money in America, and who isn't from this country, must get one of these H-1 permits, which allows "any person or persons to perform a specified temporary service of a highly skilled nature while in this country."

**THREE GROUPS CANCELLED**

The news meant the cancellation of tours by three groups already in this country . . . the Nashville Teens, The Hullabaloos, and the Zombies. The three groups were forced to leave their tours and fly back to England. The Beatles and Rolling Stones, who hold H-1 visas at this time, are also threatened. Under the new law, these visas could be cancelled at any time, which would mean that the Beatles and the Stones could not perform in this country.

**TRADE AGREEMENT**

According to a trade agreement worked out between Britain and America, one American recording artist tours England for each English star who comes to this country. The new law would put an end to this too, since Fats Domino, who was to perform in England in exchange for the Nashville Teens, had to cancel out when the 'Teens' visa was pulled.

The only forseeable way to overcome the new rule is by using the H-2 visas, which would mean

*Continued on Page 4*

## KRLA TOP THIRTY

1. LOST THAT LOVIN' FEELIN' ........ Righteous Bros.
2. DOWNTOWN ........ Petula Clark
3. THE NAME GAME ........ Shirley Ellis
4. LAUGH, LAUGH ........ The Beau Brummels
5. MY GIRL ........ The Temptations
6. THE "IN" CROWD ........ Dobie Gray
7. COME SEE ABOUT ME ........ The Supremes
8. LOVE POTION NO. NINE ........ The Searchers
9. KEEP SEARCHIN' ........ Del Shannon
10. ALL DAY AND ALL OF THE NIGHT ........ The Kinks
11. GOIN' OUT OF MY HEAD ........ Anthony & Imperials
12. I FEEL FINE/SHE'S A WOMAN ........ The Beatles
13. OH NO, NOT MY BABY ........ Maxine Brown
14. THE RICHEST MAN ALIVE ........ Mel Carter
15. TELL HER NO/LEAVE ME BE ........ The Zombies
16. HOLD WHAT YOU'VE GOT ........ Joe Tex
17. THE JERK ........ The Larks
18. NEEDLE IN A HAYSTACK ........ The Velvelettes
19. LAND OF 1000 DANCES ........ Cannibal, Headhunters
20. WILLOW WEEP FOR ME ........ Chad & Jeremy
21. THIS DIAMOND RING ........ Gary Lewis & Playboys
22. WALK AWAY ........ Matt Monro
23. HOW SWEET IT IS ........ Marvin Gaye
24. LAND OF 1000 DANCES ........ The Midnighters
25. I GO TO PIECES ........ Peter & Gordon
26. I'LL BE THERE ........ Gerry & The Pacemakers
27. AS TEARS GO BY ........ Marianne Faithful
28. MR. LONELY ........ Bobby Vinton
29. DEAR HEART ........ Andy Williams
30. THE JOLLY GREEN GIANT ........ The Kingsmen

## TOP TEN ALBUMS

1. BEATLES '65
2. WHERE DID OUR LOVE GO — Supremes
3. THE BEACH BOYS CONCERT
4. THE BEATLES/HARD DAY'S NIGHT
5. ROUSTABOUT — Elvis Presley
6. THE ROLLING STONES 12 x 5
7. COAST TO COAST — Dave Clark Five
8. BOBBY VINTON'S GREATEST HITS
9. THE BEATLES' STORY
10. A BIT OF LIVERPOOL — Supremes

## TOP TEN OLDIES

1. Devil or Angel — Bobby Vee
2. Point of No Return — Gene McDaniels
3. Ghost Riders in the Sky — Ramrods
4. Whole Lotta' Shakin' Goin' On — Jerry Lee Lewis
5. Heartbreak Hotel — Elvis Presley
6. He's Sure the Boy I Love — The Crystals
7. Tutti-Fruitti — Little Richard
8. Kisses Sweeter Than Wine — Jimmie Rodgers
9. Why Do Fools Fall in Love — Frankie Lymon
10. Rock Around the Clock — Bill Haley

## TOP TEN UP AND COMERS

1. Heart of Stone — Rolling Stones
2. Hear My Heartbeat — Herman's Hermits
3. Across Mersey — Gerry & Pacemakers
4. The Boy Next Door — Standells
5. Fannie Mae — Righteous Bros.
6. Boy From New York — The Ad Libs
7. For Lovin' You — Peter, Paul & Mary
8. Born to Be Together — The Ronettes
9. At the Club — The Drifters
10. Little Red Rooster — Rolling Stones

## HI, HULLABALOOERS!

*Did you see me on tv the other day? Boy, was I great! In fact, I was so good that I got an offer from a movie company to be the understudy to one of their top stars. But I turned it down. I never liked Lassie that much anyhow. Seriously though, that show was so much fun to do that I wish all of you could have been there. "HOW COME I WASN'T INVITED?" Oh, no! It's Maud Skidmore again! Thank goodness she wasn't at the tv show . . . one look at her and the cameramen would have run screaming out into the street! Anyhow, before I go . . . so many of you KRLAers have written asking for more English pen pals that I went out and rounded up some more for you . . . so turn the page and sit down and write!*

## STARS VISIT ENGLAND

ENGLAND — "You've Lost That Lovin' Feeling" is making lots of hits in England! Cilla Black covered the Righteous Brothers' version over there, and so did Barbara Ann. Both records were taking off with a leap . . . and then the Righteous Brothers version hit town, along with the Righteous Brothers! The boys got there last week, and today the song (by them) is number twelve, jumping up past both female versions. The boys are really tearing them up in Beatle land. Every one of their shows have been sold out with standing room only.

Other American artists currently in England are Chuck Berry and Del Shannon.

# KRLA ARCHIVES

## D.J. SPOTLIGHT AT THE REVELAIR

Reb Foster's Revelaire certainly put Redondo Beach on the map! Here, Reb stands outside the Revelaire and looks at the "program." The club is on Catalina Street.

Inside, the place is swinging! You can always be sure of meeting groovy people, and every Friday and Saturday the club is jam packed. Everyone has a real blast!

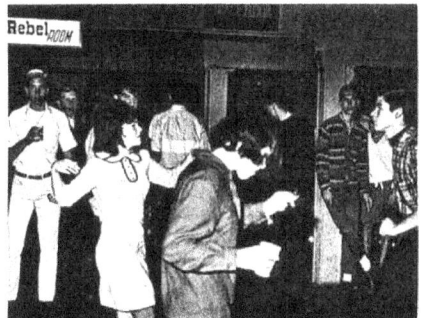

In the back of the club is the famous Rebel Room, with a snack bar and groovy private tables where you can sit and talk. If you can't dance, someone is sure to teach you!

Here Reb sits with some friends in the Rebel Room. Between sets, everyone gathers here to make friends and get to know each other. The snack bar serves sandwiches and cokes.

After announcing Reb, the Showmen stand ready to back the acts appearing. This week it was Joey Paige and Kathy Marshall. Soon, it might be Reb doing his record!

Joey proceeds to wipe everyone out! This is one singer who is going big places fast! He's the one the Rolling Stones came to America to see a few weeks ago.

Reb gets ready to introduce the next act, Kathy Marshall. That sweater he's wearing is blue suede in the front. Reb has some of the grooviest clothes around!

Kathy is one of the few girl instrumentalists in the world. She can really play, and she's only 14! She digs the Beatles and Stones, can play like them.

Photography by ROBIN HILL

# KRLA ARCHIVES

## ...RE WITH REB!

Eddie and the Showman wail out with the groovy sounds. They sound exactly like the Beatles, and are just about as good looking! They've had several hit records.

Eddie and the Showman start the nightly show. Reb always has the grooviest acts appear, and even if you can't dance, the show is worth coming to the club to see.

Joey does "Goodnight My Love" and the crowd goes wild! It's one of his most requested songs, and he may make a recording of it soon. Joey can really wail!

Joey and Reb take time out to talk to a few fans. Watch for guided tours of the Bob Eubanks' Cinnamon Cinder and Casey's dances in future issues.

## BRITAIN'S TOP TEN

So many of you have asked for the British top ten that we just couldn't resist! So here it is, the top pops in England:

1. Yeh, Yeh ..........Georgie Fame
2. I Feel Fine ................Beatles
3. Downtown ............Pet Clark
4. Somewhere ..........P.J. Proby
5. Terry .......................Twinkle
6. Girl Don't Come
   Sandie Shaw
7. Walk Tall ........Val Doonican
8. No Arms Can Hold You
   Bachelors
9. Go Now ............Moody Blues
10. I Could Easily Fall
    Cliff Richard

## RECORD REVIEW

### By BOB EUBANKS

January seems to be the month for records . . . there've been so many groovy new ones released that it's hard to know which ones to review!

Just about the best on the list is Herman and the Hermits new one, "Can't You Hear My Heartbeat." Herman's smooth sound will surely make this a good follow up to "Something Good."

"King of the Road," by Roger Miller, is causing everyone to compare him to a singing Will Rodgers! It's got a groovy beat, and the words are just too much!

For those of you who want the exclusive Rolling Stones record of "Little Red Rooster," don't fret . . . it'll be on their next album released in this country . . . along with some surprising numbers by these five gear guys.

"Fanny Mae," by the Righteous Brothers, is a good change of pace for these two. Of course, nothing can ever touch "Lovin' Feeling" in my opinion, but this new one will make both Bob and Bill established hit-makers.

Brenda Lee can become the top girl singer again with "Thanks A Lot." It's a real rocker in Brenda's old tradition.

The Searchers newest is their best so far! "What Have They Done to the Rain" is a soft, groovy ballad that the boys do extremely well.

That just about closes it for this week. Be back in two with more records to review!

## APRIL TO BE BIG MONTH FOR STARS

K*R*L*A*N*D — If the H-1 visa ban gets straightened out (and last minute flashes say it will) it looks like April is going to be the hottest month of the year as far as the group scene goes. Herman's Hermits will be here on the 16th to start the Dick Clark show, and will spend a week in K*R*L*A*N*D relaxing and doing some television shows. The Rolling Stones, who still have their H-1 permits, will start a series of concert dates across the country around the fifth of April. They would also like to spend at least three weeks here in California, their favorite place!

The Manfred Mann will definitely be back, whether the visa ban is off or not. They will come in on the fifteenth to tape the Shindig show, and will spend a few days relaxing in town before flying to New York. Scheduled for the same type of tour are the Kinks, who have wanted to come to this country for a long time, and should arrive around the 20th.

Gerry and the Pacemakers may be the first group to lead the parade . . . plans are underway for Gerry to return during the last week of March. It isn't known yet whether Billy J. Kramer and the Dakotas will accompany him, but it looks as though he might. Keep reading the BEAT for more news of when your favorite stars will be here in K*R*L*A*N*D!

## BEATLES TO DO SIX NEW SONGS

LONDON — If you want to get in touch with the Beatles . . . by phone, that is, get ready to place a call to London on February 16th! That's the date the four groovy guys will be recording six songs for their upcoming movie. The recording session will take place in studio two at EMI, starting at 3:00, London time. The six songs were written by, of course, John and Paul. And here's a little scoop . . . a lot of you have been wondering which part Paul writes and which part John writes. Here's the lowdown . . . Paul writes the words and John writes the melody! Walter Shenson, the producer of the film, said that there is no title or release date yet, but the film will definitely be in color. Shenson was also the producer of "Hard Day's Night."

## GROUPS IN TOWN

Get set for stars! Freddie and the Dreamers, the newest rage in England, make the local scene on February 11th. They will tape

# KRLA ARCHIVES

the Shindig and Dick Clark show for future showings, and will spend a week relaxing before leaving for Hong Kong.

Tony Hatch, one of the most famous producers and A and R men in England will also be in K*R*L*A*N*D in February. He'll get here on the 15th, joined later by Petula Clark, who's hit recording of "Downtown" was also written and produced by him. On February 17, the Rolling Stones will fly in for one day to stay with friends before going back to England. However, they are tentatively scheduled for a concert tour in April, and if possible, will be back then for a longer stay.

## FAX... ON... WAX!

### By REB FOSTER

It's super scoop time in wax land, so let's go!

The Standells, those four groovy guys who've flipped all you girls all over the southland are really becoming movie stars! Their first try was in "Get Yourself a College Girl," with the D.C. 5 and the Animals, and now they've been signed to sing the title song in MGM's "Zebra In The Kitchen"!

If you want to make a hit with Keith Richards of the Rolling Stones, tell him you dig listening to Irma Thomas. She's one of his favorites!

Speaking of the Stones, the one with the wildest sense of humor is Brian. He's also the one who likes to call his friends at 3:00 in the morning just to say hello! And when they were in town a few weeks ago, Mick Jagger dated Toni Basil, the dancer he met on the TAMI show the last time they were in town.

Bobby Vee and his wife, Karen proudly welcomed an addition to the family. Their son, Jeffrey, was born last week at St. Vincent's Hospital.

Don't tell anyone, but John Lennon is calmly looking around for an island! Yep, John wants to buy a deserted island where he and Cyn and baby John can be alone without anyone to bother them. Hey, John, if we promise not to bother you, can we come along? (In England, you can actually LEASE desert islands!)

Now that Jerry Lewis' son Gary has a hit record, we wonder if he'll be joining the rat pack!

That's about it for this week... be back in a few more with more fax on wax! Bye!

---

*Here you are, luvs! You knew we wouldn't let you down, didn't you? After all those letters we got asking for more of those groovy English pen pals, there was nothing left to do but get 'em for you! So Dave Hull went out and grabbed more gear Beatle fans just for you... and here they are!*

Miss Jacquie Edge
23, Bevington Rd.
Aston, Birmingham 6, England

Miss S. Wainwright
121, Penny Lane, Haydocie,
St. Helens, Lancashire, England

Valerie Hutton
8, Murdoch Point,
326, Aston Hall Road, Aston
Birmingham, 6, England

Eileen Elson
6, Queen Elizabeth Avenue
Bentley, Nr. Walsall,
Sraffs, England

Christine Quirke
23 Waldeck Road, Ealing
London W.D., England

Miss G. Hyman
St. Marys School,
Westwood Road, Beschill on-Seat
Sussex, England

Miss Sally Garbutt
49, Nursery Road, Knaphill
Woking, Surrey, England

Frances Morrissey
2, Beech Avenue, Higher Irlam
Manchester, Lancashire, England

Jacqueline Morgan
9, Bluebell Road, Priory, Estate
Dudley, Works, England

Eileen Bunn
164 Fawcett Estate,
Clapton Common,
London, E. 5., England

Pat Heap
4 Lawley Rd.
Blackburn Lancs
England

Kathy Jones
19 Newport St.
Oldham, Lancs
England

May Dempsey
c/o Yeasey
10 Caithness Rd.
Brook Green
London W/4, England

Mary Davis
21 Fir St.
Cadishead
Manchester, England

Ann Bennett
112 Orchard Ave.
Cheltenham
Glos, England

Penny Beech
14 Montague Sheet
Monks Rd.
Lincon, England

Miss H. Wear
37 Charville Lane West
Hillingdon, Uxbridge
Middlesex, England

Miss Ann McCartney
3, Brisco Road, Egremont,
Gumberland, England

Janet Griffin
125, Gilson Wat, Kingshurst,
Birmingham, 34 England

Linda Marron
94, Millbrook Ave., Bramblesfarm,
Middlesbrough, Yorkshire, England

Miss R. Austin
33, The New Parde, Sowerby,
Sowerby Bridge
Yorkshire, England

Miss C. Hunter
33, West Road, Crook,
Co. Durham, England

Linda Thompson
19, Stonehill Avenue, Bebington
Sheshire, Wimal, England

Margaret Hill
The Lodge, Little Canford
Nr. Wimborne, Dorset, England

Margaret A. H. Parr
21, Glenwood Road, Catford, S.E. 6
London, England

Linda Cawrytenko
23, Corwell ane
Millingdon, Midex, England

Jennifer Gadsby
28 Layton Park Ave.
Raurdon Nr. Leeds
Yorkshire, England

Christine Hilton
7 Lowgate Ave.
Bicker, Nr. Boston
Linconshire, England

Susan Birch
18 Kimberley Ave.
Newbary Park
Ilford, Essex
England

Brenda Toop
47 Haverstock Rd.
Kentish Town
London N.W. 5, England

Trina Clark
14 Windmore Ave.
Potters Bar
Middlesex, England

Anne Neve
6 The Pound
St. Audrey Lane, St. Ivers
Huntingdonshire, England

Kathy Lackey
14 Victoria Ave.
Lawden Rd., Small Heath
Birmingham 10, England

Anne Wilkinson
Langley Farm, Cowden
Nr. Edenbridge
Kent, England

# KRLA ARCHIVES

## PERSONALS

Do you want your personals printed? Each week, we'll print any messages you want to send through the KRLA BEAT! Just mail your message in on a post card to: PERSONALS, KRLA BEAT, P.O. Box 702-M, Pasadena, Calif. 91102. Keep messages about three lines. You can say anything you want (almost) . . . and it will be printed right here in the KRLA BEAT!

Call me "John"
  Elizabeth Sanchez
  of O.L.Q.A.

Brian Jones —
 I adore you.
  A Stone fan

Mick J.:
 She's a woman!!! "Ready, Steady, Go"! Great show, huh!?? "It's all over now!"
  Aaron

Eric & Wayne,
 You've got yourself 2 mo' admirers! We luv that long-hured music!
  2 Mindbenders

Prince:
 I have loved you, I do love you, I will always love you—Honest!
  All my lovin' Princess

Keith:
 To a swingin' guy—she's true—are you?
  Shrimp

T.P.:
 Don't worry—"It's all in the game." —Don't get stuck.
  "Richard's girl."

To the best bud a girl ever had—I luv you! "Susie."
  Yours, Nicky

Job emmon of the Beatles:
 I wood lick two no wear U got your Scuzzoo. Uz Eagel Rockians luv yur book and U.
  Lemmon luvers furever,

To Jim: Why don't you look my way??
  The girl in Mod. Science
  (4th seat)

Ringo, Ringo, Ringo Starr. Boy I love you wherever you are.
 Love ya —
  Joan Halpin

To Bob:
 Darling I am yours!
  Your Luv

Karynz:
 Keep your paws off him!
  Patti C.

Dave Hull:
 You're the gear! Thanks for playing all those Beatle songs. Thanks for the English pen pals.
 Love 'ya much,
  Gonks Inc.

Dave Hull: Please answer your phone— and my letters.
  S. J. Roddick
  Soledad

Dear Paul,
 (Wherever you are) I luv you
  Mrs. P. McCartney

Don't anyone luv George. He's a rat, creep, nut, and besides, he's mine.
  Shelley Janes

Coming soon! Pet and the Cynders! Watch for further details!

Hi! Bridget, Yogi, Viv, Cindy, Pat, Terri, Mary, and Sue!!!
 Love ya all,
  Judy McCartney

George and Paul are OURS!!!
  Irene (Max) and Judy

Herman's Hermits Fan Club—Dues $1.25 and 2-5¢ stamps!!
  Judy Hibbs
  631 Beatty St.
  Trenton, N.J. 08611

Mick,
 Please come back! Norma and I both love you!
  Lover

To Ken G.:
 You're the "richest man on earth," you have all my love, and Dave Hull too!!!
  A. S.

Dear Everybody:
 This is to acknowledge that I love Paul McCartney more than anything else in the world, universe even!
  Marcia Kochan

I saw the LadyBirds all girl rock n' roll band in Anaheim—They're great.
  Pat Muzik, 522 Pauline
  Anaheim, Calif.

Dona:
 I think I'm going out of my head, over you . . .
  Linda

Keith —
 Tears over Mick must seem childish to you. Thank you for being so understanding.
  Kathie green eyes

Terry Black,
 I think you are the neatest singer in the world. I luv you!
  Barb

To Barbsie Blurp: All the Redondo Union High School Sea Hawks and Hawkettes, and KRLA D.J.'s: HI!
  April O.
P.S. A ricky-ticky-tick and a fludy-utten-wosk!

Dave Hull:
 I love you dearly. Marry me and I'll make you happy!
  Sarabeth Rothfeld

Tom McGinnis of the Manfred Mann —
 I think you're the greatest! I luv you, I luv you, I luv you!
 With much luv, Barb McGrath

"How about that" Tim & Sandy are going steady. "How does that grab ya!"
  Gibuess Yibou?

Dave Hull, I'm sorry about the flash-bulbs, but I sure had a lot of fun in your arms.
  Love Donnita Moist

Brian and Keith come back! I love you both and I'll be waiting for you.
  Mickey's Pal

Dave Hull: I love you.
  A Hulabalooer.

To Cret, Andy, Joey, and Cathy: Who likes the Stones?
  Nan

To K.T.P./T.Q.R.:
 H.G.W.A.Y.
  From N.W.V.P./S.Q.R.

Peter Asher, where every you are: Doe Doe loves you! But I say up with Rolling Stones and Bobby Dale!
  Musky

Everybody support the Haunchies, 'cause they're taking over!
  A Haunchie Fan

Greetings from Florida to all Beatle fans in L.A., especially Dorothy & Criss,
  From Marlene & Debbie

B.E.:
 I'm your bottle of Pepsi forever.
  Miss Physical

I hugged Keith Richard of the Rolling Stones! Honest!!
  Elana 11

To Robert B. from Gloria K.:
 Stop taking me for granted, 'cause you'll never get to heaven if you break my heart.

To Paul McCartney:
 I love you, I love you, I love you! And Dave Hull too!
  With Luv, Donna Dolo

Paula Dempsey, I love you and always will. Your mountain of love.
  Judy Rodriguez

To Mike of La Puente: What happened between us? I'm doing the chasing this year. "Please come back!"
  Desperately Waiting

## VISA BAN...

that performers would be able to work in this country, but that they would have to get separate permission from local authorities for each single show. However, this would be so complicated and time consuming that it would be fairly impractical to do. British agents are currently trying to work something out with the American promoters that will enable English groups to come and work in this country without an H-1 permit.

## CONTEST CORNER!

*It's goodie time again, and boy oh boy, do we have a goodie this week! Of course, we always do, don't we? After all, we're just about the greatest things going. And don't ask us where we're going, either! (Some joker always wants to get technical and spoil the whole thing!) Anyhow, back to the contest. You know, every contest in the BEAT is really easy to win. You tell something in twenty-five words or less, or you guess how many of something or other is what (huh?) or you do some ridiculous easy thing that won't interfere with all that work your teacher makes you do after school. (Very unfair of her, we think) (But don't tell her we said so . . . she's bigger than we are) Anyhow . . . it's high time you had to do something constructive to win. Something creative. Something like draw a picture of Maud Skidmore! (Stop making those noises) And here's what the prize is:*

EVERY WEEK YOU SEE EXCLUSIVE PICTURES OF YOUR FAVORITE RECORD STARS AND D.J.S IN THE KRLA BEAT. EVERY WEEK YOU MUTTER UNDER YOUR BREATH THAT YOU'D LIKE TO GET YOUR HANDS ON SOME OF THOSE PICTURES. WELL NOW YOU CAN!

YES, YOU CAN WIN TEN (10) OF THE ORIGINAL PICTURES THAT APPEARED IN THE KRLA BEAT! TAKE YOUR PICK . . . BEATLES, ROLLING STONES, D.C. FIVE . . . ANY TEN OF YOUR FAVORITE PICTURES FROM THE BEAT WILL BE FIRST PRIZE IN THIS GROOVY CONTEST! THE WINNER WILL BE NOTIFIED BY US, AND GIVEN THEIR CHOICE! AND HERE'S ALL YOU HAVE TO DO:

What does Maud Skidmore look like? Do you think you know? Okay, then draw a picture of her! That's all there is to it . . . and you might be the winner! All drawings will be sumitted to Reb Foster, who will pick the drawing that he thinks looks the most like Maud. And it might be your drawing! All entries must be in by February 15th. Winner will be notified by February 20th, and the winning drawing will be printed in the KRLA BEAT! Attach the entry blank below to your drawing.

### ENTRY BLANK

NAME:............................................ AGE:...........

ADDRESS:............................................................

PHONE NUMBER:..................................................

# BOB EUBANKS GETS HIS OWN TV BEACH SHOW

FIVE CENTS      FEBRUARY 12, 1965      (Story in Col. 1)

# KRLA BEAT

Production, Design And Content By Bonnie Golden

## RADIO STAR NOW TV STAR

KRLA — Bob Eubanks, one of the most handsome d.j.s on the air, today confirmed that he will be the host on an unusual new dance party television show. The pilot film for the show will be taped in late March at Malibu, the site of the new dance show.

### "BEACH BEAT"

The name of the new show will be "Beach Beat" and will be the only television show of its kind. The show will feature surfers and surfing, top recording stars and teens from all over doing the latest dance steps. It will be the only dance show where surfing fans all over the country can get a look at their favorite sport right at the source ... sunny California!

### RODEO RIDER

Not many people know that Bob is one of the better rodeo riders in California! He has won many contests, and recently won the Rodeo Celebrity Tie Down in Pasadena, competing against film and record stars. He is very athletic, counting horseback riding as one of has favorite sports.

Bob, 27, was born in Flint, Michigan, but has spent most of his life out here in California. He opened the first of the first teenage night clubs, the Cinnamon Cinder, which became so popular that there are now two other C.C.s in California. The main club, located in North Hollywood, is nationally famous as the spot where the Beatles held their press conference last August, and is known to always have top stars appearing every week. The C. C. has been featured in many magazines, and the club's group, the Vibrants, have appeared with top stars at many rock and roll shows.

In addition to all the other activities in this busy young d.j's life, he has also just opened up an

*Continued on Page 4*

## KRLA TOP THIRTY

1. LOST THAT LOVIN' FEELIN' ........ Righteous Bros.
2. THE NAME GAME ........ Shirley Ellis
3. DOWNTOWN ........ Petula Clark
4. MY GIRL ........ The Temptations
5. LAUGH LAUGH ........ Beau Brummels
6. LAND OF 1000 DANCES ........ Headhunters
7. THIS DIAMOND RING ........ Gary Lewis
8. LOVE POTION NO. 9 ........ The Searchers
9. ALL & ALL OF THE NIGHT ........ The Kinks
10. TELL HER NO ........ The Zombies
11. KEEP SEARCHIN' ........ Del Shannon
12. LAND OF 1000 DANCES ........ The Midnighters
13. JOLLY GREEN GIANT ........ The Kingsmen
14. HOLD WHAT YOU'VE GOT ........ Joe Tex
15. THE "IN" CROWD ........ Dobie Grey
16. I GO TO PIECES ........ Peter & Gordon
17. RICHEST MAN ALIVE ........ Mel Carter
18. COME SEE ABOUT ME ........ The Supremes
19. I FEEL FINE/SHE'S A WOMAN ........ The Beatles
20. GOING OUT OF MY HEAD ........ Anthony & Imperials
21. KING OF THE ROAD ........ Roger Miller
22. OH NO NOT MY BABY ........ Maxine Brown
23. THE JERK ........ The Larks
24. GIVE HIM A GREAT BIG KISS ........ The Shangri-Las
25. PAPER TIGER ........ Sue Thompson
26. WHERE LOVERS GO ........ The Jaguars
27. AS TEARS GO BY ........ Marianne Faithful
28. WALK AWAY ........ Matt Monro
29. HOW SWEET IT IS ........ Marvin Gaye
30. NEEDLE IN A HAYSTACK ........ The Velvelettes

### TOP TEN ALBUMS

1. BEATLES' 65
2. WHERE DID OUR LOVE GO — Supremes
3. 12 x 5 — Rolling Stones
4. BEACH BOYS IN CONCERT
5. ROUSTABOUT — Elvis Presley
6. GOLDFINGER — Soundtrack
7. LOST THAT LOVIN' FEELIN' — Righteous Bros.
8. YESTERDAY'S GONE — Chad Stuart/Jeremy Clyde
9. HARD DAY'S NIGHT — Beatles
10. A BIT OF LIVERPOOL — Supremes

### TOP TEN OLDIES

1. Hurt — Timi Yuro
2. Twist and Shout — Beatles
3. Tragedy — The Fleetwoods
4. Hot Pastrami — Dartells
5. Hold Your Hand — Beatles
6. Beep Beep — Playmates
7. April Love — Pat Boone
8. Runin' Scared — Roy Orbison
9. There's A Moon Out Tonight — The Capris
10. Stay — Maurice Williams

### TOP TEN UP AND COMERS

1. The Boy Next Door — The Standells
2. Heart of Stone — Rolling Stones
3. Fannie Mae — Righteous Bros.
4. The Boy from New York — The Ad-Libs
5. Hear My Heartbeat — Herman's Hermits
6. Across Mersey — Gerry & Pacemakers
7. Thanks a Lot — Brenda Lee
8. Born to be Together — The Ronettes
9. For Lovin' You — Peter, Paul & Mary
10. Baby — Rolling Stones

## HI, HULLABALOOERS!

Did you all send me your valentines yet? Hurry up and get busy, if you haven't! And to the one who sent me Ann - Margret, THANKS! Wow! But about those of you who have been sending me your old steadys ... I don't need them, thank you! To get serious, though, thanks to all of you who have been sending me those groovy home made valentines. They're just beautiful! "I SENT YOU ONE TOO, BIG BOY ... IT'S IN A PACKAGE AND IT TICKS!" Oh, Maud! I might have known! Geesh, you can be sure that SHE won't be getting any valentines this year! Anyhow, I hope you've got a nice valentine this year. And I hope you decide to split some of that candy he's going to give you with me! (Unless you win the candy from Freddie ... then you'll probably want to hog it all for yourself! Selfish!) Oh, before I forget ... next week Dee-Dee's column starts! So if any of you have questions about any stars, send 'em in to DeeDee here at the BEAT, and she'll answer them for you! See you in a week ... and goodnight, Dave Clark ... wherever you are!

Address all mail to:
KRLA BEAT
P.O. BOX 702-M
PASADENA, CALIFORNIA

If you wish to order the latest issue of the KRLA BEAT, send a self-addressed stamped envelope and five cents for each issue. Back issues of the KRLA BEAT are ten cents and a self-addressed, stamped envelope.

# KRLA ARCHIVES

KRLA was the first radio station in the world to have its very own tv spectacular ... and what a spectacular it was! The audience started coming to the studio hours before the taping ... no one wanted to miss getting a good seat.

Outside the studio, in the hall, fans risked not getting a seat to get Dave Hull's autograph. Dave was mobbed by fans! But he wasn't the only one ... our d.j.s signed more autographs than the stars on the show!

Off in the dressingroom, Dick Moreland, who show, goes over the line up with Hank Mancin The show had the highest ratings of any show i

Emperor Hudson ("You don't push an emperor around") introduced the 'King' ... Presley. He had everyone in stitches with his jokes and stories! He even got a special cheer when he mentioned the KRLA BEAT! He's wearing his gold robes.

Reb Foster sits on a handy box while they get the cameras in position. (His new record, by the way, is a gas!) Then he talked about the 'golden years of rock & roll' ... bringing back memories for all of us. He introduced Duane Eddy.

Duane was wearing a groovy leather suit th first big hit, "Rebel Rouser." Duane was th opened up a whole new field of music. He's

Next it was Dick Moreland's turn. It's too bad he couldn't wear his John Lennon hat so that you all could get to see it! Dick is looking better than he ever did, and wasn't nervous about being on television ... he introduced the Ventures.

The Ventures are local boys, and every one of their albums has been a hit. Like Duane Eddy, they've had a lot of influence on popular music ... especially the guitar side! They've also done a lot of shows at Bob's Cinnamon Cinder nite club.

Gary Mack, our 'meet 'em at the airport' d.j on-the-air man, and is also president of the his first time on television, and he loved it

Casey Kasem stole the whole show! He talked about the many wonderful stars who are no longer with us, and everyone said that he was so good they couldn't believe it! Casey always knows unknown facts about top recording stars!

Photography by ROBIN HILL

Casey introduced Bobby Vee, and told of how Bobby became a star through tragedy. Bobby is married, recently became a proud papa! He did "Take Good Care of My Baby," one of his many big hits.

Then Dave Hull came on ... with Roger Mil be found! Dave and Roger entertained for ho tape ... and everyone was laughing so l

# KRLA ARCHIVES

eland, who wrote much of the script for the
iank Mancini, the host on the 90 minute bash.
any show in KCOP's history! And no wonder!

The taping starts! All the KRLA d.j.s were together on stage as a groovy background for the opening shot. Henry Mancini opened the show by introducing our fine nine, and the swinging show was ready to start! Everyone was excited.

First off was Bobby Dale, who knows more about music than just about anybody! Bobby talked about the early beginnings of rock and roll back in 1955 ... when he was one of the first people to jump on the beat bandwagon.

ther suit that turned everyone on! He did his
ine was the first guitar instrumentalist, and
nusic. He's one of George Harrison's favorites.

For the first time in history, it's Charlie's turn to introduce Dick Clark as a guest on HIS show! And while Dick was talking, Charlie rolled Dick's pant leg up to the knee! (He was getting even for all the time Dick's done it to him!)

Dick, naturally, introduced the dancers on the show. They did all the old dances, like the stroll and jump, right up to the new ones like the jerk and monkey. The Vibrants, Bob Eubanks' C.C. group, backed the dancers and all the acts.

airport' d.j. was next. Gary is KRLA's youngest
lent of the Tommy Quickly fan club. This was
he loved it!

Bob Eubanks talked about his second favorite sport ... surfing. Here, Adrian models show the latest swimwear while Bob discusses the finer points of shooting the curl! After some groovy surfing film, Bob introduced Jan and Dean.

Although the two can't surf that well, they sure know how to sing about it! Dean is the more athletic of the boys, and also the one with the wildest sense of humor. He sings the high part on all their songs, and the girls love him! Jan too!

Roger Miller! A funnier combination couldn't
ined for half an hour while they rewound the
ghing so hard that they had tears running!

Then Roger did "Dang Me," the record that introduced him to the pop world. He's becomming known as the new Will Rogers ... one of the funniest men on record! He and Dave caused permanent laugh wrinkles on everyone there!

Then Dave introduced ... well, can't you guess? A film clip was shown of their press conference, and Dave told of the gear four's fantastic impact on today's music. Next week, the BEAT wil has a fantastic scoop about Dave!

# KRLA ARCHIVES

## PERSONALS

Do you want your personals printed? Each week, we'll print any messages you want to send through the KRLA BEAT! Just mail your message in on a post card to: PERSONALS, KRLA BEAT, 1401 South Oak Knoll Rd., Pasadena, California. Keep messages about three lines. You can say anything you want (almost) ... and it will be printed right here in the KRLA BEAT!

Janie,
Want an exclusive? You can have four Beatles I.A.D.R. — I'll take my 5 any time! (hic)   Stones Rule

To Tommy Quickley and the Very Gear Beatles: Please come back we all miss you (at least I know I do).
Shelly Heber

To the Funny Boy in the Record Store who sells me "Beats" — "Hall"

To George Harrison —
Hi Bird! (?) I love you more than Elaina does!   Marilyn

To Gary in Downey:
"Howdy from the Farm!"
Linda Seed-bag from Tarzana

Beatles forever, Dave Clark never.
From a Beatle Lover    R.H.

To Dave Clark 5:
Why did you copy the Beatles?
A Beatle People, Becky

Paul, Paul, your mind, mind, all mind, aren't you?
Jane Asher C.O.D.

## BEATLE BITS

**by Dick Moreland**

I've gotten a lot of letters asking what kind of guitars the Beatles play, so instead of bits about the boys this week, I'll tell you about the Beatle guitars!

Paul, who plays bass, uses a Hofner Violin bass guitar. On records, he also plays piano and organ.

Ringo's drum setup is composed of a Ludwig 22 inch Super Classic and two 20 inch Downbeat drum kits. His cymbals are Avedis Zildjian 18 and 20 inch, and he uses a 15 inch Hi-hat.

George, who is lead guitar, uses several different kinds on stage. The two he uses most often are the Rickenbacker No. 1993 twelve string and the Gretch Tennessean, which is used for the "Nashville" sound.

John plays rhythm of course, and uses three different guitars. He plays the 12 string used by George, along with the Rickenbacker No. 1996 six string and the Gibson Jumbo guitar. On stage and records he also plays the Hohner Super Chromonica, Echo Super Vamper, and Basil harmonicas.

For amplifiers, both John and George use the Vox AC 100-watt Super De Luxe amplifier with one extension cabinet containing four 12 inch and two Midax speakers. It was built especially for the Beatles. Paul uses the same type amplifier with a bass speaker cabinet with two 15 inch speakers.

## EUBANKS...

agency of his own in Hollywood. One of the people working for him will be Derek Taylor, former Beatle press agent, who will arrive to start his new job later this month.

Bob is currently the number one d.j. in his time slot, 6:00 to 9:00, a rating he is sure to hold for a long time to come.

In answer to the many letters asking how you can join the Dave Hull fan club, here's the info:

Club members are given top priority when any English group gets into town. They get to see and many times talk to the group, and are informed in advance when any star is coming to California. Club members also get to go to the taping of Shindig any time they wish, and a certain number of tickets to the show is set aside each week for their use. Upon joining the club, each member receives a fan club card and autographed picture of Dave. In addition to this, you also receive a monthly bulletin with inside scoops about all the English groups including the Beatles! Information in this bulletin is for club members only, top secret facts that no one else knows. All members are informed at all times of Dave's activities, and are given special invitations to things like KRLA's spectacular two weeks ago, press conferences, etc. To join, send one dollar ($1.00) to Colleen Ludwick, president, 6231 Ivar, Temple City, California.

## CASEY'S CORNER

**by Casey Kasem**

You keep asking for those likes and dislikes of your favorite stars, so here are some more for you:

The Righteous Brothers both dig girls who know the music business and can talk about it intelligently. Bill likes quiet girls ... Bob likes talkative ones.

Gerry Marsden can't stand snowy weather ... he likes the hot sun of California!

Peter Asher likes to talk about philosophy with a girl ... and one way to get a smile out of him is to give his sister, Jane a compliment. They are very close.

Dick St. John, of Dick and Dee-Dee likes to go horseback riding ... DeeDee likes going out to a club where she can get all dressed up!

Herman of Herman's Hermits likes to be called by his real name ... Peter. He loves a good joke, and can tell a lot of them.

Brenda Lee hates anyone to say something about how small she is ... she's self conscious about her height.

Brian Jones loves to go clothes shopping ... and he loves long hair on girls.

That's it for now ... see you in two weeks with more inside news about your favorite stars!

## CONTEST CORNER!

*You all know that Freddie and the Dreamers will be in town on the 14th of February. (You do if you've been reading the BEAT!) Anyhow, the 14th of February is also a day to celebrate for another reason ... and don't try to fool us, we know that you know it's Valentine's day! Anyhow, is there anyone out there who's not going to have a Valentine? Tsk, tsk, tsk. That's awful! Can't tell you how bad we feel 'bout that. In fact, we feel so bad that we just might do something about it. (Then again, we might not. Never can tell about us!) What's that? You want us to do something about it? You want us to find you a Valentine? Alrighty. Anything you want! (Greedy little nits) (See, we saw Hard Day's Night too!) Anyhow, here it is:*

### YOU CAN WIN FREDDIE AND THE DREAMERS FOR YOUR VALENTINE!

Freddie will call you and introduce himself. You'll get to talk to him and all the Dreamers for as long as you want! And that's not all. He'll give you one of his favorite pictures of himself, and he'll sign it with a special Valentine message just for you! And even that's not all ... he'll also pick out a special Valentine box of candy for you! Freddie will be your very own Valentine! And here's all you have to do to win:

**Just tell in twenty five words or less why you want Freddie to be your Valentine. We'll pick the ten best entries, and Freddie and the Dreamers will pick the winning one. You'll be notified by phone on the 15th, and told when Freddie will call you. And that's all there is to it! Be sure and get your entry in by February 15th! You can enter as many times as you wish, but all entries must be accompanied by an entry blank. Entries will be judged on basis of neatness and originality. (Except by Freddie. He'll probably pick the mushiest one. Men are all alike!) (And we love 'em that way!) Anyhow, get busy! Freddie could be YOUR Valentine!**

### ENTRY BLANK

NAME: ............................................................ AGE: ...............

ADDRESS: ..........................................................................

PHONE NUMBER: ..................................................................

# KRLA ARCHIVES

# THOUSANDS ENTER KRLA HEART ART FESTIVAL

GRAHAM'S PIPER MUSIC CO.
9612 E. LAS TUNAS DRIVE

FIVE CENTS — FEBRUARY 22, 1965 — (Story in Col. 1)

KRLA BEAT
© COPYRIGHT 1965

The KRLA BEAT is owned and published by KRLA. All material therein is the property of KRLA, as is the name "BEAT" and/or the KRLA BEAT.

## OVER 5,000 RECEIVED

KRLA — One of the most successful contests in radio history was held by KRLA this month. The Valentine Art Festival, which started in late January, saw over 5000 hand made valentines sent or brought to KRLA's studios in Pasadena!

The valentines all showed great imagination and creativity. Some of them were so unusual that the d.j.s they were sent to decided to take them home and save them!

### PIZZA AND CAKE

It looks as though a lot of you believe the old saying "The way to a man's heart is through his stomach"! So man, cakes were brought to the station that KRLA could have opened up its own bake shop! Many of the cakes were in the shape of hearts, and all of them were beautifully decorated. You can be sure that everyone at the station gained at least ten pounds! One of the most unusual valentines was a four foot pizza in the shape of a heart! The pizza was decorated with sausage, mushrooms, anchovies and green peppers, and looked simply delicious! Other valentines were made of cardboard, wood, and paper. They were decorated with sequins, artificial flowers, tissue paper roses, glitter, and paint. Most of them had some kind of lace trim, and all of them showed hours of hard work.

### THE WINNERS

The two d.j.s who got the most valentines were Emperor (Beautiful Bob) Hudson, and the winner, Dave Hull. So many valentines came for Dave that a special room had to be set aside for his valentines only! The happy winners will appear next week in the KRLA BEAT, along with their winning valentines. And if you didn't win this time . . . there's always next year!

## KRLA TOP THIRTY

1. LOST THAT LOVIN' FEELIN' .......... Righteous Bros.
2. DOWNTOWN .......... Petula Clark
3. THE NAME GAME .......... Shirley Ellis
4. LAND OF 1000 DANCES .......... Headhunters
5. MY GIRL .......... The Temptations
6. LAUGH LAUGH .......... The Beau Brummels
7. THIS DIAMOND RING .......... Gary Lewis
8. LAND OF 1000 DANCES .......... The Midnighters
9. TELL HER NO .......... The Zombies
10. JOLLY GREEN GIANT .......... The Kingsmen
11. LOVE POTION NO. 9 .......... The Searchers
12. ALL DAY & ALL OF THE NIGHT .......... The Kinks
13. KEEP SEARCHIN' .......... Del Shannon
14. I GO TO PIECES .......... Peter & Gordon
15. RICHEST MAN ALIVE .......... Mel Carter
16. TWINE TIME .......... A. Cash & Crawlers
17. HOLD WHAT YOU'VE GOT .......... Joe Tex
18. KING OF THE ROAD .......... Roger Miller
19. PAPER TIGER .......... Sue Thompson
20. BOY FROM NEW YORK CITY .......... The Ad-Libs
21. THE BIRDS & THE BEES .......... Jewel Atkins
22. THE "IN" CROWD .......... Dobie Grey
23. HEART OF STONE .......... Rolling Stones
24. WHERE LOVERS GO .......... The Jaguars
25. GOING OUT OF MY HEAD .......... Anthon & Imperials
26. I FEEL FINE/SHE'S A WOMAN .......... The Beatles
27. LOOK OF LOVE .......... Lesley Gore
28. NEW YORK'S A LONELY TOWN .......... The Trade Winds
29. VOICE YOUR CHOICE .......... The Radiants
30. WALK AWAY .......... Matt Monro

## TOP TEN ALBUMS

1. BEATLES '65 — THE BEATLES
2. WHERE DID OUR LOVE GO — THE SUPREMES
3. BEACH BOYS IN CONCERT — THE BEACH BOYS
4. GOLDFINGER — SOUND TRACK
5. ROUSTABOUT — ELVIS PRESLEY
6. COAST TO COAST — DAVE CLARK FIVE
7. 12 x 5 — ROLLING STONES
8. VINTON'S GREATEST HITS — BOBBY VINTON
9. LOST LOVIN' FEELIN' — RIGHTEOUS BROTHERS
10. YESTERDAY'S GONE — CHAD & JEREMY

## TOP TEN OLDIES

1. Walking to New Orleans — Fats Domino
2. Let the Good Times Roll — Shirley & Lee
3. I'm Available — Margie Rayburn
4. Tragedy — The Fleetwoods
5. Smokie (pts. 1 & 2) — Bill Black Combo
6. Butterfly — Charlie Gracie
7. My True Love — Jack Scott
8. Stay — Maurice Williams
9. There's a Moon Out Tonight — The Capris
10. Guess Things Happen That Way — Johnny Cash

## TOP TEN UP AND COMERS

1. 8 Days a Week — The Beatles
2. I Need You Baby — Rolling Stones
3. Across Mersey — Gerry & Pacemakers
4. Fannie Mae — Righteous Bros.
5. Hear My Heartbeat — Herman's Hermits
6. Boy Next Door — Standells
7. For Lovin' Me — Peter, Paul & Mary
8. Ask the Lonely — Four Tops
9. At the Club — The Drifters
10. Little Things — Bobby Goldsboro

## HI, HULLABALOOERS!

Well, I've finally made the big time! If you don't believe me, look inside for the scoop! Tell me what other d.j. could do that . . . and be so modest, too! Anyhow, to all you scoffers out there, I DO have a few friends. "HERE'S TWENTY CENTS, BIG BOY . . . CALL BOTH OF THEM!" Oh, Maud, your jealousy doesn't even bother me any more . . . not when the Scuzzys are Casey's pick to hit! (I would have made it my own pick, but how conceited can you get!) Actually, I can't tell you how excited I am about the record! It really makes me feel good. Now, don't all of you go writing songs for me just because you want a hit record! After all, Ringo, you really don't need another hit! By the way, did you know that for some strange reason, the record is a KRLA exclusive? Yep, we get 'em all first! And another thing, thanks for all those nice valentines, you all! I'm going to take them home and paste them on my wall . . . it's high time I took down all those Christmas cards! Anyrode, goodbye for this week . . . but don't fret, I'll be back next week, you lucky t h i n g s! And goodnight, Dave Clark . . . whatever you are!

## JOHN HATS

LONDON — If you've wanted a cap just like John Lennon's, now you can get one! KRLA BEAT tracked d o w n the store where John bought his Beatle hat and got some information about it for you!

The cap is handsome of soft top quality leather, lined with red satin. They come in black and brown, and John has bought over eight of them so far, all black. The satin inside is stainproof, and

Continued on Page 4

# KRLA ARCHIVES

By day, Dick Moreland is KRLA's record librarian, listening to the hundreds of records brought to KRLA each week to see if they have that "hit" potential. But during the TAMI show, mild mannered D.M. went to the show ...

... and had the time of his life! He knew most of the artists on the show, and it was great to see them all together again. Here he talks to the M.C.s of the show, Jan and Dean. They were really funny during the taping!

Dick meets one of the Miracles, one of his all time favorite groups. You can hear Dick's groovy show every weekend ... and some of his funny jokes about the top stars will have you in stitches!

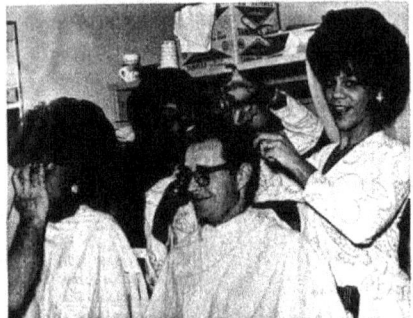

Uh, oh, what's this! We all thought that Dick's hair looked fine, but it looks like the Supremes didn't! Actually, they did, but they all have secret desires to be hairdressers and decided to experiment on Dick!

Gab time! One of the Beach Boys takes time out to talk to two of his friends with the same first name. Dick St. John, of Dick & DeeDee, stopped by to say hello and catch the show. DeeDee couldn't make it.

In case you're wondering where Dick got all those groovy scoops on the Beach Boys, now you know ... right from the source! The Beach Boys recently finished a tour of England and said that it was a gas.

Dick talks with the man that stole the show ... James Brown. Dick says that he is one of the greatest r & b entertainers out today, and anyone who saw the TAMI show will surely agree with him. He was great!

During a break in the taping, Dick relaxes with some of the KRLAers who attended the show. Over 3000 free tickets were given away by KRLA for this groovy show! It has now been turned into a film and will be out this month.

This is one of the most famous pictures to ever appear in the KRLA BEAT. Dick and Gerry Marsden grin from ear to ear and manage to look like twins doing it! Gerry completely cracked up when he saw this picture.

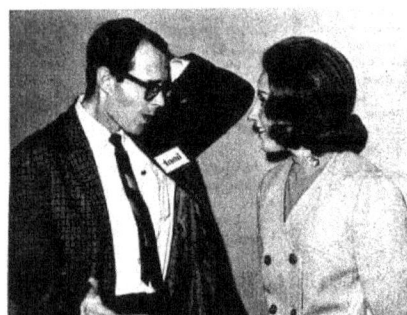

Dick talks to one of his favorite girls, Lesley Gore. Leslie loved being in the show, and said that the next time she came out to California, she would make a special trip to Pasadena to see KRLA.

Here Dick is with the king ... Chuck Berry! Chuck is coming to town on the 24th of this month for a show, and you can bet that Dick will be there ... along with Bobby Dale, of course! A new TAMI show will be filmed in April.

After the taping, there was a big banquet for everyone at the show. The informal fun after the show was even more fun than the show itself! Dick said that he had more fun there than at any other show he's ever been to!

Photography by ROBIN HILL

# KRLA ARCHIVES

## LEADER GETS MARRIED

ON—Ray Davies, leader nks, was married December in Bradford, England. The is Rasa Davies, 18, from Ray met Rasa over a year n she was singing folk a party. The two started on after, and became engaged September. The new Mrs. a natural blonde, with that she wears straight. ables Jackie DeShannon, o one of her idols. Rasa's be heard on a record that leased in an album in this country, "Come On Now." She background. The record is currently on the other side of est single in England.

Now there's an addition to the Kinks . . . (See Story)

isn't think that his marriage will hurt the group's popularity. as our records are good, I think teenagers will accept us." up was formed three years ago in Muswell Hill, London. members, Ray, his brother Dave, Mick Avory, and Pete ere art students at the Croydon School of Art. They decided group to help earn money for their studies, and the Kinks Ray plays rhythm guitar and harmonica, while Dave is ad lead guitarist of the group. Pete, who also sings, plays bass le Mick is the group's drummer. The boys designed their age uniforms themselves, and the clothes have now become mark.

nes from a big family . . . five brothers and one sister. His is snobs, and he likes to spend his spare time sleeping. "I lf out on stage," he grins. He flips for r&b, but also knows t about classical music. Even though the group's success has em from continuing their studies at the Croydon art school, eps his hand in, and loves to draw quick sketches of people ay the time backstage at performances.

ant to send a congratulatory card to Ray and his new wife, ss is Collingwood Avenue, Muswell Hill, London, England.

## Like Lennon, Like Stone!

LONDON—John Lennon isn't the only musical author . . . as Charlie Watts of the Rolling Stones proved when his book, "Ode to a High Flying Bird" was released last week in England!

The book is a tribute to Charlie's idol, Charlie "Bird" Parker the late sax player who is one of the lengendary greats of jazz. (Charlie has always been a jazz fan). It consists mainly of Charlie's drawings with handwritten captions. The drawings are in color, and show quite a bit of talent. Since Charlie was a commercial artist before he became a Stone, they are imaginative and professional.

"I wasn't trying to write a book . . . in fact, I did this years ago, way before there was any 'beat' sound. It was something I felt, and I just put it down in drawings on paper. There's hardly any actual writing in it, in fact. It's only about 30 pages. I'd nearly forgotten I'd ever done it, and then mentioned it to a friend who asked to see it. When he said he wanted to publish it, it knocked me out!"

The book has gotten very good reviews so far. It's not known yet if Charlie plans on following up with another book, as has Lennon, but if the good reviews continue, he probably will!

***

If you wish to order the latest issue of the KRLA BEAT, send a self-addressed stamped envelope and five cents for each issue. Back issues of the KRLA BEAT are ten cents and a self-addressed, stamped envelope.

***

## RECORD REVIEW
### By BOB EUBANKS

Before I start reviewing records this week, I want to ask you if you've noticed something I've been noticing . . . there's a new trend in music! Both English and American artists are getting down to the roots of rock . . . blues! I'm glad of it, too, because records are sounding better than ever!

To start off, KRLA's exclusive by the Rolling Stones, "Need You Baby," should be released as their next single in this country. It's caused more reaction than any other record by the group, and is one of their best so far.

The Animals have a hit with "Don't Let Me Be Misunderstood," their newest. It's a gas of a song, and should start climbing.

Maxine Brown, one of the fastest rising blues singers, follows up her last hit with a real goodie, "It's Gonna Be Alright." She really wails on this one, and it could happen for her.

Reb Fosters' newie, "Something You Got," is a real winner! No one at the station knew he could sing with so much soul! Looks like our boy is going to be a star!

The Dave Clark Five get off the beaten path with "Come Home." It's more of an American sound than an English one, and entirely different from the group's past efforts.

Terri Black should really make the top of the charts with his new one, "Everyone Can Tell." It's a real rocker, with lots of beat behind it.

That cools it for this week. I'll be back with more records to review in two!

## Dave In Magazine

KRLA—Teen Screen Magazine, the top selling, biggest teenage fan magazine on the stands, is doing a two page article on . . . none other than Dave Hull! They have done short articles on Dave before this, and he has also been their d.j. of the month. Janey Milstead, editor of the magazine, said that "Dave has shown much more potential than most of the d.j.s in this country. We get letters asking about him from as far away as New York, and many of the top groups that stop into the office mention that he is their friend. When we saw the pictures of Dave with the Hullabaloos that appeared in the KRLA BEAT, we asked Bonnie Golden, the editor, if we could have them for an article on Dave."

## FAX... ON... WAX!
### By REB FOSTER

Paul McCartney must be thinking of becoming a racing driver! His new car, an Aston Martin, goes over 150 miles per hour! The car is dark blue and has black leather upholstery, and includes a record player which was custom built for the car!

Bass player for the Hollies, Eric Haydock, got married on January 23rd to Pamela Done, 20, in Stockport, England.

Chad and Jeremy have turned to acting! The gear twosome from you-know-where have been signed for a dramatic role on the Patty Duke show. Stay tuned and we'll tell you when the show will be on.

Brian Epstein flew to New York last week to discuss the summer tour by the Beatles. He now says that the boys won't do the same grinding type of tour they did last year, but will do only about 15 days of concert dates. AND . . . they're going to take a short vacation in this country . . . right here in K*R*L*A*N*D!

The next Dick and DeeDee record will be the one that was written especially for them by Mick Jagger and Keith Richard! But they aren't the only Stones who can write a song . . . Bill Wyman also wrote Joey Paige's new one, "I'm In Love With You. It was recorded two weeks ago and will be out later this month.

Dave Davies of the Kinks bought George Harrison's old guitar. Kink, by the way, is English slang for wild, weird, and wonderful!

That's it for this week . . . see you in two with more fax on wax!

## SHOW SKIING TRIP FOR BEATLE

vision, the firm who first TAMI show, has how to American In-films, who are re-as a full length movie le. The film is now re-der the name of "The ck and Roll Festival," rently playing in New ould reach here later h. A new TAMI show to be filmed in April, star eleven groups. f the groups aren't at this moment, but definite that the show n be filmed out here.

John Lennon has announced that he will take a short vacation from Beatle activities this week to go on a skiing trip to the Alps. His wife, Cynthia, will go with him, along with George Martin, his recording manager. Although John has never skied before, he has always wanted to try his luck at the sport and feels that he will learn enough this trip so that he'll at least be able to make it down one of the slopes!

## BBY IS V ACTOR

WOOD—Bobby Vin-ly riding the charts ording of "Mr. Lonely," hard on scaring peo-right . . . scaring! He's lead roll of a baby-r on the Alfred Hitch- This isn't Bobby's first to the film world. He's n several movies and a tv shows, but says that career will always be ortant than his film far, he's doing a good mbining both! After n the show, which will in two months, you can Bobby a letter telling you thought of the home address is 7100 os Angeles 46, Calif.

## REB'S RECORD

HOLLYWOOD—Reb Foster, popular KRLA d.j., is well on his way to being a new singing sensation! His record, "Something You Got," was released last week and is starting to take off like a bird! The record is on the Loma label, and is backed by "Quetzel and Jude," an instrumental. Sonny Buono, of Sonny and Cher, directed the recording session, and also played harmonica on it. Last month, the KRLA BEAT printed pictures taken at the session, and you were able to see the singing side of Reb for the first time. The record has a blusey, funky sound with plenty of soul! Cashbox and Billboard, the two record industry trade magazines, both picked the record as a "Best Bet," which means that they think the record will be a hit. After listening to it, so do we!

## VISA BAN GETS GROUP

NEW YORK — The power of the H-1 Visa ban was felt once more when another of England's top groups was forced to cancel a personal appearance just a few minutes before they were to go on stage. The incident happened in New York, where the group, the Animals, were scheduled to record an album live at the Apollo Theatre in Harlem. The Apollo is the home of rhythm and blues, and it had been the ambition of the whole group to someday work there. They had arrived in New York on January 18th for two days work at the famous theatre, and were also going to shoot part of a movie during that time. After their show at the Apollo, they were to tape an Ed Sullivan show on the 24th and fly out to California.

Unfortunately, these arrangements were made without the permission of the American Federation of Musicians, who have to give the okay on all overseas groups who appear in this country. The Animals had done one of the four shows a day they did at the Apollo when they received a call from their agent stating that unless they left the theatre immediately, their visas could be withdrawn and they would have to leave the country that day. The boys left, and then discovered that the AFM had also withdrawn permission for them to appear on the Sullivan show. The group and their manager, Mike Jeffries, along with their lawyer and agents then met with officials of the union to discuss this, and permission was finally granted for them to appear on the Sullivan show, barely 24 hours before the show was to be taped. They did one number on the show, "Don't Let Me Be Misunderstood," which is their latest record.

The group's trip to California is now being delayed until Mike Jeffries can make arrangements with the union to have their visas restored. If the visas are not given back to the group, they will have to go back to England immediately and won't be able to come back to this country until April.

# KRLA ARCHIVES

## PERSONALS

Do you want your personals printed? Each week, we'll print any messages you want to send through the KRLA BEAT! Just mail your message in on a post card to: PERSONALS, KRLA BEAT, 1401 South Oak Knoll Rd., Pasadena, California. Keep messages about three lines. You can say anything you want (almost) ... and it will be printed right here in the KRLA BEAT!

Diana and Sandy—Best "Birds" In La Habra. Thanx to Dave Hull?
*Phyllis and Fraya, Winnipeg, Canada*

To Sara C.:
I love you a whole awful lot.
*Mike C.*

Mick — Janie thinks of you when she opens her closet, but I think of you when I see cookies! (or half)

To John Stevenson of Alhambra High.
I like you a lot!!
*A Alhambra Admirer*

Pat:
J.P. will be as famous as the R.S. and B. Just takes time.
*The girl at the TAMI show*

To All Stone Fans:
My friends in the U.S.A., this is being sent by one of my friends in the U.S.A. So that you won't know my street number, but Michael Phillip Jagger is mine!
*HIS BIRD in Manchester*

Hi Linda! Give Scott my best.
*Luv, D.W.A.*

To Mike Gillum of La Puente:
You are a tootie rat.
*Toot the 1st & Toot the 2nd*

To Mike Smith — Don't let anyone tell you they love you more than me!
*Luv, G.E.*

Mark Lane—Keno:
Thanks for writing—they believe me now. See you this summer.
*KRLA JoAnne*

Cheryl:
Please call me at CL 5-4191⁴.
*Jack, the boy at the Rose Parade*

To Teri Smith—
You can have Paul McCartney but just stay away from Ringo!
P.S. Thanks for the Pen-Pals Dave Hull!
*Luv ya, Joan Starkey*

Dave Hull —
I love you, I love you, I love you— Yeah, Yeah, Yeah!
*A Dave Hull Maniac*

To Mike Sheggles —
Teri loves you almost as much as Paul McCartney!
*A Traitor*

To the Scuzz:
We used to love you but it's all over now (DC5 Forever).
I remain unknown and still loyal (I guess) *A Hullabalooer*

To Joy and Margi:
I love Mike Smith more than anything else in the world. Do you?
*D.C.5 Lover*

G. E. of Whittier:
Will you Please finish that story— and hurry!
*You-know-who*

To Colleen, Rhio, Judy and Derra,
You're so 'lucky' I could break down and cry.
*Love Beatles & DC5*
*From Whittier and La Habra*

To Dave Hull:
Need any fan club members to take Peter & Gordon to Marineland? We're available!
*Love ya, Diana & Greer*

Bobby I am sorry. Hope you're not mad. I love you.
*Yours 4ever, Angie*

Charlie Watts
We hope he rots! (he got married)
*Suzanne & Kathie*

Phil —
I want my eye liner back!
*Kathie S.*

---

To DC5 — You're the greatest! Don't let anyone tell you different. Even the no-good, Dum Dum, head, scuzzy Hullaballooer.
*Love G.E.*

Dear Sue — I'm so sorry that you lost, but so did I! If Dave Hull knew, he would dedicate, "I'm a Loser" to us. You're not reall, though. Better luck in next year's elections.
*A good friend, Ruth*

## DATE WITH DEEDEE!

*By DeeDee Sperling*

Hi, everyone!

Gee, I can't tell you how excited I am to have my own column in the BEAT! I'll be here once a month from now on, and I'd really like to hear from every one of you . . . just send your letters to me, DeeDee Sperling, here at the KRLA BEAT.

A lot of you have been wondering if Dick and I are related or going steady or what. Actually, Dick and I met in high school and were always good friends. Dick wanted to cut a record, and asked me to sing on the other side of it. I did, and our first record, "Mountains High" was a hit. Dick and I have been singing ever since!

Now I'll answer a few of the letters I've received from you:

To Franny, L.A.: Yes, we just came back from a tour of England, and can't wait to go over again. It was our first trip, and we loved it.

To Tom, Encino: You heard right, I am serious about being a writer. I've been working on some serious stories, and someday hope to write a book.

To Ginny, Pasadena: Wow, that's a hard question to answer! I really can't describe which group I've enjoyed working with the most! We did the Rolling Stones show in Long Beach, and they are simply fantastic . . . one of the greatest groups in the world. Gerry and the Pacemakers are also too much . . . in fact Gerry is one of the friendliest people I've ever met! Tell you what . . . if Dick and I are ever lucky enough to work with the Beatles, maybe I'll be able to answer your question. Right now I just can't decide!

Whoops, I've run out of room! Guess I'll have to say goodbye for this month . . . in the meantime, why don't you drop me a line? I'd love to hear from you!

## HATS...

the leather is waterproof and never needs shining or polishing. It can be cleaned with a damp cloth. If you want one, write to: "The Bazaar," 46 Brompton Road, London SW3, England. Here's the catch . . . the cap costs 15 guineas English money . . . and that figures out to be about $44.10 American! However, if the cost hasn't thrown you already, and you DO want one, please write to the store for information before you send any money!

---

## CONTEST CORNER!

*Every week, when the KRLA BEAT comes out, do you rush right down to your neighborhood record store, only to find out that they were sold out five minutes ago? And so do you rush back to your house, cram a nickle and self addressed stamped envelope into another envelope, and rush right down to the post office for your copy? Tsk, tsk. That's awful. This is the way it should be: You're lying on your silk sheets in your heart shaped bed ... the maid comes in and asks you if you feel like having a delicious steak before you hop into your private chauffered limousine to be taken to school. When the maid brings your breakfast, the butler comes in and hands you your own copy of the KRLA BEAT ... hot off the presses. Doesn't that sound great? How would you like it to come true? Well, it can! All you have to do is find the silk sheets, heart shaped bed, chauffered limousine, butler and maid. We'll do the rest!*

**Yes, You Can Win Your Very Own Copy of the KRLA BEAT, Mailed to Your Home the Minute It Gets Off the Press! Every Week Your Copy Will Be Delivered Right to You, and You'll Get Your's Before Anyone Else!**

Just think how everyone will scoot over to your house to find out all the scoops! Just think of how important you'll feel as you carry your exclusive copy of the KRLA BEAT down the street for all the world to see! Boyohboy, could you ask for anything more? (And stop yelling Ringo at us ... we want him too!)

*How many issues have there been of the KRLA BEAT so far? Twenty? Ten Fifteen? Forty? Do you know? If you do, jot the answer down on a postcard and mail it to Conest Corner. You might just be the winner! Entries must be in by March 1st. Winner will be decided by earliest post mark.*

### ENTRY BLANK

NAME:........................................................ AGE:..............

ADDRESS:...........................................................................

PHONE NUMBER:................................................................

# KRLA BEAT

*In This Issue:*
ROLLING STONES
RIGHTEOUS BROS.
BEAU BRUMMELS

RINGO
Before & After

February 25, 1965 — Los Angeles, California — Ten Cents

# BEATLE-BALL AT KRLA!

## Hull, Taylor To Visit Beatles During Filming

KRLA explodes another Beatle bombshell!

And all of you have a chance to get in on the excitement.

Dave Hull, the world's biggest Beatle booster, and Derek Taylor, the Beatles' press agent and liaison man before coming to KRLA, are flying to Nassau for a series of exclusive interviews with John, Paul, George and Ringo as they film their latest movie.

**Fun For You**

Here's where you come in.

Through Dave and Derek, you can ask the questions! Just jot them down on a postcard and mail them to BEATLE QUESTIONS, KRLA, PASADENA. But hurry — there isn't much time left.

Here are some that have already been submitted:

What does Ringo think of married life? What does Maureen think of John, George and Paul? What's it like to be married to a Beatle? What do the other Beatles think of her? What is their reaction to Ringo's marriage? Do they think it will hurt the Beatles' popularity? Does Maureen want Ringo to stay with the group?

**Lots of Questions**

What special activities do they plan during their next visit to Los Angeles? How long will they be here? With John and Ringo married, are Paul and George thinking about giving up their bachelor life? What is the truth about the latest report that Paul may be altar-bound? Who is the man trying to break up the Beatles, and for what purpose?

Keep your ears glued to KRLA for the FIRST and ONLY answers to such questions — by the Beatles themselves.

Derek Taylor and An Unidentified Friend

## Beatles' August Tour To Include L.A. Show

We can't give you any official word yet, but negotiations are almost completed to bring the Beatles back to Los Angeles for another live concert spectacular.

Word of a final agreement is expected to be announced any day now . . . and KRLA and the Beat will be first to announce it, naturally!

They are expected to do two concerts this time, so that a lot of people who missed out on their first performance will have a chance to see them in person.

The boys have expressed a preference for Los Angeles, and they have reserved two open dates on the schedule for their American tour this summer — Aug. 29 and 30.

Revealing his plans for the Beatles for the rest of 1965, Brian Epstein indicates they will make the third of their three-picture commitment for United Artists this year.

The Beatles are starting their second film this week. They have flown to the Bahamas for location shooting which will take almost three weeks. Then they fly to Austria to film there for about ten days before returning to London to complete the picture.

They will begin their European tour in July with a major concert in Paris, likely to be combined with a TV show over the Eurovision link from the French capital. Other concerts will follow in Barcelona, Madrid, Milan and another Italian city to be named later.

Then comes the big trip American fans are anxiously awaiting. They will leave London for the U.S. on Aug. 13, and the following day tape a spot for the Ed Sullivan show.

The four Liverpool lads have selected nine cities for concerts, including Los Angeles. Others are expected to be Atlanta, San Francisco, Toronto, Minneapolis, Houston, Chicago, Detroit and Mexico City.

They are to begin their U.S. tour Aug. 15 in New York and will probably conclude it with the two shows here.

## DEREK TAYLOR, BEATLE ASSOCIATE NOW EXCLUSIVE KRLA REPORTER

KRLA has again made Beatle history!

It's not only the talk of the Beatle world, but the sensation of the radio world.

KRLA has employed the man who helped make the Beatles the most popular entertainers in the history of the world, Derek Taylor — press agent, liaison man, confidant and companion to the Beatles during and after their climb to the pinnacle of stardom — has moved to Los Angeles and will report exclusively for KRLA.

While Derek was with the Beatles, every piece of official news on the group was released by him. In the past he has been quoted and interviewed by everyone — including KRLA — who wanted to know anything about them. Aside from the Beatles themselves, he is the world's greatest authority on them.

And now he will report such news directly and exclusively to KRLA.

He will also provide KRLA listeners with exclusive reports on other British entertainers and has arranged to get us even more exclusive records from England before they are released to other stations in the U.S. You can easily see why

— Turn to Page 4

## KRLA TUNEDEX

1. MY GIRL .......................................... The Temptations
2. DOWNTOWN .................................... Petula Clark
3. YOU'VE LOST THAT LOVIN' FEELIN' ........ Righteous Brothers
4. LAND OF 1000 DANCES .................. Cannibal & Headhunters
5. THE JOLLY GREEN GIANT ..................... The Kingsmen
6. THIS DIAMOND RING ................... Gary Lewis & Playboys
7. LAUGH, LAUGH ............................ The Beau Brummels
8. FERRY ACROSS THE MERSEY ........... Gerry & The Pacemakers
9. THE NAME GAME ............................ Shirley Ellis
10. THE BOY FROM NEW YORK CITY ................ The Ad Libs
11. TELL HER NO/LEAVE ME ME .................. The Zombies
12. KING OF THE ROAD .......................... Roger Miller
13. 8 DAYS A WEEK/DON'T WANT TO SPOIL PARTY....The Beatles
14. NEW YORK'S A LONELY TOWN ............. The Tradewinds
15. LAND OF 1000 DANCES .................... The Midnighters
16. CAN'T YOU HEAR MY HEARTBEAT ..... Herman's Hermits
17. ALL DAY AND ALL OF THE NIGHT ............. The Kinks
18. TWINE TIME ....................... Alvin Cash & Crawlers
19. PAPER TIGER ............................... Sue Thompson
20. KEEP SEARCHIN' ............................. Del Shannon
21. I GO TO PIECES .......................... Peter & Gordon
22. HOLD ON TO WHAT YOU GOT .................. Joe Tex
23. LOVE POTION NUMBER NINE ............... The Searchers
24. GOLDFINGER ............................. Shirley Bassey
25. THE BIRDS AND THE BEES ................... Jewel Akens
26. HE WAS REALLY SAYIN' SOMETHING ....... The Valvelettes
27. THE IN CROWD .............................. Dobie Gray
28. HURT SO BAD ............................ Little Anthony
29. FOR LOVIN' ME ................... Peter, Paul & Mary
30. LEMON TREE ............................... Trini Lopez

### CLIMBERS

1. FANNIE MAE ........................... Righteous Brothers
2. BORN TO BE TOGETHER ..................... The Ronettes
3. LITTLE THINGS ........................ Bobby Goldsboro
4. YEH YEH ................................ Georgie Fame
5. ASK THE LONELY ......................... The Four Tops
6. WHAT HAVE THEY DONE TO THE RAIN ....... The Searchers
7. I'VE GOT A TIGER BY THE TAIL ............. Buck Owens
8. IF I LOVED YOU ....................... Chad & Jeremy
9. COME HOME ........................... Dave Clark Five
10. GO NOW .............................. The Moody Blues

### ALBUMS

1. BEATLES '65 .............................. The Beatles
2. WHERE DID OUR LOVE GO ................... The Supremes
3. BEACH BOYS IN CONCERT .................. The Beach Boys
4. GOLDFINGER .............................. Soundtrack
5. ROUSTABOUT ............................ Elvis Presley
6. COAST TO COAST ..................... Dave Clark Five
7. 12 x 5 ............................... Rolling Stones
8. VINTONS' GREATEST HITS ................ Bobby Vinton
9. YOU'VE LOST THAT LOVIN' FEELIN' ....... Righteous Brothers
10. YESTERDAY'S GONE ..................... Chad & Jeremy

## STIRS LOTS OF TALK

### KRLA DJs On New Shows

The big story everyone is talking about is the "big switch" at KRLA.

It brought a promotion for Hullabalooer Dave Hull, and it brought KRLA one of the best and best-known disc jockeys in the entire world — the one and only Dick Biondi.

At the request of thousands of his fans the scuzzy one stepped into the afternoon "traffic" slot from 3-6 p.m. Daffy Dick is messing up people's minds in Dave's old period of nine-to-midnight.

While Dave had the greatest time of his life during his nightly parties on KRLA, he likes to "mix" with his listeners in public appearances and of course he wasn't able to do that with a night-time show.

But look out for him now!

The old Hullaballoer may turn up unexpectedly at your next gathering. If he does, please treat him gently, for he isn't used to being out of his cage.

Everyone is asking for information about Dick Biondi. Like . . . is he for real? Is he really human? Is he dangerous? (We're still not sure about the answer to the second question, but the answer to the other two

— Turn to Page 4

# KRLA Gets 47,000 Valentines

We didn't know there were so many valentines in the world!

KRLA received more than 47,000 hand made valentines in the Valentine Art Festival Contest. Big ones, small ones and medium-sized ones of every color, shape and description.

It kept a fleet of mail trucks busy every day just delivering them to the station.

**Full House**

After filling up every available office at KRLA and then crowding the lobby so full that people couldn't wade through them to get to work, we filled up two rooms of the Huntington Sheraton Hotel next door.

Then the mailmen kept coming with more, so the fellows at the Marine National Guard Armory in Pasadena were kind enough to let us store them there. Before it was over, even the armory was filled with KRLA valentines. If you saw the special news program Channel 7 filmed at KRLA you have some idea.

And most of them were more beautiful than you could imagine. We hope you were able to see some of them on display last week at Fashion Shopping Center.

Most people must have spent hours and hours on their entries. You just had to see them to appreciate them.

Of course the disc jockeys were competing to see who could get the most valentines, and you have never seen such confusion.

The fellows spent hours and hours counting to see who had the most, but they got so hopelessly confused that it just wound up in a big argument. But everybody finally agreed that Dave Hull got the most and that Emporer (Beautiful Bob) Hudson was second.

**Tough To Choose**

Needless to say, the judges had the toughest job imaginable, trying to pick a winner from all those beautiful valentines. They even got into an argument!

But somehow they did settle on a winner, who receives a beautiful Magnavox console stereo set valued at $595, 20 record albums and a dinner date for herself and a friend with the Hullabalooer, Dave Hull.

She is Celeste Susany of 7447 Luxor Street in Downey. Celeste sent Dave Hull a giant red heart, trimmed with intricate white lace, with pink and white simulated flowers held by two golden cherubs.

Here are the runners-up, who receive a Panasonic portable AM-FM shortwave radio.

Judy Yothers, 8447 Shulman, Whittier. Judy sent Bob Eubanks a scale model of the KRLA studios, with working parts and lights, against a background replica of the Sierra Madre Mountains.

Daniel K. Hayashi, 7873 Ethel Avenue in North Hollywood. He sent Emporer Hudson a framed and textured cut-out of a girl in handmade clothes with a life-like hairdo, displaying a red valentine on a black and white textured background.

Kit Jackson of 6667 Zumirez Drive, Malibu. Kit sent Dave Hull a 48x18 inch scroll of modern comic art, depicting the oddities and characteristics of the Dave Hull Show — in full color with captions. The scroll was originally a window shade.

Richard House of 426 S. Hill Street in Los Angeles. He sent Emporer Hudson a full color, etched comic valentine showing Emporer Hudson in crown and robes beside his lavish, golden Rolls Royce—with Lieutenant Cavendish as a hood ornament.

Mel Hall, the KRLA program director, says our next project will be an elephant contest. The disc jockey who receives the most elephants . . . HELP ! ! !

## Winning Entries On View

Large crowds gathered in Fashion Square to view some of the finalists among more than 47,000 entries in the KRLA Valentine Art Festival Contest. Above, the first prize, a giant red heart submitted by Celeste Susany of Downey. Her prizes included a beautiful stereo console. Two runner-ups are also pictured . . . a window-shade scroll to Dave Hull designed by Kit Jackson of Malibu and a scale model of the KRLA studios, with working parts and lights, submitted by Judy Yothers of Whittier.

## Beat Gets New Look

As you can plainly see, there are a lot of changes in this week's KRLA Beat.

We hope you will like them. The newspaper is larger, and there are more stories, many new special features and pictures of a lot more people.

It's your newspaper, and we will continue making every change that we think will make it a better one. Please give us your suggestions, criticisms and comments.

We have a new mailing address. Send all correspondence and material for the Beat to 6290 Sunset Blvd., Suite 504, Hollywood, Calif.

### LOST AND FOUND

Five years ago, Emperor Bob Hudson lost an expensive diamond ring from his royal collection and had given up any hope of finding it again. Last week Lt. Cavendish noticed a glittering object at his feet and picked it up. As he suspected, it was a piece of broken glass.

### SECRET RECORD

Although most people are not aware of it, Bob Eubanks has a long record. It is an entire Beatle concert on one disc.

# Letters

We hear a lot about the English groups. How 'bout putting some light on the American groups now and then. A. S., Pasadena

*How about looking through the Beat now and then. Do you think all those guys and gals are from England?*

We were so heartbroken when we heard Ringo was married! We just couldn't believe it. It still doesn't change our opinion of him or the other Beatles at all! They are still the greatest and the gearest! They'll always be on top! Best of luck to you, Ringo! D. K., Norwalk

Really glad to hear the Dick Biondi sound again. He's a gear guy. Another #1 for KRLA. J. B., Los Angeles.

*Another "One" is right. By the way, Dick says your check is in the mail.*

What in the world is going on? I turned on my radio today and couldn't believe my ears. Dave Hull was on in the afternoon and a maniac named Biondi was on in the Hullabalooer's regular spot. Is this for real? E. C., Los Angeles

*Yes . . . REAL groovy.*

I really luv the Beat! I wanna hear more about the Beatles and the gear guys at KRLA. Keep up the good work! C. S. F., North Hollywood

Where can I get a KRLA Beat? I went to a record store and they were out of them. I live too far from KRLA to get one there! So . . . help me, please! J C., Santa Monica

*Ask them to order more papers. Be the first one at the store next week. And just to be sure, borrow your best friend's.*

When will the new Beatles movie be out? When are they coming to LA. again? J. T. B., Los Angeles

*Beatle movies will never be "out"!!! Release date — dunno. The Beatles wil be in Los Angeles on the the 29th and 30th of August.*

I just want to say — I love the Beatles and even Ringo, altho he let us down. But we luv him anyway. B. A., San Gabriel

Dick Biondi is mad, mad, mad. But he is also great, great, great. Sorry to repeat but this letter is from three of us. K. H., Alhambra

*Good thing it wasn't from your whole class.*

# Scoops & Flashes...

THE BEAU BRUMMELS, who have ben breaking attendance records throughout Northern and Southern California, are presently in New York taping Hullabulloo, which is to be aired Feb. 23rd. They will also be seen March 10th on Shindig.

Their record of "Laugh Laugh" took off with amazing speed across the country, but it is their personal appearances that really make us state with certainty that they are very shortly going to be one of the top groups in the country. Watch for their new LP on Autumn label soon. We promise you it will be out of sight.....

The Shindig ABC people had a surprise this week when FREDDIE & THE DREAMERS unexpectedly arrived in town to do the show. Although they had been previously scheduled, there was supposedly a hang-up in securing their visas and they were not going to be able to come. From Los Angeles, they will be going to Australia for a 3 week tour.

Producer JACK GOOD is on vacation and his chores are being ably handled by his new assistant, recently arrived from London, DAVID MALLET. NEIL SEDAKA in town for Shindig Show, and JERRY NAYLOR, with a new release "I Found You" on Smash, airing on the February 24th show. This is JERRY's first release as a single artist on Smash. He has, and still does, record with the CRICKETS for Liberty and was largely responsible for the CRICKETS' great success with personal appearances both in the United States and abroad...

THE RIGHTEOUS BROTHERS (BILL & BOB), who got their start right here in Southern California by way of Orange County, are now one of he top record attractions in the world. Their recording "You've Lost That Lovin' Feeling" passed CILLA BLACK's cover record in England and knocked her out of the Number One spot.

### Freddie Calls KRLA

Freddie & The Dreamers, one of the most popular new English groups, arrived here last week to tape appearances on both Shindig and Hullabaloo. While at the airport, Freddie placed a call to KRLA and did a live interview with Deejay Gary Mack.

## BEFORE... AND AFTER

Ringo Starr broke millions of hearts last week when he added a fifth ring — a gold wedding band. He married Maureen Cox, a hairdresser whom he began dating three years ago, at the same time that he joined an unknown group of long-haired singers called The Beatles. As you can tell from the picture on the right, he was delighted to give up his bachelorhood.

## Derek Taylor's Report

by Derek Taylor

Great to be back!

Back in California . . . in Hollywood . . . in KRLA-land.

I love this station. Does this sound like a plug? It isn't. I was talking like this back in August when I didn't know Dave Hull from Bob Eubanks.

I just think it's a great station. It is up with what's happening. The Beatles think so too. When they came to Hollywood to play the Bowl one station was like any other. But they liked KRLA's style and tuned in most hours of their day, which stretches from 2 a.m. till dawn.

They pulled Dave Hull's leg a bit for giving away their home addresses but it was all in fun. Dave became a good friend. Of theirs and mine.

I got radio-happy when I was here. If time dragged a bit I'd call Dave and talk to him — on any subject from Beatles to Beethoven.

The Beatles he could talk on. Beethoven he didn't seem to know too well. He claims to have met him. Maybe he did, maybe he didn't . . .

He knows most people.

I'm also happy to be working permanently with Bob Eubanks. I met him first in his Cinnamon Cinder Club at the Beatle press conference. A straight man, and he did a great promotion job for the Beatles . . . and for Tommy Quickly when I came over with Tommy just before Christmas. Tommy sends his love, by the way. Hollywood "knocked him out," he said.

Talk of Tommy reminds me of England . . . and his home town and mine . . . Liverpool. The beat scene is still swinging in Britain but something awful just happened to the man who owns the Cavern Club where the Beatles got their start in Liverpool.

He is "in the red." In debt. No one knows how or why. It seems the kids aren't as Cavern-minded as they were. That was where it all started in 1960 but somehow the scene there isn't as lively.

One of our top groups now, far and away, is the Animals from Newcastle. The Beatles admire them tremendously.

The Rolling Stones continue to run the Beatles not too close as second group. They don't sell nearly as many discs but they have a massive following. And they're good. The US thinks so too, I'm told.

That's about it for now. Thanks for having me with you. If there's anything you want to know about England, write and let me know. I'll do my best to tell you.

Goodbye for now.

**ADVERTISERS**
For rates and information call the KRLA BEAT at 469-3641.

## John and Paul Sell Stock Fast

LONDON — If you'd like to make a million dollars in a hurry, two young men have discovered the way. All you do is sell 1,250,000 shares of stock at a dollar each.

Of course, it helps if your name is John Lennon or Paul McCartney.

Last Thursday the two Beatle businessmen did just that, offering stock in their music publishing company for $1.09 each.

The public grabbed up the stock — Paul and John picked up another million bucks — and the whole thing took only 60 seconds!

### MORELAND HOST

KRLA Deejay Dick Moreland will host the festivities and crown a king and queen for Pasadena High Schools "Story Book Ball" February 26th at the Altadena Country Club.

## Rolling Stones Roll Into L-A

The Rolling Stones paid a surprise visit to Los Angeles last week to visit recording star Joey Paige and other friends here, including the KRLA Deejays. The boys will be back May 16 for a return engagement at the Long Beach Auditorium, presented by KRLA's Bob Eubanks. Their first performance here last fall was a sell-out, and their fans have been clamoring for more.

# KRLA ARCHIVES

## LURKING IN THE BACKGROUND
### New KRLA Program Director Has Found His Own Niche

Meet Mel Hall, the man behind the scenes at KRLA.

Nationally known for various things in the broadcasting field, Mel has joined KRLA as program director.

A native of Long Beach, he began his broadcasting career in the U.S. Army, where he served with valor and was awarded a Gold Microphone Cluster for bravery under fire. Mel had the only portable record player in his barracks and used to announce the titles of records as they dropped from the spindle.

Displaying extreme heroism under fire, Mel stuck by his record player despite a blistering barrage of boots and curses when he mistakenly played a Roy Acuff record after introducing Dave Brubeck.

From the Army he vaulted through a series of deejay jobs in major markets such as Mobile, Ala., and Ontario, Calif., before going into the advertising field in Los Angeles.

After developing several new concepts in that field, he found another job in radio, working on several occasions at a Los Angeles station before moving up again — this time to San Diego.

Employed by his brother-in-law at WJJD in Chicago as disc jockey and program director, Mel found himself in direct competition with the man who has just taken over the nine-to-midnight show at KRLA, Dick Biondi.

Although Biondi received all the publicity, Mel did very well, too. With no challenges left unconquered, Mel gave up his disc jockey show and moved to another Chicago station as program director.

Later he moved back to San Diego, as program director of Channel 6, where he spent the last three years before joining KRLA.

Denying any hidden desires to go back on the air and ignoring the lure of the spotlight, Mel toils vigorously in the background — directing programs, formulating new policies, writing important memos and attending to all the other important details which occupy the time of a busy executive.

Shying away from such descriptions as handsome, rich or loveable, Mel modestly states that when he is not directing programs or working behind the scenes he lives a quiet, retiring life in his bachelor apartment.

## Crowds Hunt Head Beatle

KRLA was the object of another Beatle rumor recently . . . and this one almost got us in trouble with our landlord.

A report was circulated that John Lennon was in town, along with Cynthia and their "Junior Beatle," staying at the Huntington - Sheraton Hotel while negotiating a business transaction with KRLA.

The hotel was flooded with callers and visitors asking about John . . . and they thought hotel officials were "putting them on" when they denied the Lennons were staying there.

We're sorry to report that John and his family were in England all the time . . . it was just a false alarm.

But if and when John-John does come over to see us about those negotiations, we'll give you the full story over KRLA . . . and the full story in pictures right here in the Beat.

## NEXT WEEK IN THE KRLA BEAT

THE BEATLES ON LOCATION
*Special Report from Nassau*

HOW TO BE A DEEJAY

AN EXCITING NEW BEATLE CONTEST

AND MUCH, MUCH MORE!
**LISTEN TO KRLA FOR DETAILS**

### More About
## DEREK
(From Page 1)
we're all so excited!

One other KRLA bonus — Derek will do a special column every week in the KRLA Beat, giving us behind-the-scenes information from the personal lives of the entertainers, new trends in music and accounts of his own experiences with the greatest names in the entertainment world. You'll find his first column in this issue.

A celebrity in his own right, Derek is recognized as one of the sharpest publicity and promotion men anywhere. He has helped form a new company in Hollywood — Prestige Promotions — to represent American as well as English acts.

We asked him why he had selected KRLA.

"In our previous tours, the Beatles & everyone travelling with them were greatly impressed by KRLA," he said. "Of course you have a world-wide reputation as the top Beatle station anywhere, but aside from that, all of us — especially John, George, Paul and Ringo — enjoyed listening to KRLA more than any other radio station we had ever heard. I'm looking forward to being associated with such a station."

## Righteous Bros Soar To Top As New Hit Tops Them All

THE RIGHTEOUS BROTHERS' "You've Lost That Lovin' Feelin'" has set a record at KRLA for holding the top position on the KRLA survey longer than any other record during the history of the survey.

They are now one of the most famed "brother" teams in the world — and they aren't even brothers.

Bob Hatfield and Bill Medley are, in fact, just good friends who happened to get up in a club in Orange County one night two years ago and sing together.

Both boys had their own groups at the time and it was just by chance, or fate, that they discovered they had a good blend and a tremendous amount of "soul."

Their first professional appearance was at the Rendezvous Ballroom in Balboa Beach and they were an instant success. Soon over-flowing crowds were pouring into the Rendezvous to hear the Righteous Brothers and appearances in other Orange County clubs and ballrooms and the Cinnamon Cinders followed.

At the Rendezvous they attracted the attention of Ray Maxwell of Moonglow Records which ultimately resulted in their recording of "Little Latin Lupe Lu," which was penned by Bill. At this time, their trademark was black suits with preacher-like collars.

The success of "Latin Lupe Lu" led to an appearance on Dick Clark's American Bandstand in Philadelphia — their first national television exposure. After "Latin Lupe Lu" came a succession of West Coast hits such as "My Babe" and "Koko Joe," and their popularity grew in leaps and bounds. Soon they were outdrawing any other recording artist — including the big names from the East coast.

When the Beatles made their first appearance in the United States (in Washington, D.C.), the Righteous Brothers were on the show and created a great deal of interest among young and old alike. The Beatles and Brian Epstein were also impressed, and the boys were signed for the 30-day U.S. tour.

Prior to Jack Good making the rock and roll pilot for the proposed ABC Shindig tour, he witnessed an appearance of the boys in Hollywood and immediately signed them for the pilot, along with Little Richard and Jody Miller.

Although this show was never shown, the ABC executives in New York were also quite taken with the Righteous Brothers and they were signed for the next show.

The rest is history, as they are now regular performers on Shindig and are tremendously popular with viewers throughout the country.

### More About
## BIONDI
(From Page 1)
is yes.)

Dick came to KRLA from the frozen wastelands of New York, where he did a daily show over the Mutual radio network which was broadcast over 105 stations. He was the first modern radio disc jockey ever to be given a show by a major network.

Before that he worked at WLS in Chicago, where he earned some of the higest ratings ever recorded in a major city. For two years in a row he was named the nation's top deejay of the year in popular music.

A word of comfort to all Beatle fans (isn't everyone?) . . . Dick is not only a maniac, but a BEATLEmaniac. He did several live interviews with them over his network show and is the only other deejay in America who can compete with Dave Hull in his knowledge of the group and scoops on what they are doing.

We had planned to run a picture of Dick in this issue of the Beat, but he screamed and turned purple at the thought of it. The last time his picture was run in a newspaper he was arrested for inciting a riot.

## Beau Brummels Walk Into Busy Month

The Beau Brummels ("Laugh, Laugh") are going places, but they're usually running instead of walking. Acclaimed as among the most talented and exciting new discoveries in years, they will stop here March 1 to reveal plans for a whirlwind of activities during the month. Plans include a new single, an album, a tour of England and appearances on Shindig, Hullabaloo and the Dick Clark Special. March will be a busy month for the boys from San Francisco.

# KRLA BEAT

**WIN BEATLE AUTOGRAPHS** SEE PAGE 4

**HOW TO BE A DEEJAY** SEE PAGE 3

March 10, 1965 — Los Angeles, California — Ten Cents

# BEATLES PRAISE L.A.!

## Derek Taylor Reports

Gerry and the Pacemakers are in town . . . on celluloid. In their first movie, "Ferry 'Cross The Mersey."

I haven't seen it yet, in full — tho' I saw it many times in the creative stage. I saw the rushes and the eerie silent stages when it was movement without sound-track.

And I remember the day when Gerry came up with the theme song. We were both in Liverpool to meet with the producers (they also made "Tom Jones") and the director.

Gerry had promised to bring the theme with him. He did. Plus his acoustic guitar. And over a glass of Guinness Stout — his favorite drink — he first launched the haunting notes of "Ferry 'Cross The Mersey."

**Nice Lad**

We all liked it. So, thankfully for Gerry, do the record-buyers.

Gerry is a nice lad. Tough and forthright; happy and straightforward. He is every bit as pleasant as he seems in his performances. His engagement to his fan-club secretary proves that he doesn't go hunting for

—Turn to Page 4

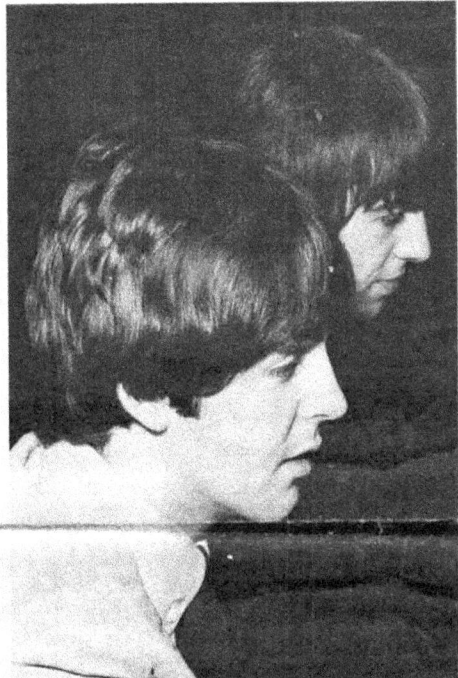

The Bachelors . . . What Are Their Plans?

## HULL, TAYLOR VISITING SCENE OF BEATLE MOVIE

*(KRLA's Dave Hull and Derek Taylor are on Nassau, guests of the Beatles during filming of their second movie. Their reports and interviews are being broadcast daily over KRLA.)*

### by Derek Taylor

This is where I came in. Interviewing the Beatles.

It's surprising how soon you can adjust. Three months ago I was sifting through inquiries from people who wanted to meet them. Now I've been sifted myself.

The Beatles are fine. They never change. Their millions of dollars, yens, kroners, marks, rupees and pounds — their multi-million fans, their ceaseless success . . . none of these things alter their basic down-to-earth, rough-and-ready ap-

— Turn to Page 4

### KRLA TOP TEN

1. MY GIRL
2. I DON'T WANT TO SPOIL THE PARTY - 8 DAYS A WEEK
3. THIS DIAMOND RING
4. FERRY 'CROSS THE MERSEY
5. DOWNTOWN
6. JOLLY GREEN GIANT
7. YOU'VE LOST THAT LOVIN' FEELIN'
8. KING OF THE ROAD
9. BOY FROM NEW YORK CITY
10. RED ROSES FOR A BLUE LADY

(Complete Listing Page 4)

### by Dave Hull

Hi, Hullabalooers!

Right now Derek and I are relaxing beside the pool here at the beautiful Balmoral Country Club after our first get-together with out hosts — four fellows named George, John, Paul and Ringo.

You probably never heard of them, but they're singers. Also movie actors. Their group is called . . . let's see, is it the Bugs? No, that doesn't sound right. Maybe they're the Insects. No, that's not right either. Surely I haven't forgotten.

Here it is . . . I wrote it down so I wouldn't forget. THE BEATLES! Isn't that a funny name? They couldn't amount to much with a name like that. They're nice boys, though.

Seriously, it was a great thrill seeing them again after their visits to Los Angeles last summer.

They said to tell all of you hello and that they were looking forward to their next trip to Southern California Aug. 29 and 30. They regard last year's

— Turn to Page 3

The Worrier . . . What's Bothering Him?

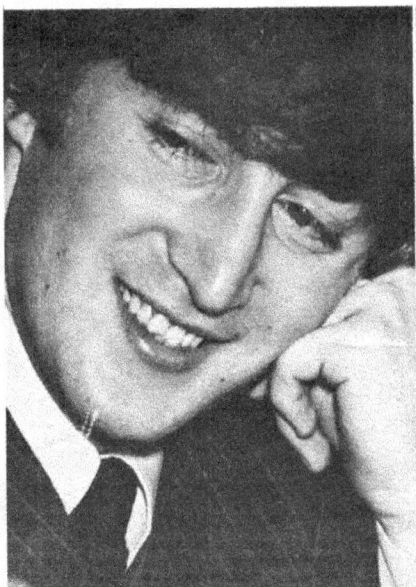

The Married Men . . . Check Ringo's New Ring

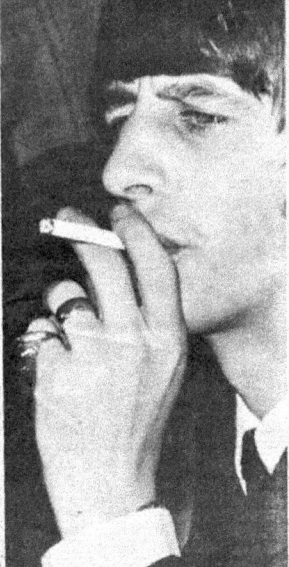

# KRLA ARCHIVES

MUSICAL INDEPENDENCE

## Paul Revere & Raiders Carry Fight to British

by Derek Taylor

Watch for the world-wide ride of Paul Revere!

In three-cornered hats, ruffled shirts and startling frock coats, these five swinging lads, from the Northwest corner of the Union are about to do battle with the British.

And I think they are going to give a very good account of themselves.

While I will be specializing in information — both old and new—about the English groups, it is also my pleasure as a new resident of this country to keep an eye out for promising American entertainers.

I'm happy to report I have found an excellent group, and I'd like to tell you about them.

### Paths Crossed

At about the time I was leaving the Beatles to come to America, Paul Revere and the Raiders were also on the move . . . flanked by a remarkable young man named Roger Hart.

A manager - guide - friend, man-about-Hollywood, producer and disc jockey and a devout believer in the Raiders, he brought them south from Portland, Oregon.

Our paths crossed for the second time a few days ago. I was greatly intrigued by their determined and promising assault on showbusiness — and ironically, on the British dominance of the disc scene.

We had met the first time during the heat and turbulence of the Beatles' tour when it hit Denver in a screaming holocaust last fall.

At the time Roger was a disc jockey for a leading Portland station, but there were dozens of disc jockeys all about and I probably wouldn't have distinguished him from the others had I not heard a couple of fellows talking about Roger's group.

I learned they had awakened the Northwest as surely as the first Paul Revere had awakened the Minutemen in his famous midnight ride.

At Roger's invitation I saw and heard Paul Revere and the Raiders, and I was immediately impressed.

The modern-day Paul Revere is a blond, handsome 24 year-old human dynamo who rides a rocking piano just as hard as his namesake rode a horse acros the New England countryside.

Who are Paul Revere and the Raiders?

Well, Paul himself is using his real name. It is no stunt. He is from a small town in Idaho, Caldwell. He is a natural-born musician, can play a bass guitar but mainly performs on piano and organ. He is a long-time admirer of Jerry Lee Lewis and could compete with his idol . . . and win.

Next . . . Mark Lindsay. He is 22, darkly handsome with a good face. Strong-jawed Mark is a single and lead singer with the Raiders. He plays saxophone and rhythm guitar. From Boise, Idaho, Mark is the exciting spark which ignites the group — the McCartney if you will, to Revere's Lennon.

Drummer Mike Smith looks a drummer. He is just built that way. He is short, alert, sharp and 21. Plus married. Like Ringo. Mike is from Portland.

The group has two "babies." Musical twins almost. They are lead guitars Drake Levin and Phil Volk. Both 18. Phil plays bass guitar (right-handed!).

Both are from Idaho, both travelled parallel paths which led them to Paul Revere and the Raiders. They are single and handsome.

The thing which impresses me about all five is that they are natural talents.

That and the fact that they are genuine. And this, ultimately, is the thing that matters most in any business.

Even showbusiness.

Paul Revere and the Raiders . . . Charge!

### Mack Fan Club Tours KRLA Studios

It was an exciting afternoon when the Gary Mack Fan Club, as a special treat to its members, conducted a tour of the KRLA studios.

The visitors each received a new record from KRLA, all the autographs they could carry away, and a peek at Dave (Scuzzy) Hull in action as he did his show.

Well over a hundred members turned out to be shown through the station and learn all about it from their guide, KRLA Deejay Gary Mack.

### Gary Mack Fan Club

## Scoops & Flashes...

We are happy to see that GLEN CAMPBELL is such a big success on Shindig. GLEN, one of the most talented musicians in the country, has long been over-due for national recognition. There is no limit to this boy's talent. He can sing a hillbilly, pop, jazz, or blues tune equally well. The majority of hit rock and roll and country records that come out of Hollywood feature GLEN's guitar or banjo. His new Capitol recording, a beautiful ballad, "Tomorrow Never Comes," is doing quite well . . . . .

THE FOUR SEASONS, in town for DICK CLARK'S television spectacular "Where The Action Is," had an exciting ride to Big Bear where they were locationing. The driver of their chauffeured limousine got lost and the two and a half hour drive took them six hours. They arrived late for their call and a bit shakey after maneuvering long, winding and narrow mountain roads . . . and, brrr, you couldn't convince them they were in sunny California. They were freezing to death in the snow, after just having left more of the same in New York. Guess the SUPREMES and BOBBY FREEMAN were better off by riding in the bus. "Where The Action Is" is scheduled for airing in late Spring, hosted by FRANKIE AVALON.

We understand from president AL BENNETT of Liberty Records that GARY LEWIS & THE PLAYBOYS will be making a ten day promotional trip to England the first of March in conjunction with the release of their stateside hit, "This Diamond Ring," which is presently #1 in the nation . . . . .

### *P*ersonals

Derek Taylor:
Hurry and give Jeanie A. some stuff on Tommy Quickly. Glad you came here. Luv from Ricki and Cyn.

Dear Fans:
We're looking forward to seeing you again and we hope you like our new book.
The Scooters

Joey Paige,
The pics I took of you backstage are selling like crazy. I'll never forget you.
Brenda Royer, El Segundo

Vanda,
Hear what the BEAT said about the TAMI show in April? The Stones will be in town! . . . You're still the best R. S. Fan Club president. Drop me a line.
Diane

The Animals rule.
San Diego Zoo Keeper

MORE ABOUT

## DEREK TAYLOR
(From Page 1)

proach to life.

As I was saying, this interview trip takes me back a year or two. They were on the climb which finally took them to unbelieveable heights.

I first saw them in a cinema in Manchester.

I had never seen anything like the audience reaction and I believe that except for the Beatles, we never will again. I wrote in the Daily Express — a London newspaper: "Something wonderful has happened to pop music . . ."

And it had.

It is still happening here in the Bahamas. They have some great new songs, recorded in England the week before they came out here. They are far more mature and ready for filming than they were in "Hard Day's Night."

As John said last night, "we were doing the unknown then. Now we've all our mistakes to learn from."

What's the title of the film? Your guess is as good as mine. "Bahama Ball"? Maybe. "Beatles Two"? I doubt it.

I wouldn't be at all surprised if the title wasn't delayed until the film's completely in the can. Then one of the Beatles will come up with a brainwave. Like Ringo's "Hard Day's Night."

ADVERTISERS
For rates and information call the KRLA BEAT at 469-3641.

# KRLA ARCHIVES

## EXPERT ADVICE
## YOU WANT TO BE A DEEJAY? THERE'S REALLY NOTHING TO IT

They remain decent, simple people. What Americans would call "regular guys."

Perhaps the question we hear the most at KRLA is, "How do you get to be a deejay?"

It's a good question, and to get a good answer, we asked the experts — the KRLA Deejays. Here's what they said:

EMPORER HUDSON: "Well, when I was just a four-year-old emporer, I was given a small radio station for a birthday present. The thought occurred to me, 'What better way to make the people happy than by letting them hear the magnificent voice of their own Beautiful Bob.' Since I owned the station, I hired myself . . . and the rest is history."

CHARLIE O': "Not being an emporer, I didn't get a radio station for my birthday, but I did get into radio at an early age. I was fortunate enough to get my start as a child actor on radio when I was 12 years old, and have been in the business ever since."

CASEY KASEM: "Like Charlie, I started as a radio actor. It all began back in 1950 with such unforgettable shows as The Lone Ranger and The Green Hornet. Those early days, filled with priceless experience, gradually changed into modern radio as we know it today, and I rode right along with it to KRLA."

DAVE HULL: "Before I answer the question, may I award Casey a honk on the Hullaballooers' horn? (HONK) Thank you. Now then, I got to be a deejay . . . believe this or not . . . simply by walking up to the manager of a small town radio station, and insisting that he hire me because I was the greatest deejay in the world. He hired me. And just because Clarence was twisting his arm had nothing to do with it."

BOB EUBANKS: "I'm afraid my story is not quite as unbelievable as the Hullaballooer's. I got into radio by studying all about it before I looked for my first job. I enrolled in a school for announcers here in California, and it was a great help. And, by the way, Dick Moreland was one of my classmates in that school."

DICK BIONDI: "I just hung around the radio station in my hometown getting coffee for the deejays, running errands, and stuff life that. Then, all of a sudden, there I was playing records on the radio myself."

BOBBY DALE: "Are you serious? Do you think the old Benevolent One is going to go around spilling secrets that could flood the market with millions of potential deejays, all looking for work? Haven't you heard of job security, man?"

DICK MORELAND: "I was able to land a part-time job at a station while still in high school, and later went to a school for announcers. After graduation, I became a teacher at the radio school before getting out for that first full-time job."

GARY MACK: "While I was still in the Air Force, a buddy of mine who worked for a station in town noticed my interest in radio. He taught me the basics of announcing and running the controls. After months of practice, I landed my first job, which paid $15 a week."

That's how they got to be deejays . . . the BEST deejays in the world. Sounds simple, doesn't it.

## MANY NEW DANCES TO LEARN IF YOU WANT TO STAY 'HIP'

If you really want to be "In" during the weeks and months ahead, you have a flock of new dances to learn.

The Swim, the Surf, the Frug, the Watusi and the Bird will soon be as old fashioned as a 1964 calendar.

The coming dance crazes will have names like the Bostella, the Twine and the Ski.

Of the current favorites, only the Jerk seems destined to hang around for awhile, for it has fallen into the category of a classic.

### Bostella Newest

The Bostella, which originated in France, is the newest of the new. It is the first foreign dance to become popular in this country since the Limbo caught fire several seasons ago with the help of Chubby Checker.

The Bostella is a wild dance which started in a small Paris club late one night when somebody put on a far-out record with a strong beat and a group of tourists laughingly began dancing to it with vigorous gyrations and violent contortions. They wound it up by throwing themselves to the floor and rolling about convulsively.

As you may gather, the Bostella is a wild scene.

### Twine Time

Then there's the Twine, already the subject of four new records — "Twine Time" by Alvin Cash and the Crawlers, "Jerk and Twine" by Jackie Ross, "Woodbine Twine" by the Five Du-Tones, and "Let's Twine" by Dee Dee Sharp.

Experts say the Twine is best described as a maneuver where the dancers "unwrap each other like packages."

Another new dance recently introduced is the Mlle (pronounced Millie), which is described as the first real 'touch' dance in seven years. It has already been demonstrated on TV in the New York area and plans are underway to issue both an album and a single record featuring it.

Finally there's the Ski, an athletic-type dance along the order of the Swim and the Surf. United Artists has issued a record called "The Ski," by the Kinks & Queens, complete with instruction leaflets.

One other new dance on the horizon has a name, but the movements and steps are still a mystery. Elvis Presley will introduce it with his next single record, called "The Clam."

## KRLA Still Tops By Big Margin Thanks To You!

Thanks to the help of all our loyal listeners, KRLA has done it again!

Latest ratings released by C. E. Hooper and Pulse, Inc., show KRLA is still the "Giant" in Southern California. Our ratings are bigger and better than ever.

The December - January Hooper rating shows KRLA with almost half-again as many listeners as our closest competitor — 20.3 to 14.6.

The latest Pulse rating gives us an even bigger edge!

### Rolling Stone Turns Deejay

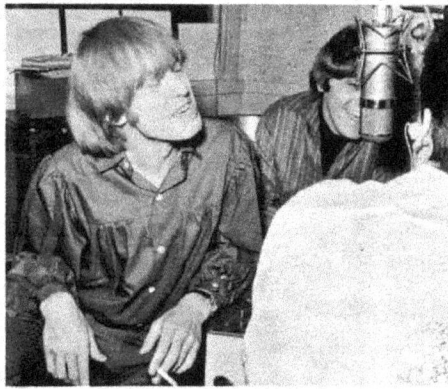

## Rolling Stone Plays D-J On KRLA Show

Brian Jones of the Rolling Stones pulled the surprise of the year when he became an honorary KRLA Deejay.

Brian, here in Los Angeles for a vacation, thought it might be fun to be a disc jockey — especially on KRLA, his favorite station.

Brian, his best friend Joey Paige, and Gary Mack went on the air at midnight with one of the wildest hours ever broadcast.

Brian and Joey picked out all of the music, read all the announcements, and ran the whole show. The only sad note was that Bobby Dale, probably the worlds' greatest Rolling Stones' fan, was ill and unable to be there for all the fun. The hour was over all too soon, and KRLA's first Rolling Stones Disc Jockey had to leave. As he headed for the door, Brian said that it had been wonderful, and that when the Stones were back in LA next time, he'd like to try it again.

As for becoming a deejay permanently, it looks rather doubtful. As Brian said, "If it's all the same to you, I'll keep *making* the records, and let you keep *playing* them."

### Boy, What Strategy!

The KRLApes call "time out" during a recent basketball game, evidently for a strategy session with the cheering section. From the look on Dave Hull's face, it's evident the fans have come up with a devilish plot. Casey Kasem and Dick Moreland conspire in the background.

## More About DAVE HULL
(From Page 1)

performance at the Hollywood Bowl as the highlight of their tour.

Derek and I saw them for only a few minutes today between scenes for their movie. We have a longer meeting scheduled tomorrow, and at that time we'll start asking them the questions many of you sent in to us before we left KRLA.

It was like old home week when they saw Derek. He had been their long-time press officer before leaving the group to move to Los Angeles, and Paul said things didn't seem the same without him.

### Congratulates Ringo

I congratulated Ringo on his marriage and didn't have the nerve to tell him what a lot of you said about that!

Neither Maureen nor John's wife, Cynthia, came with them to Nasau and they're razzing Ringo about the nightly calls he makes to her in England. He's been away from her for more than a week now . . . almost half their married life.

Everything is so British here in the Bahamas. It's a British possession, you know, and I feel a little out of place. But Derek feels right at home. In fact, I may have to tie him up to get him back to KRLA.

### Beatle Answers

In next week's issue of the Beat we'll have transcripts with our interviews with the Beatles, including their answers to some of the questions you have been asking . . . such as how the other boys are reacting to Ringo's mariage . . . what effect they think it will have on their popularity . . . any possible wedding plans for the two bachelors — Paul and George — plus more information about the movie and what they are doing in it. We will also have more pictures of the boys here in Nasau.

### Autographs

One other thing . . . they have promised us some autographed pictures which we will be bringing back to give away as prizes, plus some of the things they have used on their trip.

Well, Hullabalooers, Derek and I will soon been calling in some Beatle interviews over KRLA. Hope you get a chance to hear them.

And don't miss our complete report in next week's KRLA Beat.

### LONG FLIGHT

After flying non-stop from Chicago to Los Angeles to be on time for his first show on KRLA, Dick Biondi was barely able to make it. He could hardly lift the records because his arms were so tired.

### FEARLES FIREMAN

As a volunteer fireman, Bobby Dale once climbed a ladder and carried a screaming girl down from the fifth floor.

He was ordered never to do it again unless the building was on fire.

# KRLA ARCHIVES

## Beatle Scrambled Features Contest

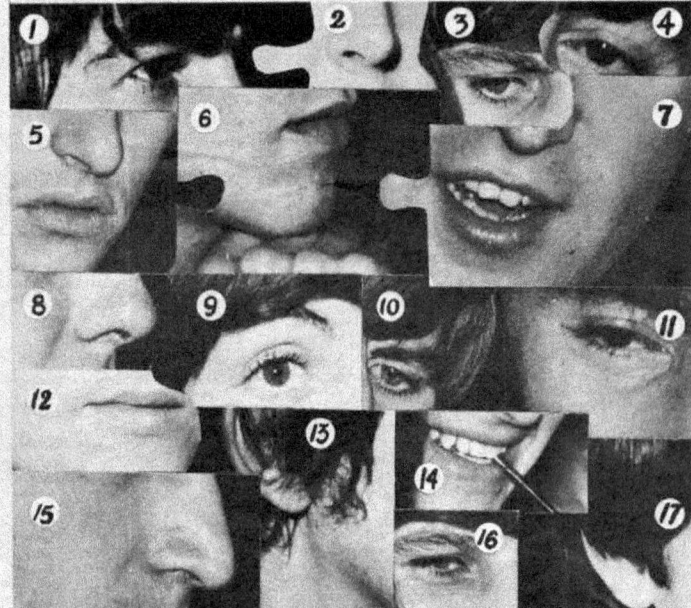

**My Answers to the Beatles Scrambled Features Contest:**

1. _____   10. _____
2. _____   11. _____
3. _____   12. _____
4. _____   13. _____
5. _____   14. _____   Name _____
6. _____   15. _____   Address _____
7. _____   16. _____   City _____
8. _____   17. _____   State _____
9. _____                  Phone _____

Mail Entry to:
KRLA BEAT
6290 Sunset Blvd., Suite 504
Hollywood, California

## Test Your Beatle Skill – Autographs For The Winner

ATTENTION Beatlemaniacs: Here's the contest you been asking for ... *The Beatles Scrambled Features Contest.* And the grand prize is something out of this world — An Autographed Picture of the Beatles!

Derek Taylor and Dave Hull are bringing back the prize when they return from Nassau — personally autographed by John, Paul, George and Ringo.

If you know the Beatles as well as you think you do, then you may be the winner. And the owner of one of the few autographed pictures of the Beatles in the entire world!

Look at each of the scrambled features in the picture layout to the left. If you think that's Paul nose in No. 2, then write his name beside that number on the entry blank below.

When all the blanks are filled, send in your entry and wait for the results to be announced in the KRLA Beat. You may enter as many times as you like. All entires must be postmarked before March 15, 1965, and in case of a tie, the earliest postmark wins.

Good Luck!

**ADVERTISERS**
For rates and information call the KRLA BEAT at 469-3641.

## More About DEREK TAYLOR
(From Page 1)

false glamour. He will be marrying a decent, pretty girl-next-door type.

A lot of people in the pop world are marrying in England. Ringo of course is the obvious example. But there are many others. Charlie Watts of the Stones just recently.

**British Bits**

Latest news from the British pop-scene: Top of the charts is a disc by The Seekers, an Australian group never before in England or in the record-leaders. Which just shows that anything can happen.

There's another new name in the No. 2 spot: Tom Jones, a handsome Welshman. The Beatles don't show anywhere in the top 20 single list. They saturated the market with "I Feel Fine" and unlike America, that was their last release.

The British Beatle releases of singles never exceed four per year. But in the US their albums have only 12 songs against 14 in the British albums. This leaves two songs which go out as American singles, "Eight Days a Week" is an example.

The scene here is pretty exciting. I'm very interested in two groups. The Beau Brummels and Paul Revere and the Raiders, both of whom have done wonderfully well in their own home areas — the West Coast and the North West respectively.

## KRLA TUNEDEX

| | | | |
|---|---|---|---|
| 1. | (1) | MY GIRL | The Temptations |
| 2. | (14) | I DON'T WANT TO SPOIL THE PARTY/ EIGHT DAYS A WEEK | The Beatles |
| 3. | (6) | THIS DIAMOND RING | Gary Lewis & Playboys |
| 4. | (8) | FERRY ACROSS THE MERSEY | Gerry & Pacemakers |
| 5. | (2) | DOWNTOWN | Petula Clark |
| 6. | (5) | THE JOLLY GREEN GIANT | The Kingsmen |
| 7. | (3) | YOU'VE LOST THAT LOVIN' FEELIN' | Righteous Bros. |
| 8. | (12) | KING OF THE ROAD | Roger Miller |
| 9. | (10) | THE BOY FROM NEW YORK CITY | The Ad Libs |
| 10. | (13) | RED ROSES FOR A BLUE LADY | Vic Dana |
| 11. | (15) | NEW YORK'S A LONELY TOWN | The Trade Winds |
| 12. | (19) | TWINE TIME | Alvin Cash and the Crawlers |
| 13. | (11) | TELL HER NO/LEAVE ME BE | The Zombies |
| 14. | (4) | LAND OF 1000 DANCES | Cannibal & Headhunters |
| 15. | (20) | PAPER TIGER | Sue Thompson |
| 16. | (29) | HURT SO BAD | Little Anthony & The Imperials |
| 17. | (17) | CAN'T YOU HEAR MY HEARTBEAT | Herman's Hermits |
| 18. | (26) | THE BIRDS AND THE BEES | Jewel Akens |
| 19. | (22) | I GO TO PIECES | Peter & Gordon |
| 20. | (7) | LAUGH, LAUGH | The Beau Brummels |
| 21. | (45) | STOP! IN THE NAME OF LOVE | The Supremes |
| 22. | (27) | HE WAS REALLY SAYIN' SOMETHIN' | The Velvelettes |
| 23. | (41) | GO NOW | The Moody Blues |
| 24. | (16) | LAND OF A THOUSAND DANCES | The Midnighters |
| 25. | (30) | FOR LOVIN' ME | Peter, Paul & Mary |
| 26. | (25) | GOLDFINGER | Shirley Bassey |
| 27. | (27) | LOVE POTION NUMBER NINE | The Searchers |
| 28. | (9) | THE NAME GAME | Shirley Ellis |
| 29. | (18) | ALL DAY AND ALL OF THE NIGHT | The Kinks |
| 30. | (21) | KEEP SEARCHIN' | Del Shannon |

### CLIMBERS

| | | |
|---|---|---|
| (1) | BABY, PLEASE DON'T GO | Them |
| (2) | COME HOME | The Dave Clark Five |
| (3) | LEMON TREE | Trini Lopez |
| (4) | IF I LOVED YOU | Chad & Jeremy |
| (5) | YEH, YEH | Georgie Fame |
| (6) | GOODNIGHT | Roy Orbison |
| (7) | (HERE THEY COME) FROM ALL OVER WORLD | Jan & Dean |
| (8) | MIDNIGHT SPECIAL | Johnny Rivers |
| (9) | COME TOMORROW | Manfred Mann |
| (10) | IT HURTS ME | Bobby Sherman |

## Dinner With Dave

One of the prizes Celeste Susany of Downey won for placing first in the KRLA Valentine Art Festival was a dinner with Dave Hull. But Celeste (standing next to Dave) didn't count on the Hullabalooer's fans getting into the act. They had to cross this "picket line" before entering the restaurant.

## NEXT WEEK IN THE KRLA BEAT

**REPORT FROM NASSAU:**

- Exclusive Beatle Pictures!
- The Beatles Answer Your Questions!

Dave Hull and Derek Taylor report the latest news from the Beatles themselves.

---

**KRLA DEEJAYS ON TELEVISION**

A preview of three exciting new TV shows.

---

AND MUCH, MUCH MORE!
**LISTEN TO KRLA FOR DETAILS**

## DENTAL HEALTH

Visiting the dentist recently for his semi-annual check-up, Dave Hull was assured he had a perfect set of 32 teeth. Thirty-one on top and one on the bottom.

**KRLA ARCHIVES**

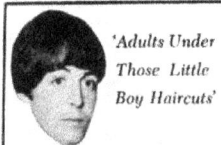
'Adults Under Those Little Boy Haircuts'

# KRLA BEAT

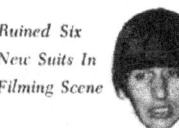
Ruined Six New Suits In Filming Scene

March 17, 1965 — Los Angeles, California — Ten Cents

# BEATLE MOVIE A BLAST!

## Derek Taylor's Report

The Beatles are fine. They feel fine, they look fine, act brilliantly, sing better than ever. On and off-set they have the air of assured young men who have it made. They may not ever claim to be the greatest act showbiz has ever known, but they certainly look it and certainly are. I hadn't seen seen them for three months and of course, they hadn't changed too much. But the feature which struck me most was that they looked more mature. They have more assurance than ever; they are no longer boys.

As Peter Evans, Britain's most important entertainment columnist wrote in the London Daily Express: "They are man-talking adults beneath those little-boy haircuts."

Evans came away from meeting them in the Bahamas, soured. He wrote a biting attack on their off-stage attitude to the press and described them as "rude and arro-

**Turn to Page 2**

## VISITORS TO MOVIE LOCATION TELL OF BEATLEMANIA ANTICS

### By Dave Hull

If I wasn't a complete raving, total Beatlemaniac before, then I certainly am now!

What an experience! After spending four days with them in the Bahamas while they filmed portions of the second movie, I feel as wrung out as a piece of laundry.

There is so much to tell I'm sure neither Derek Taylor nor I will be able to do much more than scratch the surface during this edition of the Beat. But we'll continue it from week to week until you have the whole story . . . the whole *book* is more like it, because anyone could write a book after spending a few days with those guys.

They are so full of life and mischief that they're perpetual motion machines. They really wear a person down — even the old Hullabalooer himself.

### Different Atmosphere

My p r e v i o u s associations with the Beatles had mostly been in situations where there were crowds all about or near-impossible schedules to meet so that we were unable to really sit down and talk for more than a few minutes at a time.

But this trip was completely different. Although they are working about 12 hours a day on the movie, there is a much more relaxed and casual atmosphere.

After inviting Derek and me to visit them, they were great hosts. Completely friendly, relaxed and outgoing.

To our surprise, Derek and I found that anyone going to the Bahamas where they're shooting the film is allowed to see the Beatles. This includes visiting them on the set!

### Friendly to Visitors

Tourists w e r e constantly snapping pictures of them, and the Beatles actually seemed quite happy about it. They even took the time and trouble

—**Turn to Page 4**

Here they are! The Beatles in the Bahamas on location for their new film. You will see this picture later in other publications, but this week it is a world-wide exclusive for the KRLA Beat . . . a gift from the Beatles to KRLA's Derek Taylor and Dave Hull. Other exclusive pictures of the Fab Four on page 3.

### KRLA TOP TEN

1. STOP IN THE NAME OF LOVE
2. EIGHT DAYS A WEEK/I DON'T WANT TO SPOIL THE PARTY
3. MY GIRL
4. THIS DIAMOND RING
5. THE BOY FROM N. Y. CITY
6. RED ROSES FOR A BLUE LADY
7. HURT SO BAD
8. DOWNTOWN
9. FERRY ACROSS THE MERSEY
10. GO NOW

(Complete Listing Page 4)

# KRLA ARCHIVES

*The Beau Brummels — Declan Mulligan, Ron Elliott, John Petersen, Sal Valentino and Ron Meagher.*

## FRESH, ORIGINAL STYLE
## Beau Brummels Zoom Toward Top

The freshest and most original new sound of the past year originated in San Francisco and is rapidly spreading throughout the land.

It came from the Beau Brummels, a group which has captivated the enthusiasm of West Coast fans like no other entertainer since Elvis Presley.

The Beau Brummels combine a colorful, stylish appearance with a solid, imaginative new musical sound which needs no "gimmicks." They are big league professionals, and the smash success of their first release, "Laugh, Laugh," was no one-shot accident.

Four of them are from the San Francisco area; lead guitarist Ron Elliott, singer Sal Valentino, bass guitarist Ron Meagher and drummer John Petersen. The fifth, rhythm guitarist Declan Mulligan, came to the bay area in 1963 from his home in County Tipperary, Ireland.

Enthusiastic fans of the Beatles, Rolling Stones, Searchers and other top English groups, the Beau Brummels originally patterned their overall style after the "English Sound" that has dominated the American market.

In so doing, they became the first American group to successfully interpret that sound — rather ironic since the British groups admit they derive their sound and style from the American groups that were popular in the late fifties.

### Distinctive Style

But the Beau Brummels have also developed a style which is distinctively their own, a style best illustrated by

### "I'VE FORGOTTEN MY NAME!"

*Mobbed by autograph fans after a recent game with the KRLApes, one of the players appears to have forgotten something. Fortunately, one of the girls reminded him that he was Casey Kasem.*
*Photo by Jerry Long*

their recording of "Laugh, Laugh."

The Beau Brummels had been organized a few weeks when they were discovered by Bob Mitchell and Tom Donahue of KYA in San Francisco, who were immediately impressed by the fledgling group's distinctive style and showmanship.

While the boys have always been stylishly attired, their manager, Carl Scott is capitalizing further upon their namesake — Beau Brummel, the English aristocrat who gained a worldwide reputation in the early 19th century for his colorful fashionplate attire.

Scott went to the very top and asked Hollywood's Sy Devore to create new wardrobes for them.

Devore, whose male fashion creations for filmland celebrities sets the trend throughout the world, had previously refused a similar request by the Beatles.

### Finally Agreed

But Devore agreed to Scott's request, intrigued by the thought of outfitting five contemporary Beau Brummels and further motivated by the urging of his 14-year-old daughter, Lisa, an ardent fan of the group.

March is a big month for the Beau Brummels. During this month they are releasing their second single, an album, appearing on the Hullabaloo, Shindig and Dick Clark television shows and doing a series of public appearances in England, where "Laugh, Laugh" has just been released.

## Jerry Naylor Wins Acclaim In Solo Duet

Handsome singing star Jerry Naylor, former lead vocalist with the fabulous Crickets, now appears well on his way toward becoming one of the top single artists.

With the ink hardly dry on a new contract with Smash records, his first solo offering has just been released . . . "I Found You," coupled with "I'll Take You Home."

Jerry has a busy new schedule which includes a recent appearance on Shindig and future appearances on Country Go Go, several TV commercials and roles in two forthcoming movies, "Just For You" and "Girls on the Beach."

Jerry has long been a favorite with other entertainers, who admire both his personality and ability.

Among his early admirers were four English singers who were so impressed by the Crickets — then at the height of their popularity — that they tried to come up with a similar name.

They finally decided to name their group after another insect — the BEATLES!

By the way, girls, Jerry lives in Los Angeles and is single.

## Scoops & Flashes

### DC-5 Due Back In June or July

All you DAVE CLARK FIVE fans will be happy to know they're coming back. They're due in the States between June 19 and July 21 . . . PAUL PETERSEN recently got his Cobra back after having the front end completely replaced. He's going right back to racing it.

RAY PETERSON is currently at the Hideaway in Palm Springs . . . JOHNNY RIVERS will do his third Hullabaloo appearance on April 27 . . . JAN AND DEAN just signed to appear on the first Dean Martin show this year . . . THE BIG BEATS in town to promote their new album "The Big Beats — Live!" — they're on their way to an engagement in Hawaii . . .

MARK LINDSAY of PAUL REVERE AND THE RAIDERS out of the hospital and doing fine following throat surgery . . . LESLIE GORE in town for Shindig . . . BOBBY VEE leaves March 13 for a tour of Europe . . . WAYNE FONTANT & THE MIND BENDERS in town to promote their new release.

### PEN PAL

Maureen O'Brien is English and would like to have an American pen pal. Her address is 57 Seymour Road, Broadgreen, Liverpool 14, England.

### ETERNAL DEBT

KRLA owes a lot to Emporer Hudson. He keeps forgetting to pick up his paychecks.

MORE ABOUT
## DEREK TAYLOR
(From Page 1)

gant."

The Beatles were quite unworried by this. They shrugged their shoulders and forgot about it. But a lot of people around them (who know what the Beatles go through in the way of pressure, strain, travelling, heat and so on, were very annoyed by the article.

Said the film's publicity officer, Tony Howard — a good man and an honest one — "I like Peter Evans and he is entitled to his views."

But Peter's views are not shared by the other journalists who came here to the Bahamas.

### Beatles Patient

Tony Howard told me: "You know yourself that the Beatles are extremely patient. They are particularly nice to unimportant people from small newspapers or radio stations. The only thing they ask of people is that they should be as honest and direct as them.

"We had 45 press-men and radio people here in five days. The Beatles met them all. And out of those 45, only Peter Evans attacked them. Maybe he had a difficult time with them. Maybe he didn't. Whatever happened, it was unusual. The journalists have been thrilled with the Beatles' co-operation."

Well, Dave Hull and I were very, very happy with the way things went. The Beatles were great.

### Big Welcome

They gave me a wonderful welcome and it was just like old times. We went out to dinner together under the blue Bahamian skies, visited clubs, laughed about funny things that had happened in the past.

The film should be marvelous. It is full of action. Paul is shrunken to thumb-size for one wild scene. There are four Ringos at one time.

Also, there are 11 songs, the Bahamas background; scenes in the Alps and in London. Ringo is nearly murdered for his precious ring. The film is shot in colour and it will be one of the huge events of the cinema in 1965. Release-date USA and UK: around August 1.

Watch out for more film news and some inside news on the Beatles' lives in next week's KRLA Beat.

## KRLA ARCHIVES

BEATLE PHOTOS BY CURT GUNTHER

# Behind The Scenes With Beatles ... Exclusive Photos

A Hard Day's Night Enroute to Nassau

"Looking for Somebody, Stranger?"

Showdown at the OK Corral

"Please, Ringo, Keep Me In Mind, Anyway"

# KRLA ARCHIVES

## KRLA TUNEDEX

1. (21) STOP IN THE NAME OF LOVE .......... The Supremes
2. ( 2) EIGHT DAYS A WEEK/
         I DON'T WANT TO SPOIL THE PARTY .... The Beatles
3. ( 1) MY GIRL .................................................... Temptations
4. ( 3) THIS DIAMOND RING ............................ Gary Lewis
5. ( 9) THE BOY FROM NEW YORK CITY ...... The Ad Libs
6. (10) RED ROSES FOR A BLUE LADY .............. Vic Dana
7. (16) HURT SO BAD ............ Little Anthony & Imperials
8. ( 5) DOWNTOWN ................................................ Pet Clark
9. ( 4) FERRY ACROSS THE MERSEY .... Gerry & Pacemakers
10. (23) GO NOW ............................................ The Moody Blues
11. (17) CAN'T YOU HEAR MY HEARTBEAT ... Herman's Hermits
12. (11) NEW YORK'S A LONELY TOWN ...... The Trade Winds
13. (12) TWINE TIME .......................... Alvin Cash & Crawlers
14. ( 8) KING OF THE ROAD ............................ Roger Miller
15. (43) SHOT GUN ................................................ Jr. Walker
16. (44) TIRED OF WAITING FOR YOU .............. The Kinks
17. (18) THE BIRDS & THE BEES ...................... Jewel Akens
18. (15) PAPER TIGER ...................................... Sue Thompson
19. (13) TELL HER NO/LEAVE ME BE .............. The Zombies
20. ( 7) YOU'VE LOST THAT LOVIN' FEELIN' .... Righteous Bros.
21. (19) I GO TO PIECES .............................. Peter & Gordon
22. (31) BABY PLEASE DON'T GO .......................... Them
23. ( 6) THE JOLLY GREEN GIANT ........................ Kingsmen
24. (25) FOR LOVIN' ME .................... Peter, Paul & Mary
25. (34) IF I LOVED YOU .......................... Chad & Jeremy
26. (14) LAND OF 1,000 DANCES .... Cannibal & Headhunters
27. (22) HE WAS REALLY SAYIN' SOMETHIN' .... The Velvelettes
28. (20) LAUGH LAUGH ............................ The Beau Brummels
29. (26) GOLDFINGER .......................... Shirley Bassey
30. (37) KEEP SEARCHIN' ............................ Del Shannon

## EUBANKS, KASEM AND HULLABALOOER
## KRLA Deejays To Host TV Shows

You'll soon be able to see three of your favorite KRLA Deejays on television — each with his own regular show.

Bob Eubanks, Casey Kasim and Dave Hull have been selected as hosts of separate TV shows, and all three sound exciting.

Bob was tabbed several weeks ago to host "Beach Beat," a nationally syndicated dance party variety show to be aired on Saturday nights. Casey and Dave were selected for their shows only a few days ago.

Casey will host a daily hour - long TV program called "Shebang," to be produced by Dick Clark Productions a program that will be aired Monday through Friday at 5 p.m. Locally it will be seen on KTLA, starting March 22.

### Truly Unique

Bill Lee will be executive producer, with Hall Galli as producer.

Lee says it will be truly unique, featuring not only top artists and lively musical entertainment, but interviews with interesting people who do unusual things. The program will also feature a lot of contests in which the viewers can participate.

Many guest artists have already been scheduled, including Dick and DeeDee, Bobby Freeman, the Ikettes, Cannibal and the Headhunters and Freddie Cannon.

The shows will also feature filmed flashbacks of hit songs of the past, performed by such artists as Connie Francis, Frankie Avalon and Paul Anka.

### Final Stages

Dave's show is still in the final production and planning stage, but it has encountered enthusiastic response from all who have heard the format.

It will be a form of daily quiz show -- probably to be shown in the afternoons — to be called "Quick as a wink." We'll have more information about it in the KRLA Beat just as soon as all the arrangements are completed.

For those who missed our previous description of Bob Eubank's show, it will be the only television program of its kind. "Beach Beat" will be taped on the Southern California beaches and it will feature not only surfers and surfing, but top recording stars and teens from throughout the country doing the latest dance steps.

It will be a real swinging beach party, and sounds like loads of fun.

The pilot is to be taped at Malibu the latter part of this month.

### ALL THE ANSWERS

Casey Kasim knows more than anyone else about little things in the lives of the recording artists. He is now trying to find out some of the big things.

---

### More About
## DAVE HULL
(From Page 1)

to speak to a lot of the visitors. I'll pass along a few of the experiences that occurred while we were there.

At one point, Ringo, who plays a very unusual role — is painted by a savage. That particular scene had to be shot six times, and each time an expensive suit was ruined.

The script called for a giant idol to rise out of the sea on cue. For some reason, the thing fell over, breaking off two of the arms. With boats, a blimp and helicopter required to set it right again, the arms were finally welded back on at a tremendous cost.

### Sea Monster

While Malcolm Evans, the Beatles' road manager, was filming a bit as a channel swimmer, a huge sting ray came in close to shore — evidently to see what was going on (You find Beatlemaniacs in every form).

The director quickly ordered Malcolm and the Beatles out of the water. A diver was sent out to scare it off. I didn't envy the diver a bit, because that thing was about 20 feet in diameter and was so huge that everyone on shore could see him out there.

### Good Times

We had some great times with John, Paul, George and Ringo and other members of the company. We asked them every question we could think of and got replies to almost all of them. Derek is covering some of those points in his report in the Beat this week . . . and together we'll take up some of the questions and answers, item by item, next week.

Right now I have to sit back and catch my breath while trying to recuperate from an acute attack of Beatlemania.

---

### EUROPEAN TOUR RESULTS
## Opportunity Comes Knocking When Stones Visit Joey Paige

The Rolling Stones' visit to Los Angeles recently has provided a real boost for their host here, singer Joey Paige.

The Stones, who became close friends with the Southern California singer when they met in England last year, have been touting Joey as one of the most talented and promising male vocalists in the world.

Before they returned to England, their manager, Eric Easton, asked Joey to return the visit and do a promotional tour. He agreed, arranging to make the trip on March 12.

When VeeJay Records President Randy Wood heard of the tour he liked the idea so much that he made plans to accompany Joey personally. His main interest will be to help promote Joey's first record release in England. Incidentally the record, "Cause I'm In Love With You," was written by Bill Wyman of the Rolling Stones. It is also being released in the U.S. this month.

Joey is already scheduled for a number of radio and television appearances in England, and a news conference is to be held in his honor several days after his arrival. There now also appears to be a good possibility that he will do a series of personal appearances in London, Copenhagen and West Germany before he returns to Los Angeles.

Not bad for a trip which began simply as a personal visit by a group of friends.

### FAN CLUBS

**CHARLIE O'DONNELL**
Vivian Morales, President
O'Donnell Fan Club
430 E. Elm Avenue
Fullerton, California

**THE HIDEAWAYS**
Susan Franklin
22858 Gault
Canoga Park, California

**BEAU BRUMMELS**
Sally Schumacher, Pres.
261 Atherton Avenue
Atherton, California

**DAVE CLARK FIVE**
Margie Naumann, Pres.
Dave Clark Fan Club
11006 Foxcroft Drive
Whittier, California.

Send Fan Club information to KRLA Beat, 6290 Sunset Blvd., Suite 504, Hollywood, Calif.

---

**NEXT WEEK**
IN THE
**KRLA BEAT**

EXCLUSIVE BEATLE PHOTOS
*While Movie-Making in Bahamas*

---

DEEJAY'S FAVORITE ARTISTS
*You May Find Some Surprises*

---

ARE BRITISH GROUPS FADING?
*A Report on Popularity Trends*

---

AND MUCH, MUCH MORE!
LISTEN TO KRLA
FOR DETAILS

---

"And If I'm Elected, I Promise . . ."

### Personals

Dave Hull,
Why did you have to go and change your time? Now you can't sing me to sleep anymore.
Sleepless

The Beau Brummels,
Our parents took us to see you in San Francisco. Only two words to say . . . gear and fab! Come to Los Angeles to live, please.
Pat and Sally

Dear Ringo and Maureen,
I hope you have a lifetime of happiness. Best wishes always. I'm still a fan.
G. W., Los Angeles

Gary and the Playboys:
Saw you at Disneyland. We screamed our lungs out for you. Now we've got sore throats and headaches, but it was worth it.
Viv and Yogi

Dick Biondi,
You're the groove! Glad you're back.
Cathie, Sandi and Clarence

Dear Derek Taylor,
Welcome to K-R-A-L-A-N-D!! We're all glad to have you here.
April, January and Barbs

# KRLA BEAT

**KRLA D-J's Pick Favorite Artists**
—See Page 3

SCRAMBLE FEATURES ANSWERS!
(See Page 2)

INTIMATE BEATLE PHOTOS
(See Page 3)

March 24, 1965 — Los Angeles, California — Ten Cents

## HULL REJECTS FILM OFFER!

BY DAVE HULL
(KRLA 3-6 P.M.)

FLASH — It's still not definitely decided, but a new name has been tossed into the hat for the new Beatle movie. They are strongly considering "8 Days a Week" as the title.

George is apparently still holding out for the name he suggested while Derek Taylor and I were visiting them in the bahamas — "Who Fell Into My Porridge?"

You have to admit his title sounds more glamorous.

Several people have asked me about reports that I turned down an offer to appear in the new Beatles movie.

True, while I was in Nassau, United Artists did offer me a part. It's also true that I declined that exciting offer. And I've been crying in my root beer ever since.

Let's face it — I'd like to be a movie star as much as the next guy, but there were reasons for not taking them up on it (aside from the fact that I might break their lenses!).

Derek and I were there visiting the Beatles at their personal invitation and as their guests. Even though United Artists assurred me that the two scenes they offered could be shot while we were there, I was afraid John, Paul, George and Ringo would put me in the same class with the rest of the people in this business who try constantly to use the Beatles for their own personal gain.

They would probably have thought, "Look at Dave Hull. We invite him to visit us and immediately he horns in on our movie. He must be just like the rest of these people who shake hands and then try to shake us down for whatever they can get."

Much as I would like to be in their movie, I value their friendship more. No personal thrill could ever be worth the price.

A disc jockey named Murray the K arrived there before we left and didn't hesitate to take a bit part in the movie. I envied him in a way, and if the circumstances were the same I would have glady done the same thing.

When they finally release "Eight Days a Week" or "Who Fell Into My Porridge" — or whatever they decide to name it — I'll probably walk around telling everyone, "Gee, I was almost in this movie with the Beatles."

One thing I noticed about the guys . . . particularly Paul and George: During the past few months since they were in Los Angeles they have grown and matured.

Those two have filled out physically and put on a few pounds. But they are no longer the awestruck, starry-eyed boys getting their first look at the wonders of the world.

They now seem more poised and have a more mature and adult outlook.

Maybe this is good, in a way . . . as long as they don't ever lose the enthusiasm and excitement which seemed to spill over and infect their fans with such joyous hysteria everywhere they appeared.

## Derek Taylor Reports

While the Beatles are making their film, the Rolling Stones are making the British disc charts. They are on top of the English "Melody Maker" list — having taken over from Tom Jones, the Welsh newcomer.

The Stones chart-topper is The Last Time. It leapt to the top on advance sales, proving that the group's popularity is as strong as ever.

Generally, however, groups are not as powerful as they used to be in England. Too many poor groups saturated the market and now only the best succeed.

You in America are fortunate because you only see and hear the cream of the British groups — people like Freddie & the Dreamers. Herman, Manfred and so on. In the U.S., therefore, the British remain strong.

Talking of Herman . . . his Mrs. Brown disc is an example of the freak hit. It has nothing to do with rock'n'roll. It is not even well sung. But it has a wonderful North-British appeal and it is a certainty for the Top Ten.

The attraction lies in the Lancashire accent (which is Herman's birth-right) and in the simplicity of the melody. We had an artist in England called George Formby who made a million dollars in the thirties and forties singing just this sort of song.

If only he'd lived to see how commercial his songs had become.

In the old days few of us cared to admit we had Northern accents. Now they're fashionable beyond belief. Anyone who speaks like the Beatles has it made!

I called London today to see what was happening. They tell me PJ Proby has another hit. Called I Apologize. This shot up from nowhere to 13 in the charts. It will probably make the top five.

Virginia Ironside of the Daily Mail in London, a young, very hip disc-columnist, told me the

—MORE ON PAGE 2

### TOP TEN

1. STOP IN THE NAME OF LOVE
2. MY GIRL
3. EIGHT DAYS A WEEK/ I DON'T WANT TO SPOIL THE PARTY
4. BOY FROM NEW YORK CITY
5. GO NOW!
6. SHOTGUN
7. THIS DIAMOND RING
8. HURT SO BAD
9. CAN'T YOU HEAR MY HEARTBEAT
10. RED ROSES FOR A BLUE LADY

## Another Exclusive Beatle Photo

Like a postman who goes for a walk on his day off, THE BEATLES relax for a few moments by strumming their guitars. The kookie hat is a gift from an admirer who finally got to see them for a few seconds.

# KRLA ARCHIVES

## Another Exclusive Beatle Photo

ANOTHER OF THE EXCLUSIVE BEATLES photos to appear in the BEAT. The camera caught the pair in an unguarded moment inside the private dressing rooms set up for the group while they worked long hours on their island adventure story.

## Scrambled Features Winners

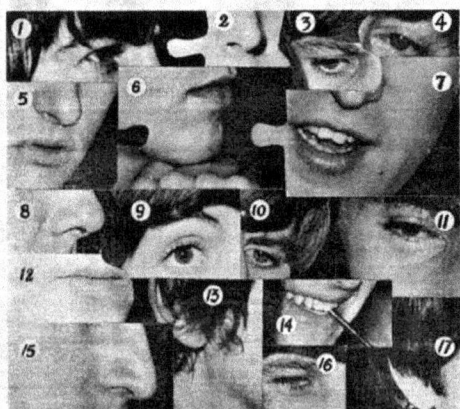

Out of hundreds of entries received, there were a number of correct answers, but an El Monte girl got in the earliest post marked entry. We'll have more BEATLE CONTESTS in upcoming issues.

The winner is Valeri Hernandez, of 4566 Esto Avenue in El Monte. Valeri is a freshman at Arroyo High School and says she really digs THE BEATLES because they're "something different" and "out of the ordinary." After she saw them on television, 14 year old Valeri knew THE BEATLES were for her!

THE BEATLES SCRAMBLE CONTEST PICTURE that brought in so many entires and deluged the offices of the KRLA BEAT. How many did you identify correctly? The actual answers are: 1—George. 2—Paul. 3—Ringo. 4—John. 5—Ringo. 6—George. 7—John. 8—George. 9—Paul. 10—Ringo. 11—John. 12—Paul. 13—George. 14—Ringo. 15—John. 16—Ringo. 17—Paul. Derek Taylor got them all the first time.

### KRLA BEAT

Published each week for Radio Station KRLA, Pasadena, California.

EDITOR ............ NORM WOODRUFF
REPORTER ......... JIM HAMBLIN
PHOTOGRAPHY ..... JERRY LONG
PRINTING ......... HENDRIX HOUSE
ARTIST ........... STEVE BELLEW
Your comments are invited. Address letters to KRLA BEAT, 6290 Sunset Blvd., Suite 504, Hollywood, California. 90028.

## Beatle Quotes
## It's Not Quiet In Studio As Beatles Make New Disc

While the Beatles filmed in the Bahamas, George Martin, (the Beatles recording manager), sat back in London listening to tapes of the last recording session.

It was at this session that the FAB FOUR recorded all the songs that will be used in the still un-named movie which will be released this summer, for all the **KRLA - BEATLEMANIACS** to enjoy.

During a lull at the recording session Paul was fooling around with an electric piano while George and Ringo danced to a playback of another soon-to-be Beatle hit.

### Still Mooches

John Lennon sits in a corner, in his own little world. John is the mastermind of the Beatles.

Although a millionaire, John carries little money, and is always scrounging cigarettes. He still uses matches instead of a flashy lighter.

Taking advantage of the lull in the session, John gave his thoughts to the KRLA BEAT, about the Beatles, recording stars, and film stars.

### Lennon Talking

"We'll be pop stars as long as we continue making records, and that will be quite awhile. We regard filming," John says, "as a bit of a giggle, too. We're film stars, and pop stars, we hope."

The KRLA BEAT got this quote of John, when asked about rumors that the end of the line has been reached, and the Beatles will disband soon:

"Why are these things even considered? They suppose that just because we've done well, we might as well pack it in. We'll never pack it in completely, because we've made so much money, and we're still making it.

### Rubbish Talk

"People talk a load of rubbish about us. We have no plans to break up. We may be interested in more than filming and making records, but the Beatles will always be the Beatles."

John goes on to reveal some of the plans for the future.

"I'm going to do some A&R work. I want to be an independent record producer. I'd like to find someone as good as Tom Jones and record them. Probably, Paul and me will work together."

### Friendship

There is an indestructible bond of warm friendship between Paul and 24 year old John Lennon.

John goes on, "Until now, there's never been time for other work, but there might be now.

I was going to have a recording studio built at my house. But I gave up the idea. It couldn't work. Good lord, I can't even work a bloody tape recorder, so I can't see myself doing the big equipment bit.

"I'm getting this shed built," John says, "at the back of the house. I'll discover people, then hire a studio to record them.

"This won't be for some time yet, so I don't want hundreds of people imagining that I'm walking around with a big cigar and open to offers.

### What Type?

What variety of talent would John like to discover?

"I've been thinking about this. I'd like to discover someone with the looks of Bardot, and the voice of Dionne Warwick."

Do you like Dionne?

"Her voice is OK. I'm not exactly crazy about her, but that's the sort of combination I'm thinking of. A big symbol. A girl who looks great, and sings wild. She's got to be somewhere. There's never been someone like this as I can remember."

"The sort of girl I'd be interested in would be someone with such a voice that the fellas look up to see what she looks like and then when they see her . . ."

### Companys Taken

Does this interest in a single star mean groups are fading?

John says, "This year the record companies will not be signing up all the lousy groups like they did last year. There was a time when the companies would sign up anybody who made a noise like four men with guitars. They were taken and deserved to be taken. They signed up rubbish, and when they didn't get hits they starting running. Can't blame them, but they should have been more sensible."

Does John still get a kick out of recording?

"Yeah," he says, "more now than before. When we started, I didn't know much about it. What to do and what to expect at the end. But, now that we know a bit more, it's much more interesting."

## More About
### DEREK TAYLOR
#### FROM PAGE ONE

Beau Brummel's disc Laugh Laugh was causing some excitement over there.

"They sound very British," she said. "And very good." Virginia was wild about another American artist — Roger Miller. "Absolutely fabulous," she shouted over the 8,000 miles of Post Office cable. "When is he coming over here?"

The answer is "soon," both for Roger and the Brummels. Each has yet to dent the British charts. But when the personal contacts are made with fans over there, expect an entirely different story.

The Beatles left the Bahamas a few days ago. Their tropical segment of the film is complete and everyone is very happy. You can still hear them on KRLA. Stay tuned. See you soon.

# KRLA ARCHIVES

## KRLA TUNEDEX

| THIS WEEK | LAST WEEK | TITLE | ARTIST |
|---|---|---|---|
| 1. | 1. | STOP! IN THE NAME OF LOVE | The Supremes |
| 2. | 3. | MY GIRL | The Temptations |
| 3. | 2. | EIGHT DAYS A WEEK – I DON'T WANT TO SPOIL THE PARTY | The Beatles |
| 4. | 5. | THE BOY FROM NEW YORK CITY | The Ad Libs |
| 5. | 10 | GO NOW! | The Moody Blues |
| 6. | 15 | SHOTGUN | Jr. Walker & All Stars |
| 7. | 4. | THIS DIAMOND RING | Gary Lewis & Playboys |
| 8. | 7. | HURT SO BAD | Little Anthony |
| 9. | 11. | CAN'T YOU HEAR MY HEARTBEAT | Herman's Hermits |
| 10. | 6. | RED ROSES FOR A BLUE LADY | Vic Dana |
| 11. | 14. | KING OF THE ROAD | Roger Miller |
| 12. | 17. | THE BIRDS AND THE BEES | Jewel Akins |
| 13. | 16. | TIRED OF WAITING FOR YOU | The Kinks |
| 14. | 9 | FERRY ACROSS THE MERSEY | Gerry & The Pacemakers |
| 15. | 12. | NEW YORK'S A LONELY TOWN | The Trade Winds |
| 16. | 13. | TWINE TIME | Alvin Cash & The Crawlers |
| 17. | 22. | BABY, PLEASE DON'T GO – GLORIA | Them |
| 18. | 42. | I'M TELLING YOU NOW | Freddie & the Dreamers |
| 19. | 8. | DOWNTOWN | Petula Clark |
| 20. | 19. | TELL HER NO – LEAVE ME | The Zombies |
| 21. | 43. | WHEN I'M GONE | Brenda Holloway |
| 22. | 45. | NOWHERE TO RUN | Martha & the Vandellas |
| 23. | 24. | FOR LOVIN' ME | Peter, Paul & Mary |
| 24. | 20. | YOU'VE LOST THAT LOVIN' FEELIN' | Righteous Brothers |
| 25. | 34. | GIRL DON'T COME | Sandie Shaw |
| 26. | 31. | DO YOU WANNA DANCE? PLEASE LET ME WONDER | The Beach Boys |
| 27. | 26. | LAND OF 1,000 DANCES | Cannibal & Headhunters |
| 28. | 27. | HE WAS REALLY SAYIN' SOMETHIN' | The Velvelettes |
| 29. | 18. | PAPER TIGER | Sue Thompson |
| 30. | 32. | DON'T LET ME BE MISUNDERSTOOD | The Animals |

### CLIMBERS

| | | | |
|---|---|---|---|
| 1. | HERE THEY COME FROM ALL OVER THE WORLD | | Jan & Dean |
| 2. | IF I LOVED YOU | | Chad & Jeremy |
| 3. | STRANGER IN TOWN | | Del Shannon |
| 4. | THE RACE IS ON | | Jack Jones |
| 5. | LITTLE THINGS | | Bobby Goldsboro |
| 6. | IT HURTS ME | | Bobby Sherman |
| 7. | PEOPLE GET READY | | The Impressions |
| 8. | LONG LONELY NIGHTS | | Bobby Vinton |
| 9. | IF I RULED THE WORLD | | Tony Bennett |
| 10. | I KNOW A PLACE | | Petula Clark |

## Exclusive
### HERE FOR FIRST TIME KRLA DEEJAYS REVEAL FAVORITE ENTERTAINERS

Disc jockeys are constantly being asked to name their favorite artists.

Small wonder, since they play such a vital role in the shaping of record hits, and since they play thousands of records from hundreds of artists every year.

This week the Beat asked KRLA dee-jays to name their favorite recording artists and to explain the reason for their choice. Here's what they told us:

**EMPEROR HUDSON** — "I can't really give you an overall answer because there are so many different categories. But I can tell you my favorite new group. They record under the name of "Them" and their recording of Baby Please Don't Go is going to be a nationwide smash.

"It takes something mighty good to satisfy the taste of an emperor, and from the very beginning this record has knocked me out."

**CHARLIE O'DONNELL** — "My all-time favorite single performer is Elvis Presley. Although he may not have had quite the world-wide impact of the Beatles, he has done more for promoting the cause of modern-day pop music than any other entertainer in the history of the recording business. There has never before been a young people's idol of his stature or popularity in this country, and there may never be again."

**CASEY KASEM** — "My favorite entertainer is a man who has more talent in one package than any other entertainer in history. He is a wonderful singer, an excellent dancer, a fine actor and one of the finest mimics in the world. It seems like he can do everything, and do it all unbelievably well. You must know by now that I'm talking about Sammy Davis, Jr."

**DAVE HULL** — "You must be out of your mind to ask me a question like that! As president of the Southern California Beatle Fan Club, the official Beatle Rumor-Buster and a man who lives, breathes and exists for nothing but the Beatles, you have a lot of nerve to ask me to name my favorite entertainers. Actually, I'm really glad you asked me, though. Because my favorite entertainers are really the Scuzzies!"

**BOB EUBANKS** — "Definitely the Beatles. That's not to take anything away from any of the other groups or single artists, but based upon their impact on the recording business and the effect they have had upon their millions of fans the world over, there's just no one else to compare with them at present."

**DICK BIONDI** — "Man, I'm hung up on the Beatles too, but my favorite over the past several years has to be Elvis Presley. One reason for this is not only his talent, but a kind of sentimental attachment. I was getting my first big breaks as a disc jockey at just about the same time he made his first big hit as a recording star and was privileged to have met him several times along the way. He's not only a great star, but an extremely nice guy."

**DICK MORELAND** — "The Righteous Brothers are one of my favorites. Not only because of their great talent, but because they're from this area and we've been able to watch them on their climb to the top."

DEREK TAYLOR AND THE HULLABALOOER step off a sleek jet after an exciting trip to the Bahamas for visits with the BEATLES.

# KRLA ARCHIVES

## At Deadline

Nashville teens propose turn about is fair play, so the British should ban the American groups. Seems the whole controversy arose when the Americans wouldn't allow *Sandi Shaw* to come to America because she isn't well enough known. So say they.

The poor quality of *Elvis Presley's* new one — *Do The Clam* — has many fans turning in their membership cards.

Wonder who plays motorcycle on *Leader of the Pack?*

It is now an official million seller: *Downtown* by *Petula Clark.*

The *Searchers* are turning down more and more tours. They want more and more money.

One of *Mike Jagger's* pet hates are artists who talk about how bad pop music is, then talk about how much money they are making at it.

*P. J. Proby* was banned for being too obscene on stage. The *Rockin' Berries* did a comedy take off on *P. J.* and got themselves banned.

Favorite singers of *Tom Jones: Brook Benton, Jerry Lee Lewis,* and *Ben E. King.*

*Kay Davis* of the *Kinks* has written a special number for the *Honeycombs.*

Twenty-six stitches on one arm, six stiches on one finger, and a gash on the leg. This is the result of *Freddie,* the drummer for *Freddie and the Dreamers,* walking through a plate glass door.

Did you know *Roy Orbison* is younger than *Elvis Presley?*

The first *Beatles* release in East Germany will be *Ain't See Sweet.*

*Memphis,* by *Chuck Berry* was recorded in his home. He wrote the song after a girl called him while on a St. Louis DJ's show asking that he write a song for her. No, her name is not Marie.

The new *Herman's Hermits* record will be *Silhouettes.* It's already a hit over there. The flip side in England is *Can't You Hear My Heartbeat,* which is a hit here by *Herman. Can't You Hear My Heartbeat* is a hit in England by *Goldie and the Gingerbreads* who were discovered by the *Animals* in New York. It's groovy to see the record business is so simple.

*John Lennon* and *Paul McCartney* are writing a song for *Keeley Smith.*

*Del Clusky* of the *Bachelors* is having his tonsils removed.

*Julie Roger's* new single will be *Andy William's* old hit, *Hawaiian Wedding Song.*

*Shindig* will probably go to one half hour again.

*Freddie and the Dreamers* will be on *Ed Sullivan* April 25th. This, if they can get out of some filming commitments.

Newest group from England is called the *Measles.* A discovery of *Mickey Most.*

Tracks of the new *Rolling Stones* LP from the American to English versions are quite different. Much shorter, too.

## Righteous Disc Ready

THE RIGHTEOUS BROTHERS have returned from their London tour and now are making several personal appearances here in California. Bob and Bill set a new all-time record at KRLA when their recording YOU'VE LOST THAT LOVIN' FEELING lasted EIGHT STRAIGHT WEEKS as Number One! They told us that they have finished their newest recording, but the title is still a SECRET, while a release date is determined. It should be another smash for the Anaheim pair.

## Beatles Head Home From Bermuda

GOODBYE FOR NOW, say THE BEATLES. And off they go, after hectic filming on the newest film for the group. Just what the title will be is still uncertain, but DAVE HULL has an inside scoop in his column for this week's KRLA BEAT!

## Stones Set Date For Swingin' Show Sunday, May 26th

The Rolling Stones will be in Long Beach May 16th, according to KRLA's Bob Eubanks.

And that's the good news that everyone has been waiting for.

Bob told the KRLA Beat, the Stones will be in the 13-thousand seat Long Beach Arena, Sunday afternoon at 4 p.m.

Already, ticket requests are rolling in by the bagfull, but Bob says they won't go on sale for a couple of weeks.

Starting April 10, they will be available at Wallich's Music City, Mutual Agencies, and at the Long Beach Arena box office. The tickets will sell for $2, $3, $4 and $5. They are all reserved seats. So, be sure to get in line on April 10, so you won't miss this big show of '65.

Since the last Los Angeles visit by the Rolling Stones, Eubanks has been flooded with calls wanting them back, and he has been working on a date ever since. Now, it's here.

On the same show with the Stones will be a good friend of their's from Los Angeles, Joey Paige. Also, all the Cinnamon Cinder bands: The Vibrants, and Don and the Deacons.

Bob says there will still be more talent added to the show soon, and the KRLA Beat will let you know right away.

Be sure to hear Bob on KRLA each night from 6 to 9 p.m., for more details.

## KRLA NEWS

In our first report for the KRLA BEAT, let's get acquainted. The KRLA newsroom provides the newcasts heard every 30 minutes on the station. The men who report the news spend their day gathering the news stories together, and then as the KRLA disc jockey ends each portion of the show, controls are switched to the main newsroom, where the reports are made. In the early morning, we regularly hear Richard Beebe report the news. If you happen to peek into the studio sometime, Richard is the tall one with the bushy beard! Also working with Beebe every morning is the boss, Cecil Tuck, who as News Director administers the News Department, figures out how much money can be spent by the station for covering news, and what hours each newscaster works. Cecil also reads many of the newscasts each day, himself.

Later in the day you might hear Carl Mesmer, whose big bass voice has been heard for many years on KRLA News. Carl works late afternoons and nights, keeping Los Angeles informed. Also heard is Jim Steck who everybody knows interviewed the Beatles many times, and was the man who stowed away on the Beatles' private plane, all the way to Denver! Jim still wears the black knit tie that Ringo gave him, although Jim says it's about a foot longer now, 'cause everybody is always pulling on it!

The outside news reporter who covers activities as they happen in Los Angeles is rotund Jim Hamblin, who makes several "beeper" reports every day — and can be seen almost anywhere news is happening carrying a portable tape recorder with the KRLA sign on it.

Also working the night shift back at the studio is jolly Thom Beck who recently took a second lok at the Surgeon's General's report, has been diligently sticking to his decision to stop smoking ever since. He now brings a suitcase full of bagels and cream cheese to work every day.

During the Bobby Dale show, newsman Mike Allen works by the KRLA world-wide teletype service, which prints all the news 24 hours a day. Mike selects the most important and interesting stories, and reports them on the news all night. Mike, by the way, has quite a bit of trouble getting through doors in the studio . . . he is almost 7 feet tall! In his spare time he is writing a book about famous bandleader Glenn Miller.

These 7 men work carefully every day to bring to KRLA listeners the most up to date and comprehensive news reports on radio.

# KRLA ARCHIVES

## Derek Taylor Reports

Cilla Black and Sounds Incorporated are due in Hollywood at the end of March.

Coming into Southern California at the same time will be their manager — my former boss — Brian Epstein.

### Is A Star

Cilla, persistent hit-songstress in England, has yet to persuade American record-buyers that she is a star. But this will come, because the girl has tremendous quality in her presence and personality. And when her voice is more mature, she will be a considerable singer.

Already she has sold far more than a million discs. Cilla is an extremely nice girl, unspoiled by her immense, almost over-night, success.

Sounds Incorporated, the most
—MORE ON PAGE 2

# KRLA BEAT

March 31, 1965     Los Angeles, California     Ten Cents

## BEATLE TITLE CHOSEN!

**By Dave Hull**

The report that the Beatles planned to name their second movie "Eight Days a Week" proved to be about 25 per cent correct. The first word was right — "Eight."

Derek Taylor called me while I was on the air last week to give KRLA a world-wide exclusive.

He had just received a call from the Beatles' camp in Austria saying that the boys had finally hit upon a title . . . Eight Arms to Hold You.

You can look for a song by that same title in the movie, and that will probably also be the title for the Beatle record album to accompany the movie.

### Sacrificial Ringo

The "Eight Arms" applies to John, Paul, George and Ringo, of course, but it also fits portions of the movie. The giant idol to which Ringo is to be sacrificed in the movie also has eight arms. Another exclusive for KRLA and the Beat!

We have received many, many requests to repeat the questions and answers from the interviews Derek and I did with the Beatles on Nassau. There is not enough space to print the entire three hours of tape recorded interviews, but we are going to print the highlights.

We're starting this week with Ringo, and we'll take each one of the Beatles in the following weeks. As the scene opens in this one, I had just finished talking to John and walked up as Derek was interviewing Ringo down on the beach near the area where they were filming. Ringo was a strange sight, dressed in a handsome suit which was splattered with red paint.
—MORE ON PAGE 2

### TOP TEN

1. STOP! IN THE NAME OF LOVE
2. GO NOW!
3. MY GIRL
4. EIGHT DAYS A WEEK—I DON'T WANT TO SPOIL THE PARTY
5. SHOTGUN
6. TIRED OF WAITING FOR YOU
7. CAN'T YOU HEAR MY HEARTBEAT
8. BABY, PLEASE DON'T GO
9. BOY FROM NEW YORK CITY
10. THIS DIAMOND RING

—SEE PAGE 3

## Leisure Hour in Life of a Beatle

## Derek Taylor Reports

**FROM PAGE ONE**

musicianly big brass-and-string group in Britain, have also waited a long time for a hit in the United States.

They are almost always included on Beatle tours, in Britain, Europe, and Australia.

### Landing Here

They will fly into Los Angeles International Airport with Cilla from Perth, Australia, after their "downunder" tour. The tour opened on March 8th in Auckland, New Zealand, and they are now basking their way 'round the sun-scorched southern coast of Australia.

I was with the Beatles — and Sounds Incorporated — in Australia last year. It is a great land with lovely people.

Cilla makes her Ed Sullivan TV debut in New York on Sunday, April 4th.

### Quickly on TV

Tommy Quickly, you will be glad to know, has now completely made it in England. He has been selected as host of a major twice-weekly television show called "Five O'Clock Club" — in the Lloyd Thaxton idiom. Tommy tells me he bought a suit of black kid mohair with a wide velvet collar, elaborate stand-out wide gauntlet cuffs. He wears it with a black velvet waistcoat and opera-style cloak.

The cloak is cut circular and can be thrown over the shoulder to display a lavender-colored satin lining.

Don't worry. He still goes out with girls.

### Raiders Rested

Paul Revere and the Raiders are back in business again this week after a 21-day rest enforced by the illness of their handsome lead singer, Mark Lindsay.

The Raiders received a letter from Dick Clark Productions thanking them for their contributions to his "Where the Action Is" show.

The Beau Brummels are leaving for England very soon and a big welcome is being prepared for them. They will be leaving behind their splendid $450 Beau Brummel suits because an English pop singer of the same name wears them too. And as the Englishman has not yet been successful as an artist, the conflict of names would be no help to our excellent San Franciscan group.

### No Damage

Sorry to hear the Beatles were booed when they got into Austria. It means nothing. And it cannot damage the Beatles. When I was with them in Europe, I always detected an undercurrent of resentment, which has nothing to do with the Beatles. There is, on the Continent of Europe, a persistent envy and resentment of the British. Britain should worry.

Still top of the British charts: The Rolling Stones with The Last Time.

### Proby Dropping

I was wrong about P. J. Proby's latest British release, I Apologize. It suddenly stopped climbing and is now on the way down from No. 13, its highest point.

Amazing.

So what else is new?

Oh, yes. Gerry and the Pacemakers are hitting thirty key cities throughout the States between April 29 and May 27, in the "Shindig" road show. Alas, they may not be coming into Southern California.

Thank you for all your letters. I am still trying to answer them. Bear with me.

## Popular Girls

**PETULA CLARK** (left) **AND SHIRLEY ELLIS** (right) both have new releases promising to duplicate the success each has had with former hits. SHIRLEY is coming on strong with THE CLAPPING SONG, hard on the heels of her smash NAME GAME. Meantime, PETULA is hitting it big with follow-up to DOWNTOWN — this time it's I KNOW A PLACE. Read about reaction to PETULA CLARK described in Louise Criscione's column ON THE BEAT.

## Continued

### HULLABALOOER AND RINGO

**FROM PAGE ONE**

**DEREK:** Good morning, Ringo.
**RINGO:** Good morning, Derek. Good to see you again.
**DEREK:** Good to see you, Ringo, particularly in weather like this. Is it too hot for you?
**RINGO:** Uh . . . it gets a bit hot when you're staked in the sun and have to lay there for half an hour or so, fully dressed.
**DEREK:** Why the red paint all over your suit, Ringo?
**RINGO:** Well, it's . . . the film is basically a chase film and it's about a ring, and it starts off where they're going to sacrifice a girl, and they paint everyone they sacrifice red, you see . . . this tribe . . . but they can't sacrifice the girl because she hasn't got this magic ring on which she sent to me because I wear rings. And so they're after me now and they can't get the ring off and so they're going to sacrifice me . . . and that's why I'm red.
**DEREK:** And the paint has been put on you so they could sacrifice you?

**RINGO:** Yes.
**DEREK:** How many times have you been painted up to now?
**RINGO:** Oh, about four or five times.
**DEREK:** Do you like filming? It seems hard work for you. You always seem to be the one out on your own while all the other Beatles are in bed.
**RINGO:** Not all of the time. Some of it. I've enjoyed filming anyway. It's just that I hate to get up in the mornings. That's the only drag.
**DEREK:** What time to you have to get up in the morning, Ring?
**RINGO:** Malcolm woke me up at 25 to seven this morning.
**DEREK:** How do you stand the separation so soon after getting married?
**RINGO:** Oh, you know, you just when we were getting married that I would have to leave to come out here for the film, and we just got used to the idea. It's a bit of a drag,

**ADVERTISERS**
For rates and information call the KRLA BEAT at 469-3641.

y'know. But there was no point fetching Maureen because we're working like lunatics and we don't have a day off when we're on location.
**DEREK:** It wasn't a question then, really, of having a Caribbean honeymoon, which is many people's dream?
**RINGO:** No, no. Well, we didn't have an English one . . . never mind the Caribbean one.
**DEREK:** How long were you actually away from London?
**RINGO:** We got married on a Thursday and went back on a Sunday night.
**DEREK:** It was quite a dramatic story, which broke at a very good time of day, too. How long was it planned before it happened?
**RINGO:** Well, we decided to get married two weeks to the day, and it started getting planned from then.
**DEREK:** Well, let me say congratulations because everyone who knows you, and knows you both, is delighted. I think it was a marvelous move and I'm sure you thought so too or you wouldn't have done it.
**RINGO:** Well, thanks a lot, Derek. I thought it was a good move.
**DEREK:** It means that at last we won't have to deny or confirm the queries "Is Ringo married," so will you now say into the mike something for all time, on record, "I married Maureen Cox."
**RINGO:** I married Maureen Cox. I'm very happy . . . and her name is now Maureen Starkey.
**DEREK:** Which is no bad name and we're all very happy. Tell me, the other Beatles in the film . . . are they detached from you for a time as they were in "Hard Day's Night?"
**RINGO:** Yes, just a short time. Not too long this time, though.
**DEREK:** In this film there's no question of you falling out at all?
**RINGO:** No, no. Well, as I say, I get captured and things and they're looking for me, and when they're looking for me you won't see me on the screen, and when I'm sort of being captured and taken away, you'll see me and not them.
**DEREK:** Is the film in Technicolor?
**RINGO:** Yes, yes. Well, it's in some color. I don't know if it's

in Technicolor or one of the other colors.
**DEREK:** It's a beautiful day, Ringo.
**RINGO:** It's marvelous. I think it must be getting 75 or 80 degrees.

## Crowded?

**FREDDIE & THE DREAMERS** found out about the new $1 rate for long distance calls, and are really cashing in! Group is also cashing in on their national hit I'M TELLING YOU NOW! The sloe-eyed beauty is Cathe Cozzi, kibitzing with Freddie.

**DEREK:** It's a different climate from California, of course, because I think there is more humidity coming in from Florida.
**RINGO:** Well, it's very hot if you get into the sun. It's not so bad while you're on the beach, but while you're in town it's hard going, y'know . . . you sweat like a pig.
**DEREK:** This sort of climate suits me very well, which is really why I came to live in California. Dave Hull just walked up.
**RINGO:** Yes, I've noticed. Hi, Dave.
**DAVE:** Hi, Ringo. I think it's my turn to toss a few questions at you.
**RINGO:** Yeah, I sort of expected that.
**DAVE:** Speaking of Maureen again, are you happily married?
**RINGO:** Yes, very happily, thank you.
**DAVE:** Good. That's very good. I know all of your fans . . . there are a few dissenters but I'm sure most of your fans . . .
**RINGO:** I hope I haven't upset anyone too much.
**DAVE:** No, I don't think it has. Most of your fans are quite happy if you're happy. I know that's the way they feel.
**RINGO:** Well, that's good. Thank you.
**DAVE:** The last time you were in the States, in Hollywood, and in Los Angeles in particular, I asked you a question: "What about Maureen? and your answer was: "Maureen who?" Do you know the Maureen that I meant now?
**RINGO:** Yes, yes. Yes, but I mean . . . when I was last in the States there was nothing . . . no thought about getting
**—MORE ON PAGE 4**

# KRLA ARCHIVES

## New Show
### Kasem Readys TV Debut As Great New Show Organized

Millions of Southern California viewers found both a surprise and a threat on their television screens this week.

KRLA's Casey Kasem, whose top-rated early afternoon radio show is one of the most popular in the nation, made his debut as a TV star.

He is host of a highly acclaimed new program called "Shebang," shown from 5:00-6:00 p.m. on KTLA (Channel 5).

Produced by Dick Clark Productions, the show has a number of unusual and highly entertaining features.

Casey's accounts of little-known episodes in the lives of pop recording stars have long provided an extra spark to his radio shows on KRLA. But now television viewers can watch Casey, and the stars he talks about.

"Shebang" features actual films of the performers doing the big hits for which they are noted.

"But the real stars of the show," says Casey, "are the teenagers who appear on the program each afternoon." In addition to music, dancing and interviews, "Shebang" also features several entertaining contests.

For the studio group, "Wisk-a-Disc" is one of the most unusual contests ever seen on television. Contestants try to identify records played at the wrong speed.

"For the viewers, 'Name-A-Disc' offers a challenging and exciting opportunity to compete for prizes," says Casey. "While a record is playing, ten pictures are flashed on a screen. From those pictures, the viewers try to guess titles for the records."

Future plans call for the show to be syndicated nation-wide. It represents a well-deserved break for Casey, one of the most popular and best-liked disc jockeys in the country.

## KRLApes Back to Trees

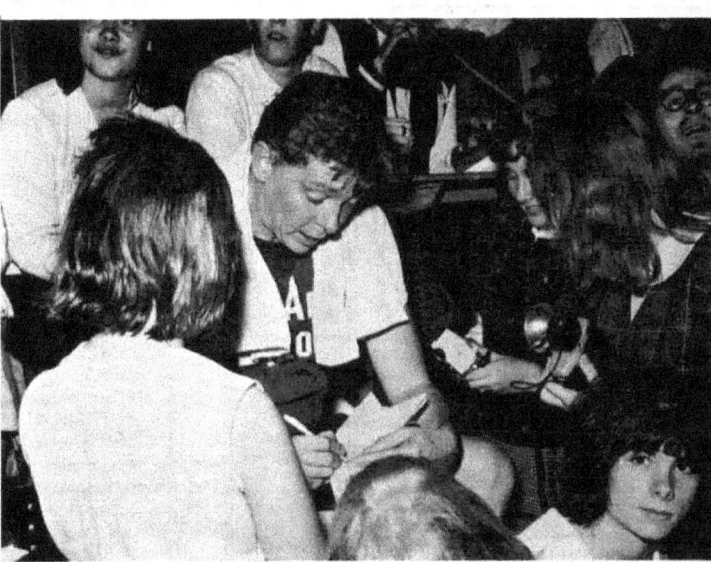

**DISILLUSIONED TEAM MEMBER CHARLIE O'DONNELL** in state of shock after major upset of year — pondering accidental victory of KRLApes. In game with San Fernando Youth Center, Apes stumbled into win column, 32-15, in first game ever won by the "team" in 2 years of play. O'Donnell pegged responsibility for win on Dick Diondi, Dave Hull, and Bob Eubanks. None of them showed up!

## KRLA TUNEDEX

| THIS WEEK | LAST WEEK | TITLE | ARTIST |
|---|---|---|---|
| 1. | 1. | STOP! IN THE NAME OF LOVE | The Supremes |
| 2. | 5. | GO NOW! | The Moody Blues |
| 3. | 2. | MY GIRL | The Temptations |
| 4. | 3. | EIGHT DAYS A WEEK — I DON'T WANT TO SPOIL THE PARTY | The Beatles |
| 5. | 6. | SHOTGUN | Jr. Walker & All Stars |
| 6. | 13. | TIRED OF WAITING FOR YOU | The Kinks |
| 7. | 9. | CAN'T YOU HEAR MY HEART BEAT | Herman's Hermits |
| 8. | 17. | BABY, PLEASE DON'T GO — GLORIA | Them |
| 9. | 8. | THE BOY FROM NEW YORK CITY | The Ad Libs |
| 10. | 7. | THIS DIAMOND RING | Gary Lewis & Playboys |
| 11. | 18. | I'M TELLING YOU NOW | Freddie & The Dreamers |
| 12. | 14. | FERRY ACROSS THE MERSEY | Gerry & The Pacemakers |
| 13. | 8. | HURT SO BAD | Little Anthony |
| 14. | 10. | RED ROSES FOR A BLUE LADY | Vic Dana |
| 15. | 11. | KING OF THE ROAD | Roger Miller |
| 16. | 22. | NOWHERE TO RUN | Martha & the Vandellas |
| 17. | 21. | WHEN I'M GONE | Brenda Holloway |
| 18. | 41. | GAME OF LOVE | Wayne Fontana & the Mindbenders |
| 19. | 15. | NEW YORK'S A LONELY TOWN | The Trade Winds |
| 20. | 12. | THE BIRDS AND THE BEES | Jewel Akins |
| 21. | 16. | TWINE TIME | Alvin Cash & the Crawlers |
| 22. | 40. | I KNOW A PLACE | Petula Clark |
| 23. | 30. | DON'T LET ME BE MISUNDERSTOOD | The Animals |
| 24. | 25. | GIRL DON'T COME | Sandi Shaw |
| 25. | 20. | TELL HER NO — LEAVE ME | The Zombies |
| 26. | 26. | DO YOU WANNA DANCE PLEASE LET ME WONDER | The Beach Boys |
| 27. | 19. | DOWNTOWN | Petula Clark |
| 28. | 35. | LITTLE THINGS | Bobby Goldsboro |
| 29. | 23. | FOR LOVIN' ME | Peter, Paul & Mary |
| 30. | 42. | I'LL NEVER FIND ANOTHER YOU | The Seekers |

### CLIMBERS

1. HERE THEY COME FROM ALL OVER THE WORLD ........ Jan & Dean
2. NOT TOO LONG AGO ........ Uniques
3. THE RACE IS ON ........ Jack Jones
4. IT'S NOT UNUSUAL ........ Tom Jones
5. LONG LONELY NIGHTS ........ Bobby Vinton
6. SEND ME THE PILLOW YOU DREAM ON ........ Dean Martin
7. I MUST BE SEEING THINGS ........ Gene Pitney
8. CHIM, CHIM, CHEREE ........ New Christy Minstrels
9. IT HURTS ME ........ Bobby Sherman
10. ANGEL ........ Johnny Tillotson

## On The Beat

Petula Clark really "tore up" the Ed Sullivan audience Sunday night. This girl sure swings; she even had the sedate adult audience clapping their hands to the beat of I Know a Place which will probably be another big one for Petula.

**Name By Derek**

We noticed the phrase "Cellarful of Noise" comes up twice on Petula's song. This is the title of Brian Epstein's autobiography, a name chosen for the book by Derek Taylor (who also helped in the writing of the book). The "cellar," of course, is Liverpool's Cavern. And the "noise" was the noise of the Beatles.

Word to the Austrian Beatlebooers: you're showing your ignorance, not to mention your bad manners.

**Great Sound**

Wayne Fontana and the Mindbenders have come up with a great sound in the "Game of Love." It's way up there in the British charts.

We've completely flipped for Mrs. Brown, You've Got A Lovely Daughter by Herman's Hermits. Sorry to report that the record is not available as a single, but is on their fabulous album, Introducing Herman's Hermits. Another potential hit by these boys is Silhouettes, their new single.

Expect more "Mrs. Brown" type songs from Herman. I, for one, can't have too many of them.

Have you heard Allan Sherman's take-off on Downtown? It's done in that inimitable Sherman style and is really hilarious.

**Too Much Exposure?**

It's a pity Sherman is less fashionable than he was a year ago. Perhaps it was a case of too much exposure and too many discs too quickly.

Note to those who think the English are taking over the world: The American artists are as popular in England as the English groups are in America.

Another note: Some of the English groups popular over here are not so popular over there. Namely, the Dave Clark Five, Peter and Gordon, Chad and Jeremy, and the Zombies.

Looks like "Them" has a big two-sider in Baby Please Don't Go and Gloria.

Please Let Me Wonder by the Beach Boys reminds us of their summertime hit Don't Worry Baby.

Did you know that Bobby Goldsboro's recording of Little Things is one of Brian Jones' favorites? We heard Brian say so himself. Also overheard: Besides the blues (Rolling Stones' style), Brian likes jazz and classical music.

That's it for this week. If you have any views, write and let me know.

'Bye for now.
—Louise Criscione

 **BEATLE PHOTOS BY CURT GUNTHER**

---

**MAKE THE**
# LEWIN
**Record Paradise**

6507 Hollywood Blvd.
(at N. Wilcox)
HO 4-8088

**Your Headquarters For All Your Favorite**

## 45's and L.P.s

ALL ENGLISH GROUPS
ALWAYS IN STOCK

*Our Prices Will Please You
Everything Here Real "Neat"*

# KRLA ARCHIVES

## Bahamas Beatle Battle

## FAN CLUB INFORMATION

**THE DAVE CLARK FIVE**
Miss Billie Jo Heltne
2725 Chromite Drive, Apt. A
Santa Clara, California.

**PAUL REVERE & THE RAIDERS**
Miss Kylie Scheibner
7216 S. E. 30th St.
Portland, Oregon.

**JOEY PAIGE INTERNATIONAL FAN CLUB**
c/o Frankie Horvath
171 E. Walnt Street
Costa Mesa, California.

**DAVE HULL FAN CLUB**
c/o Colleen Ludwick
6231 Ivar
Temple City, California
(Dues — $1.00 per year to cover mailing costs)
Includes monthly newsletter

**ROLLING STONES FAN CLUB OF SOUTHERN CALIFORNIA**
c/o Vanda Dixon, President
157 Ardmore
Los Angeles, California
90004

**JERRY NAYLOR INTERNATIONAL FAN CLUB**
c/o John Beecher
4 Hazel Way
Fetchum, Leatherhead, Surrey
England

**GERRY AND THE PACEMAKERS**
c/o Barbara Crouch
2207 Duell
Glendora, California
Dues are $1.00
Includes an 8" x 10" picture
plus fact sheet & newsltter

## King Cole Honored

SINGER NAT KING COLE will be paid tribute on an upcoming nationally televised network spectacular. Still in the planning stage, the show was announced by (Mrs.) Maria Cole, who is heading a drive for funds for a Nat Cole Memorial Cancer Hospital, to be built by public subscription in Los Angeles. An appeal for funds is being made nation-wide. Contributions can be mailed to the NAT KING COLE FOUNDATION, Hollywood, Calif.

## At Deadline

"HULLABALOO," which was to have been cancelled next fall, will be back — but only with a half-hour show. Monday night — instead of Tuesday — 7:30 to 8:00.

CHAD AND JEREMY signed a new record contract. They should make a minimum of $500,000 in the next seven years — plus their television and movie appearances.

GERRY AND THE PACEMAKERS will arrive in America in April to do the Ed Sullivan Show (April 11) and a Shindig tour. In case you didn't know, the movie "Ferry Cross the Mersey" is the real story (as it happened) of their lives.

FREDDIE AND THE DREAMERS will be on the Sullivan show next month, too — April 25. They are now making "TOAD" Awards for people who help them with their careers. (TOAD means Thespian Order of Acerbated Dreamers). Although it is confusing, there are many readers of the BEAT who are entitled to the award — whatever it is. FREDDIE and his group are very popular here.

The SUPREMES, 4 SEASONS and the RIGHTEOUS BROTHERS will *all* be in the new movie "Beach Ball."

The CASCADES are in Hawaii for 6 weeks. They should have a new BIG record out very soon.

BOBBY GOLDSBORO in town for "Shivaree." You can see him on April 3.

Also in town, MARVIN GAYE — for "Shindig." His latest release, "I'll Be Doggone," has been rumored to be a sure hit. Listen for it.

DENNIS WILSON, one of the Wilson Brothers of the Beach Boys, now gazing over the jeweled lights of Southern California from his Hollywood home. Dennis can now be seen driving around the city in the late Sam Cooke's Ferrari, which he recently purchased.

JAN & DEAN, top singing duo for years, have turned to the writing side of life. These two are currently cooking-up a book called "Jan & Dean's Fun and Games Book For Delinquent Litle Old Ladies and Their Sewing Circle Cohorts!" Wonder if the book's as long as the title!

## More Ringo Answers

**FROM PAGE ONE**
married or anything. I just used to take her out a lot, and other people as well, you know. And I got back and about November/December we sort of went out together, just the two of us, all the time. I didn't go with anyone else or anything, and then three weeks before we got married I asked her to marry me. And then two weeks from the day before we got married we started setting the wedding up.

**DAVE: How did she feel about not being with you on this particular trip?**
RINGO: I don't know, really. I don't think she likes it . . . When I phone her she says, you know, "I miss you," and things like that. And I miss her. But you know, we're working every day and there would be nothing for her to do and she's busy with all the family, because none of the family came to the wedding, only her mother and father and mine, and she's sort of going around being congratulated by the aunties and uncles, you know. So she's doing that job while I'm doing mine.

**DAVE: That's good. Yesterday — to get back to the movie for just a moment — yesterday there was . . . not a mishap . . . but the car in which they were shooting you and John and Paul and George, slammed into the tree a little hard. Is that correct?**
RINGO: Yesterday? That was about four days ago — three days ago. None of us were in the car. George was on top of it when it smashed into the tree, and it's all part of the film, so . . .

**DAVE: Oh, it is.**
RINGO: So there was no great danger.

**DAVE: They are shooting some of this in Austria.**
RINGO: Next Wednesday we go back to Britain for two days, and then we fly out to Austria for eight days, and then we finish the film in Britain the next two months.

**DAVE: Listen, it has been awfully nice of you to take this time, Ringo.**
RINGO: It's my pleasure.
**DAVE: Best of luck to Mrs. Starkey.**
RINGO: Thanks very much. I'm still not really used to that name, Mrs. Starkey.

## Winner

Valeri Hernandez—winner of the Beatles scramble contest last week. Valeri, 14, has become the envy of her whole area. Her prize was a big picture of The Beatles, actually autographed personally by the international stars!

# KRLA ARCHIVES

# BEATLE PLANS REVEALED

## More of Hull-Tayor Interview Tells About Beatles' Life

# KRLA BEAT

April 7, 1965     Los Angeles, California     Ten Cents

The recent Beatle interviews by Derek Taylor and Dave Hull — broadcast over KRLA — have attracted widespread interest and enthusiasm.

Because of the close friendship between Dave and Derek and The Beatles, they were able to obtain intimate, personal insights into the lives and personalities of the four lads from Liverpool who have become the most popular entainers in history.

Radio stations across the nation have requested tape recordings of the exclusive interviews. The Beat has also been beseiged by requests to print them in their entirety.

This is the second in a four-part series. The subject this week is George Harrison. The setting is Nassau, the Bahamas, where the Beatles were filming a segment of their second movie — "Eight Arms to Hold You." Derek begins the interview:

**DEREK: With the gentle swish of the Caribbean behind me, this is Derek Taylor sitting thankfully in the sun on the beach of Nassau with George Harrison, who's wearing a straw hat and blue jeans, and looks extremely well. His long, dark hair is curly. He's, of course, one of the two single Beatles and I think the first to buy a house. He bought a house in Surrey which he takes considerable interest in. Anyway, George, let's say first it's nice to see you after about three months away.**

GEORGE: Nice to see you again, Derek.

**DEREK: How do you like it here?**
GEORGE: I like it fine except that we're up at 7:00 in the morning every day on the set filming. It's good really because
—MORE ON PAGE 2

### TOP TEN

1. STOP! IN THE NAME OF LOVE
2. BABY, PLEASE DON'T GO — GLORIA
3. GO NOW!
4. MY GIRL
5. TIRED OF WAITING FOR YOU
6. SHOTGUN
7. CAN'T YOU HEAR MY HEARTBEAT
8. I'M TELLING YOU NOW
9. EIGHT DAYS A WEEK—I DON'T WANT TO SPOIL THE PARTY
10. NOWHERE TO RUN

## Derek Taylor Reports

Freddie & the Dreamers' success in America, though late, comes as no surprise.

What had amazed me was that he hadn't made it earlier over here for he has been a very big act in England for two years or more.

### Beatles Share
The Beatles themselves chose Freddie and his lively friends for their recent three-week Christmas Show in London.

Also — and this is more important, since the Beatles are very careful about sharing their humor — they included Freddie in a number of their skits on stage.

The hit song the States have just discovered — "I'm Telling You Now" — was released in England more than eighteen months ago and was a very big seller. Deservedly so.

Freddie is not as light-hearted off stage as on. He takes his work pretty seriously. Like many other pop stars, he wants to expand and become more than just a teenage idol. Unlike many other pop stars, however, he may well do it because he is an able dancer and a very good comedian. As I say, like a lot of clowns, a little melancholy at times.

"I'm Telling You Now" should pass the million mark over here. I'm very glad.

Freddie lives a couple of miles from my old home in Manchester and I used to see a lot of him and the Dreamers in days gone by. Nice to see them again when they were in Hollywood a month ago.

### Potential
And Chubby Checker has a disc out called "Let's Do the Freddie." Mr. Checker is very fast to see potential in a new craze.

Had a marvelous phone call last week from an American who said his name was Chuck, and he was —MORE ON PAGE 4

## Recording Star Holds Press Fete: Chats With Derek

Marvin Gaye hosted a dinner for Hollywood press, held at the Sunset-Vine Tower. KRLA BEAT columnist Derek Taylor chatted with Marvin, who will be seen soon in virutally every major network musical show on the air, including AMERICAN BAND-

STAND, and SHINDIG. Derek talked about Marvin's albums, and Marvin autographed one just for Derek!

Newest album features selections from top Broadway shows, and will include HELLO, DOLLY; PEOPLE, and many of the other big songs from the most famous productions. Marvin can perform a beautiful ballad as well as he can belt out the most finger-snapping R & R tune!

Now living in Detroit, he wishes he could move to Los Angeles because he likes it better out here, but for the time being he will just have to commute as often as he can.

### His Start
Marvin really "soloed" when he was 3 years old, singing in his father's church. But in 1958, he joined the MOONGLOWS, a popular vocal group, and toured the country. Later a recording executive saw him entertaining at a party, and asked Marvin to record a song. It was STUBBORN KIND OF FELLOW, and went straight to the top. So have all the other big ones for Marvin.

We all wish Marvin even bigger success in the future. (See another photo on Page 3.)

### PEN PALS

MISS IAN ANDERSON
70, Wrotton Road
Welling, Kent
England

JULIE WEBB
740 Seven Oaks Way
Saint Paul's Cray
Kent, England

## The Supremes --- America's Number One Girls!

**TOP RECORDING TRIO — THE SUPREMES,** as they appeared on last week's "Hollywood Palace," on ABC Television. Show was hosted by film star Tony Randall. SUPREMES are rated as the number one female vocal group in the nation since THE ANDREWS SISTERS and THE McGUIRE SISTERS. Their top hit STOP! IN THE NAME OF LOVE has hit the top. (l-r) Florence Ballard, Diana Ross, and Mary Wilson.

# KRLA ARCHIVES

## More Beatle Answers

**FROM PAGE ONE**
if you're off work there's nothing much to do. It gets boring just sitting in the sun, and we'd all prefer to be up and working.
**DEREK:** I asked you because it may seem like a paradise to people who can't get into the sun to think of spending two or three weeks in the Bahamas. But of course you are working very hard all day.
**GEORGE:** Yeah, that's right. Well, we get up at 7:00 and we usually start about 8:00 or 8:30, right through and then have lunch for about a half hour, and then we work right through until the sun goes and there's no more light, which is usually about 5:30.
**DEREK:** The pattern of your life now seems to be with not so much touring. Now that you can record 11 numbers in five days you can have an awful lot of leisure. Do you have too much leisure, do you find?
**GEORGE:** No. We haven't had a great deal, really. This year, maybe, because after the film I'm not too sure what we're doing. I think we may have a week or so and then we go to Europe for about a week.
**DEREK:** Are you touring Europe?
**GEORGE:** I think we're doing six concerts — two in France and two in Italy and two in Spain.
**DEREK:** You've been in France. You haven't been to the other places before?
**GEORGE:** We've been to Spain — Paul, Ringo and I went.
**DEREK:** You didn't play there, though.
**GEORGE:** No.
**DEREK:** When that tour is over you presumably will then have a lot of time before visiting America.
**GEORGE:** That's August. I think in the meantime we'll have a new record out, doing TV and things in England. And then with a bit of luck the film will probably be out around about that time. So then we'll have the film songs out to plug and we'll have a premiere. And then I think it'll be the American trip. Or maybe the premiere will be after the American trip, which is in August.
**DEREK:** So in fact the pace in life seems to be almost as hot as it was. It appears deceptive.
**GEORGE:** We can't tell, really, because we haven't really been told exactly what's happening. We just vaguely know that it's America, and then for all we know we may start on our third film after the American trip, in which case, you know, we'll be ...
**DEREK:** I notice that ... you seem to be doing two films in one year.
**GEORGE:** We're trying to. I hope so because we enjoy it so much more than anything else.
**DEREK:** You prefer films?
**GEORGE:** Yeah, it's great. And when the film's finished you get more satisfaction from it. You feel as though you've done something worthwhile more so than a tour.
**DEREK:** Brian Epstein did say once — I don't want to commit you to anything that you don't want to talk about — but he did say once that it might be you'd go more and more into filming, and into isolated shows. Is this going to be sooner than we expected?
**GEORGE:** I don't know. This depends on when we expected it.
**DEREK:** He means in terms, I think, of next year.
**GEORGE:** We'd like to do more films and naturally a little less touring because ...
**DEREK:** Touring's tiring.
**GEORGE:** Yes, it is. People don't realize that each day you jump

out of bed onto an airplane and fly two thousand miles to do a show ... You know that's not much fun, really.
**DEREK:** The American trip destroyed almost everybody. Everybody was a bit off their heads when it was over.
**GEORGE:** Yeah.
**DEREK:** Now going back to leisure, how do you spend your free time when you're home? Like spend a Sunday off?
**GEORGE:** On Sunday I have a lie-in, I suppose, and then ...
**DEREK:** You're a great sleeper ... a sleep worshipper, really.
**GEORGE:** Yeah, but I do like it if I can. It's just trying to get up. Since I've gotten my house I used to just lie around in the backyard last summer when it was quite hot. But now, as it's sort of freezing cold in England, on a Sunday I just get up and have a late breakfast about 12 o'clock.
**DEREK:** Have you got help in the house?
**GEORGE:** I've got a woman who comes in each day. She cooks dinner for me and keeps the place tidy.
**DEREK:** What's her name?
**GEORGE:** Margaret. Mrs. Walker. I read the Sunday papers and go out for a drive, and sometimes go out for lunch with some people.
**DEREK:** Do you eat more out than you do in?
**GEORGE:** Uh ... I think so because I usually just eat in on the weekends. I usually, on a Sunday, have friends over and just stay in and have dinner and watch TV.
**DEREK:** You've got a pretty good garden. You don't do it yourself, do you?
**GEORGE:** No.
**DEREK:** Do you like gardening?
**GEORGE:** Well, I like a sort of nice garden but it's too much trouble really. But the good thing about my garden is that most of it just lawn. It's just lots of big lawn with trees and things.
**DEREK:** It's a new house though?
**GEORGE:** It's a bungalow, actually, just a big long bungalow.
**DEREK:** Bungalow is what we call a one-level house, I think.
**GEORGE:** Anyway, originally the fellow who built it is the fellow I bought it from was an Australian. He built it like an Australian ranch bungalow. It's about ten years old. Two years ago he had a new part built on the end so it's ten and two years old.
**DEREK:** Do you take an interest in the house in improving it or is it simply a place to live?
**GEORGE:** I like it.
**DEREK:** Are you a house-proud man? Do you talk about your house to other people?
**GEORGE:** Well, to friends and things I suppose. I like the idea of it looking great in the way I like it.
**DEREK:** Are your tastes in interior decorating simple?
**GEORGE:** Really being the first house ever of mine I've just tried to get it so that it pleases me. At first I got some fellow to get some furniture and he bought a lot of rubbish. Since then I decided I didn't really like it. He just bought odd stuff just so I could move in straight away. Since then I've changed it around a lot. Things I'd like to do if ever I buy another house is stay in this one until I get the new one furnished just how I like it and then move. I'm not a great believer in interior design and all that because it ends up you're living in the designer's house and I'd much rather do it myself.
**DEREK:** Yes, I quite agree. You were going to have a pool put in, I think, the last time I saw you. Is that still happening?
**GEORGE:** They started about two weeks before we left England, and actually the morning we left the airport there was a massive great hole dug out and mud all over the place, and one of these big diggers in the backyard. The workmen have got sheds built up. Everytime I go out there I just hear music in the little shed and they're all playing cards and singing. They never seem to do any work. I'm hoping by the time I get back most of the mess will be gone.
**DEREK:** Have you spent a lot of money on the house since you got it?
**GEORGE:** Uh ... not really, no.
**DEREK:** What's it called, by the way, has it a name or a number or what?
**GEORGE:** It has a name but somebody pinched it.
**DEREK:** The fans know where it is, do they?
**GEORGE:** Well, some of them do. Actually there's a girls' school right next to it but the head mistress was good and she told the kids to give me a bit of privacy.
**DEREK:** Pursuing the point of leisure but now forgetting about the house, it has for a long time been quite easy for you in certain places to move around London as a normal human being in your own car. Can you explain how you've been able to do this because I've never never known how you managed it, how you park and how you get from the car to the theatre?
**GEORGE:** The thing is, if we're doing a show then that's the only time there is going to be thousands of people, really. If we're not doing a show and just going out for the night somewhere, there's not liable to be millions of people waiting for you to arrive at the restaurant
**—MORE ON PAGE 3**

# KRLA ARCHIVES

## KRLA TUNEDEX

| THIS WEEK | LAST WEEK | TITLE | ARTIST |
|---|---|---|---|
| 1. | 1. | STOP! IN THE NAME OF LOVE | The Supremes |
| 2. | 8. | GLORIA — BABY, PLEASE DON'T GO | Them |
| 3. | 2. | GO NOW! | The Moody Blues |
| 4. | 3. | BY GIRL | The Temptations |
| 5. | 6. | TIRED OF WAITING FOR YOU | The Kinks |
| 6. | 5. | SHOTGUN | Jr. Walker & All Stars |
| 7. | 7. | CAN'T YOU HEAR MY HEART BEAT | Herman's Hermits |
| 8. | 11. | I'M TELLING YOU NOW | Freddie & The Dreamers |
| 9. | 4. | EIGHT DAYS A WEEK / I DON'T WANT TO SPOIL THE PARTY | The Beatles |
| 10. | 16. | NOWHERE TO RUN | Martha & The Vandellas |
| 11. | 18. | GAME OF LOVE | Wayne Fontana & The Mindbenders |
| 12. | 17. | WHEN I'M GONE | Brenda Holloway |
| 13. | 22. | I KNOW A PLACE | Petula Clark |
| 14. | 9. | THE BOY FROM NEW YORK CITY | The Ad Libs |
| 15. | 12. | FERRY ACROSS THE MERSEY | Gerry & Pacemakers |
| 16. | 15. | KIND OF THE ROAD | Roger Miller |
| 17. | 32. | NOT TOO LONG AGO | The Uniques |
| 18. | 30. | I'LL NEVER FIND ANOTHER YOU | The Seekers |
| 19. | 7. | RED ROSES FOR A BLUE LADY | Vic Dana |
| 20. | 13. | HURT SO BAD | Little Anthony & The Imperials |
| 21. | 10. | THIS DIAMOND RING | Gary Lewis & The Playboys |
| 22. | 24. | GIRL DON'T COME | Sandi Shaw |
| 23. | 23. | DON'T LET ME BE MISUNDERSTOOD | The Animals |
| 24. | 26. | DO YOU WANNA DANCE / PLEASE LET ME WONDER | The Beach Boys |
| 25. | 21. | TWINE TIME | Alvin Cash & The Crawlers |
| 26. | 45. | THE LAST TIME — PLAY WITH FIRE | Rolling Stones |
| 27. | 28. | LITTLE THINGS | Bobby Goldsboro |
| 28. | 34. | IT'S NOT UNUSUAL | Tom Jones |
| 29. | 19. | NEW YORK'S A LONELY TOWN | The Tradewinds |
| 30. | 20. | THE BIRDS AND THE BEES | Jewel Akins |

### CLIMBERS

1. THE CLAPPING SONG ............ Shirley Ellis
2. PEACHES AND CREAM ............ The Ikettes
3. I'LL BE DOGGONE ............ Marvin Gaye
4. SEE YOU AT THE GO-GO ............ Dobie Gray
5. POOR MAN'S SON ............ The Reflections
6. CRAZY DOWNTOWN ............ Allan Sherman
7. CHIM, CHIM, CHEREE ............ New Christy Minstrels
8. I CAN'T EXPLAIN ............ The Who
9. ALL OF MY LIFE ............ Lesley Gore
10. THE RECORD (BABY I LOVE YOU) ............ Ben E. King

## Beatles' Favorite Singer!

**MARVIN GAYE ENTERTAINS** private party. It was just such a party that led to his fabled success as singer both in ballads and rockers. Watch for Marvin's new album, and read about his meeting with DEREK TAYLOR on Page 1.

## Best Man Soon A Groom?

**FROM PAGE TWO**

because they don't know where you're going.

**DEREK:** But you still have the autograph books.

**GEORGE:** Oh, yeah.

**DEREK:** How do you avoid that? Do you go to selected places?

**GEORGE:** Now, you know, through experience, you just do it by . . . if you go to a place and have quite a good time and you're treated all right, then naturally you go back again. And usually the managers of places like you to go there so it's in their own interest, really, to make sure you're having quite a good time. But generally in London it's quite good.

**DEREK:** You're very fond of London, I think?

**GEORGE:** Yeah, I thing it's fabulous.

**DEREK:** Do you go home very often?

**GEORGE:** To Liverpool? I went there about three weeks ago. I was up there for a week . . . my brother got married.

**DEREK:** I saw the picture in the paper.

**GEORGE:** Yes. Really, there are so many people and friends to see in the short time I was there.

**DEREK:** You're like most people you left the place you were born and you've grown very fond of London. It happens in most countries of the world. You probably grow away from places and grow up a bit. Never been any suggestion of your living outside England?

**GEORGE:** No.

**DEREK:** This is a good place to live here, of course.

**GEORGE:** Thing is, with a place like, say this beach, we're sitting on now, I think it's marvelous and I'd love a house . . . but probably after two or three weeks of this I'd get fed up. I wouldn't mind living in a place like this . . . nice beach, nice sea, and sort of hot climate. But it's so boring after two weeks. But still I wouldn't mind a place like this say . . . every time I got fed up with the cold in England you could just fly out here. But still I prefer to live in a place like London anytime.

**DEREK:** Well, there's an awful lot happening in London and in Los Angeles, where your voice will be heard pretty soon — as soon as Dave Hull and I get back there. Los Angeles has a climate similar to this only cooler in winter and always much drier. Well, George, I won't keep you any more because I know you have to get on the set. It's been nice to see you and I'll see you later on today. I'll turn you over to Dave Hull now.

**GEORGE:** Okay, see you, Derek. Bye, Bye.

**DAVE:** How're you, George?

**GEORGE:** Hello, Dave, how're you?

**DAVE:** Good. You look comfortable, you've got on a pair of faded blue Levi's and an old straw hat . . .

**GEORGE:** They're not Levi's.

**DAVE:** Well they're jeans. In America we call them Levi's. That's what we call anything that's blue and faded. You got a straw hat on. Where'd you find that straw hat?

**GEORGE:** Just bought it here.

**DAVE:** I see you stole my dark glasses.

**GEORGE:** They're yours, are they?

**DAVE:** Yeah.

**GEORGE:** No they're not . . . I bought them.

**DAVE:** No you didn't, you just stole them from me. I just set

them on the sand.

**GEORGE:** No you didn't, they're mine.

**DAVE:** No they're not.

**GEORGE:** They're not . . . I've had these on for days.

**DAVE:** Listen . . .

**GEORGE:** Don't believe this man . . . they're mine.

**DAVE:** Listen, this idol out there in the water that we're watching, is going to be a one-shot take, and it comes up and it's got ten arms. What has this got to do with the movie?

**GEORGE:** This is Kali, and . . . it's the sacrificial god or something. It's a bit involved. I'll wait until they finish making the film and then I'll go and see it and then I'll know what's happening.

**DAVE:** How come it has to be a one-shot take?

**GEORGE:** This thing is 20-foot high and it's taken them two hours to submerge it under the water. They can do it again but they'll have to wait another two hours before they can get the thing down on the bottom again. It's a lot of work, so if they can do it in one take it saves a lot of time and trouble.

**DAVE:** How do you feel about this movie compared to "A Hard Day's Night." Is the script different? Is there a lot of spontaneity?

**GEORGE:** The only thing, really, that's the same as "Hard Day's Night" is the fact that we're still playing ourselves. But I mean, this has got a story line to it whereas "Hard Day's Night" didn't, really. It was more or less like a documentary.

**DAVE:** You mean this one's got a plot?

**GEORGE:** Yeah, this one's got a plot.

**DAVE:** Are you ad-libbing a lot of lines? A lot of scenes that were in "A Hard Day's Night" were spontaneous and when you had to go back and cut the scene came out completely different from the way it was before. Is this happening now or not?

**GEORGE:** Yeah, there's lots of things that if we think of on the actual day of shooting — if the director can think of something or we can — that will make it a little bit better, then we'll change it a little bit. But, you know, so far we seem to be sticking to the script.

**DAVE:** I didn't ask John or Paul or anyone about the songs in the movie, but can you give me an idea . . . You have seven new ones, is that correct?

**GEORGE:** Well, we recorded 11 the last week before we left England.

**DAVE:** But you're only using seven, are you?

**GEORGE:** We'll only use about seven in the film, but even if we use only about five in the film, we'll still have about 10 or 12 tracks on the L.P.

**DAVE:** Can you tell me what the titles are . . . I bet you can't, can you?

**GEORGE:** I can't, no.

**DAVE:** Can you give us a hint, then, what they're like?

**GEORGE:** It's so hard, really, because when you record eleven all in one week, you just work on one until you've finished it then completely disregard that and go on to something else. By the time the week's over, you've forgotten, really, what you've done. You know vaguely, but not until we start doing

—MORE ON PAGE 4

## At Deadline

BRIAN JONES of the ROLLING STONES is hosting JOEY PAIGE at his home in England.

The Stones invited Joey to visit them while they were here recently. To quote Joey's letter to the Beat: "I'm living with Brian. He has a groovey place. It's a little house. All the boys are fine and are getting ready to go on tour for two weeks. Saw a few of their shows here in England and they were just great. They did a live album that should be out in America in a month or so. They're the hottest act going here (London) right now."

Joey has been mobbed in London since his arrival there. He will no doubt be a top artist in England by the time he returns to the U.S.

The BEAU BRUMMELS were in town recently to appear at the Cinnamon Cinders. While there, photographers and writers from Look Magazine saw their show, photographed and interviewed them. The June 1 issue of Look will have the full story. Their new record is really great. It is taken from their first album, "Introducing the Beau Brummels," which will be available very soon and includes 10 original songs.

The BEATLES will play their August 15 concert in New York to nearly 60,000 fans. ED SULLIVAN will introduce them and the event will be filmed for release throughout the world within days. Of course we expect to see them in person in Los Angeles soon after.

ROGER MILLER who is nearing the million record mark with *King of the Road* is in Europe to appear on several TV shows and make personal appearances in England and France.

FREDDIE AND THE DREAMERS will join Dick Clark's "Caravan of Stars," a tour which begins on April 30. Also, they will appear on Ed Sullivan's show on April 25.

PETER AND GORDON were in the U.S. during the last week of March to tape for "Hullabaloo." They begin a six day visit to Japan on April 19.

Also scheduled for a tour of Japan by way of California are THE ANIMALS. They will arrive in the U.S. on May 19 and be in California a few days after.

The DAVE CLARK FIVE's film will be released this summer. To assure all the fans which film is theirs, the title selected was "The Dave Clark Five Runs Wild."

WAYNE FONTANA and the MINDBENDERS will appear on "Hullabaloo" on April 20. Their first American release, "Game of Love" keeps on a steady climb toward the top of the charts.

DEL SHANNON is drawing capacity crowds in England. He will return to the U.S. in mid-April.

BOBBY SHERMAN who is a regular on "Shindig" is on a cross-country tour. Bobby is a very handsome and talented artist and should gain a lot of fans by making personal appearances.

BEATLE JOHN LENNON ordered *contact sunglasses*, while filming on sunny snowslopes in Alpine segs of *Eight Arms To Hold You*.

## FAN CLUB INFORMATION

**BOBBY SHERMAN**
c/o Barbara Schare
P.O. Box 3187
Hollywood, California
(Dues — $1.25. Members receive a fact sheet, 8"x10" picture and a monthly call from Bobby)

**BEATLES**
Judy Doctor, Vice President
401 S. Barrington Avenue,
Apt. 116
West Los Angeles 90049
(Dues — $2.00. Members receive quarterly newsletter, picture and exclusive Beatle book)

**ROLLING STONES**
c/o Debbie Kelley
11360 Harvard Drive
Norwalk, California

**BEATLE BOBBIES, INC.**
11122 S. Corley Drive
Whittier, California 90604
(Members must be over 13)

**BOB EUBANKS**
c/o Janet Wolfe
7839 Beckett St.
Sunland, Calif. 91040

### READER'S NOTE
So that you could read every word of the GEORGE HARRISON interview as it was recorded, Louise Criscione's column ON THE BEAT has taken a vacation for one week, because of space limitations.

## More Derek Taylor

### FROM PAGE ONE

with one of the Animals, the drummer John Steele.

They were, he said, stranded without money at Los Angeles International Airport. He added, "Eric Easton (Rolling Stones' manager) and Brian Epstein flew off in a private plane taking all our money and passports with them to the Bahamas."

"Oh," said I. "That means you want money."

He muttered, "Yes," and put 'John Steele' on the line.

"Hello, John," I said.

In what he believed to be a North British accent he grunted, "Hello there."

And I said, "Where are you from, John?"

He replied, "From Liverpool."

I asked him what part of Liverpool and he said, "Near where John Lennon lives."

I said, "Now listen, the Animals, as you should have known, come from Newcastle-on-Tyne, which is a very tough seaport 170 miles from Liverpool, another very tough seaport. And no Newcastle man would ever say he came from Liverpool, or vice versa."

I advised him to go off, rehearse his accent, check his facts, and then try the trick somewhere else.

Nice to see the success of "Red Roses For a Blue Lady." There are three versions in the national top 20 — proof that a good song can always stand revival by any number of artists. It was a great hit fifteen years ago when melody was in fashion, long before the days of rock 'n roll and big beat.

The Righteous Bros. had a successful tour with the Beau Brummels. More than that, it has been a happy, friendly tour. The Bros., after their experience on the Beatle tour, take great pains to make all the other artists on the bill feel happy and comfortable.

You may remember that the Righteous Bros. left the Beatle tour in the east because Beatlemaniacs refused to give them a chance. The Beatles themselves were fine to the California twosome, but the fans weren't. Now that the Righteous Bros. are at the top, they always go on stage at the opening of the show and appeal for a fair hearing for the other artists.

Watch for "Cast Your Fate to the Wind." This is a beautiful instrumental with a dominant piano. It leapt up the British charts without warning, with little promotion, and is in direct contrast to the pounding beat of most chart-toppers.

The pianist, by the way, is Johnny Pearson, musical arranger for Cilla Black. The record will be a big hit.

That's all for now. Keep smiling.

## More Beatle Answers

### FROM PAGE THREE

the songs do we remember them one at a time. It's a mixture.

DAVE: I want to ask you a question about your mother and father, if I may for a moment. They had planned on coming to America and to Hollywood. Do you know if your mother and father have continued with their plans?

GEORGE: I don't know... don't think so. I think they'd like to go for a holiday. They've mentioned to me that they may go. I don't think they've made any sort of definite plans.

DAVE: You probably haven't seen them for some time anyway.

GEORGE: I saw them three weeks ago when I went to Liverpool for my brother's wedding.

DAVE: Oh, that's right. Your brother Peter, is it not?

GEORGE: That's right.

DAVE: You were best man?

GEORGE: That's right.

DAVE: When did that all take place?

GEORGE: It was January.

DAVE: Well, you've been a best man now. What about your plans? Do you have any plans for the future as far as Pattie Boyd or anything like that, can you say?

GEORGE: Well, you know, I wouldn't make sort of long arrangements long before hand. At the moment I have nothing in mind at all.

DAVE: Have you talked to Pattie recently?

GEORGE: Not since I was in England.

DAVE: You haven't called her then?

GEORGE: No, not yet.

DAVE: We'll be seeing you tonight. I see you've got your feet buried in the sand. It'll cool you off a bit.

GEORGE: Okay, see you then, Dave.

DAVE: Thank you very much.

## Beatles Booty Bag

WATERPROOF—WASHABLE—STRONG

### TOTES-ALL
—YEAR ROUND—

*"Stylishly Carries"*

- SHOPPING
- OVERNIGHTING
- PICNICKING
- BEACHING
- BALL GAMING
- BOATING
- TRAVELING
- CAMPING
- BOWLING
- SPORTING

Foods and Drinks • Toiletries • Swim Suits • Towels • P.J.'s • Records • Blankets • Books • Gym Clothes • Cameras • Radios • Tennis Shoes • Tennis Balls • Raincoats • Art Supplies

CARRIES THREE WAYS

DETACH AND SEND

TO: BEATLES, BOX C, CULVER CITY, CALIFORNIA
PLEASE RUSH... Beatles Booty Bag at $1.00 ea., incl. tax OR 4 Beatles Booty Bags for only $3.00, incl. tax.
ENCLOSED FIND $_____
NAME_____ ADDRESS_____
CITY_____ STATE_____

# KRLA BEAT

April 14, 1965          Los Angeles, California          Ten Cents

## BEATLE RUMORS ENDED!

(Editor's Note: This is the third in a series of Beatle interviews by Dave Hull and Derek Taylor, who talked to John, Paul, George and Ringo at length while they were in the Bahamas filming scenes for their second movie. The recorded interviews were originally broadcast over KRLA.

In this interview Derek and Dave are talking with John Lennon while sitting on the beach at Nassau.)

**DEREK:** John Lennon, in dark glasses, white trousers, blue Plimsolls, black socks, lilac shirt, and multi-colored jacket. Lovely to see you again, John, after about 3 months.
**JOHN:** Good to see you, Derek, in your grey shirt, blue tie, grey trousers and the tweedy thing.
**DEREK:** How many songs have you written for the film, John?
**JOHN:** Altogether we've written fourteen but only seven will be in the film, Derek.

**DEREK:** Could I have a few titles?
**JOHN:** Uh, no.
**DEREK:** Why?
**JOHN:** Because they don't like giving titles out until they're published. People might write songs with the same title and confuse the market.
**DEREK:** How many songs were there in "Hard Day's Night," how many originals?
**JOHN:** I can't remember. They were all originals.
**DEREK:** What I meant by originals was, how many were created especially for the film?
**JOHN:** Oh. I don't know how many of them were. Say eight out of ten, if it was ten. But all of these are for the film in this one.
**DEREK:** Are you taking the same pains to introduce the songs naturally as part of the plot?
**JOHN:** I think it's very easy in this film. A lot of them are going to be behind-the-scene,

like the running in the field in "Hard Day's Night."
**DEREK:** Sort of background music?
**JOHN:** Yeah, and a lot of them are going to be just potty. We've done a lot of mad stuff.
**DEREK:** The script, which I had a look at this morning, looks rather eccentric. The end of the operation, I presume, is to get a different sort of film from "Hard Day's Night."
**JOHN:** Yeah, and we've done it, haven't we?
**DEREK:** Well, from the look at the set you have — sitting on the beach in holes in the sand and people in khaki uniforms, red sashes and red turbans . . . some of them carrying guns and some of them carrying shovels. Over by the water's edge Leo McKern, the British actor, is standing looking like a Polynesian high priest. The whole
—MORE ON PAGE 2

## Derek Taylor Reports

The record charts are the most fascinating feature of the pop music scene — and the strangest aspects in the whole intricate fabric of this industry.

Also — because immediate and conspicuous success depends entirely on the fate of an artist's records — no one in the business can ignore them.

But which chart do you follow? I never did know just what to accept in England. The New Musical Express — with a circulation of 250,000, Britain's biggest-selling pop newspaper — frequently showed an artist at

### KRLA 1110
### TOP TEN

1. GLORIA —
         BABY, PLEASE DON'T GO
2. STOP! IN THE NAME OF LOVE
3. TIRED OF WAITING FOR YOU
4. WHEN I'M GONE
5. GO NOW!
6. GAME OF LOVE
7. SHOTGUN
8. NOWHERE TO RUN
9. I'M TELLING YOU NOW
10. EIGHT DAYS A WEEK—I DON'T WANT TO SPOIL THE PARTY

TUNEDEX ON PAGE 4

No. 1 when the Melody Maker, the second biggest weekly pop journal, didn't even show the group in the top 30.

Yet both newspapers are utterly reliable and honest. In Britain, these are the most important charts. Some national daily newspapers in London follow the New Musical Express, others the Melody Maker. But Brian Epstein and I and other people closely concerned with the charts waited until both charts showed our artists at No. 1 before we relaxed and congratulated ourselves.

Over here, show-business people — and fans — rely on trade papers like Billboard, Cash Box, Record World, and so on. But this week, for instance, Cash Box shows Herman's Hermits at the top with "Can't You Hear My Heart Beat." While Record World and Billboard still have the Supremes in the No. 1 position.

Well . . . take your pick.

Some interesting things are happening with albums. Gerry and the Pacemakers' long player has jumped nine places in Record World — from 20 to 11. Cash Box shows it with a one-place move from 14 to 13.

Herman's Hermits—now fighting Freddie and the Dreamers for top British group in the U.S. — have their album at No. 19 in Cash Box — from 30. This success is largely due to the freak popularity of the catchy "Mrs. Brown . . ."

It was a pity Cilla Black couldn't make it to Los Angeles. She flew directly from Australia to London because of the death of the father of her road manager, Bobby Willis.

This also meant that her manager, Brian Epstein, cancelled his trip to Hollywood. He had planned to guide Cilla's five-day holiday-and-promotion stay here. Now, both go direct to New York for the Ed Sullivan Show.

(Incidentally, that flight from Sydney to London is some trip, you pass through nineteen hours of night. If, for instance, you board a plane in Sydney on Tuesday afternoon, you do not arrive in London until Thursday morning.)

It was marvelous to meet Sounds Incorporated again. I joined them for a wild reunion at the Red Velvet Club on Sunset Boulevard the night they came in and introduced them to the Beau Brummels. As both groups are intensely musical, very intelligent and humorous, the meeting was very happy and profitable.

There is an awful lot of excitement about the new Beatles' single. A Beatle release has become the major event of the recording world. I have never known anything like the tense feeling of expectation in the days preceding release date. Every deejay in the world is clamoring to get his hands on the disc first.

The title, as Dave Hull told you on KRLA and as you should all now know, is "Ticket to Ride." With the other side, "Yes It Is," it will be featured in their second movie, "Eight Arms to Hold You."

By the way, note that neither title contains a personal pronoun. This is unusual for a Beatle song. That's it for this week.

### Radio Star Takes To TV For Exciting New Show

CASEY KASEM, top rated KRLA dee-jay, as he appears on the new television show starring the personable and informative man of music. The show, "SHEBANG," is seen daily on Channel 5, KTLA. Viewers actually participate in show with contests, and performers appearing recently include some of top stars in show biz. Casey combines live talent with special film clips of outstanding performances. Popular show is produced by Bill Lee and Hall Galli and film is syndicated nationally by television star Dick Clark.

# KRLA ARCHIVES

# Another New Book From Beatle

**FROM PAGE ONE**
scene is pretty wild. John hasn't been doing too much this morning. I presume you got up later than Ringo?
JOHN: Ringo got up about 7:00. I got up at about 9:00, which is late for a film. It's early for me.
DEREK: How do you come to terms with getting up so early when normally you are late risers and late to bed?
JOHN: Well, we just go to bed about 12:00 every night. We go out at 6:00 and pretend it's 11:00 at night, and come in at 12:00, you see.
DEREK:: Are you finding it fairly easy to move around in the Bahamas?
JOHN: Oh yeah, it's not bad at all. Just the usual tourists. Aside from that it's not bad.
DEREK: Did you have a big send-off at London Airport?
JOHN: Yes. It was very big because it was a half day for the schools. There were about eight or ten thousand there. It was like the crowd we had when we got back from America. It was very good.
DEREK: That's probably the biggest send-off . . . Well you have had huge crowds going in. Normally you don't get a big crowd to see you out.
JOHN: No, that's right. That's probably the biggest send-off we've had.
DEREK: The Beatlemania level in England, if you'll forgive the phrase, I know you don't like the phrase, is still pretty high. It's very high in America, too.
JOHN: Good.
DEREK: When are you due back in America?
JOHN: I think it's about the autumn or fall, as they call it, I think.
DEREK: There are a few other things I would like to talk to you about, John. Like killing a few rumors. Is it still true that you have only one child?
JOHN: I have the only one child and none on the way.
DEREK: There are an awful lot of rumors about your having been in Hollywood recently, with Cyn, and that wasn't true either?
JOHN: No, I haven't been in America since we were last there.
DEREK: When you leave here where will you be going?
JOHN: To England for two days and then to Austria for a week, and then back to England for the rest of the film.
DEREK: Thank you very much, John. I'l turn you over to Dave now.

DAVE: How are you, John?
JOHN: Fine, Dave, how are you?
DAVE: How's Cynthia?
JOHN: She's great.
DAVE: Good, good. How do you like the weather down here? I understand you're not too happy with it.
JOHN: It's too humid for me. It's not bad . . . it's better than rain, I suppose.
DAVE: The weather's quite different back in England right now. Rather grey, isn't it?
JOHN: I think they're having a bit of snow here and there.
DAVE: What about the movie. How do you feel about it compared to "Hard Day's Night." Is it somewhat the same for you? Are you having less work to do?
JOHN: So far we've had less to do but it's only in the first week. But you know, it's okay.
DAVE: What about your part in "Hard Day's Night." You know a lot of it was spontan-

eous. The part in the bathtub, you recall you talked to me last time . . . are you doing the same here or are you sticking to the script?
JOHN: We're sticking to the script until there's an opportunity of, you know, going away from it. We've done a bit that has nothing to do with the script . . . filmed little bits that the director thought might come in handy for something or other. Whenever a situation arises we do it.
DAVE: Are you thinking of a great deal of things yourself, John?
JOHN: Well, we've hardly done anything on it. It's mainly been people chasing Ringo. So far we haven't done much at all.
DAVE: What about your new book? "A Spaniard in the Works" is the title. It's being published by whom?
JOHN: Simon & Schuster, I presume.
DAVE: They're the ones who published your other one. Is it almost the same as your other one?
JOHN: Well, it's pretty similar, yeah. Better, I think, because it's developed a bit bigger. The drawings are better and it's longer . . . there's more of it.
DAVE: Well that's good. I know it will make your fans happy.

Your other one was a very successful book. Is this one done on short stories again?
JOHN: Yeah, but the stories . . . but there are none that are really short, they're all about four or five pages long.
DAVE: Are these new stories, or are they ones you did a long time ago?
JOHN: They're brand new.
DAVE: The titile is "A Spaniard in the Works." Now, you've made a play off the word spanner.
JOHN: Spanner is a wrench in America. When you "put a spanner in the works" you louse everything up. In America you say "put a wrench in the works."
DAVE: Yes, toss a wrench in the works. How do you use the play off words for the title of the book?
JOHN: It's the title of one of the stories about a Spaniard who gets a job in Scotland, that's all. I thought everybody knew the expression. I didn't know they had a different expression in America.
DAVE: Well, we do. Usually we say "don't throw a monkey wrench in the works," or don't throw a monkey wrench in the machine." But now we understand. You use "a spanner" and "a Spaniard" to play off words. It's very clever.
JOHN: Thank you.
DAVE: What about the sales? The book is published?
JOHN: No, it's not published yet. Won't come out for another month, I don't think. It's finished and everything's done. They're just putting it together in the publishers.
DAVE: Did Paul get a chance to write the front . . .?
JOHN: There's no introduction on this one. They're thinking of putting the same introduction again exactly. They thought it didn't need one this time or they didn't want one. There were enough pages as it was.

DAVE: What about the people here? Have you had many problems getting around the Bahamas?
JOHN: No, it's not bad at all. There are not many people here.
DAVE: What about your night life. Are you enjoying any night life here?
JOHN: We've been to a couple of places. The club's aren't sort of wild. We wouldn't bother normally with them but they're the only places to go so we have to go to them.
DAVE: You and Paul and George are more or less protectors during the movie. You're trying to keep him from being chased by these different people?
JOHN: He comes in possession of this ring and whoever wears it has to be sacrificed by this big mod that Derek described before, and we're trying to save him and get this ring off his finger. They're other people trying to get it off for various reasons. It's very complicated. Basically what it is is to stop him getting sacrificed.
DAVE: John, there's been a controversy in the States concerning one tune out of your recent "Beatles for Sales" album. The tune was also on the "Beatles '65" album released in the States. Most magazines say that it's Paul doing the tune "Rock 'n Roll Music" and I've continued to say it's you. Will you please straighten this out for us once and for all?
JOHN: It's definitely me. There's only one voice on it and it's me. On the British album, you see, they explain who sings what exactly, and who sings the harmony. They seem to miss it off in the American one, which is silly. It saves all the messing. I heard one on the radio last night who said George was singing and it was me and Paul. There were about eight voices on it and it's all me and Paul. It's mad. They should print it on the album like they do in England and there wouldn't be any messing.
DAVE: On these trips that take you away from your family . . . don't you miss Cynthia and Julian a great deal?
JOHN: Yeah, I miss them like mad. I was going to bring them out here but they'd just be hanging around all the time because that's all there is.
DAVE: You've kept your son out of the press. Has that been your own doing or is it that the press is not really interested in your son?
JOHN: I don't know. They want pictures, I suppose, but I'm . . . you know . . . he's going to have enough problem as it is being my son without getting pictures in when he's a kid. I don't like family pictures anyway.
DAVE: When you go away for any length of time and return, do you find he's de-

—MORE ON PAGE 4

# KRLA ARCHIVES

# On The Beat

Did you know that the Searchers and their former lead singer, Tony Jackson, have split? Tony has his own group, the Vibrations. An unusual position for Tony: he is lead vocalist on the Searchers' version of "Love Potion No. 9" and also on his own version!

Did you know American-born P. J. Proby, born James Marcus Smith, formerly known as Jet Powers, split his pants in several appearances in his adopted England? He seems to be quite popular over there which is all right with THE BEAT because P. J.'s brand of "entertainment" we can do without.

THE BEAT hopes you realize how lucky we are to have KRLA twenty-four hours a day. Liverpool listens to Radio Caroline (a pirate ship) from 6 a.m. to 7 p.m. and then switches to Radio Luxembourg from 7 p.m. to 3 a.m. And if anyone's up from 3 a.m. to 6 a.m. — tough luck!

That handsome English fella, Adam Faith, was in our town recently. He has a new record scheduled for release by the time you read this. It's a real swinger entitled, "Talk About Love." Reminds THE BEAT of Adam's old one, "It's All Right."

THE BEAT wonders why the Blossoms are featured so little on "Shindig"? These girls are great and should be given more opportunity to solo on the show. You listening, Mr. Good?

Be informed that a new folk singer is on the English scene. His name's Donovan; he's Scotch; and he has printed on his guitar, "This Machine Kills." Donovan appeared three times in a row on "Ready Steady Go" and made a lot of friends and enemies in the process. His enemies' reasoning: mere copy of Bob Dylan — complete with hat, harmonica, and guitar.

A three-toot salute to our own Dave Hullabalooer because he got us an EXCLUSIVE in "Cara Bella" and "Soldiers of Love." Did you know they have never even HEARD them in Liverpool? They were recorded in pre-Epstein days. In far off 1961.

### Two-Month Stay

Herman's Hermits and the Rolling Stones will hit L.A. about the same time. The Hermits will land on U.S. soil on April 18 for a TWO-month stay. They will be touring with the Dick Clark Caravan of Stars which will play Melodyland on May 17. Did you know this marks the first time an English group has ever got out with the Caravan?

The Stones will roll into town to do a one-nighter at Long Beach on May 16. Note to you Stonelovers: Your boys will be featured in a seventeen minute short subject film to be out around Easter vacation! It's a United Artists release, and will be similar to "The Beatles Come To Town" which was shown in the theaters last year.

### Playboys New Disc

Gary Lewis and his Playboys have come up with a fabulous follow-up to "This Diamond Ring." This new one, "Count Me In," is VERY VERY reminiscent of the Bobby Vee sound. From our observation post, it looks like a sure winner for Gary and the Playboys.

Another Beatle note: They have received EIGHT Grammy Award nominations! These awards are the recording industry's answer to the motion picture Academy Awards, so you should be proud of your boys. The winners will be announced on April 18, and again the Beat wishes the Beatles good luck.

### Bound To Go

A record really breaking in England right now is "Concrete and Clay" by the Unit Four Plus Two. We think this record is going to GO Stateside. It's a little different sound, a little hard to dance to, but it's good, it's catchy, and it ought to sell.

Did you know the British Immigration Service may tighten it's entry requirements for American acts wishing to perform in England? This is, of course, in retaliation for the slap-in-the-face the British groups got from the U.S. government by our refusal to issue work permits to the English entertainers.

### May Be Cheated

We don't know what is behind all this, but we think it is certainly unfair that BOTH American and English teens may be cheated out of seeing their favorite groups. The Beatles and Rolling Stones are safe, it's the lesser-known performers who are having all the trouble.

The Righteous Brothers have done it again with "Just Once In My Life."

We liked the "old" Jan & Dean better. You remember them: They wore suits, white shirts and ties (or at least, matching sweaters). Now they look like a couple of rejects from the very first Surf Fair.

I'll say BYE for this week.
— Louise Criscione

## Sport?

THE KRLApes begin another losing streak as they fall to the Aviation High School student council, at Redondo Beach. Score was Aviation 26, the KRLApes 24. Game played, by the way, on donkeys. No puns, please.

DICK MORELAND said he had no trouble with basketball, but got no co-operation from the animal!

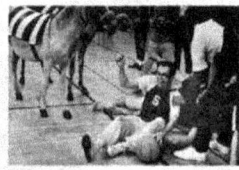

GAIL GOODRICH OF UCLA is nationally famous basketball star, who is not shown in this picture because he would naturally have nothing to do with this rag-tag outfit! Dick Biondi tried for kick to get ball and fell flat on his attempt.

ANOTHER VIEW of KRLApes, head for basketball history as they lose the game. After one accidental win, confidence of team was shaken, but on March 29 a game ON DONKEYS straightened them out. They lost to San Gabriel High Faculty.

## New Guy

The host for night people is Bill Slater. Bill in 1963 worked in Houston at the very same time as two other KRLA personalities, newsmen Cecil Tuck and Thom Beck — and now 2 years later they meet at KRLA.

Bill lives in Covina with his wife and 2 children, along with "Pebbles," a one-year-old pup. Bill, working at a Buffalo, New York television station, left the studio one night and was confronted by a "dirty-faced crying boy, who told me the landlady made him get rid of the dog, and wanted me to take care of him." (He did.) Bill's hobbies: flying and photography.

SHEBANG is produced by Dick Clark Productions, headed by AMERICAN BANDSTAND star Dick Clark, shown on left above. Dick talks over particular problem with Casey Kasem, who emcees the show, seen daily on KTLA. Soon the two agree, and the cameras roll on another show, bringing recorded and live entertainment to your living room. Casey is famous for his intimate insights and anecdotes of the lives of popular performers.

## FAN CLUB INFORMATION

**HERMAN'S HERMITS, USA**
c/o Sue Chelius, President
341 Palos Verdes Drive, W.
Palos Verdes Estates
California 90275

**HERMAN'S HERMITS**
679 Thayer Avenue
Los Angeles, Calif. 90024
(Send a self-addressed, stamped envelope)

**KINKDOM KOME (The Kinks)**
765 Holmby Avenue
Los Angeles, Calif. 90024

**JAN AND DEAN**
c/o Barbara Magee
18335 Malden St., Apt. 10
Northridge, California

**GERRY & THE PACEMAKERS**
c/o Diane Marienthal
7307 W. 91st Street
Los Angeles, Calif. 90045
(This is a chapter of the National Gerry and the Pacemakers Fan Club)

**BOBBY PICKETT**
c/o Shery Dodd, President
6615 Franklin Ave., Apt. 118
Hollywood 28, California

**BEATLES**
c/o Rhonda Fernandez
207 S. Benton Way
Los Angeles, Calif. 90057

**ROLLING STONES**
c/o Cheryl Keitel
2139 W. 160 Street
Gardena, California

**DEREK TAYLOR**
c/o Shelly Heber
6087½ Alcott Street
Los Angeles 35, California

**THE DENNISONS**
c/o Judy Hibbs
631 Beatty Street
Trenton, New Jersey

**THE DEL-RAYZ**
c/o Linda Semon
371 Ashwood Avenue
Ventura, California

## Beatles' Ski Talent "Eager ad Lazy" Instructor Reports

OBERTAUERN, AUSTRIA — Filming another segment of their second movie, "8 Arms to Hold You," the Beatles have been the center of attention on the ski slopes.

How do they rate as skiers? Observers say John Lennon isn't bad. He's had private lessons and spends most of his time on the slopes.

But George has apparently been having a difficult time. Ski instructors are required to catch or tackle him at the bottom of the hill to keep him from coming to grief.

Franz Lang, who has been teaching skiing fundamentals to the Beatles, put it this way: "Some of them are very eager, but others are rather lazy."

He did not name names.

---

**25 - 30% DISCOUNT ON ALL RECORDS**

Complete Stock Of All The Latest Hits, Both In 45 RPM and ALBUMS

### GOIN'S Record Shop

12908 Venice Blvd.
Los Angeles    Ph. 397-7842

# KRLA ARCHIVES

## Top Group Soon In Movies

**CLIMBING THE CHARTS**, is POOR MAN'S SON, by The Reflections, pictured here. Left to right are Tony McCale, lead singer; Danny Bennie; Johnny Dean; and Phil Castrodale. Group is working on Columbia Pictures' WINTER a-GO-GO, cutting songs for the sound track. Quartet also has appeared on the Casey Kasem TV show.

## KRLA TUNEDEX

| THIS WEEK | LAST WEEK | TITLE | ARTIST |
|---|---|---|---|
| 1. | 2. | GLORIA — BABY, PLEASE DON'T GO | Them |
| 2. | 1. | STOP! IN THE NAME OF LOVE | The Supremes |
| 3. | 5. | TIRED OF WAITING FOR YOU | The Kinks |
| 4. | 12. | WHEN I'M GONE | Brenda Holloway |
| 5. | 3. | GO NOW! | The Moody Blues |
| 6. | 11. | GAME OF LOVE | Wayne Fontana & The Mindbenders |
| 7. | 6. | SHOTGUN | Jr. Walker & All Stars |
| 8. | 10. | NOWHERE TO RUN | Martha & The Vandellas |
| 9. | 8. | I'M TELLING YOU | Freddie & The Dreamers |
| 10. | 9. | EIGHT DAYS A WEEK / I DON'T WANT TO SPOIL THE PARTY | The Beatles |
| 11. | 13. | I KNOW A PLACE | Petula Clark |
| 12. | 4. | MY GIRL | The Temptations |
| 13. | 17. | NOT TOO LONG AGO | The Uniques |
| 14. | 7. | CAN'T YOU HEAR MY HEART BEAT | Herman's Hermits |
| 15. | 18. | I'LL NEVER FIND ANOTHER YOU | The Seekers |
| 16. | 21. | IT'S NOT UNUSUAL | Tom Jones |
| 17. | 26. | THE LAST TIME - PLAY WITH FIRE | Rolling Stones |
| 18. | 22. | GIRL DON'T COME | Sandi Shaw |
| 19. | 15. | FERRY CROSS THE MERSEY | Gerry & Pacemakers |
| 20. | 24. | DO YOU WANNA DANCE / PLEASE LET ME WONDER | The Beach Boys |
| 21. | 20. | HURT SO BAD | Little Anthony & The Imperials |
| 22. | 16. | KING OF THE ROAD | Roger Miller |
| 23. | 42. | SILHOUETTES | Herman's Hermits |
| 24. | 23. | DON'T LET ME BE MISUNDERSTOOD | The Animals |
| 25. | 25. | TWINE TIME | Alvin Cash & The Crawlers |
| 26. | 31. | THE CLAPPING SONG | Shirley Ellis |
| 27. | 32. | PEACHES N' CREAM | The Ikettes |
| 28. | 47. | JUST ONCE IN MY LIFE | Righteous Brothers |
| 29. | 19. | RED ROSES FOR A BLUE LADY | Vic Dana |
| 30. | 27. | LITTLE THINGS | Bobby Goldsboro |

### CLIMBERS

| | | | |
|---|---|---|---|
| 1. | 41. | OOH, BABY, BABY | The Miracles |
| 2. | 33. | I'LL BE DOGGONE | Marvin Gaye |
| 3. | 46. | COUNT ON ME | Gary Lewis & The Playboys |
| 4. | 35. | POOR MAN'S SON | The Reflections |
| 5. | 38. | I CAN'T EXPLAIN | The Who |
| 6. | 43. | GOT TO GET YOU OFF MY MIND | Solomon Burke |
| 7. | 34. | SEE YOU AT THE GO-GO | Dobie Gray |
| 8. | 34. | ALL OF MY LIFE | Lesley Gore |
| 9. | 37. | CHIM, CHIM, CHEREE | New Christy Minstrels |

## More Beatle Answers

**FROM PAGE TWO**
veloped new traits that you weren't aware of before?

**JOHN:** Oh, yeah, they change all the time at that age. He's only two. Mainly new words he's learned. Quite good fun to see what he's learned.

**DAVE:** You made a statement that I understand was more a put-on than anything else. I thought at the time it was a John Lennon put-on, but most of the American press are not aware of your talent of kidding and that was when at the marriage of Ringo and Maureen when you and your wife drove up in your Rolls-Royce, and you said that George had driven over on his bicycle. You were putting on the world, weren't you?

**JOHN:** Yeah. Did that get around? I didn't know it.

**DAVE:** Yes, it made press all across the nation. Everybody was saying "which was the Beatle who arrived on a bicycle?". But he really didn't, did he?

**JOHN:** No, it was just a joke. He came with me in the Rolls. We just said it to a friend of ours, Maureen Cleve, on the phone and we thought she'd know. But it was so early in the morning that she probably didn't think. She just wrote it down. I forgot to apologize to her, but it's got around the world.

**DAVE:** Well it was a surprise to everyone, Ringo's marriage. I know it wasn't a surprise to the Beatles because I knew for some time he's been very much in love with her. How long was it before they really got married did they plan on it ... actually the marriage date?

**JOHN:** I haven't a clue. I knew there was something in the air but I went on holiday so I was way out of touch ... nobody was in touch. And I just got back and they suddenly said the date is in two days' time. I said, right. It was quite a shock to us, too, because we knew he was going to get married but not exactly when.

**DAVE:** Your last holiday was spent where?

**JOHN:** St. Moritz, Switzerland, skiing.

**DAVE:** The fact of the matter is, I saw a picture of you sitting down in the snow ... you had fallen while skiing. Did you take your wife? And Julian?

**JOHN:** I didn't take Julian because he's too young to learn to ski. They learn about four. I'll take him about four. I took my wife. It was great.

**DAVE:** Was it a publicity set-up or did you really fall down?

**JOHN:** Well I fell down a few times but that actual photograph I couldn't fall over. When they waited for the fall, I kept doing it right, so the skiing instructor told me I had to go downhill and fall over as well. So I did fall over. I did fall over a lot. Obviously everybody does.

**DAVE:** Are you really a good skier? An average skier? How do you rate yourself?

**JOHN:** Well, both my wife and I did well because we had a private instructor, you see. The people who were in big classes were doing the same stuff at the end of two or three weeks. And we were going down from the tops, so I suppose we were above average. It takes a long time if you're in a big class of forty. They can't teach you properly.

**DAVE:** Well, I don't want to bug you anymore. I know you'd like to relax for a second. Thank you so much, John.

**JOHN:** Good to see you again, Dave.

**CASEY KASEM WONDERS** whatever happened to vaudeville ... and who knows? — he may bring it back himself. "The Caser" is seen on SHEBANG. Hear him daily on KRLA.

# KRLA ARCHIVES

**FROM LONDON,** the singing group SOUNDS INCORPORATED meet for an evening of relaxation with the fabulous San Francisco group, the BEAU BRUMMELS. The two pretty girls are fans who joined the meeting of Anglo-American friendships recently at a Hollywood nitery. KRLA BEAT columnist Derek Taylor described the meeting of the two groups as humorous, happy, and profitable. The Beau Brummels met quite by accident with the English group and introduced themselves while at the club.

# KRLA BEAT

April 21, 1965 — Los Angeles, California — Ten Cents

## Derek Taylor Reports

So Ringo Starr is going to be a father. This was confirmed in the British press — who know everything almost as soon as it happens — a couple of days ago. I am sure everyone in the world who cares about the Beatles will be happy for Ringo and Maureen

### New Group

More exciting news from England — though an a different level. A wonderful new group called Unit Four Plus Two have crashed on the scene with something approaching the impact of the early Liverpool bombshells.

They have a song called "Concrete and Clay" which is a huge hit in England and will most certainly claw its way up the charts here.

This was a much needed injection of new vitality in England where fans were growing a little tired of old faces.

### Jostling

A friend of mine in London — Don Short, show-business reporter of the Daily Mirror — phoned me today to say that the Yardbirds and Cliff Richward were also jostling for the top of the charts.

The Yardbirds are a very strong London group and play with the Beatles on their Christmas Show. I don't think they have made too much noise over here yet. Nor has Cliff Richard, the most consistent British solo star and — with Adam Faith — the only pop star to make the transition from the 1950s to the 1960s successfully. He earns something like $6,000 a week and was only unseated as top British rave when the Beatles finally made it in 1963.

### Herman's Love

Sad news for Herman fans. The London Daily Express quotes girl singer Twinkle saying, "You can say Herman and I are in love."

Twinkle has the fashionable long blonde hair, tiny face, and round, round eyes of the Mod Londoner, and made an overnight name for herself with a song called "Terry," which was about a boy who was killed on his motorcycle. A morbid, unattractive song which gained the distinction of being banned from several television shows.

However, one of my London friends says the Twinkle/Herman romance may be brief. Both are very young.

Cilla Black finally made it to Los Angeles. She flew in from New York after the Ed Sullivan Show with her road manager, Bobby Willis, and Brian Epstein's personal assistant, Wendy Hanson.

Cilla was, I thought, pretty good on the Sullivan show though she and Willis were unhappy that she was announced suddenly and without warning before the dancers were ready and before the scenery was properly in place.

### Why Here?

They were in Hollywood for "Shindig." Wendy Hanson, who had worked for the late President Kennedy and several senior American executives, became Epstein's assistant late last year. She is tall, handsome, blonde, very charming and efficient.

Paul Revere and the Raiders are due back in town any day now to promote their new record "Sometimes." The flip side is a new arrangement of "Oopoopado." The disc is expected to sell well — deservedly because the group is very experienced and take their music seriously.

### New Task

I became a manager this week — for the first time. I signed a great young singer called Thomas James Turner, 21, with the most beautiful voice. He was Dallas born but has lived in California for most of his life.

He attended high school here
—MORE ON PAGE 3

### TOP TEN

1. GLORIA — BABY, PLEASE DON'T GO
2. WHEN I'M GONE
3. GAME OF LOVE
4. STOP! IN THE NAME OF LOVE
5. TIRED OF WAITING FOR YOU
6. GO NOW!
7. I'M TELLING YOU NOW
8. NOT TOO LONG AGO
9. NOWHERE TO RUN
10. I KNOW A PLACE

—TUNEDEX ON PAGE 4

# LET'S TALK WITH PAUL

(Editor's Note: This is the fourth in a series of Beatle interviews by Dave Hull and Derek Taylor, who talked to John, Paul, George and Ringo at length while they were in the Bahamas filming scenes for their second movie. The recorded interviews were originally broadcast over KRLA.

In this interview Derek and Dave are talking with Paul McCartney while sitting on the beach at Nassau.)

**DEREK:** Paul McCartney just came down on the sands. He probably looks the smartest of the three this morning. He's got on grey trousers, light blue jacket, blue checked shirt, deep tan film makeup, and I think his feet are bare. Good morning, anyway, Paul.

**PAUL:** 'Morning, Derek.

**DEREK:** How have you been?

**PAUL:** Well, you know, Derek, what it's like . . . fine, dandy, everything's going great. You knew I'd say that, didn't you?

**DEREK:** Well, you see, I just sort of let you walk through the opening, because I don't need to tell you what to say, and never did. Or did I.

**PAUL:** No. Of course you didn't, no.

**DEREK:** How many people are in this film who were in the last film besides you, Paul, besides the Beatles?

**PAUL:** Victor Spinetti was in the last one — he was the TV producer — and this time he's one of the baddies. Dick Lester and Walter Shenson, really, I think that's all. The actors are all different except for Victor Spinetti.

**DEREK:** I don't know whether the plot has ever been published so I don't want to go into tremendous detail because it would spoil things, but could you just give me a brief run-down what it's all about?

**PAUL:** Yeah, it roughly people trying to get hold of Ringo's ring for some reason or other, so that he can be sacrificed or something. It's very funny. And they keep trying to get ahold of him and get the ring and we keep trying to rescue him, etc., etc., and it goes on. It fills ninety minutes worth of screen time.

**DEREK:** There are a lot of new songs. I think in "Hard Day's

Night" there were six or seven brand new ones. How many in this one?

**PAUL:** There'll be about the same — six or seven new ones. In actual fact I don't think we'll stick in old ones like we did in "Hard Day's Night." I think it's better if we got completely new songs.

**DEREK:** You mean you wouldn't use any old ones as background music?

**PAUL:** I don't think so. We might as well . . . We've recorded eleven new songs.

**DEREK:** Those are actually already on tape are they?

**PAUL:** Yes, and they could all be done for the film. What Dick Lester is going to do is pick the best seven—the seven he likes best—or that fit best in the film. And if we do need any background music we'll put the others in.

**DEREK:** George Martin, presumably, is cooperating completely on the score and the background and that sort of thing, is he?

**PAUL:** Nobody's got round to the score yet because we've only just done the numbers and he'd have to write the score around the numbers. Anyway we've only just started filming so there's no particular panic for that.

**DEREK:** No. I think when I last saw you when I left you in December, there were no songs at all. Is that right?

**PAUL:** Right.

**DEREK:** You must have worked pretty hard since then.

**PAUL:** No, not really. We just sort of did a couple a week. I know I wrote a couple on holiday and John wrote a couple on holiday too. And we did a lot together. So when we go back we have quite a bit ready. We have about fourteen songs in all to record. We've done about eleven of them. There are still one or two that we haven't done actually. Might do those when we get back to England.

**DEREK:** It's widely known now that a lot of the songs which bear both your names were, in fact, written by one or the other on your own, and then arranged jointly later. Of the songs in the film, are several of them single records or have you written them alone or are they joint endeavors this time?

**PAUL:** Well, there are a couple of single efforts and couple of joint. What we normally do,
—MORE ON PAGE 2

# KRLA ARCHIVES

# More Beatle Answers

**FROM PAGE ONE**

though, even if I go away and write a song . . . normally the reason I write it on my own or John writes it on his own is 'cause it's daft to sit around waiting for the other one to come up and finish the song. If you happen to be off on your own you might as well finish it off yourself, cause we don't have words and music, as you well know. So what normally does happen is that if I get stuck on the middle of a song, I'll give in, knowing that when I see John he'll finish it off for me. And it'll be a fifty-fifty thing. That's what happens with a lot of them. That's what happened even with a lot of the single efforts. I just sort of forget about the middle eight until I see John, and then say "I need a middle eight for this one," and he says, "Right, okay." And it works.

**DEREK:** I think "I Saw Her Standing There" was written almost entirely by you, but John put in one word which sort of made it right.

**PAUL:** Yeah, that's it. What happened was, he took out one word which would have made it very wrong. The first two lines . . . I did it going home in a car one night, so I wasn't really thinking too much about it. The first two lines, originally, were "she was just seventeen and she'd never been a beauty queen," which just sounded like it rhymed to me.

**DEREK:** How'd you happen to write a line like this?

**PAUL:** You try writing a song going along in a car and, I don't know, you sort of think of things like that. Anyway, when I saw it the next day and played it through to John, I realized it was a useless line. So we sat down and tried to think of another line which rhymed with "seventeen" and meant something. We eventually got "you know what I mean," which means nothing . . . completely nothing at all.

**DEREK:** On the other hand it's not an embarrassing line like 'beauty queen' would have been.

**PAUL:** No, but on the other hand it could have been a deep and sort of involved line — "you know what I mean," you know, seventeen-year-old girls . . . you know . . . great . . . you know what I mean. You see. It's just a Liverpool expression, as it were, Derek.

**DEREK:** That's what I thought, a Liverpool expression. A lot of your songs could actually be conversation pieces in Liverpool — "She Loves You," "I

## PEN PALS

Clare Davies and Janice Alford
4 Updale Close
Potters Bar
Middlesex, England

Saw Her Yesterday," and that sort of thing.

**PAUL:** Yeah. Actually, there was some fellow in England who was thinking of doing that, speaking our songs just to use them. Called John Junkin. Do you know him? He was in our last film, played "Shake," the road manager.

**DEREK:** Yes.

**PAUL:** He wanted to do a record of something like "She Loves You . . . Yeah . . . Yeh?" etc.

**DEREK:** Probably work, I think.

**PAUL:** It might do, yeah.

**DEREK:** But it seems to me it might be the only thing left to do now . . . an exploitation of Beatle material. I would like to say that during the time I was with the Beatles I never ever saw any professional jealousy. Paul came along with a song that became the "A" side, and John had one which he thought might have been the "A." There was never any sort of nonsense or back-biting or

jealousy. Paul, for instance, came up with "She's A Woman" and thought it was an "A" and other people did, and then John came up with "I Feel Fine" so Paul's "She's A Woman" went on the back. Did you mind?

**PAUL:** I didn't mind at all. In fact, I wouldn't have liked it to have been an "A." As it happened afterwards, it was quite well received. A lot of people just thought I was singing too high. They thought I'd picked the wrong key.

**DEREK:** Probably less commercial anyway.

**PAUL:** Yes, might have been, I don't know. You get those people who come up and say, "Why did you sing it that high, you should have done it in a lower key," because it sounded like I was screeching it. But, ladies and gentlemen, that was on purpose, honest. It wasn't a mistake, honest.

**DEREK:** Maureen Cleve, who is a London journalist, had a very good line in a piece on this disc when she wrote, "How can a dirty great voice like that come out of such a face?" I think it's often surprising that with a face like yours . . . sort of angelic face . . . the face of a delinquent choir boy, someone once said . . . that you have actually got many voices. One of them you might call a "colored voice." That was your "colored voice" in "She's A Woman," wasn't it?

**PAUL:** No, it was my green voice.

**DEREK:** What would you call your anti-lovely voice?

**PAUL:** I don't know . . . soppy, I suppose.

**DEREK:** Away from song-writing since you're now actors . . .

**PAUL:** Me James Cagney one, isn't it?

**DEREK:** Yeah, he's playing a James Cagney face, which isn't recording too well on tape. Could you give us a James Cagney line?

**PAUL:** No, I'm afraid not.

**DEREK:** Would you do us a quick imitation of any of your friends?

**PAUL:** Any of my friends? I couldn't, really, I'm not very good on these imitations.

**DEREK:** You don't like being prompted to do it.

**PAUL:** You're right.

**DEREK:** I see Bob Freeman over there.

**PAUL:** He's done the cover for our latest album in England. I don't think it was in America, was it?

**DEREK:** No, it wasn't, but the disc is on sale in America.

**PAUL:** But they changed the cover.

**DEREK:** They did. But the English disc has another name, "Beatles For Sale," and has a bonus of two numbers over and above the American album.

**PAUL:** That's it, you see, better value. Buy Britain, folks, buy Britain!

**DEREK:** When you come back to America, you know you're going to Hollywood again . . .

**PAUL:** Yes, see you there.

**DEREK:** Well, I'll see you there if not before. Thank you very much, indeed, Paul, and it's nice to see you again.

**PAUL:** Okay, Derek, see you.

**DAVE:** Hi, Paul.

**PAUL:** Hi, Dave.

**DAVE:** The last time you were in Hollywood you appeared to be a little put out with me because of the addresses I gave out.

**PAUL:** I was, yes.

**DAVE:** Are you still put out with me?

**PAUL:** Well for that, yes.

**DAVE:** You still think I'm a rotten guy, do you?

**PAUL:** No, I just didn't like the idea of your giving everybody's addresses out just because if you're trying to keep quiet ever — not that I particularly am — but if I was trying to keep quiet and you were giving the addresses out it would be a big drag, you know.

**DAVE:** Really the addresses I gave were your folks' addresses, as you know, and not your hotel.

**PAUL:** That doesn't matter at all, I don't mind. It's just that I know a lot of people who have sort of been cursing you because it's caused them a lot of inconvenience. It's okay, and it's good news for you to give our addresses out, I agree. I would probably do the same thing if I were in the same position. But if you were in my position and other people's position, you'd probably think the same of me giving out addresses as I thought then. Actually it doesn't worry me too much. I don't hate you or anything because of it. In fact, we're quite good friends.

**DAVE:** What about your getting around the islands here. Have you been other places besides Nassau? Have you been jumping around the island?

**PAUL:** Well, we've been out here on Paradise Island and to Nassau and a little bit around the island on location with the film. We've been out to nightclubs in the town. It's pretty quiet here, you know. Nobody seems to bother you. There doesn't seem to be an awful lot of people actually on the island. It's a quiet place. So we're having it pretty easy.

**DAVE:** The people who do bother you, are they mostly Europeans or Americans?

**PAUL:** Mostly Americans, really. I think mainly because the main lot of the tourists here are American. The natives here don't bother much. They just sort of go out and . . . "Ho-ho, the Beatles." And they have big grins on their faces. That's good enough for them. But the people ask you for autographs I think mainly are Americans or Americans living here or American tourists.

**DAVE:** Do you have many problems getting around when you're on vacation?

**PAUL:** It depends on where you go. Last time I went to Tunisia and had no problems at all. It's so quiet here, really.

As I was telling Derek before about the phones. They're so cut off in Tunisia it's ridiculous. I mean a man from a newspaper came around when we were in Tunisia and spoke to me and everything, and it didn't get back to England. It was ridiculous.

**DAVE:** You mean nothing of the material got out?

**PAUL:** No, because all the lines were so bad. I couldn't speak to anyone in England. It was a fluke if you managed to get a good line to England.

**DAVE:** Isn't it a pleasure, though, if you're on vacation? You get away . . .

**PAUL:** Yeah, right, it was this time. I enjoyed it. Went away for two weeks, lazed around, went to the little soukhs, which are little market places the Tunisian's have. In fact, this very pair of sandals was bought for one dinar. It's about fifteen shillings in English — I think about two dollars.

**DAVE:** When you go on vacation do you turn into a tourist like most tourists do?

**PAUL:** Yes, mainly. Like Tunisia I did. Sometimes you don't. You go to somewhere where it's not so quiet, then you don't really get a chance to go out and turn into a tourist. I was completely tourist with a movie camera and snapshots.

**DAVE:** When you are returning to Hollywood — of course the itinerary hasn't been planned yet, meticulously — but I understand you're going to do a couple of shows in Hollywood, then you're going to San Francisco, then you're returning to Hollywood for a couple of days' vacation. Is that true?

**PAUL:** I think that's true. I'm not really sure about the itinerary myself yet, but that sounds like it.

**DAVE:** Were you interested in seeing Hollywood? Remember last time you didn't get a chance to see much. You were locked in the house and really didn't . . .

**PAUL:** Well that was good

—MORE ON PAGE 3

# KRLA ARCHIVES

## Hullabalooer Accepts Award For KRLA

**PROUDLY DISPLAYING A BEATLE AWARD,** which was given to Radio Station KRLA is Dave Hull. The award is, "in recogniton of outstanding promotion, programming, and merchandising of the BEATLES during BEATLE YEAR 1." This week's BEAT has all of the Dave Hull and Derek Taylor interview with BEATLE PAUL McCARTNEY. Read the full interview transcript beginning on Page 1.

### FROM PAGE TWO

enough really. We saw Bel-Air and we stayed in a nice house in Bel-Air and we enjoyed ourselves. That was good enough. That was really all I wanted. Like when I went to New York we saw skyscrapers. That's about all we wanted to see in New York. In Hollywood we wanted to be in Bel-Air for a bit.

**DAVE:** When you returned, Derek told me you were impressed with the performance in Hollywood and also that you were impressed with one other place, and that was the Red Rock Stadium in Denver. Is that correct?

**PAUL:** Yes, actually we were impressed with a lot more places than that. But we enjoyed Red Rock. It was funny playing there because it's the mile-high city and the air is different a mile high. It's much harder to breathe. We felt sort of drunk or something on stage. We were sort of falling about.

**DAVE:** Because of the oxygen, I suppose?

**PAUL:** Somebody said it was that. Sounds feasible. Might not be true. Might be we were just imagining it. Very hard to sing. I couldn't get any breath. None of us could get any breath.

**DAVE:** When you return to Hollywood, a great many stars, as you know, listen to KRLA . . . any particular stars you're looking forward to seeing this time. You really didn't get a chance last time . . .

**PAUL:** We met Burt Lancaster last time and he's a great fellow . . . marvelous bloke, and his kids great.

**DAVE:** What about some of the others . . . of course during the lawn party in Beverly Hills you met a lot of them. But are you looking forward particularly to being with some particular star, this time around?

**PAUL:** Well, I'll tell you . . . I'm just like anybody else. When I meet any stars . . . I haven't changed that much that it doesn't impress me. I always say "Great," you know, seeing them in the movies or "I saw him on television." But I'm always impressed. So it doesn't matter, really, who I meet.

**DAVE:** We're on the air at this time, broadcasting to Hollywood. Is there anything particularly you can think of to say to the fans — the millions of fans in Hollywood and Los Angeles and Southern California?

**PAUL:** All I can say is — it sounds corny—but just thanks for being nice last time and wanting to come and see us. Because it still knocks me out if people want to come and see us. It's great. I don't think anyone can get that blase that they don't care who comes to see them. So I just like to say thanks to everybody and everybody who looked after us while we were there, and to people like Burt Lancaster who invited us over to his house. We had a great evening. In fact, to everybody in Hollywood who came to see us or who met us at one time or another. Even the people who didn't meet us who bought our records. Great.

**DAVE:** I want to thank you, too, Paul, for taking a moment out to talk with us.

**PAUL:** Okay, Dave.

## More Derek Taylor

### FROM PAGE ONE

and majored in music. Recently he has been singing with the Coasters. Nothing in the world can stop him from being a tremendous success and both he and I are full of optimism.

Watch out for the Byrds. They

were retained for a third week at Ciro's on Sunset Strip and I hear that the "Shindig" people have become very excited about their first record, "Tambourine Man." This song was written by Bob Dylan who attended the Byrd's recording session and gave their version his personal approval.

By the time you read this the Beatles, no doubt, will be No. 1 all over the world with "Ticket to Ride."

Georgie Fame's new one, "In the Meantime," is not moving as swiftly as "Yeh Yeh." I, personally, don't like it as much though his voice is as interesting as ever. His sound isn't pretty but it's very compelling.

They tell me the Righteous Brothers' latest, "Just Once In My Life," is also struggling a little in Britain. This isn't serious, however, because "You've Lost That Loving Feeling" took some time to catch on.

Jerry Naylor, former member of the Crickets, has a new disc upcoming. Tower Records — his new label — are keeping the title a pretty tight secret but I

suspect it's a revival of a good oldie.

Well, as people write when thye can't think of anything else to say in a letter, I must close now.

See you next week.

## Fan Club Information

**FREDDIE & THE DREAMERS**
c/o Carol Moody
2145 Las Lunas
Pasadena, California
Phone: 795-7802

**HERMAN'S HERMITS**
c/o Diane Gourley, President
505 Via Alcance
Palos Verdes Estates, Calif.

**BEATLES**
c/o Mary Ann Geffrey, Pres.
1122 W. Desford Street
Torrance, California 90502

**ROLLING STONES**
c/o Debbie Kelley
11360 Harvard Drive
Norwalk, California

**THE MERSEYBEATS**
c/o Janice Sutliff
5336 N. Noel Drive
Temple City, California.

**PETER AND GORDON**
c/o Pam Lord
2120 Santa Lucia Avenue
Oxnard, California 93032

**CHALLENGERS**
Southern Calif. Fan Club
c/o Barbara Kidman
200 E. 20th Street
Costa Mesa, California

**BEAU BRUMMELS**
San Bernardino Chapter
c/o Nan Wright, President
2052 Mallory Street
San Bernardino, Calif. 92405

## Girls -- You Have A Fan

**SKYROCKETED TO THE TOP** by such records as WILLOW WEEP FOR ME, and IF I LOVED YOU, Chad and Jeremy strike a serious pose for BEAT photog. Chad first worked as a record store clerk before becoming a recording star. Chad goes canoeing with his wife, Jill, for relaxation. Jeremy says he likes girls, clothes, girls, girls and movies — if there are girls in it! Look for CHAD and JEREMY soon in other roles besides singers.

# KRLA ARCHIVES

## On The Beat

Ed Sullivan is really the groove. In about a month's span, he will have had Petula Clark, Bobby Vinton, Little Anthony and the Imperials, Cilla Black and Freddie and the Dreamers on his Sunday night show. This summer he will present the Beatles not only at Shea Stadium to an expected audience of 60,000, but also to the entire nation on his TV show in September. Our hat's off to you Mr. Sullivan because after all YOU are one of the people who started this whole thing.

QUICK ONES: A British music paper, Melody Maker, thinks the Beatles should be feted at Buckingham Palace . . . Sandie Shaw claims her gimmick of wearing no shoes is not a gimmick at all — she just likes to sing bare-footed . . . When the Beatles' contract with EMI Records expires in about 18 months, rumor has it the boys will form an independent company . . . The Righteous Bros. are due in London April 19 to promote their new record, "Just Once In My Life."

SAW: Gordon Waller wearing four rings. What does this mean, Gordon? Looks suspiciously like a steal from that other guy!

Puzzle of the week: What English group, who recently acquired a new lead singer, seems to be getting a bit swell-headed? Turned down three seperate offers to tour America. Stated reason: The money wasn't good enough for them. Great way to make fans, boys!

Note to Joe Agnello, director of "Hollywood A Go Go": We'd like to see more of the performers and a lot less of the dancers. You have so many trick camera shots that we NEVER do get a clear picture of the guest artists!

### Great Sound

Lesley Gore has come up with a great sound in "All of My Life." She says she "Loves California" and is trying to talk her parents into moving out here. Lesley's plans for this summer are not definite yet, but she is considering doing either a summer replacement for a TV show, a movie, or a cross-country tour.

Remember Soupy Sales? Well, he's back on the scene with a new record called "The Mouse." Soupy is now New York based, where he has completely captured the skyscraper crowd. We're glad for Soupy, but we wish he was hurling his pies back in L.A.

### Teens Here

The Nashville Teens have made it back to the U.S. for about a three week visit. As you probably know, the boys' last American tour was cancelled because of work permit trouble. The Teens were pretty upset about it, and we don't blame them because it was a LOUSY deal. But it is all straightened out now (we hope!). Anyway, a BIG welcome to the Nashville Teens, and we hope this time your visit will NOT be cut short.

### Magic?

England's puzzle of the week: Where, oh where, are those pirate radio stations getting their records? They are NOT recognized by the British government, and the recording companies SAY they do not deal with them either officially or unofficially. Yet, the pirates manage to get ALL the records they want, and they aren't telling on their sources. So, for the time being, the mystery of the pirate stations remains a mystery.

Appears too many recording companies are vying for the services of Chad & Jeremy. The boys recently filed legal action in New York to void their contract with Ember Records. In the middle of the problem is Columbia Records, who were apparently under the impression that THEY had Chad & Jeremy entirely to themselves. Must be terrible to be so popular!

Well, that's all for this week— Bye now.

—Louise Criscione

### Beatles in Nassau

ANXIOUS MOMENT IN NASSAU as two BEATLES watch Ringo flounder in surf during filming sequence with stone idol. Photo snapped by SANDY FRAZER of Palos Verdes Estates — whose exciting vacation with the BEATLES will be seen next week!

## KRLA TUNEDEX

| THIS WEEK | LAST WEEK | TITLE | ARTIST |
|---|---|---|---|
| 1. | 1. | GLORIA — BABY PLEASE DONT GO | Them |
| 2. | 4. | WHEN I'M GONE | Brenda Holloway |
| 3. | 6. | GAME OF LOVE | Wayne Fontana & The Mindbenders |
| 4. | 2. | STOP! IN THE NAME OF LOVE | The Supremes |
| 5. | 3. | TIRED OF WAITING FOR YOU | The Kinks |
| 6. | 5. | GO NOW! | The Moody Blues |
| 7. | 9. | I'M TELLING YOU NOW | Freddie & The Dreamers |
| 8. | 13. | NOT TOO LONG AGO | The Uniques |
| 9. | 8. | NOWHERE TO RUN | Martha & The Vandellas |
| 10. | 11. | I KNOW A PLACE | Petula Clark |
| 11. | 17. | THE LAST TIME — PLAY WITH FIRE | The Rolling Stones |
| 12. | 28. | JUST ONCE IN MY LIFE | Righteous Brothers |
| 13. | 23. | SILHOUETTES | Herman's Hermits |
| 14. | 15. | I'LL NEVER FIND ANOTHER YOU | The Seekers |
| 15. | 7. | SHOTGUN | Jr. Walker & All Stars |
| 16. | 16. | IT'S NOT UNUSUAL | Tom Jones |
| 17. | 12. | MY GIRL | The Temptations |
| 18. | 10. | EIGHT DAYS A WEEK — I DON'T WANT TO SPOIL THE PARTY | The Beatles |
| 19. | 27. | PEACHES 'N' CREAM | The Ikettes |
| 20. | 26. | THE CLAPPING SONG | Shirley Ellis |
| 21. | 18. | GIRL DON'T COME | Sandie Shaw |
| 22. | 50. | MRS. BROWN, YOU'VE GOT A LOVELY DAUGHTER | Herman's Hermits |
| 23. | 14. | CAN'T YOU HEAR MY HEART BEAT | Herman's Hermits |
| 24. | 32. | I'LL BE DOGGONE | Marvin Gaye |
| 25. | 31. | OOO BABY BABY | The Miracles |
| 26. | 19. | FERRY CROSS THE MERSEY | Gerry & Pacemakers |
| 27. | 20. | DO YOU WANNA DANCE — PLEASE LET ME WONDER | The Beach Boys |
| 28. | 46. | JUST A LITTLE | The Beau Brummels |
| 29. | 41. | COME BACK BABY | Roddie Joy |
| 30. | 35. | POOR MAN'S SON | The Reflections |

### CLIMBERS

| | | | |
|---|---|---|---|
| 1. | 38. | SEE YOU AT THE GO-GO | Dobie Gray |
| 2. | 37. | GOT TO GET YOU OFF MY MIND | Solomon Burke |
| 3. | 34. | COUNT ON ME | Gary Lewis & Playboys |
| 4. | 42. | JUST YOU | Sonny and Cher |
| 5. | 33. | CRAZY DOWNTOWN | Allan Sherman |
| 6. | 43. | IT'S GROWING | The Temptations |
| 7. | 47. | CAST YOUR FATE TO THE WIND | Sounds Orchestral |
| 8. | 44. | SHE'S COMING HOME | The Zombies |
| 9. | 45. | BUMBLE BEE | The Searchers |
| 10. | 40. | TICKET TO RIDE — YES IT IS | The Beatles |

## At Deadline

Ringo had agreed to appear with the other Beatles in an edition of BBC-TV's new "This Is Your Life" series but the idea had to be scraped when one person refused to appear — his mother.

Petula Clark has been recording in France recently — for release in that country — where she makes her home.

The Hollies, another top British group will arrive in the U.S. around April 15. Following a 10-day engagement in New York (at the Paramount) they will film "Hullabaloo" and "Shindig."

In addition to all of the other stars already scheduled for the "Ed Sullivan Show" this summer a film of Dusty Springfield is being considered for the June 13 show. The film was made of Dusty in London last August.

The Seekers will tour their native Australia beginning May 25. Their record "I'll Never Find Another You" has won them a Gold Disk, a "Hollywood Palace" appearance and a guest spot on the "Jack Paar Show." In case you haven't read, there are 3 guys and a gal in the group.

Roger Miller will appear at the Santa Monica Auditorium on May 28 and in Pasadena the following night.

Jackie and Gayle will make their acting debut in a new movie, "Beach House Party."

Gerry Marsden is "made up" (Mersey language for very happy) about his upcoming American trip. The thing he wants most while he is here is to live in a house with a swimming pool — and no telephone. His new single is "I'll Be There" — a song he used to close his act even before he hit the big time.

# KRLA BEAT

**BACK ISSUES AVAILABLE** *(See Page 2)*

April 28, 1965 — Los Angeles, California — Ten Cents

**NASSAU BEATLE PHOTO** *(See Page 3)*

## CHIMP EXCITES TEEN FAIR!

**HULLABALOOER A DISBELIEVER** — In an amazing conclusion to the excitement of the 1965 Teen-Age Fair in Hollywood, Dick Biondi's chimpanzee "GOLDFINGER," actually typed the letters K-R-L-A!

Murmurs rippled throughout the tense crowds pushed around the special booths as Goldfinger poised thoughtfully for a moment, raised to look around . . . and moved toward the keyboard.

A hush fell over the audience. Will he do it? Yes — HE DID!

Most surprised of all was KRLA dee-jay DAVE HULL, pictured at left, who daily had kept insisting that the chimp would never type the right letters. Hull was almost right. Goldfinger frequently appeared to be ready for the great moment, only to casually rip out the typewriter ribbon, or tear up the paper. Chimp is resting comfortably after fantastic feat before thousands that gathered at the Teen-Age Fair.

### Crowds Flock to Exposition

**BIONDI FANS WATCH GOLDFINGER** as he performs his amazing feat. KRLA BEAT photographer nearly captured DICK BIONDI (in sweater) on film, but fingerprint smudge blurs face. Biondi has never been photographed. For the reason, see inside.

### Derek Taylor Reports

Shout it from the canyons and from the orange groves. From the beaches and the boulevards. Herman's Hermits are taking over! They now have three of their recent American releases in the national top 20. No British group before or since the Beatles has achieved placings like this. Not the Rolling Stones, not Peter and Gordon, not Gerry and the Pacemakers. Nobody.

And because their management in England — and the Dick Clark office here — are very much on the ball, Herman has been sent over here at precisely the right time. He's here in the U.S. right now, as you know.

Apart from the Beatles, I have never known anything like Hermanmania. Ninety per cent of the queries I am receiving either by phone or by mail, are for Herman.

**Not Overtaken**

The other ten per cent are largely for the Beatles. But, of course, this does not mean that the Beatles have been overtaken by Herman or Freddie, or anybody else.

The Beatles are the Beatles, and so far as I can see, no one will ever match their peak of popularity, their appeal, their talent, or their fame.

**Above Competition**

So we shouldn't include the Beatles in any comparison we may make between one set of pop stars and another. They are really above competition now — part of the folklore and legend of show business. And, in my opinion, the best group in the world.

**Little Boy Charm**

What is Herman's appeal? So far as young fans are concerned, probably his appearance. He has the little-boy charm of the 17-year-old who looks younger. He has that "mother-me" look which made Ringo Starr so popular over here. Also, he has an unusual voice. His sound is not musical but it has a lot of rhythm. And

—MORE ON PAGE 2

### KRLA 1110 TOP TEN

1. GLORIA / BABY PLEASE DON'T GO
2. GAME OF LOVE
3. WHEN I'M GONE
4. TIRED OF WAITING FOR YOU
5. THE LAST TIME / PLAY WITH FIRE
6. JUST ONCE IN MY LIFE
7. MRS. BROWN YOU'VE GOT A LOVELY DAUGHTER / I GOTTA DREAM ON
8. SILHOUETTES
9. STOP! IN THE NAME OF LOVE
10. IT'S NOT UNUSUAL

—TUNEDEX ON PAGE 3

### DISNEYLAND DOINGS

Under a beautiful California sky, thousands saw the annual Easter Parade — complete with Mickey Mouse, Donald Duck, Goofy, and the great cast of Disney characters.

Headed by the Disneyland Marching Band, the paraders were all dressed in styles of the 1900's for an old fashioned Easter Parade.

The Magic Kingdom was open special hours during the Easter week, and the park has many new features planned for this summer, including mermaids in the submarine lagoon. Officials have announced that this year's budget for dance groups and teen entertainment has been raised to an all-time high of $330,000.00.

## More Derek Taylor
### FROM PAGE ONE

whoever chooses his songs has a keen ear for the ingredients of a hit.

His record sales over here are obviously going to be in the millions before high summer. And, Freddie and the Dreamers apart, I can see no challenger from England. The Rolling Stones run everyone pretty close but I would think that the age level of their fans is rather higher than that of Herman's fans. And everyone knows that the biggest record buyers are the younger teenagers.

#### Busy Managers

Herman's management — Kennedy Street Enterprises from Manchester — must be tremendously pleased with themselves. For they also manage Freddie and the Dreamers, and Wayne Fontana and the Mindbenders. Wayne has an excellent group and was one of the first non-Liverpool groups to get on the move nationally in Britain. But he never quite achieved the fame of Gerry and the Pacemakers, Billy J. Kramer, the Searchers, or his two Manchester companion groups.

You really have to come from either Liverpool or Manchester to appreciate the rivalry between the two cities. Though they are only about 40 miles apart, the way of life is entirely different. Liverpool is the city of comedians, song and, very often, poverty. Manchester is the solid, stolid city of manufacturers, businessmen and prosperity.

#### Upsurge Reasons

One of the reasons for the upsurge of groups in Liverpool was there were so many teenagers without work, or hope of work. Locally, more American groups are attracting notice. The Byrds have been bringing large crowds into Ciro's nightclub on the Strip in Hollywood — which is a new experience for Ciro's. Down at the Red Velvet the Guilloteens came into their own this week — as a paid booking. Previously they had been working there for nothing — presumably because they enjoy performing.

Talking of groups of the future, the Beatles' "Ticket to Ride" coupled with "Yes It Is" has not come in the charts as high as one would expect.

I should have thought that advance orders would have guaranteed entry somewhere in the top 50. Particularly as KRLA had the disc several days before the official release date on April 7th.

#### "Weirdest Sound"

Paul is quoted as describing the sound of "Yes It Is" as, "The weirdest sound we have ever got on records — it's perhaps our most unusual disc yet." I think he's right, and I personally prefer it to the official "A" side. I hear a whisper that it may not — after all — be included in the movie.

Two groups with the same name have emerged in these parts. One is the Missing Links; the other is the Missing Links. Both claim to be the original Missing Links. But since neither has the money to fight a million-dollar court action, a compromise has been reached and one group has added the prefix "American."

#### Confusing?

The American Missing Links operate from the Pacific Coast — the other Missing Links are now Los Angeles based and originated in Australia.

Word reaches me from England that P. J. Proby is due here in the summer for "Shindig" and to work on a movie. He remains very powerful in England and Liberty Records are optimistic that he may soon have a hit here.

Tommy Turner, the 21-year-old singer about whom I told you last week (he is the first artist I have signed as manager), is to appear on "Shindig." He sang two numbers at an audition for Jack Good and he was immediately hired. Date to be fixed.

Jan and Dean have been signed by Paramount Pictures, as headliners for their up-coming movie "You Really Know How to Hurt Me," scheduled to start production on June 15th. This comedy will also star Soupy Sales and Edie Adams.

Thank you for all your letters. I am still attempting to reply to all of them.

## Will The Real Ones Please Stand

**THE BEATLES IN HOLLYWOOD.** Experts put finishing touches on amazingly realistic wax figures of the Liverpool Four. When wax figures were delivered to TUSSAUD'S in Hollywood, hundreds of excited fans stood in rain to watch the figures carried in and set in place. After the final touches were made on THE BEATLES set, doors were opened. Although exhibit is behind heavy glass, special guards are on duty at all times to protect the visitors — and the museum!

**WHICH IS THE REAL** Jean Harlow? Amazing life-like quality of movie siren of the 1930's is apparent in this photo, taken of TUSSAUD's Wax Museum. (Girl on right is real-life actress Joi Lansing. Sleepy fellow is ALLAN SHERMAN. "Wax figure" is Spoony Singh — the owner!

**HERE'S SPOONY AGAIN** — talking to actress CAROLYN JONES, who appears regularly on TV series, The Addams Family. The pretty witch added just the right touch of mystery to opening of TUSSAUD'S WAX MUSEUM, 6767 Hollywood Boulevard, near Highland. Museum features Chamber of Horrors, Movie Monsters, and many presidents of the U.S. In addition, DaVinci's LAST SUPPER, and Liverpool's THE BEATLES. Museum is open 7 days a week 'til 2:00 a.m. — but if you go, watch out for KING KONG — who roams the dark corridors silently and swiftly.

## Joey Paige: "Great To Be Back!"

After three weeks of tours, radio interviews and photo sessions in England, Joey Paige says, "No matter how great they say England is, it's still great to be back in Southern California."

Joey, sitting with friends at Hollywood's Ciro's, was very excited over the success of his current record, "Cause I'm In Love With You," which is making big jumps up the English record charts.

"You know, the English music industry is a lot fairer towards artists than ours is over here. Perhaps it's because they're going through a great social change; I don't know. Being an entertainer in England is definitely a status symbol," answers Joey when asked about the differences between the recording industry in England and The States.

"The average unkown group is lost, you know, because the kids would rather listen to the discotheque," adds Joey. The kids themselves go wild for American records, and will listen to them all night, but it's the English records that they buy."

While there, Joey stayed with his friend, Brian Jones, and joined Brian one day on a shopping spree to the fashionable Mod center of London, Carnaby Street. Both Joey and Brian walked out of smart Lord John's with an armful of modern-styled clothes.

When asked by THE BEAT who, in his estimation, was the most promising English artist, Joey immediately answered, "Without a doubt, it's got to be The Hollies. For my money, they belong right on top with the Stones."

Until July, when Joey returns to England for another tour and some tv exposure, our young friend will be touring the U.S. with the "Shindig Tour," stopping occasionally to make a guest appearances on local television stations.

Until then . . . welcome home!

## Starr Checks Cues

**RINGO STARR CHECKS SCREENPLAY** — As crucial scene is set for cameras in a few minutes, BEATLE RINGO reads the "bible," the script for the film, which outlines camera angles and actors' lines, as well as directions for action. Photo shows how close lucky Susan Frazer of Palos Verdes came **each day** to THE BEATLES. Susan spent her whole vacation in the Bahamas watching the Fab Four.

---

Advertising space is available for some of the forthcoming isues of THE BEAT. For information, call the Hollywood office at 469-3641.

---

Back issues of the KRLA BEAT are still available, for a limited time. If you've missed an issue of particular interest to you, send 10 cents for each copy wanted, along with a self-addressed stamped envelope to:

KRLA BEAT
Suite 504
6290 Sunset Blvd.
Hollywood, California 90028

**ISSUES AVAILABLE —**

2/25 — BEATLE BALL AT KRLA
3/10 — BEATLES PRAISE L.A.
3/17 — BEATLE MOVIE A BLAST
3/24 — HULL REJECTS FILM OFFER
3/31 — INTERVIEW WITH RINGO STARR
4/7 — INTERVIEW WITH GEORGE HARRISON
4/14 — INTERVIEW WITH JOHN LENNON
4/21 — INTERVIEW WITH PAUL McCARTNEY

# On The Beat

"Shindig" producer, Jack Good, and Andrew Oldham, Rolling Stones' recording manager, are apparently on different wave lengths as far as live television shows are concerned. As you know, "Shindig" is almost completely live — very rarely is the lip-syncing device used — and this is the way Mr. Good likes it. He thinks lip-syncing is "fake and phoney." Mr. Oldham, on the other hand, is against live tv shows because he thinks they kill the incentive for record production. We're inclined to go along with Mr. Good (providing, of course, a live show IS possible), but you can choose your own side.

Did you know Ian Whitcomb is primarily a pianist and he says he can't really sing at all. Ian has been visiting our town and reports that long hair on English groups is on its way out, and now the "in" thing is to cut your hair and dress smartly. By the way, Ian has a follow-up to "This Sporting Life" which is entitled, "You Turn Me On."

Here's a fair exchange for you: At the end of this month, we will trade Bob Dylan for Donovan. As THE BEAT reported earlier, Donovan is being BOTH praised and criticized in England. His record "Catch The Wind" is doing quite well over there, and it will be interesting to see how Donovan fares Stateside.

For his part, Dylan will begin an English tour on April 30, and most of his concerts are already sold out! He has a new record with a way-out title, "Subterranean Homesick Blues." After watching and listening to both Dylan and Donovan, make up your mind and let me know which "D" will it be?

Looks like movies and recording artists are THE THING. Leading off were the Beatles and "A Hard Day's Night." Next came Gerry and the Pacemakers and "Ferry Cross The Mersey." Freddie and the Dreamers have already made a movie, "Every Day's A Holiday," which is scheduled for release in the near future. We Americans will be represented by the Righteous Brothers, who will begin filming their movie in May; it's tentatively titled "You've Lost That Lovin' Feeling" and will be a Dick Clark production. And the latest artist to enter the screen scene: Herman. Nothing is definite yet, but it is a strong probabiliy. Imagine having your life story filmed when you're only seventeen!

Puzzle of the week: How come Bobby Sherman, tremendously popular regular on "Shindig," CANNOT come up with a hit record? "It Hurts Me" looked like a sure-fire winner, but after giving off a few initial sparks it simply fizzled and died.

Quick Ones: The Beach Boys have a new one, "Help Me Rhonda" b-w "Kiss Me Baby" . . . The Beatles are going to Italy for a three day tour in late June. Cities on the agenda: Milan, Genoa, and Rome . . . Georgie Fame has a new album out titled after his hit, "Yeh Yeh" . . . Ditto for Wayne Fontana and the Mindbenders . . . The Rolling Stones are having the same trouble in Denmark that the Beatles had in America: hotels cancelling their reservations . . . Gerry and the Pacemakers will be in the U.S. until the end of May; THE BEAT hopes they will be able to make it to the Southland on this trip.
—Louise Criscione

## KRLA TUNEDEX

| THIS WEEK | LAST WEEK | TITLE | ARTIST |
|---|---|---|---|
| 1. | 1. | GLORIA/BABY PLEASE DON'T GO | Them |
| 2. | 3. | GAME OF LOVE | Wayne Fontana & Mindbenders |
| 3. | 2. | WHEN I'M GONE | Brenda Holloway |
| 4. | 45. | TIRED OF WAITING FOR YOU | The Kinks |
| 5. | 11. | THE LAST TIME/PLAY WITH FIRE | The Rolling Stones |
| 6. | 12. | JUST ONCE IN MY LIFE | The Righteous Brothers |
| 7. | 22. | MRS. BROWN YOU'VE GOT A LOVELY DAUGHTER/I GOTTA DREAM ON | Herman's Hermits |
| 8. | 13. | SILHOUETTES | Herman's Hermits |
| 9. | 4. | STOP! IN THE NAME OF LOVE | The Supremes |
| 10. | 16. | IT'S NOT UNUSUAL | Tom Jones |
| 11. | 9. | NOWHERE TO RUN | Martha & The Vandellas |
| 12. | 6. | GO NOW! | The Moody Blues |
| 13. | 10. | I KNOW A PLACE | Petula Clark |
| 14. | 8. | NOT TOO LONG AGO | The Uniques |
| 15. | 28. | JUST A LITTLE | The Beau Brummels |
| 16. | 7. | I'M TELLING YOU NOW | Freddy & The Dreamers |
| 17. | 14. | I'LL NEVER FIND ANOTHER YOU | The Seekers |
| 18. | 40. | TICKET TO RIDE/YES IT IS | The Beatles |
| 19. | 15. | SHOTGUN | Jr. Walker & All Stars |
| 20. | 25. | OHH BABY, BABY | The Miracles |
| 21. | 20. | THE CLAPPING SONG | Shirley Ellis |
| 22. | 19. | PEACHES 'N CREAM | The Ikettes |
| 23. | 45. | WOOLY BULLY | Sam the Sham & the Pharoahs |
| 24. | 24. | I'LL BE DOGGONE | Marvin Gaye |
| 25. | 33. | COUNT ME IN | Gary Lewis & The Playboys |
| 26. | 21. | GIRL DON'T COME | Sandie Shaw |
| 27. | 34. | JUST YOU | Sonny & Cher |
| 28. | 18. | EIGHT DAYS A WEEK / I DON'T WANT TO SPOIL THE PARTY | The Beatles |
| 29. | 27. | DO YOU WANNA DANCE / PLEASE LET ME WONDER | The Beach Boys |
| 30. | 51. | BABY THE RAIN MUST FALL | Glenn Yarborough |

### CLIMBERS

| | | | |
|---|---|---|---|
| 1. | 42. | SHE'S ABOUT A MOVER | Sir Douglas Quintet |
| 2. | 35. | CRAZY DOWNTOWN | Allan Sherman |
| 3. | 32. | GOT TO GET YOU OFF MY MIND | Solomon Burke |
| 4. | 41. | THE ENTERTAINER | Tony Clark |
| 5. | 43. | IKO IKO | The Dixie Cups |
| 6. | 44. | CONCRETE AND CLAY | Unit Four Plus Two |
| 7. | 36. | IT'S GROWING | The Temptations |
| 8. | 37. | CAST YOUR FATE TO THE WIND | Sounds Orchestral |
| 9. | 39. | BUMBLE BEE | The Searchers |
| 10. | 31. | SEE YOU AT THE GO-GO | Dobie Gray |

## Beatles in Nassau

**ANOTHER BEATLE PHOTO** from the dream vacation of Susan Frazer. The teener, from Palos Verdes Estates (near Redondo Beach) spent her vacation in the Bahamas — at the same time as the fabulous BEATLES were filming their second movie on location. Imagine waking up every morning — and knowing that you'll spend the day with the BEATLES! Susan's big problem now is how to ever top that wonderful vacation she took at Nassau.

---

**THE BYRDS • • LIVE!**
Tuesday, April 27 — Wednesday, April 28 — Thursday — April 29
FIRST SHOW AT 7:30 P.M. AT THE
**TROUBADOUR CAFE THEATRE**
9083 SANTA MONICA BOULEVARD, BEVERLY HILLS

## At Deadline

The KINKS are all seriously ill. Singer Ray Davies was the first to be stricken with a suspected fever, later diagnosed as pneumonia. Now the entire group and their road manager are ill with the same serious fever virus.

All of the group's dates have been cancelled for a month. There have been many offers for them to tour the U.S. including an appearance on **Hullabaloo** but all tentative plans for an American tour have been delayed until their health improves.

Recently someone in a crowd at a dance they were to play set fire to Dave's (one of the KINKS) hair and as a result their manager has insured each of them for $360,000 against injury. The BEAT hopes they will recover soon and fulfill their plans to tour America.

ELVIS just celebrated his 10th year in the entertainment business. He stars in three films a year and they are released during the Easter, summer and Christmas vacation times. Scheduled for release this summer is "TICKLE ME," with a follow-up at Christmas of "HAREM HOLIDAY."

GEORGIE FAME has bought a new car — a Jag (the most popular car among the recording artists, it seems).

The ROLLING STONES are almost certain to make their first full-length film in July or August — scheduled to be a true story of the STONES' life. They are also appearing in "TEENAGE COMMAND PERFORMANCE" along with Gerry and the Pacemakers, Chuck Berry and Billy J. Kramer. The latter film should be released here in the summer. "The Last Time" by the STONES has just passed the million mark in sales. This is the "first time" for them to have a record in the million category.

P. J. PROBY'S next release will be "Hold On To What You've Got" — which was a recent hit for Joe Tex. P. J. begins a tour of Scotland this month.

WAYNE FONTANA is recovering from the collapse he suffered due to nervous exhaustion. His first hit, "Game of Love," was so successful that his new album has been titled the same.

---

**NEXT WEEK IN THE KRLA BEAT**
EXCLUSIVE BEATLE PHOTOS
Taken By Susan Frazer

A HALF PAGE PICTURE OF PAUL McCARTNEY

THE RIDDLE OF BEATLEMANIA
AND MUCH, MUCH MORE!
**LISTEN TO KRLA FOR DETAILS**

## At the Fair

**CHARLIE O'DONNELL AT THE FAIR.** The famous KRLA Man of Song signs autographs for admiring fans. Charlie made several personal appearances at the Teen-Age Fair, held at the Hollywood Palladium.

**ROYALTY REIGNS** as four of Big Town's most listened to disc jockeys chat at the Teen-Fair. Pictured are Casey Kasem, Dick Moreland (with glasses) fuzzy scuzzy Hull, and the benign one, blue-eyed, hairy-chested, broad shouldered Emperor Bob.

# KRLA ARCHIVES

## West Germany Fans Mob Rolling Stones

How does a fan meet a Stone? And having met one, what does she do? Techniques and responses vary, but here is what happened to little Liz at Los Angeles Airport recently . . . in her own words.

"When the Rolling Stones were leaving Los Angeles, me and two friends decided to go to the airport to see them. When we got there we didn't know where to go so we began walking around. Soon we became lost in a huge crowd and before long I discovered that Terri and Kathy were missing. As my Dad and I turned back to look for them, I thought I saw Mick walk into a little room near the coffee shop. I was too scared to go in even though my Dad kept pushing me toward the door.

"When I got up enough nerve, I pushed open the door and saw the Stones and their manager on six chairs in a circle. I just stood there in complete shock not believing that these five beautiful Stones were within touching distance from me!! They were looking at me and I was looking at them.

"I kept telling myself to go get their autographs or something, but I just couldn't move. I mumbled out "Hi!" But that was all I could say cause Mick got up, took my hand and led me straight out the door. Once outside, I ran and told Kathy, Terri and my Dad all about it.

"Just as we were leaving, we saw the Stones running to their plane. We ran up quickly and got their autographs. Then they ran in the plane, turned around to wave, and disappeared behind the doors."

"It was thrilling."

## Turtle Shell Glasses, Too?

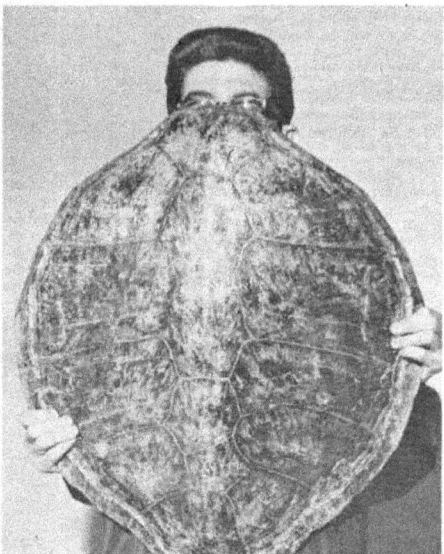

**ONLY KNOWN PHOTOGRAPH** of Dick Biondi. The Wild Italian refuses to pose for photographers, says he has a very SPECIAL REASON for staying away from cameras — and will not allow any picture of him to be published. This rare photo is only likeness in existence of the mysterious dee-jay. Why won't Dick Biondi let us take his picture?

## FAN CLUB INFORMATION

**HERMAN'S HERMITS**
c/o Carole Winder
5901 W. 7th Street
Los Angeles, Calif. 90045
(Dues — $1 and 2 5-cent stamps).

**BEATLES**
c/o Richard Rivera
1936 East 75th Street
Loes Angeles, Calif. 90001
(Dues — $2.00)

**ANIMALS Official Fan Club**
101 Dean Street
London W. 1, England

**BILLY J. KRAMER & DAKOTAS**
c/o Pat Strong
Second Floor
Service House
13 Monmouth Street
London W. C. 2, England

**(AMERICAN) MISSING LINKS**
c/o JoAnn Matrone
1917 Condon Avenue
Redondo Beach, Calif.

**SONNY & CHER FAN CLUB**
c/o Gene Daniello
7715 Sunset Blvd.
Los Angeles, California

**WORLD WIDE BEATLE ASSN.**
c/o Cindy Kelly
3600 Fairmeade Road
Pasadena, California 91107
(Dues — 50 cents)

**RIGHTEOUS BROTHERS**
c/o Carol Marburger
301 East 91 Street
New York, New York 10028
(Dues—$1.00 plus a stamped, self-addressed envelope)

## Beatle Manager Signs Group As Folksinger Battle Rages

The prediction that folk music is taking up where rhythm and blues or "rock" is leaving off has become a popular topic lately.

Britain has been taken over and is currently watching the battle for the top spot between Bob Dylan and Donovan. Bob Dylan has been well known in this country for quite a long time. Donovan is an 18-year-old boy-hermit from Glasgow.

The only criticism given Donovan so far is that he sounds too much like Dylan — and this similarity is making a lot of money for both of them.

The trend was started in London when the Seekers, an Australian group, settled there six months ago and were produced on "I'll Never Find Another You," by Dusty Springfield's brother, Tom. The record — their first single — won a Gold Disk for them on world sales with 700,000 selling in London alone.

Dylan's first British concerts have been selling out as fast as the Beatle concerts do — at an unusually high price of $3.00 per ticket. The Beatles have bought tickets — so has Donovan.

Donovan will visit New York later this month for TV appearances and he hopes to have the same success in Dylan's home country that Dylan is now having in Britain. The name of his most popular single is "Catch the Wind."

So as "Times They Are A-Changing" is selling well in London plans are being made to release a second single "Subterranean Homesick Blues," of which he has never written down the lyrics twice in the same way.

So as the see-saw continues — men watch. Including Brian Epstein who has expressed an interest in the world of folk by signing a new group, the Silkie.

Since the U.S. had a wave of folk-mania recently there is no real doubt that Dylan, Donovan, the Seekers and all the soon to be familiar groups will enjoy a lot of success in this country, too.

---

**MAKE THE**

# LEWIN
### Record Paradise
6507 Hollywood Blvd.
(at N. Wilcox)
HO 4-8088

**Your Headquarters For All Your Favorite**

## 45's and L.P.s

ALL ENGLISH GROUPS
ALWAYS IN STOCK

*Our Prices Will Please You
Everything Here Real "Neat"*

# KRLA ARCHIVES

## How The Beatles Struck It Rich!
• See Page 5

# KRLA BEAT

May 5, 1965 — Los Angeles, California — Ten Cents

# HERMANIA SPREADS

**THE LOVELY DAUGHTER OF MRS. BROWN** has just the Liverpool touch, apparently, and has skyrocketed this quintet to the dizzy heights of America's Number One group. PETER NOONE (Herman) first joined the group almost by accident. Known then as the HEARTBEATS, the boys were short a singer one evening. Peter happened to be in the audience, sang that night, and is still singing! Many changes have come about, and only KARL GREEN remains of the original association. Others of the HERMITS include 21 year old DEREK LECKENBY, who wants to be a civil engineer, 18 year old BARRY WHITMAN, who joined the group the night they changed their name to HERMAN'S HERMITS. Also shown is 17 year old KEITH HOPWOOD. The Hermits will appear in L. A. this summer.

One day, three young girls from Manchester decided to write to their local musical paper. "We are always hearing about Beatlemania," they complained. "Well, we've got 'Hermania.' What about giving HIM some publicity!?"

### Tops In England

They were talking about a young gentleman by the name of Herman, who, with his group the Hermits (they call themselves simply Herman's Hermits) have become one of the most popular groups in Manchester and the North of England in the space of nine months.

Their following is a big one. The staunchest fans have pioneered their admiration which they call 'Hermania' and the word has spread. White sweaters and waistcoats with inscriptions like 'We love Herman,' 'Hermania' and 'Herman's Hermits' are to be seen in abundance at every concert they do in the North.

The present line-up has only been together for 3 months. Herman joined them when they were called the Heartbeats. The group was playing at a youth club that Herman frequented one night and were short of a singer. He stepped in and sang and hasn't looked back. The personnel of the group has changed around a bit since its formation. Karl Green (bass guitar) is the only member of the original group. As people left, Barry Whitman (drum) was the first to join, then Derek 'Lek' Leckenby (lead & rhythm guitar) and last Keith Hopwood (lead & rhythm guitar).

### How The Name?

The rather unusual name of Herman comes from a cartoon character. In a cartoon show on TV called "The Bullwinkle Show" was a boy called Sherman. The rest of the group were amused at the similarity of the character and their lead singer. Mistaking the name of Sherman for Herman, they christened him. They chose The Hermits because it fitted the first name. First going out as Herman and the Hermits, it was later shortened to Herman's Hermits.

The group was brought to the attention of independent record producer Mickie Most, the man most responsible for the hits of the Animals and the Nashville Teens. He travelled to see them at a concert in Bolton, was immediately impressed by their stage show and signed them to a recording contract. He did however point out many of their faults and the boys have tremendous confidence in him. In fact, he saw them, signed them, recorded them and got the record released in the space of three weeks.

Mickie Most was completely responsible for a choice of material on the debut disc by Herman's Hermits. Title — I'm Into Something Good.

### Backgrounds

Herman (real name Peter Noone) is a mere 16 years old and was born in Manchester on November 5th, 1947. He had sung a little at school and although at first just having drama lessons he combined these with singing lessons. He attended the Manchester School of Music for both drama and singing classes when he was 14. He has appeared in several stage plays and has done considerable work on TV.

Karl Green (bass guitar) is 17 years old and was born in Salford, Manchester on July 31st, 1947. He worked with a group, the Balmains, before becoming a member of the Hearbeats, predecesor of Herman's Hermits.

### Varied Beginnings

Derek Leckenby (lead and rhythm guitar) is 21 years old and was born in Leeds on May 14th, 1943. Nicknamed 'Lek', he attended Manchester University where he studied Civil Engineering, a field in which he hopes to enter.

Barry Whitham (drums) is 18 years old and was born in Manchester on July 21st, 1946. After engaging in various non-show biz jobs he joined the Hermits when he found that he had taught himself to play the drums with tremendous success.

Keith Hopwood (lead and rhythm guitar) is 17 years old and was born in Manchester on October 26th, 1946. He bought his first guitar at 14 and joined a local group at 16 before becoming the finishing touch to the newest sensation in the music world.

The group is very popular now, everywhere.

## Derek Taylor Reports

The Byrds will, I believe, be No. 1 nationwide with "Mr. Tambourine Man" — their first recording now on general release here and zooming up hundreds of local charts.

Dave Hull, who misses very little in the way of new sounds and fresh trends, was smart enough to pick it as a hit on KRLA. In Pittsburgh, it was selected as Hit of the Day by a vast listening audience.

I personally think it is a marvelous disc. But then, I am a little prejudiced because I started taking an interest in the group some time before the disc was made.

### Can Recognize

Having heard it, however, I am now convinced it has limitless potential. It's different, sympathetic and gentle. It has a plaintive, melodious insistence which means that once having heard it, you recognize it the first few seconds when it is replayed.

It is very difficult to know how to put the right hit-ingredients into a disc, and there is never a guarantee ever that you will achieve the right mixture. Only the Beatles and Elvis Presley in his hey-day could be sure of automatic Number Ones.

But there are, I am quite sure, conspicious hits. The sort of discs which, if you know anything about sounds, you are certain will make it.

### Examples

There are fair hits, good hits and great hits. "Pretty Woman" was a great hit. "You've Lost That Loving Feeling" was another. "She Loves You," by any group, deserves to reach the top.

I believe "Mr. Tambourine Man" is in this bracket. And if it doesn't make it, I'll print my picture upside down!

### Beatles Wrong

So, the Beatles — for the first time in my recollection — have changed their minds and admitted they were wrong on an important issue.

As you will have learned from Dave Hull's broadcast, the foursome decided they didn't like the title they had chosen for their new movie.

Though it is scarcely relevant, I didn't like it either and I am glad they agreed to change it.

To date there is no substitute title but United Artists will, no doubt, be very glad when the Beatles make up their minds.

It will be interesting to see if they come up with something as clever as "A Hard Day's Night."

—MORE ON PAGE 8

### KRLA 1110 TOP TEN

1. WOOLY BULLY
2. GLORIA / BABY PLEASE DON'T GO
3. WHEN I'M GONE
4. MRS. BROWN YOU'VE GOT A LOVELY DAUGHTER / I GOTTA DREAM ON
5. GAME OF LOVE
6. JUST ONCE IN MY LIFE
7. TIRED OF WAITING FOR YOU
8. THE LAST TIME / PLAY WITH FIRE
9. TICKET TO RIDE / YES IT IS
10. IT'S NOT UNUSUAL

—TUNEDEX ON PAGE 8

# KRLA ARCHIVES

## Still The King

**TENTH ANNIVERSARY CELEBRATION** — Elvis Presley has come a long way since the time he drove a truck for a living. Always interested in singing, Elvis managed to cut a record for SUN RECORDS in Nashville. Colonel Tom Parker heard it — and dollar signs rang up in his eyes. The experienced showman took over management of the hip-swinging country boy, and molded him into one of history's brightest show business personalities. RCA Victor signed Elvis and bought some master tapes from Sun Records. One of them was HEARTBREAK HOTEL — and the rest of the story is paved in gold, literally. Elvis has more than 20 Gold Records — each representing sales of a million or more records of a song. With the first flush of success, the personable Elvis bought 7 Cadillacs — to fulfill a childhood ambition. He also purchased a beautiful new home near Memphis, Tennessee, for his parents. Everyone who works with Presley always comes away, with the same impression: a soft-spoken, hard-working, congenial professional. Elvis begins his 11th year as a star.

## British Coming
### Southlanders Eagerly Await Arrival of Rolling Stones

As reported earlier in the BEAT, the Rolling Stones expect to make their first full-length feature film in July or August. Now comes word that it will be about the Stones themselves — a chronicle of their life — and should be in the movie houses by next January or February.

**Scandinavia Filming**

Currently they're looking for a producer, director and other co-stars but it has already been decided that the film will be in black and white and will contain at least two full-length concerts featuring the Stones. It will probably be filmed in Scandinavia, where the boys received a fantastic reception during their recent tour.

Although this will be their first regular full-length movie, the Stones are no stranger to motion picture cameras. Along with Gerry and the Pacemakers, Chuck Berry and Billy J. Kramer they recently made a film called "Teenage Command Perform-ance" which is now ready for release.

It's a two-hour film of an American stage show.

Incidentally, the Stones recently reached another milestone. For the first time, one of their records—"The Last Time" — passed the million mark in sales.

The Rolling Stones, next big pop act on the Ed Sullivan Show, have stood their ground and forced Sullivan to back down from an earlier ultimatum.

The Stones will appear on May 2 — the day after starting a U.S. tour which will bring them to Southern California — and Sullivan had ordered their manager, Eric Easton, to have them dress more neatly before his TV cameras. Easton refused to budge.

"They will appear dressed in whatever each of them feels like wearing that day," he says.

## On The Beat

Parlez Vous Francais? Well, you'd better, because France is now importing something besides perfume — GIRLS! Two of the "Ye Ye" girls—Sylvie Varton and Francoise Hardy — have been receiving plenty of American exposure via the big tube.

Will France replace England in the hearts of U. S. teens? We doubt it. But as all the boys agree, the little French girls are much easier on the eyes than say, the Hullabaloos!

Too bad for Sylvie and Francoise that the American girls and NOT the American boys buy the majority of records!

In case you're wondering exactly who the Guess Who are, they are Chad Allen and the Expressions. That should clear up the mystery for you. Now all you have to find out is — who are Chad Allen and the Expressions? Whoever they are, we like their sound of "Shakin' All Over."

QUICK ONES: "Shindig" will go the movie route in August... Chad and Jeremy have settled their legal hassle with Ember Records; they now belong to Columbia... The Tamla-Motown tour of England, starring the Supremes, Martha and the Vandellas, the Miracles, and Little Stevie Wonder, received wild acclaim but did NOT do as well as expected at the box office... Radio Caroline (British pirate radio station) is AMERICANIZING their programs.

**PUZZLE OF THE WEEK:** What exactly is it that makes a star? What separates our local L.A. groups from the Beach Boys of five years ago? Obviously, there is no set answer; if there were, theoretically all groups would enjoy the same success.

Still, it's interesting to ponder, and who knows, maybe the gang down the street from you who practice the same off-key song OVER and OVER will one day set the record world on its ear?

**Note To Dave**

Dave Hull should be interested in knowing that "Fabulous," an

English fan magazine, credits him with phoning Mrs. Louise Harrison once a week and broadcasting the conversation "live." Although most of those conversations have been on tape, the old Scuzzy is gaining a world-wide reputation as the most avid Beatlemanic in existance.

Since that British music paper introduced the idea of having the Beatles feted at Buckingham Palace, reaction from the British populace has been terrific.

Most of the other English newspapers shout a vehement NO, but the majority of teens seem to think the Beatles should be honored in SOME WAY, and they were quick to offer their suggestions: Liverpool should have Ringo Road, George Grove, John's Avenue, and Paul Parade... The British Post Office should issue Beatle stamps... They should name the Liverpool College of Art after John Lennon... They should make John director-general of the BBC... and they should make the Beatles directors of the Bank of England since they have got most of the money anyway!

**Fun To Dream**

We seriously doubt if any of their suggestions will be adopted, but they seem to be having a ball thinking them up!

WATCH OUT FOR: Herman's Hermits on "Shindig" in early May... A half-hour Beatle special, "Big Night Out," on TV later this spring... "Letkiss" — a song and dance which is taking the Continent by storm.

**Follow The Leader?**

The Shadows, Cliff Richard's backing group, signed with Epic Records here in the U.S. The group's first release on Epic is "Mary Ann," which was a fair-sized hit in England. Richard failed to make it Stateside; will the Shadows follow suit?

We think Brian Epstein's decision to have the Beatles make more movies and fewer personal appearances is one he is going to regret. Once a group — ANY group — loses personal contact with their fans, their fans lose interest in them. A case directly on point — Elvis.

Sure, Elvis makes plenty of money for those movies he makes, but isn't he sacrificing fans to do it? Elvis was once a consistent chart-topper, now he's rarely on the survey at all!

BEATLES TAKE NOTE — it COULD happen to you — if you are not careful. And anyway, why can't Epstein strike a happy medium and please everybody?

—Louise Criscione

## Beatle Movie Plot

The Beatles are off on another series of European concerts after completing three months of difficult filming for their second movie.

Back in London, the 90-minute film spectacular is being edited, dubbed and prepared for release later this year.

Now that "8 Arms to Hold You" has been scrapped as the title (See Derek Taylor's column) everyone connected with the film is competing to see who will be the first to dream up an acceptable new title.

For those of you who missed the exclusive Beatle interviews by KRLA's Dave Hull and Derek Taylor — in which most of the plot was revealed — here's a recap:

**Opens With Song**

The beginning of the movie starts with a song penned by Paul McCartney. The opening scene shows the preparation of a priestess for sacrifice to the gods of a Far-Eastern temple.

Careful attention is given to the fact that she is wearing the ceremonial ring, a precious collection of exotic stones carrying a high religious and financial value.

As could only be expected, the ring slips from the priestess' finger... and into the hands of Ringo Starr.

From this point on the movie is filled with high comedy and un-Beatle-like chases, as our "fearless foursome" speed back to England, pursued by ruthless-looking hired gangsters.

**Beatles Disguised**

Throughout the movie, John, Paul, George and Ringo wear different disguises in an effort to elude their pursuers.

Somehow The Beatles manage to escape to Austria, where they are seen in some comical daring-do as they speed down a mountain slope, with the crooks hot on their heels!

Through scenes that the viewer can hardly believe, our intrepid do-gooders make their way back to England, where Ringo finally manages to get the ring off his finger.

As fate would have it, the ring then falls into the hands of a very unlucky young man. As the Beatles un-knowingly walk away whistling, he is seen running like mad from the ever-present crooks intent on retrieving the ring.

It all shapes us as exciting entertainment for millions of Beatle fans around the world.

---

**ADDRESS ALL BEAT MAIL TO:**

**KRLA BEAT**

6290 Sunset Blvd., Suite 504

Hollywood, California

All back issues of the BEAT are 10 cents each. Also send a stamped, self addressed envelope.

---

**DICK CLARK**
**CARAVAN of STARS**
*STARRING*
**DICK CLARK**
MONDAY, MAY 17
*TWO PERFORMANCES*
5 & 9 P.M.
**ONE NITE ONLY!**
FEATURING 15 OF THE
NATION'S TOP RECORDING ACTS!
DEL SHANNON
The ZOMBIES
The SHANGRI-LAS
JEWEL AKEN
The LARKS
TOMMY ROE
DEE DEE SHARP
MEL CARTER
The AD LIBS
The VELVELETTES
JIMMY SOUL
MIKE CLIFFORD
The IKETTES
The EXECUTIVES
DON WAYNE

PRICES... $2.50, $3.50, $4.50
TICKETS AT BOX-OFFICE, BY MAIL AND ALL SOUTHLAND AGENCIES

**MELODYLAND THEATER**
OPPOSITE DISNEYLAND

FOR INFORMATION CALL
ANAHEIM (714) 776-7220

# KRLA ARCHIVES

## KRLA Beat Exclusive -- Portrait of a Beatle

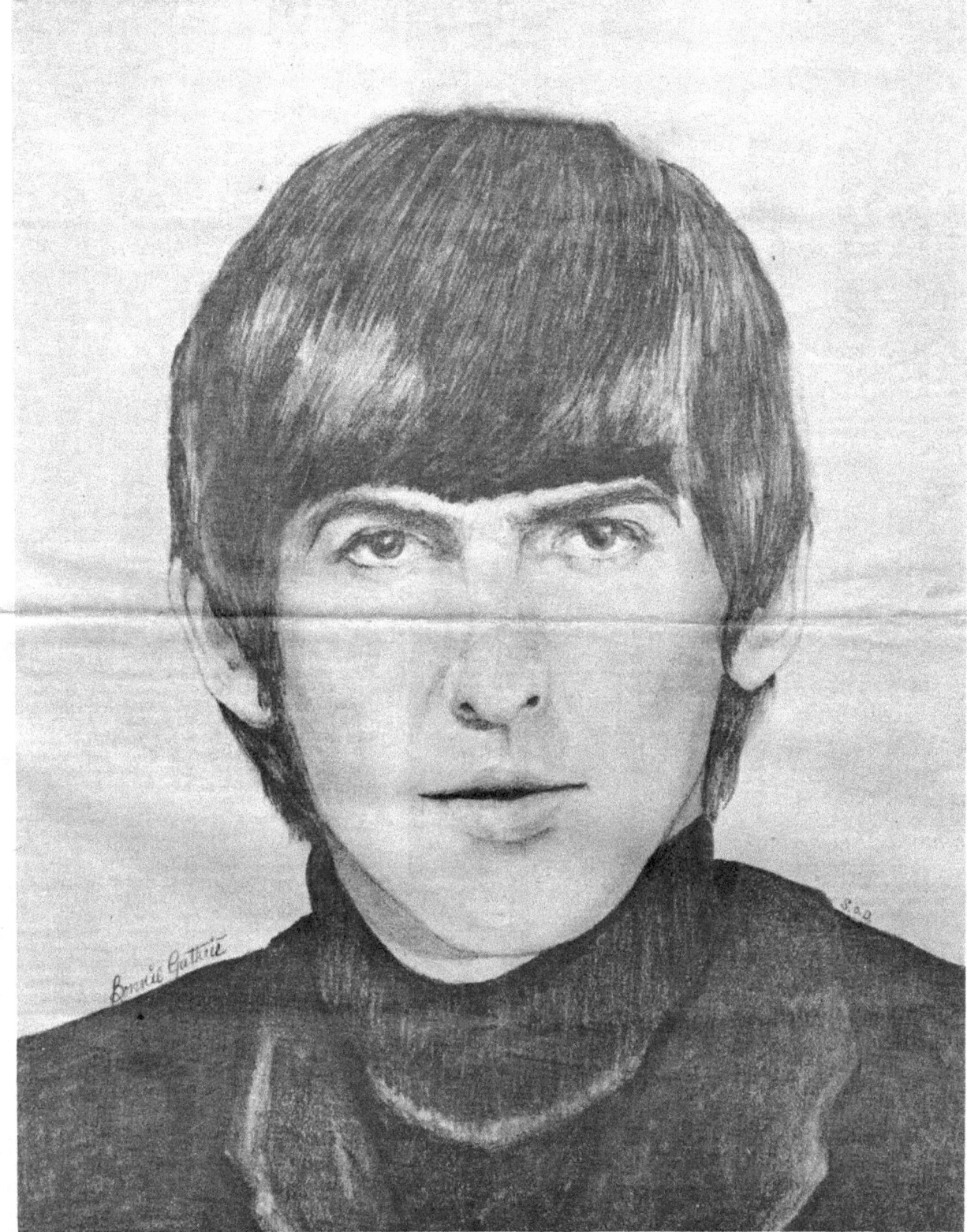

**THIS MAGNIFICENT PENCIL DRAWING OF GEORGE HARRISON** is the work of BONNIE GUTHRIE, 16-year-old San Diego high school girl, who has already presented several of her drawings to other leading world artists. She is planning to take up art as a career. In December, Bonnie presented a splendid drawing to a famous man — a portrait of BRIAN EPSTEIN. It was handed over to the BEATLES' manager when he was here with his singer TOMMY QUICKLY. Bonnie does not trace over a photograph — she draws from models or just simply recollection, and has produced some startling results. In addition to Bonnie's obvious talent as an artist, she also sings rhythm and blues, and has done some work in that field. But her first love is her work with art. Watch for other impressive exhibitions of Bonnie Guthrie's work, coming soon in the KRLA BEAT.

# KRLA ARCHIVES

## Rolling Stones Here Soon

**THIS IS WHERE A POP SINGER LIVES** when he has it made. This is the home of a Rolling Stone, in London. It is in Chelsea — a cute, neat little refuge behind a bland brick wall. A Mews cottage, it costs a mere $90 a week. And long, long ago, horses used to live there. The STONES "have it made" for sure. The featured group will make personal appearances in California.

**AS A PLATFORM** for a Stones' elbow, is a hitching post for horses. BRIAN JONES can afford to relax. And JOEY PAIGE, though bemused by the antiquity of it all, looks much at home.

**RINGO STARR** lived on such a road until well-meaning excited fans coming round at all hours drove the BEATLES' drummer off to another hideaway somewhere in England.

## At Deadline

Wayne Fontana is anxious for his fans in America to know his recent illness was nothing serious. "All I needed was a good rest," he told the BEAT. "I've been out every night for two and a half years and the strain finally got to me — I just had an attack of nerves." After a four-week lay-off he is now accepting bookings again. Wayne is pleased with his success in the U.S. "It's a nice tonic," he said, "and I believe I'll be going over to America with Herman and Freddie.

Herman is wearing a cast on his thumb. A policeman who had helped him through a mob of fans and safely into his waiting car was so anxious to get Herman on his way that he slammed the car door on the head Hermit's thumb and broke it in three places. The injury doesn't prevent him from his peculiar "addiction," though. Herman is, by his own admission, a "coke addict" and drinks six at a sitting — more than once a day.

Peter Asher recently did a solo on television, performing "True Love Ways" without Gordon. Gordon says his car broke down on his way to the studio. It could have been even more serious. The gear box fell apart while he was driving 75 m.p.h., but Gordon was able to stop it without mishap.

The Rolling Stones are the objects of a fierce controversy in England. Seems they've been ejected from a few clubs and restaurants because of the way they dress and their fans are up in arms about it. Friends of the Stones say they have a right to dress however they please — and besides that, some of their "seedy-looking" clothing is actually very expensive.

Similarly, the Pretty Things, whose unkept appearance strongly contrasts with their name, have encountered a housing problem in England. Because of their long hair, landlords slam the door in their faces. As a result, all but two of them are homeless. "We couldn't get a flat together now if we tried," says Phil May. "Once they realize we're the Pretty Things that's it. Or they try to stick us for double rent. "It seems if you belong to a long-haired group, nobody wants you."

Elvis Presley will be on "Shindig" May 5. Unlike most of the artists appearing on the popular television show he will be featured not as an "up-and-coming" star but as a veteran of the entertainment business. It will be a celebration of his 10th year — all of them as a star — in the world of music.

Dobie Gray's apartment was burglarized and his gold record received for "The In Crowd" taken as part of the loot.

The Beatles are dog lover. John has a red setter and Ringo has an apricot colored poodle, a wedding gift.

Tom Jones has been signed for five "Ed Sullivan" shows, the first of which will be aired on May 2. Unfortunately, three "Shindig" appearances scheduled for him had to be cancelled due to a conflict in dates.

Cliff Richard has been popular in England for many years — even before the Beatles. However, his No. 1 record in Britain, "The Minute You've Gone" was recorded in Nashville, Tenn.

And then, there's the conflicting situation regarding P. J. Proby, an American who was a virtual unknown until recording in England.

Californian Bob Dylan, the brilliant folksinger and composer, has become a smash during his current tour of England. Ticket demands for his concerts are fantastic, and he has been forced to schedule extra performances. Among those grabbing tickets for his London concerts are the Beatles. Donovan, the fast-rising young English folksinger who is often accused of copying Dylan's style, also plans to see him perform.

NEW RELEASES: TOM JONES — "Once Upon A Time"; KINKS — "Everybody Is Gonna Be Happy"; IAN WHITCOMB — "You Turn Me On"; SEEKERS — "A World of Our Own"; and MANFRED MANN — "Oh No Not My Baby."

---

**Long Beach Arena – Sunday, May 16**

## THE ROLLING STONES
### IN CONCERT

CHOICE SEATS STILL AVAILABLE AT
LONG BEACH ARENA, WALLICH'S MUSIC CITY
AND ALL MUTUAL TICKET AGENCIES

# KRLA ARCHIVES

# Making A Gold Record

**By Derek Taylor**

St. John's Wood is very much London. Solid and a little old. But nice and comfortable, and not yet shabby. The buildings h a v e dignity and an elderly charm. And people still clean their windows.

If a horse-drawn cab clattered up Abbey Road, it wouldn't seem too unusual. Somewhere far away there is still a faint rustling of crinoline.

It is 2 o'clock in the afternoon in Abbey Road in St. John's Wood. The leaves are flickering from the sycamore trees, and George Harrison is late.

John Lennon's Rolls-Royce glides by and the blue uniformed doorman straightens his tie.

### Teenagers Gather

Around the wrought-iron gates of the EMI Studios in St. John's Wood, flushed and flustered knots of teenagers gather, clutching ballpoint pens and rolled-up drawings, newspapers, magazines and autograph books.

Paul McCartney's Astin-Martin is snaking its way through the lunch-hour traffic of London's chollied West End. Paul is still battling his way. He isn't worried because he knows he won't be late. He never is.

And miles away, deep in the heart of the Surry countryside, George Harrison is trying to buy a swimming pool.

### Ringo To Reality

Ringo Starr has just this minute passed his driving test and Bert, the Beatles' general chauffeur, is waiting by the huge black Austin Princess to take Ringo away from his dreams of Italian cars to the realities of the studio.

Another Beatle recording session is about to begin. Around the corner and only a few weeks away, lie a brace of golden discs, hundreds of thousands of dollars, and fresh glory in the perilous world of recordings.

Paul and John are usually early. Particularly Paul. He is the eager Beatle and, in any case, he has neither wife nor domestic involvements to hold him back.

### Midnight Deadline

In the No. 2 Studio in St. John's Wood, the thin, stooping figure of George Martin is hunched over the control panel. He knows the Beatles may be a few minutes late, but he knows, too, that as an "A" side must be recorded by midnight, then an "A" side will be recorded by midnight.

Also, he knows it will be a worldwide hit. And this helps him to relax.

The doorman salutes John, who steps from his Rolls-Royce, says goodbye to his chauffeur — John doesn't drive yet — and walks with that curious, swift loping Beatle walk up the steps into the hallway of the cream - painted building.

"John," the fans wail plaintively, waving and dropping their pens and books, their pictures and magazines.

### Professional Fans

Neil Aspinall, the taciturn Beatles road manager waves back. "He'll be back later, he assures them. Neil doesn't worry because he knows that these fans have three or four dozen sets of autographs already. They are the professional hunters—they have kept a vigil outside the studio and outside the Beatles' homes for the past eighteen months.

It is n o w 2:20 p.m., and George is still talking swimming pools in Surrey. Little Ringo bustles in from his Princess and joins John and Paul in the control room.

John tells him, "We've got the single, Ring."

And R i n g o says, "Great." Which is the optimum in Beatle enthusiasm.

### "It's Gear"

The single is called "I Feel Fine," and John says, "It's gear, except for one thing. We've got the phrase 'diamond ring' in again. But we can always change that."

I'm there, too, smoking and a little worried because a nervous photographer is waiting to take arty pictures of the Beatles' hands for a way-out European magazine.

The Beatles want to get on with their music, and I want them for pictures. Not a new dilemma.

### How?

Curious how the Beatles get away with it. As someone once said of a great politician, "He can charm the birds out of the trees and yet remain, himself, totally unmoved."

George Martin knows the session must start soon and the Beatles, being basically diciplined people, get down to business. George has still not arrived but John and Paul have to get together on "I Feel Fine" because Paul has never heard the tune and there is no middle eight'.

Within minutes the two of them are leaping about the studio in delight. Paul says he is quite happy for "She's A Woman" to go on the "B" side. "I Feel Fine," he agrees, is a far more commercial number.

### Where's George?

"Okay, Beatles," says George Martin amiably. "Let's have something on tape. Where's George?"

"Here, Mr. M a r t i n ," says George, unwrapping himself from a gigantic black wollen scarf. "I've got a gear swimming pool."

The four most expensive artists in the world are now in position in the spot where they first stood two-and-a-bit years ago to play the first tentative bars of a song called "Love Me Do." Which is where they and we all came in.

### John Thrilled

One hour later, without studio m u s i c i a n s , without benefit of tricks or gimmicks, the next Beatle single is on tape. John is thrilled, because not only has a song—born that morning—grown into a fully developed recording, but he has achieved a unique effect on the first note.

Paul, it seems, has stepped between two pieces of equipment to produce a weird twanging sound. John, with his odd, off-beat view of life, thinks this is great. A hit with a differential, he says ?????.

And, of course, a few weeks later that twang will become world famous. And because the Beatles are exceptional, they were able to reproduce this sound on stage as well.

### Beatles Happy

So, with an "A" side of a new single in the bag and the "B" established as "She's A Woman," the Beatles are now completely happy. Any other group would have settled for any one of the four or five songs already recorded "No Reply," "Eight Days A Week," "I Don't Want to Spoil the Party," or "I'm A Loser."

But the Beatles are not any other group, and their aim is to make every track on an album a potential single.

This is why they are great. This is why they are different. This is why they are millionaires.

### Professionals

The atmosphere in the studio is marvelous. To watch the Beatles at work is to watch great sportsmen in an arena. It is — without overstating the case — like sitting in on a group of scientists talking about space, or time. They are total professionals and they could, no doubt, produce hits in somebodys back kitchen.

George Martin is thrilled with them, but because he is an austere Englishman, he plays it very cool. "Would the great and famous Beatles," he asks, "run through 'I Feel Fine' once again?"

### Tea Time

"Yes," says John, "If the great and famous George Martin would let us have a cup of bloody tea."

The faithful Neil Aspinall shoots off for tea and for cheese sandwiches. And sitting in a corner, mending guitar strings and reading a detective novel, massive Mal Evans, the Beatles' equipment manager, smiles to himself. He turns to me and says, "This is when you get proud of them. They can be difficult but when you see how good they are, you forgive them everything."

You do!

# KRLA ARCHIVES

## Number One On The Tunedex

**FROM THE PRESIDENT'S HOME STATE** of Texas, comes SAM THE SHAM and the PHAROAHS. Their M-G-M- hit "WOOLY BULLY" has launched the exciting group on the road to stardom. Group drives a new black hearse to carry all their instruments on the road! Sam (whose real name is Domingo Samudio) carries around an electronic organ to keep the unusual sound of the five musicians.

**ONE OF THE GREAT** all-time name groups, THE BEACH BOYS will always be remembered for their overnight rise to fame and their fantastic holding power.

**THE FAMOUS FUNNY MAN** — whose records have hit the Top Ten — is ROGER MILLER. A real country boy, Roger used to pick guitar in band for western singer RAY PRICE, and entertain his friends at parties. Those same ditties now entertain millions. Roger is a natural talent who has written his hits himself.

## Legend In Music Industry Is 24-Year-Old Genius

**By Rod Alan Barken**

Phil Spector, at 24, is already a legend in the music industry. The most controversial and colorful figure on the current scene, he is a diminutive giant, an eccentric genius, a self-made millionaire. And one of the most dominant men in the field of pop music.

Songs like "You've Lost That Lovin' Feeling," and "Just Once In My Life" — both performed by the Righteous Brothers — are a perfect illustration.

**SPECTOR**

Spector tasted his first major success in 1958 when he and some high school friends wrote and produced a song that sold over a million records in 30 days. "To Know Him Is to Love Him," a ballad by the Teddy Bears, was the stepping stone to stardom for a bright-eyed young man of 17.

### Other Hits

In the years that followed, he produced such hits as "Da Do Ron Ron," "And Then He Kissed Me," "The Boy I'm Gonna Marry" and "Zipee Da Doo Dah."

Who will ever forget the classic written by Phil for Ben E. King, "Spanish Harlem"? Or "Pretty Little Angel Eyes" by Curtis Lee?

"Corina, Corina" by Ray Petersen was another of his classics.

A few critics describe the Spector sound as nothing more than "A huge echo chamber of reverberating noise."

But others point out that he possesses a unique combination of talents to select the right instrumentation, the proper microphone placement and the ideal arrangements — and the ability to use multiple recording processes to build an ordinary song into an almost overpowering production.

No one can deny that the Spector sound has been amazingly successful. And no one has ever succeeded in imitating it.

---

Lucky Southland ticket-holders to the May 13th taping of the "Shindig" television show are in for quite a treat. On that night, visitors to the audience will see The Rolling Stones "live" on stage as they tape their appearance for a future air date, May 26.

Security precautions are reportedly doubled for that night only.

Persons wanting to obtain tickets for future Shindig tapings should write their requests to: Shindig, ABC TV Center, 4151 Prospect Ave., Hollywood 27. You must enclose a stamped, self-addressed envelope . . . and then be patient. There is a waiting list.

## FAN CLUB INFORMATION

**TOMMY QUICKLY**
Official National Fan Club
Jeanie Anderson, Nat'l Pres.
Kirby Johnson, Nat'l Sec'ty.
P. O. Box 966
Glendale, California 91205

**DEREK TAYLOR FAN CLUB**
c/o Shelly Heber
6087½ Alcott Street
Los Angeles 35, California

**PETER & GORDON**
c/o Diana Klass
441 N. Fonda Street
La Habra, California 90632

**ROLLING STONES**
c/o Vanda Dixon
157 S. Ardmore Avenue
Los Angeles 90004

**SONNY & CHER**
c/o Becky Vancoorkees
P.O. Box 84
Montrose, California

**THE STANDELLS**
c/o Lee Jacobs
7251 Willoughby
Los Angeles, California
(dues — 50 cents)

**THE BYRDS**
Official National Fan Club
Nancy Migdol and Kathy McIntyre, Joint Presidents
6290 Sunset Boulevard,
Suite 504
Hollywood 28, California
(send $1.00 plus two 5 cent stamps for photos, biographies, fact sheet and newsletter; include date of your birth).

## PEN PALS

**Clare Davies and Janice Alford**
4 Updale Close
Potters Bar
Middlesex, England

**Carol Metcalf**
515 W. Derby Road
Tuebrook, Liverpool 13
Lancaster, England

## Dobie

Dobie Gray is known internationally as Leader of the "In" Crowd. In an exclusive interview with the talented singer, we asked him to describe the "In" Crowd.

"It's difficult to explain," he said. "Actually the term 'In Crowd' represents different things to different people. For me, it's being with people you dig and are able to communicate with.

"We are all part of individual groups. Once you have found the group that you feel most comfortable in, that's when you can consider yourself part of the 'In' Crowd."

I asked the lithe, handsome young singer with the big brown eyes and warm smile if he felt that being part of one of these groups is a bad idea — whether it might destroy a person's own individuality.

"Not at all," he replied. "Many people make the mistake of thinking that all the kids today are just a bunch of conformists and can't think for themselves. This isn't true."

# KRLA ARCHIVES

## There's Something Missing Somewhere!

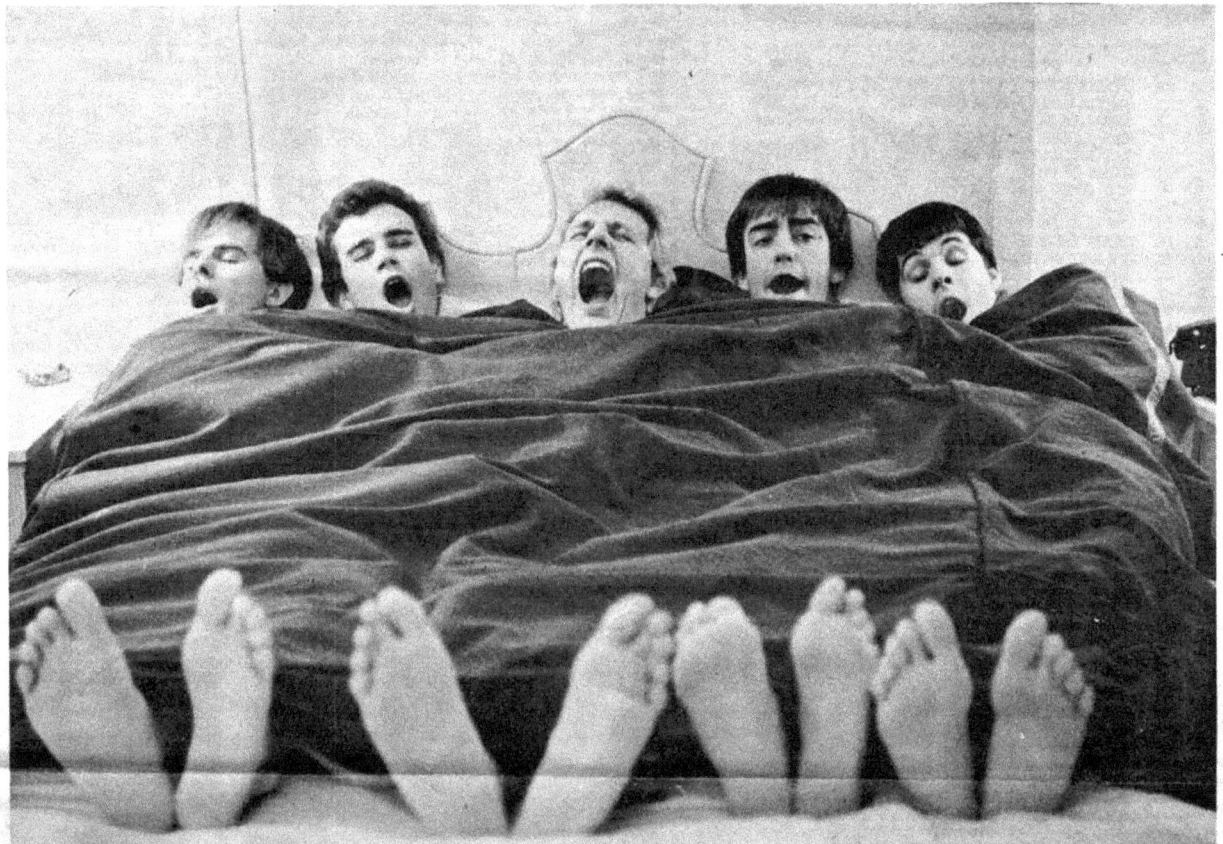

**THERE IS SOMETHING WRONG WITH THIS PICTURE.** Have you spotted it? Write and let us know if you can find the flaw. The tops and toes belong to PAUL REVERE AND THE RAIDERS. They are doing very nicely with their latest Columbia release "SOMETIMES" — a double pick on KRLA. The disc was named as a hit by DICK MORELAND, KRLA librarian — a man with a great ear for a successful record — and by CASEY KASEM. Up to now, the disc is only on release in the West and in the Raider's own home territory in Oregon. There the sales have been exceeding 2,000 daily! Group back in the Southland again a few days ago. They came in for television work, to promote the record, and to plan their summer programs. The mouths belong to (l-r) MIKE SMITH, DRAKE LEVIN, PAUL REVERE (who has the widest yawn west of the Mississippi), MARK LINDSAY, and PHILIP VOLK.

## Did You Know This?

While John Lennon, Paul McCartney, George Harrison and Ringo Starr continue soaring to new heights in popularity, a former Beatle has hit rock bottom.

Before Ringo joined the group Pete Best was the Beatle drummer. He's on several of their early records which have been featured on KRLA.

After parting company with John, Paul and George, Pete formed a group of his own, the Pete Best Combo. But while the Beatles, sparked by Ringo's driving arms, skyrocketed to become the most popular entertainers in the history of the world, Pete Best struggled to find bookings for his group.

The handsome ex-Beatle has finally given up, disbanding the Pete Best Combo for lack of work.

Behind that brief story lies an even greater story. It is one which should be told, and will be told — soon — in the KRLA BEAT.

## EXCLUSIVE

As a KRLA BEAT exclusive, here is a reprint of a letter received by an English girl from Beatle Paul McCartney while he was in Nassau.

"Dear Sue,

"How are you? Hope this finds you as it leaves me. Wish you were here. Weather fine. All the best to all at number twelve. Your policemen are wonderful.

"Anyway — at the moment we're making a fillum (of the same name.) — and we're having a laugh (to boot.)

"Love from your old pals."

The letter is signed: "The Bottles — John, George, Ringo & Harold."

## High Numbers — Who?

Who has one of the most unusual names and unusual sounds among the new British vocal groups?

The "Who," that's who!

The Who zoomed into international popularity with their recording of "I Can't Explain."

But even before their success in records, the group was well known in English clubs.

They began with a name almost as unusual as their present one, calling themselves The High Numbers. Hearing that name, customers in the clubs immediately asked, "The Who?"

So The High Numbers promptly changed their name to The Who.

Adding to the distinction of their name, the boys ignored the popular long hair styles and sported short, moddy-type mops. But despite their club popularity, their first record failed to sell.

Then their lead guitarist, 19 year old Pete Townsend wrote "I Can't Explain." Their recording of it became an instant hit on both sides of the Atlantic and now music fans throughout Europe and the United States are clamoring for personal appearances.

Now it's no longer "the who?" but "The Who!"

**PRETTY THINGS** is what this group is called as they pick flowers on a typical Sunday outing. Group has record in the top five in merrie England.

---

**FUTURE D.J.'S**
Join the Ranks of
**DON MARTIN GRADS**
YOU WILL FIND THEM ON
EVERY MAJOR STATION
IN
LOS ANGELES
"A Career In A Year"
— Jobs Assured —
**DON MARTIN
SCHOOL OF RADIO
& TV**
Call or Write for Information
**1653 N. CHEROKEE AVE.
HOLLYWOOD**

---

**BANDS, GROUPS**

HAVE YOU FOUND THE SOUND?

**WE RECORD HITS!**

**EMPEROR PRODUCTIONS**

1721 N. VERMONT AVE.    PHONE 662-4373

*Finest Reproduction Facilities In Los Angeles
Expert Engineering and Recording Services
Reasonable Rates*

# KRLA ARCHIVES

## KRLA TUNEDEX

| THIS WEEK | LAST WEEK | TITLE | ARTIST |
|---|---|---|---|
| 1. | 23. | WOOLY BULLY | Sam The Sham & The Pharoahs |
| 2. | 1. | GLORIA/BABY PLEASE DON'T GO | Them |
| 3. | 3. | WHEN I'M GONE | Brenda Holloway |
| 4. | 7. | MRS. BROWN YOU'VE GOT A LOVELY DAUGHTER/I GOTTA DREAM ON | Herman's Hermits |
| 5. | 2. | GAME OF LOVE | Wayne Fontana & Mindbenders |
| 6. | 6. | JUST ONCE IN MY LIFE | The Righteous Brothers |
| 7. | 4. | TIRED OF WAITING FOR YOU | The Kinks |
| 8. | 5. | THE LAST TIME/PLAY WITH FIRE | The Rolling Stones |
| 9. | 18. | TICKET TO RIDE/YES IT IS | The Beatles |
| 10. | 10. | IT'S NOT UNUSUAL | Tom Jones |
| 11. | 11. | NOWHERE TO RUN | Martha & The Vandellas |
| 12. | 8. | SILHOUETTES | Herman's Hermits |
| 13. | 20. | OOO BABY BABY | The Miracles |
| 14. | 15. | JUST A LITTLE | The Beau Brummels |
| 15. | 49. | STOP! IN THE NAME OF LOVE | The Supremes |
| 16. | 25. | COUNT ME IN | Gary Lewis & The Playboys |
| 17. | 13. | I KNOW A PLACE | Petula Clark |
| 18. | 17. | I'LL NEVER FIND ANOTHER YOU | The Seekers |
| 19. | 12. | GO NOW! | The Moody Blues |
| 20. | 31. | SHE'S ABOUT A MOVER | Sir Douglas Quintet |
| 21. | 49. | I DO LOVE YOU | Billy Stewart |
| 22. | 27. | JUST YOU | Sonny & Cher |
| 23. | 24. | I'LL BE DOGGONE | Marvin Gaye |
| 24. | 14. | NOT TOO LONG AGO | The Uniques |
| 25. | 53. | BACK IN MY ARMS AGAIN | The Supremes |
| 26. | 36. | CONCRETE AND CLAY | Unit Four Plus Two |
| 27. | 19. | SHOTGUN | Jr. Walker & All Stars |
| 28. | 30. | BABY THE RAIN MUST FALL | Glenn Yarbrough |
| 29. | 21. | THE CLAPPING SONG | Shirley Ellis |
| 30. | 16. | I'M TELLING YOU NOW | Freddie and The Dreamers |

### CLIMBERS

| | | | |
|---|---|---|---|
| 1. | 35. | IKO IKO | The Dixie Cups |
| 2. | 34. | THE ENTERTAINER | Tony Clarke |
| 3. | 42. | IT'S GONNA BE ALL RIGHT | Gerry & The Pacemakers |
| 4. | 47. | CATCH THE WIND | Donovan |
| 5. | 45. | SHAKING ALL OVER | Guess Who |
| 6. | 43. | REELIN' AND A'ROCKIN' | The Dave Clark Five |
| 7. | 48. | SWING ME | Nino and April |
| 8. | 46. | MISSION BELL | P. J. Proby |
| 9. | 58. | WOMAN GOT SOUL | The Impressions |
| 10. | 60. | NOTHING CAN STOP ME | Gene Chandler |

## Group Stricken

Fans of the Kinks can relax. The crisis seems to be over and there is good news on two fronts.

First, the Kinks are recuperating rapidly from the pneumonia attacks which struck the entire group during a tour of Scotland. Doctors were worried for a time, but they all pulled through in fine shape.

As the BEAT reported earlier, Ray was the first to fall ill. Appearing against doctors' orders, he collapsed during one of their performances and was immediately rushed back to London in a special compartment of an express train under strict medical care. Shortly afterward the others were stricken.

Although they were forced to cancel future engagements for several weeks, they're up and about again.

The second item of good news concerns a widespread rumor that the Kinks were disbanding. This is strongly denied by all the boys, and the denial is echoed by their management.

No matter how popular the Kinks become, one of them will never have any worries about fans or autograph hounds pestering him at his home.

Pete Quaife is getting a cheetah!

Pete, bass guitarist with the Kinks, says he's always wanted one as a house pet. The manager of South Africa's top singing group, The Shangaans, has promised to bring him a cheetah when the group visits England for a series of personal appearances.

According to Pete, Cheetahs can be house-trained and make fine pets. We'll take his word for it — from a distance.

---

**BECOME A MEMBER IN THE WORLD'S MOST FUN-FILLED FAN CLUB**

Send $1.00 plus two 5-cent stamps to

**THE BYRDS Official Nat'l Fan Club**

SUITE 504, 6290 SUNSET BOULEVARD

Receive Photos, Letters, Fact Sheets, Contests,

**FREE BYRDS CONCERTS — HURRY!!**

---

## BEATLEMANIA RIDDLE

There are millions of Beatlemaniacs throughout the world, but few can provide a definition of Beatlemania.

Kathy Klar of Redwood City, an ardena Beatle fan recently set her own definition down on paper. Apparently many others share her feelings, for Kathy has been besieged by requests for copies of it. She offered to share it with other readers of THE BEAT this week. As you will see, Beatlemania is many things. It is . . .

● "Fun . . .
● Laughing at one's own mistakes, and then trying to correct them . . .
● Enjoying life immensely and getting a lot out of it . . .
● Being an individualist . . .
● Dignity . . .
● Good manners . . .
● Courtesy to everyone, no matter who they are . . .
● Hard work, and appreciation of hard work . . .
● Demanding perfection of one's self . . .
● Willingness to sacrifice . . .
● A hard struggle to the top. . .
● Respect — for friends, parents, other young people, other performers, the Beatles themselves and even the policeman—but most of all, respect for one's self . . .
● Respecting other peoples' views on the Beatles . . .
● Appreciation of other performers . . .
● Appreciation of what is happening on the stage when one is attending a concert . . .

Beatlemania also is:
● Loyalty . . .
● Being strong in the face of criticism . . .
● Standing up for what one believes is right . . .
● A strong, quiet determination . . .
● A reward, or two rewards, or three . . .
● A dream . . .
● Understanding . . .
● Something different to every person . . .
● A person's own beliefs and feelings about a very deep subject. However, after all this, I have found that — to me, at least — Beatlemania is not:
● Standing in line for four days to get a Beatle concert ticket . . .
● Crying over the Beatles . . .
● Screaming . . .
● Fainting . . .

Really?

## POPULARITY?

Is Brian Epstein losing his popularity in the United States?

Some people seem to think so. Including the producers of "Hullabaloo," who have quietly dropped the segment that was taped in England and m.c.'d by the recently-popular Mr. Epstein.

Although many critics thought the English portion of the show "dull" and poorly handled, most of the young audience seemed to find it the most interesting part of the show.

Perhaps many of the viewers expected to see the Beatles appear on the T.V. screen, and resented his failure to produce any comparable talent.

That's the generally-accepted reason for the change in "Hullabaloo."

Whether the decision was actually made by Brian Epstein or by "Hullabaloo," there will most certainly be strong protest from the many Beatle and Epstein fans.

## More Derek Taylor

### FROM PAGE ONE

There seems no reason why they shouldn't because their intuitive skill is boundless.

### English Guides

Now that it has become fashionable to be British — and, more particularly, to come from the north of England — people are putting out all sorts of guides to Englishness — slang, clothes, boots, and so on. I have a list of what the publishers describe as "Beat Bash" of slang. This lists words like "gear," "fab," "kip," and other Liverpool phrases which have now passed into world-usage.

There are some in the list, however, which are absolute rubbish. Such as "Mersey Beat," which is described as "in" music. No self-respecting Liverpudlian (and everyone in Liverpool has the greatest respect for himself) would ever use a phrase like "Mersey Beat" because he knows there is no such thing. The Mersey Beat is simply a description of a beat which happened by accident in Liverpool.

Brian Epstein pointed out this in his book "Cellarful of Noise."

### At The Top

"Music Business," a very good trade publication, has "Mrs. Brown, You've Got A Lovely Daughter" at the top of the charts. Inevitable. This may be the biggest seller of the year — always, as I keep saying, excepting the Beatles.

Herman's Hermits were allegedly seen at the Teenage Fair last weekend, along with the ghosts of Ringo Starr, Mick Jagger, Billy J. Kramer, Freddie of the Dreamers, Donovan, and others too illusory to mention.

In fact, none of these people made the Teenage Fair because they were a few thousand miles away. This is a familiar story — while the Beatles were on tour over here, they were rumored to be seen in Houston, Little Rock, Hartford, and Denver all at the same time.

### Start A Rumor

A roumor is a fascinating thing. You can start one at 2 p.m. in Los Angeles and have it broadcast as far as three thousand miles away an hour later. If you have a spare moment, try it.

I am not sure that I like the new Roger Miller record as much as the last one. His voice is still enriched by his sense of humor, but I don't think the appeal of "King of the Road" has been matched this time.

Roger must be delighted — deservedly so — by his 100% success in the country and western section of the awards granted by the National Association of Recording Arts and Sciences (The "Grammy" Awards).

### Shindig Quality

The Rolling Stones will be seen on "Shindig" soon. Excellent. The group is well up to the standard demanded by jolly Jack Good and his team.

"Shindig" maintains a tremendous pace and quality. And I think "Hullabaloo" is vastly improved.

The producers have found a very nice balance between newcomers to show-business and established artists.

Sammy Davis, Jr., for instance worked wonderfully well with the Animals on last week's show. Mr. Davis' presence on the show guarantees that older people will tune in. And the show, of course, already has an assured audience of young adults.

### Tour Set

The Beau Brummels go out on tour shortly with the Righteous Brothers — the first time the Brummels have made major personal appearances outside the western states. They will travel to Ohio, Tennessee, Kentucky, and to Canada. As forecast, and rightly so, "Just A Little" succeeds "Laugh Laugh" as a major chart leader.

The Brummels' album is also moving very well.

Forgive me, for a moment, if I boast. But "Cast Your Fate to the Wind" by the British Sounds Orchestral is now on the threshold of the Top 20. I forecast this success a month ago.

As I said then, the chief strength of the record lies in the use of the piano. The piano contributed substantially to the success of "Downtown" and to Petula Clark's latest, "I Know A Place."

Watch, therefore, for increasing use of the piano until everyone becomes so sick of it that another instrument will take its place.

Aren't you glad to see eight pages in the BEAT?

# KRLA BEAT

**FREE TRIPS TO LONDON!**
(See Page 4)

May 12, 1965 — Los Angeles, California — Ten Cents

**BEAT SUBSCRIPTIONS AVAILABLE!**
(See Page 5)

# HERE COME THE BEATLES!

## Contract Signed -- Preparations Underway

**PLANNING THE CONCERT** — Promoter Bob Eubanks discusses 1965 Beatle tour with KRLA's Dave Hull and Derek Taylor. With the famed Hollywood Bowl as a backdrop, the three music and public relations experts talk over the unending details required to present THE BEATLES effectively and still provide for everyone's safety and enjoyment. This year's show will feature performances on both August 29th and the 30th.

### Fans Eager
## Liverpool 4 Here In August

Now it's official! The Beatles will return to Southern California this summer for two concerts at Hollywood Bowl —Aug. 29 and 30. They will be presented by the same sponsors who brought them here last year — KRLA and Bob Eubanks. Ticket applications will be taken by mail only this year. You'll find the information, including a ticket application coupon, on page 7 of this week's KRLA Beat.

Their performances here will climax a North American tour that will take the Beatles from New York to Mexico City.

Bob Eubanks began negotiating with the Beatles for this year's performances immediately after their concert at Hollywood Bowl last year. But so did dozens of other people, including a number of other radio stations who offered them almost unbelievable sums of money for the privilege of sponsoring their Hollywood Bowl concerts.

However, the Beatles were so impressed by KRLA's reputation as the Beatle station in America and by Eubanks' handling of their 1964 performance that they rejected all other offers.

Last year at this time — before he joined KRLA — Derek Taylor was working with the Beatles as their press officer. Below you'll find his interesting account of their first visit to Southern California, which John, Paul, George

—MORE ON PAGE TWO

## ENTRY INTO STATES IS SERIOUS PROBLEM FOR BRITISH ACTS

Organized protests are under way, trying to force the U.S. Immigration Department to allow more British recording stars to make personal appearances in this country.

At present the U.S. allows only a few "alien" performers to obtain work permits to perform over here.

The restrictions are particularly frustrating right now, since British artists are completely dominating pop music in America. Recently only two American artists were on the top 10 and the rest were English.

Many critics say the problem was caused by our government "passing the buck" and delegating its powers to the various entertainers unions to judge the performers' merits for work permits here.

### Dislike Pop
The unions, often unfamiliar with recent pop music trends and openly showing a strong dislike for this type music, are rejecting many performers on grounds that they are not good enough or not well known.

The situation has gotten so bad that some American TV producers are threatening to tape their shows in England.

And to make matters worse, KRLA Beat sources in London say the British are threatening to retaliate by clamping down on American artists who try to perform in England.

Many in the business feel the present turmoil and hardships could be avoided if the U.S. Immigration Department w o u l d bring in one person with some background and knowledge of the music business to handle the work permit applications.

## Derek Taylor Reports

So we have the Beatles. It is all over. We have them for KRLA. Bob Eubanks has done it again — against fierce, frightening opposition. I'm naturally delighted and although I knew that Brian Epstein strongly favoured Bob and KRLA as promoters, I couldn't say so for certain until all the signatures were inked. Elsewhere in this issue I've attempted to capture the details of our stay here last year when the Hollywood Bowl erupted in Beatlemania. It has one advantage over all the other various versions of those four frantic days. It's true!

"Go Now," a wonderful disc and a smash in England and over here for the Moody Blues, has not been followed up as well as expected. Their other disc is crawling feebly up the charts in the UK. Maybe it will do better here.

There is, of course, no guarantee that one smash will be followed by another. I can't see the Righteous Bros. making No. 1 with their latest.

Personally — and regretfully— I find it rather dull and shapeless. I think the able Mr. Spector has over produced it. A pity because

—MORE ON PAGE 8

### TOP TEN
1. WOOLY BULLY
2. GLORIA — BABY PLEASE DON'T CRY
3. MRS. BROWN
4. WHEN I'M GONE
5. TICKET TO RIDE/YES IT IS
6. JUST ONCE IN MY LIFE
7. OOH BABY BABY
8. THE LAST TIME — PLAY WITH FIRE
9. GAME OF LOVE
10. NOWHERE TO RUN

—TUNDEX ON PAGE 4

The latest listenership ratings are out of sight!

Both Pulse, Inc., and C. E. Hooper show that KRLA has increased its first place rating and is now even farther out front than before — the most popular major radio station in the United States!

The new Pulse report shows that KRLA has more than twice as many listeners as any other radio station in Los Angeles or Orange counties.

This includes all age groups with KRLA leading in both adult and teenage listeners.

All of us at KRLA are deeply gratified by your support. We will continue to do our best to merit it.

# KRLA ARCHIVES

# The First American Beatle Trip

**FROM PAGE ONE**
and Ringo regarded as the highlight of their tour.

**by Derek Taylor**

The Beatles and I have lost count of the rumors, mis-statements and guesses about our stay in Hollywood when they appeared at the Bowl last year.

In fact, we had a very peaceful working vacation. We arrived here in the small hours of the morning at Los Angeles International Airport. We were met notably by Dave Hull — plus Bob Eubanks — who, with KRLA, was promoting the show. We had come many hundreds of miles throught the night on our Electra turbo-jet after an open air concert in Vancouver, British Columbia. Though we were tired, we were sufficiently excited by the prospect of seeing Hollywood properly that we kept alert. And when we arrived at the house in Bel-Air, John and I went for a dawn swim in the pool.

The house in Bel-Air was no disappointment. It was as large and luxurious as any house we ever saw in the movies. With two-level rooms, gigantic beds, mirrors covering whole walls.

**Finally Sleep!**

After our swim, John and I joined the other Beatles and our touring managers for breakfast. Then we went to bed for a few hours sleep.

The Beatles were up early — early, that is, for them — at about 1 p.m. and we all spent the afternoon by the pool.

In the evening we drove to Bob Eubanks' Cinnamon Cinder in North Hollywood for a wild, unruly news conference attended by hundreds of teenagers and adults — who seemed almost as excited as the younger Beatlemaniacs.

The news conference lasted an hour. The Beatles then shot off for the Hollywood Bowl in their limousine. I stayed behind to comfort a mother and daughter, both of whom were in tears because they had come from Pheonix by bus to present a plaque to Ringo. But because of the crush they hadn't been able to get near him.

The story of the actual concert is legend. As soon as the last echoing notes of "Long Tall Sally" had died in the hills above the Bowl, The Beatles were driven off by Jim Steck, KRLA newsman.

**Unusual Night**

There were many human interest stories in the Bowl that night. One man had his leg broken by a run-away car tire. An emotional girl threw herself into the Bowl fountain after the concert.

The press and TV cameramen were having a hard time moving among the audience, for police officers had strict instructions to prevent movement and keep order at all costs.

I experienced the greatest difficulty getting in the Bowl at all. I had to empty my pockets to produce four or five forms of identification. My English accent — normally a guarantee of access to any hall where the Beatles were appearing — wasn't enough because the police thought it was phony. Finally, I got in by producing two sets of Beatle autographs.

Back at the house, we spent a quiet hour or so talking and reminiscing. Paul played the piano.

I suppose most people would call it a dull evening, but anyway it was nice to relax.

**More Reporters**

The following day we spent more hours at the pool and photographs were taken which eventually found their way into publications all over the world. Col. Tom Parker, manager of Elvis Presley, arrived to take Brian Epstein to lunch. The Beatles and I lunched with their road managers Neil Aspinall and Mal Evans.

Col. Parker and Brian returned in good spirits after a nice lunch. They had discussed the problems and delights of managing the hottest show-business acts in the world, and Col. Parker's aides presented us all with gunbelts, magnificent toy pistols, and models of old pioneer covered wagons.

The Beatles then went off to wash, shave and dress themselves in their best suits for the charity garden party held nearby at the home of the mother-in-law of Mr. Alan Livingston, president of Capitol Records.

This was the most glamorous affair — guests paid $25 a head to be there and the profits went to the Hemophilia Foundation. Hundreds of young people were meekly lined up to meet The Beatles, who sat on high stools in a reception area.

Again I had difficulty getting into the grounds. This time Brian Epstein was with me, and we both found the way barred by stone-faced guards.

"I'm Brian Epstein," said Brian gently. And the guard laughed and said, "I'm Errol Flynn." We finally got in because our credentials were vouched by a man called Hal York, who was organizing arrangements inside the gate. This was odd since Hal York had no credentials whatsoever and was, in fact, a notorious —though amiable—gate crasher.

**Stars Attend**

There were many famous faces at the garden party: Edward G. Robinson and his granddaughter, Mrs. Dean Martin and her beautiful children. Jack Palance was there, along with Lloyd Bridges, Shelly Winters, Eva Marie Saint, Hedda Hopper and her hat; Gary Lewis — this was long before The Playboys — and many others.

It was a wonderful day and everyone was thrilled with The Beatles and their impeccable couduct. They were on their best behaviour that day. They looked well and they had a great time.

There was, of course, no work that night so we had a party at the house. Bobby Darin and Sandra Dee came. So did Paul and Paula and many other of the Hollywood younger set. The party lasted 'til dawn.

At 10 a.m., I was awakened by John Lennon who decided he wanted to go out shopping. So with a cameraman friend of ours, Ron Joy, John, Neil Aspinall and I drove down to Beau Gentry where we all bought light-weight jackets. John picked up a couple of cowboy shirts and arrangements were made for Beau Gentry to send other samples to the house.

The other three Beatles were up by the time we returned and we spent the remainder of the day by the pool.

In the meantime, Jayne Mansfield had expressed a desire to meet The Beatles, and they thought it would be interesting to meet her. So I was asked to telephone her. Miss Mansfield was playing at a nearby theatre and she said she would love to meet The Beatles. I said The Beatles would prefer not to have a cameraman present because it would look like a publicity stunt. They simply wanted Miss Mansfield and her escort to be their guests for cocktails by the pool. Miss Mansfield thought a photographer would enhance the occasion and a compromise was reached when it was decided we would all meet at the Whisky-a-Go-Go at midnight.

The Whisky-a-Go-Go was asked to provide privacy and security, but, alas, we achieved neither. And when John, George and Ringo met with the glamorous star, there was mass pandemonium, noise and panic, and the meeting ended in complete disorder.

**Confused Facts**

The story of this has been accurately described in many magazines — with the untrue embellishment that George Harrison threw a beverage over a photographer. What happened was that George tossed a couple of ice cubes in the direction of the camera. I don't blame him.

Earlier that evening, Paul and I had gone to Burt Lancaster's magniifcent home at his invitation for a private viewing of "A Shot in the Dark." This was a wonderfully relaxed evening and Paul wisely decided not to go to the Whisky-a-Go-Go.

The following morning, tired but sunburned and pretty fit, we left Los Angeles for the next stage of the tour — for Denver, Colorado.

Though we didn't spot them then, Dave Hull and Jim Steck astutely stowed away on our plane and revealed themselves in Denver. Smart work in the best tradition of news gathering.

Thus, Hollywood 1964. No one can guess what it will be like this year.

But I anticipate that the highways, byways, fields, hedges, and hills for miles around will again be swarming with Beatle-hunting youngsters.

---

**DICK CLARK**
**CARAVAN of STARS**
STARRING
**DICK CLARK**
MONDAY, MAY 17
TWO PERFORMANCES
5 & 9 P.M.
ONE NITE ONLY!
FEATURING 15 OF THE
NATION'S TOP RECORDING ACTS!
DEL SHANNON
The ZOMBIES
The SHANGRI-LAS
JEWEL AKEN
The LARKS
TOMMY ROE
DEE DEE SHARP
MEL CARTER
The AD LIBS
The VELVELETTES
JIMMY SOUL
MIKE CLIFFORD
The IKETTES
The EXECUTIVES
DON WAYNE
PRICES . . $2.50, $3.50, $4.50
TICKETS AT BOX-OFFICE, BY MAIL
AND ALL SOUTHLAND AGENCIES

FOR INFORMATION CALL
ANAHEIM (714) 776-7220

---

**FUTURE D.J.'S**
Join the Ranks of
**DON MARTIN GRADS**
YOU WILL FIND THEM ON
EVERY MAJOR STATION
IN
LOS ANGELES
"A Career In A Year"
— Jobs Assured —
**DON MARTIN**
**SCHOOL OF RADIO**
**& TV**
Call or Write for Information
1653 N. CHEROKEE AVE.
HOLLYWOOD

---

**23 SKIDOO**
Dancing to Live Name Bands
2116 Westwood Blvd., West Los Angeles
Girls 18, Guys 21
23 Skidoo Dancers are now seen on TV's
Hollywood A'GoGo Saturday on Channel 9 at 9:00 p.m.
**Closed Mondays**

# KRLA ARCHIVES

## Son of Comedian Becomes Musician And Sells Millions

A few weeks ago Gary Lewis had a problem — what to do for an encore to his hit record, "This Diamond Ring."

The answer was simple — record another hit.

And young Lewis, the talented son of Jerry Lewis, did just that. He and his group, the Playboys, now have another nationwide smash, "Count Me In."

A college student until recently, Gary now finds himself and his quintet among the nation's top recording stars.

"This Diamond Ring" was Gary's first disk, and it sold a million copies to become the nation's number one song almost overnight.

In the highly competitive recording business, it is rare that a singer's first record becomes number one. Even rarer is to follow with a second hit. "Count Me In" could well become as big a record as his first one.

**Disneyland Debut**

Gary started playing the drum and singing with his group at private parties. Last summer the boys auditioned for Disneyland and were hired for six weeks. It was sometime later — when Jerry Lewis visited his son during a session at Disneyland — before officials there discovered he was the young singer's father.

It was then that Gary's mother encouraged the boys to make a recording. She paid for the recording sessions, a cost of approximately $1,000. Executives at Liberty Records agreed to distribute "This Diamond Ring," but with little hope that it could become a hit.

Gary Lewis and the Playboys got their biggest boost last December when they appeared on the Ed Sullivan Show. "This Diamond Ring" was already climbing on the KRLA Tunedex, but with the Sullivan exposure it became a nationwide hit.

After the Sullivan show Gary intended to return to his studies at Los Angeles State College. However, personal appearance offers began coming in so fast that he asked his parents' permission to withdraw from college. He plans to return later. Gary also studied at the famed Pasadena Playhouse.

**Aspiring Comedian**

Gary, who learned the meaning of show business perfection from his father, looks forward to something more than a couple of quick record hits.

Speaking of his future, he told the KRLA Beat:

"I'd like to go into movies as a comedian. I've got a great teacher. I hope that being a comedian runs in the family."

Gary's parents are pleased that their first son (they have five boys) has become a success in the record business.

"Nothing makes me happier than pleasing mom and dad," says Gary. "They did it all for us. They bought us instruments and let us rehearse. The money has

---

**THE PYRAMIDS**
Stars of
"BIKINI BEACH PARTY"
Hit Record: Penetration
Available For Bookings
Call: (213) 591-3046

---

all been paid back and it's good to be making some money on our own."

The "us" in this case refers to the other members of his quintet. They are Dave Costell, Dave Walker, Al Ramsay and John West — all from Pasadena.

There is another aspect to Gary's success. It is not often that the son or daughter of a Hollywood star is such an instant success in the recording field.

**Boost From Dad**

Gary's father claims that he would not have helped him get on Sullivan's show if Gary didn't have the talent necessary for such important television exposure.

Jerry has described Gary's comedy as "better funny" than his own talent was at 19 years of age.

Gary is the third generation of the Lewis family to enter show business. Jerry's father was a performer. And Patti Lewis was once a singer.

Gary will probably be compared to his famous dad as he progresses in his career, especially when he appears in comedy routines.

But Jerry says, "He sure won't be a second Jerry. He's a first Gary. Here's a case where the name won't hurt or hinder. He has a wonderful, eager, giving-of-himself kind of humor. He's funny and has infinite timing."

No one could ask for higher praise.

---

UCLA Committee on Fine Arts Productions
presents

**3rd ANNUAL UCLA**

**FOLK FESTIVAL**

May 14-16, Royce Hall, UCLA

with

| | | |
|---|---|---|
| Jimmy Driftwood | Sam Hinton | Ruth Rubin |
| Dave Fredrickson | Dr. Howard Hopkins | Bookmiller Shannon |
| Ollie Gilbert | Son House | Vern and Ray |
| Bess Hawes | Glenn Ohrlin | Hedy West |

All Evening Concerts at 8:30 p.m. (Plus Song Swap 11:15 p.m., May 15)
SPECIAL AFTERNOON CONCERTS: Children's Concert, Saturday 2:45 – Religious Folk Music, Sunday 2:30.
Workshops and lecture-demonstrations, Saturday & Sunday from 9:30 a.m.–6:00 p.m. Admission: $1.00 each.
Series tickets (including workshops) $11., 9., 8., 6.50. Prices for all concerts from $2. to $4. (children $1. & $1.50). Call GR 8-7578 for info. Tickets at UCLA and ALL MUTUAL AGENCIES.

---

## At Deadline

The Dave Clark Five were presented with a gold record award in London for their best-selling LP "Glad All Over." The presentation took place at the Oasis Swimming Pool in Holborn, London, where the new D.C. picture, "Having A Wild Weekend," was being filmed. They will return to the U.S. in June for their third American tour. On July 10 they will appear in San Diego, and in Anaheim on the 12th. Gerry and the Pacemakers, now on the East Coast beginning their third American tour, have completed their first recording session in the U.S. They recorded two sides, one especially for British release and the second designed for their American fans.

And here's good news for all their fan club members. They also recorded a special seven-inch disc for fan club members only. It features informal conversations by Gerry and other members of the group.

Peter and Gordon set aside their guitars temporarily and produced a record for another performer. The song, "Always At A Distance," featues guitarist-vocalist Eddie Young, who has been working with them as an accompanist.

Jan and Dean picked up a rich assignment, recording five Coca-Cola commercials.

Look for a flock of "Letkiss" albums to follow the newest (and happiest) dance craze. At least five record companies are quickly turning out albums on it.

Jerry Lee Lewis, rocking like the days of old, has signed for a fourth appearance on Shindig and they're dickering on a fifth. Before the filming dates June 15-17 Lewis will fill a series of one-nite engagements in California, starting June 7.

After losing his spot on "Hullabaloo" Brian Epstein is co-hosting a new BBC series, "Ten Years of Pop" (1955-1965), in England. The show is scheduled for three dates.

Bobby Vinton did a dramatic part on a recent Alfred Hitchcock production.

Gerry Marsden has a new Volvo which he has driven 115 miles per hour on the Motorway (near Liverpool) but says he doesn't do any drag racing on the highway. Also, he has a new 14-foot Viking speed boat, is interested in horses and skin dives as deep as 40 or 50 feet. Wonder what Gerry does for kicks?

Johnny Rivers will be singing weekly on TV. He's been signed to sing the title song in the new CBS-TV series, "Secret Agent."

The Standells have just opened at the Tiger A Go-Go Room in San Francisco. Their new single, "Big Boss Man," looks like it's going to be a big hit.

Gary Lewis isn't the only new recording star with a famous father. Two sons of famous show business performers from England have jumped into the recording act. Noel Harrison, son of actor Rex Harrison, made his television debut on "Hullabaloo" recently with his recording of the folk song, "Barbara Allen." Michael Chaplin, son of comedian Charlie Chaplin, has released a record called "I Am What I Am." It was produced by Larry Page, who also produces the Kinks' disks.

---

**OFFICIAL ENTRY BLANK**
FOR REVLON'S BIG 'SWINGSTAKES'
'NATURAL WONDER'

**WIN**
A FREE WEEKEND
(FOR 2) IN LONDON
WITH THE
**DAVE CLARK FIVE**

**9,225 OTHER BIG PRIZES!**
GE PORTABLE TV SETS!
RCA STEREO RECORD PLAYERS!
GE TRANSISTOR RADIOS!
SCHICK ELECTRIC HAIRDRYERS!

EASY! Just follow the simple directions on the back of this entry. Complete and mail it right now to your local radio station (listed on the back). Enter as often as you like!

NAME _____

ADDRESS _____

PHONE NUMBER _____

NAME OF YOUR SCHOOL _____

STORE WHERE YOU OBTAINED THIS ENTRY BLANK: _____

BONUS PRIZE: You will win a free Dave Clark Five record album if your local "SWINGSTAKES" disc jockey phones you! If he does, may he use the recorded conversation on the air? YES ☐ NO ☐

(your signature)

# KRLA ARCHIVES

## KRLA TUNEDEX

| THIS WEEK | LAST WEEK | TITLE | ARTIST |
|---|---|---|---|
| 1. | 1. | WOOLY BULLY | Sam The Sham & The Pharoahs |
| 2. | 2. | GLORIA/BABY PLEASE DON'T GO | Them |
| 3. | 4. | MRS. BROWN/I GOTTA DREAM ON | Herman's Hermits |
| 4. | 3. | WHEN I'M GONE | Brenda Holloway |
| 5. | 9. | TICKET TO RIDE/YES IT IS | The Beatles |
| 6. | 6. | JUST ONCE IN MY LIFE | The Righteous Brothers |
| 7. | 13. | OOH BABY BABY | The Miracles |
| 8. | 8. | THE LAST TIME/PLAY WITH FIRE | Rolling Stones |
| 9. | 5. | GAME OF LOVE | Wayne Fontana & The Mindbenders |
| 10. | 11. | NOWHERE TO RUN | Martha & The Vandellas |
| 11. | 12. | SILHOUETTES | Herman's Hermits |
| 12. | 20. | SHE'S ABOUT A MOVER | Sir Douglas Quintet |
| 13. | 10. | IT'S NOT UNUSUAL | Tom Jones |
| 14. | 22. | JUST YOU | Sonny & Cher |
| 15. | 26. | CONCRETE AND CLAY | Unit Four Plus Two |
| 16. | 17. | I KNOW A PLACE | Petula Clark |
| 17. | 25. | BACK IN MY ARMS AGAIN | The Supremes |
| 18. | 7. | TIRED OF WAITING FOR YOU | The Kinks |
| 19. | 16. | COUNT ME IN | Gary Lewis & The Playboys |
| 20. | 43. | HELP ME RHONDA | The Beach Boys |
| 21. | 18. | I'LL NEVER FIND ANOTHER YOU | The Seekers |
| 22. | 21. | I DO LOVE YOU | Billy Stewart |
| 23. | 28. | BABY THE RAIN MUST FALL | Glen Yarbrough |
| 24. | 14. | JUST A LITTLE | The Beau Brummels |
| 25. | 23. | I'LL BE DOGGONE | Marvin Gaye |
| 26. | 24. | NOT TOO LONG AGO | The Uniques |
| 27. | 34. | CATCH THE WIND | Donovan |
| 28. | 33. | IT'S GONNA BE ALRIGHT | Gerry & The Pacemakers |
| 29. | 37. | SWING ME | Nino Tempo & April Stevens |
| 30. | 35. | SHAKIN' ALL OVER | Guess Who? |

### CLIMBERS

| | | | |
|---|---|---|---|
| 1. | 55. | YOU TURN ME ON | Ian Whitcomb |
| 2. | 46. | MR. TAMBOURINE MAN | The Byrds |
| 3. | 39. | WOMAN'S GOT SOUL | The Impressions |
| 4. | 42. | TRUE LOVE WAYS | Peter & Gordon |
| 5. | 40. | NOTHING CAN STOP ME | Gene Chandler |
| 6. | 41. | DO THE FREDDIE | Freddie & The Dreamers |
| 7. | 54. | QUEEN OF THE HOUSE | Jody Miller |
| 8. | 51. | GOOD LOVIN' | The Olympics |
| 9. | 47. | FOR YOUR LOVE | The Yardbirds |
| 10. | 49. | ENGINE ENGINE NO. 9 | Roger Miller |

**DAVE HULL AND DARLENE LARRIE** entertain Bessie the Cow, as last minute touches are given to the 1965 Great Western Fair and Dairy Show. With apologies to the discotheque houses, DARLENE will call hers "dis-COW-theque." DAVE is holding record player — proving once again that he forgot that May is National Radio Month! Show, at Great Western Exhibit Center, is held May 27th thru the 31st.

## English Top Ten

The Beatles' "Ticket to Ride" zoomed to the top the week after it was released in England.

Cliff Richards' "The Minute You're Gone" climbed upward a notch to the second spot and would have been tops except for the Beatles.

The only new entry on the Top-Ten is a red-hot one by the Animals, "Bring It On Home to Me," which climbed all the way up from 27th place.

| | | |
|---|---|---|
| 1. | TICKET TO RIDE | The Beatles |
| 2. | THE MINUTE YOU'RE GONE | Cliff Richard |
| 3. | HERE COMES THE NIGHT | Them |
| 4. | FOR YOUR LOVE | The Yardbirds |
| 5. | CONCRETE AND CLAY | Unit 4 + 2 |
| 6. | CATCH THE WIND | Donovan |
| 7. | THE LAST TIME | The Rolling Stones |
| 8. | STOP! IN THE NAME OF LOVE | The Supremes |
| 9. | BRING IT ON HOME TO ME | The Animals |
| 10. | THE TIMES THEY ARE A-CHANGIN' | Bob Dylan |

## You Could Win!

The thrill of a lifetime may be awaiting two people who read this.

Thirty-eight lucky girls from KRLAnd have already won Dave Clark Five record albums, "Weekend In London," and are finalists in the drawing for a real weekend — a free weekend for two in London as guests of the Dave Clark Five.

There are 9,225 other big prizes, including G-E portable TV sets, RCA stereo record players, G-E transistor radios and Schick electric hairdryers.

It's all part of Revlon's "Natural Wonder" Weekend in London contest on KRLA. The following first round winners have been selected so far:

**Album Winners**

Karolyn Williams, Los Angeles; Carol Ann Maxwell, El Monte; Johnny Sedwick, La Habra; Christine Bowers, Burbank; Rossie Birnbaum, Los Angeles; Sharise Milne, Santa Monica; Kathy Francis, Pacific Palisades; Leigh Kruckman, North Hollywood; Janice Ferguson, Pasadena; Trina Josephson, Fontana; Nancy Anton, North Hollywood; Mady Ridley, Van Nuys; Debra Smith, West Covina and Susan Rosen, Gardena.

More winners are Janet Gellman, Granada Hills; Brenda Rodgers, Van Nuys; Janice Green, Bakersfield; Veronica Arnett, Monterey Park; Cheryl Weadon, Whittier; Tobi Bronstein, Sherman Oaks; Cathye Burton, Encino; Sherry Donaldson, Los Angeles; Kathy Hession, San Marino; Illi Raid, Los Angeles, and Sally Weiland, Encino.

Completing the list of winners are Deborah Casey, Glendora; Sandra Gilbert, Los Angeles; Patty Miller, Pomona; Mathy Hession, San Marino; Barbara Moss, Northridge; Elizabeth Field, Glendale; Stephanie Thompson, Cypress; Candy Cummings, La Canada; Marion Folson, Coalinga; Pam Oliphant, Costa Mesa; Linda Jamroz, West Covina; Carla King, Pacific Palisades; Joan L. Cox, Los Angeles; and Sylvia Haimoff, Beverly Hills.

The contest is still open, so hurry and get your entry in before the deadline.

All you need do to enter is pick up an entry blank at any store where Revlon cosmetics are sold, or from KRLA. Then tear off the words "Natural Wonder" from any "Natural Wonder" package (or hand print the words "Natural Wonder" in block letters on a 3x5 inch piece of paper), fill in the entry blank and mail them to KRLA, 1401 S. Oak Knoll, Pasadena, 91106.

Enter as often as you wish, but each entry must be mailed separately.

Hurry — all entries must be postmarked by May 15.

## WIN

A FREE WEEKEND IN LONDON! FOR 2 WITH THE

### "DAVE CLARK FIVE"

ENTER REVLON'S

### 'NATURAL WONDER'

### 'Swingstakes'

Get your entry blank today! It's yours FREE at any fine drug or department store where you see Revlon's big 'Natural Wonder' display!

### 9,225 OTHER BIG PRIZES!

GE Portable TV Sets!
RCA Stereo Record Players!
GE Transistor Radios!
Schick Electric Hairdryers!
Special 'Dave Clark Five' Albums!

### KEEP TUNED TO KRLA 1110

---

Here's all you do to enter: 1. Tear off the words 'Natural Wonder' from any 'Natural Wonder' package (or hand print the words 'Natural Wonder' in block letters on a 3" by 5" piece of paper), fill in this entry blank, and mail them to the radio station nearest to you.

| | | |
|---|---|---|
| WHLO — Akron, Ohio | KLIF — Dallas, Texas | WKY — Oklahoma City, Okla. |
| WPTR — Albany, N.Y. | KFJZ — Ft. Worth, Texas | WIBG — Philadelphia, Pa. |
| WAEB — Allentown, Pa. | WSBA — Harrisburg, Pa. | KRIZ — Phoenix, Ariz. |
| WQXI — Atlanta, Ga. | WDRC — Hartford, Conn. | KQV — Pittsburgh, Pa. |
| WCAO — Baltimore, Md. | KILT — Houston, Texas | KISN — Portland, Ore. |
| WSGN — Birmingham, Ala. | WIFE — Indianapolis, Ind. | WICE — Providence, R.I. |
| WMEX — Boston, Mass. | WHB — Kansas City, Mo. | WBBF — Rochester, N.Y. |
| WKBW — Buffalo, N.Y. | KFWB — Los Angeles, Cal. | KROY — Sacramento, Cal. |
| WIST — Charlotte, N.C. | KRLA — Los Angeles, Cal. | KTSA — San Antonio, Texas |
| WLS — Chicago, Ill. | WAKY — Louisville, Ky. | KGB — San Diego, Cal. |
| WSAI — Cincinnati, Ohio | WMPS — Memphis, Tenn. | KYA — San Francisco, Cal. |
| WHK — Cleveland, Ohio | WDGY — Minneapolis, Minn. | WARM — Scranton, Pa. |
| WCOL — Columbus, Ohio | WTIX — New Orleans, La. | KJR — Seattle, Wash. |
| WING — Dayton, Ohio | WABC — New York, N.Y. | KXOK — St. Louis, Mo. |
| KIMN — Denver, Colo. | WINS — New York, N.Y. | WOLF — Syracuse, N.Y. |
| WKNR — Detroit, Mich. | WMCA — New York, N.Y. | WEAM — Washington, D.C. |
| WXYZ — Detroit, Mich. | WGH — Norfolk, Va. | WPGC — Washington, D.C. |

If you live in an area not serviced by any of the above radio stations, mail your entry to: "SWINGSTAKES", BOX 548, NEW YORK, N.Y. 10046. (Do not mail your entry to Revlon.)

2. Enter as often as you wish, but each entry must be mailed separately. Entries must be postmarked by May 15, 1965 and received by June 1, 1965.

3. Winners of record albums will be selected from entries received by participating radio stations. All entries will be forwarded to the D. L. Blair Corporation, an independent judging organization, who will select the Grand Prize winner and all other major prize winners. No substitutions will be made for any prize offered.

4. "SWINGSTAKES" is open to any girl 13 years of age and over in the United States except employees and their families of Revlon, Inc., its advertising agencies, participating radio stations and their respective "SWINGSTAKES" agents. The Grand Prize winner, if under 21, must be accompanied by a guardian. The Grand Prize flight and weekend will be during the Summer of 1965 and the winner will be notified as far in advance as possible, as to the arrangements.

5. Offer void for residents of Florida and Wisconsin, and where prohibited or restricted by law, and is subject to all Federal, State and local regulations. Residents of Missouri just mail filled-in entry blank and disregard other provisions of Rule #1. Winners will be notified by mail, as soon as possible after June 1, 1965. Taxes on prizes, if any, are the responsibility of the winners.

# KRLA ARCHIVES

## On The Beat

Democrats and Republicans beware: According to "Teen Screen" there is a new political party on the U. S. scene — the American Teenage Party! It's headed by President Ringo Starr, Vice-President Paul McCartney, Sec. of State John Lennon, Sec. of the Treasury George Harrison, and Sec. of Health, Education, and Welfare Dave Hull!

### Likes This One

P. J. Proby is going to begin filming a movie this summer in Britain. Proby reveals that he has had movie offers but has turned them all down because they were not suitable. He has finally found two that are to his liking and he states, "people will be surprised by my first film because it won't be the Proby they know." And just what does that mean?

The Yardbirds have been waiting quite awhile for a hit, and it looks like they finally made it with "For Your Love" which has already topped the British charts. The song was written by two Manchester boys and features an instrument seldom used on pop records — the harpsichord. There are five Yardbirds, one with relatively short hair and another who looks a bit like Brian Jones.

QUICK ONES: When asked his phone number by a fellow Britisher, Mick Jagger replied: "It's off the hook" . . . Pint-sized Rita Pavone has more energy than any five other girls in the business . . . Joey Paige reports probably the only two consistent sell-outs in England (excluding the Beatles) are the Rolling Stones and Herman's Hermits . . . Finally saw a picture of the Rats, yet another English group, and they don't look a bit like their furry namesakes . . . . The Everly Brothers are currently touring Europe, and will hit Germany, Italy, Sweden, France, Holland, and England before returning stateside on May 13 . . . If everything goes as planned, the Righteous Brothers will play Carnegie Hall later this year . . . Petula Clark is coming to L.A. in the near future for a screen test and recording session . . . Sylvia Varton recently married Johnny Hallyday, one of the most popular singers in France.

### New Take-Off

The Detergents, who specialize in take-offs such as "Leader of the Laundromat," have come up

with yet another, "Mrs. Jones ('Ow About It)." Quite obviously, it is a take-off on Herman's "Mrs. Brown." It might go, but with a novelty record it's hard to tell. If they happen to catch the public's fancy, they're a huge success, but if not they're the biggest kind of bomb.

ON THE BEAT has flipped for Roger Miller's new one, "Engine Engine No. Nine." This man is absolutely fantastic; he received FIVE Grammy Awards while such artists as the Beatles received only two!

A note to you who are under the impression the Byrds are English: they are not, they're very much American. They have a fabulous record out, "Mr. Tambourine Man," which is a good-sounding, nicely produced record.

### Town Without Pitney

Gene Pitney is a very busy man these days. He has just embarked on a 40-day tour which will hit some twenty-three states. At the end of the tour, in early June, Gene will make a movie. And sandwiched in there somewhere are scheduled appearances on "Hullabaloo" and the "Jimmy Dean Show." A special honor for Gene: he was voted the number ONE male singer by "Disc Weekly" a British magazine. The number two man was Roy Orbison. ON THE BEAT congratulates both Gene and Roy!

WATCH OUT FOR: Some very good new records — "Stop, Look, and Listen" by Wayne Fontana and the Mindbenders; "Here Comes The Night" by Them; and "Now That You've Gone" by Connie Stevens.

Freddie and the Dreamers have started an independent production company, Dreamers Records. Their debut number will be "How Can I Hide From My

Heart" by a seventeen year old discovery of Freddie's, Maxine Darren. Predictions are that Freddie's new one, "You Were Made For Me" will out-sell ALL his others!

PUZZLE OF THE WEEK: Why the shortage of air play for Cilla Black's records? Cilla's last single was "Is It Love," but unless you diligently search through every single 45 in your record store, you will probably not even know it was released! Cilla has tremendous talent; the people of England recognized it and made her a star. What's taking America so long to catch on? Cilla introduced a new song on "Shindig," a different sound which really grows on you. It's entitled "I've Been Wrong Before."

Previous publicity about Tom Jones indicated he was 22 years old and single. Then his record caught on, he had a hit, and the secret was out — Tom Jones was neither twenty-two nor single. The fact of the matter was, he was not near twenty-two, he was very much married and also the father of a seven year old son!

THE TIME IS PAST when marriage must be "hushed-up." Some of today's most popular performers are married; the most obvious examples being John Lennon and Ringo Starr. Or how about Gregory Peck and Rex Harrison, who did not lose fans because of their honesty. Whenever something like this Tom Jones' thing comes up, it leaves the record-buying public with a persistent lingering doubt if other performers are trying to pull the same trick. It's a disturbing thought. But perhaps it is all the idea of the publicists who are paid for such things.

—Louise Criscione

## Dave Clark

The Dave Clark Five finished their movie, "Having a Wild Weekend," just in time to receive the most coveted award in the record industry.

They were presented with a certified gold record for over $1,000,000 in sales for their "Glad All Over" album.

Dave was still wearing a rubber skin-diving suit he used for underwater scenes in the movie when the presentation was made at the Oasis swimming pool in London.

The DC-5 also have completed arrangements for their U.S. tour this summer.

After several concerts on the East Coast they will make their fifth appearance on the Ed Sullivan Show. Then their schedule brings them to the West Coast for a series of appearances and two more television shows, "Shindig" and the Dean Martin show.

The Dave Clark Five will appear in San Diego July 10, in Anaheim July 12, in Sacramento July 14 and in San Carlos July 19.

---

Back issues of the KRLA BEAT are still available, for a limited time. If you've missed an issue of particular interest to you, send 10 cents for each copy wanted, along with a self-addressed stamped envelope to:

KRLA BEAT
Suite 504
6290 Sunset Blvd.
Hollywood, California 90028

ISSUES AVAILABLE —
2/25 — BEATLE BALL AT KRLA
3/10 — BEATLES PRAISE L.A.
3/17 — BEATLE MOVIE A BLAST
3/24 — HULL REJECTS FILM OFFER
3/31 — INTERVIEW WITH RINGO STARR
4/7 — INTERVIEW WITH GEORGE HARRISON
4/14 — INTERVIEW WITH JOHN LENNON
4/21 — INTERVIEW WITH PAUL McCARTNEY
4/28 — CHIMP EXCITES TEEN FAIR
5/5 — HERMANIA SPREADS

---

## KRLA BEAT SUBSCRIPTION

Order By Mail Now—Save Over 40%!

Please Rush Me the KRLA BEAT at Your Special Introductory Subscription Rate

☐ 1 Year—52 Issues—$3.00      ☐ 2 Years — $5.00

Enclosed is $_____
Send To:_____ Age_____
Address:_____
City_____ State_____ Zip_____

Please be sure to include your Zip Code number!
MAIL YOUR ORDER TO:
KRLA BEAT
1401 South Oak Knoll Avenue
Pasadena, California 91106

---

## YEAH-YEAH WHISK

### IT'S NEW!

You Have Seen It On National TV!

Now Twisk YOUR Whisk And Add

New Excitement To Your Dancing!

Available At:

**BROADWAY DEPT. STORES**

**WALLICHS MUSIC CITY**

**FEDCO, UNIMART, AND CORNET STORES**

## KRLA ARCHIVES

### Here to Stay
### World of Folk Entertainment

The world of pop music is changing! From the established pounding beat of the Elvis Presley-era, to the hop-skip-and-a-jump rhythm of The Beatles, tastes in music are being drawn back into the folds of the world of folk music.

Folk music, too, has recently seen great changes within its own ranks. There are two basic breeds of folk singers: the purists, and the commercialists. As often must be the case, one style must adopt the attributes of another to reach a certain goal. Such is the case today.

**Honesty**

Some of today's groups may be commercializing the songs, their presentation, et cetera, but they are striving to keep the true basic honesty. (A case in point could well be THE BYRDS.) They have to, for today's young adults know the world of music, and can spot a phony a mile away.

Peter, of Peter, Paul and Mary,

is a little frightened when he thinks of the tremendous drawing power that folk music has. He recognized how easily the youth of America can be mobilized through this type of music.

**It's Your World**

If you have ever been to a true folk concert, you know how gripping the generated excitement can be. If you haven't been able to feel this pull, then you have, so far, missed out on a wonderful experience.

The music style that is now beginning to sweep this nation is a style that is proving to teens everywhere that this is their world, and if that world rears back its head and hits them pretty hard, they still have pride.

How long will it last? Pete Seeger, long time disciple of the true meaning of folk music, sums it up by saying, "We'll have real folk music as long as we have real folks."

An interesting new dance which originated in Finland is taking the U.S. by storm after sweeping Europe.

It's called the Letkiss and it's just as intriguing as it sounds. Soon you'll be hearing and seeing it constantly as the record companies begin releasing a flood of Letkiss albums as well as singles.

A hop and a kiss away from a polka, the Letkiss has already swept across Europe, much to the dismay of many doctors who feel that the kissing aspect may help spread an epidemic of Asian flu.

Originally there was no kissing involved in the Letkiss b u t enterprising teenagers quickly began utilizing the name as a means of legalized kissing on the dance floor. From that point on there was no stopping it.

Reprise has issued the original record which started the European craze, by the Finnish Letkiss All Stars. Along with the record, Reprise is issuing a four-page instruction sheet illustrating the dance and containing step-by-step details.

Letkiss, anyone?

### English Teens Dig California

While American teens fall in love with England, the English are falling in love with America's Southern California. For Pat Rhodes and David Stebbing, the transition from foggy skies to those of sunshine is a pure delight!

Patricia Rhodes, pert, blue-eyed Mod who used to live near Westminster Bridge in London, and David Stebbing, now a hairdresser here in Los Angeles, moved to America on January 30, 1964, right at the crest of Beatle popularity in England.

Recently, these two handsome young adults became well known to Southern California through a series of interviews on Casey Kasem's daily TV program, "SHEBANG." Letters started to pour in, and in no time at all, Pat and David found themselves surrounded by questioning faces.

Pat and David are boyfriend and girlfriend, and met in one of London's many small French coffee bars about two years ago. Pat now works as a secretary, and moved to this area because she wanted to see how the other half lives. In her own words, "... they live!!"

They are both devout fans of The Rolling Stones, but Dave confides in THE BEAT that he's also very keen on Gerry & The Pacemakers, Gerry being a personal friend since childhood.

They are both typically-Mod, but not beatnik-ish. Pat has straight, blonde hair, soft, light skin, pretty eyes and light thin lips. David is soft-spoken, alert, a very good dancer, and can almost always be found wearing the very popular wide-ribbed Corduroy pants.

---

### PEN PALS

**William Wonderly**
6 Wykeham Street
Kirkdale
Liverpool 4, Lancashire
England

**Persons interested in English, Swedish, or Australian Pen Pals:**
LPL Inc.
67, Longton St.
Blackburn
Lancs, England

---

## SUZUKI LIGHTWEIGHTS SWEEP DAYTONA-AGAIN!

**RESULTS: AMERICAN GRAND PRIX AT DAYTONA**

**125cc CLASS**
1. Hugh Anderson — Suzuki
2. Ernest Degner — Suzuki
3. Frank Perris — Suzuki
  (and 2 laps behind)
4. Rick Shell — Honda

**50cc CLASS**
1. Ernest Degner — Suzuki
2. Hugh Anderson — Suzuki
3. M. Ichino — Suzuki
4. M. Koshino — Suzuki
  (one lap ahead of field)

### HAIL TO THE CHAMP!

Points piled up in the American Grand Prix put Suzuki in the lead for another World Championship trophy from the International Motorcycle Federation in 1965.

**1962**- Suzuki 50cc proclaimed Champion du Monde (World Champion) by the Federation Internationale Motorcycliste.

**1963**- Suzuki 50cc *and* 125cc awarded World Championship trophies by the Federation Internationale Motorcycliste.

**1964**- Suzuki runs away with the First American Grand Prix. Awarded its third World Championship Trophy in the 50cc class by FIM.

**1965**- Suzuki again makes astounding sweep of 50cc and 125cc races at the American Grand Prix.

*Champion Anderson accepts his wife's congratulations as Champion Degner discreetly turns away.*

**WHERE DID EVERYBODY GO?** *A smooth 1, 2, 3 Suzuki finish. two laps ahead of the field.*

### ASTOUNDING Suzuki Two-Stroke

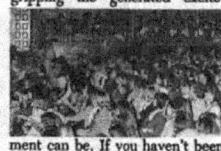

*(or hup, two; hup, two...)*

The hot power plant in the World Champion 50cc motorcycle is the astounding Suzuki two-stroke, the most efficient small displacement engine ever crafted.

Because it fires more frequently, it creates more usable horsepower and more spirit than a four-stroke. Also runs smoother, quieter and has more torque at low speeds and under adverse conditions.

For the second year in a row, Suzuki took all the marbles in the lightweight classifications at the 2nd racing of the American Grand Prix at Daytona.

In the 50cc class, the world champion Suzuki swept all of the first four places. In the 125cc class, Suzukis roared into first, second and third spots. The third Suzuki finished two full laps ahead of the fourth place cycle, a Honda.

From start to finish, the lower displacement categories were clearly Suzuki's. Though competing against cycles and riders from all over the world, the Suzuki team was never seriously challenged. The thrills and excitement, from the sound of the gun to the sweep of the flag, centered on Suzuki riders duelling each other.

In 1964, both the 50cc and 125cc races at Daytona were also swept by Suzuki. If the trend continues, which it probably will, they'll be calling Florida the Double-S State—Sunshine and Suzuki.

The essence of simplicity with only seven (count 'em, seven) moving parts, the Suzuki two-stroke is the most reliable motorcycle available to the American consumer.

*The World's Champion lightweight motorcycle designed to fit the requirements of American riders by America's most experienced team of motorcycle men—that's Suzuki!*

**U. S. SUZUKI MOTOR CORPORATION        200 W. CENTRAL AVE. SANTA ANA, CALIFORNIA**

# KRLA ARCHIVES

# THE BEATLES RETURN!
## HOLLYWOOD BOWL AUGUST 29 - 30

Radio Station KRLA and Bob Eubanks Proudly Present Two Concerts By The Fabulous Beatles AT HOLLYWOOD BOWL AUG. 29.30

Tickets are available by mail **only**. Applications will be filled by date of receipt. No ticket applications accepted before May 8.
1. **No more than six tickets to any one person.**
2. **Tickets are $3, $4, $5, $6 and $7.**
3. **A self-addressed, stamped envelope must be included with your order.**
4. **Tickets will be mailed July 15.**
5. If tickets are not available at the price you order, you will be sent tickets for the alternate date. If tickets at that price are not available for either date, you will be sent tickets at the next lowest price, along with a refund.

**MAIL TO:**

HOLLYWOOD BOWL
P.O. BOX 1951
LOS ANGELES, CALIF., 90028

**ON OR AFTER MAY 8**

### TICKET APPLICATION

I have enclosed a check or money order (NO CASH) payable to HOLLYWOOD BOWL, plus a self-addressed, stamped envelope. Please send me the following BEATLE TICKETS:

- ☐ 1 TICKET   ☐ $3.00   ☐ AUGUST 29
- ☐ 2 TICKETS  ☐ $4.00   ☐ AUGUST 30
- ☐ 3 TICKETS  ☐ $5.00
- ☐ 4 TICKETS  ☐ $6.00
- ☐ 5 TICKETS  ☐ $7.00
- ☐ 6 TICKETS

SEND TO .................................................
ADDRESS ................................................
CITY ................... STATE ....... Zip Code ......
TELEPHONE NO. ................

## KRLA ARCHIVES

# An English Success Story

**By LOUISE CRISCIONE**

The city of Manchester, England, lies east of Liverpool by some 31 miles of rail. It is the leading textile manufacturing city in England and the greatest cotton-textile center in the world.

Manchester is noted for the John Rylands library, for the Halle concerts, for the Manchester Academy of Fine Arts . . . and for the three fastest-rising English groups on the American scene: Hermans Hermits, Wayne Fontana and the Mindbenders and Freddie and the Dreamers.

The three groups share a common heritage, but there the comparison ends, for each group has its own distinctive style.

### HERMAN'S HERMITS

Leading off the Manchester parade were Herman's Hermits. It was around November of last year when their first hit, "I'm Into Something Good," reached that coveted number one position on the charts. About the same time, the Hermits visited our town, did a "Shindig," and appeared on several local TV shows.

These appearances netted the boys quite a large following in and around L.A. It was only a matter of time before the rest of the U.S. discovered the fresh appeal of the Hermits. By the time of their next release, "Can't You Hear My Heartbeat," America had indeed fallen for Herman's Hermits, and the boys had a second national chart-topper.

Next came the release of their first album, "Introducing Herman's Hermits," with a cut on it which was to be the boys THIRD number one record in a row! That cut, of course, is "Mrs. Brown," an old music hall song with enough novelty appeal to send it to the top of the national charts in just three short weeks!

The Hermits are five in number: real name Peter Noone, 17 year-old lead singer noted for his "tooth"; Karl Green, 17-year-old bass guitarist; Barry Whitman, 18-year-old drummer; Derek "Lek" Leckenby, 21-year-old lead and rhythm guitarist; and Keith Hopwood, 17-year-old lead and rhythm guitarist.

Herman and the Hermits are looking forward to surfing when they visit L.A. this time. On their last trip to the Southland, they met "some swinging girls who are mad keen surfers." So, this time if the weather's okay and they get the chance they're going to try it themselves.

If you happen to see five long-haired Englishmen getting wiped-out, don't laugh — it may be Herman and his Hermits!

### WAYNE FONTANA

Wayne Fontana and the Mindbenders were introduced to the American audience via Brian Epstein's segment of "Hullabaloo" some months back. Their sound, "Game of Love," climbed steadily up the national charts, reaching the number one position several weeks ago. However, it was not an overnight success for Wayne. He had been singing all over England for two and a half years prior to "Game of Love."

Wayne joined a group called the Jets when he was 16 (he's now 19), and after plenty of hard work the boys managed to get themselves an audition with Fontana Records. But when the agent for the record company showed up Wayne was minus two Jets! Desperate, Wayne borrowed two members from a couple of other local Manchester groups, and the Mindbenders were born!

The Mindbenders include Wayne Fontana, real name Glyn Geoffrey Ellis, lead singer; Eric Stewart, lead guitar; Bob Lang, bass guitar; and Ric Rothwell, drums.

### FREDDIE

Freddie and the Dreamers have quite a success story here in America. They were virtually unknown until they made appearances on "Shindig" and "Hullabaloo." Then their record, "I'm Telling You Now," shot to number one on the national charts. They currently have three records going for them.

There they are, the three Manchester groups — Herman's Hermits, Wayne Fontana and the Mindbenders, and Freddie and the Dreamers. All controlled by Danny Bettesh, head of Kennedy Street Enterprises, a man who is threatening to give Brian Epstein a real run for his money!

## More Derek Taylor
### FROM PAGE ONE

the Brothers R. and their eccentric A&R (artists and repertory) man are a very fine trio; nice men as well as great artists.

#### In's Out

I hear from England that Bob Dylan is having a wonderful time. His concerts have been sell-outs and this time the audiences have been all-age, all-type. On his previous trip only the very "in" folk crowd went to see him. He has since won for himself a wide following from the rock'n'roll and R&B fans, thanks mainly to the public relations work of John Lennon.

I don't care what Donovan says . . . He must have got his clothes and his style from Dylan.

#### About The Tube

Can you blame groups for objecting to appearing on "live" television?

Freddie and the Dreamers sang three songs on Ed Sullivan's key TV show a few days ago and I could hardly hear them. Fortunately, Freddie is now sufficiently established to survive the impression of inadequacy which lingered after the performance.

But a new act could have been destroyed by that one show. The sound system simply was not good enough. The poor lad was having a hard enough time dancing with a hand microphone without having to fight the system.

The Beatles were not happy with their Ed Sullivan sound though they thought Ed himself was a gas. And fortunately their discs and their personalities helped them to convince the public that they really were the greatest show business act in th world.

I hear there are three groups of Ikettes touring America . . .

#### Up They Go

Up and up the charts come the Beau Brummels. No. 56 and climbing fast in Cashbox at the time of writing. And into the Top Ten soon expect my tip of a few weeks ago "Cast Your Fate to the Winds."

Looks as if Gary Lewis is going to make it to the top again with "Count Me In." Not bad for a young lad with his first group and only his second disc. Whose son did you say he was?

#### Terpsichorean Trouble

The "Freddie" is an impossible dance. Despite the publicity and Freddie's charm, despite C. Checker and the British influence, the dance isn't going to catch on.

It was a good try.

May I say that one of the nicest things about the charts at the moment is that two of the songs from "Mary Poppins" are well placed. "Chim Chim Cheree" and 'Supercalifragilisticexpialidocious.' Strange that "Spoonful of Sugar" didn't catch on so much here. It was very big in England. Sugar sales were trebled.

#### Taylor Predicts

Forecast: "Mrs. Brown" is going to outsell every other 1965 record. Excepting the Beatles.

There's an extraordinary young man making a name for himself in club circles in Hollywood. He calls himself the Wild Man and he can say that again. His real name is Larry Fischer. He's 21 and he has a cabaret act. This consists of making a terrifying variety of noises and movements. He mesmerises audiences, nervous people clutch each other for safety.

The Wild Man writes his own material and calls each item in his act by weird names: "The Mopey People," "the Popers," "The Mope." I was asked to manage him but I have enough problems. He's a delightful man and very talented. He'll either be another Danny Kaye or he'll be arrested. There won't be any half measures.

That's it for this week. Short perhaps. But I've a lot of writing to do for the other pages. See you there.

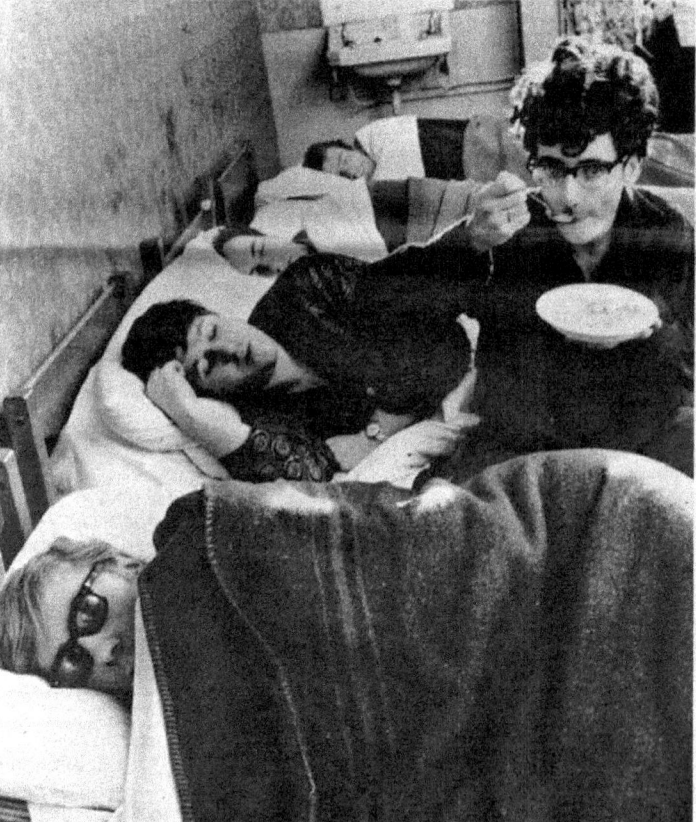

**FREDDIE AND THE DREAMERS** were last seen in the BEAT stuffed into a phone booth with a comely lass. Now we see them in a more relaxed fashion — as a matter of fact Freddie's the only one awake. (He's eating ice cream.) Boys are Dreamers, all right, with visions of success for their own new label.

---

**Long Beach Arena – Sunday, May 16**

## THE ROLLING STONES
### IN CONCERT

CHOICE SEATS STILL AVAILABLE AT
LONG BEACH ARENA, WALLICH'S MUSIC CITY
AND ALL MUTUAL TICKET AGENCIES

---

## WAREHOUSE IX
2214 Stoner Avenue
off Olympic in West Los Angeles

**Dancing to Live Name Bands**

Los Angeles' Unique Young Adult Nite Club
*Girls and Guys 18 and Over*
**Big Sunday Afternoon Dance Sessions from 4 to 10 p.m.**
Closed Tuesdays

# KRLA ARCHIVES

## Beatle Bowl Tickets Going..... Going.....

—SEE PAGE 5

Volume 1, No. 12　　　Los Angeles, California　　　Ten Cents　　　May 19, 1965

## Derek Taylor Reports

What on earth is going on between the British and American immigration authorities and the musical unions of the two nations?

The situation would be laughable if it were not so serious, so stupid and so sad.

I remember the enormous excitement in England when we were able, once again, to hear the majestic American swing bands in the mid-1950's.

Up to then, visas had not been granted to American greats like Armstrong, Goodman, Basie, Teagarden, and Woody Herman.

The visas were granted, the ice was broken, and the hungry British public gobbled up American talent with immense relish.

And then we sent you our best performers. Unhappily, few of them made it over here until the invasion spearheaded by you-know-who from Liverpool.

**Ridiculous**

The irony of the situation is made more ridiculous by the Early Bird Satellite which makes trans-Atlantic television possible 24 hours of the day.

The motto of the British Broadcasting Corporation (the only official radio station in the U.K.) is "Nation shall speak peace unto nation."

Yet the two greatest English-speaking nations in the world cannot even speak peace on the exchange of innocent young pop singers.

We are all the losers in this matter. It makes me tired.

**Breakthrough**

One man who did break through the immigration-union blockade recently was Ian Whitcomb, a charming English lad who, though he was unknown in England, made a great impression in Hollywood both in person and on "Shindig."

He would, I'm sure, be the last to claim that there is any music in his voice in "You Turn Me On." But the disc is going to be a hit. And, probably a real big one.

While we are talking about voices, I should say that Donovan is a great disappointment in "Catch the Wind." This, too, is a hit. But there is a profound lack of voice.

The boy's no Bob Dylan.

Jody Miller has made a lovely job of "Queen of the House." A certain smash and a pretty good achievement so soon after the Roger Miller hit.

Saw the Ed Sullivan Show again on Sunday — I try not to miss it when there are English acts. Some comedian friends of mine were on the show—(Morecambe and Wise, very big stars in England!

Plus the delightful Tommy Cooper, also a top-liner from England, who was waving from the audience.

Stars of the show, of course, were the Rolling Stones. The sound was pretty good and they themselves were excellent, I thought. I wonder why Mick Jagger didn't do his little dance? Too provocative for network TV perhaps.

**Ruggedness**

Tom Jones I hadn't seen before. His first disc — the majestic "It's Not Unusual" — was just moving up the charts when I came over here. It's easy to see why he has become so popular on personal appearances. He has a very strong masculine presence, and there is obviously a lot of hard experience there. He has the characteristic ruggedness of the south Welshman and, I am told, a lot of the intensive training in music which is inherent in being a Welshman.

Jackie De Shannon has, I hope and believe, a hit in "What the World Needs Is Love." The title is wonderfully apt and the song has all the fashionable hit ingredients.

Recent releases include The Standells' "Zebra in the Kitchen," (from the MGM movie of the same name. I like it very much.) and Gene Chandler's "Nothing Can Stop Me", which is also very good.

I hope The Impressions have a massive hit with their latest "Woman's Got Soul."

LOCALLY: the Whisk — a plastic-handled tassel used in current dances — is catching on. It has already been featured on the Casey Kasem show and looks like a promising novelty.

. . . The American Missing Links had a substantial success at the plush Teen Beat Nightclub in Las Vegas.

. . . Jerry Naylor's first single for Tower Records — "Only Make Believe" — is now gracing local disc stores.

AND — The Beatles are coming.

**TOP TEN**

1. WOOLY BULLY
2. GLORIA/ BABY PLEASE DON'T GO
3. MRS. BROWN/ I GOTTA DREAM ON
4. TICKET TO RIDE/YES IT IS
5. JUST ONCE IN MY LIFE
6. OOO BABY BABY
7. HELP ME RHONDA
8. THE LAST TIME/ PLAY WITH FIRE
9. WHEN I'M GONE
10. SHE'S ABOUT A MOVER

—TUNEDEX ON PAGE 7

# EXCITING CONTEST OFFERS BEAT READER VISIT WITH BEATLES

How would you like to interview the BEATLES for the KRLA BEAT? Silly question! But you may have that opportunity, provided you know the BEATLES well enough. That's the prize in the BEAT'S BEATLE INTERVIEW CONTEST.

The winner will interview John, Paul, George, and Ringo, for the BEAT, when they arrive for their Hollywood Bowl concerts in August. Here is how it will work:

Each week for the next 10 weeks, the BEAT will ask a series of questions about the BEATLES. Send in your answers on the special form which will be provided each week, and at the end of 10 weeks the contestant with the most correct answers will win the thrill of a lifetime.

An example of the kind of questions that will be asked will include:

● When did Ringo join the BEATLES?

● In what city outside England did they first gain recognition?

● Who was their drummer when they first played at the tavern in Liverpool?

● What is the name of John's wife?

Entries will be judged for accuracy by Derek Taylor, former press agent for the BEATLES and close friend from England, now a KRLA BEAT columnist in Hollywood.

In case of a tie, a drawing will be held to determine the winner. It starts next week in the BEAT, so be ready for the first set of questions!

### First KRLA BEAT Subscriber

**GIRL ON RIGHT WAS FIRST TO SIGN UP** for subscription to the KRLA BEAT. Pictured are (l-r) KRLA Program Director Mel Hall, Music Man Dick Moreland, and DEREK TAYLOR. Accepting last week's BEAT is 15 year old ROSIE HESSION of San Marino. Rosie signed for the introductory offer of 52 issues of $3. Now she gets THE BEAT by mail every week direct to her home!

# Letters Flood Beat Office

Last week's announcement in the KRLA BEAT that subscriptions were being taken for the first time, met with wild enthusiasm from teenagers throughout Southern California, and, surprisingly, from much of the western United States.

Ever since the initial announcement on KRLA Radio and in the pages of the KRLA BEAT of subscriptions being taken, mail has been pouring in to the KRLA BEAT offices.

Two secretaries have been hard at work trying to open all the mail. And, what a deluge of mail it was!

Obviously the loyal listeners of KRLA Radio are eager to learn more about their favorite artists. Particularly about the BEATLES. Derek Taylor, former press agent for the Beatles, can always be depended upon for the very latest word on where the Beatles are and what they are doing. And, it's **inside** information!

As yet we have no count of the total number of new BEAT subscribers. Mailing lists are being prepared, and the new subscribers can expect their first copies to arrive at home in just a couple of weeks.

You can subscribe too!

An order blank is on Page 4 of this week's KRLA BEAT.

Fill it out and you too will soon have the convenience of getting your BEAT, at home right off the press.

# KRLA ARCHIVES

## What Drives "The Groupies" To Their Strange Behavior?

By Rod Alan Barken

Los Angeles has it's own brand of teenage "happiness hounds." They are . . . "the groupies." To a hundred or so English entertainers who have visited the sunny Southland during the past year, these energetic young girls represent today's own personal style of youthful exhuberance and feminine excitement.

From the moment that the huge jet plane lands at the Los Angeles Airport, to the very last avalanche of multi-colored jellybeans thrown with affection from a loving audience, our intrepid English entertainers scarcely find free moments away from this travelling band of adoring teenage girls. And everybody loves it!

### Definition

A "groupie" is a young girl, usually in her mid-teens, intent on meeting and greeting the many pop music groups visiting the city.

To become a "groupie," or group-chaser, a spirited young girl needs no membership cards, no secret whistle, no compass, or any knowledge of an intricate code or spy-type language. She must possess, though, a very keen wit (to match same with the very witty British), a great sense of humor (to keep from crying when disappointment strikes), a very fast mind (to guess the security guards and the other girls), and a strong pair of legs.

And, above all else, the group-chaser must definitely want to have a good time. She must be willing to sacrifice hours of sleep, good food, pocket money, and steady nerves. For the game of "group-chasing" is more complicated and involved than most any other game played before.

### Rules of Sport

How does a "groupie" meet her favorites?

Some use the direct approach of walking up with their hands extended. Most use devious methods, applying all of the female tricks of her trade. Some of these methods are as complicated and involved as a military operation, and, at times, contain the secrecy of a jewel theft.

One pact of girls once dressed as maids to reach a certain floor in the Hollywood Roosevelt Hotel. When Peter and Gordon visited Hollywood this past December, two young ladies camped overnight by their patio door, then burst inside when the two Londoners awoke.

Many "groupies" carry press cards from assorted publications, but they are soon finding that these cards give no real guarantees.

### Stones Started It

Where did it all begin? For Southern California, at least, it began in June of last year, when the Rolling Stones paid their first visit to the West, and appeared at a show in San Bernardino. Constant mention of the huge crowds of fans in England seemed to ignite the fuse for Southern California youngsters, and by the time the show was over, thousands of fans were mobbing the back door to the Swing Auditorium to catch a glimpse of, and perhaps to touch, their favorite idols.

When The Beatles came to Los Angeles for their concert last August, they were constantly being turned out to witness the huge mobs that had met their plane, followed them about town, jammed the entrance to the Hollywood Bowl, and completely taking over the streets leading to their fashionable residence in Bel-Aire.

Since that time, a number of English artists have appeared on the sidewalks of Los Angeles. Most specifically, the city of Hollywood. The Rolling Stones are now due for their fourth appearance in this area. Chad and Jeremy live here for the better part of their trips to America. Ian Whitcomb (currently hot with the record, "You Turn Me On") is making plans to settle here during the coming summer.

Why do they want to keep coming back? "Because of the fantastic receptions," states Peter Asher, of Peter and Gordon. "We love the way people accept us here on the West Coast."

Every English group, from The Beatles to Manfred Mann, have all gone home talking about "the groupies."

For the Englishman, the "groupies" have become a way of live, and an occupational hazard that they face each time with a broad grin.

### Fun Lovers

There are hazards for the group-chaser to face, too. Hazards like: How can I meet them? Where are they staying? Will my mother let me go to the airport?

As a rule, the majority of the girls that flock to the hotel corridors and lobbies are great fun-lovers, bent not towards malicious mischief, but rather towards good, clean wholesome fun. The huge crowds that fill the hotel entrances have caused many of the better hotels to refuse rooms to the visiting entertainers.

Security precautions are always taken to protect not only the traveling group, but the traveling group-chaser as well. Recently, as co-promoter of a Rolling Stones Concert in San Diego, I was faced, personally, with an unfortunate incident that has probably happened elsewhere a thousand times over.

Two young girls, both from Riverside, in love with The Stones, thought it a great idea to hitch-hike the one hundred-odd miles to San Diego to see their idols perform.

When 48 hours had elapsed, and their frantic parents had heard no word from their daughters, a statewide police broadcast was sent out. That same afternon found me — as a contact of the Stones — being questioned by not only the juvenile authorities, the San Diego Police, the Highway Patrol, but the FBI as well!

### Ends Well

The girls were found, nine days later, staying at a girl friends house not three blocks from their own homes. As the story unfolded, everyone learned that these two innocents, bright-eyed and not even slightly tired, had managed to hitchhike and walk, ride buses and run, through over sixty seven Southern California cities. When asked why they, at 15 years old, wanted to do such a thoughtless thing, they replied, "Why to meet the Rolling Stones, of course." They never did meet their idols.

It's great fun, but it's also dangerous if proper precautions are not taken. If you are inclined to be a "groupie," be one, but please be careful. Consider others. If you live by the following simple saying, things will always work out for the best.

"May you live as you want, and never want as long as you live. Live it up, but don't live it up so high that you can't live it down 'cause that's bad jazz."

Was it Shakespeare who said that?

---

**KRLA BEAT**

The KRLA BEAT is published weekly by Prestige Publishing Company; editorial and advertising offices at 6290 Sunset Boulevard, Suite 504, Hollywood, California 90028.

Single copy price, 10 cents.

Subscription price: U.S. and possessions, and Canada, $3 per year or $5 for two years. Foreign rates upon request.

# KRLA ARCHIVES

## Inside KRLA

TIME MAGAZINE paid KRLA a great honor this week. TIME is preparing a cover story on modern music, and selected KRLA as the most outstanding popular music station in the United States. Tentatively scheduled for the May 14th issue, a major news break may delay it. But watch for KRLA in TIME MAGAZINE!

CASEY KASEM felt that last week's shows on SHEBANG were the best yet. He was completly "knocked out" by the performance that Timi Yuro turned in for that week. Timi is an exciting performer. Casey's show is seen daily on Channel 5.

EMPEROR HUDSON is currently dickering with the TV networks for a new idea for a show he has. All 3 networks have shown interest, but no deal has been signed as yet. Details are secret, but the BEAT knows it has something to do with golf.

 ROCK HUDSON (no relation) is starring in the new CHARLIE O'DONNELL movie titled, BLINDFOLD, and many feel it's the big break ROCK has been looking for! Watch for pictures of both of them in next week's BEAT.

DICK (The Wild Italian) BIONDI, the famous animal lover, has been moping around the studios with a long face all week — one of his dogs had to undergo surgery. The patient and doctor are doing fine, according to the reports just in.

NIGHT PEOPLE BILL SLATER is presently out in front of the "Pick Race," having selected the most number of songs that actually became hits. Included are Count Me In (Gary Lewis & Playboys) Concrete And Clay (Unit Four Plus Two), You Turn Me On (Ian Whitcomb), Back In My Arms Again and Just You (Sonny & Cher).

NEW SOUNDS ON THE AIR this week include Last Chance To Turn Around, another Gene Pitney smash; 3 O'Clock In The Morning by Bert Kaempfert; Goodbye, So Long by Ike and Tina Turner; Bring It On Home To Me by The Animals; Keep On Trying by Bobby Vee; and Voo-Doo Women by Bobby Goldsboro.

THE KRLApes ARE REALLY OFF on a real trip for their next game. They'll board a bus for Palmdale on May 18th, to meet the Palmdale High School faculty. The APES are humiliated by their present record — 2 wins and 51 losses — wondering how they ever won those two games!

THE KRLA STAFF and several lovely young secretarial assistants imported for the job have been trying to dig out from under the SEND ME MINE mail response this week. KRLA has received over 30,000 requests for "SEND ME MINES," and we thank you for joining the fun.

THE HULLABALOOER is heading up a folk concert in Brea for Jack Linkletter on May 21st.

KRLA AND ALL THE DEE-JAYS are participating in the FREEDOM FROM HUNGER drive. We've scheduled a giant benefit show June 6th at the Hollywood Bowl starring Gary Lewis and The Playboys, Dick and DeeDee, Jan and Dean, The Kingsmen, The Byrds, Jackie De Shannon, Steve Allen, Jerry Lewis (Gary's dad), Bob Newhart (with-the button-down mind), Joey Bishop, and Bill (Jose Jiminez) Dana. Still more stars will be added this week.

---

**23 SKIDOO**
Dancing to Live Name Bands
2116 Westwood Blvd., West Los Angeles
Girls 18, Guys 21
*23 Skidoo Dancers are now seen on TV's*
*Hollywood A'GoGo Saturday on Channel 9 at 9:00 p.m.*
**Closed Mondays**

---

## Two Famous Sons Start Careers

**THIS TRIO WAS FORMED** on a Beverly Hills Little League diamond. DINO, DESI, AND BILLY began recording for Reprise Records after Frank Sinatra heard them singing in an upstairs bedroom of Dean Martin's home. Dino is 13, son of Martin, while Desi, also 13, is son of Desi Arnaz. Third member of trio is Billy Hinshe. They'll have a new release soon.

### Premiere Soon

The Paramount Studios in Hollywood have announced completion of their new film, GIRLS ON THE BEACH, and what a cast has been assembled!

Starring are THE BEACH BOYS, in an exciting movie all about summer fun. We'll be able to tell you all about it next week, after our Movie Editor attends a special showing of the film at the studio.

---

**WAREHOUSE IX**
2214 Stoner Avenue
off Olympic in West Los Angeles
**Dancing to Live Name Bands**
Los Angeles' Unique Young Adult Nite Club
*Girls and Guys 18 and Over*
**Big Sunday Afternoon Dance Sessions from 4 to 10 p.m.**
Closed Tuesdays

---

## YEAH-YEAH WHISK

**You Have Seen It On National TV!**

**Now Twisk YOUR Whisk And Add**

**New Excitement To Your Dancing!**

ORDER NOW BY MAIL!
NAME_____
ADDRESS_____
CITY_____ ZIP CODE_____

Check Color Preference:
Red ☐   White ☐   Blue ☐   Yellow ☐
         Orange ☐  Green ☐

Send $2.00 (includes postage and tax) to:
"WHISK"
1800 No. Argyle, Suite 510
Hollywood, California

# KRLA ARCHIVES

*Interview:*
## Stones Answer Questions From Beat Staffer Barken

### By ROD ALAN BARKEN

Five intense young men with a purpose — Mick Jagger, Bill Wyman, Brian Jones, Keith Richards, Charley Watts — England's phenomenal, controversial . . . Rolling Stones!

When you first meet The Rolling Stones, you find them to be everything that their advance publicity has said they were; long haired, not-too-healthy looking, out-spoken, and fantastic entertainers. Their presence on stage is as electrifying and captivating as any performance you've ever seen. The emotion is swept from the huge audience to the five young men on stage, and, in less than a flashing heartbeat, shown reappeared anew in their music. Their show is, without a doubt, the most invigorating and refreshing piece of showmanship ever.

Here are just a few of the questions I asked of The Stones during their previous visits to Southern California. Their candid answers can well speak for themselves.

DO YOU LIKE THE BEATLES? AND WHAT DO YOU THINK OF THEM?

MICK: Yes, we do like them . . . and we think of them . . . a lot.

WHAT DO YOU THINK OF EACH OTHER?

MICK: We like each other, you know, otherwise we would not be a group.

HOW DID YOU ARRIVE AT THE NAME, "THE ROLLING STONES"?

MICK: We needed a name for our group, and we saw this song called "Rolling Stones' Blues," and we thought it was a good name so we called ourselves The Rolling Stones.

WHERE DID ALL OF THE LONG HAIR COME FROM?

MICK: We've always had it, ever since we began. Even before The Beatles.

CHARLEY: We picked it up from those people at the art schools. That's the same place that The Beatles got it.

OF THE THREE GROUPS—THE BEATLES, THE DAVE CLARK FIVE, AND THE ANIMALS — WHICH GROUP TO YOU LIKE BEST?

MICK: The Beatles.

BRIAN: The Beatles.

CHARLEY: The Beatles.

IS THIS SOCIALLY OR PROFESSIONALLY?

(Chorus): All!

WHO IS ANDREW LOOG OLDHAM?

MICK, BRIAN, KEITH, CHARLEY, BILL (in chorus): Andrew Loog Oldham is the greatest record producer in the world!

HOW DID YOU MEET ANDREW LOOG OLDHAM?

MICK: He came to see us . . . at this club.

WHAT WAS THE NAME OF THIS CLUB?

CHARLEY: The Craw Daddy, in Richmond (pause) surrey.

WHAT DO YOU THINK OF ED SULLIVAN?

BRIAN: I think he was a very nice fellow. He took the time to talk to us.

WHAT DO YOU THINK OF AMERICAN RADIO AND TELEVISION?

BILL: I'm not too keen on the old movies, but the radio's okay. I like them.

These, then, are The Stones . . . five exciting young men. As The Rolling Stones roll towards Southern California, and their subsequent appearance at the Long Beach Auditorium, anxious fans and music lovers alike, await their arrival with baited breath.

## Folk Singers Move To Rock Beat

JOE AND EDDIE HAVE ANOTHER ONE that may climb the charts, called DEPEND ON YOURSELF. They have recently appeared on the ED SULLIVAN SHOW, SHINDIG, and HULLABALOO. Now touring in the east, Joe and Eddie have moved slightly from the folk sound to the modern rock beat.

## Fan Club Report

**CANNIBAL AND THE HEADHUNTERS**
c/o Miss Margie Martinez
5160 Whittier Blvd.
Los Angeles, Calif. 90022

**STANDELLS**
c/o Lee Jacobs
7251 Willoughby Avenue
Los Angeles, California

**SONNY & CHER**
c/o Miss Jane Lee
P.O. Box 84
Montrose, Calif.

**THE BYRDS**
c/o Kathy McIntyre
Suite 504
6290 Sunset
Hollywood, Calif.
Dues—$1.00 plus 2 five-cent stamps)

**DAVE CLARK FIVE**
c/o Lenore Longpre
346 Oak Cliff Road
Monrovia, California
(Dues $1.25 and 4 stamped self-addressed envelopes)

**GERRY & THE PACEMAKERS**
c/o Tina Di Florio
702 Lime
Brea, California 92621
(Dues — 50 cents. You receive monthly bulletins, pictures, membership card, contests, etc.)

**IAN WHITCOMB**
c/o Kathie Raisler
14720 Gandesa Road
La Mirada, California 90638
(Send a self-addressed and stamped envelope)

**JOEY PAIGE**
c/o Linda Kirk
6372 Antioch
Riverside, Calif. 92504
(Dues — $1.00 Members receive 8x10, wallet picture, membership card, fact-sheet and news letters)

**DOBIE GRAY**
c/o P.O. Box 1446
Studio City, California

**SIMI MUSIC CENTER**
*Headquarters For*
Top Records-Music Lessons
Large Jam Room
10 Yrs. In Business
853 Los Angles Ave.
Simi, California

The KRLA Beat is now accepting subscriptions!

Due to overwhelming response during its first few months of operation, the Beat has been unable to keep up with the demand through its regular outlets at newsstands and record shops.

If you're one of the thousands who have found a "sold out" sign when trying to find a copy of the Beat, you'll be happy to learn you can now receive it in the mail at your home each week.

You'll find a subscription coupon and a special introductory subscription offer on page 4 of this issue.

## KRLA BEAT SUBSCRIPTION
Order By Mail Now–Save Over 40%!

Please Rush Me the KRLA BEAT at Your Special Introductory Subscription Rate

☐ 1 Year—52 Issues—$3.00   ☐ 2 Years — $5.00

Enclosed is $_____

Send To:_____ Age_____

Address:_____

City_____ State_____ Zip_____

*Please be sure to include your Zip Code number!*
MAIL YOUR ORDER TO:
KRLA BEAT
1401 South Oak Knoll Avenue
Pasadena, California 91106

# KRLA ARCHIVES

## On The Beat

ON THE BEAT welcomes the Rolling Stones to our town and hopes their visit will not be marred by any unpleasant incidents.

The boys' other visits have not been so marked and lets not make this one an exception. In England, the Stones had girls falling out of the balconies! It's a long way down, so I advise you lucky Long Beach ticket-holders not to try it. Anyway, a BIG Southland welcome to the Stones.

Best quote of the week comes from Georgie Fame concerning remarks that he is a pop singer and not an R&B singer: "I endeavor to sing the blues to the best of my ability and people that knock are narrow minded twists." You tell 'em, Georgie!

### Invitation

The Swinging Blue Jeans accepted an invitation to play with the Royal Liverpool Philharmonic Orchestra for the first performance of a work by an American composer, Carl Davis. It's entitled "Symphony Orchestra and Beat Group." What else? I, for one, wish I had the necessary capital to make it to Liverpool for this one! It ought to be WILD. Just picture the sedate Philharmonic Orchestra and the denim-clad Blue Jeans on the same stage at the same time!

ON THE BEAT has it straight from the Dick Clark office that the plans for the Righteous Brothers movie have ben dropped. I'm sorry to hear that; it would have made quite a movie. Dick Clark Productions will do a movie which may feature several pop artists, but the emphasis will be on the plot and not the singers.

### Warmongers

A bit of philosophy from Donovan: "You don't have to follow the philosophy (of folk music), but if you don't follow what you think it can only be painful to you in the end." Very well put by a young man who is getting plenty of criticism heaped on him for allegedly imitating Bob Dylan. Donovan declares this criticism does not bother him and he doesn't lose any sleep over it. ON THE BEAT reported earlier that Donovan has printed on his guitar "This Machine Kills". Well, now we know who it is supposed to kill — warmongers!

Apparently, I confused a number of people by stating in my column on April 14 that Herman's Hermits would be touring with the Dick Clark Caravan of Stars, and that the Caravan would be playing Melodyland on May 17. Well, the Hermits ARE appearing on the Caravan, but it is NOT the Caravan which will play Melodyland on the 17th. The one the Hermits are on is touring in the Eastern part of the U.S. The one playing Melodyland will star the Zombies. My apologies to all you Herman fans. Sorry if I misled you.

The Searchers' favorite TV show is "The Fugitive". Mike says: "Wherever we go, we always look out for the Fugy." That's the Searchers' nickname for the extremely popular TV "Fugitive", David Janssen. The Searchers are tentatively set for a summer tour of America.

QUICK ONES: Adam Faith has been offered a movie role . . . Peter Asher denied a rumor that he and Gordon were planning to settle permanently in America by stating: "I wouldn't dream of becoming an American citizen" . . . Both sides of Dick & DeeDee's new one were written by the Jagger/Richard team . . . A group called The Liverpools have been discovered in Hong Kong . . . Bobby Rydell's absence from the pop scene can be explained quite easily — he's in the Army . . . Gerry and the Pacemakers have a new album which compiles all their hits onto one record for those of you who may have missed them the first time around.

ON THE BEAT has flipped for that knockout of a record by Them, "Here Comes The Night". Kind of an ironic situation for these boys: While their fantastically popular "Gloria" was number one in L.A., it wasn't even in the top 100 on the national charts! Hope the new one goes nationally like "Gloria" went locally.

— Louise Criscione

**THEY'LL BE IN HOLLYWOOD** in August, and response to ticket availability has been overwhelming. A full-page advertisement, both in THE BEAT, and in the May 8th edition of the Los Angeles Times, brought deluge of applications to the Hollywood Bowl. Management at Bowl is pleased with the KRLA promotion and the amazing response. Perhaps the most exciting news is that THE BEATLES will take a 10-day vacation in Los Angeles in September.

---

# THE BEATLES RETURN!
## HOLLYWOOD BOWL AUGUST 29 - 30

### Radio Station KRLA and Bob Eubanks Proudly Present Two Concerts By The Fabulous Beatles AT HOLLYWOOD BOWL AUG. 29 . 30

**MAIL TO:**

**HOLLYWOOD BOWL**
**P.O. BOX 1951**
**LOS ANGELES, CALIF., 90028**

Tickets are available by mail **only**. Applications will be filled by date of receipt.

1. No more than six tickets to any one person.
2. Tickets are $3, $4, $5, $6 and $7.
3. A self-addressed, stamped envelope must be included with your order.
4. Tickets will be mailed July 15.
5. If tickets are not available at the price you order, you will be sent tickets for the alternate date. If tickets at that price are not available for either date, you will be sent tickets at the next lowest price, along with a refund.

### TICKET APPLICATION

I have enclosed a check or money order (NO CASH) payable to HOLLYWOOD BOWL, plus a self-addressed, stamped envelope. Please send me the following BEATLE TICKETS:

- ☐ 1 TICKET    ☐ $3.00    ☐ AUGUST 29
- ☐ 2 TICKETS   ☐ $4.00    ☐ AUGUST 30
- ☐ 3 TICKETS   ☐ $5.00
- ☐ 4 TICKETS   ☐ $6.00
- ☐ 5 TICKETS   ☐ $7.00
- ☐ 6 TICKETS

SEND TO ............................................
ADDRESS ...........................................
TELEPHONE NO. ................
CITY ................ STATE ....... Zip Code ......

# KRLA ARCHIVES

## TALENT IMMIGRATION DISPUTE CONTINUES

By LOUISE CRISCIONE

It appears that the Government is not giving in after all, and is still making it plenty rough on British acts trying to get into the U.S. Besides making the American teens, record companies, promoters, and TV producers furious, their tactics are damaging our image abroad.

Earlier in the year, the trouble flared up with the news that the Zombies and Nashville Teens' tours were cut short because of work permit trouble. Several other groups were refused permits resulting in hard feelings on both sides of the Atlantic. The furor enjoyed a few weeks of relative quiet, but now it is bubbling up again and it is even more rancid than before. The latest victims were Wayne Fontana, Sandie Shaw, and Twinkle.

### Yankee Position

The American side of the story goes something like this: The U.S. Government, and more particularly the U.S. Immigration Department, has taken it upon themselves to judge the merits of each performer wishing to enter the United States. These duties have been delegated to several performing unions, and this is where the trouble lies.

There are two kinds of permits which can be issued to foreign artists: the H-1 permit, which is granted to performers of distinguished merit and ability, and the H-2 permit which is granted to performers whose services are unique and cannot be duplicated by an American act. Now, it is up to these unions to decide who possesses "distinguished merit and ability" and who has a "unique" act. The Government then relies heavily on the unions' appraisal in issuing permits.

### Unions Criticized

These unions have been deluged with criticism because they pay absolutely no attention to what the American public likes and who they want to see. The unions are admittedly ignorant when it comes to popular recording artists. When a union official recently rejected an English performer, he suggested two "American" substitutes. As it turned out, both these "American" substitutes were also English! And these are the people who are being asked to pass judgment on who should and who should not be admitted to America.

The unions wish to protect their own and this is a fine and noble idea, but by carrying it too far they have inadvertently thrown Americans out of work. The demand for English performers is tremendous. Since many performers are refused entry into the U.S., the TV people have been forced to go to England and with them have gone salaries which otherwise would have gone to American musicians and television crews.

### Lack of Agreement

The unions do not even agree among themselves as to the merits of a particular performer. Take the case of Wayne Fontana. Wayne was at first refused an H-1 permit, then he was given an H-2 permit, and then they decided his act was "unique" for night clubs but not for TV! Thus, the film clip of Wayne on "Shindig" a few weeks back. Later, they did a turnabout and okayed Wayne for TV and he was able to appear on Hullabaloo "live".

The English are getting fed up to here with the banning of their acts. So far, there has been plenty of criticism, hard feelings, and a lot of talk of retaliatory measures. Now, it looks as if the talking is leading to action. The British Agents Association sent a delegation to the Ministry of Labour on May 5. They are demanding a tight Government clamp on the unknown American performers who continue to stream into England.

The English do not mind the "swapping idea" whereby we trade one American act for one British act. This is quite fair to both sides. What is making the British particularly angry, and rightly so, is the fact that before the Beatles hit our shores the American artists had an absolute monopoly on the American record business plus a very sizable hunk of the British market. There was no trouble about swapping artists then because American unions were quite satisfied with their share of the pie.

So who is winning in this battle? The answer is NO ONE. American record sales are down in Britain, and if the English Government decides to retaliate we will lose even more. It is a sad situation; one which could, and should, be resolved in a big hurry if only the unions and Immigration Department would grow up and start acting like responsible, reasonably intelligent adults instead of like little children mortally afraid of competition. Keep the "swap system" if you like, but get rid of the ridiculous ban. It is way beneath us.

### Appearing At KRLA Benefit

IT TOOK JUST TEN DAYS for their first recording to be a smash hit. DICK AND DEE DEE have been going strong ever since. Watch any live show of theirs — and you will see why they're so popular. They sing, twist, shout, twist, and stomp. And everybody has fun. Duo records for Warner Brothers-Reprise, and will appear at the KRLA Hollywood Bowl Show on June 6th.

---

IAN WHITCOMB

Turns Everyone On With

His New One

"YOU TURN ME ON"

exclusively on tower

---

## The Latest On Herman

Herman of Herman's Hermits may become a controversial figure if he follows his present plans. He's writing a book. It's about other pop music stars, but not just an ordinary book. Herman says it will include stories about stars that have never been printed before.

He told the BEAT, "I'm writing about how they really are and not what they seem to be to the public — false images and all that sort of thing."

"This surely will be the most controversial book of the year when it comes out."

But before rushing out to the newsstand to buy a copy, read what else he has to say:

"When it's published I'll probably be sued by everyone I've written about, so I'll probably have to wait until I finish in pop music."

In that case, despite strong curiosity, we hope the publication date is a long time off. And judging by his current popularity, it will be.

The hottest group in the U.S. at present, Herman's Hermits, will spend several weeks in Hollywood this fall.

Following the lead of the Beatles and the Dave Clark Five, they'll star in a movie. It will be produced by Dick Clark Productions.

Clark set it up on his recent European tour. He told the Beat it will feature them in a mystery story, starring Herman but featuring the group in a number of songs.

The script is being written in England, but filming will be done here, probably starting the third week in September.

---

**THE BYRDS**
Official National
**FAN CLUB**

Suite 504
6290 Sunset Blvd.
Hollywood

Send $1.00 plus two 5-cent stamps and receive photos, fact sheets, biographies. Fun contests each month.

Free Concerts Planned
For Members Only

Be a chapter president. Enlist ten (10) new members now!

**The BYRDS Are Great**

---

Back issues of the KRLA BEAT are still available, for a limited time. If you've missed an issue of particular interest to you, send 10 cents for each copy wanted, along with a self-addressed stamped envelope to:

KRLA BEAT
Suite 504
6290 Sunset Blvd.
Hollywood, California 90028

ISSUES AVAILABLE —

4/14 — INTERVIEW WITH JOHN LENNON
4/21 — INTERVIEW WITH PAUL McCARTNEY
4/28 — CHIMP EXCITES TEEN FAIR
5/5 — HERMANIA SPREADS
5/12 — HERE COME THE BEATLES

# KRLA ARCHIVES

## KRLA TUNEDEX

| THIS WEEK | LAST WEEK | TITLE | ARTIST |
|---|---|---|---|
| 1. | 1. | WOOLY BULLY | Sam The Sham & The Pharoahs |
| 2. | 2. | GLORIA/BABY PLEASE DON'T GO | Them |
| 3. | 3. | MRS. BROWN/I GOTTA DREAM ON | Herman's Hermits |
| 4. | 5. | TICKET TO RIDE/YES IT IS | The Beatles |
| 5. | 6. | JUST ONCE IN MY LIFE | The Righteous Brothers |
| 6. | 7. | OOH BABY BABY | The Miracles |
| 7. | 20. | HELP ME RHONDA | The Beach Boys |
| 8. | 8. | THE LAST TIME/PLAY WITH FIRE | The Rolling Stones |
| 10. | 12. | SHE'S ABOUT A MOVER | Sir Douglas Quintet |
| 11. | 14. | JUST YOU | Sonny & Cher |
| 12. | 17. | BACK IN MY ARMS AGAIN | The Supremes |
| 13. | 11. | SILHOUETTES | Herman's Hermits |
| 14. | 24. | JUST A LITTLE | The Beau Brummels |
| 15. | 31. | YOU TURN ME ON | Ian Whitcomb |
| 16. | 15. | CONCRETE AND CLAY | Unit Four Plus Two |
| 17. | 9. | GAME OF LOVE | Wayne Fontana & Mindbenders |
| 18. | 23. | BABY THE RAIN MUST FALL | Glen Yarbrough |
| 19. | 32. | MR. TAMBOURINE MAN | The Byrds |
| 20. | 13. | IT'S NOT UNUSUAL | Tom Jones |
| 21. | 21. | I'LL NEVER FIND ANOTHER YOU | The Seekers |
| 22. | 30. | I DO LOVE YOU | Billy Stewart |
| 24. | 16. | I KNOW A PLACE | Petula Clark |
| 25. | 10. | NOWHERE TO RUN | Martha & The Vandellas |
| 26. | 27. | CATCH THE WIND | Donovan |
| 27. | 19. | COUNT ME IN | Gary Lewis & The Playboys |
| 28. | 28. | IT'S GONNA BE ALL RIGHT | Gerry & The Pacemakers |
| 29. | 18. | TIRED OF WAITING FOR YOU | The Kinks |
| 30. | 25. | I'LL BE DOGGONE | Marvin Gaye |

### CLIMBERS

| | | | |
|---|---|---|---|
| 1. | 38. | GOOD LOVIN | The Olympics |
| 2. | 39. | FOR YOUR LOVE | The Yardbirds |
| 3. | 37. | QUEEN OF THE HOUSE | Jody Miller |
| 4. | 29. | SWING ME | Nino Tempo & April Stevens |
| 5. | 44. | HERE COMES THE NIGHT | Them |
| 6. | 40. | ENGINE ENGINE NO. 9 | Roger Miller |
| 7. | 36. | DO THE FREDDIE | Freddie & The Dreamers |
| 8. | 34. | TRUE LOVE WAYS | Peter & Gordon |
| 9. | 46. | YOU WERE MADE FOR ME | Freddie & The Dreamers |
| 10. | 42. | SOME THINGS JUST STICK IN YOUR MIND | Dick & Deedee |

## What An Emperor Must Do!

EMPEROR BOB, that blue-eyed boon to radio, has situation well in hand as he checks out final details. The Emperor wanted to make sure everything was OK for DAVE HULL, when both made appearance recently. It just shows you what the long-suffering Emperor will do for his fellow man. If we're lucky, HUDSON will return to the air tomorrow morning for more exciting hours of pure joy.

## "Queen of the House"

"QUEEN OF THE HOUSE" is big hit for JODY MILLER. The record is a parody of Roger Miller's KING OF THE ROAD, but oddly enough the two artists have never met. She's not related to him.

---

**FAMOUS!  100  FAMOUS!**

### MOVIE STAR'S HOME ADDRESSES

Send $1.00 Cash, Check, or Money Order.

**NO C.O.D.'s**

### V. M. ENTERPRISES

9201 SUNSET BOULEVARD, SUITE 104
HOLLYWOOD, CALIFORNIA 90069

---

## WHILE THEY LAST!

### BEATLE BOOTY BAGS

*If you don't own an autographed picture of the Beatles . . . this is the next best thing.*

Fully emblazoned with pictures of
**GEORGE, JOHN, RINGO & PAUL**

**Strong. Reinforced Vinyl. Waterproof. Washable**

PERFECT CARRY-ALL FOR . . . BEACH-GEAR, CAMERAS,
PORTABLES . . . SNACKS . . SWEATERS
(IN AN EMERGENCY . . . EVEN SCHOOLBOOKS)

Full Size: 10½" x 15". Lightweight. Closes Tight. Beatle approved and just right.

**Limited Supply. First Come, First Serve!**

- - - - - - - - - - - - DETACH AND MAIL - - - - - - - - - - - -

MAIL TODAY TO:
BEATLES, BOX C, CULVER CITY, CALIFORNIA
PLEASE RUSH ME the Beatle Booty Bags at $1.00 each (including tax)
ENCLOSED find $............. for (quantity) ............. Beatle Booty Bags
Send To:
NAME ........................ ADDRESS ........................
CITY ........................ STATE ............. ZIP .........

# KRLA ARCHIVES

### A Friend of Emperor Hudson Comes To Call

**IT WAS A STRANGE PAIR** that recently visited the KRLA studios in Pasadena. HERMAN MUNSTER chats in parking lot with DAVE HULL (who's not sure what may happen) and BOB EUBANKS. That wild car is what HERMAN uses to fling along the Sunset Strip. EMPEROR HUDSON, who authorized this rare informal picture, seems pleased by the antics of good-natured Herman. At least HULL hopes he's good-natured!

# New Formula "S" sports package gives Barracuda added sizzle. Ouch.

A hot Commando 273-cu.-in. V-8 engine, with 4-barrel carburetor; 10.5:1 compression ratio; high lift, high-overlap cam. Heavy-duty shocks, springs and sway bar. A tachometer, wide-rim (14-in.) wheels, special Blue Streak tires, and simulated bolt-on wheel covers. Barracuda. The fast moving fastback that seats five! Seven feet of cargo space – great place for surfboards!

**Served *hot* at your nearby Plymouth Dealers.**

## HAVE YOU HEARD???? GOT THE WORD????
## Your Plymouth Dealer is a DEALIN' MAN!

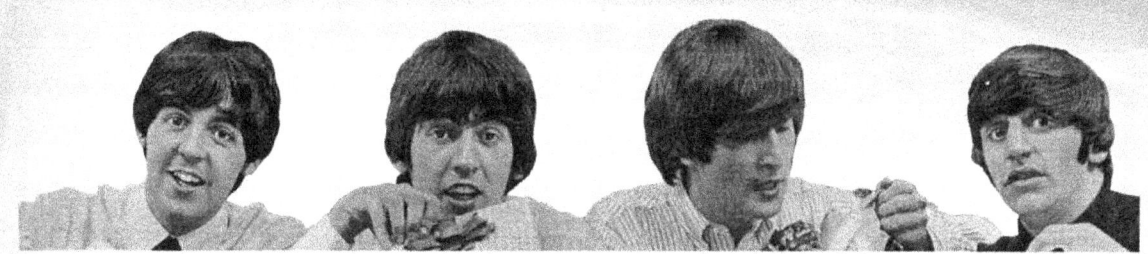

**EARN TOP MONEY WHILE HAVING FUN** (See Page 5)

# KRLA BEAT

**ENJOY A LAUGH ON THE BEATLES** (See Page 7)

Volume 1, No. 13 — Los Angeles, California — Ten Cents — May 26, 1965

## Derek Taylor Reports
## Byrds Hit Sour Note

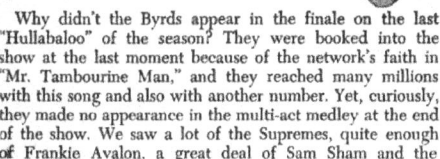

Why didn't the Byrds appear in the finale on the last "Hullabaloo" of the season? They were booked into the show at the last moment because of the network's faith in "Mr. Tambourine Man," and they reached many millions with this song and also with another number. Yet, curiously, they made no appearance in the multi-act medley at the end of the show. We saw a lot of the Supremes, quite enough of Frankie Avalon, a great deal of Sam Sham and the Pharoahs, more of Barbara McNair and Joannie Sommers.

But no Byrds.

**Refused**

So why? I hear the Los Angeles Fivesome were asked to join in the medley by singing "This Diamond Ring," and they didn't want to do it.

Well, it's their decision, but I think it was a wrong one because the eyes of practically everybody in America who cares or knows about pop music were on the screen for the final "Hullabaloo."

And those closing moments are vital if a group is to make any sort of lingering imprint. Sam Sham benefitted by the absence of the Byrds and will, as a result, probably take "Wooly Bully" very close to the top of the national charts.

The Byrds, of course, are still zooming to the elite cluster of artists who will sell a million records.

I believe they are still in with a good chance of a No. 1.

**Premature**

But at this stage in their career, it seems a little early to be turning down opportunities to appear in front of major network television cameras.

Enough of that. "Mr. Tambourine Man" remains a beautiful record.

So, the Rolling Stones came in and were absolutely charming with everyone. Dick Biondi went overboard just before midnight on the day of their arrival to thank them for their cooperation and their warmth.

It was quite obvious that he meant what he was saying. And having travelled appalling distan—

**—MORE ON PAGE TWO**

## Thanks For Your Great Response On Subscriptions

Subscriptions continue to flood the KRLA BEAT office, and we couldn't be happier.

It means that everyone now has a chance to receive the BEAT, America's fastest-growing newspaper and the leading publication for teens and young adults.

Our special introductory offer, introduced two weeks ago when the KRLA BEAT first began accepting subscriptions, is still in effect. You can have the BEAT delivered to your mailbox for just $3 per year, or $5 for two years.

You'll find a subscription coupon inside. You will begin receiving your copy from the mailman within one or two weeks.

## BEATLE WRITER REVEALS STORY BEHIND FILMING OF NEW MOVIE

"The size of the ten-armed image of the terrible Goddess of Kaili looming above the high walls surrounding London's Twickenham Film Studios was such that, as each of her giant arms was dismantled by crane one chilly February morning of this year, rumor had it that the Beatles' second movie had been scrapped."

Thus begins publicist Tony Howard in the opening paragraph of an interesting behind-the-scenes story of what really happened during the often-hectic and sometimes-dangerous three months of filming by John, Paul, George and Ringo.

Next week the KRLA BEAT will carry every word of Tony Howard's revealing and exclusive account. Subscribe now and have next week's BEAT delivered to your home by mail. You'll find a subscription blank in this issue.

## Winner Gets Interview
## Fab New Beatle Quiz!

Have you done your Beatle homework?

Then get ready for the most fabulous contest ever offered. The KRLA BEAT's "BEATLE QUIZ" starts this week.

The winner will receive the thrill of a lifetime, interviewing the Beatles for the BEAT when they arrive for their Hollywood Bowl concerts in August! Here's still more:

The Winner — if he or she doesn't collapse from excitement — may invite a friend and both will be special guests of the KRLA deejays and the BEAT at a Beatle concert.

Additional prizes will be announced later for runners-up. We're still dickering on them at the moment, but we promise you they will also be fabulous.

**CONTEST DETAILS:**

Here's how it will work:

Each week, until the Beatle invasion in August, the BEAT will ask a series of questions about the "Fab Foursome" — the Beatles.

Contestants will send in their answers each week on a special form to be provided in each issue (starting with this one). When it's all over, the contestant with the most correct answers will see a Beatle concert and interview John, Paul, George and Ringo (and may take a friend along on both occasions).

Nothing like this has ever been offered before!

The questions are being provided by Derek Taylor, who was a key member of the official Beatle organization before joining KRLA and the BEAT and knows more about them than anyone else in the world. Derek will also judge the answers for accuracy and his decisions will be final.

In case of a tie there will be either further questions for those still competing or a drawing to determine the winner.

**HERE'S A TIP**

One helpful hint in advance: Many of the answers have appeared in previous issues of the KRLA BEAT. A limited number of back issues are still available. Elsewhere in the BEAT you'll find special information on obtaining back issues.

Another point: Each person may send in only one set of answers per week. However, if you have friends who don't know about the contest, tell them about it and urge them to enter. If they're luckier than you and should win first prize, they just might take you along as their guest.

Take a look at the questions now and start racking your brain and going through all your Beatle material for the answers.

Good luck!

**— SEE CONTEST ON PAGE 3 —**

### Bowl Acts

## Star-Studded Benefit At Bowl To Aid 'Freedom From Hunger'

The lineup is nearly completed for one of the most fabulous shows ever staged at Hollywood Bowl — and one which will give every Southern California teenager a chance to make a worthwhile contribution toward ending human suffering.

It's the Freedom From Hunger Show of Stars on Sunday, June 6. KRLA is pleased to be a participant.

Among the stars appearing on the giant benefit show will be Steve Allen, Bob Newhart, Joey Bishop, Bill (Jose Jiminez) Dana, Gary Lewis and the Playboys, Dick and DeeDee, Jan and Dean, the Kingsmen, the Byrds and Jackie De Shannon.

Other top names are expected to be added within the next few days, donating their services to help feed hungry children and ease human suffering. Tickets may be ordered now. You'll find an order blank in this issue of the KRLA BEAT.

The Freedom From Hunger campaign in southern California is being watched closely by officials of the organization in Washington and in Rome, the site of the international headquarters.

If the fund-raising drive is successful here it will be attempted nationwide. The Freedom From Hunger campaign was founded by the late President Kennedy to help backward nations develop an agricultural system capable of feeding their starving millions.

**KRLA 1110**

### TOP TEN

1. WOOLY BULLY
2. HELP ME, RHONDA
3. GLORIA/ BABY PLEASE DON'T GO
4. BACK IN MY ARMS AGAIN
5. YOU TURN ME ON
6. TICKET TO RIDE/YES IT IS
7. OOH BABY BABY
8. MRS. BROWN
9. MR. TAMBOURINE MAN
10. THE LAST TIME/PLAY WITH FIRE

—TUNEDEX ON PAGE 6

# KRLA ARCHIVES

## More About
### DEREK TAYLOR

ces in all conditions with the Beatles, Tommy Quickly and others, I know how difficult it can be even looking an interviewer in the eyes, never mind answering questions and creating a good impression.

**Marathon**

Probably the worst trip is the flight from London to Los Angeles.

It lasts 13 hours. If one leaves at 11 o'clock in the morning, one arrives in Los Angeles at 3 p.m. in the afternoon. It is, in fact, 1 a.m. the following day in England. So you can imagine how full of vigor and energy a pop star feels when he steps off the aircraft. Still . . . that's show-business. The money is good.

One of the weirdest names in the business is Sir Raleigh and the Cupons.

Sir Raleigh is, really, an amiable young Canadian called Dewey Martin, with a large voice and a big grin. He has been on the Hollywood scene for a few weeks now, singing now and again at the Red Velvet Club and recording.

He is due to work for Tower Records soon. Meanwhile, his latest release is "Tomorrow's Gonna Be Another Day," It's not at all bad.

**Fine Act**

Talking of the Red Velvet, the other night I saw one of the best acts in the world — the Checkmates, a fivesome playing organ, drums, brass, guitars, and singing better than most other groups I've ever heard.

The leader is a man called Bobby Stevens, facially the double of Sammy Davis Jr., but more heavily built.

The musicianship, vitality, personality and humor of the group is an object lesson in entertainment. You have to be 18 to visit the club, but try and catch this group. They come from Seattle.

What ever happened to Tommy Quickly? It's now five months since the BEAT quoted Brian Epstein as saying, "He is going to be bigger than the Beatles." To the best of my knowledge, this claim has scarcely been justified.

**No Hits**

This Liverpool 19-year-old — the first male soloist to be signed by Brian — is an extremely good live entertainer. But he cannot, for the life of him, make a hit record.

However, I learn that he is due in the States in July for a Dick Clark Caravan of Stars. I'm looking forward to seeing him again because he is a cheerful companion and a very hard worker, utterly dedicated to show-business.

**Another Tommy**

How wonderful to see that Tommy Steele, first and greatest of the British Rock 'n' Rollers, has had a Broadway triumph in "Half a Sixpence."

This excellent, unpretentious musical — adapted from H. G. Wells' "Kipps" — had a successful run of over two years in London's West End and now looks set for a prolonged stay in New York.

Tommy Steele was Britain's answer to Presley in 1955. He was then a thin, pale boy with a wide, wide smile and a tumult of golden hair.

He did with Rock what the Beatles did with Beat — he made it respectable and acceptable to adults.

Now, ten years later, he has successfully crossed the treacherous gulf from pop star to legitimate artist.

## Charlie Chides Petula Clark

AFTER RECEIVING A GOLD RECORD and a Grammy Award for "DOWNTOWN," the English thrush made a confession to KLRA's CHARLIE O'DONNELL. She is frightened by all the downtown traffic.

### Backstage Report
## Pet Clark A Hit At Party

One of the record world's most popular attractions is the meet-the-press party for a performer whose records are bursting through the charts.

To those who have been in the news profession for years, such functions may eventually get to be "old hat." But I find them to be entertaining, sometimes a little bewildering and often quite exciting.

I'll share the experience with you, recounting last week's session with the very popular and charming Petula Clark.

The backdrop is the plush Rodeo Room of the Beverly Hills Hotel. A small table, with press biographies and publicity pictures piled high, is startegically placed just inside the door. The room itself is filled with small groups of people — eating, drinking, "talking shop" and blowing cigarette smoke into the already hazy atmosphere.

**Hidden**

The star herself is hidden by towering reporters — some with tape recorders, such as KRLA's Jim Hamblin who seems to be everywhere all the time.

The question of the hour seems to be, "Which one is she?" I decided to try the direct approach.

In the middle of a knot of reporters, photographers, record executives and assorted hangers-on I finally spot the extremely petite Petula Clark. She speaks in a soft British clip, and one has to listen closely to hear her above the general uproar. Her first name is pronounced "Pa-chew-la," with the emphasis on the second syllable.

**False Report**

It quickly becomes apparent that the press release which said she was in town for a screen test was false.

Miss Clark says she did not start out as an actress, and if she does make a movie she wants it to be a good one. She doesn't mind if it's only a small part, just as long as it is a small part in a good movie. But as of now there is no movie — either good or bad — in the offing.

At this point, after some man snatches Petula away from me, I penetrate further into the mass confusion of the Rodeo Room. I spot a few familiar faces in the crowd. Jack Good, "Shindig's" very capable producer is on hand. KRLA is represented by Charlie O'Donnell, Dick Moreland, Derek Tayor, and the ever-present Jim Hamblin.

Several disc jockeys from "rival" radio stations are there. (You might be interested in knowing that there is no active warefare between disc jockeys and their "rivals." In fact, some of them are the very best of friends.)

**Big Moment**

Then comes the highlight of the evening — the presentation of a gold record signifying record sales totaling one million for Petula's "Downtown." Pet reports that although she felt "Downtown" would be a hit, she had no idea it would be such a big hit.

Next, Petula is presented with her grammy award for the Best Rock and Roll record of 1964 — "Downtown." She steps to the microphone, thanks everyone for their support, and says she hopes she will be doing a lot more performing for American audiences in the future.

There are more pictures, more questions, and more answers. Petula made her debut on the BBC when she was nine years old, and by the time she had reached 12 ances on television! She has also made over 25 movies, but she says singing is her real love.

As her favorite groups Petula lists the Beatles, Rolling Stones, and Beach Boys. Among other things, she dislikes getting up in the morning, snakes, and people who don't dig Peter Sellers. She lives in Paris with her French husband and two daughters. Her personal ambition: to have a son.

Finally, about three hours after it began, it's all over. The guests begin drifting out as they had come in — in pairs, in groups, or alone. Some hurry — they have deadlines to meet. Others saunter out slowly, stopping at each group to say their good-byes. Still others hang around, apparently dreading the return to the office, home or traffic-jammed streets.

The red-jacketed waiters begin their enormous task of cleaning up, and restoring the Rodeo Room to its original splendor. The Petula Clark party is over, but another star is scheduled for another star later in the evening.

—Louise Criscione

## FAN CLUBS

**PRETTY THINGS**
c/ Sue Bray
627 E. Dalton
Glendora, California

**DONOVAN FAN CLUB**
c/o Mary Curry
617 W. 107 Street
Los Angeles, Calif.

**HERMAN'S HERMITS**
c/o Sandi & Shar
21722 Anza Avenue
Torrance, Calif. 90503

**WE APPRECIATE THE TALENTED ROLLING STONES**
c/o Elaine Romero
323 N. Marfguerita Ave.
Alhambra, Calif. 91801
For information on any of the Fan Clubs be sure to send a stamped, self-addressed envelope.

**IAN WHITCOMB**
c/o Kathie Raisler
14720 Gandesa Road
La Mirada, California 90638
(Send a self-addressed and stamped envelope)

**DOBIE GRAY**
c/o P.O. Box 1446
Studio City, California

**CANNIBAL AND THE HEADHUNTERS**
c/o Miss Margie Martinez
5160 Whittier Blvd.
Los Angeles, Calif. 90022

**THE BYRDS**
c/o Kathy McIntyre
Suite 504
6290 Sunset
Hollywood, Calif.
Dues—$1.00 plus 2 five-cent stamps)

**JOEY PAIGE**
c/o Linda Kirk
6372 Antioch
Riverside, Calif. 92504
(Dues — $1.00 Members receive 8x10, wallet picture, membership card, fact-sheet and news letters)

**THE SPATS**
SHOWS-DANCES
FAN CLUB
P.O. Box 12
Stanton, Calif.
Tel. (714) 539-5980

---

**23 SKIDOO**
Dancing to Live Name Bands
2116 Westwood Blvd., West Los Angeles
**Girls 18, Guys 21**
*23 Skidoo Dancers are now seen on TV's
Hollywood A'GoGo Saturday on Channel 9 at 9:00 p.m.*
**Closed Mondays**

---

**WAREHOUSE IX**
2214 Stoner Avenue
off Olympic in West Los Angeles
**Dancing to Live Name Bands**
Los Angeles' Unique Young Adult Nite Club
*Girls and Guys 18 and Over*
**Big Sunday Afternoon Dance Sessions from 4 to 10 p.m.**
Closed Tuesdays

# KRLA ARCHIVES

## KRLA TUNEDEX

| THIS WEEK | LAST WEEK | TITLE | ARTIST |
|---|---|---|---|
| 1. | 1. | WOOLY BULLY | Sam The Sham & The Pharoahs |
| 2. | 2. | GLORIA/BABY PLEASE DON'T GO | Them |
| 3. | 3. | MRS. BROWN/I GOTTA DREAM ON | Herman's Hermits |
| 4. | 5. | TICKET TO RIDE | The Beatles |
| 5. | 6. | JUST ONCE IN MY LIFE | The Righteous Brothers |
| 6. | 7. | OOH BABY BABY | The Miracles |
| 7. | 20. | HELP ME, RHONDA | The Beach Boys |
| 8. | 8. | THE LAST TIME/PLAY WITH FIRE | Rolling Stones |
| 9. | 4. | WHEN I'M GONE | Brenda Holloway |
| 10. | 12. | SHE'S ABOUT A MOVER | The Sir Douglas Quintet |
| 11. | 14. | JUST YOU | Sonny & Cher |
| 12. | 17. | BACK IN MY ARMS AGAIN | The Supremes |
| 13. | 11. | SILHOUETTES | Herman's Hermits |
| 14. | 24. | JUST A LITTLE | The Beau Brummels |
| 15. | 31. | YOU TURN ME ON | Ian Whitcomb & Bluesville |
| 16. | 15. | CONCRETE AND CLAY | Unit Four Plus Two |
| 17. | 9. | GAME OF LOVE | Wayne Fontana & The Mindbenders |
| 18. | 23. | BABY THE RAIN MUST FALL | Glenn Yarbrough |
| 19. | 32. | MR. TAMBOURINE MAN | The Byrds |
| 20. | 13. | IT'S NOT UNUSUAL | Tom Jones |
| 21. | 21. | I'LL NEVER FIND ANOTHER YOU | The Seekers |
| 22. | 22. | I DO LOVE YOU | Billy Stewart |
| 23. | 30. | SHAKIN' ALL OVER | Guess Who? |
| 24. | 16. | I KNOW A PLACE | Petula Clark |
| 25. | 10. | NOWHERE TO RUN | Martha & The Vandellas |
| 26. | 27. | CATCH THE WIND | Donovan |
| 27. | 19. | COUNT ME IN | Gary Lewis & The Playboys |
| 28. | 28. | IT'S GONNA BE ALRIGHT | Gerry & The Pacemakers |
| 29. | 18. | TIRED OF WAITING FOR YOU | The Kinks |
| 30. | 25. | I'LL BE DOGGONE | Marvin Gaye |

### CLIMBERS

| | | | |
|---|---|---|---|
| 1. | 34. | SWING ME | Nino Tempo & April Stevens |
| 2. | 38. | TRUE LOVE WAYS | Peter & Gordon |
| 3. | 27. | COUNT ME IN | Gary Lewis & The Playboys |
| 4. | 41. | CRYING IN THE CHAPEL | Elvis Presley |
| 5. | 46. | ENGINE ENGINE NO. 9 | Roger Miller |
| 6. | 39. | YOU WERE MADE FOR ME | Freddie & The Dreamers |
| 7. | 43. | GOOD BYE, SO LONG | Ike & Tina Turner |
| 8. | 42. | YOU REALLY KNOW HOW TO HURT A GUY | Jan & Dean |
| 9. | 43. | PEANUTS (LA CACAHUATA) | The Sunglows |
| 10. | 45. | LAST CHANCE TO TURN AROUND | Gene Pitney |

## English Top Ten

1. TICKET TO RIDE ............................ The Beatles
2. KING OF THE ROAD ........................ Roger Miller
3. THE MINUTE YOU'RE GONE ............. Cliff Richard
4. HERE COMES THE NIGHT ........................ Them
5. POP GO THE WORKERS ............... Baron-Knights
6. BRING IT ON HOME TO ME ........... The Animals
7. A WORLD OF OUR OWN ................ The Seekers
8. CATCH THE WIND ........................... Donovan
9. LITTLE THINGS ............................. Dave Berry
10. CONCRETE AND CLAY ............... Unit Four + 2

### FREDDIE MAKES 'CUKOO' MOVIE

What better title for a movie starring Freddie and the Dreamers than "Cuckoo Patrol."

As you might suspect, it's a comedy. Freddie and the boys supplied many of the ideas for it.

Freddie told the Beat it's based on the style of the Three Stooges several years ago.

Freddie's sidekick Derek explained, "Being idiots, we decided to center the plot around five boy scouts, a scoutmaster and cook. Since we all look marvelous in shorts, we play the boy scouts."

"We're the type of boy scouts who can do nothing right and have all their good deeds misfire," added Freddie.

And leaping into the air he shouted, "I've always wanted to be a boy scout rubbing sticks together in the woods."

### Donovan

ENGLAND'S UNUSUAL and controversial young folk singer, Donovan, sings "Catch The Wind." He's never without his familiar cap. That's a harmonica under his chin.

## The Week That Was
### 'CELLAR FULL OF NOISE' SET FOR EARLY RELEASE

The BEATLES' second film, officially titled "Help!", will be premiered at the London Pavillion on July 29.

Like we said . . . "Help!", because we can't be there.

BRIAN EPSTEIN'S best-seller, "Cellar Full of Noise," is to be released in paperback form in July. It's his story of discovering the BEATLES and other top English acts.

DONOVAN hats, tunics and sweaters may be on sale in the near future. It remains to be seen how they will fare over here, but in England many predict sales will be as large as they were for Beatle jackets.

BILLY J. KRAMER has an unusual title for his new song—"Trains, Boats and Planes." It's a slow ballad written by Burt Bacharach. Discouraged by the failure of his last record, "It's Gotta Last Forever," Billy had been looking for months for the right song to record. At one point earlier he found a number by JACKIE DeSHANNON, featured it in his act, and decided to record it upon returning from Australia. Returning to England on the plane, he read where the SEARCHERS had beaten him to the punch. The song was "When You Walk in the Room."

Speaking of unusual titles, MANFRED MANN just released "Watermelon Man." And the group also recorded the background songs for the United Artists move, "What's New Pussycat?"

The RONETTES have recorded their first British album —"The Fabulous Ronettes."

BOBBY RYDELL proves he's not only a leader in the entertainment field, but in anything he undertakes. The popular vocalist, serving a hitch in the Army, has just been selected as one of the top two men in his group completing basic training at Fort Dix, N.J.

The YARDBIRDS' manager is in this country arranging dates for their first U.S. tour.

While much has been said about the British influence on American music, one-third of the songs on the English charts are by American artists. And a large number of the British hits were written by Americans.

Despite the English craze of the past year or so, BOBBY VINTON'S popularity has remained at its peak. His string of hits began in the summer of 1962 with "Roses Are Red." Since then he's hit with "Blue on Blue," "Blue Velvet," "My Heart Belongs to Only You" and "Clinging Vine." His latest, "L-O-N-L-Y," also appears to be a solid hit. Incidentally, DANNY THOMAS has signed Bobby for one of his TV specials in the fall.

The ANIMALS will wind up their current U.S. tour by appearing on the Ed Sullivan show May 30.

### THE BYRDS
Official National
FAN CLUB
Suite 504
6290 Sunset Blvd.
Hollywood

Send $1.00 plus two 5-cent stamps and receive photos, fact sheets, biographies. Fun contests each month.

Free Concerts Planned For Members Only

Be a chapter president. Enlist ten (10) new members now!

The BYRDS Are Great

## Who Says Today's Recording Stars Don't Have Talent?

Many people in the cube-shaped world like to criticize pop music stars as "no-talents" and ignoramuses. If such people listened more and talked less they would discover:

That hundreds of today's pop music figures are just as talented away from the microphones as they are in front of them.

That John Lennon has world popularity as an author.

That Peter Noone (Herman) is drafting a forthcoming novel about the pop music industry that is already being touted as a best-seller.

Twinkle and Bob Dylan are also writing novels.

That Charley Watts has received rave reviews for his first book of prose and drawings, and is now preparing a series of childrens' books.

That Mick Jagger, Brian Jones, Les Chadwick and Paul McCartney are also widely known for their photography.

And that Wayne Fontana and Sandie Shaw are accomplished at sketching and designing.

Speaking of outside talents, what can the critics do besides gripe?

### Herman To Star In Clark Film

The hottest group in the U.S. at present, Herman's Hermits, will spend several weeks in Hollywood this fall.

Following the lead of the Beatles and the Dave Clark Five, they'll star in a movie. It will be produced by Dick Clark Productions.

Clark set it up on his recent European tour. He told the Beat it will feature them in a mystery story, starring Herman but featuring the group in a number of songs.

### KRLA BEAT

The KRLA BEAT is published weekly by Prestige Publishing Company; editorial and advertising offices at 6290 Sunset Boulevard, Suite 504, Hollywood, California 90028.

Single copy price, 10 cents.

Subscription price: U.S. and possessions, and Canada, $3 per year or $5 for two years. Foreign rates upon request.

## BEATLE QUIZ

Beatle Quiz
KRLA BEAT
Suite 504
6290 Sunset Blvd.
Hollywood, Calif. 90028
CONTEST EDITOR:

Below are my answers to the first five questions in the BEATLE QUIZ CONTEST.

My Name .................................................. Address ..................................................

City .................................................. State .................................. Zip Code ..............

I (☐ am) (☐ am not) presently a subscriber to the KRLA BEAT.

### QUESTIONS:

1. Of those who performed in "A Hard Day's Night," how many acting roles in the Beatles' second film, "Help!"? ..............................
2. Who is Malcolm Evans? ..............................
3. In what country have the Beatles performed most, outside England? ..............................
4. How were Paul and George travelling when they first met? ..............................
5. In what part of Liverpool were the Beatles raised? ..............................

# KRLA ARCHIVES

## DUBLIN'S IAN WHITCOMB IS A STRANGE MIXTURE

Ian Whitcomb is certainly full of contrasts. To begin with, he is English but the name "Ian" is Scottish for John. He goes to Trinity College in Dublin where he studies American History. And as a topper, he spends most of his free time in Seattle, Washington!

Ian was born in Working county of Surrey on July 10, 1941 (that makes him 23, girls). He likes "coarse" music of all types, but no opera and no art music.

By all rights, Ian should be enjoying the "good" life of the higher-ups; his one grandfather was offered a peerage, and the other is an oil magnate! But this "good" life of coming-out parties etc., holds no charm for him and so he sings and plays the piano.

### Many Bands

During his twenty-three years, Ian has formed a number of bands. He once had a skiffle group, a "Dave Brubeck" group, a jazz group, and a rock 'n roll band. This last one called Bluesville, does great business in and around Dublin and is the only beat group of its kind in Ireland. The members of Bluesville are all Irish except for one lone Yankee who plays sax for the group.

Besides going to school and singing, Ian has also managed to do some film editing at Pinewood Studios where he worked on "Tune of Glory" with Alec Guinness. He then moved to documentaries where he pieced together a ragtime sequence and also acquired quite an attachment for that kind of music.

He likes playing ragtime best, but since it is currently unpopular he confines himself to playing it only as a hobby.

### High Voice

Ian was just fooling around when he came up with the idea of singing in that high voice. It seemed to work all right in "This Sporting Life", so this time Ian went all the way and sang "You Turn Me On" entirely in his high voice.

It looks like it worked all right on this one too as it made its initial appearance on the survey at number fifteen and is 15 and is the fastest climbing record on the charts!

Ian is primarily a pianist, and it is he who does all that wild piano playing on his records. Ian says he has been playing the piano for about ten years. Besides that, he began playing the accordian when he was twelve, went on to the kazzoom, ukelele, the tub bass, and the jug!

### Song Writer

Ian is also a song writer both the "A" and "B" side of his new record were penned by Ian himself. Ian reports that "You Turn Me On" was a one-take record. In fact, right in the middle of the song he knocked an ash tray off the piano, and the crash was picked up by the sensitive microphone. That didn't bother Ian; he kept right on singing!

He thought perhaps they had left that little extra noise in the final product, but this reporter listened intently and failed to hear it, so the record producer must have decided the ash tray added nothing to the record and cut it out. What a pity!

In the vital statistics department, Ian is good looking (just look at his picture), has a fabulous sense of humor, and is single! And if that isn't enough, Ian says he "likes American girl because they are more attractive than English girls!"

### Long Hair

Ian has the traditional long hair, but he says he doesn't know what he will do with it because now the trend in England is toward shorter hair. If he doesn't play the piano in his act, he does a weird bit with the microphone. It must be seen to be believed because it is absolutely impossible to describe with mere words!

Among his favorite recording artists, Ian lists the Beatles, Roy Orbison, Chuck Berry, and Sophie Tucker. (Seems these English boys still like Sophie!). As for the future, Ian is in his last year at Trinity College. After graduation, he hopes to work for his Ph.D. at an American University.

After watching Ian Whitcomb perform and after listening to him talk, it is a pretty safe assumption to say that this Englishman with the Scottish name, who goes to school in Ireland, and likes American girls will go just as far as he wants to in this business.

## It Works Both Ways
# U.S. Still Music Capital

By LOUISE CRISCIONE

The subject of the British influence on American record charts and recording artists has been overdone to the point where most people are sick unto death of it.

The other side of the story, the American influence on British record charts and recording artists, has been strangely ignored. No one, it seems, cares to discuss the fact that Americans have contributed heavily to the pop scene all over the world, and the British pop scene in particular.

British singers rely heavily on American composers for their material. If the Beatles don't write their own songs, they are apt to use Chuck Berry ("Roll Over Beethoven", "Rock And Roll Music") or Carl Perkins' ("Honey Don't", "Everybody's Trying To Be My Baby") compositions.

Ditto for the Rolling Stones ("Carol", "Down The Road Apiece"). Jackie DeShannon wrote Marianne Faithful's hit "Come Stay With Me" and the Searchers' "Needles and Pins" and "When You Walk In the Room".

Quite a few Buddy Holly compositions have been redone successfully by British artists. The Beatles did "Words Of Love", and the Rolling Stones did "Not Fade Away". The current example of the late Holly's work is Peter & Gordon's "True Love Ways".

Then there is the popular composing team of Goffin/King. These two Americans wrote three of the songs on Herman's tremendously popular album, "Introducing Herman's Hermits". "Chains" featured on one of the Beatles' first albums was also penned by the Goffin/King team.

Two Sam Cooke compositions are currently heading for high positions on American charts by way of the Animals new one, "Bring It On Home To Me", and Herman's latest, "Wonderful World". Both of these records have already hit the British charts in a big way.

And so the list of American penned compositions goes on and on and would probably run the entire length of the Sunset Strip if one were ambitious enough to write them all down!

Another interesting note is that many English groups would rather fly the several thousand miles to record in an American studio than to use the more convenient but less well-equipped English studios. The Rolling Stones are the big case-on-point.

So, one would do well to remember that behind the facade of the British taking over the pop scene there beats a VERY American heart, not to mention an American pen and recording studio!
—Louise Criscione

---

**KRLA BEAT SUBSCRIPTION**

Order By Mail Now—Save Over 40%!

Please Rush Me the KRLA BEAT at Your Special Introductory Subscription Rate

☐ 1 Year—52 Issues—$3.00    ☐ 2 Years — $5.00

Enclosed is $_____

Send To:_____ Age_____

Address:_____

City_____ State_____ Zip_____

*Please be sure to include your Zip Code number!*

MAIL YOUR ORDER TO:

KRLA BEAT
1401 South Oak Knoll Avenue
Pasadena, California 91106

---

Back issues of the KRLA BEAT are still available, for a limited time. If you've missed an issue of particular interest to you, send 10 cents for each copy wanted, along with a self-addressed stamped envelope to:

KRLA BEAT
Suite 504
6290 Sunset Blvd.
Hollywood, California 90028

ISSUES AVAILABLE —

3/31 — BEATLE TITLE CHOSEN
4/7 — BEATLE PLANS REVEALED
4/14 — INTERVIEW WITH JOHN LENNON
4/21 — INTERVIEW WITH PAUL McCARTNEY
4/28 — CHIMP EXCITES TEEN FAIR
5/5 — HERMANIA SPREADS
5/12 — HERE COME THE BEATLES
5/19 — EXCITING CONTEST —
         VISIT WITH BEATLES

---

# YEAH-YEAH WHISK

**You Have Seen It On National TV!**

**Now Twisk YOUR Whisk And Add**

**New Excitement To Your Dancing!**

ORDER NOW BY MAIL!

NAME_____

ADDRESS_____

CITY_____ ZIP CODE_____

Check Color Preference:
Red ☐    White ☐    Blue ☐    Yellow ☐
         Orange ☐   Green ☐

Send $2.00 (includes postage and tax) to:
"WHISK"
1800 No. Argyle, Suite 510
Hollywood, California

# KRLA ARCHIVES

## PAY FOR YOUR SUMMER VACATION

### And WIN

### FABULOUS PRIZES

AS A SPECIAL REPRESENTATIVE

FOR THE

# KRLA BEAT

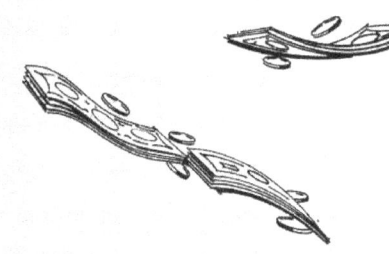

**6 STUDENTS IN EACH SCHOOL**

*May Qualify to Accept Subscriptions*

**FIRST PRIZE!**
YOU AND A FRIEND WILL BE GUESTS OF KRLA AT A
**BEATLE CONCERT!**
And a Beatle Press Conference!
You will also receive
A Beautiful WRIST WATCH!

## IT'S FUN AND PROFITABLE

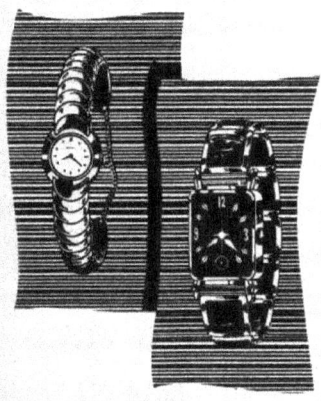

The KRLA BEAT is the NATION'S TOP NEWSPAPER for young Americans, and it is NOW ACCEPTING SUBSCRIPTIONS FOR THE FIRST TIME. Now you can become a circulation representative in your school.

HERE'S ALL YOU HAVE TO DO: Send your name, address, telephone number and the school you attend to KRLA BEAT, 1401 S. OAK KNOLL, PASADENA, Calif. But do it fast — first come, first served. We will send you all the necessary information to become a successful KRLA BEAT representative. You will learn handsome profits on each subscription. Earnings are unlimited, because EVERY TEENAGER SHOULD BE A SUBSCRIBER!

AND THERE ARE SPECIAL PRIZES FOR THOSE WHO SELL THE MOST SUBSCRIPTIONS BETWEEN NOW AND THE END OF THE SEMESTER!

**10 Second Prizes:**
BEAUTIFUL, ENGRAVED
**WRIST WATCHES!**
(Winners may choose between second and third prizes.)

**10 Third Prizes:**
AUTOGRAPHED
**BEATLE ALBUMS!**

### Don't Wait! Join the Fun and Earn Money as Well!

Remember: We Can Only Appoint Six Students From Each School
SEND IN YOUR APPLICATION TODAY

## Inside KRLA

BOB EUBANKS is by far the most popular man in town these days. Bob had no idea he had so many friends until he booked THE BEATLES for Hollywood Bowl. Even though tickets for both concerts are being handled by the Bowl, Bob is still besieged by telephone calls begging him to dig up a couple of ducats — "just for old times" sake."

CHARLIE O'DONNELL AND DICK MORELAND attended a Warner Bros. Record party for PETULA CLARK and came away very impressed with the lovely songstress from England. PETULA was in town for the Grammy show, in which she received an award for 'DOWNTOWN.'

SATURDAY, MAY 29, is the date of the annual goat-milking contest among the KRLA deejays at the Great Western Fair & Dairy Show. After watching the practice sessions it looks like a toss-up between the HULLABALOOER and the EMPOR-ER. BEAUTIFUL BOB seems to have more "pull" but DAVE has an advantage even though he's a city boy. He's been practicing all his life by squeezing nickels.

CHARLEY O' and DAVE are large with bunnies as well as goats. Elsewhere in this week's issue you'll see them awarding the KRLA "Bunny" to the contest winner at the Playboy Club (was he surprised when the "life-sized and loveable bunny" he won turned out to be a huge stuffed one instead of the Playboy-type.

CASEY KASIM would have gone to the Playboy Club with them, but got lost on the way. He had a package of carrots in his hand and walked all up and down the Sunset Strip asking directions to the "Rabbit Club." NEWSMAN RICHARD BEE-BE is back on the job, although still limping noticeably, after routine surgery recently. You should hear him talk about his operation.

## What Did You Expect?

"A LIFE-SIZE, CUDDLY BUNNY OF YOUR VERY OWN." That was the big prize in the KRLA Bunny Contest, and CHARLIE O'DONNELL and DAVE HULL give winner JAMES PATRICK HARBUCK his "bunny" in ceremonies at the Playboy Club. Mrs. Harbuck seems quite happy over the way things turned out, but her husband — perhaps expecting the other kind of "bunnie" — manages only a weak smile. KRLA Program Director MEL HALL, who dreams up such gimmicks as this, is currently in hiding from enraged listeners. Wait 'til you see what's in those "Send Me Mine" envelopes.

---

**PETE SEEGER**
JUNE 11 — SANTA MONICA CIVIC AUDITORIUM
JUNE 12 — PASADENA CIVIC AUDITORIUM
TICKETS: $2.50, $3.50 AND $4.00 AT
THE ASH GROVE, BOX OFFICES, & ALL AGENCIES

---

## 2 'Shindig' Shows Fight Legal Battle

Is Irving Weinhause's face ever red! It appears Mr. Weinhause is the loser in the "Battle of the Shindigs". Weinhause is the producer of a touring show called "Shindig 65"; a name which is naturally being confused with ABC-TV's "Shindig". And to add to the abundant confusion, the TV "Shindig" (a Selmur Production) has a show currently touring cross-country under the name "Shindig"!

The battle has already generated three legal suits charging, among other things, restraint of trade and infringement. It has also left Weinhause with a huge flop in Phoenix. Weinhause had booked his show, starring Paul Peterson, into Phoenix. Selmur Productions got wind of this, and bought time on the local radio stations to announce that the show was not in any way connected with the nationally televised "Shindig". It worked beautifully, and Weinhause and his "Shindig 65" were a big bomb. This, of course, caused Weinhause to be particularly upset, and thus the lawsuits.

---

### FREEDOM FROM HUNGER
# SHOW OF STARS
Hollywood Bowl, Sunday, June 6
GIANT BENEFIT SHOW STARRING:

1. Please include a stamped, self-addressed envelope.
2. If tickets are not available at the price you order, you will be send ticket sat the next lowest price, along with a refund.
3. MAIL TO: Freedom From Hunger
   KRLA Radio
   1401 S. Oak Knoll
   Pasadena, California

★ The Byrds
★ Jan And Dean
★ Dick And DeeDee
★ Gary Lewis and The Playboys
★ The Kingsmen
★ Jackie De Shannon

PLUS
★ Steve Allen
★ Bob Newhart
★ Joey Bishop
★ Bill (Jose Jiminez) Dana

**TICKET ORDER**
I HAVE ENCLOSED A CHECK OR MONEY ORDER PAYABLE TO "FREEDOM FROM HUNGER." PLEASE SEND ME THE FOLLOWING TICKETS:
(NO.) ............ TICKETS AT
☐ $2.00
☐ $3.00
☐ $5.00
SEND TO: ...........
ADDRESS: ...........
CITY: ........... STATE ...........
ZIP CODE ........... TELEPHONE ...........

"FREEDOM FROM HUNGER" HELPS THE STARVING HELP THEMSELVES

---

### NEXT WEEK
IN THE
**KRLA BEAT**

MORE QUESTIONS IN BEATLE QUIZ

FASCINATING NEW PICTURES FROM ENGLAND

AND MUCH, MUCH MORE!
LISTEN TO KRLA

# KRLA ARCHIVES

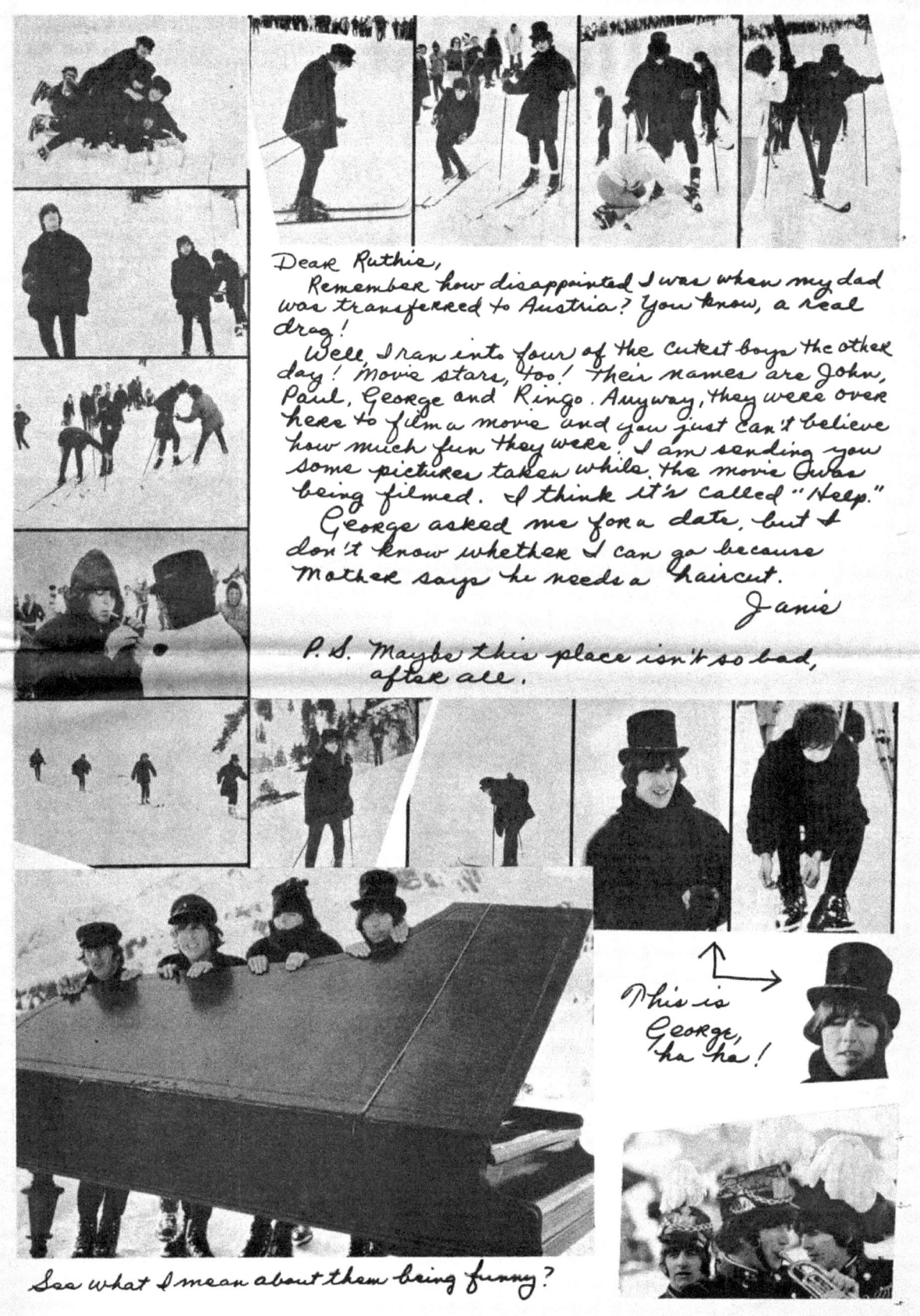

Dear Ruthie,
  Remember how disappointed I was when my dad was transferred to Austria? You know, a real drag!
  Well, I ran into four of the cutest boys the other day! Movie stars, too! Their names are John, Paul, George and Ringo. Anyway, they were over here to film a movie and you just can't believe how much fun they were! I am sending you some pictures taken while the movie was being filmed. I think it's called "Help."
  George asked me for a date, but I don't know whether I can go because Mother says he needs a haircut.
                                    Janie
  P.S. Maybe this place isn't so bad, after all.

This is George, ha ha!

See what I mean about them being funny?

# On The Beat

Always quick to spot potential, Walt Disney has jumped on the bandwagon and will book rock 'n roll acts into Disneyland!

The weekly shows will be tabbed "Humdingers" and will also feature jazz and folk music to appease the older folks. The traditional big bands and gospel singers will also be performing throughout the Magic Kingdom.

On the subject of the rock groups Mr. Disney says "at least they must be reasonably scrubbed and barbered." Anyway, the invasion of Disneyland by rock 'n roll acts will undoubtably attract legions of Southland teens to the famed park and I, for one, can't wait for the season to open! A *very* good move by a very *smart* man.

### Big Hit

I'm going to stick my neck way out and predict that the Animals latest, "Bring It On Home To Me", will be a BIG hit! It's an old Sam Cooke song, and the five Animals really do it justice. These boys have never been able to top their "House of the Rising Sun" although "Please Don't Let Me Be Misunderstood" was certainly a good try.

I will not go so far as to say "Bring It On Home To Me" will either out-sell or outlast "House", but it's the best attempt the Animals have made so far.

The Best Quote of the Week comes from Paul McCartney on how to play the bass guitar: "The best thing to learn about bass guitar is to learn when to shut up."

### Jackie Clicks

Blonde singer, composer, record producer, etc., etc., Jackie DeShannon has come up with a fabulous sound in "What The World Needs Now Is Love." It's the kind of song which haunts you for hours after you've heard it. Anyway for what it's worth, it merits the official ON THE BEAT stamp of approval.

QUICK ONES this week is devoted entirely to the girls on the scene: Cilla Black says she is going to trade in her straight hair style for a curly one like Petula Clark's... And Pet Clark herself will open at the famous Copacabana in November... Francoise Hardy definitely does have a forehead—I saw it... Congratulatitons to Jody Miller, 'cause she really is "Queen of the House" and also the mother of a brand-new baby girl... Sandie Shaw has released an album entitled simply "Sandie Shaw"... Our own tiny, big-voiced girl, Brenda Lee, has a very good new single "Too Many Rivers"; hope it is a big hit for Brenda 'cause she deserves one.

### Animal Photos

Sidenote on the Animals: Eric Burden, lead singer for the group, is a photography nut. Saw some of the pictures he took in New York, and they are really quite good and very professional looking. The line forms on the right for you girls who would like Eric to take your picture—I imagine he could drum up quite a bit of business that way!

WATCH OUT FOR: "Born To Be With You" by the Capital Showband. These showbands are very popular in their native Ireland, but they are having a difficult time duplicating this popularity in England. So, it should be interesting to see how they fare here in America.

ON THE BEAT congratulates those swingin' Beach Boys for having surpassed the ten million mark in record sales! Quite an achievement for these boys and quite a way up from their very first hit, "Surfin."

The Beach Boys' newest addition to their unbroken string of hits, "Help Me Rhonda", has been rapidly ascending the national charts. It looks as if it could go all the way to the top, but then that's nothing new for the five Beach Boys!

### Herman Movie?

PUZZLE OF THE WEEK: Well, will he or won't he? That's the big question this week. Will Herman and his Hermits make a movie or not? Quite sometime ago, Herman announced that he was interested in making a film. Then the news came out that Dick Clark Producttions had signed Herman for a mystery-type movie to begin shooting in September. (But then D.C. Productions was also scheduled to make a Righteous Brothers movie and these plans were dropped. So . . .)

Now, Unger Productions has announced it will begin filming "Pop Goes The World" which will feature, among others, Petula Clark, Rita Pavone, AND Herman's Hermits! All this time, there has been no official word from either Herman or Kennedy Street Enterprises.

So, will he or won't he?

The Chad Mitchell Trio, popular folk singing team, will be doing without their leader, Chad Mitchell, as of July 5. There was no big rift or anything like that—Chad just wants to give acting a try. He will make his debut in a Broadway play, "Postmark Zero". The group will replace Chad but will still keep the name "Mitchell Trio".

Apparently Chad does not intend to abandon singing because he has said: "I don't plan to give up singing. I love it." The Trio has enjoyed plenty of success with their albums and are very much in demand on college campuses throughout the nation.

Our best wishes to Chad on his acting career and to the Mitchell Trio without Chad.

Almost forgot—add Peter & Gordon and the Kinks to your list of English performers scheduled to tour the U.S. this summer.

—Louise Criscione

### Beat Exclusive: Stones Tell All

The Rolling Stones have provided an exciting two weeks for their Southern California fans.

It was exciting for them, too, for all seem to have fallen in love with this area and some of them are seriously planning on making their homes here in later years.

From the moment the Stones arrived to the final note of their latest appearance on "Shindig" KRLA Beat Reporter Rod Barken was constantly with the fun-loving entertainers.

In next weeks' KRLA BEAT Rod recalls all the exciting moments — public and private — as the most controversial act in the entertainment field staged a memorable visit.

A full report on the fabulous Rolling Stones — their opinions, feelings and plans as well as their activities — will be in next week's KRLA BEAT!

## Another Smash Hit For Beach Boys

**THE FABULOUS BEACH BOYS** have done it again! They have a new smash record, "HELP ME, RHONDA," and a top-selling album, "The Beach Boys Today." They earned nearly a million dollars last year in less than 80 concerts, and the Southern California stars should do even better this year.

If you were a KRLA Beat subscriber your name and address would be printed here and you would receive your copy at home, saving 40%. See page 4.

BULK RATE
U.S. Postage
PAID
Permit No.
25497
Los Angeles
California

# KRLA ARCHIVES

**ROLLING STONES**
Unguarded Moments
In Their L.A. Hideaway

# KRLA BEAT

**THE BYRDS**
Why They're Flying
So High and Fast

Volume 1, No. 13 — Los Angeles, California — Ten Cents — June 2, 1965

# L.A. ROCKS AS STONES ROLL

KRLA BEAT
6290 Sunset, #504
Hollywood, Cal. 90028

BULK RATE
U.S. Postage
PAID
Permit No.
25497
Los Angeles
California

## INSIDE THE BEAT

> THE ROLLING STONES - As YOU'D Like To See Them!
> "HELP" - Behind The Scenes In Beatle Film
> BEATLE QUIZ, Part 2 - WIN A BEATLE INTERVIEW
> A BEAT EDITORIAL - Are You Hurting Your Idols?
> HOW TO START A FAN CLUB
> SEND A KISS TO JOHN, PAUL, GEORGE or RINGO

— also —

DEREK TAYLOR, HERMAN AND THE HERMITS,
ELVIS PRESLEY, SONNY & CHER, IAN WHITCOMB,
THE KRLA DEE JAYS, SCRAMBLED GROUPS

If you were a KRLA Beat subscriber your name and address would be printed here and you would receive your copy at home, saving 40%. See page 4.

# KRLA ARCHIVES

## HARD WORK, DANGER FOR BEATLES IN 'HELP'
### Press Officer Tells Of Problems Encounted In Filming Movie

(Editor's note: Seldom if ever has any movie caused such world-wide excitement as the second Beatles film. Tony Howard was in charge of publicity, and press relations and travelled with the film company from the sunny Bahamas to the frozen Alps. Howard, a friend of KRLA's Derek Taylor, has written the following account for the KRLA BEAT.)

**BY TONY HOWARD**

The size of the ten-armed image of the terrible Goddess of Kaili looming above the high walls surrounding London's Twickenham Film Studios was such that, as each of her giant arms was dismantled by crane one chilly February morning of this year, rumour had it that the Beatles' second movie had been scrapped.

If it was a bad day for the local fans, for Producer Walter Shenson it was not. After many a hard day's night — preparations for his second Beatles film — this Sphinx-like idol was merely being "disarmed" for transportation to the Bahamas in order to be "re-armed" on arrival there for the astounding finale.

Producer Shenson chartered a BOAC Boeing 707 to transport the cast, unit and very piece of equipment to the Bahamas, but there was the extra passenger with more room than any first class traveller — it was Kaili, whose dismembered body, adorned in white sheets, was stored in every free corner of the plane. Her torso, however, was too big for any luggage rack or spare seat, so Kaili made the trip along the gangway, much to the chagrin of the stewards carrying their trays through the plane.

**From Icebox to Oven**

Artists and crew, muffled in coats and scarves to combat the wintry February weather in London, landed in Nassau to the temperature of 90 degrees in the shade.

For weeks before, Shenson's location manager had been battling with the accommodation problem which confronted him in this popular resort.

**BEATLES IN SCENE FROM NASSAU LOCATION**

How were 700-odd extra people going to be housed in Nassau, which was already bulging at the seems with its usual influx of high season tourists? That his efforts met with success was largely due to the enthusiastic co-operation of American Bob Rowley, chief of the Bahamas Tourist Board.

Next day was spent unpacking and getting ready for shooting. Nearly everyone assembled on the magnificent beach outside the Balmoral Club Hotel. Julie Harris, the costume designer, set about giving the Beatles their final costume fittings. The immense generator was moved into position and Director Richard Lester roamed about, deep in thought, picking the best spots for the next day's filming.

All this activity was accompanied by the cries of fans spotting their

**TURN TO PAGE 9**

---

## FIRST PRIZE!
YOU AND A FRIEND WILL BE GUESTS OF KRLA AT A
**BEATLE CONCERT!**
And a Beatle Press Conference!
You will also receive
A Beautiful WRIST WATCH!

## EARN FAB MONEY, PRIZES AS A BEAT REPRESENTATIVE

### 6 STUDENTS IN EACH SCHOOL
*May Qualify to Accept Subscriptions*

# IT'S FUN AND PROFITABLE

The KRLA BEAT is the NATION'S TOP NEWSPAPER for young Americans, and it is NOW ACCEPTING SUBSCRIPTIONS FOR THE FIRST TIME. Now you can become a circulation representative in your school.

HERE'S ALL YOU HAVE TO DO: Send your name, address, telephone number and the school you attend to KRLA BEAT, 1401 S. OAK KNOLL, PASADENA, Calif. But do it fast — first come, first served. We will send you all the necessary information to become a successful KRLA BEAT representative. You will learn handsome profits on each subscription. Earnings are unlimited, because EVERY TEENAGER SHOULD BE A SUBSCRIBER!

**AND THERE ARE SPECIAL PRIZES FOR THOSE WHO SELL THE MOST SUBSCRIPTIONS BETWEEN NOW AND THE END OF THE SEMESTER!**

## 10 Second Prizes:
**BEAUTIFUL, ENGRAVED WRIST WATCHES!**
(Winners may choose between second and third prizes.)

## 10 Third Prizes:
**AUTOGRAPHED BEATLE ALBUMS!**

I would like to be a KRLA BEAT REPRESENTATIVE in ................ ☐ Jr. ☐ Sr. High

School in the city of: ................

Please send me additional information and forms for selling subscriptions.

Name ................ Age ................

Address ................ City ................

Phone ................ Zip Code ................

# KRLA ARCHIVES

## BYRDS FLYING HIGH

### SKYROCKET TO SUCCESS
## Byrds Utilize Work, Talent

The Byrds are currently one of the hottest groups in the country and some may say they're also one of the luckiest.

One month after their first public performance they have a skyrocketing hit record, "Mr. Tambourine Man," and are attracting swarms of new-found fans — including other artists — for their night club, television and concert performances.

But if luck is one of the ingredients in their recipe for success it must be matched by equal portions of skill, experience and a generous helping of hard work.

The Byrds are often mistaken for a British group. They certainly look the part, from their Beatle-type haircuts to their English-cut clothes. And their sound often has the ring of Liverpool or Manchester.

But at other times it varies from the raw, "gutsy" beat of rhythm and blues to the haunting, delicate sound of folk balladry — a style best illustrated by their recording of "Mr. Tambourine Man."

### No Accident

The Byrds' unique blending of all three styles is not something they hit upon by accident. It is a product of their varied musical backgrounds, since each was an accomplished performer in another field before joining the Byrds. It is also the result of months of rehearsal and practice while they worked tirelessly to develop just the right material, style and blend — before even accepting a club engagement.

It has paid off, for their impact on the American music scene has been more immediate than any other group in years.

It began in August, 1964, when Jim McGuinn, a former accompanist for the Chad Mitchell Trio, worked up some songs with the idea of forming his own group. Three days later David Crosby, a folk singer, joined him to sing harmony. The third member to join the group was Gene Clark, formerly with the New Christy Minstrels.

Some time later David met Michael Clarke, the drummer, at Big Sur in Northern California. Mike joined the group at the same time as Chris Hillman, who formerly had his own bluegrass music group. Now there were five of them and their closed-door practice sessions really began in earnest.

Gene wrote 16 songs for the group and they also worked on material that Bob Dylan wrote for them.

They began their first public performances at Ciro's on the Sunset Strip, a once-proud nightclub which attracted big names from the film colony until a few years ago but was now suffering from a slump in which the performers often outnumbered the customers.

Soon, however, the Byrds caught on with their distinctive infectious sound and their newfound fans began filling up the tables and the dance floor. The crowds were usually sprinkled with other entertainers who had heard of the Byrds and came in to hear them . . . many returning night after night.

Among those who began boosting the Byrds were such artists as Peter, Paul and Mary, Bob Dy-

TURN TO PAGE 10

---

**KRLA BEAT**

The KRLA BEAT is published weekly by Prestige Publishing Company; editorial and advertising offices at 6290 Sunset Boulevard, Suite 504, Hollywood, California 90028.

Single copy price, 10 cents.

Subscription price: U.S. and possessions, and Canada, $3 per year or $5 for two years. Foreign rates upon request.

---

### KRLA BEAT SUBSCRIPTION

As a special introductory offer — if you subscribe now you will save 40% of the regular price.

☐ 1 YEAR — 52 Issues — $3.00        ☐ 2 YEARS — $5.00

Enclosed is $..........

Send to: .......................................... Age: ..........

Address: ..........

City: .......................... State: .................. Zip: ..........

MAIL YOUR ORDER TO: **KRLA BEAT**
1401 South Oak Knoll Avenue
Pasadena, California 91106

---

### Derek Taylor Reports
## 'Wooly Bully' Mystery; Why's It Successful?

Who buys "Wooly Bully?" Here, staring us in the face and outselling the Beatles in Los Angeles, is this first major chart disc by the unknown Sam the Sham and the Pharaohs leaping up every national chart and top of the Tunedex for four weeks.

As far as I can see there was no sustained advertising campaign to launch the record; the group is not particularly handsome; the name is old-fashioned and cumbersome.

So what is selling the record:

It's pure rock n' roll content. It has the pounding beat which has dominated the record scene for 11 years, and for many fans — both in their teens and 20's — it is a welcome return to the raw shouting of the early rockers. A throwback to Little Richard, Carl Perkins or, if you like, Elvis in the good days.

Times are gentler now with Herman singing "Mrs. Brown" and the Beatles writing songs like "If I Fell," and "Yes It Is."

### Room For Something Different

"Wooly Bully" proves that there is always room for something slightly out of step with the trend. On a different level, but proof of the flexibility of the charts, is the current success of Dean Martin, Vic Damone and Patti Page. Patti Page, for example, is bounding up the top 100's on an average of about fifteen places a week with a song called "Hush, Hush, Sweet Charlotte."

It's strange, then, that Frank Sinatra, biggest of them all, fails to make the charts.

One of the penalties of working late into the evening is that one often misses many of the better musical shows on television. I was very disappointed, for instance, to miss the Beatles talking to Peter Sellers on the Grammy Award presentations last week. I'm told the Beatles were as spontaneous and amiable as ever. I didn't think that Sammy Davis sang the late, great Nat King Cole's numbers too well.

It's very difficult for an artist in one mold to do justice to another's songs.

### Jolson The Greatest

Nobody does justice to Jolson like himself. Incidentally, he must be the greatest entertainer of the century. For nearly 40 years after his prime and more than a decade after his death, he is the singer whose great hits are still sung in television medleys.

In my opinion, for what it's worth, he was the star to end all stars. This is not to diminish the importance or talent of Crosby, Sinatra, Eddie Cantor or others who made their names long before big beat took over. Enough reminiscing.

Elvis is back in the charts with "Crying in the Chapel." This is what we English would term a very "American" number.

Rarely does anything about "chapel," "church," "mother," or "God" make any imprint on the British charts.

There are exceptions—Wink Martindale's "Deck of Cards," the song "I Believe," and Julie Rogers' "The Wedding" were three of them. But they were rare. This is not because Britain is a pagan country but because the English are a more inhibited race than the Americans — slightly embarrassed by obvious references in pop music to religion, motherhood, or excessive sentiments.

### Beatles Songs Direct

Hence the immediate success of the Beatles with their direct everyday messages in "She Loves You," "Love Me Do," "I Want to Hold Your Hand," and "Money Can't Buy Me Love."

It's worth making the point, by the way, that the Beatles — apparently so rare and unique with their wit and honesty — are very typical of millions of young Englishmen. Their speed with a joke or a response to practically any good line is amazing.

Nice to see . . . the Beau Brummels heading for the Top 10 nationally.

. . . Jackie DeShannon doing so well again.

# KRLA ARCHIVES

## AUSTRALIA'S SEEKERS BIG HIT

THE SEEKERS may have found what they were seeking. The Australian group has a smash hit in "I'll Never Find Another You."

## A KRLA BEAT EDITORIAL -
## Crowd Violence

This isn't going to be easy to say. Important things never are.

There were no casualties at the Rolling Stones Concert in Long Beach. Or were there?

Out of all the girls who rushed for the stage and for the Stones, all managed to survive. All the same, something died that afternoon.

The acts of violence were physically dangerous for everyone concerned. To the girls who committed them, to everyone around them, the Stones included.

But there's a new kind of danger now. A part of the fun and excitement is dead because in the middle of all the chaos of that Sunday afternoon, everyone knew this could never happen again.

They knew there would be no more concerts. Ever. Unless the violence stops now.

Violence is like a weed. Once it firmly takes root, it grows and overpowers everything in its path. If that Sunday afternoon were to ever happen again, the violence would be even stronger. Next time more girls would make it to the stage. Next time someone might succeed in wrenching a car door open and dragging a group of terrified singers into the middle of a howling mob. If this happened, someone would not live to remember it.

You can stop the crop of violence from completely taking over and destroying everything. We feel you will do everything in your power to stop it. People you care about are in danger. We feel confident you'll come to the rescue and put an end to the danger.

## A KRLA BEAT EXCLUSIVE -
# Life With The Rolling Stones—Off Stage

By ROD BARKEN

Bill Wyman: "Where did you come from?"

KRLA BEAT'S Rod Barken: "From the KRLA Beat."

Bill Wyman: "Come in, then."

That's how it began on Tuesday, May 11, at The Ambassador Hotel, just outside Room 21-B. For almost all of the next ten days Rod Barken was the constant companion of five unusual and talented young men who call themselves . . . . The Rolling Stones.

Here is his exclusive report to the KRLA BEAT:

### STONE-AGE FACTS

Did you know that:

Charlie Watts was born less than six miles from London's Picadilly Circus.

Keith left school because of bad truancy reports.

Charlie spends more money than the rest of The Stones on clothes.

Keith's grandfather used to play in a dance band.

Brian was best at English and music, but was asked to leave school because he was a "trouble-maker."

Charlie used to earn $46.40 per week as an advertising agency assistant.

Mick, Keith and Brian used to share an apartment in Chelsea which seldom saw food in the cupboards.

Charlie used to flirt with models from Christian Dior's London office, which was located next door to his.

Ian Stewart kept The Rolling Stones fed during the early days. Now he's one of their road managers.

Keith almost quit The Stones during the early days. "The strain was too great," says he.

The Rolling Stones got their start on an Everly Brothers —Bo Diddley Show.

The Rolling Stones' first record, "Come On," got as high as number 20 in the British charts.

The Rolling Stones want to do at least two United States tours per year, and hope to be back here in the Fall.

The Rolling Stones are great!

At 2:15 p.m., just four minutes after The Rolling Stones landed, I received a telephone call that was to mark the beginning of a very exciting period in my life.

A voice, female, and clearly out of breath, said, "They're here . . . they've finally arrived . . . Oh, Rod, you should see them!" Then the receiver clicked off, and I was rushing for the front door and The Stones' hotel on Wilshire Blvd.

When I arrived, a security lieutenant ushered me into an office. I identified myself. A fast telephone call cleared me through, and I was taken to the rooms.

Once inside, I shook hands with Moe Shulman, of London Records, and Bob Bonis, road manager for the boys from London. It was good seeing them again, having met them last year.

### Meets Stones

I then went off to meet The Rolling Stones.

I passed Mick while walking to Keith's room. He was dressed in a sweater and a pair of wool slacks. We said hello, shook hands, and exchanged brief greetings.

Keith was in his room, and answered my knocking at the door while still brushing his teeth. There then came one of those unique moments when you are able to see a Stone completely relaxed. After a moment, we started to laugh at the toothpaste that was dripping onto Keith's hand.

As I walked back to the other bungalow, I passed Charlie Watts, the drummer. Charlie is the pensive one of the Rolling Stones, and passed me staring intently at the ground. I said "Hi," being answered by a silent nod of recognition. (This is as good as an enthusiastic, back-pounding hello.)

Brian was standing in the center of a crowd of girls, signing autographs. Bill Wyman came out of his room just as I walked up to the door, and invited me to accompany him to the coffee shop downstairs.

### Crowds Grow

The crowds of fans on the grounds of the hotel had started to grow by this time, and the security officers had started to give out a few elementary safety rules. They involved the strict rules that The Stones themselves had laid down, along with a few that were added to protect the property of the hotel.

Ian Stewart joined me a bit later, and we sat and chatted about incidentals. Ian's from England, and travels with The Rolling Stones as their equipment manager.

After our short conversation, I wandered into the hotel and talked to a few of The Stones' fans. Through these devoted people, I came to learn much about what makes Mick, Brian, Keith, Bill, and Charlie, seem irresistible to so many.

### Why They're Popular

At first it was their rebellious attitudes, their "who cares" impression. Then it became their music, their deep-down struggle for identification with what they wanted and believed in. I think now is the time for the real answer that explains the "why" of The Rolling Stones.

They are very honest.

"If a man can't get on with a job, then let him say so. Don't lie and make excuses," said Mick Jagger one morning. "If he doesn't like what he sees, he should say so, instead of being phony on it."

Bill Wyman dislikes people who insistently try and impress him with what they've accomplished.

### Basically Honest

The simplicity of this outspoken sincerity has reached deeply into the feelings of many people, teenagers and young adults alike. Most young people are basically honest, and are quick to recognize this admirable quality in others. It is my own personal feeling that this is the strongest reason for The Stones' popularity.

Anyway, back at The Ambassador . . .

Bill Wyman was standing in his doorway, saying, "I can't find a record player — Do you know where I can get one?"

In less than 30 minutes, with the help of a young man named Bill Kane, I came back with a record player used in The BEAT offices. We sat in Bill's room and listened to records for awhile, then said good night, and went home.

I was completely exhausted, and looked forward to a good night's rest before rejoining them the following day.

### Album Session

Wednesday the Stones did a recording session at the Hollywood studios of RCA Victor. It was a "closed session," and the songs that were recorded are scheduled to go into a forthcoming album.

That night found all but one of The Rolling Stones thoroughly ex-

**TURN TO PAGE 12**

---

**THE SPATS**

SHOWS-DANCES
FAN CLUB:
P.O. Box 12
Stanton, Calif.
Tel. (714) 539-5980

---

**23 SKIDOO**
Dancing to Live Name Bands
2116 Westwood Blvd., West Los Angeles
Girls 18, Guys 21
23 Skidoo Dancers are now seen on TV's
Hollywood A'GoGo Saturday on Channel 9 at 9:00 p.m.
**Closed Mondays**

## ON THE BEAT

Herman has lots of plans for the future — if he makes a lot of money, that is. First of all, he would like to open a hotel. "With traveling around the country I've got to know all the bad points about hotels — I think if I were to open one of my own I'd know what not to do." Then if he had some more money, Herman would open a few clubs — one where he would charge five pounds to get in, another especially for teenagers, one with gambling tables for adults, and one for babies where they could buy milk!

And there is one more thing Herman would like to do. "I get so much crummy food in restaurants that I'd like to have one of my own in each town so that wherever we play I'd be certain of getting a decent meal."

Okay, so it's all in the dreaming stage right now — but if Herman keeps turning out those hit sounds, babies may be sipping milk in the Herman Club before too long!

### Irish Peeve

Them are "sick of being tagged Irish." According to the five-man group: "It gives the impression we've just come over on the late cattle boat." Well, well! Seems kind of a small thing to be so upset about, but then we're all entitled to our own pet peeves.

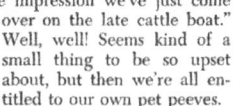

The Best Quote of the Week comes from Mickie Most, independent record producer, concerning English-made records: "We don't want them too good. What we try to get in a record is 'magic' — something to make the kids want to buy the record."

Evidently, Mickie Most has found just such "magic" because he has produced hit records for such people as Herman's Hermits, the Animals, Bobby Vee, and Brenda Lee!

The three Bobby's — Vee, Goldsboro, and Sherman — have all come up with good new records. Bobby Vee's "Keep On Trying" is the best he's done in a long time. It very well could be that this one will once again establish Bobby Vee as a consistent chart-topper; hope so anyway.

Bobby Goldsboro's "Voodoo Woman" is a catchy one and a natural follow-up to "Little Things." In England, Bobby got cheated out of a hit with "Little Things" because a popular British singer, Dave Berry, covered the record and made a fair-sized hit out of it. Maybe Bobby can click on both sides of the Atlantic with his "Voodoo Woman."

As for Bobby Sherman, he has come up with his best sound to date in "Well All Right." With a little promotion and a little air play, this one could go in a big way. Again, I hope so — it's about time Bobby had a hit.

### Quick Ones

The Walker Brothers, formerly of "Hollywood A Go Go", are doing big business in England . . . Bobby Vee is scheduled to make a color movie . . . Marianne Faithful's first album has been released — it's titled "Marianne Faithful" and features "I'm A Loser" . . . The Animals are scheduled for the Ed Sullivan Show on May 30 . . . Pete Quaife of the Kinks wants to add a cheetah to his list of pets which already includes a poodle, a tortoise, a goldfish, and a cat!

Trini Lopez's promoters are really going all out for their boy. They recently bought 21 ads in one issue of "Billboard"! That's a lot of adverts — could it be they're trying to tell somebody something?

Looks like the Rolling Stones did all right on their recent tour of Canada — they toppled ALL the attendance records set by the Beach Boys, Gerry and the Pacemakers, Billy J. Kramer, and the Dave Clark Five! Only group the Stones failed to top—the Beatles! The Stones did all right in Long Beach too!

WATCH OUT FOR: Georgie Fame on an Alka-Seltzer commercial! He's the one playing "In The Meantime".

I managed to get some pertinent facts for you from Mick: He definitely does want to be a serious actor; the Stones ARE going to make a movie but no particulars are available yet; and the sound on the Ed Sullivan Show didn't bother Mick because he couldn't hear it!

—Louise Criscione

## CHARLIE "O" COACHES ROCK HUDSON

IT'S EASY TO RECOGNIZE THE MAN ON THE RIGHT — He's Charlie O'Donnell, the KRLA Man of Music. But the one on the left obviously enjoying himself is Universal Pictures' star ROCK HUDSON, embracing CLAUDIA CARDINALE, co-star of new film "BLINDFOLD," soon to be released. The comedy plot involves Rock as a doctor, and Claudia about to say something she shouldn't to Charlie, who plays a newspaper reporter. And Rock is using a very effective silencing device!

## BEATLE QUIZ

Here they are — the second set of questions in the big KRLA BEAT Beatle Quiz!

If you've answered the first five questions from last week (they weren't really hard, were they?) then start digging up the answers to the next five. For those who missed last week's KRLA BEAT we have repeated the first set of questions . . . so you still have time to enter.

The contest will continue for ten weeks, and the winner will receive the thrill of a lifetime, interviewing the Beatles for the BEAT when they arrive for the Hollywood Bowl concerts in August!

The winner and a friend will also be special guests of the KRLA deejays and the Beat at a Beatle concert. Additional prizes will be announced later for runners-up.

In case you've forgotten the contest details, all you have to do is fill in the entry blank each week and mail it in. At the end of ten weeks, the contestant with the most correct answers wins. In case of a tie there will be further questions for those still competing, or a drawing to determine the winner.

The questions are being provided by Derek Taylor, who will judge the answers for accuracy.

Beatle Quiz
KRLA BEAT
Suite 504
6290 Sunset Blvd.
Hollywood, Calif. 90028
CONTEST EDITOR:

Below are my answers to the first five questions in the BEATLE QUIZ CONTEST.

My Name ............................................. Address ...............................................
City .......................................................................... State ........................... Zip Code ............
I (☐ am) (☐ am not) presently a subscriber to the KRLA BEAT.

### QUESTIONS FROM LAST WEEK

1. Of those who performed in "A Hard Day's Night," how many have acting roles in the Beatles' second film, "Help!"? ...........
2. Who is Malcolm Evans? ...........
3. In what country have the Beatles performed most, outside England? ...........
4. How were Paul and George travelling when they first met? ...........
5. In what part of Liverpool were the Beatles raised? ...........

### NEW QUESTIONS

6. What percentage of the Beatles' income does Brian Epstein receive? ...........
7. Who is the Beatles' music publisher? ...........
8. Where did the Beatles go shopping for clothes in Hollywood? ...........
9. Who was the Beatles' press office before Derek Taylor was appointed? ...........
10. Who wrote all but one line of the lyrics to "I Saw Her Standing There"? ...........

MORE QUESTIONS IN NEXT WEEK'S BEAT

# KRLA ARCHIVES

## THEY RAISED THE ROOF AT LON[G BEACH]

Photos by [...]
and Ted S[...]

Sell out crowd greets BOB EUBANKS' Rolling Stones show with stone-age enthusiasm. Entire show was packed with talent... and the crowd loved it.

SORRY ABOUT THAT, MICK!

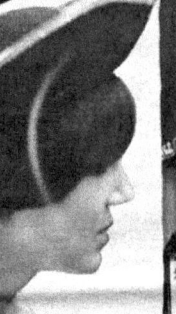

DINA MARTIN - Dean's daughter back stage in a Raider Hat

TALENTED JERRY NAYLOR has re-organized the famed Crickets. He sings here with Keith Allison, a dead ringer for Paul McCartney.

KRLA DEEJAYS Bob Eubanks, Bill Slater, Charlie O'Donnell, Dick Biondi and Dave Hull - backstage with The Rolling Stones. You'll notice several of the DeeJays need haircuts.

THE KRLA DEEJAYS ham it up on stage at Long Beach Arena

DAVE HULL gives the KRLA BEAT a boost, announcing that subscriptions are available.

# KRLA ARCHIVES

## G BEACH
### a KRLA spectacular

*obin Hill*
*chultz*

**LOUISE CHATS WITH MICK**

THE BYRDS were cheered almost as wildly as The Stones

"THE BRITISH ARE COMING!" (warns Mark Lindsay, A Raider.*)

( * Turn Out to be Stones)

PAUL REVERE AND THE RAIDERS - colorful, exciting entertainers.

## STONES SHOW WAS REALLY A ROCKER

**BY LOUISE CRISCIONE**

Long Beach thought it had rocked before.

It had hosted a combined Gerry & the Pacemakers — Billy J. Kramer show, not to mention a previous Rolling Stones' show. But as it turned out, Long Beach hadn't seen anything like the May 16 Rolling Stones' Concert!

By three o'clock, the doors to the enormous Long Beach Arena had opened and the crowd had begun streaming in. Backstage, things were relatively quiet; most of the performers had not yet arrived.

Fans were stationed outside the stage door; some had been there since seven o'clock that morning.

Shortly after three, their faithful vigil began to be rewarded. Paul Revere and the Raiders arrived, followed in short order by The Byrds. Both groups evoked screams from the girls and some fancy footwork from the police, who were trying to get the groups in and keep the girls out!

**All Present**

By four o'clock, all performers (except the Stones) were present and accounted for, empty seats were nonexistent, and the show was about to begin.

Bob Eubanks started the giant, excitement-packed show by introducing the Cinnamon Cinder bands — Don and the Deacons and the Vibrants. Both groups were great and set the pace for the rest of the show.

Next, Charlie O'Donnell introduced that fabulous singer, Jerry Naylor. Jerry did four songs, the best of which was his brand new record "Make Believe". It's the old Conway Twitty song, and Jerry really did it justice.

The Dartells were next on the agenda. They also did four numbers and managed very nicely to get tremendous audience response, especially for "Hot Pastrami" and "Land Of A Thousand Dances."

The old Hullabalooer himself, Dave Hull, was the next one out. He succeeded in doing two things: literally blowing his horn, and introducing The Byrds!

**Byrds Great**

The Byrds were fantastic and the crowd went absolutely wild for them! Flashbulbs flashed and jelly beans flew through their entire performance, especially when the boys started into their hit "Mr. Tambourine Man".

At about this time, backstage got that hectic look because the Rolling Stones had just arrived! The Stones went directly to their dressing room where they "tuned up" in privacy.

Charlie Watts wandered out of the dressing room for a few minutes and when he tried to get back in, the guard informed him that the Stones weren't allowing anyone in there just yet and so he would have to wait!

Charlie protested that he WAS a Stone, but the guard seemed not at all impressed. So a gentleman and myself volunteered the information that Charlie was indeed a Rolling Stone. We must have had honest faces because the guard grinned sheepishly and let Charlie in!

**Door Opens**

After the "tuning up" process was over, the Stones opened their dressing room to a selected few. The boys were all sipping Cokes. Mick was reading a handwritten fan letter marked "Personal" in big bold print. Charlie was looking at a book about the Civil War. Brian was checking the line-up and inquiring about The Byrds. Keith was making funny remarks, and Bill was simply sitting there.

A helmeted policeman stood inside the dressing room to see that no unauthorized personnel managed to sneak in. None did. What did get in, however, was a horde of photographers. Flashbulbs flashed continually, but the Stones seemed to pay little attention and went on about their business.

Out front, Paul Revere and the Raiders were doing their stuff, and doing it very well. What a reaction this group got, and no wonder! Besides wailing such songs as "Money" and "Big Boy Pete", the Raiders also did acrobatics!

The two lead guitarists stood on their amplifiers, and the lead singer balanced himself on the top of the piano. A fabulous group, these Raiders.

**Stones On**

The KRLA disc jockeys then made their way to the stage and introduced the group which was to close the show — THE ROLLING STONES! Since the Stones were scattered throughout the backstage area, it took them a few seconds to get regrouped and climb the six steps onto the stage.

Mick was the first Stone on stage, and when the audience caught sight of him a roar went up which in all probability was heard all the way into L.A.!

Altogether, the Stones did nine songs, including some of their very biggest hits, such as "Time

**TURN TO PAGE 11**

# For Girls Only

**By SHEILA DAVIS**

If you're a boy and you're reading this, I think I'd better give you fair warning. This column is For Girls Only and we really wish you'd let us have this one little corner of the Beat all to ourselves.

If you won't and you absolutely insist on getting in on our weekly-from-now-on gab fest, you'd better batten down a few hatches and get prepared to hear a few things you didn't know we knew about you.

Just don't say I didn't warn you! And away we go!

Now that we're on the subject of boys, let's stay there for a moment. You know what really cracks me up? The way most of them snicker about the way we "fall in love with one groovy singer after another." Well, I have news for them!

I was sitting behind two perfectly normal looking boys at the Stones concert. Until the Stones came on stage, they spent most of their time making "clever" remarks about the "ridiculous" girls in the audience who were letting out war whoops every time anyone so much as mentioned the Stones.

### What A Change

The boys really changed their tunes when Mick and company came on stage, and joined right in the applause and the shouting for more.

What really made me laugh was the way the two of them would pause every now and then, and glance furtively about to make sure no one was seeing them joining in.

The poor dears. Don't they know that we know what they're all about? Guess not. And maybe it's just as well. This way we get the chance to really surprise them every once in awhile!

The English trend in fashions is still reigning throughout the country. But I have noticed a noticeable lack of boots lately. I hope this is just because it's summer and boots are a bit hot this time of year. I started being boot-happy long ago, and never had the nerve to wear them until everyone else started to. So here's hoping this type of footwear will be the big thing again come fall.

Have you heard what some boot wearers are doing in the Mid-West? They're buying leather boots and dyeing them a different color practically every day. You know, to match whatever outfit they're wearing. I know it must be simple to do with all the new shoe-coloring equipment on the market, but it sounds just a little too simple to me (if you know what I mean). I just can't imagine pink boots. Oh yes I can, come to think of it. I just don't want to have to.

Picked up a pointer about the long hair look the other day. The warm iron treatment works great, as we all know, UNLESS you have a tangle of split ends. Then it just makes them worse. Something else about shoes, too, before we go on to greater things. Don't forget to watch out for shoes with straps now that "Mr. Sunlight" (Sorry, Beatles, about the not-very-brilliant paraphrase) is back with us again. Just walking to the corner newsstand to pick up a copy of the Beat (plug, plug) can give you the weirdest marks across the top of your feet. This can happen even if you're wearing nylons. The sun goes right through them!

Things really get weird if you have several different types of strap shoes. A few walks in the sun and you have a pattern and a half, and a lot of strange looks when you go to the beach!

### Bikini Blitz

Now that it's bikini time again, it's also diet time. If you know someone who's having a rough time staying on the cottage cheese and lettuce route, come to the rescue and make them a Diet Scrapbook.

Paste a "before" photo on the first page and continue snapping pix throughout their diet (you know, the sort of photo that will make their weight loss obvious) and pasting them in the book.

Then, if your friend starts nibbling at a chocolate pie (in a weak moment) present the scrapbook and save the day. When she sees how much progress she's already made, she'll put that pie down fast.

Now that I'm about to run out of room, I'd better say farewell for all the things I was going to mention here. As usual, I got carried away and didn't mention nearly all of them. Guess they'll have to wait until next time.

Just one before I go. If you're one of the no-lipstick crowd, I'd like to recommend a boss (I don't like that word . . . I only said it to see how it would look) (ech!) product you'll soon be needing. It's called Blistex, and it's great protection against chapped lips and all those terribly unattractive things.

Now that I really am out of room, I'd better say farewell for now. I'll see you in the next Beat, and I'll be hoping to hear from you soon. Drop me a line and let me know what's happening and all that, and also let me know what you'd like to read about in our For Girls Only column.

Meet you here next week!

---

**WAREHOUSE IX**

2214 Stoner Avenue

off Olympic in West Los Angeles

**Dancing to Live Name Bands**

Los Angeles' Unique Young Adult Nite Club

*Girls and Guys 18 and Over*

**Big Sunday Afternoon Dance Sessions from 4 to 10 p.m.**

Closed Tuesdays

---

## FREEDOM FROM HUNGER

# SHOW OF STARS

### Shrine Auditorium, Sunday, June 6

### GIANT BENEFIT SHOW STARRING:

1. Please include a stamped, self-addressed envelope.
2. If tickets are not available at the price you order, you will be send ticket sat the next lowest price, along with a refund.
3. MAIL TO: Freedom From Hunger
   KRLA Radio
   1401 S. Oak Knoll
   Pasadena, California

★ The Byrds
★ Jan And Dean
★ Dick And DeeDee
★ Gary Lewis and The Playboys
★ The Kingsmen
★ Jackie De Shannon

**PLUS**

★ Steve Allen
★ Bob Newhart
★ Joey Bishop
★ Bill (Jose Jiminez) Dana

**"FREEDOM FROM HUNGER" HELPS THE STARVING HELP THEMSELVES**

### TICKET ORDER

I HAVE ENCLOSED A CHECK OR MONEY ORDER PAYABLE TO "FREEDOM FROM HUNGER." PLEASE SEND ME THE FOLLOWING TICKETS:

(NO.) .......... TICKETS AT
☐ $2.00
☐ $3.00
☐ $5.00

SEND TO: ..........
ADDRESS: ..........
CITY: .......... STATE ..........
ZIP CODE .......... TELEPHONE ..........

---

## personals

Barb Bradwell of San Diego: Wish you weren't retiring as president of the "Beatle Birds". Thanks for doing such a great job of running our club. Please keep in touch with us.
*Your L.A. Members*

To Derek Taylor: We'll never forget how you smiled and waved back at us the night we drove by you on Sunset. Next time we'll try not to scream so loud.
*The Girls In The Red Mustang*

To Bill of Marshall High: You are for the birds, and I don't mean Byrds. (I'm for them!)
*You Know Who*

To Mr. & Mrs. G. of Sunland: I heard you listening to KRLA when I was supposed to be asleep. Thanks for being teenagers at heart.
*Your Daughter*

Sandra of Pasadena: Remember that Beatle record you liked so much called "I Don't Want To Spoil The Party"? Listen to the words and take a hint.
*Hostess*

To M.N. of Van Nuys: I'll bet you a subscription to the KRLA Beat this time. Anyone can afford that.
*"Welcher"*

To Dave Hull of KRLA: Next time you're in Glendale, stop by Bob's and we'll treat you to a free hamburger. Please bring Clarence.
*Five Scuzzy Fans*

To Dave Hull of KRLA: On second thought, please do NOT bring Clarence. Pretty please?
*Us Again*

To "Scotty" of North Hollywood: Stop talking about wanting to go to England. Are you forgetting we have plans?
*Unsteady Steady*

To Marv of Los Angeles: Keep your shirt on and you'll learn to dance a lot faster.
*"Arthur Murray"*

To George Harrison of Liverpool: Please give me a ring when you get to Calif. I want to introduce you to someone who looks exactly like you.
*The Girl You Met In Beau Gentry's*

To Dick Biondi of KRLA: I sit by my radio every night and listen to your show. (I think they are coming for me soon.)
*Nancy Moss*

To Carter of Orange High: I am going to hold my breath until you call me. (Please hurry.)
*G-l-o-r-i-a*

To "English" of Redondo Beach: What color are your eyes? Your bangs are so long I can't tell.
*Red-Blooded American*

To Bobby Sherman of "Shindig": Thanks for stopping to give us your autograph. Too bad the light turned green so fast. (Remember us? You know, the four girls with blonde hair.)
*Your Fans Forever*

## DREAM VACATION

For Sandra Frazer of Palos Verdes it was a dream vacation - a dream come true. A trip to Nassau where the Beatles were on location shooting the tropical segment of their new movie. As you can see from these pictures she made the most of the opportunity - and became the envy of every other girl in the world.

PAUL looks up to say goodbye to Sandra before driving back to the Balmoval Club after a long day of filming.

JOHN looks like a typical beachcomber sitting on the White Sandy beach.

HERE'S SANDRA IN PAUL McCARTNEY'S SPORTS CAR

### MORE ON BEATLES MOVIE

# Days Spent Filming - But Nights Delightful

CONTINUED FROM PAGE 2

favorite Beatle, tourists taking photographs, a 50-strong group of pressmen and photographers from all over the world, plus a small army of extra policemen. It looked like unbelievable chaos. How could anyone hope to make a film under those conditions? But next day's shooting commenced without a hitch, although the number of fans and spectators had doubled.

#### Queen Mother Passes

During the days that followed, over 40 sequences were filmed in public places in and around Nassau, and – although most of the Island and tourist population were there at one time or another – there were very few interruptions of any consequence. The most notable incident that held up shooting for a while was when her Majesty the Queen Mother came into shot as she and her entourage of cars and outriders passed by on their way to the airport, homeward bound after her Jamaican tour.

At night, most of the unit took advantage of the delights available in this picturesque spot – the calypsos, the steel bands for moonlight dancing, the exotic menus and the inate gaiety of the native population. Most members of the unit had to take their swims at night since there was never time for bathing in the famous blue waters during the day.

The Beatles would dodge the fans congregating outside their luxurious beach bungalow, and race to the capital in their open sports cars to live it up for awhile after the gruelling day's work under the burning sun. But most of the time they would stay at home and continue working on the musical score for the picture, music and lyrics by Beatles Paul McCartney and John Lennon – seven new numbers in all.

The last sequences to be shot in the Bahamas were to take place on Paradise Island, by kind permission of Huntington Hartford, who owns the island. While Director Lester supervised the crew on the beach, further activity was going on under the sea a few hundred yards out.

Almost very skindiver in the vicinity, whether they were treasure hunters or underwater guides, were operating from the sea bed, trying to stage the dramatic rising out of the water of the great Image of the Goddess of Kaili – now complete again. Richard Lester was in constant touch by radio with the divers handling the air tanks and pressure bombs needed to make the slow appearance of the 40-foot high idol.

Mr. Huntington Hartford, with his entourage, watched the scene with great interst. His beautiful wife, Diane, was even persuaded to play a small part in the movie.

#### Kaili Finally Filmed

It took three whole weary days to get Kaili to come out of the water at the right time, at exactly the right place, and by that time the entire unit was glad to see the back of her as she was towed away by a specially hired Navy salvage vessel.

But with the disappearance of the Goddess, an airborne, monster-shaped object became an equally startling sight to the islands. It was the famous Goodyear blimp which was transported from Florida for a spectacular scene in the film.

By now most of the unit was in various stages of sun tan and sun burn, except for the Beatles who had to keep out of the sun throughout the location. Since the Bahamas sequences were actually the last scenes in the completed film, audiences would find it rather odd to watch the boys in varying skin colours without explanation. However, the run on sun tan products and the sale of soft drinks was formidable. It was estimated that some 700 bottles of soft iced drinks were consumed by the unit each day.

When artists and crew finally said goodbye to the Bahamas, unwillingly sweltering in their London clothes, they were given a rousing sendoff by the Bahamanians, for these islands are new ground for film producers and it may well be that Walter Shenson has started up a new profit sideline for them. Indeed, shorter afterwards a 150-strong film unit arrived in Nassau to film exteriors for United Artists' fourth James Bond film, "Thunderball."

London was cold but the unit hadn't much time to notice it because, before two days had passed, they were on their way once again by chartered plane to another extreme of climate – the Austrian Alps!

(In next week's KRLA BEAT, Tony Howard tells of the complications and dangers of filming in the avalanche-threatened Austrian Alps, of the night the Beatles surprised everyone with a performance and of the assault by Beatle fans upon their return to London.)

# KRLA ARCHIVES

## GO CART A GO-GO

SONNY AND CHER whose recording of "Just For You" is a nationwide hit. Prepare for another kind of spin.

## Try This Quiz

Here's something to do in study hall (besides snore)! The following is a list of singing groups, and if it sounds a bit odd, that's only because it is a bit odd. All the names have been scrambled to protect the eggs, or some such thing.

If you'll go over the list carefully, you'll be able to pick out 27 of today's top groups, and one of the top twosomes in the singing world.

The quiz shouldn't take more than a few minutes to do (which makes us livid because it took two hours to make up), and once you've finished you can pass notes around the hall, bragging about your score! (You can also get expelled if you start taking very much of our advice.)

The correct answers to the Scrambled Groups are printed right here, upside down, so you won't be tempted to sneak any peeks.

SCRAMBLED GROUPS: (1) The Moody Mindbenders (2) Cannibal & The Animals (3) The Pretty Hermits (4) The Rolling Kinks (5) The New Christy Cups (6) Herman's Headhunters (7) The Nashville Things (8) The Swinging Stones (9) Paul Revere & The Boys (10) The Four Teens (11) Gary Lewis & The Dreamers (12) The Beach Beatles (13) Sam The Sham & The Zombies (14) The Dave Clark Raiders (15) The Blues Brothers (16) Freddie & The Blue Jeans (17) The Five Supremes (18) The Dixie Tops (19) Jay & The Pacemakers (20) The Righteous Playboys (21) The American Minstrels (22) The Beau Byrds (23) Billy J. Kramer & The Pharoahs (24) Wayne Fontana & The Brummels (25) Gerry & The Dakotas.

HOW TO SCORE: Your Scrambled Group Quiz that is, of course. If you managed to unscramble at least 25 of the groups (or more) you're practically perfect. If you guessed correctly on between 19 and 24 of them, people aren't exactly going to be going around whispering about how brilliant you are. If you guessed right on 18 or less, you'd better brush up on your groups before people start pointing!

ANSWERS: HALT! YOU ARE READING THIS UP-SIDE DOWN AND YOU HAVEN'T EVEN TAKEN THE QUIZ YET! TAKE THE QUIZ THIS INSTANT! Groups mentioned are Cannibal & The Headhunters, Herman's Hermits, The Animals, The Pretty Things, The Rolling Stones, The Swinging Blue Jeans, The Nashville Teens, The Kinks, The Four Tops, Gary Lewis & The Playboys, Freddie & The Dreamers, The Moody Blues, Sam The Sham & The Pharoahs, Wayne Fontana & The Mindbenders, The Zombies, The Dave Clark Five, The Beatles, Paul Revere & The Raiders, The Beach Boys, The Byrds, Billy J. Kramer & The Dakotas, The Beau Brummels, The Supremes, Gerry & The Pacemakers, Jay & The Americans, The New Christy Minstrels, and the Dixie Cups. The twosome was the fabulous Righteous Brothers.

## More About THE BYRDS

CONTINUED FROM PAGE 3

Ian, Odetta, Sonny and Cher and Jackie DeShannon. From a tentative booking at Ciro's, the Byrds extended their stay for four weeks and packed the place.

Then the Byrds were able to interest Columbia Records' inspired young producer Terry Melcher — son of Doris Day — to record them on "Tambourine Man," a number which Dylan had written and recorded himself on a recent album.

### Personal Interest

Dylan attended the Byrds' recording session and gave his personal approval to their version. Melcher devoted hours of overtime to perfecting the sound of the disk.

And all of this personal interest is reflected in the quality of the recording and the speed of its success.

They come from a variety of places across the United States. Gene is from Kansas City; Dave, Santa Barbara; Mike, Greenwich Village; Chris, San Diego; and Jim, Chicago. Mike is the drummer; Gene writes some of their songs, sings and plays the harmonica; Dave plays the rhythm guitar and sings; Jim sings and plays both the five and 12 string lead guitar; Chris is bass guitar player.

## PEN PAL

JOHN A. ISAAC
57 Gladeville Road
Aigburth,
Liverpool 17
Lancaster, England
(6 ft. tall, born in Liverpool and met the Beatles at the Cavern before they turned pro)

## Inside KRLA

The KRLA-APES finished off their basketball season in a blaze of glory this week by dropping two games. The season road trip was a great success with everybody involved having a great time. At the Palmdale High School, faculty defeated the APES 74-61. The final game of the season at Gardena High School against the Gardena Pacers had the APES a bit worried and they had to go into overtime to lose 37-36. All the deejays can hang up their tennis shoes for another year.

The giant Freedom from Hunger Show to be held at the Shrine June 6, is really shaping itself into the show of the year. Jack Good, producer of "Shindig," has now agreed to produce the show for KRLA.

• • •

The strange voice that comes in every now and then on Emperor Hudson's 6-9 a.m. show claiming to be the Program Director and asking some favor from His Majesty, is really the Program Director, Mel Hall.

• • •

It now looks as if Dick Biondi is going to get some of Dave Hull's money. Dick, being a giant Elvis Presley fan, made a bet on his latest, "Crying in the Chapel." And the disc, much to Dave's dismay is really beginning to move, debuting on the Top 30 at 27 this week.

• • •

What does Casey Kasem do on a day off? He tapes five 1-hour TV shows and throws a dance at the Rec Center in Thousand Oaks. And this kind of schedule is not unusual among KRLA deejays. So it's really a rare case when they get a chance to spend some leisure hours together. When it does happen, it goes something like this: Dick Moreland's house with Charlie O'Donnel and Dave Hull playing English darts and listening to the stereo, playing the Rolling Stones, the Righteous Brothers and Hank Williams records . . . with Dave asking, "Where are the Beatle albums?" And Dick and Charlie in unison saying, "We knew you were coming Dave. They're locked up."

## Host

MAJOR LANCE, popular recording artist, recently feted the staff and crew of "Shindig" to a party following his apearance on the show. It was held at fashionable Ciro's, in Hollywood, and was attended by more than 150 people. In attendance were The Shindogs, Sonny & Cher, Jack Good, almost all of the "Shindig" dancers; members of the "Shindig" Band; Bill of The Righteous Brothers; and a member of the KRLA BEAT staff.

Major Lance, The Vibrations, The Dave Clark Five, Bobby Vinton, Adam Wade, Billy Butler, and The Yardbirds

congratulate
**THE KRLA BEAT**
on its first 12-page edition

EPIC
AND
OKeh

---

THE SPATS

SHOWS–DANCES
FAN CLUB:
P.O. Box 12
Stanton, Calif.
Tel. (714) 539-5980

### 'WOOLY BULLY'
TO THE
### SETTING SUN

Hollywood's
Land of 1,000 Dances

1642 N. Cherokee
(½ Block So. of M'Goo's)

Thurs.-Sunday 9-2
Live Music & Dancing

---

Back issues of the KRLA BEAT are still available, for a limited time. If you've missed an issue of particular interest to you, send 10 cents for each copy wanted, along with a self-addressed stamped envelope to:

KRLA BEAT
Suite 504
6290 Sunset Blvd.
Hollywood, California 90028

ISSUES AVAILABLE —

4/7 — BEATLE PLANS REVEALED
4/14 — INTERVIEW WITH JOHN LENNON
4/21 — INTERVIEW WITH PAUL McCARTNEY
4/28 — CHIMP EXCITES TEEN FAIR
5/5 — HERMANIA SPREADS
5/12 — HERE COME THE BEATLES
5/19 — EXCITING CONTEST —
VISIT WITH BEATLES

# KRLA ARCHIVES

## How To Start A Fan Club

The Beat has received so many letters asking just how to go about starting a fan club for a special favorite, we've decided to answer all of them at once, through this article.

Many of those letters have contained a measure of disappointment, because a lot of you have already written to your favorite, asking for their permission and their help, and received no answer.

First of all, we'd like to tell you why this happens.

Unless your favorite star has a king-sized staff of secretaries (and very few do), answering each letter he receives would be impossible. It isn't that he just doesn't care, and doesn't want your help. There just isn't enough time in the day.

### Get Permission

Writing to the star for permission should be your first step all the same. Address your letter to his studio or record company. Some personalities do send out letters of permission, and some will provide you with materials to help run your club. A fan club that has the financial backing of the star is simpler to organize, so don't leave this stone unturned.

If you receive no reply, just keep in mind why you didn't, and try writing to the president of another of his clubs. You'll find fan club listings in most teenage magazines, and also in the Beat. The president may be able to help you get started, and may also be able to help put you in direct contact with the star.

If all else fails, and you are completely on your own, here's where to begin.

### Kind of Club

Begin by deciding what kind of club you want to organize.

In order to start a national club, and have a chance of competing with other clubs for members, you will need to provide the following materials: A membership card, photos of the star, a fact sheet, a fan club bulletin at least every three months, and any extras you can think of. The average membership price for this amount of material would be between $1 and $1.50 per year, plus four stamped, self-addressed envelopes (for your bulletin mailings).

These materials are paid for with the membership dues you receive, and if you have enough members, the club shouldn't cost you any money. You may have to make an original investment, but you'll make it back as your membership increases.

### Find Printer

Membership cards can be purchased for a reasonable price from a number of printers. Look in the yellow pages (under Printers) for companies that specialize in this sort of thing (business cards, etc.), then call and ask for a price list. Decide what you want printed on the card before you begin shopping around, because the amount of words will help determine the price.

To have photos made, you should first have a negative of the photos you want duplicated. If this isn't possible, you will have to pay to have a negative made. (A charge of a few dollars.) Beginning on page 1379 in the Los Angeles Yellow Pages, you'll find a listing of photo reproduction companies. Again, shop around by phone until you find the most for your money.

### Fact Sheet

The fact sheet, which should contain all available material on the star's background can be mimeographed, and so can your quarterly bulletins.

If you don't have access to a mimeo machine, ask around among your family and friends. Someone may know of a machine you could use free, or for a small fee. There are also services that do this type of work for not too much money, so if you can't locate a mimeo, try the Yellow Pages again.

The bulletins will be composed of the latest news about the star, fan clubs projects, names and addresses of members (so members can write to each other), contests, etc. If you're completely new at all this, it would be to your advantage to join a fan club just to see what type of material you receive.

### Big Undertaking

This kind of club is, of course, on a large scale and can be quite an undertaking. It will take a great deal of your time, but the project can be well worth the time spent. You'll be doing a lot to help your favorite star, and meeting hundreds of new friends with similar interests.

Another type of club you can start is the sort that either costs nothing to belong to, or costs 25 to 50 cents. A completely free club usually provides nothing more than a membership card and the President (if she doesn't have star backing) has to personally assume the costs of the cards. When advertising for members in a free club, don't forget to ask them to send a stamped, self-addressed envelope for the mailing of the cards. A five cent stamp doesn't sound like much until you get into the realm of hundreds and thousands. If you were to mail out a thousand membership cards, using your own money for postage, it would cost you forty dollars for stamps alone.

### Free Clubs

A free club is the easiest of all, but because it is free, you are able to contact your members only once (when you send them the card), unless you ask for another stamped, self-addressed envelope.

A club that charges 25 to 50 cents can afford to send out a fan club package containing some of the materials we've already mentioned. But you wouldn't be able to afford more than one photo (if any) and probably would not be able to send out more than one bulletin per year.

Also remember that clubs which charge less money draw more members, and you'll really be kept hopping.

There you have it. How to start a fan club. The next step is to make your club appealing and intriguing and different by coming up with interesting extras and fun projects.

We'll be exploring that portion of the fan club subject in the next issue of the Beat. If you're still in a starting-a-fan-club-mood, our list of extras and projects and possible ways to meet your favorite will be invaluable to you. So don't miss it!

## Send A Kiss To The Beatles

Have you ever wished you could walk right up to your favorite Beatle and give him a great big kiss?

What a question?

Well, you'd better stock up on lipstick because that wish is about to come true.

Half of it is, anyway. We just can't think of a way for each one of you to walk right up to your favorite Beatle, aside from getting in line and waiting your turn until you're about forty years old.

But the great big kiss part? That's simple!

Just plant that great big smooch on the KRLA Beat-le Kiss Coupon and send it off to John, Paul, George or Ringo c/o The Beat.

When the Beatles arrive in town, we'll personally deliver all your smooches. Your favorite Beatle is really going to flip when he finds out how kissable he is. He's going to feel so welcome here, he may never want to leave. Especially if you make him feel even more welcome by enclosing a personal note with your smooch.

Doesn't this whole fabulous idea make your heart want to skip a beat?

We hope so! (Just as long as it isn't the KRLA Beat.)

Subscribe Now to the Beat

## Raise Money For Your Club

Want to raise extra money for your club treasury? You could easily make several hundred dollars.

For information write Fan Club Funds, KRLA, Sunset-Vine Tower, Suite 504, Hollywood, California—90028.

### More About LONG BEACH SHOW

CONTINUED FROM PAGE 7

Is On My Side", "Off The Hook", "Little Red Rooster", and their current smash, "The Last Time". Pandemonium broke loose, and bedlam reigned! The Stones got pelted with jelly beans, flash bulbs, lipstick, and anything else the audience could lay its hands on.

At another point, a young fan raced to the balcony overlooking the stage, and unfurled the British flag. A loud cheer went up from the audience, but a quick-footed policeman evidently did not appear impressed with this patriotic testimonial and unceremoniously yanked both the girl and the flag down from the balcony!

A half hour later, the Stones were finished and the show was over. At least, most people thought it was over. The Stones rushed off the stage and into a black station wagon parked inside the building directly behind the stage. The get-away plans had been carefully laid, but somebody goofed somewhere.

The black wagon was in motion a split second after the Stones had jumped aboard, but it was moving in the WRONG direction! After proceeding half way around the Arena, the car could not get out, was spotted by throngs of screaming fans, and was forced to turn around and began backtracking.

Once outside, the car was engulfed in a mass of surging bodies. The Stones were trapped inside the station wagon behind locked doors and rolled-up windows. Policemen and officials did their best to untangle the crowd and get the Stones safely out of the parking lot. It was a tough assignment, but about fifteen anxious minutes later they had succeeded, and the Rolling Stones were gone.

No, Long Beach had never seen ANYTHING like this before!

## Fan Club Information

**DEREK TAYLOR FAN CLUB**
c/o Shelly Heber
6087½ Alcott Street
Los Angeles 35, California

**THE AMERICAN MISSING LINKS**
c/o JoAnn Matrone
1917 Condon
Redondo Beach, California

**BEATLES (U.S.A.) LTD.**
c/o Mary Ann Geffrey
1122 West Desford Street
Torrance, California 90502

**HERMAN'S HERMITS**
c/o Kathy Madrigal
Port Hueneme, Calif, 93031

**MISSING LINKS NATIONAL FAN CLUB (FROM AUSTRALIA)**
c/o Laura Best
3125 S. Crescent Heights
Los Angeles 34, California

**BILLY J. KRAMER (And THE DAKOTAS)**
c/o Miss Lorraine Cicarone
538 Chestnut Street
Orange, New Jersey

---

### KRLA BEATLE KISS COUPON

Dear ......John,......Paul,......George,......Ringo,...All Four Beatles:

I've been wanting to do this so bad, I could almost taste it. (Yum.) Now I'm finally going to get my chance to give you the great big kiss I've been dreaming about! After all, it's only fair. I have so much to remember you by. It's about time you had something of mine to remind you of me. Take a deep breath now, because HERE GOES!!!!!!

Plant Beatle Kiss Here

Wow! I hope you liked stealing a kiss as much as I did. You better have, or else! Or else what? I dunno. This is my first (lip) stick up.

Name ............................................................ Age ............
Address ........................................................................
City ............................................................................
P.S. — I luv you

---

### THE BYRDS
Official National
FAN CLUB
Suite 504
6290 Sunset Blvd.
Hollywood

Send $1.00 plus two 5-cent stamps and receive photos, fact sheets, biographies. Fun contests each month.

Free Concerts Planned
For Members Only

The BYRDS Are Great

---

### Richard J. Shepp's
Top 40 Productions

has available for dances and shows, the finest Top 40 talent. If you and your organization need and want, the very best in talent, call or write today, to:

Top 40 Productions
P.O. BOX 8244
Universal City
Telephone 985-1911

# KRLA ARCHIVES

## TUNEDEX

| | | ARTIST |
|---|---|---|
| | | Sam The Sham & Pharaohs |
| | | The Beach Boys |
| | AGAIN | The Supremes |
| | | Ian Whitcomb & Bluesville |
| | IAN | The Byrds |
| | | Sonny & Cher |
| | | The Miracles |
| | SE DON'T GO | Them |
| | | Guess Who? |
| | | The Beatles |
| | EEDS | |
| | | Jackie De Shannon |
| | | The Olympics |
| | GHT | Them |
| | F | Four Tops |
| | WITH FIRE | Rolling Stones |
| | TA DREAM ON | Herman's Hermits |
| | IFE | Righteous Brothers |
| | ER | Sir Douglas Quintet |
| | | Donovan |
| | ST FALL | Glenn Yarborough |
| | | The Beau Brummels |
| | Y | Unit Four Plus Two |
| | | The Yardbirds |
| | | Billy Stewart |
| | | Brenda Holloway |
| | | Herman's Hermits |
| | PEL | Elvis Presley |
| | SE | Jody Miller |
| | | Peter and Gordon |
| | | Ike and Tina Turner |

### BERS

| | | | |
|---|---|---|---|
| 1. | 45. | ENGINE ENGINE NO. 9 | Roger Miller |
| 2. | 42. | BRING IT ON HOME TO ME | The Animals |
| 3. | 39. | PEANUTS | The Sunglows |
| 4. | 38. | YOU REALLY KNOW HOW TO HURT A GUY | Jan and Dean |
| 5. | 48. | WHITTIER BOULEVARD | Three Midnighters |
| 6. | 49. | THE CLIMB | The Kingsmen |
| 7. | 47. | YOU CAN HAVE HER | Righteous Brothers |
| 8. | 41. | THREE O'CLOCK IN THE MORNING | Bert Kaempfert |
| 9. | 43. | KEEP ON TRYING | Bobby Vee |
| 10. | 40. | LAST CHANCE TO TURN AROUND | Gene Pitney |

### ENGINE No. 9

ROGER MILLER HAS DONE IT AGAIN. His "Engine, Engine No. 9" is one of the hottest on the charts.

## English Top Ten

1. TICKET TO RIDE .................. The Beatles
2. KING OF THE ROAD ............. Roger Miller
3. A WORLD OF OUR OWN ........ The Seekers
4. TRUE LOVE WAYS ........... Peter & Gordon
5. HERE COMES THE NIGHT ............. Them
6. BRING IT ON HOME TO ME .... The Animals
7. WHERE ARE YOU NOW ......... Jackie Trent
8. POP GO THE WORKERS .... The Barron Knights
9. THE MINUTE YOU'RE GONE .... Cliff Richard
10. SUBTERRANEAN HOMESICK BLUES .... Bob Dylan

## STONES DISLIKE INSINCERE PEOPLE

CONTINUED FROM PAGE 4

hausted. That one was Bill Wyman. After a full day's work behind the microphones, Bill still wanted to sit around, chat, and listen to records.

Bill seemed to be the most open-hearted of The Rolling Stones, and our relaxed conversation was interrupted many times when he would stop to invite a fan inside.

Both Bill and I discovered a mutual interest in science fiction books, and we enjoyed talking about books we had both read. It was after three a.m. when I finally shook hands, and headed for home.

### Mick Tired

I telephoned the boys three or four times Thursday. Mick was starting to feel a bit tired, having been touring the U.S. since April 30. They had started this tour on April 11 at Wembley, England, and were all beginning to feel the strain of more than a month on the road. They had played club and concert dates in England, Germany, France and Canada.

Saturday was quite a day. San Bernardino's Swing Auditorium, with the thermometer above 80! The crowds formed their lines early in the day, many curled up with pillows under their heads and thermos bottles full of lemonade by their side.

By showtime the huge auditorium was filled. There were three acts on before The Stones. One of them, The Byrds, completely brought down the house with their hit, "Mr. Tambourine Man."

### Stones Arrive

The Stones arrived in a white sedan, and sauntered into their dressing room. Mick nearly lost a handful of hair when a zealous fan broke through police lines and grabbed at his head.

Backstage, Keith was sitting in a corner, staring out at the people milling about.

Mick was pacing the floor, anxious to get on the stage that proved to the United States that the boys with the long hair were really valuable.

Bill, dressed in denim pants and a black leather coat, was happily chatting away with questioners.

Brian sipped a drink from a paper cup, and shot back icy stares at people pulling at his clothing. Charley had wandered off somewhere, making it difficult for photographers to get a decent group shot of The Stones together.

### Strange Bump

After the show there was a frightening moment. As the car pulled away, a bump was felt. All The Stones were sure that an innocent fan, (one of thousands jammed around the car in San Bernardino,) was caught underneath. It proved to be nothing more than a huge boulder placed in the roadway by a quick-thinking, but not-too-thoughtful fan.

The car managed to get free, and sped off to the freeway.

Back at the hotel there was a cluster of fans, asking for autographs. The Stones signed a few, then dashed to their rooms. They were definitely tired, and had an important show due next day ... The Long Beach Arena, for KRLA's Bob Eubanks. (The story of that show is in this issue of THE BEAT . . . . reported by Louise Criscione.)

After the show and the drive back, they lounged about, watching television and swapping jokes with fans outside. The guards cleared everyone away and the boys went to sleep early.

Monday was spent much as Sunday was, with everyone making preparations for the trip to San Diego. The show there went well, save for a few fights between girls in the audience. The "escape" went just as planned, and the boys drove off before the fans reached them.

Tuesday, Wednesday and Thursday were spent at ABC-TV, either rehearsing or taping. On Thursday night a rather large crowd lined at the entrance, but doubled-up security precautions had been made and the efficient ABC guards kept the fans contained.

The shows elsewhere in California went well, The Stones drawing capacity in every city in which they played. A far cry from their first tour in the early summer days of 1964, when they had to share the bill with tumblers, trick riding horses, and an insulting emcee on The Hollywood Palace.

Thousands saw The Rolling Stones, either on stage or in person, and hundreds of thousands more have fallen in love with them.

Anyone who gets to know these five young "rebels with a cause" must immediately feel a strong liking and respect for them. I certainly fit into that category.

## IAN WRITES

## Ian Sings High Just As A Gag

(As an exclusive to the KRLA BEAT, here is a reprint of a letter received by Ian Whitcomb's friend, Reporter Rod Barken:)

Dear Rodney:

Hello mate, how are you? Thanks for the copies of your paper (THE KRLA BEAT). They're great! The kids here at school didn't believe me when I said that America had a pop-music paper, but sure changed their tune when I flashed the ones you sent.

So now you're wondering about the song. That figures. It's a funny sort of a thing to explain, but that voice style that I used on "You Turn Me On" was something that we came up with on the day of the recording. I just started fooling around, and that's the way it came out.

. . . Many thanks to every one of you there in Hollywood for the great way you all treated me. The people up at Tower Records sure showed me about in royal style, and I especially enjoyed meeting Derek.

Everybody in England is talking about Dylan and Donovan. That Donovan's unbelievable.

You can't believe how they treat me back here at Trinity College. I'm a bloody star! Some of the English press got those pictures we took at Shindig, and reports that my record has started to make points on your charts have caused everybody to talk. I love it! Girls that I used to date ask for my autograph.

Right now I'm studying hard, and playing a few clubs around Dublin on the weekends. I'm told (just a minute ago) that I'm coming back to tape another "SHINDIG" and spend a few weeks in Hollywood in June.

Let's get together then, okay?

Ian

"LITTLE LONELY ONE"
TOM JONES

# KRLA ARCHIVES

## KRLA BEAT

**BEATLE TICKETS** — Win Free Passes To Hollywood Bowl

**BIRDS-EYE VIEW** — A Hilarious Chat With Tambourine Men

Volume 1, No. 14     Los Angeles, California     Ten Cents     June 9, 1965

## BEATLES VI
**THE WORLD'S MOST POPULAR FOURSOME! JOHN • PAUL • GEORGE • RINGO**

YOU LIKE ME TOO MUCH • TELL ME WHAT YOU SEE • BAD BOY • DIZZY MISS LIZZIE • EIGHT DAYS A WEEK • YES IT IS
WORDS OF LOVE • KANSAS CITY • I DON'T WANT TO SPOIL THE PARTY • EVERY LITTLE THING • WHAT YOU'RE DOING

RECORDED IN ENGLAND

*Capitol Records*

*Here's Exclusive Preview of Beatle's New Album*

### Worldwide Premiere
## KRLA First With Beatles' Album

KRLA scored another world-wide "first" last week. And as a result, KRLA listeners became the first anywhere to hear the exciting new Beatles' album, "BEATLES VI!"

Ignoring the red "on the air" sign, KRLA's Dave Hull and Von Filkins strolled calmly into the studio as Dick Biondi was in the middle of his nightly nine-to-midnight riot act.

Unwrapping an ordinary-looking record album, they placed it on a turntable and suggested that Dick play it as his next record.

The sound that came forth — broadcast over KRLA — had never before been heard by any radio audience on earth. And with that world-wide exclusive, KRLA maintained a perfect record of being the first to broadcast every major new Beatles disc — including both 45 r.p.m. singles and albums.

No wonder were recognized as the world's foremost Beatles station. Although the KRLA deejays do not attempt to impose upon their personal friendships with the Beatles, John, Paul, George and Ringo seem to have gone out of their way to provide any possible favors.

Judged on overall sound, this is one of their finest albums. It provides a good cross-section of the unique musical abilities which have made the Beatles the most popular entertainers in history.

Capitol Records scheduled it for release to the public on June 14. Advance public reaction from its international premiere over KRLA indicates it will be another number-one smash for the Fab Foursome.

It contains two fantastic songs which have never

**—MORE ON PAGE 11**

### INSIDE THE BEAT
★ THE BEATLES — An Autographed Picture
★ "HELP" — Beatles Face Danger in Austria
★ FREDDIE — Zany Scenes From His New Movie
★ ROLLING STONES — Tell All In BEAT Exclusive
★ DEREK TAYLOR — "My Life With the Beatles"

*also*

THE ZOMBIES, THE KINKS, SANDIE SHAW
BEATLE QUIZ, KRLA DEEJAYS, TUNEDEX,
BRITISH TOP 10, PICTURE PUZZLE

# DEREK TAYLOR'S LIFE WITH THE BEATLES
## Recalls First Meeting When He Marveled At Their Magnetism

**AS BEATLE PRESS OFFICER**

By DEREK TAYLOR

On May 30, 1962, I telephoned the manager of the Odeon Cinema in Manchester, and told him that I was interested in a touring show due at his cinema that night.

The manager — a gloomy, pessimistic man like a lot of his kind in England — was not impressed because he knew that newspapermen working for daily publications were of no use to him so far as 1-night stands were concerned.

The reason for this is that by the time the journalist's report on the show is published, the show has moved to another town and the publicity is, therefore, of no help to his cinema.

### KRLA BEAT

The KRLA BEAT is published weekly by Prestige Publishing Company; editorial and advertising offices at 6290 Sunset Boulevard, Suite 504, Hollywood, California 90028.

Single copy price, 10 cents.

Subscription price: U.S. and possessions, and Canada, $3 per year or $5 for two years. Foreign rates upon request.

So he merely grunted when I asked for a couple of tickets. He said, "There are no free ones for the press." Journalists, such is their temperament, detest paying for admission to anything, whether to a cinema, theatre or a nightclub.

But as this was to be no ordinary show, I said, "Well, how are you fixed for tickets if I pay?"

He grunted a bit more and left the telephone for a moment or two. Then he returned and said, "You can have a couple on the front row for a guinea each."

"Right," I said. "I'll pick them up at the box-office for the first show."

### Turning Point

That telephone call was the turning point of my life, for the stars of the show were the Beatles.

I phoned my wife and said, "You know that group your sister told us about — the Beatles. Well, they're in Manchester tonight and I've got a couple of tickets."

She hustled about, found some babysitters, and at five minutes to 6:00 we were in our seats among the most nervous audience I'd ever seen.

I had been to pop shows before — not many, for the popular music scene in England up to that time had held little appeal for anyone above teen age — but I had neevr sensed such urgency and excitement in any audience.

There were banners everywhere. Everyone was sitting on the edge of his seat, and I said to my wife, "There's something happening in this theatre and whatever it is, it's new to me. Can you feel it?"

### Like Sinatra

She said she could, and we both agreed the nearest we had come to it was in the early 1950s when Sinatra — during his fall from grace — had toured England, playing in old-fashioned vauderville shows with the top seat price less than a dollar. But neither Sinatra, nor Danny Kaye in the wild days of 1949, had caused such extraordinary tension in any theatre.

On the bill with the Beatles were Roy Orbison, Gerry and the Pacemakers, and a few other acts whose names I have now forgotten.

The show opened with the lesser-known acts and then, to a storm of applause, little Gerry Marsden burst onto the stage in a tight suit and pounding into the first bars of "How Do You Do It."

His reception was enormous and I remember thinking that if the Beatles were going to top it, they had better be pretty good.

Gerry was a delightful artist and his personality and energy were something completely new in popular music, which had become very jaded and static.

Remember that at that time the major recording stars of England were Cliff Richard and the Shadows who, though experienced and established, were hardly electrifying on stage.

### Teen Idols

The Beatles by then had a huge teenage following but were scorcely known to adults. This was not the fault of the Beatles, for they had already made three records — "Love Me Do," which had reached No. 17 in the British charts, "Please Please Me" and "From Me To You," both of which had made No. 1.

It was simply that most adults didn't concern themselves with the teenage world or its idols.

Perspiring and obviously delighted by his reception, Gerry finished his act in a hailstorm of jelly babies and I slipped out for a drink during the intermission.

After the break, the extraordinary Orbison strolled up to the microphone to a hushed, almost reverent reception.

**—MORE ON PAGE 6**

---

## THE CINDERS

*The One and Only*
### CHUCK BERRY
**SUNDAY, JUNE 20**
North Hollywood Cinnamon Cinder

**WEDNESDAY, JUNE 23**
Long Beach Cinnamon Cinder

## HAVE THE ACTION

*The Fabulous*
### CRYSTALS
**SUNDAY, JUNE 27**
North Hollywood Cinnamon Cinder
**WEDNESDAY, JUNE 30**
Long Beach Cinnamon Cinder
AGES 18-25

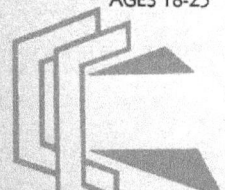

### CINNAMON CINDER
11345 Ventura Blvd., North Hollywood
4401 Pacific Coast Highway, Long Beach

### FREE BEATLE PIN-UPS
(Regular 50¢ Each)

TO EVERY CUSTOMER WHO PRESENTS

THIS AD AT:

### HOLLYWOOD WAX MUSEUM
HOLLYWOOD BLVD. AT HIGHLAND AVE.

# KRLA ARCHIVES

### KRLA's James Bond

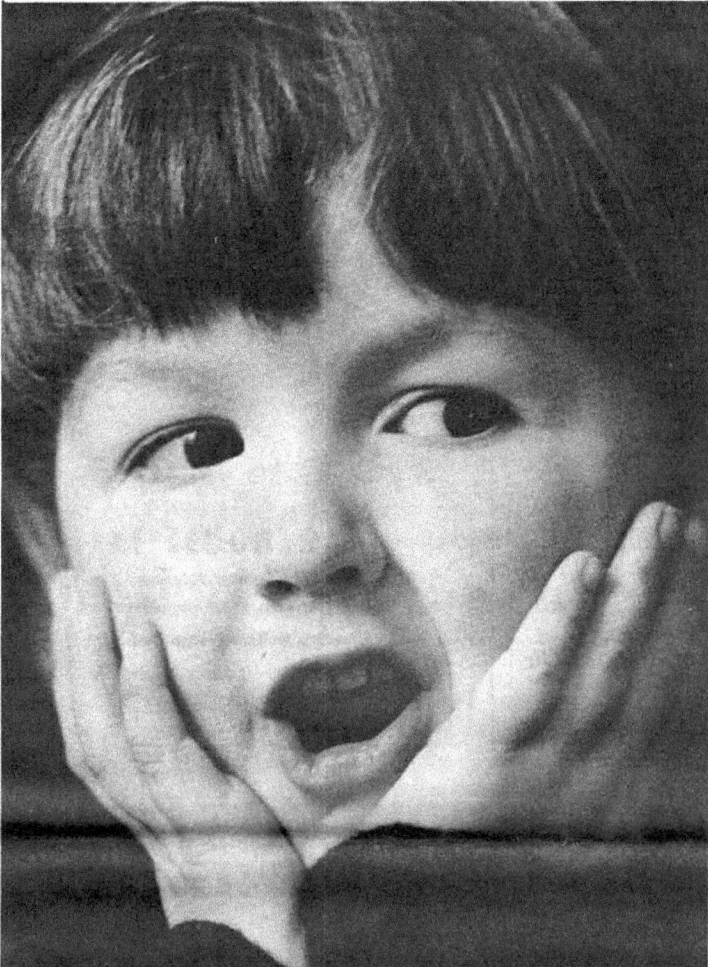

**THIS TOUGH-LOOKING MYSTERY MAN is KRLA's** James Bond, the English adventurer who often takes breathtaking chances by listening to the radio when he is supposed to be taking a nap. James Bond is a fictitious name. He is forced to use an alias because relatives are not allowed to work together at KRLA. Do you think he resembles the man whose column is to your right?

### Comer

**THOMAS TURNER,** Derek Taylor's protege, has been signed for two appearances on "Shindig." At present he sings with the Coasters, and music experts are predicting a great future for the talented young tenor.

### A KRLA BEAT Editorial

## Move Over, Beethoven

A very recent issue of Time Magazine had a very interesting cover. And very interesting contents.

A number of rock and roll singers were featured outside, and seven of the inside pages were devoted to that subject.

In case you didn't read the article, the gist of it was this: Rock and roll, questionable as its value may be, is undoubtedly here to stay. Today's music and dances are nearly as popular with adults as they are with teenagers. In fact, an amazingly large percentage of hit recordings are purchased by the 20-40 age group.

Several other national magazines — including Life and Look — are running similar articles.

We usually hate to say I told you so. But not this time. Adults have been saying rock and roll was on its way out since the day it came in.

It's been over ten years since then, and rock and roll is still having its day. Makes you stop and think, doesn't it.

It now takes less and less time for the adult population to learn to enjoy our ever-changing fads and fancies. Makes you wonder why they don't just admit they like them right at the beginning instead of under-going a massive "change of heart" later in the game.

The Beat of the sixties may not outlast the four B's.

But let's face it, Beethoven. Roll over. Right now there's room for one more.

## Derek Taylor Reports
## We'll Miss Jack Good; His Kind Hard To Find

It's a pity about Jack Good. In a few days' time he leaves "Shindig." Hollywood, "Shindig," the record industry and the worldwide pop scene are the poorer.

This is not to diminish his successor, Dean Whitmore, who will soon step in as producer, doubling up on his current duties as director. I simply want to make the point that you do not pick Jack Goods off trees.

Whatever happens to Rock 'n' Roll, the Go-Go shows in general, and "Shindig" in particular, Jack Good can be assured of some place in show business history.

He was the only important man on the English Rock 'n' Roll scene in the mid-1950s.

Why?

Beacuse he had been properly educated at a good English school, further matured and schooled at university, and because, after all this valuable conditioning, he was able to superimpose a rebellious and creative talent.

### Early Rock Supporter

The young, pink-cheeked Jack Good was not ashamed to admit — in 1955 when Rock 'n' Roll was not respectable in England — that he admired Elvis Presley, Gene Vincent, Little Richard and Chuck Berry.

To the early British rock shows he brought his education, his zeal, and his outgoing honesty. Then he came to America and showed the Americans how to create a full, fast and rich hour of pop music.

Now that "Shindig" is assured of a huge all-age audience, Jack feels the time has come to move away and apply his creative instincts elsewhere. Anyone who cares about popular music will wish him well.

But make no mistake. Show-business is not as generous a sphere as it seems. There are those who will be glad that his outspoken non-conformity will no longer be around to confound the smooth-talking slogan-mongers.

### Beatles Missed

So the Beatles failed to make it in Los Angeles with "Ticket to Ride." Even on our own Tunedex the greatest group the world has ever known could get no higher than No. 4. For the Beatles to be out-sold by Sam the Sham and the Pharohs is incomprehensible. But it happened. So that's that.

The Beach Boys are No. 1 in the very reliable national music charts with "Help Me, Rhonda." Personally, I loathe the record because I think it lacks heart and warmth. But this is only a matter of opinion, and one must concede that, musically, the piece is well constructed.

Everyone in England who buys records is conscious of the Beach Boys — and they are not without fans over there — but because England is not too well blessed with surfing beaches, Pacific Coast "surf" music never really caught on.

The Byrds — still in a position to justify the enormity of my nationwide No. 1 prediction — have jumped an average of thirty places in all the national charts this week with "Mr. Tambourine Man."

Their power in the charts lies in their coast-to-coast success.

### Tested Nationally

It's not enough — and New Yorkers are very quick to point this out — to crash dramatically into the Top Ten in the Los Angeles area. The trade newspapers and the East Coast disc jockeys are very careful to watch what they call the "West Coast freak hits."

But the Byrds qualify as hit-makers not only here but in the deep South, the Middle West, and the hard-boiled communities of the industrial East. Places like Cleveland, Pittsburgh, Detroit.

The Standells and Paul Revere and the Raiders have yet to convince the East that they are worthy hit-makers. With "Louie Louie" and now with "Sometimes," Paul Revere and the Raiders have an assured West Coast following, both north and south. The Standells with "The Boy Next Door" had a wonderful Los Angeles hit. But, so far, they have failed to penetrate the eastern charts.

Well . . . talent will always emerge. And neither group is short of ability.

### Another Motown Hit

Motown, now the label with the biggest personality-cult of its own, now has — in addition to the Supremes — the Four Tops moving smartly up the national charts in support of Detroit's proud name.

Good. The more honest R & B, the better.

Any recording artist will tell you that, though it's marvelous to have a hit record, the responsibility of securing a follow-up is enormous. As I predicted, the Righteous Brothers — legitimately claimed to be one of the hottest acts in Aemrica or Europe — did not reach No. 1 with "Just Once in My Life."

It's not too easy, positively to isolate the primary reason for failure. My view is that there was too much happening on the disc.

### Personal Choice

I don't know what the answer is to all this. The charts confuse me, not only because they vary so considerably, but because the amount of time a radio station devotes to any particular record may bear no relation to the sales of that record in the neighborhood store.

If more and more of us were to reject the commercialized and immature rubbish which creeps around every corner, we might bring some balance back to the record charts.

As I say, I'm confused.

Strange things are happening . . .

# KRLA ARCHIVES

**Win Beatle Tickets**

## Can You Identify This Picture?

*Puzzle Piece No. 1*

We've asked a lot of silly questions in our time, but this one is really going to take the cake!

Would you like to win tickets to the KRLA Beatle Concert in Hollywood Bowl??

Then stop looking so puzzled and take a look at the strange object lurking nearby. Appears to be a piece of a puzzle, doesn't it? Well, that's exactly what it is!

What does a puzzle piece have to do with winning Beatle tickets? Everything!

Here's what we've done. We took a photograph of a certain person (or persons), place or thing and cut it into ten pieces. One piece will appear in each issue of the Beat for the next ten issues, starting right now.

Here's what you have to do. Cut out the piece in this issue and start puzzling over it. Chances are you won't have much luck guessing who or what it is this week, but when you cut out the piece that will appear next week, things might not be quite so puzzling.

The first KRLA Beat reader to guess the object of the photo will win TWO tickets to the Hollywood Bowl. The next two readers to come up the right answer will each win ONE ticket to see the Beatles perform!

The fourth place winner will receive four record albums, and winners five through twelve will win a record album by a top favorite.

If you like, you can begin guessing right now! If you think you already know who or what's in the puzzle photo, send a letter (quick!) to KRLA Beat-le Puzzle, 6290 Sunset Blvd., Suite 504, Hollywood.

And don't be shattered if your first guess isn't right. Just pick up the pieces (in each of the following issues of the Beat) and keep guessing!

Don't forget to enclose your name, address, age and telephone number with each guess!

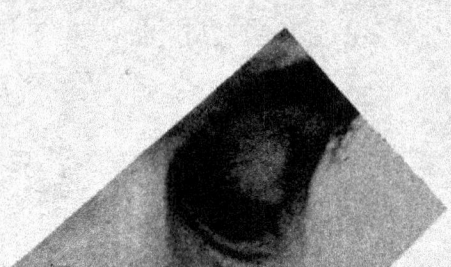

---

### KRLA BEAT SUBSCRIPTION

As a special introductory offer — if you subscribe now you will save 40% of the regular price.

☐ 1 YEAR — 52 issues — $3.00   ☐ 2 YEARS — $5.00

Enclosed is $..........

Send to: .......................................................... Age: ..........

Address: ..................................................................

City: ............................ State: ............ Zip: ..........

MAIL YOUR ORDER TO: **KRLA BEAT**
1401 South Oak Knoll Avenue
Pasadena, California 91106

---

### WAREHOUSE IX
2214 Stoner Avenue
off Olympic in West Los Angeles
**Dancing to Live Name Bands**
Los Angeles' Unique Young Adult Nite Club
Girls 18 — Guys 21
Closed Tuesdays and Sundays

---

**FIRST PRIZE!**
YOU AND A FRIEND WILL BE GUESTS OF KRLA AT A
**BEATLE CONCERT!**
And a Beatle Press Conference!
You will also receive
A Beautiful WRIST WATCH!

**10 Second Prizes:**
BEAUTIFUL, ENGRAVED
**WRIST WATCHES!**
(Winners may choose between second and third prizes.)

**10 Third Prizes:**
AUTOGRAPHED
**BEATLE ALBUMS!**

## EARN FAB MONEY, PRIZES AS A BEAT REPRESENTATIVE

### 6 STUDENTS IN EACH SCHOOL
*May Qualify to Accept Subscriptions*

## IT'S FUN AND PROFITABLE

The KRLA BEAT is the NATION'S TOP NEWSPAPER for young Americans, and it is NOW ACCEPTING SUBSCRIPTIONS FOR THE FIRST TIME. Now you can become a circulation representative in your school.

HERE'S ALL YOU HAVE TO DO: Send your name, address, telephone number and the school you attend to KRLA BEAT, 1401 S. OAK KNOLL, PASADENA, Calif. But do it fast — first come, first served. We will send you all the necessary information to become a successful KRLA BEAT representative. You will learn handsome profits on each subscription. Earnings are unlimited, because EVERY TEENAGER SHOULD BE A SUBSCRIBER!

AND THERE ARE SPECIAL PRIZES FOR THOSE WHO SELL THE MOST SUBSCRIPTIONS
BETWEEN NOW AND JUNE 23RD

I would like to be a KRLA BEAT REPRESENTATIVE in .................... ☐ Jr.  ☐ Sr. High
School in the city of: ..................................................................
Please send me additional information and forms for selling subscriptions.
Name.................................................................. Age ..........
Address .............................................. City ..........
Phone .............................................. Zip Code ..........

# KRLA ARCHIVES

## Even at Hollywood Parties

## Not All Zombies Are Weird

BY ROD BARKEN

The Zombies were recently treated to a party while staying treated to a private party while staying overnight in Hollywood.

They are currently riding the record charts with the hit, "Se'hs record charts with the hit, "She's Coming Home." They are clean cut, quiet, well-mannered, intelligent, and all very good looking.

Their d r e s s is immaculate, their speech articulate, and their conversations are not forced or rehearsed. They behave like gentlemen, and shy away from boisterous and out-of-hand affairs.

The party was hosted by record producer Steve Venet, and was held in one of those stylish Hollywood apartments that overlook the twinkling lights of the city. The first thing that struck me about these young men was their open aproach. Chris, the bass player, noticed me standing alone by a piano, and immediately came over with his hand extended.

**Introduction**

"Hello," he said. "I'm Chris— Who are you?"

Five minutes later found us talking about everything from polo ponies to sports cars (he owns a brand new Austin Healey). When I asked him how it was going, and how he liked touring the United States, he replied, "Oh, it's good enough. We miss being able to sit down and enjoy a good meal, and getting a decent night's sleep, that's all."

"How about the crowds," I asked. "Do you dig that screaming?"

To that Chris replied, "Sure we do. They're much bigger than the crowds back home in England, and the kids do yell louder, so we definitely do like it all."

After talking for a few more minutes, he introduced me to their road manager, Terry Arnold, who in turn introduced me to the rest of The Zombies.

There's Rod, the organist; Colin, the lead vocalist; Hugh, the drummer; and Paul, the lead guitarist. Chris and Rod also team up on harmonizing, and are very proud of the fact that "She's Not There" was not an over-dubbed recording. (An "over-dub" is the process of placing a recording of voices over another recording of the same lyrics.

I learned that The Zombies are somewhat renowned in England, and that three of the members could have gone on to college, but mutually decided to "pack it in" for careers in show business. This is their first tour of the U.S., and they are very encouraged by the enthusiastic reception given them.

As the sun crept over the horizon, they raveled off to a coffee shop for breakfast. Then, a few hours sleep before their bus left for Santa Barbara, and the next stop on a very successful Dick Clark Tour.

ZOMBIES — CHRIS, HUGH, COLIN, PAUL AND ROD

## BEATLE QUIZ

Here we go again! Five more questions for the KRLA Beatle Quiz.

It's evident that we have some real experts among the contestants, judging by the entires received so far. But be careful! Some of the answers are not quite as simple as they appear.

Those of you who missed the first two weeks of the Beatle Quiz may still catch up by ordering the issues of June 2 and May 26. You'll find instructions for ordering back issues elsewhere in the BEAT.

The winner, of course, will get to interview the Beatles for the KRLA BEAT when they arrive in August. The winner and a friend will also attend a Beatle Concert as guests of the KRLA Deejays.

Additional prizes will be provided for runners-up. In case of a tie there will be additional questions or a drawing to decide the final winner. The contest will cover a ten-week period, with at least five new questions asked each week. KRLA's Derek Taylor, a close friend of the Beatles and their former press officer, will judge the entries for accuracy.

Here we go with five new questions. Good luck!

Beatle Quiz
KRLA BEAT
Suite 504
6290 Sunset Blvd.
Hollywood, Calif. 90028
CONTEST EDITOR:

Below are my answers to the third set of questions in the BEATLE QUIZ CONTEST.

My Name .................................................. Address ..................................................

City .................................................. State .................. Zip Code ..............

I (☐am) (☐am not) presently a subscriber to the KRLA BEAT.

**NEW QUESTIONS**

11. What was the name of the club in Germany where the Beatles first appeared? ..............
12. Name the Beatle members at that time? ..............
13. How many songs are normally on the Beatles British albums? ..............
14. What is the name of John's and Paul's music publishing company? ..............
15. How many new songs are to be included in the Beatles' second movie? ..............

MORE QUESTIONS IN NEXT WEEK'S BEAT

## Beatles In Austria

## DANGEROUS FILMING IN AUSTRIAN ALPS

(The second and concluding portion of an eyewitness account of the problems, pleasures, thrills and dangers involved in filming the Beatles' second movie, "Help!" Publicist Tony Howard tells of the drastic change when they left tropical Nassau and moved to the snow-bound Austrian Alps.)

Things were different there. Where the generator had nearly fallen overboard during its journey from the mainland to Paradise Island, in Austria the same massive machine was frequently buried under snow and ice during blizzards. Where Princess Soraya had watched the filming in Nassau, the only visiting celebrity in Austria was Miss Austria, who was promptly engaged by producer and director for a small part opposite the Beatles. Where personnel had plodded ankle deep through silver sands, they were now working knee deep in snow. There was also a very real danger of avalanches. A week before Shenson's unit arrived an avalanche had swept a bus load of students to their death into a ravine. After this tragedy, the mountain pass to Obertauern was closed by the authorities except for four hours a day.

**Shortage**

One situation was common to both locales — lack of hotel accommodation. In Obertauern it was also high season, but camping was out; it was cold outside. The hordes of fans, sightseers and pressmen were sleeping six to a room, utilizing even billiard tables. Many bedded down in chairs in the hotel bars when the bars closed down for the night.

Filming started almost right away. And even the weather went e x a c t l y according to schedule even though the script called for tremendous physical feats on the parts of the Beatles and co-stars Leo McKern, Eleanor Bron, Victor Spinetti, Roy Kinuear, John Bluthel and Patrick Cargill. Falls from runaway sleighs, ski jumps, sprints across ice rinks — all this and more was performed by the intrepid cast. The Beatles were even required to do a musical number on a mountain top with a grand piano hauled up by eight men for the occasion, in a freezing gale.

**Fun Night**

Unlike Nassau, high life after dark in Obertauern was practically non-existent because the extremely high altitude tired people almost to the point of collapse. Towards the end of the two-week stint there was, however, one night to remember. The entire unit met at the Marietta Hotel to celebrate assistant director Clive Reed's birthday. The Beatles, perhaps tiring of the inevitable Viennesse waltzes in the band's repertoire, decided to take over. With Dick Laster at the piano, they gave a two-hour impromptu concert that nearly took the roof off.

By the last day no one had managed to get to ski but most had two layers of tan.

Back in London it was spring and the day after the chartered plane landed at London Airport, welcomed by several thousand fans, filming was resumed at Wickenham Studios. By now a lot of things had happened. George Harrison had had his 22nd birthday. Ringo's wife had announced a forthcoming baby, and brilliant British commedian Frankie Howard, star of London's long-running stage hit "A Funny Thing Happened on the Way to the Forum," had joined the cast. His portrayal of an eccentric drama coach promises to be one of the film's comedy highlights. But no one had thought of a perfect title.

**Title Change**

Ringo's "Eight Arms to Hold You" had been announced but was soon voted out again. Time passed and still no title. Then one day someone realized that the word most used in the script was "help!" So a title was born and John Lennon and Paul McCartney s t a r t e d, belatedly, to work out the title song. The boys often compose fast, and in no time the song was written and recorded.

A few problems arose — one was the inevitable fan trouble w h i c h the Beatles experience wherever they go. Twickenham's teenagers were regularly breaking into the studio or storming the gates, and it was necessary to reinforce not only the police but the very bricks and motar of the studio.

**Police Warning**

Several street sequences were on the agenda, but the London police warned the film company that they would not receive much cooperation from the overworked constabulary if the fans caused traffic obstructions. So Shenson's unit was obliged to shoot further afield and away from the crowded areas of central London.

A four-day location on Salisbury Plains was announced and with the cooperation of the war office — which supplied troops, tanks and equipment for the occasion — a near full-scale military maneuver was filmed in spite of unpredictable spring weather.

These scenes are to remain top secret—and many others in the film — until release time. Both Richard Lester and Walter Shenson feel that the plot and situa-

—MORE ON PAGE 10

# KRLA ARCHIVES

More About:

## Derek's Start With Beatles

(Continued From Page 2)

I must confess that I had never heard of him, and his appearance was, not to put too fine a point on it, unconventional for a pop star.

He wore his tinted glasses, and that smooth white face was surrounded by a halo of lacquered hair. Also, he was plump. But, of course, any early doubts were scattered by the man's enormous skill with a song and by his repose at the microphone. He was the perfect antidote to the wilderness of Gerry and the Pacemakers. And to give the audience their due, they applauded him as if he were the top-of-the-bill act.

### New Era

By this time I realized that popular music had improved beyond belief. And when the emcee came from the wings and started to say, "John, Paul . . ." the auditorium exploded in a massive scream from 3,000 throats.

It was the Beatles.

From the right-hand side of the stage came George Harrison and Paul McCartney. It was my first sight of the choir-boy countenance of Paul. Little had been written about them in newspapers, and not too much in magazines. And neither my wife nor I could identify them on sight.

But I had noticed the strong and cynical features of John Lennon on television a few days earlier and also the homeliness of Ringo Starr who, with John, pranced in from the stage-left.

By now the scream was permanent and I felt my ears would explode.

What a show! The Beatles sang ten songs and it was clear to me that we were in the presence of something quite outside normal experience.

My recollection of that first night is so clear and my assessment of the Beatles' quality was so immediate that I still see red when someone attempts to knock the Beatles' talent or personality with one of those dead-pan questions like, "What's so special about them?"

(Derek Taylor's nostalgic account of his introduction to the Beatles and of his later employment as their press officer will be continued next week.)

## LISTENERS HAVE CHOICE ON KRLA

KRLA's unequalled success story as the most popular radio station in the nation received even further recognition last week.

John Barrett, KRLA manager, was one of the featured speakers at a radio program clinic in New York sponsored by the National Association of Broadcasters.

Mr. Barrett, whose background includes extensive research in listening habits of the young adult audience, emphasized several key points behind KRLA's success.

He listed these as quality, consistency and allowing the listeners to select the music and type programs they want to hear.

## They're Still Tops

THE BEACH BOYS REMAIN AMERICA'S MOST CONSISTENT HIT-MAKERS. 'HELP ME RHONDA' IS STILL ONE OF THE TOP SONGS ACROSS THE COUNTRY.

# FREDDIE

If you think Freddie and the Dreamers are zany on TV, you should see them in their new movie 'Seaside Swingers.'

The Embassy Pictures release, a Joseph E. Levine production, is scheduled to open in the Los Angeles area shortly.

Since it stars Freddie and the Dreamers, 'Seaside Swingers' is naturally a rollicking musical. It follows a group of fun-loving youngsters who spend their vacation in madcap antics at a large seashore resort.

Other notable young British names such as John Leyton, Mike Sarne and Liz Frazer are in the cast.

Filmed in technicolor and Cinemascope, the 'Seaside Swingers' features Freddie and his cohorts in several good production numbers.

FREDDIE IS ONE OF TODAY'S TOP STARS

# KRLA ARCHIVES

## ...LAYS HIMSELF - A KOOK

ZANY FREDDIE SERVES UP A STRANGE CONCOCTION FOR RESORT GUESTS

FREDDIE AND THE DREAMERS DO SEVERAL OF THEIR BIG NUMBERS IN MOVIE

## Letters

### SOMETHING MISSING

There's only one thing missing in the Beat. A group called Them. They're my favorites and I'd love to read about Them. Will you please feature Them soon?

Please answer another question, too. When you're trying to say you like Them, do you say "Them is great" or Them are, or what? Every way you say it sounds wrong.

I asked my English teacher and all he did was stare at me and kind of moan.

D.M., Tarzana, Calif.

*Them is going to be featured in the Beat soon. No . . . Them ARE going to be . . . Them AM going to be??? Anyway, they are, and we hope that answers both of your questions.*

### DREAMBOAT

I buy the Beat every week, and I always read it just before I go to sleep.

Last night I re-read your John Lennon interview (he's my fave) and afterwards I had the greatest dream.

I dreamed I went to London as a reporter for the Beat, and John Lennon accidentally ran over me with his Rolls Royce.

It was so wonderful.

C.H., Eagle Rock

*Spoken like a Beatlemaniac! Dream on.*

### CELEBRITY TV

I recently discovered that I have the good fortune of living next door to several of Dick Biondi's relatives. Since he is my idol, I was overjoyed by my discovery.

Some people ask me if I mind living that close to the Griffith Park Zoo. Which I certainly do not.

I have never bitten anyone for asking a silly question like that, but I don't know how long I'm going to be able to hold off.

E.H., Los Angeles

*See you visiting day.*

### BACKSLAPPER

In my opinion, the KRLA Beat is Kooky, Readable, Loveable, Aware, Boss, Exceptional, Active and Terrific!

L.D., Garden Grove

*In our opinion, you are a Living Doll!*

### ABSORBING

Just a note to tell you that I find the KRLA Beat very absorbing.

It absorbs spilled milk, coke, orange juice and others.

Oh, stop looking so sad. I'm only kidding. I got the idea for this letter when my little brother spilled water all over my Beat. The whole thing was really very funny because then I hit him over the head with the soggy mess and then my mother walked in and said "Stop beating on that child."

Well, WE thought it was funny.

Anyway, I do find the Beat absorbing, in all ways.

P.L., Burbank

*We hope the Beat will continue to blot out your problems. (Sorry, we just couldn't resist.)*

# KRLA ARCHIVES

## For Girls Only

Okay, let's try it again.

Boys, keep out!! This weekly column is called "For Girls Only" and that's all it's for!

(It didn't work last week, and guess what. I think it just didn't work again. Oh well, maybe they'll learn something.)

Speaking of boys (I do have that habit, don't I?), they're all up in arms about the smock dresses that are the big deal with us at the moment. I'm afraid they're going to have to get used to it, though, as it seems this fad is here to stay awhile. Probably a long while. Besides being pretty and a whiz to take care of, they're sooo comfortable. Wildest smock dress I've seen in this area so far was made entirely of Beatle cards. You know, the kind you get in bubble gum. And I'm not kidding!

**Machine Sewn**

The girl had actually sewn the cards together on a machine. The dress hooked up the side so she wouldn't have to pull it off over her head and rumple John, George and/or Ringo (hummm, sounds like fun, doesn't it?), and it really caused a sensation on the beach.

I'd make one just like it only I don't exactly care for the idea of having to chew my way through a truck load of bubble gum.

Wow, I just had a brilliant idea! They have every kind of gum you can imagine these days. Sour orange, bananna (hope I spelled that right, if I did it'll be a first), green apple, etc. What I'm going to do is make a fortune by inventing garlic gum. Just think how handy it would come in when you're out with a boy you don't want to kiss goodnight.

**Ring Fad**

I just love the new (or is it?) fad of wearing a ring on your forefinger. Only problem is it's so hard to get used to. Even worse than that, the ring I bought to wear thereabouts turned my forefinger a delightful shade of green. Until I painted it all over with clear nail polish, that is.

I've discovered that's an answer to a lot of costume jewelry problems. It not only removes the "bath-tub ring", it also keeps settings in place, etc. If you have a pin or bracelet that just doesn't happen to be diamonds (yet!), coat the whole thing with clear polish and stop worrying about losing half of it every time you move a muscle.

What will they think of next? I just recently heard of two new products I just can't quite believe. One is spray on nylons. Sounds weird, I know, but if someone isn't putting me on, this could really be a great savings! You just whoosh on your nylons
—MORE ON PAGE 12

## Kasey's Quiz

Casey Kasem, top KRLA disc jockey, is famous for his cliff-hangers. When he starts one of his mysterious star biographies, it doesn't matter WHAT you're doing or WHERE you have to be in the next few minutes. You simply have to sit right there by the radio until you know who he's talking about. And if that isn't enough to drive you bats, now the Beat is printing a "Casey's Quiz" in every issue. So go even battier and see how well you really know the stars. You'll find the answer at the end, upside down.

1. This famous group wrote one of their biggest hit songs in a taxi cab on the way to a recording session. They have a passion for clothes, but rarely pay over a hundred dollars (apiece) for their on-stage costumes. Successful as they are, they still shine their own shoes, and do their own packing. They say they wouldn't know what to do if they had a valet, except let him "hang about." Among their many distinctions, they are the only singing group to ever be sculptured in butter. It took 800 pounds and the display was exhibited at a dairy fair in Toronto, Canada.

ANSWER: The Beatles

## Beatle Briefing

KRLA'S **BOB EUBANKS** discusses arrangements for Beatle concerts at Hollywood Bowl Aug. 29-30 with Brian Epstein.

## A RECORD MAKING ANNOUNCEMENT!

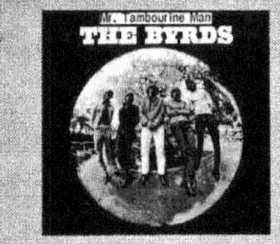

**THE BYRDS** Sing Their Smash Hit "Mr. Tambourine Man"

*Plus* It's No Use — The Bells of Rhymney — I Feel A Whole Lot Better — You Won't Have To Cry — Spanish Harlem Incident — We'll Meet Again — Chimes of Freedom — Don't Doubt Yourself, Baby — Here Without You — I Knew I'd Want You — All I Really Want To Do

**PAUL REVERE AND THE RAIDERS** Sing "Oo Poo Pah Doo"

*Plus* You Can't Sit Down — Money — Louie, Louie — Do You Love Me — Big Boy Pete — Sometimes — Gone — Bad Times — Fever — Time Is On My Side — A Kiss To Remember You By

**CHAD AND JEREMY** Sing "Before and After"

*Plus* Tell Me Baby — Why Should I Care — For Lovin' Me — I'm In Love Again — Little Does She Know — What Do You Want With Me — Say It Isn't True — Fare Thee Well — Can't Get Used To Losing You — Evil Hearted Me

## on COLUMBIA RECORDS

# KRLA ARCHIVES

### Birds of a Feather

## A Session With The Byrds

**THE BYRDS**
by
Michelle Straubing and
Susan Wylie

Q.—Who's the leader of the group?
JIM—I'm the leader, but David is mostly the spokesman.
Q.—Do you have any superstitions?
JIM—I believe if you touch a frog you'll get warts — but I trust everything will work out all right.
DAVID—I think if you kiss a frog you'll turn it into a prince and that everyone should kiss frogs.
Q.—You really want a prince?

### Barefoot Briton

That immigration bottleneck that has kept many of the top acts from England away from the United States, is beginning to free up a bit, and one of the first pleasant results will be Sandie Shaw's arrival in New York for personal appearances, including at least two TV shows.

Sandie will appear as usual without any shoes on. The Reprise Records star prefers to sing barefoot.

Her visa is good beginning in June, just as her newest hit, "Long Live Love" attracts national attention. Upcoming for Sandie: A Newsweek interview, a round of parties in New York, and for sure all our good wishes for a successful trip.

DAVID—Not much, really.
MIKE—What if you kiss a prince?
DAVID—You'll get into a lot of trouble that way — unless you're a princess.
Q.—Where did you begin your career professionally?
CHRIS—Del Mar Lanes Bowling Alley.
JIM—I started mine with the Limeliters in the 1960's. And then I worked with the Chad Mitchell Trio for two years, and toured all over except Europe and Australia. I toured all over South America also. Then I wrote with Bobby Darin for about a year and a half. I toured all over with him also. And then I got into The Byrds, and I'm glad.
CHRIS—I used to play Blue Grass-and I was a "Sparkie" for a while.
DAVID—He's probably one of the best mandolin players. One of the four or five better ones which he doesn't admit much —but he is. That's not our opinion, but the opinion of good Blue Grass people. He used to have his own group called The Hillman.
GENE—He can even play jazz on the mandolin.
GENE—I used to play in little coffee houses and stuff. Then I joined the Christy Minstrels and played with them for about a year. Then I joined The Byrds, and I'm glad — or helped start The Byrds really.
DAVID—I was playing the twelve string and singing in groups, mostly folk music, for the last five years now. I played all over the U.S., all the cities and their coffee houses and small clubs. Then I came here an started singing harmony with these guys.
MIKE—Like they told you, I was playing harmonica and conga drums and stuff for different people.
Q.—When did you begin professionally as The Byrds?
DAVID—About six months ago in a recording studio.
Q.—Are you interested in other fields of entertainment?

DAVE—Acting particularly.
GENE—Sky diving too, man.
JIM—I make good brownies.
Q.—Who wrote the song "Tambourine Man?"?
GENE—Our friend Bob Dylan wrote it.
Q.—Who arranges your music?
DAVE—It's a collective effort.
Q.—Are you planning on cutting any new records?
JIM—We're just finishing off an album now for Columbia. We're very happy about it because it's a lot of fun.
Q.—How do you feel before you go on stage?
GENE—We all get very sick.
DAVE—Impatient, shaky, green,
—MORE ON PAGE 10

### Here's A Chance To Win Stones' "Shindig" Script

Here's a treat for some lucky fan of the Rolling Stones.

A chance to win Mick Jagger's own copy of a Shindig script, autographed by the Rolling Stones and other stars who appeared on the May 26 show. Mick gave his script as a souvenir to the KRLA BEAT's Rod Barken.

Simply print your name and address on a postcard and mail to: STONES SCRIPT, Suite 504, 6290 Sunset Blvd., Hollywood, Calif. 90028.

Enter as many times as you like. The winning card will be drawn on the Bob Eubanks Show on KRLA on Tuesday, June 1.

### BEATLES 'IN'

The Beatles have finally arrived. John, Paul, George and Ringo — the most widely-publicized entertainers of this or any other century — are to appear biographically in the 1966-67 edition of "Who's Who in the U.S." This is the publication long renowned as the final authority on whether you've "made it."

What's taken them so long to recognize this? We've known it all along.

## ON THE BEAT

BY LOUISE CRISCIONE

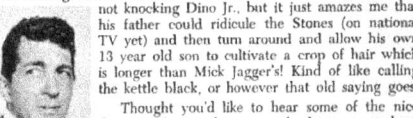

Wonder how **Dean Martin** ever had the colossal nerve to criticize the **Rolling Stones** when Dino Jr. is his own son. Understand I'm not knocking Dino Jr., but it just amazes me that his father could ridicule the Stones (on national TV yet) and then turn around and allow his own 13 year old son to cultivate a crop of hair which is longer than Mick Jagger's! Kind of like calling the kettle black, or however that old saying goes.

Thought you'd like to hear some of the nice things performers have recently done or are about to do. Some local Manchester groups have adopted the Rev. **Brian Brown** as their "pop padre." The groups have raised money for the Reverend to make a trip to Russia to take a look at the Soviet youth.

The **Beatles** will be one of the artists on a charity album, "All Star Festival" which will benefit the U.N. Fund of Refugees. The boys will receive no royalties and will foot the bill for the music themselves.

The **Rolling Stones, Animals, Kinks, Cilla Black, Sandie Shaw, Georgie Fame,** and **Tom Jones** have all ben invited to make an appearance in a movie which will go into production in July. Proceeds will go to the U.N. Children's Fund.

And that isn't all — there is a new group on the English scene called the **Envoys.** There are seven Envoys (two girls and five boys) and they have cut a record called "Door" which was inspired by a verse in the Bible. What with the Salvation Army gone beat and a beat group gone religious — that guy who said this is a mixed up world sure knew what he was talking about!

Here's a real switch for you. **Casual Records** of New York City is advertising in the British music papers for "ten unknown gear groups" to tour America. I'd be most interested in knowing how Casual plans to geth thes "ten unknown gear groups" into the United States when known groups can't even get in! And I'm not the only one who'd be interested in the answer — all those known groups would like to know too.

**Tom Jones** is scheduled for a tour with the Dick Clark Caravan of Stars and also a June 13 appearance on the Ed Sullivan Show. Don't pick Tom's new one, "Once Upon A Time", to go as far or as long as "It's Not Unusual'.

PUZZLE OF THE WEEK: How come **Alan Price** is leaving the Animals? Some reports say he simply refused to fly to Scandanavia with theg roup. Others point an accusing finger at Joan Baez. Seems Alan met Joan in England, they discussed music, and the next thing the Animals knew Alan was no longer with them! Whatever the reason, Alan Price is definitely leaving the group and will be replaced by a former schoolmate of Eric Burdons, twenty-four year old David Rowberry. ON THE BEAT says good luck to everyone involved.

**Bill J. Kramer's** new one with the weird title, "Trains, Boats, and Planes", just might get him for Billy, and people were beginning to wonder back on the charts again. It's been a long dry spell if he were still around! After hearing his new one you can be sure of one thing — he is still very much around.

With so many groups infiltrating today's pop scene, unused names are rally becoming scarce. This week's batch of new songs brought us such unusual names as Dan and the Clean Cuts, the Knights and Arthur, Patty Lace and the Peeticoats, the Riot Squad, the Goldbugs, and Grady Martin and the Slewfoot Five! (that one borrowed from way back when) Whatever happened to those nice simple names like the "Beatles" or the "Rolling Stones?"

WATCH OUT FOR: **Herman**—he's about to do it again. His new one, "Wonderful World", was the highest debuting record on the "Cash Box" Top 100. On the same survey, Herman held down the number one and number five positions as well! Looks like nothing can stop Herman and his Hermits now!

ALSO WATCH OUT FOR: **Brian Epstein** to include several of his other performers in the Beatles package which will tour the U.S. this summer. Don't hold your breath for **Gerry and the Pacemakers,** but some of Epstein's lesser-known entertainers, such as Sounds, Inc., might very well make the trek.

In just two appearances (Shea Stadium and the Hollywood Bowl) the Beatles are expected to net $190,000. After hearing that, I have definitely decided to get a Beatle hair cut, a pair of boots, and an $8 guitar; thn I intend to ask the Beatles if they can use a girl in their act!

### 23 SKIDOO
Dancing to Live Name Bands
2116 Westwood Blvd., West Los Angeles
**Girls 18, Guys 21**
Closed Mondays and Thursdays

## More About
### BYRD TALK
(Continued From Page 9)

—sometimes my leg falls off.

Q.—Is there anything that particularly annoys you while you're performing?
GENE—Bombs.
Q.—What advice would you give to newcomers who are interested in starting their own group?
DAVE—Don't quit your day job.
JIM—And persevere.
GENE—Stick with it. A little faith and perseverance.
Q.—Do you have any favorite performers?
DAVE—They sort of vary a lot. My favorite is an Indian musician named Ravi Schankar, but I also like John Coltrane and Miles Davis a lot. But I like the Beatles, the Rolling Stones, and the Manfred Mann too.
GENE—I like holes in the road.
CHRIS—John Lee Hooker and Buck Owens.
MIKE—I like John Coltrane, the Rolling Stones, and the Beatles.
JIM—We all like Bob Dylan. I like Bob Gibson.
MIKE—Joan Baez and Mary Ann Faithful.
Q.—Is there any style of clothing you prefer while on stage?
JIM—Anything we want.
DAVE—Dress creatively, you know.
GENE—Freedom. Freedom from dogma.
Q.—What is the quality in women you find most attractive?
GENE—Love.
DAVE—Love, yeah.
JIM—And long hair.
GENE—And pretty eyes.
DAVE—And intelligence.
Q.—Where did you all go to school?
GENE—A thousand different places.
JIM—I went to thirteen grammar schools for an opener.
DAVE—I was expelled from four

—MORE ON PAGE 11

## More About
### BEATLES' MOVIE
(Continued From Page 5)

tions are so explosive that to give out even an inkling of their content might spoil the impact when the film is shown.

**Broke Up**

On more than one occasion during the making of "Help!" notoriously blase film technicians had to leave the set because their vainly suppressed laughter during the shooting was coming through on the sound track.

"Help!" is essentially a holiday picture," says Producer Shenson. "It was made in two totally contrasting holiday resorts. We travelled from calypso to yodel with a lot of yeah-yeah thrown in besides. It will be released in August both in England and the States— holiday time for most people — and we hope the movie itself will be something of a holiday for everyone who sees it."

Dick Lester describes "Help!" as an adventure comedy. "The boys will play themselves again but in a completely fictitional situation, unlike 'A Hard Day's Night' which could be described best as cinema journalism."

Fimed in Eastman's Colour, Walter Shenson's and Dick Lester's second movie starring the Beatles will once again be released throughout the world by United Artists.

### Pen Pals Write, "Hi, Hullabalooer"

**KRLA'S DAVE HULL** received an autographed photo this week from four friends in England. Perhaps you'll recognize some of them. It's one of their favorite pictures and was taken as Dave and Derek Taylor interviewed the boys during filming of "Help." The photo may look familiar, since it was published earlier — without the autographs — as a KRLA BEAT world-wide exclusive.

## SHINDIG STAGES REAL CLASSIC

BY LOUISE CRISCIONE

There are not many people left who have never seen "Shindig". There are probably not many Rolling Stones fans who missed the May 26 "Shindig". But there are many who did not get to see the show in person. KRLA BEAT reporter, Rod Barken, and myself did manage to get our grubby little hands on a pair of tickets (thanks to Mr. Booker McClay), and we thought maybe you would like to know what went on behind the cameras that night.

The scene outside the ABC-TV studio was perhaps the biggest indication that something "different" was happening on the inside. The long line which habitually forms on Thursday nights (taping night for "Shindig") was there as usual. But in addition to that line was a line of ABC pages and a double force of studio police.

**Audience Excited**

Inside the studio, excited voices were raised in equally exciting chatter: "Mick's the best. I like Charlie. Everybody knows Brian's got the real talent." Jack Good came out front and welcomed the studio audience to that evening's "Shindig". Mike Dorsey, the Stones' road manager, popped his head out of the curtain just long enough to nod to Jack that the Stones were ready.

In anticipation of the Stones' appearance, screams greeted every piece of long hair which happened to wander onto the stage! Bobby Sherman opened the show, and soon thereafter the Rolling Stones made their way from the dressing rooms to the wings. They were immediately spotted, and the screaming reached the deafening level. The Stones then moved into position; Mick swung into "Down The Road Apiece". They were in great shape, as usual, and their entire number was accompanied by screams, yells, and frantic waving.

The Stones then moved off stage, and Jimmy O'Neill came on to welcome the television audience and to announce the evening's line-up. Leading off was Jimmie Rodgers (handsome in an olive green suit), and then Jackie De Shannon (stunning in a white suit). The scenery crew did themselves proud for Adam Wade's "Garden In The Rain". They provided trees, a small waterfall actually spouting water, and tall white Grecian pillars. It was beautiful.

That bulwark of American television, the commercial, came next. During this short interval, the scenery was entirely changed. The spouting waterfall, the Grecian pillars, and all the trees, save one branch, were hustled out of the stage area.

That one branch plus a replica of a haunted house were used in

—MORE ON PAGE 11

**tower**

'IT'S ONLY MAKE BELIEVE'
JERRY NAYLOR

139

# KRLA ARCHIVES

## More About
## SHINDIG-from the audience

the next number, which I considered to be the real highlight of the show. It was the opening of "Little Red Rooster" and it was fabulous! It looked for the world like an old haunted house on a stormy night, and through the open doors one could see the lone dark figure of Mick Jagger. The camera then zoomed in for a series of close-ups of Mick which were absolutely fantastic! The other Stones (except Charlie, who was continually pounding out the beat of "Rooster") stood outside the camera range and alternated between watching Mick and watching the audience, who was by this time in the clutches of pure joy. Mick himself was making faces into the camera, and Jack Good was watching the faces Mick was making! During one close-up of Mick toward the end of the song, the other Stones moved into the camera range and the number ended with all five of them in the picture. It was really the wildest number I've ever seen on "Shindig", and whoever thought it up should be rewarded with a ton of jelly beans!

Jimmie Rodgers did "Woman From Liberia" and then it was time for the finale. Jimmy O'Neill and Jack Good went through their regular routine announcing the next week's guests.

### Stones Perform

The finale belonged to the Rolling Stones. They rocked a song called "Satisfaction" as only they can do. Mick again did his dance and picked up the microphone. The cameraman captured a beautiful shot of Mick's eyes, and Brian worked his harmonica for all he was worth. The rest of the cast joined the Rolling Stones on stage, the credits came up, the song ended, and the curtain came down. The show was over.

## HOW TO START A FAN CLUB

(Editor's Note: In the last issue of the Beat we printed the first of a two part feature on how to start a fan club. If you missed last week's Beat, you can order a copy for only 10¢.)

Starting a fan club is only half the battle. Making it really matter is the other. And the most difficult.

There have never been as many fan clubs in existence as there are today. This means one thing to a new club: competition plus! Your organization will have to work at getting members and recognition, and the best way to do this is to make your club different.

Interesting club projects will make that difference.

### To Help Star

The main purpose of a fan club is to support a favorite star. To help him reach the top or to help him stay ther.

For this reason, write-in campaigns are a part of almost every fan club's duties. By having members dash off a note to a publication, TV show, any one who can aid your cause, you assure the influential people that there is a great deal of interest in your favorite.

This particular project can be done in a lot of different ways.

One of the best is to circulate a petition among the members of your club. When it's all signed, seal and deliver it. A request bearing many names sometimes has much more impact than a single opinion.

Then start all over again with another petition, aimed at another company.

Through the use of your bulletins (mailed quarterly in most clubs) you can generate interest by sponsoring membership contests. Try an art festival where everyone sketches the star, put the drawings on display at your club headquarters and give prizes for the best.

Another idea would be to have some type of contest where members would compete for "Member Of The Month" honors. The prize would be a paragraph in the next bulletin, devoted to information about the honored member.

### Contests

Contests with prizes such as the star's autograph, one of his sweaters, or a personal letter from him are extremely valuable. They're also next to impossible to sponsor unless you have the direct contact with the star or with someone in his organization.

If you don't have contact, you can buy items such as records (or any other products identified with your star) to give away. Before you buy records, try writing to the record company, telling them of your contest and your club. Some companies will be willing to sell you the records at a discount.

In order to buy prizes, you'll need to give you club fund a bit of a boost. If your club is national, it won't be easy to sponsor a nation-wide fund raising campaign. You'll have better results if you go into these projects on a local basis. (Don't forget the contribution "angle" either. By asking each member to donate a nickle, you often end up with a much fatter piggy bank.)

### Publicity

If your projects are interesting enough, they will help provide publicity for your star. And this, after all, is one of the main reasons you formed the club.

The list of possible projects, the elements that really make a club and a star important, is endless. We've only been able to list a few, and these few have probably started your mind working a mile a minute.

If you come up with bigger and better ideas for your own club, please let the Beat know about them. If there is enough interest in this subject, perhaps we can make the fine art of fan clubbing a regular feature in the Beat. It's up to you!

## Needs Love

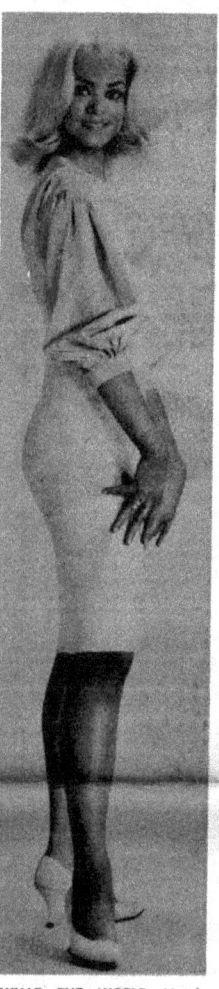

"WHAT THE WORLD Needs Now Is Love," sings Jackie DeShannon. Jackie shouldn't have any trouble finding her share of it.

## "BEATLES VI"
### (Continued From Page 1)

been heard by anyone in the world — "Tell Me What You See" by John Lennon and Paul McCartney and George Harrison's "You Like Me Too Much."

Some of the other great numbers were contained on the "Beatles for Sale" album which had been released in Great Britain but never in this country. These are "Kansas City," "Eight Days a Week," "I Don't Want to Spoil the Party," "Words of Love," "What You're Doing," "Every Little Thing" and "Yes It Is."

But two of the other songs — while heard previously in another version in some European countries after they were recorded from a live Beatles concert in Hamburg, Germany — have never been heard anywhere in their new form. The Beatles recordd "Dizzy Miss Lizzy" and "Bad Boy" especially for this album. Neither song had ever been released anywhere in the U.S. in any form.

To secure a world-wide exclusive on broadcast of an exciting new Beatles album was a proud achievement for KRLA — for which we are deeply grateful — and it was equally exciting for KRLA listeners as they heard "BEATLES VI" before anyone else in the world!

## More About
## TALKING BYRDS

high schools one right after the other.
JIM—Don't say that!
DAVE—Oops!
JIM—I wasn't expelled from anything. I just moved around a lot because my parents liked to travel.
Q.—What about Chris?
CHRIS—I went to high school.
DAVID—I graduated from high school and went right from there to one year of college and studied semantics.
JIM—I went to prep school preparing for college but I never went because I got a job with the Limeliters instead.
MIKE—Yeah, well I went to a number of high schools.
Q.—Do you like travelling?
DAVID—Very much, especially by jet.
JIM—Yeah, we want our own jet.
MIKE—I like freight trains, man.
DAVE—He's used to them.
JIM—We want our own freight train too.
DAVE—For Michael, he gets a train.
GENE—Monorail.
Q.—Where do you usually go on a date?
GENE—On a date? You mean a recording date?
Q.—No, a girl date.
DAVID—It's really kind of a hard thing you see, because most people when they take a girl out on a date, they take her out for the evening. We work all evening. I go to Gibralter a lot.
DAVE—We usually go out to eat. Sometimes if we get a night off we go to a movie or something, you know.
GENE—Or sky diving.
DAVE—Mostly we just invite them to come to the club where we're working.
JIM—We all like horror pictures.
DAVE—I like science fiction.
Q.—Do you like the dances they do now?
DAVE—Very much. I think it's an expression of individual freedom as well as being groovy to watch.
Q.—Has a string ever broken on your guitars while you were performing?
DAVE—Numerously.
JIM—Not really, though. I don't have any record of a string breaking during a performance.
DAVE—McGuinn, that's a lie.
JIM—Well Rolls Royce doesn't have any record of a car breaking down, so I don't have any record of a string breaking.
Q.—Well, what did you do when it did?
DAVE—Usually it's me t h a t breaks them and I just drop out and change it. I can change a string in about a minute and a half.
Q.—Have you ever had any really unforgettable experiences?
DAVE—The most unforgettable experience is having the people give back to you what you've given them with the music.
GENE—Eggs and apples...
Q.—How do you feel after a performance?
Q.—Have you ever been mobbed by your fans?
DAVE—We m a n a g e to avoid that.
GENE—I was in South America once, but that was with another group.
Q.—What are your plans for the future?
DAVE—To try and make The Byrds the biggest success we possibly can.
Q.—What do you think of the teenagers today?
JIM—They're groovy.
DAVE—We like them.
JIM—They're a lot more mature than anybody's ever been before in the whole history of mankind.
GENE—We hope they take over.
JIM—We love them. And besides in about 25 years they're going to be in power you know.
DAVE—And besides all t h a t they're about twice as hip as everybody thinks they are.
Q.—Now, being very objective, do you think that teenagers in America and California drink and smoke too much, etc.?

## DISC-ITIS?

---

**CASTLE ON THE STRIP**
– STRATFORD ON SUNSET –

**AGES 18-25**

**8248 SUNSET BLVD., HOLLYWOOD**
(JUST OPPOSITE CIRO'S)
**THURSDAYS – GUEST STAR NIGHT**

# KRLA ARCHIVES

## KRLA TUNEDEX

| Last Week | This Week | | |
|---|---|---|---|
| 1. | 3. | BACK IN MY ARMS AGAIN | The Supremes |
| 2. | 1. | WOOLY BULLY | Sam The Sham & Pharaohs |
| 3. | 14. | I CAN'T HELP MYSELF | The Four Tops |
| 4. | 2. | HELP ME, RHONDA | The Beach Boys |
| 5. | 5. | MR. TAMBOURINE MAN | The Byrds |
| 6. | 11. | WHAT THE WORLD NEEDS NOW IS LOVE | Jackie DeShannon |
| 7. | 9. | SHAKIN' ALL OVER | Guess Who? |
| 8. | 4. | YOU TURN ME ON | Ian Whitcomb & Bluesville |
| 9. | 6. | JUST YOU | Sonny & Cher |
| 10. | 12. | GOOD LOVIN' | The Olympics |
| 11. | 13. | HERE COMES THE NIGHT | Them |
| 12. | 7. | OOO BABY BABY | The Miracles |
| 13. | 27. | CRYING IN THE CHAPEL | Elvis Presley |
| 10. | 10. | TICKET TO RIDE | The Beatles |
| 15. | 8. | GLORIA/BABY PLEASE DON'T GO | Them |
| 16. | 19. | CATCH THE WIND | Donovan |
| 17. | 23. | FOR YOUR LOVE | The Yardbirds |
| 18. | 18. | SHE'S ABOUT A MOVER | Sir Douglas Quintet |
| 19. | 16. | MRS. BROWN/I GOTTA DREAM ON | Herman's Hermits |
| 20. | 20. | BABY THE RAIN MUST FALL | Glenn Yarbrough |
| 21. | 15. | THE LAST TIME/PLAY WITH FIRE | The Rolling Stones |
| 22. | 17. | JUST ONCE IN MY LIFE | The Righteous Brothers |
| 23. | 30. | GOODBYE, SO LONG | Ike and Tina Turner |
| 24. | 21. | JUST A LITTLE | The Beau Brummels |
| 25. | 22. | CONCRETE AND CLAY | Unit Four Plus Two |
| 26. | 32. | BRING IT ON HOME TO ME | The Animals |
| 27. | 29. | TRUE LOVE WAYS | Peter and Gordon |
| 28. | 34. | YOU REALLY KNOW HOW TO HURT A GUY | Jan & Dean |
| 29. | 31. | ENGINE ENGINE NO. 9 | Roger Miller |
| 30. | 44. | WONDERFUL WORLD | Herman's Hermits |

### CLIMBERS

| | | | |
|---|---|---|---|
| 1. | 35. | WHITTIER BOULEVARD | The Midnighters |
| 2. | 33. | PEANUTS | The Sunglows |
| 3. | 42. | LIPSTICK TRACES | O'Jays |
| 4. | 43. | VOODOO WOMAN | Bobby Goldsboro |
| 5. | 46. | LAURIE | Dickie Lee |
| 6. | 47. | L-O-N-E-L-Y | Bobby Vinton |
| 7. | 48. | SAD GIRL | The Gallahads |
| 8. | 49. | LIP SINC | Len Barry |
| 9. | 50. | THIS LITTLE BIRD | Marianne Faithful |
| 10. | 45. | ONCE UPON A TIME | Tom Jones |

### Picks To Hit

★ BEFORE AND AFTER .................. Chad and Jeremy
★ FROM THE BOTTOM OF MY HEART ........ The Moody Blues
★ TRAINS AND BOATS AND PLANES ........ Billy J. Kramer
★ I DO ................................ The Marvelows
★ GIVE US YOUR BLESSINGS ............. The Shangri-Las

**KRLA BEAT**
6290 Sunset, No. 504
Hollywood, Cal. 90028

U.S. Postage
BULK RATE
PAID
Permit No.
25497
Los Angeles
California

If you were a KRLA BEAT subscriber your name and address would be printed here and you would receive your copy at home, saving 40%.

### Kinks In California

### Raise Money For Your Club

Want to raise extra money for your club treasury? You could easily make several hundred dollars.

Write to: Fan Club Funds, KRLA, Sunset-Vine Tower, Suite 504, Hollywood, California — 90028.

### More About
### For Girls Only

in the morning and wash them off at night. I haven't seen this on the market yet, but when I do, I'll let you know. When I see it, I'll also believe it.

The other kooky idea is in the sweatshirt line. I heard some large company has just made up thousands of "Horace Wink Is A Fink" shirts. Like I said, what will they think of next? On second thought, maybe I'd better not ask.

I just discovered something about myself recently. I have telephoneitis. Once I get on the phone, it takes a charge of dynamite to get me off. It dawned on me when I realized that several of my fellow conversationalists were subtly doing their best to ring off without hanging up in my ear.

If there's a chance you may share this problem, here are the tell tale signs to watch for. If the voice on the other end of the wire says "Listen, I'll call you tomorrow," or "I have about a million things to do," stop and think how many times they may have said it while you were chattering away.

### Kinks Doing Shows, Tours, In L.A. Area

A trip around the world, and getting paid besides! That's one of the fringe benefits of this thing called show business, and brings to our shores the famous English group, the Kinks.

Ray and Dave Davies, along with Pete Quaife and Mick Avory, arrived June 3 for a personal appearance tour, including a show at the Hollywood Bowl with the Beach Boys.

The quartet, with three straight hits, plans and eight-week tour.

Scheduled on the same Bowl show will be the Righteous Brothers, and Dino, Desi, and Billy.

The Kinks told the BEAT they are very excited, and that even though they have been to Australia and France, they are very much looking forward to this first American appearance. They will be here as their newest Reprise recording, SET ME FREE, is released.

**THE SPATS**
"ATTRACTION FOR"
SHOWS-DANCES
FAN CLUB:
P.O. Box 12
Stanton, Calif.
Tel. (714) 539-5880

### THE BYRDS
Official National
FAN CLUB
Suite 504
6290 Sunset Blvd.
Hollywood

Send $1.00 plus two 5-cent stamps and receive photos, fact sheets, biographies. Fun contests each month.

**Free Concerts Planned For Members Only**

Be a chapter president. Enlist ten (10) new members now!

### BRITISH TOP TEN
1. Ticket To Ride — The Beatles
2. Where Are You Now — Jackie Trent
3. King Of The Road — Roger Miller
4. A World Of Our Own — The Seekers
5. True Love Ways — Peter & Gordon
6. Subterranean Homesick Blues — Bob Dylan
7. Bring It On Home To Me — The Animals
8. Wonderful World — Herman's Hermits
9. This Little Bird — Marianne Faithful
10. Pop Go The Workers — The Barron Knights

# KRLA BEAT

| BYRDS Follow Beatles Path To Fame —SEE PAGE 4— | | STONES Say They're Falling In Love —SEE PAGE 12— |

Volume 1, No. 15 — Los Angeles, California — Ten Cents — June 16, 1965

# BATTLE OF THE BEAT!

**DEREK PRESIDES AT NEWS CONFERENCE**

## Derek Taylor Recalls Early Beatle Appeal

(Editor's note: Last week Derek Taylor began the story of his association with the Beatles. He told of attending a concert in which he first heard and saw the four lads from Liverpool—before they were known to the adult population—and of the tremendous excitement they generated within the audience. This is part two of a three-part series).

I have never been able to isolate their primary appeal, but as Sinatra once said of someone who criticized Judy Garland, "Anyone who doesn't see her talent must have been living under a rock."

We left the theatre with our heads bursting with excitement and enthusiasm. I had convinced the news editor of the London Daily Express that it was worth making a trip to the theatre, and I was expected to turn in about five inches of copy on the concert.

I had also persuaded the picture editor to send along a cameraman just in case there were any scenes.

**Nothing Like It**

Any scenes! He was an older man than I and he joined us outside the theatre, complaining bitterly about the noise. But he had to confess that in 30 years of journalism he had never known anything like this show.

I asked, "What have you got?"

He said, "I've got three lots of pictures. I've got Gerry toweling himself after his act. I've got the screaming fans. And I've got some good pictures of the Beatles in their shirttails, pointing at the camera."

"Marvelous," I said, and the three of us went immediately into a pub.

This is the English journalist's second home where practically all the stories are written — all the best ones, anyway.

In the pub we ordered beer and a packet of potato chips. And the cameraman complained about his ears. I said, "Never mind your ears. What about the Beatles?"

**Something Happening**

"They ought to get their hair cut," he said, "But they've certainly got something."

I couldn't begin to write because I was still too excited. "Do you realize what's happening?" I asked the cameraman. "This is like nothing we've ever seen."

He said, "It's just as well it doesn't happen every night. I would go out of my mind."

My show-business colleague on the London Daily Herald (one of our rivals) wandered in. He was a middle-aged man of somber countenance with a drooping ginger

—MORE ON PAGE 6

## BEATLES vs. STONES

Have the Rolling Stones replaced the Beatles in the hearts of West Coast teens? You'll hear a lot of strong arguments on both sides.

The Stones are red-hot right now with their recordings and drew capacity attendance during their recent concerts in California.

On the other hand, interest is already at a fever pitch for the Beatles concerts scheduled in August, and their new album is causing much excitement.

Recent telephone polls by the BEAT indicate a possible trend away from the Beatles and toward the Stones. But many believe that John, Paul, George and Ringo are in a class by themselves and that any other trend can only be temporary.

What do you think? Write a postcard to the KRLA BEAT or fill out the form below and let us know whether you favor the Beatles or the Rolling Stones.

We'll keep score for the next several weeks. Here's your chance to boost your favorites and prove once and for all which one is tops. Don't let them down.

KRLA BEAT
6290 Sunset Blvd., Suite 504
Hollywood, Calif. 90028
(Check One)
☐ The Beatles are unbeatable!
☐ I vote for the Rolling Stones!

### INSIDE THE BEAT

BYRDS, P. J. PROBY
HERMAN, 4 TOPS,
SAM THE SHAM,
THE MIRACLES,
BEATLE QUIZ
PUZZLE PIC

**RECENT POLLS SHOW THEM AHEAD**

### STONES NOW 'IN THE GROOVE'

## How It All Began

By ROD ALAN BARKEN

The Rolling Stones are fantastic! They are not only great entertainers, but absolutely the greatest guys in the world.

During the time that I was with The Stones, I asked thousands of questions, and received answers to almost all of them. When The Stones left, I had pages of information.

Here is some of it. More will appear in future issues. (The scene, room in The Ambassador Hotel. There are five Stones sprawled out on two beds, sipping cokes and smoking cigarettes.)

Hello, Rolling Stones!
Mick: Hello.
Keith: Yeah . . .
Bill: Hi, Rod.
Brian: Greetings.
Charlie: Hmmph!

Today, fellows, let's start by going back to the days when it all began. Okay?
Keith: 'S'pose so.

**What was the actual start of The Rolling Stones?**
Mick: The day I saw Keith with a Chuck Berry record in his hand. That was the real beginning, when we were still going to school.

**Did you form a group?**
Keith: No, not then. We just listened to records in those days. The group and all came later.
Mick: Then we met Brian Jones, and he became "Stoned" like the rest of us.
Brian: But we didn't have a name yet.

**When did the rest join forces with you?**
Mick: After we all decided that we liked the same thing in music. There was Ian playing piano and organ for us, and a friend named Dick Taylor, who used to play bass.

**How were those first days, when it was all just beginning?**
Charlie: Rough. Nobody understood us.

Mick: They were all caught up on Elvis and Cliff Richards then . . . in 1962 . . . and they gave us trouble about our long hair.
Brian: Bill was the only one with any money to spend in those days, and he used to help us out a bit.

**What about the "long hair?"**
Mick: It was long . . . you know,
—MORE ON PAGE 12

**DEREK TAYLOR AND BRIAN EPSTEIN**

**MICK JAGGER**

# KRLA ARCHIVES

## Puzzle Piece No. 2

### Guess Who??

**HERE IT IS!** Your chance to win tickets to the KRLA Beatle Concert at Hollywood Bowl. The strange object lurking above is the second portion of the BEAT's Puzzle Piece Contest. Combine it with the piece shown in last week's issue and see if you can guess who it is. There are ten pieces in all, and we'll continue running one each week until someone guesses the name of our mystery star. The first contestant to guess who it is will win two tickets to Hollywood Bowl. The next two readers to come up with the right answer will each win one ticket to see the Beatles perform. The fourth place winner will receive four record albums, and winners five through twelve will win a record album by a top favorite. Enter as many times as you like. Send your guesses to KRLA BEAT Puzzle Piece, 6290 Sunset Blvd., Suite 504, Hollywood.

## Everything All Set For Beatles Tour

HERE IT IS! The final list of dates and cities that the Beatles will appear this summer:

New York (Aug. 15), Toronto (Aug. 17), Atlanta (Aug. 18), Houston (Aug. 19), Chicago (Aug. 20), Minneapolis (Aug. 21, Portland (Aug. 22) L.A. (Aug. 29 & 30) and San Francisco (Aug. 31).

After completing their tour they will return to Los Angeles for a few days of rest and relaxation.

Our tipsters report that they will be staying at the home of a well-known Hollywood movie star while they vacation here.

### KRLA BEAT

The KRLA BEAT is published weekly by Prestige Publishing Company; editorial and advertising offices at 6290 Sunset Boulevard, Suite 504, Hollywood, California 90028.

Single copy price, 10 cents.

Subscription price: U.S. and possessions, and Canada, $3 per year or $5 for two years. Foreign rates upon request.

"I'VE HAD IT"
"YOU DON'T LOVE ME"
THE STARLETS
144

## HERE'S HOW TO TRAVEL TO ENGLAND FOR FREE (IF YOU HAVE THE NERVE)

If you had three wishes, one of them would probably be to go to England.

Can't say we blame you, old bean. Which is why we'll be devoting portions of the summer Beats to just that very subject. How to get to England on practically nothing, and how to stay there as long as possible without draining your college fund to the last drop.

Just to get ourselves in the mood for this forthcoming feature, we sat down and let our minds wander.

### Naval Plan

(1) Build your own boat and cast off for the open sea. Swipe ... er ... purchase your materials from a reliable company. We recommend the Titantic Construction Corp.

(2) Make friends with a representative of the B. F. Goodrich Company. Talk him into building you a one hundred foot sling shot. Anchor the shot at the corner of Hollywood and Vine (never do anything small) and taking the sling in one hand, walk backwards to the Roosevelt Hotel. Aim due east, let go and you may find yourself in England before you know it. You may also find yourself in the cell next to your poor friend B. F., but that is just one of the many chances one has to take in this life.

### Diplomatic Plan

(3) Bleach your hair and let it grow until it reaches your waist. Go to the British Consulate and tell them you are one of the Hull laballoos. If they believe you, they will send you back to England. If they do not believe you, they will string you up. In either case, you will have your chance to hang around the British, which is all you really wanted in the first place.

### Group Plan

(4) Make friends with an English group about to head for home. Stow away among their equipment by setting up housekeeping in their electric piano. Pray real hard that they are not asked to perform during the trip, unless you are shockproof, that is. Then watt's the difference?

### Scientific Plan

(5) Go to the nearest satellite launching pad and convince the scientists in charge that you are an astronaut (talk about the last time you visited the moon and that kind of stuff). When you have been sealed into a space craft and sent into the heavens, keep your eye open for familiar landmarks. Bail out when you see Big Ben, but do it quick. This is no time to be monkeying around.

Fortunately, we know that none of you will take our ridiculous little ideas seriously, and that you will wait until we come up with some rational ways to get to England.

Wait a minute. We just looked out our window and there is some poor wretch at the corner of Hollywood and Vine, walking backwards with a hundred foot sling shot.

## Here's A Chance To Win Stones' "Shindig" Script

Here's a treat for some lucky fan of the Rolling Stones.

A chance to win Mick Jagger's own copy of a Shindig script, autographed by the Rolling Stones and other stars who appeared on the May 26 show. Mick gave his script as a souvenir to the KRLA BEAT's Rod Barken.

Simply print your name and address on a postcard and mail to: STONES SCRIPT, Suite 504, 6290 Sunset Blvd., Hollywood, Calif. 90028.

Enter as many times as you like. The winning card will be drawn on the Bob Eubanks Show on KRLA on July 1.

## BRIAN ROBBED

The Rolling Stones' Brian Jones received a disappointment when he returned to his hotel room following the recent concert in Long Beach.

Brian discovered that his prized record collection — which he carries everywhere — had been "collected" by overzealous record collecting fans.

# KRLA ARCHIVES

## Selecting A Harem

EMPEROR HUDSON, making a rare public appearance without his robes and crown, appears to be selecting candidates for his royal harem. As he says, "It's tough being an emperor." However, "Beautiful Bob" appears to be bearing up well under the strain.

### THE BYRDS
### Official National
### FAN CLUB

Suite 504
6290 Sunset Blvd.
Hollywood

Send $1.00 plus two 5-cent stamps and receive photos, fact sheets, biographies. Fun contests each month.

**Free Concerts Planned For Members Only**

Be a chapter president. Enlist ten (10) new members now!

**The BYRDS Are Great**

## CASEY'S QUIZ

By CASEY KASEM

This week's mystery star is a highly individual singer with only one hobby — writing songs with an equally famous collaborator. But he does have two wishes. Now that he's become a star in one area of showbusiness, he'd also like to go into acting and novel-writing. Outwardly known for his disinterest in clothes, he inwardly has a secret passion for them. The two-in-one tendency overlaps into other areas, too. On stage he is literally a ball of fire. Off stage, he's almost disturbingly quiet.
(Answer on Page 12)

## WAREHOUSE IX

2214 Stoner Avenue

off Olympic in West Los Angeles

**Dancing to Live Name Bands**

Los Angeles' Unique Young Adult Nite Club

Girls 18 — Guys 21
Closed Tuesdays and Sundays

## Derek Taylor Reports
## REFLECTIONS OF ENGLISH WEEKEND IN CALIFORNIA

Well . . . many weeks ago I made an aggressive, unqualified and, at that time, unjustifiable predication about a certain group.

"I'll say no more about it this week. But next week . . . watch out for much boasting.

KRLA did it again with the Beatle album. I was driving home when I heard the unmistakable accents of George Harrison on the car radio. He was singing a song I had never heard before and I presumed it was one of those Dave Hull "Hamburg" scoops — you know . . . one of those early Beatle discs which crop up from time to time.

But no. It was a brand new George Harrison composition — the first since "Don't Bother Me" — and on a brand new album which, to be quite honest, I didn't know Capitol was releasing.

As soon as I arrived home I phoned Dick Biondi, who was beside himself with excitement — who can blame him? — and he said, in the words of Al Jolson, "You ain't heard nothin' yet."

And promptly played a beautiful new Lennon-McCartney creation. Plus "Dizzy Miss Lizzy" and "Bad Boy" — two early rockers featured regularly in the Beatles' Hamburg stage performances.

So. A bonus Beatle album slipped dramatically onto the market two months before the breathlessly-awaited soundtrack from "Help."

It's now quite clear that the Beatles are being influenced by folk music. It's equally obvious — and I personally am glad — that they retain a nostalgic longing for hard Rock 'n' Roll.

Dick Biondi was very generous, I thought, allowing Dave Hull to take over the microphone for the last forty minutes of his show. Dave's Beatle link is now so strong that there's no separating the Liverpool four from the Hullabalooer. He was just about to go to bed when the disc became available and he dragged his levis over his pajama trousers and raced to Pasadena.

It's enthusiasm and personal involvement like this which keep KRLA ahead. Believe me. This is true.

What a "home from home" KRLA was during their English weekend. So many songs from across the Atlantic.

### American Success?

It will be interesting to see whether any of the artists previously unknown in America made an impression sufficiently strong to gather a following over here.

I'm thinking particularly of Cliff Richard — still Britain's top soloist — and the Bachelors.

Do you like Marianne Faithfull's new one, "Little Bird"? I do, but I'm not sure why since it's not very well sung. There is, however, somewhere in the production that tiny little something which makes it a hit. It's No. 6 in England, by the way, at the time of going to press.

Marianne Faithful — so the Stones' Andrew Oldham says — is now an excellent stage performer.

Marianne

But she, like Sandie Shaw, was wisely kept away from live performances until her management was sure she could impress an audience with her "live" sound as much as she did on records.

It's one thing to go into the studio and make a hit record, having spent hours experimenting, fluffing your lines, restarting, double tracking, bringing in echo, dubbing, and calling on expert engineers, trained musicians and the limitless patience of the A & R man.

It's quite another thing to stand alone in the middle of the stage, with a small group behind you and a huge okay-show-us-what-you-can-do audience of gum-chewing, popcorn-picking, wide-awake teenagers.

### Trouble In Paris

Protected though she was from this, Marianne had some unfortunate early experiences. Chiefly in Paris — quiet the toughest city in the world, not excepting New York — where pennies were thrown on the stage. This is the Frenchmen's charming way of indicating dissatisfaction.

Shock. Tom Jones didn't make it with his follow-up "Once Upon a Time". Why on earth does a thing like this happen?

"It's Not Unusual" was so good and Tom himself so strong that it seems impossible he could have failed with his second chart entry. But he did. The moral: showbusiness obeys no rules and lashes back at you just when you don't expect it.

However, it seems as if his "What's New, Pussycat?" — taken from the upcoming Peter Sellers-Paula Prentiss-Woody Allen-Peter O'Toole movie — is pretty good. Jackie, my indispensable — and some people are — secretary advises me.

Now — on the American scene — here's P. J. Proby back in Hollywood with his eccentric aide, Bongo. Nice when a local boy makes good and comes home a star.

I'm for P. J. Proby. I was as soon as I saw his potential on Jack Good's "Around the Beatles" show. How any man endured so many public disputes and damaging publicity and yet survived, and even grew in stature, I'll never know.

The lesson here is: forget the knockers — just watch your bank balance; if it grows, then you're in business.

Proby

Along with Proby, Gerry and the Pacemakers were in town for "Shindig." Les Chadwick had to rush off back to Liverpool for a fairly important appointment. His wedding! But I met the rest of them and it was great to see them all again.

Gerry has now reached the point where he no longer need work for a living. But he carries on because he's still at the top, and anyway, he enjoys performing.

# KRLA ARCHIVES

### Following In Beatles' Footsteps?

## JUST LIKE BEATLEMANIA
# Byrds Drawing Big Crowds

The skyrocketing Byrds are giving every indication of becoming a home-grown American answer to the Beatles.

Reopening at Ciro's on Sunset Strip, where large crowds have been a rarity in recent years, the Tambourine Men have been drawing overflow audiences. Passers-by were shocked to see people standing in line— clambering to get in— even on week-nights.

As the lights dimmed on opening night and the curtains parted, the first strains of the opening chords to "Mr. Tambourine Man" came pounding through to the most receptive audience that could be found in all of Hollywood.

Celebrities from all corners of the show business world were included in the audience.

As they looked out across the crowded dance floor and the enthusiastic, capacity audiences, the Byrds must have remembered their first appearance there only a few weeks ago. At that time they began their engagement as unknowns playing to audiences which often numbered no more than a dozen people.

Now they have the fastest-rising record in the nation, a highly-acclaimed new album, and Mike Clarke, Chris Hillman, David Crosby, Gene Clark and Jim McGuinn are the sensations of the entertainment world.

KRLA's Dave Hull, attending one of their recent performances, looked about at the jam-packed crowd and declared, "It's fantastic. They're starting off here just like the Beatles did at the Cavern in Liverpool. They're grabbing hold of people's imaginations, and it looks like this is just the beginning."

Coming from the Hullabalooer, that's quite a statement. It will be interesting to see what the future holds for the Byrd-men.

### Joey Paige Tells Of Zany Antics On Stones' Tour

Joey Paige, popular singer and good friend of The Rolling Stones, recently paid a visit to THE KRLA BEAT office, and spent a memorable afternoon chatting about his recent SHINDIG tour, and his weekend stay with The Rolling Stones in New York City.

"They (The Stones) looked just great, says Joey, "and I was glad to get to see them before they returned to England."

I asked Joey how The Rolling Stones liked Los Angeles, and he replied, "Just great. They were very happy about the turnouts at their shows, and were thankful to all of the people who visited them at their hotel."

While in New York, Joey Paige, The Rolling Stones, and The Animals (who were in town to do an Ed Sullivan Show) were treated to a private party by an East Coast disc jockey. Wanting to treat everyone to something unusual, this un-named di had the boys picked up at their hotels in a 35-foot yacht.

As Joey tells it . . . "It was the most fantastic thing you can imagine. Here we were, riding up the street in a huge yacht, complete with a bar, rest room, telephone, and tv. People stared at us as though we were a bit crazy.

"Of course, a truck was towing us, but Mick Jagger still played a game of pirates, and caused us all to break up laughing."

Joey is back in California for a few months before returning to England to promote his records, which seem to do all right for themselves over there.

While here, he'll be doing television shows and personal appearances, enabling thousands of fans to see him in action.

And when this young man goes into action, watch out.

### High Stepper

It's all very well being a big star at the front of the stage with a hit record going for you and the cameras playing in close-up on your famous features.

But in the background on many of the better pop shows are musicians and girls doing a great job.

Behind them they have years of training and buckets full of talent.

Here is one of them . . . Dale Vann, 18, beautiful. A dancer on "Hollywood A Go Go." Height, 5'7"; size, 8-9-10; hair, auburn, and eyes brown. Dale has had her name linked with Ian Whitcomb and Declan Mulligan of the Beau Brummels. But there's no question of romance. She is a working girl.

Without her, and artists like her, you can wave goodbye to "Shindig," "Hullabaloo," and Who-Knows-What A Go Go.

## FAN CLUBS

**TOMMY QUICKLY**

**TOMMY QUICKLY FAN CLUB**
c/o Miss Jeanie Anderson,
National President
P.O. Box 966
Glendale, California 91205
(Dues $1.00; members receive autographed picture, biography, news on contest and newsletter)

**MANDI MARTIN FAN CLUB**
c/o Miss Della Ravitz
4124 Hillcrest Drive
Los Angeles 8, California
(Dues 50 cents; members receive autographed picture, fact sheet and newsletter)

**DEREK TAYLOR FAN CLUB**
c/o Miss Shelly Heber
6087½ Alcott Street
Los Angeles 35, California

**CHAD ALLEN & EXPRESSIONS**
c/o Jane Kimak
513 Newman Street
Winnipeg 10, Manitoba
Canada

**HERMAN'S HERMITS**
c/o Merri Phillips
524 S. San Jose
Covina, Calif., 91722
(Dues $1.00; members receive pictures, bios, English pen-pals and newsletters)

**HERMAN**

# BEATLE QUIZ

Here we go again! Five more questions for the KRLA Beatle Quiz.

Those of you who missed the first three weeks of the Beatle Quiz may still catch up by ordering the issues of June 9, June 2 and May 26. You'll find instructions for ordering back issues elsewhere in the BEAT.

The winner, of course, will get to interview the Beatles for the KRLA Beat when they arrive in August. The winner and a friend will also attend a Beatle Concert as guests of the KRLA Deejays.

Additional prizes will be provided for runners-up. In case of a tie there will be additional questions or a drawing to decide the final winner. The contest will cover a ten-week period, with at least five new questions asked each week. KRLA's Derek Taylor, a close friend of the Beatles and their former press officer, will judge the entries for accuracy.

Here we go with five new questions. Join in the fun. Good luck!

Beatle Quiz
KRLA BEAT
Suite 504
6290 Sunset Blvd.
Hollywood, Calif. 90028

**CONTEST EDITOR:**

Below are my answers to the fourth set of questions in the BEATLE QUIZ CONTEST.

My Name .................................................. Address ..................................
City .......................................................... State ................. Zip Code ............
I (☐am)  (☐am not) presently a subscriber to the KRLA BEAT.

### NEW QUESTIONS

16. The Beatles stayed in a house during their last visit to the Hollywood area. On what street was it located? .................................
17. What is the largest number of records the Beatles have ever had in the American top-ten at one time? .................................
18. On what television program did America get its first look at John, Paul, George and Ringo?
19. Paul McCartney's brother now has his own group. What is the group called and what is Paul's brother's stage name? .................................
20. What Hollywood-area club promised the Beatles privacy and then notified the press they would be appearing there? .................................

**MORE QUESTIONS IN NEXT WEEK'S BEAT**

# KRLA ARCHIVES

**Sam The Sham and Pharaohs**

## 'WOOLY BULLY' MEN FIND ACTION HERE

Sam The Sham & The Pharaohs, in Los Angeles to tape a series of appearances on Dick Clark's "Where The Action Is, certainly found the "action" when they visited a popular Hollywood clothier to buy some clothes.

As these five young men, currently clicking with the hit, "Wooly Bully," waded through piles of suits, slacks, and shirts, an anxious pack of fans huddled together outside, waiting for autographs.

Inside the store, this BEAT Reporter quizzed the members of Sam The Sham's group, and came up with some interesting material. Here's what I discovered:

### Musicians

They are all accomplished musicians, each having played in at least one other group during the past ten years.

They formed the present group in September, 1963, in order to keep all of these talents together under one roof.

Though long-haired and scrubby-looking, they are all very polite, and agreed to answer practically every question thrown at them.

They are all hoping for many more hit records, and sincerely want to build strong careers in the music world.

Though not born in Memphis, Tenn, they all consider Memphis "our home town."

This is their first visit to California, and they were all disappointed that the weather couldn't have been warmer.

### Excited

They are all very excited over their hit, "Wooly Bully," and are very appreciative of the terrific response that fans have given them in Southern California.

One of their favorite groups from "back home" is The Guilloteens, who are currently making personal appearances here.

After the outfits of clothes had been selected, Sam gathered his gallant men together and dashed to their waiting car. Behind were perhaps 20 girls, autograph books still clutched in their hands.

No sooner had Sam The Sham & The Pharaohs sped off, than a car pulled up, loaded itself with giggling girls, and raced away in pursuit.

Great life, isn't it?

... Rod Alan Barken

### Stones Pen Pals

Here are the names of English pen pals that want to write to persons here in the U.S. that are sincerely interested in The Rolling Stones.

Valerie Kemp, 6 Gilchrist Ave., Hern Bay, Kent.

Tony Verguson, 115 Devonshire Hill Lane, London, N.17.

Sue Abrahams, 25 Patterdale, Robert Street, Hampstead Road, London, N.W.,1.

---

### KRLA BEAT SUBSCRIPTION

As a special introductory offer — if you subscribe now you will save 40% of the regular price.

☐ 1 YEAR — 52 Issues — $3.00 (U.S. & Canada)   ☐ 2 YEARS — $5.00 (U.S. & Canada)

Enclosed is $............

Send to: ............................................................ Age: ...............

Address: ..........................................................................................

City: ............................................ State: ..................... Zip: ............

MAIL YOUR ORDER TO: **KRLA BEAT**
1401 South Oak Knoll Avenue
Pasadena, California 91106

Foreign Rate: $9.00 — 52 Issues

---

## EARN FAB MONEY, PRIZES AS A BEAT REPRESENTATIVE

**FIRST PRIZE!**
YOU AND A FRIEND WILL BE GUESTS OF KRLA AT A **BEATLE CONCERT!**
And a Beatle Press Conference!
You will also receive
A Beautiful WRIST WATCH!

**10 Second Prizes:**
BEAUTIFUL, ENGRAVED
**WRIST WATCHES!**
(Winners may choose between second and third prizes.)

**10 Third Prizes:**
AUTOGRAPHED
**BEATLE ALBUMS!**

### 6 STUDENTS IN EACH SCHOOL
*May Qualify to Accept Subscriptions*

## IT'S FUN AND PROFITABLE

The KRLA BEAT is the NATION'S TOP NEWSPAPER for young Americans, and it is NOW ACCEPTING SUBSCRIPTIONS FOR THE FIRST TIME. Now you can become a circulation representative in your school.

HERE'S ALL YOU HAVE TO DO: Send your name, address, telephone number and the school you attend to KRLA BEAT, 1401 S. OAK KNOLL, PASADENA, Calif. But do it fast — first come, first served. We will send you all the necessary information to become a successful KRLA BEAT representative. You will learn handsome profits on each subscription. Earnings are unlimited, because EVERY TEENAGER SHOULD BE A SUBSCRIBER!

AND THERE ARE SPECIAL PRIZES FOR THOSE WHO SELL THE MOST SUBSCRIPTIONS
BETWEEN NOW AND JUNE 23RD

---

I would like to be a KRLA BEAT REPRESENTATIVE in ........................................... ☐ Jr.   ☐ Sr. High

School in the city of: ............................................

Please send me additional information and forms for selling subscriptions.

Name............................................................................................ Age ...............

Address ........................................................... City ...............

Phone ........................................................... Zip Code ...............

# KRLA ARCHIVES

## ON THE BEAT

**By LOUISE CRISCIONE**

One of the oddities of the record business is the stagnant period where good new records are kind of scarce. This is usually followed by a boom period where literally EVERYONE comes out with great sounding new ones. We are currently in just such a period, and the records hitting the market are some of the very best offerings we've ever had!

The **Rolling Stones** have come up with one of their best to date in "Satisfaction". Watch out for this one to be big — much bigger than "The Last Time." If you buy the record, flip it over and listen to "I Am The Under Assistant West Coast Promo Man." It's a tribute to George Sherlock, who was the promotion man for London records the first time the Stones made a visit to our town. They're a little bit late with their tribute because Mr. Sherlock is now with Tower Records! Oh well, it's the thought that counts.

Of course, the **Beatles** have a brand new album, "Beatles VI". Two of the cuts ("Dizzy Miss Lizzy" and "Bad Boy") are examples of raw rock 'n' roll straight out of the swinging days of Little Richard et al. Two other cuts ("Every Thing" and "You Like Me Too Much") are slower, quieter, and definitely Beatles. Adds up to a very good album and probably another million seller for the boys.

Not to be left out, **Herman** has come up with yet another one. This time he is the eighth old man of the widow next door — "Henry VIII." I like this one. It's cute, it's catchy, and it's kinda reminiscent of "Mrs. Brown".

To this list of GREAT records add "Sunshine, Lollipops, and Rainbows" by Lesley Gore—"Who'll Be The Next In Line" by the Kinks — "I'll Feel A Whole Lot Better" by the Byrds — "It's Just A Little Bit Too Late" by Wayne Fontana — "Little Bird" by Marianne Faithfull — "Seventh Son" by Johnny Rivers — "Long Live Love" by Sandie Shaw — "Trains and Boats and Planes" by Billy J. Kramer — "Where Are You Now" by Jackie Trent — and a whole lot more!

Have you heard the Rockin' Berries cover version of "Poor Man's Son"? It's a big hit in England — way up there in the top ten. The Reflections had the original sometime back. It was a good sounding record and deserved to be a hit. But, it went nowhere. So, it will be interesting to see how the Rockin' Berries do with it.

**Rockin' Berries**

The Best Quote of the Week comes from Dave Davies of the **Kinks** concerning some fans: "And then there are the rude ones who come up to you and say, 'Sign your autograph here, three times with love.' They also tell you that they want a button from your jacket and proceed to twist it off. Their attitude is that they're your bread and butter, therefore you should do what they want." Sorry to say, but such "fans" do exist.

QUICK ONES: Watch for the **Beatles** title tune "Help" to be a real Little Richard type rocker . . . The **Animals** may add a trumpet section and girl singers to their sound . . . **Tom Jones'** new record, "Little Lonely One" is really an old sound recorded in 1963, and is Tom ever mad that they are releasing it now — feels it's not up to his present standards . . . **Gerry Marsden** got hit with the weight bar in Grand Rapids, Michigan when the curtain was brought down in one big hurry to keep the fans from reaching the stage — luckily he was not seriously injured . . . **Sandie Shaw** has finally done it; she has obtained a visa and will be able to appear on American television (unless they take it away from her before she gets here!) . . . **Wayne Fontana's** shirt-maker has come up with a really fabulous idea. He has put out a line of fan proof vests which are ungrippable and assure the wearer against scratches from over-enthusiastic fans!

Back issues of the KRLA BEAT are still available, for a limited time. If you've missed an issue of particular interest to you, send 10 cents for each copy wanted, along with a self-addressed stamped envelope to:

KRLA BEAT
Suite 504
6290 Sunset Blvd.
Hollywood, California 90028

**ISSUES AVAILABLE**

4/14 — INTERVIEW WITH JOHN LENNON
4/21 — INTERVIEW WITH PAUL McCARTNEY
4/28 — CHIMP EXCITES TEEN FAIR
5/5 — HERMANIA SPREADS
5/12 — HERE COME THE BEATLES
5/19 — VISIT WITH BEATLES
5/26 — FAB NEW BEATLE QUIZ
6/2 — L.A. ROCKS AS STONES ROLL
6/9 — BEATLES VI

## Impressive Sight on Beatles Tour

AT FAMED RED ROCK STADIUM IN DENVER

## MORE ABOUT: DEREK TAYLOR'S LIFE WITH THE BEATLES

**(Continued From Page 1)** mustache.

"What on earth's going on next door?" he said. I told him the Beatles were there.

He repeated the name and asked who they were.

I said, "Get in that cinema and see for yourself."

"You know we never cover pop shows," he said. "The office isn't interested."

"Well, listen,' I said, trying to convey some of my own excitement, "You will be covering them the next time they hit Manchester."

Finally he did wander off again to watch the fans outside the theatre. In the months that followed, he and I met many times on the Beatle trail because by the end of the year, the Beatles were the biggest sensation Britain had ever known. But on our later meetings we not only had one cameraman with us, we had two or three and about four reporters per newspaper to cover every single detail and aspect of Beatlemania.

### "Let It Run"

Well, anyway, that first night I phoned my office, told them about the show and — though calmer than I was — the night editor decided to give me more space. "If it's as good as you say," he said, "Let it run." This means, "write as much as you like and we'll assess it when we see it."

I was due to cover another act at a nightclub and I was already late, so I went straight on the phone to one of the Daily Express typists who takes down the reporter's story and dictated to him the following report:

"London Daily Express — May 31, 1963.

"Measuring it word by word, let me make a solemn declaration that because of the city of Liverpool, popular music, after years of turmoil and unspeakable rubbish, has become healthy and gay and good again.

"The Liverpool Sound came to Manchester last night and I thought it was magnificent . . .

"The spectacle of these fresh, cheeky, sharp, young entertainers in apposition to the shiny-eyed teenage idolaters is as good as a rejuvenating drug for the jaded adult.

### Limitless Energy

"Their stage manner has little polish but limitless energy, and they have in abundance the fundamental rough good humor of their native city.

"It was marvelous, meaningless, impertinent, exhilarating stuff."

No other newspaper carried the story.

My next step was to see the shy, remote, young man who was said to be the genius behind the Beatles. He then had an office in Liverpool, 38 miles from Manchester. And as a Liverpool exile, I was always glad to make the trip back there, whatever the excuse.

Bear in mind that a 38-mile journey in England is quite a distance. England is not yet as blase about mileage as America.

### Saw Epstein

So I made an appointment to see Brian Epstein. He was difficult, withdrawn, and not happy to be interviewed.

He kept standing up, straightening his tie, and then sitting down again. He refused for an hour or more to be photographed, but minute by minute the cameraman and I wore him down. And taking a comb from his pocket, he said, "Very well, then. But I do hate personal publicity."

In spite of his coolness, I quite liked the man and I detected in him a desire to be liked — although he went to great pains to conceal this. Below are extracts from the interview published in the London Daily Express on June 20, 1963:

"Flanked by the symbols and symptoms of his success sits Brian Epstein, 28, ex-public schoolboy, ex-drama student, ex-furniture store boss, who suddenly owns the top three places in the nation's disc charts.

### Guiding Hand

"Epstein's is the cool, clear brain behind the extraordinary flight to stardom of the Beatles, of Gerry and the Pacemakers, and of Billy J. Kramer and the Dakotas.

"These three vocal and instrumental groups have been signed up by Epstein since October, 1961. All like Epstein are from Liverpool.

"This week Gerry, with "I Like It," Kramer, with "Do You Want to know a Secret," and the Beatles, with "From Me to You," are 1, 2, 3 in the hit parade.

"Never before have three groups — as distinct from solo performers — topped the charts. And when did any one provincial city ever figure so indestructibly in any branch of entertainment?

### Liverpool Sound

"The success of the Liverpool Sound — that curiously tough nasal vital impact of beat and voice — has been a feature of the pop music scene for some months.

"Epstein is not surprised. Not by that, or by anything.

"He is a very calm customer, a bachelor, extremely well spoken, fastidious, neat. Were it not for his buckled shoes and the royal blue initials on his white shirt, he could be in shipping or cotton. Or the bank, with an eye on the managership.

"He dislikes publicity, has a deep sense of personal privacy.

### Has An Ear

"Also he has an ear for music. Though he can't read it — like each and every one of the young men in his group — and he cannot play any musical instrument."

### So It Went On

Well, in the high summer of 1963 and in the fall, the Beatles stepped from the world of pop music into the history books. Beatlemania erupted and the Liverpool foursome became the chief talking point. As Epstein himself remarks in his book, "A Cellarful of Noise," on the writing of which I was later to collaborate, "It became impossible to have a conversation with anyone on any subject without the name of the Beatles cropping up."

(Continued Next Week)

"ATTRACTION FOR"
SHOWS-DANCES
FAN CLUB.
P.O. Box 12
Stanton, Calif.
Tel. (714) 539-5880

# KRLA ARCHIVES

## The Beat Goes To The Movies
## YELLOW ROLLS ROYCE

### By JIM HAMBLIN

"The Yellow Rolls-Royce," produced by Metro-Golden Mayer in England, is a very unusual film with an impressive cast. But they're not all in the same movie, and we'd better explain.

Yellow Rolls is actually three stories, lightly tied together by an elegant yellow sedan which plays a part in the lives of the people concerned. We follow its career from showroom to final resting place in America.

**Rex Harrison**, fresh from his amazing "My Fair Lady," and **Jeanne Moreau**, the famous French actress, pair up for the first episode in the car's life. It is in the Rolls that Harrison finds his wife playing patty-cake with another man, played by **Edmund Purdom**.

### Welcome Back

Purdom has been living in Europe making some low-budget spear-carriers, and it was a delight to see this capable man back in a significant role again. He dates back to such excellent films as "The Egyptian," in which he starred.

Following the breakup of the Harrison-Moreau episode, the car is next seen in Italy. There American ganster **George C. Scott** buys it for girlfriend **Shirley MacLaine**. The gangster's bodyguard-associate is **Art Carney** and the trio is touring Italy together.

While the boss goes back to the States to rub out some competition, MacLaine falls in love with an Italian photographer, played by **Alain Delon**. (And girls, he looks every bit as good as you expect.) That tryst also occurs in the yellow Rolls-Royce.

### Final Episode

Finally the car ends up on the Yugoslav border as Nazi Germany attacks, and American millionairess **Ingrid Bergman** meets **Omar Sharif**.

The music score is outstandingly written by Riz Ortolani, who brings Miss Katyna Raneiri back to the American screen for well-deserved exposure. Miss Raneiri may be a newcomer to most of us, but she was the singer who introduced "More" in the film "Mondo Cane." (and husband Ortolani wrote it) She appeared recently at the Coconut Grove in Los Angeles, the hallmark of success in the night club circuit.

Primarily a half-sad comedy, "The Yellow Rolls-Royce" literally lets romance, you might say, take a back seat (!) You will find it an exciting film to watch. A "jolly good show," as the saying goes.

(Reviewed at the MGM Studio Theatre in Culver City.)

MacLAINE

CARNEY

DELON

**FREE BEATLE PIN-UPS**

(Regular 50¢ Each)

TO EVERY CUSTOMER WHO PRESENTS

THIS AD AT:

**HOLLYWOOD WAX MUSEUM**

HOLLYWOOD BLVD. AT HIGHLAND AVE.

## How Now, Brown Cow?

**EVEN THE COW LOOKS AMAZED** as KRLA's Charlie O'Donnell — a city boy from Philadelphia, wins the milking contest at the Great Western Fair and Dairy Show. Dave Hull and Dick Biondi, who had trouble finding the "handles" to Bossie's hand-operated milking machine, are trying to learn his secret. Amused runner-up (in sunglasses) is Larry Berrell from KTTV. After the fun, dairy maiden Eileen Hancock took our duly impressed cow back to the sparkling clean barn.

## For Girls Only

### By SHEILA DAVIS

I'm not going to do it this time. Start my column by warning boys to stay out, I mean. This week I'm going to welcome them with open arms and invite them right into our hen party.

(Guess what. I think every boy reading this just stopped. Kill them with kindness, I always say.)

Speaking of boys (I always say that, too), I'm going to devote most of this column to a subject that is bound to come up before the summer is over, and may have already appeared on the scene. That subject being how to write to a boy.

I had to learn the hard way about what and what not to when corresponding with a member of the opposite. Two years ago this summer I was dating (semi-steady) this really gorgeous boy. I was so crazy about him I practically went around blithering when I discovered he was going to spend the whole summer on his uncle's ranch in Colorado.

### Daily Letters

We promised we'd write every day, and I didn't even wait until he'd left town to get started. I wrote a little goodbye note and secretly stuffed it in his jacket pocket. That was only the beginning. Every night I'd sit down and scribble until I got writer's cramp.

About a month later I took enough time off from my new mission in life to realize that he hadn't answered one of my letters. And what's more, he never did! And what's even more, he stayed in Colorado for a whole year!

At first I thought I was going to die, but pretty soon I met this other really gorgeous boy and forgot the whole thing. Except I always wondered what on earth I'd done to chase him away.

Quite by accident, about two months ago, I ran into my old flame. It turned out that I was with a friend of his, and he was with a friend of mine, so we sat around and talked half the night. They sat around and talked, that is. I sat around and tried to get up enough nerve to ask him what was wrong with the letters I'd written. I was really curious, and not that embarrassed to ask since the boy I was with at the time was a true creep I was trying to get rid of anyway.

When I finally did get up the nerve, he practically went into hysterics. It all started, he told me, when I stuffed that note into his pocket (I forgot to mention that it was on perfumed stationery). He went through the whole trip smelling like a florist's convention, not knowing why, and by the time he reached Colorado, people were actually starting to point. And when he got to the ranch, the cowboys (or whatever you call them) really gave him the rough time of the century. He'd found the note by then, but his jacket was to remain "delicately scented" for the next month!

This, added to the other seven million perfumed letters I sent him that summer, had the bunk house in the uproar of all time.

### Good Lesson

Funny, huh? It is now, but it wasn't very then. And I've really learned my lesson. From now on I'm never going to write to any boy that often (there really isn't that much to say anyway, except smoochy stuff boys seem to hate seeing on paper), and I'm going to save my perfumed stationery for thank you notes to my Aunt Ethel.

Guess what else I've learned recently! I've learned how to wear gloves! That might not sound like much of an accomplishment unless you happen to be one of those people who goes stark raving nuts when you have to wear anything on your hands for more than 13 seconds.

Well, I rose above it all by taking "Glove Lessons" from a friends. She started me off five minutes at a time, and now I can wear gloves for a whole evening. Without a tantrum or anything!

### Piled High

Isn't it great that those horrible high hairstyles are finally out of style? I've always disliked them, but after last week, I'm really adamant on the subject. I sat behind one of the few remaining die-hards at an Elvis movie (I don't care if he isn't English, I luv him anyway), and you've never lived until you've seen El through a mile-high film of backcoming.

I think I showed a lot of self control in the situation, though. Much as I wanted to, I didn't lean over the girl's shoulder and ask her if she'd mind taking off her head. I contented myself with an occasional moan.

I'm out of room again, but before I go, I'd like to say thanks for all the great letters my column has been receiving. "For Girls Only" is getting so much mail, the Beat has decided to separate it into two sections. One where we can rave about boys and things and another where I can answer your questions and print the beauty hints you've been sending me (and can I use them).

You'll find the other half somewhere in this issue of the Beat. Please keep those letters coming, and I'll see you next week!

# KRLA ARCHIVES

## The Many Faces of Herman

## A RECORD MAKING ANNOUNCEMENT!

**THE BYRDS** Sing Their Smash Hit "Mr. Tambourine Man"

*Plus* It's No Use — The Bells of Rhymney — I Feel A Whole Lot Better — You Won't Have To Cry — Spanish Harlem Incident — We'll Meet Again — Chimes of Freedom — Don't Doubt Yourself, Baby — Here Without You — I Knew I'd Want You — All I Really Want To Do

**PAUL REVERE AND THE RAIDERS** Sing "Oo Poo Pah Doo"

*Plus* You Can't Sit Down — Money — Louie, Louie — Do You Love Me — Big Boy Pete — Sometimes — Gone — Bad Times — Fever — Time Is On My Side — A Kiss To Remember You By

**CHAD AND JEREMY** Sing "Before and After"

*Plus* Tell Me Baby — Why Should I Care — For Lovin' Me — I'm In Love Again — Little Does She Know — What Do You Want With Me — Say It Isn't True — Fare Thee Well — Can't Get Used To Losing You — Evil Hearted Me

on **COLUMBIA RECORDS**

# KRLA ARCHIVES

## A READER WRITES
## Senior Feels Suddenly Sad As Graduation Approaches

The following letter was sent to the Beat by a Southern California teenager. It needs no explanation. After you've read it, our reason for printing it will be obvious.

"Dear KRLA BEAT:

I don't know who else to say this to. All I know is that I have to say it to someone. I'd tell my folks or my friends, but I guess I'm a little too old to be feeling the way I feel right now.

In just a few days I am going to graduate from high school. I was all for the idea at first, but I suddenly realized that a part of my world is toppling. And that none of this will ever happen to me again. I'll never lead another school cheer, or eat lunch in our crummy cafeteria, or meet my boyfriend on the front lawn, or go to a school dance or anything. It's all over and all I have left are the memories.

I probably sound like I'm feeling sorry for myself. Well, I am and I'm not. I'm sorry it couldn't have lasted longer, so I guess that's being sorry for myself in a way.

But mostly I'm sorry for the kids who don't feel the same. The members of my class, and all the other graduating classes in the world, who will accept their diploma without getting a lump in the throat. Teens who have considered these wonderful years a great big drag, and don't have any memories they'll want to press in a book and keep forever. I guess I feel even worse about the former classmates who won't be graduating at all. If only they would never have to know what they missed by not really trying to be a part of things. But I'm afraid they'll find out someday, the hard way. I finally realize the terrible truth of something I've been hearing all my life without really understanding. Life actually is what you make it. It really is up to you.

I'm so glad I made the most of my high school years. I'm proud there's going to be a lump in my throat, a kingsized one, on graduation night. When it hurts to leave a place behind you, that means you are very lucky to have been there.

I've never been happy that I'm sad before, and I don't really know how to explain it. I've never put anything this personal down on paper (I hope I didn't get too mushy), but I just had to say these things.

I hope you will print this letter in the Beat. I know a lot of teenagers feel the same way, and it might make them happy to know they aren't alone.

Thanks for listening."

Name Withheld By Request
Los Angeles, Calif.

Our congratulations to all the members of the Class Of '65, especially you. And thanks so much for writing this letter. Thanks from us and from every teenager who read it.—THE BEAT.

## JOHN LEYTON BECOMES A SINGER BY ACCIDENT WITH HIS FAB TALENT

John Leyton, who co-stars with Freddie & The Dreamers in "Seaside Swingers," became a pop singer quite by accident.

He was chosen to portray the role of a rock and roll star on an English television show. The role required him to sing a number or two, and the following morning the young actor was the toast of England's younger set.

The young actor was also quite bewildered. He had the solid acting background of a continuing role in the "Invisible Man" series (which can now be seen on Los Angeles television), and one of the leads in a famous children's series titled "Biggles." Now he was a rock and roll star? Someone had to be joshing.

**Not Dreaming**

However, he was not, as he suspected, dreaming the whole thing. The response to his performance was so overwhelming, he was rushed into a recording contract. His first four discs ("Jonny Remember Me," "Wild Wind," "Son, This Is She" and "Lonely City") held several number one slots in Britain, and totaled over two million in sales.

Swinging and swinging by the seaside aren't John's only claims to fame. He is also a gifted actor who is serious about his craft.

He has appeared in quite a number of American productions, including a "12 O'clock High" segment and movies such as "The Great Escape," "Von Ryan's Express" and "The Guns of Batasi."

John has now given up his British hit parade holdings and moved to Hollywood in search of a full-time acting career, and the Beat would like to take this opportunity to welcome him to KRLA country.

Accidents like John Leyton should happen more often!

**JOHN LEYTON**

### Bob Eubanks Aids Youth Project

## KRLA DEEJAYS WORK BEHIND THE SCENES

**By Louise Criscione**

There are quite a few people who enjoy blowing their own horn. These people love to tell all about the wonderful things they have done or which they are about to do. Then there are other people who really deserve to blow their horn, but who remain silent (or relatively so.) The KRLA disc jockeys fit neatly into this second catagory. I felt it was about time the jocks' good deeds were brought out into the open. So, I have taken it upon myself to blow their horn for them!

First off, there are those lovable losers, the KRLApes. In the past 2 years, this fantastic team played a total of 53 games of which they have somehow managed to lose fifty-one!

The Apes specialize in basketball. They're not afraid to challenge, or be challenged, by anybody. They have played against such worthy opponents as Mark Keppel, San Gabriel, El Monte, Inglewood, Valley State College, Redondo Beach, and Palmdale. There have been many many more, but I only have so much space you know!

**Charity**

The important thing about these games is that, win or lose, all the proceeds go to charity. In the past, they have benefited high schools and colleges as well as various charities.

Of course, the Apes do not restrict themselves to basketball alone. Rather, they are all-around atheletes and participate in all types of popular sports such as donkey baseball, elephant races, ostrich races, turtle races, cow milking contests, and goat milking contests! Only thing is, how come they always lose?

Remember all those KRLA signs gracing the windows of greater Los Angeles during Christmas time? Well, while Santa Claus was out looking for the daily winners, he and the accompanying disc jockeys were also visiting the children's wards of hospitals all over the Southland.

**Hootenany**

For the last two years, KRLA has put on a giant hootenany at the Pasadena Civic Auditorium. Both of these shows sold-out, netting the March of Dimes a neat $15,000.

Then there was that American Cancer Society flight over Los Angeles. Remember the skinny guy with the glasses who welcomed you aboard the plane? Well, that was our own KRLA disc jockey, Dick Biondi.

There have been numerous other benefits, among them the Heart Foundation and the Shrine Show for Cripple Children. Bob Eubanks works very hard for the Crippled Children's Society. Perhaps those of you who attended last year's Beatle Concert at the Hollywood Bowl noticed the large number of crippled children in the audience. They were there as the personal guests of Bob Eubanks.

**BIONDI**

**EUBANKS**

**Hull's Drive**

Dave Hull is the national chairman of the coast to coast drive for the Asthma Research Hospital. The drive began on June 1, and those of you who donate will receive a free box of air! It may not seem like much to you, but to those kids who have a hard time just breathing it is the most precious thing in the world.

**HULL**

Many of the KRLA personnel are active in their civic affairs as well as in their particular church groups. A notable example is Jim Steck, KRLA newsman. Jim is the sponsor of a youth group within the Catholic Youth Organization. He's the one who had all that trouble with his car washes being rained out!

All of the jocks have donated their time to speaking to the Los Angeles City College radio department. They have also spoken to classes at Pasadena City College and U.C.L.A., as well as at other Southland schools and colleges.

All of the jocks have hosted numerous dances and shows all over Los Angeles. Probably many of you have attended these shows. Just this weekend, one was held at the American Legion Hall and another at St. Paul High School. Casey Kasen hosted the first one, and the Emperor himself gave of his time and enormous talent for the second one. It's not every Emperor who'd do that!

**HUDSON**

The station itself is presently operated as a non-profit organization, donating an estimated quarter of a million dollars a year to various deserving charities.

**Stars Help**

Of course, let me make it quite clear that without the help of many recording stars, much of the money would never have been raised. These people have donated their time and talent, and they really deserve a huge share of the credit. Listed in alphabetical order are some of these generous artists: April & Nino, Frankie Avalon, Hoyt Axton, the Beach Boys, Cannibal and the Headhunters, Freddy Cannon, Jackie DeShannon, the Dillards, Dion, the Good Time Singers, Dobie Grey, Brenda Holloway, Ian & Dean, Joe & Eddie, the Kingsmen, Roger Miller, Tim Morgan, the O Jays, Bobby Pickett, the Premiers, the Righteous Brothers, the Shirelles, Connie Stevens, and Bobby Vee. And this doesn't even include the fabulous array of talent which appeared on the recent "Freedom from Hunger" show.

I realize that I have left many stars, as well as many good deeds, out of this article because of space and because of oversight. But I do think I have given you a small idea of some of the really great things our KRLA guys are doing, and on behalf of myself (and I'm sure of all their recipients) I'd like to say thanks.

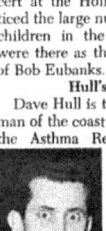

# KRLA ARCHIVES

### Gerry And The Pacemakers

**VISITING LOS ANGELES**

## GERRY AND THE PACEMAKERS ARE LIKEABLE AND FRIENDLY GUYS

Crash! Boom! Bang!

"Gerry. Oh, Gerry! Over here, Gerry!"

Looking like someone just put through a washing machine, Gerry Marsden, dripping with water from the swimming pool, towel in hand, and laughing like Crazy, came pounding into the room, and said, "Well, when do we start the interview?"

An interview with Gerry Marsden is like a young child's first visit to the toy department at Christmas; it's exciting, informative, and very rewarding, for this dimunitive carrier of happiness is as refreshing as anyone you could ever hope to meet.

My meeting with Gerry, and his Pacemakers, took place at his hotel, some three days after his arrival. He had come to Los Angeles to tape a "SHINDIG" show, and to catch a week's rest after a very hectic four weeks tour of the United States.

When I arrived at the hotel, Les Hurst, their road manager, showed me into Gerry's room. Gerry was dressing to go out for dinner, so I made my interview short. It went something like this:

Q:—How have you liked touring the States with the "SHINDIG" Tour?

A:—It's been the greatest. If all of the people in the world could be as great as those on the tour were, there wouldn't be any problems anywhere.

Q:—How do you feel about your successful movie, "Ferry Cross The Mersey?"

A:—I enjoyed making it, you know. The experience will someday prove to be very valuable. Besides, we made some good money.

Q:—How much?

A:—Can't say, exactly. It was a lot, though.

Q:—Are you excited about being on "Shindig" again?

A:—Of course. It's fun to do, and besides, Jack Good's an old friend, and he's great to work with. We all like him, and wish him luck after he leaves this post.

Q:—Where do you and your group go from here? Back to England?

A:—Yes. First we get a week's rest, then we do a week's work in different clubs in Liverpool and London, then sixteen weeks at a summer resort called Blackwel.

Q:—Are you going to make any television appearances during that time?

A:—I s'pose so, but I'm not sure. I think Brian's (Epstein) arranged some.

"I'm sorry, said Gerry, "slipping on his shoes and straightening his tie. "I've got to run. Will we see you at "SHINDIG?"

'Sure thing." I yelled, as he dashed down the staris.

I thanked Les Hurst after that, and wandered off into the hotel coffee shop, where I, and my two friends, dined with Gerry's brother Fred, and another Pacemaker, Les Maguire. While they cut through their steaks and chops, I sipped at coffee, and asked a few more questions.

I learned that Fred and Les come from an area of Liverpool known as Formby, while Gerry and the absent Les come from Ringo's community of Dingle. I told them how many of us here in the U.S. think that Liverpool is a rough, "scruffy" city, and that we were surprised to see these young men so neatly attired in conservative suits, whereas most seem to dress in the radical continental styles.

"Don't believe that we're all sloppy, please," said Fred, gulping, and almost choking, over a glass of iced tea. "We're getting pretty grown up, you know."

When I mentioned Mariann Faithful's name, Les and Fred's eyes lit up. I learned that Mariann is now definitely engaged to a college student not even remotely connected with the recording industry.

Most of our conversation at that dinner table centered around normal, everyday things; the race to the moon, economics, girls, clothes, and even race horses.

In the way of women, Gerry & The Pacemakers are very emphatic about their likes and dislikes. "None of us can stand these painted girls," said Les.

Fred interjected, "It doesn't matter if they're fantastically beautiful to us, as long as they don't wear a pound and a half of make up. So many girls lose their natural beauty — which may be a pretty mouth, or chin, or cheeks, or eyes — by putting on all of these funny colors."

As the waitress brought round the checks, I thanked these two talkative young men. I left that night thankful that things has gone so well for not only me, and my story, but for some very fine young men known world-wide as . . . Gerry & The Pacemakers.

. . . Rod Alan Barken

### Letters

I send my old copies of the Beat to my pen pal in England, and she and her mates read it to shreds. Her name in Margit Taylor (no relation to Derek, darn it) and I hope you will print this letter so she can see her name mentioned (she'll flip).

The two of us are going to meet in front of Buckingham Palace on June 30, 1966, and I would appreciate any advice you can give me on how to make extra money for my trip fund.

C.M., Rolling Hills

*Just send in the coupon on Page Five.*

**BEAT WALLPAPER**

My folks were about to paint my room a really vile shade of green, and I was about to die because they weren't going to let me put my photos back up on the walls after the remodeling.

After making several noisy protests, I came up with the brilliant idea of papering my room with the KRLA Beat. My folks made a few noisy protests, but I finally won and my room is starting to look sharp.

I buy two copies of the Beat each week so I can use both sides of each page, and in five more weeks my masterpiece will be finished. It's realy great to have wallpaper that has pix of all my favorite stars, and interesting stories, too.

I guess you could say I'm really stuck on the Beat. (Oh, brother.)

G.F., Los Angeles

*I guess you could also say the Beat is stuck on you. When your work of art is completed, invite us over. After all, this is the first time we've ever been pasted. (Oh, brother.)*

**CROSSED FINGERS**

I love your "Beatle Contest" and would give anything to meet the fab foursome.

I always have good luck when I cross my fingers, so when I heard about your contest I crossed them (on both hands) and have kept them that way every since. I'm going to keep them crossed until I find out if I won.

When people ask me why I have my fingers crossed, they won't believe I've had them this way for two weeks.

You believe me, don't you?

L.K., Long Beach

*We promise to try if you'll tell us who typed your letter for you. In any case, all the luck in the world!*

**Raise Money For Your Club**

Want to raise extra money for your club treasury? You could easily make several hundred dollars.

Write to: Fan Club Funds, KRLA, Sunset-Vine Tower, Suite 504, Hollywood, California — 90028.

---

# THE CINDERS

### The One and Only
## CHUCK BERRY

**SUNDAY, JUNE 20**
North Hollywood Cinnamon Cinder

**WEDNESDAY, JUNE 23**
Long Beach Cinnamon Cinder

# HAVE THE ACTION

### The Fabulous
## CRYSTALS

**SUNDAY, JUNE 27**
North Hollywood Cinnamon Cinder

**WEDNESDAY, JUNE 30**
Long Beach Cinnamon Cinder

AGES 18-25

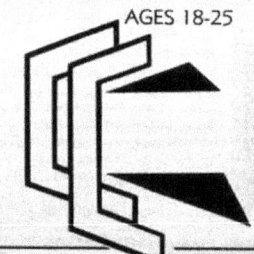

## CINNAMON CINDER

11345 Ventura Blvd., North Hollywood
4401 Pacific Coast Highway, Long Beach

# KRLA ARCHIVES

## TIPS TO TEENS

This corner of the BEAT is devoted to answering your beauty and fashion questions, and to printing the tips and hints you've been sending to our "For Girls Only" column.

If you have a tip you'd like printed or a question you'd like answered, please mail them to Sheila Davis, in care of the KRLA Beat, 6290 Sunset, Suite 504, Hollywood.

Q—I have a nice complexion and I don't want to start wearing makeup until I have to. My only problem is my nose. It wouldn't possibly shine any brighter if I stayed up nights polishing it. What can I do (Q.M., San Bernardino)

A—Go to any cosmetic counter and find a liquid makeup that blends completely with your skin tones. (Don't pay under a dollar for it as the cheaper products are often made of inferior ingredients.) Then rub a touch of the makeup into your nose before going out. If you get a shade that really blends, no one will know the difference.

Q—I've been taking guitar lessons for about a month and the fingers of my left hand look ghastly. They're all weird from holding the steel strings down. My teacher says this sort of thing has to happen or I'll never be able to chord right. Isn't there some way it can be a little less creppy looking? (B.B., Commerce)

A—File the end of your fingers with an emery board, the same way you do your nails. Sounds strange, but it works!

Q—Every time I wash my face with soap I look like a prune. Is there some product I can use that wouldn't give me so many problems? (O.E., Sherman Oaks)

A—Try washing your face with Noxzema, using it just as you would soap. If this doesn't work, you can buy a product called Phi-So-Hex in most drug stores. Both are very non-drying.

Q—I did something really stupid the other day. Instead of taking up the hem on one of my favorite cotton dresses, I cut it off and now it's too short. Now what? (S.L., Los Angeles)

A—There are two ways out of this predicament. One is to hem the portion you cut off on both edges and sew it back on. This gives the illusion of a "band" around the bottom of your skirt and can really look cute. Another is to buy a length of cotton lace, the kind that isn't transparent and hem it onto your dress.

Q—I just moved here from the Mid-West and there must be something about California that disagrees with me. I always have chapped hands. I've tried about everything, but nothing seems to help. Can you help? (R.F., Pomona)

A—Buy a jar of Johnson's White Petroleum Jelly (for babies) at the market. When you go to bed, rub it into your hands and put on a pair of white (that's important, you might have an allergy to dyes) gloves and leave them on all night. If you can't stand to wear gloves, see this week's "For Girls Only" column.

Q—I have long, straight hair and I like to backcomb the top a little because I have kind of a flat head (?). The backcombing just doesn't seem to take anymore, and the more I do it, the flatter my head looks. What am I doing wrong (F.G., Pasadena)

A—Long hair has a habit of pulling the backcombing out, probably because of the weight. If you like a semi-fluffy top, you'll need to have your top-knot thinned. You don't have to have it cut. Just having it thinned will give you enough short ends to work with.

Q—I have two problems. Perfume doesn't smell the same way on me that it does in the bottle. Sometimes it smells better, but most of the time it's pretty bad. Also, every color of lipstick I wear turns red after I've had it on a few moments. What is my problem, anyway? (R.L., Maywood,

A—These reactions are caused by the chemical balance of your skin. Solve the perfume problem by always trying a scent on the inside of your wrist before buying it (the perfume, not the wrist). Solve the other problem by testing a new lipstick on the back of your hand before making the purchase. It will turn the same color there as it will on your lips. You might also try wearing natural lipstick, which will allow your true colors to shine through.

### Hints Of The Week

I just found out something that I think everyone should know, if they don't already. I used to break out every hour on the hour, and I used to think it was just one of those teenagy things I couldn't do anything about. Well, I went to the doctor and found out otherwise. I was allergic to several foods, and when I stopped eating them, my face cleared right up. My doctor said half of the bumpy complexions among teenagers are caused by problems that can be cured. If you have a tendency like this, it would be a good idea to stop thinking it's just natural and go find out if it really is. (Barbara P., Van Nuys)

This is sort of a touchy subject, but I think you'll be interested in how I solved a big crisis with my mother. She's very pretty when she wants to be, but all of a sudden she stopped paying much attention to herself. I would rather have died than say anything, so I came up with this idea instead. I went around for about a week looking like a real mess, and she finally told me to stop it. I did, of course, and just as I suspected, she did too! I'm not going to sign my name. My mother is small but mighty. (Anonymous, Bell Gardens)

### Wild Weekend

The Dave Clark Five will arrive in New York on June 18 with a stop in California later in the summer.

This will be the group's third American tour and will include their fifth appearance on the Ed Sullivan Show on June 23. They will also tape future shows for the Dean Martin Show, Shindig and the Danny Kaye Show.

"Having A Wild Weekend" was filmed in England will be released in the U.S. late in June to coincide with their tour here.

## Glenn Yarbrough -- A Case In Point

## A KRLA BEAT EDITORIAL

### Teens Given Wrong Image

Adults may be in the process of accepting teenage music, but their acceptance of teen-slanted artists is still at low ebb.

According to most adults, a star's success with the younger set depends upon his age (preferably 13½), his physical appearance (he must have Greek God tendencies, topped with a shoulder length page boy), and his talent for keeping whatever talent he may have (the less the better) well hidden behind pounding drums and twanging guitars.

If this were the case, how would we account for the soaring record ratings of established stars like Dean Martin, Perry Como, Al Hirt, Allan Sherman, Patti Page and Vic Damone? All of them are high on the national single record charts, a portion of the market which was long ago cornered by teenage buyers.

Best of all possible examples of just how wrong the adult "teen star image" happens to be is a fantastic young man named Glenn Yarbrough. He is no teenager, pleasant in appearance rather than mop-topped, and blessed with a breathtakingly rare kind of sound.

When Glenn left his choice spot as lead singer of the popular "Limelighters" and went on his own, his vast following of fans went right with him. That following, which soon doubled and tripled, bet on his first single record to place in the highly competitive race to the top.

Glenn's entry was tagged "Baby The Rain Must Fall", and it didn't just place or show. It won, with the help of people who do know good music and who do recognize talent. Teenagers.

Baby, something besides the rain must fall, and soon. The thousand and one walls of misunderstanding between adults and teenagers have got to go.

One of them just toppled. Thanks to the teen-prompted success of a true artist like Glenn Yarbrough.

One down. One thousand to go.

---

**23 SKIDOO**
Dancing to Live Name Bands
2116 Westwood Blvd., West Los Angeles
Girls 18, Guys 21
Closed Mondays and Thursdays

---

### Miracles Click Again

**SMOKEY ROBINSON & THE MIRACLES** were one of the first groups to make the now-famous Tamila-Motown "sound" popular. Their "SHOP AROUND" was a million-seller. Now they have a brand new hit — "OOH, OOH BABY."

# KRLA TUNEDEX

## NUMBER 1

**THE FOUR TOPS – AT THE TOP**

## RED HOT

| This Week | Last Week | | |
|---|---|---|---|
| 1. | 3. | I CAN'T HELP MYSELF | The Four Tops |
| 2. | 2. | WOOLY BULLY | Sam the Sham & Pharaohs |
| 3. | 6. | WHAT THE WORLD NEEDS NOW IS LOVE | Jackie DeShannon |
| 4. | 4. | SHAKIN' ALL OVER | Guess Who? |
| 5. | 1. | BACK IN MY ARMS AGAIN | The Supremes |
| 6. | 4. | HELP ME, RHONDA | The Beach Boys |
| 7. | 5. | MR. TAMBOURINE MAN | The Byrds |
| 8. | 11. | HERE COMES THE NIGHT | Them |
| 9. | 41. | SATISFACTION | The Rolling Stones |
| 10. | 9. | JUST YOU | Sonny & Cher |
| 11. | 13. | CRYING IN THE CHAPEL | Elvis Presley |
| 12. | 8. | YOU TURN ME ON | Ian Whitcomb & Bluesville |
| 13. | 10. | GOOD LOVIN' | The Olympics |
| 14. | 17. | FOR YOUR LOVE | The Yardbirds |
| 15. | 14. | TICKET TO RIDE | The Beatles |
| 16. | 15. | GLORIA/BABY PLEASE DON'T GO | Them |
| 17. | 12. | OOO BABY BABY | The Miracles |
| 18. | 16. | CATCH THE WIND | Donovan |
| 19. | 22. | JUST ONCE IN MY LIFE | The Righteous Brothers |
| 20. | 21. | THE LAST TIME/PLAY WITH FIRE | The Rolling Stones |
| 21. | 23. | GOODBYE, SO LONG | Ike and Tina Turner |
| 22. | 19. | MRS. BROWN/I GOTTA DREAM ON | Herman's Hermits |
| 23. | 20. | BABY THE RAIN MUST FALL | Glenn Yarbrough |
| 24. | 26. | BRING IT ON HOME TO ME | The Animals |
| 25. | 31. | WHITTIER BOULEVARD | The Midnighters |
| 26. | 18. | SHE'S ABOUT A MOVER | Sir Douglas Quintet |
| 27. | 28. | YOU REALLY KNOW HOW TO HURT A GUY | Jan & Dean |
| 28. | 30. | WONDERFUL WORLD | Herman's Hermits |
| 29. | 24. | JUST A LITTLE | The Beau Brummels |
| 30. | 29. | ENGINE ENGINE NO. 9 | Roger Miller |
| 31. | 35. | LAURIE | Dickie Lee |
| 32. | 43. | HUSH, HUSH, SWEET CHARLOTTE | Patti Page |
| 33. | 36. | L-O-N-E-L-Y | Bobby Vinton |
| 34. | 37. | SAD GIRL | The Gallahads |
| 35. | 38. | LIP SYNC | Len Barry |
| 36. | 39. | THIS LITTLE BIRD | Marianne Faithfull |
| 37. | 40. | ONCE UPON A TIME | Tom Jones |
| 38. | 44. | SEVENTH SON | Johnny Rivers |
| 39. | 45. | OPERATOR | Brenda Holloway |
| 40. | 48. | TRAINS AND BOATS AND PLANES | Billy J. Kramer |

**SOUTHERN CALIFORNIA'S MOST ACCURATE RECORD SURVEY — BASED ON RETAIL SALES FIGURES**

**KRLA BEAT**
6290 Sunset, No. 504
Hollywood, Cal. 90028

U.S. Postage
BULK RATE
PAID
Permit No.
25497
Los Angeles
California

If you were a KRLA BEAT subscriber your name and address would be printed here and you would receive your copy at home, saving 40%.

**OVERFLOW CROWDS** as this one at Long Beach attest to the ROLLING STONES' popularity.

## ROLLING STONES INTERVIEW

(Continued From Page 1)

longer than most haircuts. One promoter didn't know whether to call for a stright jacket or an animal trainer when he first saw us on stage.

Bill, your hair is the longest. Has it always been that way?

Bill: Yes, but I used to comb it differently. Then, one day, my wife, Diane, washed all the grease out, and I was just like the rest . . . only shaggier.

Brian: We laughed when we first saw him with it that way.

Is that when Bill developed his "freeze" look?

Bill: Yeah, kinda'. People used to pepper us with these queer looks, so I just looked straight back at them. It sort of scared them, I guess. Pretty soon they stopped.

What about you, Charlie? Was it as rough for you, too?

Charlie: Not as bad as the rest had it. I used to stay by myself a lot . . . and besides, I used to play professionally before.

With who?

Charlie: A jazz band.

Charlie, what made you choose the drums instead of a guitar or bass?

Charlie: I don't know . . . they're fun to play . . . and I used to like Max Roach a lot.

Stones, when did you start to play before a "live" audience?

Mick: At this pub. A place called Bricklayers Arms. They didn't pay us.

Did you have any fans then?

Mick: Yes. A few would just sit around and watch us . . . and maybe dance a bit.

Brian: Our first real chance came in the summer of 1962, at a place in London . . . the Marquee Club.

What happened?

Charlie: Long John Baldry got us on the show, and we earned three pounds and four bob each! But it was fun . . . and we DID get paid.

You've come a long way since then. How does it feel?

Keith: Fantastic!

Brian: Terrific!

What's been the least amount you've ever been paid?

Bill: . . . About seven pounds, I think.

Mick: Yeah. That was the day that the bloody crowd just sat there . . . didn't say a thing. Terribly morbid lot.

What was your first record?

Mick: A song called "Come On." Andrew Loog Oldham produced it, but it didn't do too well.

Why?

Keith: It just wasn't us, that's all. It wasn't really r & b, anyway. Too commercial.

What happened then?

Mick: Andrew ran into two of the Beatles one day, and they gave us this song to consider.

Which two of the Beatles?

Mick: Oh . . . John and Paul, naturally.

Did you record it?

Brian: Yes, we did. We met in this place called the Colyer Club, in London, and went over it a bit, then decided to use it.

What was it called?

Mick: "I Wanna Be Your Man." And the rest is history.

## STONES IN LOVE?

**BRIAN JONES**

The Rolling Stones are in love! All five of them have found happiness — right here in Los Angeles.

During the past 11 months they have spent a total of 35 days in Southern California . . . and they have always gone home talking about this area.

One of the Stones, Brian Jones, is hopeful of coming back in late summer to spend some time with his friend Joey Paige. He was Joey's guest a few weeks ago and at that time told the BEAT:

"I love it here. I'd like to move here permanently."

Bill Wyman would like to bring his wife and child over because "All of this sunshine is great for little kids."

Who knows? Perhaps the day will come when you'll pass a Stone casually driving along a freeway. Let's hope so.

**British Top Ten**
1. WHERE ARE YOU NOW — Jackie Trent
2. A WORLD OF OUR OWN — Seekers
3. LONG LIVE LOVE — Sandie Shaw
4. TRUE LOVE WAYS — Peter and Gordon
5. KING OF THE ROAD — Roger Miller
6. TICKET TO RIDE — Beatles
7. THIS LITTLE BIRD — Marianne Faithfull
8. SUBTERRANEAN HOMESICK BLUES — Bob Dylan
9. WONDERFUL WORLD — Herman's Hermits
10. BRING IT ON HOME TO ME — Animals

**Casey's Quiz Answer**

(Don't peek unless you've read the question elsewhere in the BEAT) Mick Jagger of the Rolling Stones.

*Stones Lead* FIRST WEEK'S 'BATTLE' POLL

# KRLA BEAT

*Beatle Quiz* FREE TICKETS TO HOLLYWOOD BOWL

Volume 1, No. 16 — Los Angeles, California — Ten Cents — June 23, 1965

# P. J. - HERO OR HEEL?

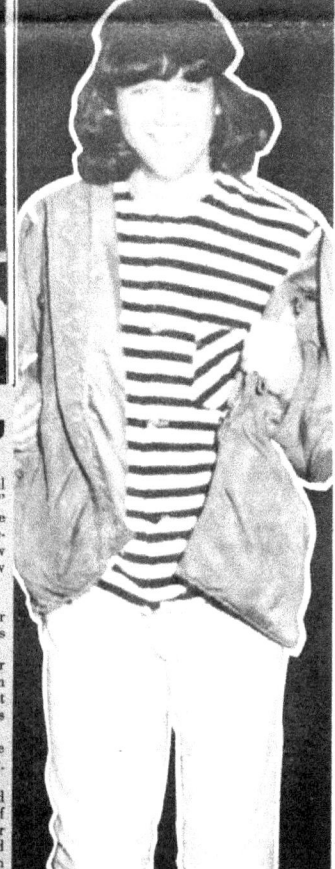

### HAD TO BE 'THE TOP STAR'
## Proby Walks Out On 'Shindig'

P. J. Proby, the transplanted Texan who *ripped* his way to stardom as a prancing English dandy by ripping his pants, is already in the middle of another controversy.

It came only a few days after he arrived here from his adopted home in England for a series of appearances on "Shindig."

After taping one performance (scheduled for broadcast this week) the unpredictable entertainer walked out at the last minute on two other scheduled performances for the network show. He felt he was not receiving sufficient recognition and respect as the "top star."

"I'm disgusted," he told the BEAT in an exclusive interview shortly afterward. "They promised me the top billing on all three shows then tried to put me in among the regular cast for the second and third performances."

#### May Hurt Career

In walking out, England's current pop music king may have shattered his dream of becoming as big a star hero in his native country as he is in England and other parts of Europe.

He also shattered his friendship with Shindig Producer Jack Good, the man he previously credited with giving him the breaks he needed to become a star.

"Now we don't even speak," said Proby in reference to his breakup with Good. "To me this is a breach of moral ethics because Jack Good and I used to be the best of friends."

The friendship had dated back two years to the time when Proby was an unknown American singer who somehow stirred Good's imagination. The English producer flew him to England and booked him on a special television show he was producing for the Beatles.

#### Much Controversy

Since then the long-haired, velvet-slippered singer's career has been spotted with controversy. But nothing stopped his streak to the top of the British popularity charts.

His walkout from Shindig leaves him few other major television outlets in either country. He was banned from all British television recently after a series of episodes at personal appearance in which he split his fancy velvet pants while cavorting about during live concerts.

Proby's only public appearance since flying here to tape Shindig was at the recent Freedom From Hunger Show. Even that appearance stirred controversy.

The star-studded show—produced by Good—was closed prematurely when Proby put on an incredible display of sensuous movements resembling a strip-teaser's dance. After "teasing" the audience for several minutes he was mobbed by a small group of girls who rushed the stage. The curtain

**TURN TO PAGE 10**

## KRLA ARCHIVES

### EPSTEIN'S PARENTS VISITING L.A.

**By Marcy Norton**

My friend, Jintz Coleman, and I recently had the pleasure of meeting the parents of BEATLE manager Brian Epstein, Mr. Henry Epstein and his lovely wife, Queenie. They were both quite charming and very candid when talking about their two sons and their vist here.

Mr. and Mrs. Epstein have been in California for two weeks. They both think it is "just wonderful". They have been sightseeing and visiting movie studios. They were also in Las Vegas where they saw Dean Martin's "marvelous" show.

While here the Epstein's have enjoyed KRLA "very much", and say they "have it on most of the time". At this point in the conversation Mr. Epstein asked if we would like to listen to the Hullabalooer. They both like pop music and Mrs. Epstein says that the British groups are "all wonderful".

Their famous son was not accompanying them on their trip here. "He is quite busy in London". As good news for all of the Brian Epstein fans who are reading this, when I asked his mother if he were engaged, as some gossip columnists have stated, she looked quite startled and said, "heaven's no, where did you ever hear that?"

The Epstein's were about to leave, but before they did I presented Mrs. Epstein with the newest KRLA BEAT because she was "very eager to read it". Mr. Epstein gave us some pictures of some of the groups that Brian manages. He and his wife autographed them.

If Brian is just half as nice as his parents he must be a wonderful man.

**GETTING READY FOR A BIG BLOWOUT**

**THE POSTER TELLS THE STORY.** The pretty young ladies are Bonnie Le Blanc (Miss Skyrocket) and Betty Rees (Miss Firecracker), both of Pasadena. The mischievous-looking fellows whooping it up in the background are (left to right) Charlie O'Donnell, Dick Biondi, Dave (Hornblower) Hull, Emperor Bob Hudson and Bob Eubanks. In addition to an awe-inspiring fireworks display, the July 4 spectacular at the Coliseum will feature a "Thrill-O-Rama" with death-defying feats of world famous stunting stars.

### The Hullabalooer

### BEATLES EXPAND U.S. TOUR

**By Dave Hull**

Hi, Hullabalooers!

Everybody else takes a summer vacation, but I take mine in the winter. So, now that summer is here I'm resuming my weekly column in the BEAT.

I'll start with a few hot items that are absolute exclusives at the time I'm writing this.

The Beatles are adding at least three appearances to their August concert schedule. They will schedule one performance in San Diego and another in Salt Lake City between Aug. 22 and Aug. 29.

In addition, they will schedule a second performance at the Cow Palace in San Francisco. At the moment, not even the radio stations and newspapers in these cities are aware of this. It will give them quite a story.

#### No Changes Here

I'm happy to report that this does not change the Beatles schedule for Los Angeles. In addition to their two concerts at Hollywood Bowl on Aug. 28 and Aug. 29, they will still be spending from seven to ten days on vacation here.

Here's a flash for Beatle fans who have not been able to obtain tickets for their local concerts. If you don't mind travelling, you can still obtain tickets for their Portland, Oregon, concert. For some reason—even though they are sold out everywhere else 10,-000 ticket are still available for the Aug. 22 performance in Portland.

Many people have asked other questions about the Beatles. I'll start answering them next week. In the meantime, if you have any questions about the Beatles or other entertainers, write me at KRLA.

See ya next week.

## BEATLE QUIZ

Here we go again! Five more questions for the KRLA Beatle Quiz.

Those of you who missed the first four weeks of the Beatle Quiz may still catch up by ordering the issues of June 16, June 9, June 2 and May 26. You'll find instructions for ordering issues elsewhere in the BEAT.

The winner, of course, will get to interview the Beatles for the KRLA Beat when they arrive in August. The winner and a friend will also attend a Beatle Concert as guests of the KRLA Deejays.

Additional prizes will be provided for runners-up. In case of a tie there will be additional questions or a drawing to decide the final winner. The contest will cover a ten-week period, with at least five new questions asked each week. KRLA's Derek Taylor, a close friend of the Beatles and their former press officer, will judge the entries for accuracy.

**KRLA BEAT**

The KRLA BEAT is published weekly by Prestige Publishing Company; editorial and advertising offices at 6290 Sunset Boulevard, Suite 504, Hollywood, California 90028.

Single copy price, 10 cents.

Subscription price: U.S. and possessions, and Canada, $3 per year or $5 for two years. Foreign rates upon request.

Beatle Quiz
KRLA BEAT
Suite 504
6290 Sunset Blvd.
Hollywood, Calif. 90028

CONTEST EDITOR:

Below are my answers to the fourth set of questions in the BEATLE QUIZ CONTEST.

My Name ............................................ Address ............................................
City .................................................... State ............... Zip Code ..............
I (☐ am) (☐ am not) presently a subscriber to the KRLA BEAT.

### NEW QUESTIONS

21. How many hats was John Lennon wearing during his bubble bath scene in "Hard Day's Night?" ...................
22. Who has taken Derek Taylor's place as Beatle Press Agent? ...................
23. According to their hair dresser, which Beatle's hair is the softest? ...................
24. The Beatles had a name for the pointed-toe shoes they wore in the old days. What was it? ...................
25. When the Beatles first landed in New York, their arrival was picketed by a group of local union members. What was the purpose of the picket and what union participated?

**EPIC** Dave Clark Five's "I LIKE IT LIKE THAT"

### KRLA BEAT SUBSCRIPTION
Order By Mail Now—Save Over 40%!

Please Rush Me the KRLA BEAT at Your Special Introductory Subscription Rate

☐ 1 Year—52 Issues—$3.00  ☐ 2 Years — $5.00

Enclosed is $...................
Send To:................................................Age..........
Address:.........................................................
City......................State......................Zip..........

*Please be sure to include your Zip Code number!*
MAIL YOUR ORDER TO: KRLA BEAT
1401 South Oak Knoll Avenue
Pasadena, California 91106

# KRLA ARCHIVES

## WHICH ONE IS THE THIEF?

ONE OF THESE STARRY-EYED FIGURES IS A THIEF! Elvis steals a few kisses but that doesn't count, so we'll let you in on a secret—the sticky-fingered one is gorgeous Brenda Benet, a former "Shindig" dancer. This shot was taken during a scene from "Harem Scarem", a new MGM movie scheduled for release this fall. Elvis plays a James Bond-type secret service agent who is faced with a spine-chilling decision.

## ARTISTS DISAGREE OVER REASON FOR RECORD RECESSION

Why are record sales in England way down? Everyone seems to have come up with a reason why.

The majority blame the sales drop on the pirate radio stations. Before the pirates, the British had only Radio Luxembourg and the BBC.

If they wanted to hear a record, they were practically forced to buy it! Now with several pirate stations, they are forced to do nothing but turn the radio on.

Other people have different ideas. *Ringo* and *Cilla Black* both agree that the English record scene is getting Americanized— more albums are being sold, and there are more changes at the top of the chart.

*Sandie Shaw* thinks "there were too many tours recently with too many rubbishy acts. So-called showmen tried to cash in on the kids. So it didn't last as long as they thought."

*Billy J. Kramer* feels that "there is always a bit of a lay-off in the summer and I can't see any real recession."

Jimmy Savile, popular British DJ, has come up with the most clever remark on the subject: "If record sales are down that's just too bad. It's up to us DJs to put them up again. If there's a slump in the business there isn't one in mine. I've just had a raise!"

Wonder who's right?

## CASEY'S QUIZ

By CASEY KASEM

Up until two years ago, all this artist wanted to do was grow up in a hurry. One of his greatest fears was being called a "kid." In 1965 he stopped being one at the ripe old age of nineteen and became an international sensation. He has five brothers, all younger than himself, and he made his television debut singing a duet with his father. His first professional "live" appearance was made at Disneyland, and in addition to his vocalizing, he plays drums, guitar, clarinet and sax.

ANSWER ON PAGE 12

## FAN CLUBS

(For information from any of the listed fan clubs enclose a self-addressed, stamped envelope.)

**THE CALIFORNIA ROLLING STONES**
c/o Debbie Kelley
11360 Harvard Drive
Norwalk, Calif.

**LESLIE GORE**
c/o John Beach
1925 E. Glenoaks
Glenoaks, Calif. 91206

**HERMAN'S HERMITS**
c/o Greer Eagleson
9191 Randall Avenue
Whittier, Calif. 90603

**JOEY PAIGE**
c/o Mary Lutes
7311½ Seashore
Newport Beach, Calif.

**PETER & GORDON**
c/o Norma J. Reill
9744 Mango Drive
Fontana, Calif. 92335

**SONNY & CHER**
c/o Barbara Messer
2829 East Walnut
Orange, California

**DICK BIONDI**
c/o Nancy Smith
4427 N. Sierra Madre
Baldwin Park, Calif. 91706

**UNITED BEATLES FANS**
c/o Laura Springer
1151 Brewster Drive
Pomona, Calif.

**BEATLE LUVERS, LTD.**
c/o Barbie Hines
1045 W. Deodar
Oxnard, Calif. 93032

The above information is provided us a service to our readers. Accuracy of the information you receive is the responsibility of the officials of each club.

LESLIE GORE

## Derek Taylor Reports
## THE BYRDS FLY HIGH AND IT'S TIME TO CROW

For the Byrds, the time has come.
The time is now.
Now it is time to say that the Byrds will be the showbusiness sensation of the United States by the fall of this year.
Now it is time to say I was right.
Now it is time to say that I knew I would be right because I had seen it all before. In Manchester, England—long, long ago.
Now listen:
On May 5 of this year the Byrds had a record called "Mr. Tambourine Man" climbing certain local charts. Dave Hun had picked it on KRLA. A man called Jim Dickson who manages the Byrds had visited my office and had murmured that his Byrds were pretty good.
Also, I had seen the Byrds.
So in this KRLA Beat newspaper I wrote the following words:
"The Byrds will, I believe, be No. 1 nationwide with "Mr. Tambourine Man" — their first recording now on general release here.
"I personally think it is a marvelous disc. But then, I am a little prejudiced because I started taking an interest in the group some time before the disc was made.
"Having heard it, however, I am now convinced it has limitless potential. It's different, sympathetic and gentle. It has a plaintive, melodious insistence which means that once having heard it, you recognize it the first few seconds when it is replayed.
"It is very difficult to know how to put the right hit-ingredients into a disc, and there is never a guarantee ever that you will achieve the right mixture. Only the Beatles and Elvis Presley in his hey-day could be sure of automatic Number Ones.
"But there are, I am quite sure, conspicuous hits. The sort of discs which, if you know anything about sounds, you are certain will make it.
"I believe "Mr. Tambourine Man" is in this bracket. And if it doesn't make it, I'll print my picture upside down!"
So that is what I wrote.
And all I want to say now is that I was right—for next week the wonderful Byrds, the fivesome from right here in your own smog-ridden, talent-laden, wayward, sprawling Los Angeles will be Number One in the nation. I will not have to print my picture upside down, although it might be an improvement.
This week the Byrds are Number 2 in "Billboard" magazine. This is the trade newspaper sold and respected worldwide from its New York publishing office.
This week they are Number 3 in "Cashbox" magazine. This is where the Beatles first hit No. 1 with "I Want To Hold Your Hand".

**Also In England**
And without any noise or pandemonium, the Byrds are heading the British Top Five.
So far so good. Wait for the next single. Listen to the album. See the Byrds at Ciro's. Experience the dancing. Marvel at the line outside Ciro's . . . the people who can't get it.
And hear this: the Byrds will fly across the world.

**European Tour**
Because of their English success, the Byrds are now contemplating an early visit to Europe. Already a coast to coast tour is planned for next month—the Byrds are playing in dance halls and theaters and will take with them in their tour-bus a number of their dance-crazed followers.
On July 16 the Byrds visit Miami for a Columbia Records Convention. So, too, do Paul Revere and the Raiders, now well on with their new network TV show "Where the Action Is".
They are booked for 65 of the shows which are to be presented by ABC Television and produced by Dick Clark Productions.

**Other Tidbits**
Dick and Deedee have a European trip planned. And Joe and Eddie return from the East very soon to play concerts in Southern California. Ian Whitcomb is due back in Los Angeles next month.
So much for comings and goings. Now a word or two about ups and downs.
The Everly Brothers became No. 1 on the English charts last week. And about time, too. Tom Jones, who failed with his follow up to "It's Not Unusual", is making headway with "What's New Pussycat?", the flip side of "Once Upon a Time".
Herman's Hermits are moving toward No. 1 again with "Wonderful World".

# KRLA ARCHIVES

## A KRLA BEAT EDITORIAL
### IRRESPONSIBLE RUMORS

The rumor-mongers are at it again.

Their latest contribution — actually broadcast over another radio station which obviously didn't take the trouble to check the facts — speaks of Paul McCartney's "official" engagement to Jane Asher.

According to the slip-shod report in question, Paul made the announcement himself. That's a lot of hooey — the result of an over-active imagination on the part of someone. Paul made no such announcement. You will not find it in any major or responsible publication.

Ordinarily the BEAT could care less what other radio stations or other publications have to say on any subject. They have a right to say whatever they please.

However, freedom of speech does not include the right to mislead the public — whether intentional or the result of lazy reporting.

Eventually people will reach the point where they are so fed up with untruths that they will refuse to believe anything. When and if that should occur, our entire system of communications will have been destroyed.

For every right there is a responsibility. With the right to free speech goes the responsibility for truth and integrity.

##  TIPS TO TEENS

If you have a question you'd like answered in this beauty and fashion corner of the Beat, or a tip you'd like to share with our readers, send your letters to Sheila Davis, c/o The Beat, 6290 Sunset Blvd., Hollywood.

Q: This is an old question, but I'm hoping you'll have a new answer. How can I stop biting my fingernails? I don't even know when I bite them, so how can I quit?
(P. B., Anaheim)

A: If you're not aware of when you bite your nails, you probably do your gnawing when your attention is focused on something like television. Start stopping this habit by having a professional manicure, which will make your hands look too nice to chew on. Then wear gloves when you watch TV or movies.

Q: I need to go on a diet because I'm 15 pounds overweight, but my mother is such a great cook, I can't stand not to eat. My folks think I look fine the way I am.
(F. S., San Fernando)

A: The best way to solve this is to go to your doctor and see if you really are overweight. If he says diet, then do it. Your parents will gladly cooperate if the suggestions comes from him.

Q: I must have tender eyebrows or something, because I about die when I have to pluck them. Is there some way this could be less painful?
(J. L., Westwood)

A: There is a product you spray on that deadens the area around your brows, but I've forgotten what it's called. Ask at the drug store, they'll know. It works great!

Q: I'm sixteen and I don't understand how you go about shading your face with different colors of makeup. I don't even exactly know how to explain it, so I hope you know what I mean.
(O. A., Inglewood)

A: I do know what you mean. Different shades of makeup are used to remove facial shadows, etc. Don't worry about not understanding the process involved. I don't either, and it'll be a few more years before we'll need to.

Q: Please settle an argument. I made a three-tone dress. The top is light yellow, the skirt is kind of a pastel orange and the tie belt is brown. My girlfriend says this is the most horrible color combination she's ever ever heard of. Is it?
(N. C., Santa Monica)

A: The colors you mentioned are harmonious, so you just won the argument. And I think your girlfriend is a stinker.

### WEEKLY HINT

If curlers keep you awake, make rollers out of tightly packed cotton, cover them with wide tape and set your hair the same as always. You can make them any size you want, and they're not the least bit uncomfortable.
(K. D., Los Angeles)

## 'MY LIFE WITH THE BEATLES'
# Beatlemania Grips England

(Editor's Note: This is the third and concluding installment of Derek Taylor's life with the Beatles, first as a newspaperman covering their exciting rise to world fame and later as their press officer.)

The Beatles returned to Manchester in November of that year at the height of Beatlemania and again I was on the scene. Here are some extracts of that report:

"Beatlemania, in its sobbing, throbbing extremities, gripped Manchester last night.

"It captivated the teenagers of the city and far beyond. It drew 5,000 of them inside the Apollo Cinema to share the thumping ecstasy of their electronic excitement.

"It tore half the city's police force — men and women — from normal duties. It totally mobilized the first-aid resources of South Lancashin — men and women, even earnest children.

"At noon in a curiously apprehensive atmosphere, in places far from the Apollo, plans were rehearsed. St. John's paraded their staff with first aid kits. So did the Red Cross.

### Bedlam

"The police were given their final orders. A mobile headquarters — last used in a murder hunt last month — was set up outside the cinema. . . .

"Many girls fainted. Thirty were gently carried out, protesting in their hysteria, forlorn and wretched in an unrequited love for four lads who might have lived next door.

"The stalls were like a nightmare March Fair. No one could remain seated. Clutching at each other, hurling jelly babies at the stage, beating their brows, the youth of Britian's second city surrendered themselves totally.

"It is, quite simply, the ultimate phenomenon of show business."

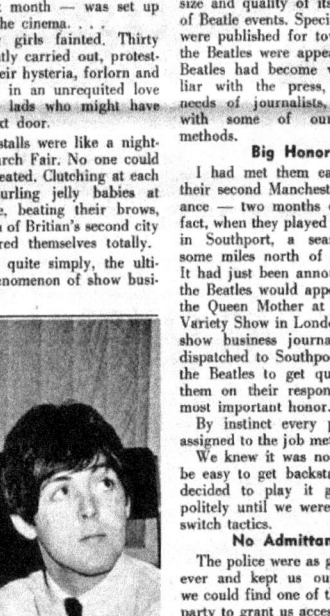

### National Heroes

They were extremely cooperative, envy friendly, and the press was very much in favor of all four of them. There was no question at that time of attempting to knock them. Everyone was in love with all that the Beatles stood for — their gaiety, their honesty, and their enormous commercial value.

Every newspaper by then was boosting its circulation by the size and quality of its coverage of Beatle events. Special editions were published for towns where the Beatles were appearing. The Beatles had become very familiar with the press, with the needs of journalists, and also with some of our strange methods.

### Big Honor

I had met them earlier than their second Manchester appearance — two months earlier, in fact, when they played at a dance in Southport, a seaside town some miles north of Liverpool. It had just been announced that the Beatles would appear before the Queen Mother at the Royal Variety Show in London. All the show business journalists were dispatched to Southport to meet the Beatles to get quotes from them on their response to this most important honor.

By instinct every press man assigned to the job met in a pub. We knew it was not going to be easy to get backstage, so we decided to play it gently and politely until we were forced to switch tactics.

### No Admittance

The police were as gracious as ever and kept us outside until we could find one of the Beatles' party to grant us access.

Finally we got into the Beatles' dressing room, grabbed a few quick quotes before they were due to stage.

But most of us felt we hadn't enough to write a decent story so we returned to the dressing room. This time the door was held firm against us. Neil Aspinall, the Beatles' road manager, said, "I'm sorry, the Beatles leave almost immediately and there's no time."

There was a smaller, older man there and we persuaded him to let us in. He, it seems, was the company manager.

We again hammered on the door and Neil reappeared and said, "I'm awfully sorry but we can't give any more interviews." I pointed to the company manager and said, "He said we can."

Neil muttered, "He has nothing to do with it," and closed the door. I told the company manager, "Neil Aspinall says your word doesn't count," starting a beautiful row between Neil and the company manager.

Because of the diversion caused by the row, we all burst into the Beatles' dressing room and secured our further interviews.

They really were remarkably patient.

But when I met Neil and the Beatles at that second Manchester concert, they pointed at me and said, "Hey . . . you're the one who kicked the door in in Southport." They have good memories.

### Join Beatles

Well, to cut a long story short, I became more and more friendly with them. And when the Daily Express decided to pay a Beatle as a weekly columnist, I asked for George Harrison. Brian Epstein and I negotiated a fee of $300 a week (we had offered $90 but the shrewd Epstein wasn't having that!) and I was assigned to help George to write it.

I traveled to Europe with them and in March of last year, Brian Epstein asked me to help him with his book. While we were completing the taping of interviews for the book, Brian finally invited me to join him as his personal assistant and press and promotions officer for the Beatles.

This was what I had been after for six months, and after a short discussion on salary — in which, I might add, Epstein emerged victorious — I left the Daily Express and journalism for a hot-seat at the center of the biggest show business storm of all time.

### Lasted Nine Months

Nine months later it was all over. Brian Epstein and I — though we remain friendly and share considerable mutual respect — cannot get on together as employer and employee.

I still believe the Beatles to be the best thing in show business and marvelous companions.

Epstein I will always admire very much. They are a magnificent fivesome and let nobody tell you that there is any fifth Beatle other than Brian Epstein.

PAUL and RINGO

# KRLA ARCHIVES

## For Girls Only

**By Sheila Davis**

This column isn't really for girls only. It's for boys only. And this week we're going to be discussing many masculine subjects—such as keeping a diary and sewing.

There, I think we just lost them for good. Fine with me! Now we can talk about them.

Do you know what makes me furious about boys? The icy stares they give a girl if she so much as LOOKS like she's going to giggle. What do boys have against girls having a good time, anyway? You'd think boys never so much as cracked a smile.

Well, I happen to know better. My brother is always inviting his nutty friends over to our house and all they do during their bull sessions (which are certainly aptly named) is laugh themselves silly. Sillier than they already are, that is.

I'll never understand boys. But never let it be said (or thought) that I'm not perfectly willing to learn.

**Style Shifts**

Remember when I told you about the girl who made a beach shift by sewing Beatle bubble gum cards together? Well, I've just seen it topped. Not in originality, but in style. Saw a girl the other day on the beach wearing a white lace shift over a red one-piece bathing suit, and did it look sharp!

I asked her where she bought it and she told me she sewed it herself. In an hour and a half! Some people have all the talent.

Do you keep a diary? I used to, but I'd always forget to write in it, or sometimes I just would not have anything to say. Now I've found an easier way to keep track of where I was when. Our cleaners gave us this big ugly calendar, and my mom was about to hurl in into the garbage can when I grabbed it and ran.

**Calendar Dairy**

Now I write a little note on it every night about what I did, or how I feel at the moment, and it's just great. I'm going to keep doing it and then save all the calendars to look at when I'm real old. About 40 or so.

I had a birthday not long ago, and I got the nicest present I've ever received in my entire life. It only cost a dollar, but I would not take a million of them for it. A close friend of mine (who's just as poverty-stricken as I am) made a scrapbook for me that covered the entire school year.

If your bank account is suffering from similar difficulties, keep this gift idea in mind. A summer scrapbook, starting now and ending when school starts is another fabulous idea, and if anyone would like to make one for me, I'm available!

**Painted Cast**

Talk about loyalty! I was walking down Hollywood Blvd. the other day and I noticed (I couldn't HELP but notice) a girl wearing a cast on her ankle. (She was also wearing a "Pray For Surf" sweatshirt, so I can about imagine what happened.) Only it wasn't just an ordinary cast.

She'd painted it red and pasted Union Jacks all over it. That's such a clever thought, I almost want to go out and break a leg. But not quite!

Do you know what I just can not BEAR? Those very fashionable shoes with the little squatty heels. I must really be out of it, but something about them just turns me off. Does anyone else feel this way, or am I THAT out of it?

**Watch Moms**

Something else I've been meaning to tell you. Do you know why a boy once broke up with me? Because I got too chummy with his mother! Oh, brother, how ridiculous can you get. I suppose he thought she was telling me all kinds of "cute" little things he used to do or something. I'd ask him about it (it's been over a year) but I'm STILL not speaking to him.

Let me see if I have this straight now. Don't get friendly with your boyfriend's mother unless the two of you are engaged (you and your boyfriend, not you and his mother) or he'll never marry you. And do get very friendly with your fiancee's mother or he'll never marry you.

As I once said (about three million times), I will NEVER understand boys!

Also, I will never be able to thank you for all the letters you have been writing me. I know I've said that about three million times, too, but I mean it. I have to stop now, but don't you do the same!

## Guess Who??

**Puzzle Piece # 3**

**HERE IT IS!** Your chance to win tickets to the KRLA Beatle Concert at the Hollywood Bowl. The strange object lurking above is the third portion of the BEAT'S Puzzle Piece Contest. Combine it with the pieces shown in the past two week's issues and see if you can guess who it is. There are ten pieces in all, and we'll continue running one each week until someone guesses the name of our mystery star. The first contestant to guess who it is will win two tickets to the Hollywood Bowl. The next two readers to come up with the right answer will each win one ticket to see the Beatles perform. The fourth place winner will receive four record albums, and winners five through twelve will win a record album by a top favorite. Enter as many times as you like. Send your guesses to KRLA BEAT Puzzle Piece, 6290 Sunset Blvd., Suite 504, Hollywood. A HINT: THE MYSTERY MAN (OR WOMAN) IS **NOT** ONE OF THE BEATLES.

---

## EARN FAB MONEY, PRIZES AS A BEAT REPRESENTATIVE

### FIRST PRIZE!
YOU AND A FRIEND WILL BE GUESTS OF KRLA AT A **BEATLE CONCERT!**
And a Beatle Press Conference!
You will also receive
A Beautiful WRIST WATCH!

### 10 Second Prizes:
**BEAUTIFUL, ENGRAVED WRIST WATCHES!**
(Winners may choose between second and third prizes.)

### 10 Third Prizes:
**AUTOGRAPHED BEATLE ALBUMS!**

**6 STUDENTS IN EACH SCHOOL MAY QUALIFY TO ACCEPT SUBSCRIPTIONS**

## IT'S FUN AND PROFITABLE

The KRLA BEAT is the NATION'S TOP NEWSPAPER for young Americans, and it is NOW ACCEPTING SUBSCRIPTIONS FOR THE FIRST TIME. Now you can become a circulation representative in your school.

HERE'S ALL YOU HAVE TO DO: Send your name, address, telephone number and the school you attend to KRLA BEAT, 1401 S. OAK KNOLL, PASADENA, Calif. But do it fast — first come, first served. We will send you all the necessary information to become a successful KRLA BEAT representative. You will learn handsome profits on each subscription. Earnings are unlimited, because EVERY TEENAGER SHOULD BE A SUBSCRIBER!

AND THERE ARE SPECIAL PRIZES FOR THOSE WHO SELL THE MOST SUBSCRIPTIONS BETWEEN NOW AND JUNE 30th

I would like to be a KRLA BEAT REPRESENTATIVE in ................................................. ☐ Jr. ☐ Sr. High

School in the city of: ...............................................

Please send me additional information and forms for selling subscriptions.

Name................................................................................................................ Age ..............

Address .......................................................................................... City ........................

Phone .......................................................................................... Zip Code ..................

# KRLA ARCHIVES

## FREEDOM FROM HUNGER BENEFIT
## Most Fantastic Show Ever!

PRODUCER JACK GOOD WITH KRLA'S DAVE HULL, CHARLIE O'DONNELL, BOB EUBANKS AND DICK BIONDI.

In those "olden" days when our parents were teenagers, there used to be such things as marathon dances. They're ancient history now. In fact, marathons of any kind are rarely heard of. But one of those rarities did occur on June 6 at the Shrine Auditorium. It was the giant excitement packed Freedom From Hunger Benefit, and it lasted approximately three and a half hours!

Jack Good produced the entire affair in the same style for the tremendously popular "Shindig" television show. Very few introductions, just continuous entertainment.

The fantastic Byrds opened the show with both sides of their new record, "All I really Want To Do" and "I'll Feel A Whole Lot Better". And from then on everything was "go".

Gary and the Playboys (looking sharp in red jackets and black turtle neck sweaters) performed both their hit songs, "This Diamond Ring" and "Count Me In".

Blonde and bubbly, Jackie De-Shannon was tremendous and beautiful, but then she always is. She sang her current smash, "What The World Needs Now Is Love". During the last part of her song, she had everyone join in singing the now familiar words of what has got to be Jackie's biggest hit to date.

Sonny and Cher entertained in that casual yet exciting way for which they are so well noted. Their outfits were terrifically way-out. Sonny wore what looked like a sheep hair vest, made out of about six sheep! Cher wore another wild bell bottom outfit out of her equally wild collection of pants. Anyway they were great sounding too!

Those fabulous Everly Brothers were next on the bill. They are without a doubt one of the best American acts in the entire U.S., or in the entire world for that matter. They appeared several times throughout the evening and sang some of their biggest hits such as "Dream, Dream, Dream" and "Lucille". The two Everlys have influenced many of the top English groups, and after seeing them perform "live" it is certainly easy to see why!

Johnny Cash, the popular Western star, was next up. He sang one of his biggest hits,

EVERLY BROTHERS

"Ring Of Fire", and also several other songs.

The entire "Shindig" crew, including the band, the dancers, the Blossoms, the Wellingtons the Chamber Brothers, and Willy Nelson were on hand the entire evening to perform solos or to back up the other entertainers. The easiest way to describe the whole group is simply to say — they were at their usual "Shindig" best!

Ray Peterson was also there, and he did a really magnificent job of singing "Ebb Tide". It was the best, and most exciting, rendition of the old masterpiece that I have ever heard. What a voice this man has!

The Crickets caused quite a sensation when the light came on them. For two reasons. First off, they are a good sounding group. And secondly, they possess a guitar player named Keith Allison who is a dead look alike for Paul McCartney. The shrieks and screams of "It's Paul" which inevitably greet Keith are unbelievable! Watch out for this group — they're going to go places.

Jody Miller looked like a little doll in a pink chiffon dress, and she is too. She sang her smash hit of "Queen of the House".

Also on the show and doing a great job were the Bitter End Singers, Dick and DeeDee, Jackie and Gayle, Sal Mineo, and the Kingsmen (who did their hit "Louie, Louie" and their

**TURN TO PAGE 10**

SAL MINEO CHATS WITH DICK BIONDI AND CHARLIE O'DONNELL BACKSTAGE.

---

## A RECORD MAKING ANNOUNCEMENT!

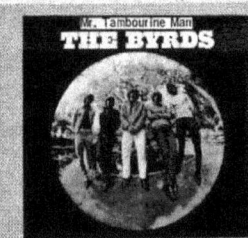

**THE BYRDS Sing Their Smash Hit "Mr. Tambourine Man"**

*Plus* It's No Use — The Bells of Rhymney — I Feel A Whole Lot Better — You Won't Have To Cry — Spanish Harlem Incident — We'll Meet Again — Chimes of Freedom — Don't Doubt Yourself, Baby — Here Without You — I Knew I'd Want You — All I Really Want To Do

**PAUL REVERE AND THE RAIDERS Sing "Oo Poo Pah Doo"**

*Plus* You Can't Sit Down — Money — Louie, Louie — Do You Love Me — Big Boy Pete — Sometimes — Gone — Bad Times — Fever — Time Is On My Side — A Kiss To Remember You By

**CHAD AND JEREMY Sing "Before and After"**

*Plus* Tell Me Baby — Why Should I Care — For Lovin' Me — I'm In Love Again — Little Does She Know — What Do You Want With Me — Say It Isn't True — Fare Thee Well — Can't Get Used To Losing You — Evil Hearted Me

**on COLUMBIA RECORDS**

# KRLA ARCHIVES

## THE BEAT GOES TO THE MOVIES

### "GIRLS ON THE BEACH"

#### by JIM HAMBLIN

"Girls On The Beach", a Paramount Picture, stars those unbelieveable Beach Boys and Noreen Corcoran in a colorful panorama of flesh and singing, sun and sand. It's a good entry for this season's bill of fare.

Made more than a year ago, it has been held on the shelf until now, for the best timed summer release. And in its current run it is something of a bargain, as it is being shown on a triple feature bill in some locations.

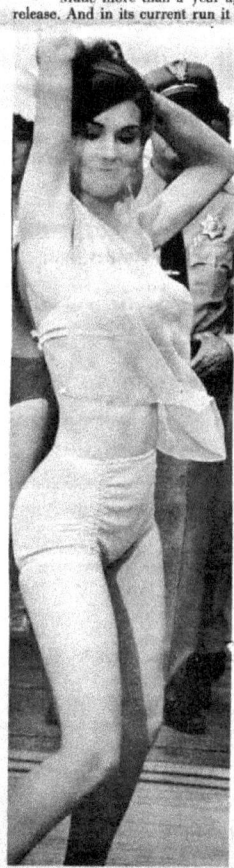

Because it was shot some time ago, the Beach Boys will be singing a couple of older tunes, but the music is fine anyway, and there is pretty little Leslie Gore, who wanders through the film with several numbers of her own.

The plot has something to do with a phony report that THE BEATLES are coming to Beachtown, and the girls' sorority house, thinking the Fab Four are on the way to do a benefit show just for them, get a real promotion campaign underway.

Naturally the BEATLES do not show up, and finally the fellows who started the whole hoax confess, and then things end happily when the gals themselves handle the show.

Aside from some awkward moments brought on by the understandable inexperience of some of the cast, the film is really a lot of fun and is a summer treat—especially if you happen to be a boy!

There is a lovely sea of feminine charm all around, and the Eastman color does justice to them all.

The Crickets appear in the film, with their featured singer Jerry Naylor, now on his own with a contract at Tower Records in Hollywood.

Our favorite is an elaborate surf board that includes what appears to be its own navigation system, and,—if you can believe it—a vintage automobile horn. The belly laughs come when the picture features its own "masked grandma".

"Girls On The Beach" is an unlikely contender for any major awards, but it does entertain the surfers as well as the ho-

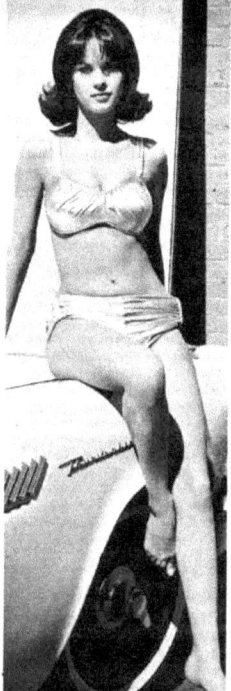

dads with some fun and a lot of music . . . and oh, those girls! What more can be say?
(Reviewed at Paramount Studio Theater in Hollywood.)

**YOU PROBABLY WON'T BELIEVE IT** (above) but there is a logical explanation for the lovely clothes the boys are wearing. Martin West, Aron Kincaid, and Steve Rogers are trying to bail themselves out of trouble with the girls. Below, a happier moment from the colorful film, with Linda Saunders, Jerry Naylor, and Noreen Corcoran in scene from Paramount flick.

# KRLA ARCHIVES

## ON THE BEAT

**By Louise Criscione**

If this doesn't beat everything. *Billy J. Kramer* and *Cilla Black*, in London, were signing autographs for fans in New York! The autograph requests were telephoned to the Africa House in London, Cilla and Billy signed them, they were reproduced, and sent across the ocean by Electrowriter. Pretty wild idea, huh?

The riddle of why *Alan Price* left the *Animals* has finally been resolved by Alan himself. "I can't stand the pressure of the pop world any longer; I've been to see a doctor and I was told the usual thing—mental breakdown and nervous exhaustion unless I gave up the pace. Let's get this clear as well—there was no bad feeling between me and the others." As for the future, Alan just doesn't know. Right now, he is having himself a well-deserved rest.

QUICK ONES: *Brian Jones* bought himself a new sweater which he wore on stage for two shows before someone spotted the price tag still hanging on the back of it . . . *Joey Paige* is getting some nice publicity out of his recent trip to England . . . *Marianne Faithful* likes Femme perfume by Marcel Rochas . . . *Peter Quaife* of the Kinks washes his hair in beer and drys it with a hand-dryer . . . *Gerry Marsden* likes to skin dive in his "holiday haunt" in Anglesey, Wales . . . *The Yardbirds* want to buy a tropical island . . . *Stones* possibly in California in October.

*Ray Davies*, lead singer of the Kinks, is the proud papa of a brand new baby girl, Louise Claire . . . *Sandie Shaw* sketches her own clothes and then has her dressmaker make them up to her design . . . *Bobby Jameson*, an American who lives in England and is trying to make it on the pop scene, wears a black glove on his right hand which he never takes off—reminds him he has a purpose in life . . . Did the *Kinks* really have a fight on-stage?

Never thought this would happen, but when *John Lennon* appeared at the Cannes International Film Festival no one even recognzied him! Without his three side-kicks, John looked just like any other long-haired Englishman.

When *Marianne Faithful* and *Andrew Oldham* parted company (he used to produce all her records), he went out and made a brand new discovery. Her name is *Vashti Bunyan*, and she is a 21 year old ex-art student of Oxford University. Oldham discovered her singing at a London club called the Dark Room.

Vashti has written 18 folk songs, but she chose to make her disc debut with a Jagger/Richard composition, "Some Things Just Stick In Your Mind". You might have heard the song before—Dick and Dee Dee recorded it.

*Brian Jones* says the *Stones* like Southern California better than any other place in the U.S. And as for himself, Brian declares "Los Angeles is definitely my number one place."

Another note on the Stones: If you have a friend in England, ask them to pick up a copy of the *Rolling Stones* new EP, "Got Live If You Want It" for you. It was recorded "live" at the Liverpool Empire and the Manchester Palace. *Andrew Oldham* has this thing about all the Stones' records being different. "That's why this is a 'live' session." It was an attempt to capture the great excitement of the Stones on stage, and it has done just that.

The EP was originally scheduled for release on June 11, but the demand was so tremendous that they were forced to release it early. Some of the cuts might be used on an up-coming LP to be released in America, but then again they may never be released here in the U.S.

WATCH OUT FOR: Some very good new albums—"Herman's Hermits On Tour", "Tom Jones", "This Is New—Righteous Brothers", "Unit Four Plus Two #1", and "Chuck Berry In London".

---

### WAREHOUSE IX
2214 Stoner Avenue
off Olympic in West Los Angeles

**Dancing to Live Name Bands**

Los Angeles' Unique Young Adult Nite Club

Girls 18 — Guys 21

Closed Sundays

---

## 'THE TIGER'

### Tom Jones IS Unusual

Tom Jones, the guy they call "the tiger", was really born Thomas Jones Woodward. He's from a Welsh town called Pontypridd.

Tom says everyone in South Wales is always singing, and he was no exception. "I sang at school, kids' parties, weddings — anywhere. Later on I used to sing on the job when I started working."

Tom was married when he was 16. His wife's name is Milanda, and they have a seven-year old son, Mark.

Tom sang around Wales, but he was getting nowhere. "Now, of course, pop groups are a big thing around Pontypridd. But a few years ago pop acts couldn't get into the clubs there."

**Tried London**

He talked it over with his wife and decided that his only chance of success was to go to London. And so an eager and enthusiastic Tom Jones made his way to the foggy capital city. He auditioned, but nothing happened, and he returned to Wales terribly disappointed.

After some more serious thinking, Tom decided to make the trip again. This time he cut seven sides, but nothing really "happened".

Back in Wales, Tom finally caught up with that elusive lady luck. Gordon Mills, the man who penned "It's Not Unusual", had made a trip to Pontypridd to visit his mother.

**Turning Point**

Mills saw Tom and his group, the Senators, performing in a local club. And that was the turning point in the career of Tom Jones.

Tom liked "It's Not Unusual" the minute he heard it. "When I heard the playback of the demo I knew I must get this song."

The rest, of course, is history. Tom got the record, made a tremendous smash out of it, and is now one of the most sought-after performers in the world.

Tom Jones has come a long long way from Pontypridd, Wales, but "as far as I'm concerned, I'm still Tommy Woodward from down the road."

### BEST QUOTE OF THE WEEK

The *Best Quote of the Week* comes from Peter and Gordon regarding who is the leader on stage.

Peter: "Gordon makes the decisions on stage."

Gordon: "I make most of the mistakes on stage as well! In Japan I sang the verses in the wrong order and Peter sang some other verses from nowhere; it was so funny we just laughed."

---

## SNEAK YOUR WAY INTO BEATLE SHOW

If you weren't able to get tickets to the Beatle concerts at Hollywood Bowl, all is not lost. The KRLA Beat is going to come to your rescue and help you see the concert another way. One of five other ways to be exact!

Are we kidding? Would WE do a thing like THAT? Stop being so suspicious and read our helpful hints!

1. Buy several yards of yellow cotton, cover it with feathers and dress up like a 500 pound canary. The day of the concert, roost cofortably in a tree near the stage. (On a low branch, please.) If you are shortly thereafter hauled off to the nearest cage, don't fret. The experience was "cheep" at half the price.

**Down The Wire**

2. You've all been to Disneyland and seen Tinker Bell "fly" down from the Matterhorn, right? Well, rig up a similar type wire, don a sheet and a pair of wings and float gracefully into the concert.

3. Build a huge plaster statue leaving two peep holes, and a hollow place. Transport the statue to the Bowl, fill it with several boulders, several cokes and yourself. Then have a friend cement you inside. Since no one will be able to lift the statue and cart it away you can peacefully watch the concert while drinking cokes on the rocks. Your friend won't be able to get near the stage to let you out after the concert, but what does that matter? Haven't you always wanted to be plastered?

**Salad Bowl**

4. Locate a large vat and fill it with salad greens. The night of the concert, hide under the vegetables and have the bowl delivered to the Bowl. (Attach a note saying it has been ordered by the Beatles for a backstage snack.) There is a slight possibility that the tomato at the bottom of the salad might be discovered and delivered to the can, "lettuce" hope not.

5. Construct a large rubber kite and fill it with helium. The night of the concert, hold on tight and have a friend fly you over the Bowl. You should be able to see the festivities quite well. If anything goes wrong and something brings you down out of the clouds, don't let anyone give you a lot of hot air.

Well, why are you snarling. We may have ASKED if you thought we'd kid you about something like this, but we did not ANSWER!

Seriously, although this feature was all in fun, all is still not lost if you weren't able to get ticket to the Beatle concerts. You can still win one of our Beatle Ticket contests, and there is another thing in your favor. The Beatles are going to be in Los Angeles for EIGHT WHOLE DAYS! You just never know WHERE you might run into them.

See next issue of the Beat for what to do if you do bump into a Beatle.

### ANOTHER 'BIRDIE'

"Birdies" for Jay and the Ams.

Jay and the Americans have captured roles in a revised version of the hit Broadway show and movie, "Bye Bye Birdie". The new one is entitled "Bye Bye Birdies". It will open August 24 for a two week run at the Tenthouse Theatre in Highland Park, a surburb of Chicago.

On the record scene, Jay and the Americans are doing good business with their new single, "Cara Mia".

The boys also have a new album out called "Blockbusters"

---

**THE BYRDS**
Official National
**FAN CLUB**
Suite 504
6290 Sunset Blvd.
Hollywood

Send $1.00 plus two 5-cent stamps and receive *photos, fact sheets, biographies.* Fun contests each month.

**Free Concerts Planned For Members Only**

Be a chapter president. Enlist ten (10) new members now!

**The BYRDS Are Great**

---

Back issues of the KRLA BEAT are still available, for a limited time. If you've missed an issue of particular interest to you, send 10 cents for each copy wanted, along with a self-addressed stamped envelope to:

KRLA BEAT
Suite 504
6290 Sunset Blvd.
Hollywood, California 90028

**ISSUES AVAILABLE**
4/14 — INTERVIEW WITH JOHN LENNON
4/21 — INTERVIEW WITH PAUL McCARTNEY
4/28 — CHIMP EXCITES TEEN FAIR
5/5 — HERMANIA SPREADS
5/12 — HERE COME THE BEATLES
5/19 — VISIT WITH BEATLES
5/26 — FAB NEW BEATLE QUIZ
6/2 — L.A. ROCKS AS STONES ROLL
6/9 — BEATLES VI
6/16 — BATTLE OF THE BEAT

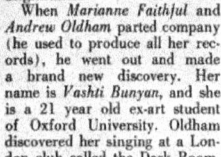

# KRLA ARCHIVES

# SECOND HIT A JINX FOR MOST ARTISTS

Whatever happened to those one-shot wonders who rode in on the second wave of the Beatle invasion? There were plenty of them. They made good records, and they created a lot of hits. But where are they now?

There was one group which really caught the public's fancy, he five-man group with the one-man name, *Manfred Mann*. They had a gigantic hit with "Do Wah Diddy", and it looked as if the Mann would be around for quite awhile. They appeared on "Shindig" and stirred up plenty of excitement both in the studio audience and in the television audience at home.

The Manfred Mann followed up "Do Wah Diddy" with a s l o w e r, altogether different sounding record, "Come Tomorrow". It was a good record which looked like a second chart-topper for the group. But unfortunately it went like a bomb, and the Manfred Mann have not since been heard of in America.

However, they are still doing well in their native England where they currently have a hit in "Oh No, Not My Baby."

### Honeycombs

Then there were the *Honeycombs*. They enjoyed a tremendous hit with "Have I The Right". Besides having a good sound they also possessed a rather unique item — a girl drummer! The b o y s sang, Honey beat on her drums for all she was worth, and it looked like this group had found a home at the top of the charts.

But again the second record failed miserably. The Honeycombs did release a follow-up, but no one heard it, and they soon faded into oblivion.

How about the *Swingin' Blue Jeans?* They're the ones who made "Hippy Hippy Shake" such a big hit. They then proceeded to follow in the path the Honeycombs had carved out. They released a follow-up, nobody heard it, exit the Swingin' Blue Jeans.

### Nashville Teens

There were also the *Nashville Teens*, who had lots of success with their "Tobacco Road". It went soaring up the charts like nobody's business. It was a chance hit, a one in a million shot which just happened to go in a very big way. With their second try, the Teens did not have such luck. On top of this, the Teens got caught in the work permit mess and so were unable to really promote their second sound, "Google Eye".

They are currently attempting a comeback with a cover version of *Marianne Faithful's* "Little Bird". Even though their version was produced by Andrew Oldham (producer of all the Stones' hits) it looks like Marianne, and not the Nashville Teens, is going to come out with the winner.

### George Fame

It's a shame, but it looks as if *George Fame* also fits into this category. His "Yeh Yeh" was one of the really big hits of a few months back. It was an original sound, kind of a mixture of jazz and rock 'n' roll. It caught on in a big way, and it appeared that Georgie was about to start a whole new thing.

But once again, that second record got in his way. "In The Meantime" was the one Georgie chose as a follow-up. It wasn't a half bad record either, but it was not a record the kids were about to buy. So Georgie Fame has left the American scene, at least for the time being.

### Cilla Black

The girls have had their share of trouble too. *Cilla Black*, that redheaded wailer, had a hit going for her in "You're My World". Although the music business is reluctant to allow any feminine voice to roost permanently in the charts, it certainly looked as if Cilla Black had taken up residence and was not about to leave.

To insure that second hit, Brian Epstein got *Paul McCartney* and *Jon Lennon* to pen a follow-up for Cilla. They did as they were told. They came up with a sure-fire hit, "It's For You". And that's not all. They also taped an introduction to the record saying what a fabulous singer Cilla is (and she is too), and that everyone rush out and buy the record. With the official Beatle stamp of approval on it, "It's For You" was bound to go all the way to the top.

But somebody goofed. It did not go anywhere near the top—on most charts, it didn't even go near the bottom!

### Millie Small

And then there was that little Jamacian swinger, *Millie Small*. She had a freak hit with "My Boy Lollipop". It was another one of those cute, catchy, and slightly different sounding records which become huge hits. When Millie tried to capitalize on this sound with her second record "Sweet William", it went like a bomb. Nothing.

Even though Millie has made visits to the States and appeared on national television, she has so far been unable to come up with that all-important second hit.

What is the secret of a successful follow-up? How can one performer make a hit, follow it up with a similar sounding record, and fail to make even a dent in the charts?

### Oddities

First of all, many of these hits (like "My Boy Lollipop") have been freak hits. The time was right and so the record was a smash. If it was released today, or even two months later, it might have been a terrific bomb.

Some records just possess that certain something called "novelty appeal." But novelty wears off. If *Herman* had released nothing but "Mrs. Brown" records, he probably would not be enjoying so much success.

The second reason appears to be in direct opposition to the first one, but actually it is not. In the U.S. if we like a sound we stick with it. If we like an artist's first record, we expect his second record to sound similar. Because the Supremes have stuck with basically the same sound, they have been rewarded with five hits in a row!

### Not In England

On the other hand, in England they try for a different sounding record each time. When the Mann tried to follow-up "Do Wah Diddy" with "Come Tomorrow", U.S. teens turned thumbs down on it but the English teens dug it.

*The Righteous Brothers* tried to follow-up "Lovin' Feeling" with "Just Once In My Life". It worked fine in America, but the English didn't like it at all.

**ANIMALS' ERIC BURDON**

Eric Burdon of the *Animals* had this to say about it: "I think they made it after 'Lovin' Feeling'. It's a typically American habit of producing records with the same sound. This maddens me about American artists who have one big hit and their second record is just the same."

Of course, this can work both ways. The same sound time and time again gets repulsive, but then a radical change on each record can make for bombs instead of hits.

### No Formula

As you have probably guessed by now, there is no tried and sure formula for producing hit records. And that is because there is one factor involved here that is impossible to predict. That factor is the record-buying public. No one yet has been able to figure them out. They change their minds almost hourly.

What they like today they may despise tomorrow.

—Louise Criscione

MANFRED MANN    CILLA BLACK

MILLIE SMALL    GEORGIE FAME

**RIGHTEOUS BROTHERS STAY WITH WINNING SOUND**

**THE RISING SUNS**
ASH GROVE    8162 Melrose Ave., Los Angeles    OL 3-2070
JUNE 29 - JULY 11 — (NO MINIMUM AGE LIMIT)

**THE NASHVILLE TEENS ARE STILL LOOKING**

# KRLA ARCHIVES

## People May Control Their Own Dreams

While the nation's astronauts have been spending their time rolling Heaven all day, a group of mere earthlings have also been devoting their efforts to scientific pursuits.

These particular earthlings aren't missle experts or research chemists. Rather, they are six very inventive teenagers from Alhambra who have been conducting a study in what they call "Dream Science".

If you're thinking this all sounds a lot like science class, think again, for the project was an effort to prove that it's possible to dream the dream of your choice, about the person of your choice!

### Harrison Dream

It all began when the project's "president" couldn't get to sleep one night and began to think of what she'd say to George Harrison if they chanced to meet. She drifted off right in the middle of the imaginary conversation, but woke up the next morning to find the conversation had continued in her dreams!

Together with five of her friends, she began an experiment to see if the miracle could be worked again, and they were finally able to come up with a method that really works.

Here, in their own words, is their "Dream Science" theory.

### Dream Science

*If you want to dream about your favorite star, on a special someone, brushing with Crest should no longer be the last thing you do before going to sleep.*

*Turn out all the lights, completely clear your mind of all thought, and start concentrating on the name of the person you want to dream about. Don't say the name. Think it!*

*After you've slowly repeated the name in your mind at least five times, picture it in giant red letters inside your mind's eye.*

*While all this is going on, remain perfectly still, completely relaxed, and don't open your eyes. Then float into the beginning of the story you'd like to dream. Picture whatever situation you prefer and imagine what you and the person would say to each other, word for word.*

*We've found that by falling asleep in this fashion, you will pick up where you left off once you're asleep, and have the greatest dreams imaginable. It won't work every time, and if you're really worried about something, you'll probably end up dreaming about cleaning out the basement, but it works often enough for us to think we've really discovered something.*

*All we ask is that you don't laugh, and that you let us know if it works for you.*

### Doctor's Approval

All the Beat asks is that you don't go around whispering about our sanity until you've tried "Dream Science", Alhambra style. The project committee members all asked their family doctors if this could hurt anything, and according to the members, they all laughed.

So, since it isn't harmful, sounds like fun and just might work, why not try it?

Don't forget to let us know if it does work so we can pass the news along to the inventors (and rush home and have a go at it ourselves).

Until then, see you in your dreams.

## Most Fantastic Show Ever

*(Continued from Page 6)*

latest, "Do The Climb").

Two of the giants of the entertainment field, Steve Allen and Bob Newhart, also gave of their time to help fight the hunger in the world today. Both men were brilliant in the very best tradition of their profession — making people laugh!

The man who closed the show and who caused a heck of a lot of excitement was P. J. Proby. As a matter of fact, he caused so much excitement that the curtain was brought down prematurely! However, contrary to certain newspaper reports "several hundred teenagers" DID NOT rush the stage, two policemen were NOT "bowled over", and the statement by Harrison Carroll that "even the Beatles never topped the wild hysteria with which fans greeted singer P. J. Proby" is a lot of rubbish. It was nothing, and I do mean NOTHING, like what greeted the Beatles, the Stones, or Gerry and the Pacemakers when each of these groups played L.A.! I know because I saw all four of these shows.

What did happen was this. Several (not several hundred) fans did rush the stage. About ten girls did actually get on the stage. No one was hurt. No one was bowled over. When the girls reached the stage, the show was stopped and the evening's performance was over.

—Louise Criscione

## P. J. Proby Walks Out On "Shindig"

*(Continued from Page 1)*

was dropped immediately, ending the show.

### Hired Shills?

Other entertainers and observers backstage—many of them obviously angered by what they considered poor taste in Proby's performance—insist they saw a member of his group hand money in advance to four girls who later led the rush to the stage as Proby performed.

With many of his bridges blazing behind him, Proby's Shindig caper may have blown his chance to achieve national popularity in the U.S. On the other hand, some believe he will still become as big a sensation over here as he is in Europe.

Reporter Rod Barken spent an entire day with Proby recently. You'll find his interesting interview plus other stories and pictures of this strange and unusual personality elsewhere in this issue.

Whether you like him or dislike him, chances are you will be hearing more about P. J. Proby. But the question is, what will you be hearing?

## At Home With Sonny & Cher

By Louise Criscione

I have just spent the last hour in a beautiful apartment with a huge picture window which overlooks Hollywood. The occupants of this hideaway are Mr. & Mrs. Bono, better known to you as Sonny & Cher.

This talented couple has made a profitable business out of marriage by being two of the most popular entertainers on the scene today. Actually

the whole thing came about as an accident. Sonny was producing records, and occasionally Cher would go along to the sessions.

On one of her visits, a member of the backing group failed to appear. Sonny needed another voice. He turned to Cher. Could she sing? Well, she said she was a pretty fair "shower singer" and could carry a tune. And that's how it all began.

### First Hit

Sometime later, Sonny told Cher he felt she was ready to make a record of her own. He penned "Baby Don't Go", sang harmony with Cher, liked the sound, and so they both recorded the record. The hit-producing singing team of Sonny & Cher was born.

Perhaps the most unique thing about Sonny & Cher is their clothes. Cher always appears in pants, and for a very good reason too—"I dig 'em." She feels more comfortable in them and, in fact, she says she has only two dresses to her name! Besides being more comfortable in pants, Cher confesses that she can't really find any dresses which she likes enough to buy.

Although her closet is almost devoid of dresses, Cher has all kinds of pants. "I especially like bell bottom pants. I've been wearing them for two years now."

Those of you who also dig Sonny & Cher's outfits will be interested to know that they are thinking seriously of opening a dress shop. It will be named "Just You", and will feature exclusives by Sonny & Cher.

### Hates Barbers

As for Sonny, his hair (which is long) is more of a talking piece than his clothes. The reason for his long hair is simple—he just doesn't like barbers (or dentists either!). Sonny says he used to get quite a few stares before the Beatles and company appeared on the scene. Now long hair is pretty commonplace, and the stares have been replaced by accusations of copying the Beatles hair style.

Let's settle this once and for all: Sonny really did have his first. Or at least, he had his before anyone in America ever heard of the Beatles!

Now that we have that straightened out, we can go on to other things, such as the Beatles themselves. Both Sonny & Cher think they are the greatest thing going! And they state with a pretty strong conviction that no one will EVER outdo the Beatles.

As for their favorite singers, Cher's favorites at the moment are *Sandie Shaw* and *Dionne Warwick*. Sonny says: "I don't really have one favorite singer. I go for the records themselves. Right now my favorite is 'Here Comes The Night'."

### Made a Movie

Sonny & Cher have already made one movie, "Beach Ball", which should be released shortly. And they are planning on making another one, "Dr. Rock and Mr. Roll". It's a take-off on Dr. Jekell and Mr. Hyde. You know, everytime this guy hears rock 'n' roll he turns into some kind of a nut. It ought to be a really wild picture!

Sonny & Cher are also planning on doing a tour of England. Cher says: "I can hardly wait to get to London. I'm going to throw out all my old clothes and buy a whole new wardrobe!" Sonny had no comment on Cher's last comment.

Sonny feels the hardest part of the recording business is finding good material. He has solved this problem quite nicely by writing his own.

"Just You" was written by Sonny himself and was one he really liked. Apparently you liked it too because it made it way up into the top ten. It's just about time for another release. So as I left, Sonny was going to sit down and write their next record. If it is anything like "Just You", I can guarantee one thing—it will be the third hit in a row for Sonny & Cher! Hope so anyway. They're nice—I like them.

**DANCING IN THE DARK.** That's what Dave Hull and Singer Joey Paige were doing (with female partners, of course) while attending the Byrds' re-opening at Ciro's. Suddenly Dave and Joey collided on the dance floor. There was a moment of instant recognition, and at that moment our KRLA BEAT photographer caught them.

# KRLA ARCHIVES

## Controversial P. J. Proby-The Pros and Cons

**P. J. PROBY OFFERS A MODEST PREDICTION THAT HE WILL SOON BE RECOGNIZED AS "THE GOD OF POP MUSIC."** Until Television Producer Jack Good befriended him last year with an appearance on a Beatles' show, Proby was unknown. Now England's most popular single performer, last week he walked out on two appearances on "Shindig" because he didn't think Good was treating him with enough recognition and respect as "The top star."

### IN A WHITE ROLLS ROYCE
# HE LAUGHS ON WAY TO BANK

**By Rod Alan Barken**

I have just interviewed England's current Number One single artist. Talking in his hotel suite, sitting by the swimming pool, at parties in the Hollywood hills, driving to Newport to charter a 65-foot yacht for a day's relaxation and at Shindig I asked these questions:

Q. P. J., What Is Your Real Name?
A: James Marcus Smith, but most of my old friends still call me "Jet".

Q: When Were You Born?
A: On November 6, 1938, in Houston, Texas.

Q: How Does It Feel To Return To America — Or More Specifically, Hollywood — As A Star?
A: I don't know . . . great I guess. I was a bit apprehensive. I was here for years and nothing happened.

Q: Are There Ever Any Doubts?
A: Sure, I feel out of my element, that's all. England made me a star, not America.

Q: How Did It All Begin?
A: It began just over seventeen months ago, when Jack Good asked me to come to England to do a Beatle spectacular, a thing called "Around The Beatles".

Q: Why Do You Think You Made It Over There Instead Of Here In The States?
A: The English and European kids are more "hip" than they are over here. They were just more ready for me, that's all.

Q: How Do English Girls Compare With American Girls?
A: American girls are much more on the defensive, and have that attitude that they must 'put you down before you put them down'.

Q: Is There Really Any Difference In People Around The World?
A: No, not really. They're all the same, just using different languages.

Q: How Do You Feel About Entertainers That Want To Go To England Now In Order To Become Successful?
A: A day late and a dollar short.

Q: What Do You Mean By That?
A: It's much harder to make it there, now, because of all of the new talent.

Q: How Much Do You Earn Per Night?
A: One thousand pounds per night, five nights a week. (A pound is equal to about $3.)

Q: What About Your Being Banned From Theaters?
A: That's only in England. I still appear in Sweden and Denmark, and throughout the rest of Europe.

Q: What Exactly Caused This Ban?
A: My pants ripped across the knee and up the thigh, but it
**TURN TO PAGE 12**

## P. J. HAPPY AFTER GIRLS SWARM HIM ON STAGE

"Unbelievable!"
"Those kids were great."
"Utterly fantastic!"

These were the first words spoken by P. J. Proby after he returned to his dressing room backstage, following a dynamic performance that ended almost as soon as it began.

"What a way to return to America," P. J. Proby said, as he pranced merrily about the room, obviously delighted "I love it."

**Successful Return**

In the spirit of frivolity, with people patting him on the back and with teenage fans waiting outside, it was obvious that all doubts that had run through P. J.'s mind prior to the performance were removed. He moved from person to person, shaking hands, laughing, and thoroughly enjoying himself.

Old friends stopped in to say "Congratulations", and to wish him the best.

Photographers and reporters stood outside the dressing room door, waiting for an interview session that would never come.

**Door Barred**

Policemen barred the entrance from the most zealous fans, allowing none to enter.

Inside, Robin Hill of KRLA snapped the only photographs of P. J. in his relaxed poses.

It was a grand reunion for P. J. Proby and his parents, Mr. and Mrs. Smith, of Santa Barbara, who came to see the show. P. J. joked with his younger brother and sister, then bid farewell as road managers completed escape plans, and the subsequent ride back to the hotel.

The show was over.

## Proby Angers Some With Crude Antics

"I can't believe that teenagers actually think this is talent," flatly declared one woman, as she dragged her 15-year-old daughter out of the Shrine Auditorium during the middle of P. J. Proby's act.

"His hip-shaking movements are the most suggestive and sensuous I've ever seen. No child of mine belong in this atmosphere," said an irate father whose teenage girl had rushed onto the stage, hugging and kissing England's most controversial and sensational entertainer.

In the wings off stage, a police officer who had guarded the Beatles at The Hollywood Bowl, stated, "Is he kidding? I don't believe it. That man can't be for real! If that's talent . . . you can forget it."

So excited P. J. Proby, one of the world's highest-paid young performers, from the stage of KRLA's Freedom From Hunger Show. Teenagers and adults alike stood momentarily shocked from the scene they had just witnessed.

One 13-year-old girl was in tears over him. "He's so great. He's greater than the Beatles, even if he doesn't really come from England."

"I think I love him," said another.

Something new has been added to the world of American show business.

P. J. Proby.

It remains to be seen whether this will prove to be a blight or a blessing.

**THE SPATS**

"ATTRACTION FOR"
SHOWS-DANCES
FAN CLUB:
P.O. Box 12
Stanton, Calif.
Tel. (714) 539-5880

---

**THE ARROWS**
"BABY RUTH"
b/w "FOUR LEAF CLOVER"

---

**23 SKIDOO**
Dancing to Live Name Bands
2116 Westwood Blvd., West Los Angeles
Girls 18, Guys 21
Closed Mondays

# KRLA ARCHIVES

## KRLA TUNEDEX

**#1 RED HOT**

| This Week | Last Week | | |
|---|---|---|---|
| 1. | 9. | SATISFACTION | Rolling Stones |
| 2. | 1. | I CAN'T HELP MYSELF | The Four Tops |
| 3. | 3. | WHAT THE WORLD NEEDS NOW IS LOVE | Jackie De Shannon |
| 4. | 2. | WOOLY BULLY | Sam The Sham & The Pharaohs |
| 5. | 5. | BACK IN MY ARMS AGAIN | The Supremes |
| 6. | 4. | SHAKIN ALL OVER | Guess Who? |
| 7. | 6. | HELP ME RHONDA | The Beach Boys |
| 8. | 7. | MR. TAMBOURINE MAN | The Byrds |
| 9. | 10. | JUST YOU | Sonny & Cher |
| 10. | 8. | HERE COMES THE NIGHT | Them |
| 11. | 13. | GOOD LOVIN' | The Olympics |
| 12. | 12. | YOU TURN ME ON | Ian Whitcomb & Bluesville |
| 13. | 11. | CRYING IN THE CHAPEL | Elvis Presley |
| 14. | 14. | FOR YOUR LOVE | The Yardbirds |
| 15. | 17. | OOH BABY BABY | The Miracles |
| 16. | 31. | LAURIE | Dickie Lee |
| 17. | 28. | WONDERFUL WORLD | Herman's Hermits |
| 18. | 20. | THE LAST TIME / PLAY WITH FIRE | The Rolling Stones |
| 19. | 25. | WHITTIER BOULEVARD | The Midnighters |
| 20. | 37. | ONCE UPON A TIME | Tom Jones |
| 21. | 32. | HUSH, HUSH, SWEET CHARLOTTE | Patti Page |
| 22. | 21. | GOODBYE, SO LONG | Ike and Tina Turner |
| 23. | 36. | THIS LITTLE BIRD | Marianne Faithfull |
| 24. | 18. | CATCH THE WIND | Donovan |
| 25. | 27. | YOU REALLY KNOW HOW TO HURT A GUY | Jan & Dean |
| 26. | 15. | TICKET TO RIDE | The Beatles |
| 27. | 19. | JUST ONCE IN MY LIFE | The Righteous Brothers |
| 28. | 24. | BRING IT ON HOME TO ME | The Animals |
| 29. | 46. | I'M A FOOL | Dino, Desi & Billy |
| 30. | 38. | SEVENTH SON | Johnny Rivers |
| 31. | 52. | YES, I'M READY | Barbara Mason |
| 32. | 40. | TRAINS AND BOATS AND PLANES | Billy J. Kramer |
| 33. | 34. | SAD GIRL | The Gallahads |
| 34. | 42. | SUNSHINE, LOLLIPOPS & ROSES | Lesley Gore |
| 35. | 41. | BEFORE & AFTER | Chad & Jeremy |
| 36. | 51. | THE DIP | The Whispers |
| 37. | 45. | GIVE US YOUR BLESSING | The Shangri Las |
| 38. | 43. | FROM THE BOTTOM OF MY HEART | The Moody Blues |
| 39. | 44. | I DO | The Marvelows |
| 40. | 47. | I LIKE IT LIKE THAT | The Dave Clark Five |

**SOUTHERN CALIFORNIA'S MOST ACCURATE RECORD SURVEY — BASED ON RETAIL SALES FIGURES**

KRLA BEAT
6290 Sunset, No. 504
Hollywood, Cal. 90028

U.S. Postage BULK RATE PAID Permit No. 25497 Los Angeles California

If you were a KRLA BEAT subscriber your name and address would be printed here and you would receive your copy at home, saving 40%.

### BRITISH TOP TEN
1. THE PRICE OF LOVE — Everly Brothers
2. KING OF THE ROAD — Roger Miller
3. LONG LIVE LOVE — Sandie Shaw
4. THIS LITTLE BIRD — Marianne Faithful
5. THE CLAPPING SONG — Rockin' Berries
7. TRAINS AND BOATS AND PLANES — Burt Bacharach
8. CRYING IN THE CHAPEL — Elvis Presley
9. TICKET TO RIDE — The Beatles
10. MARIE — The Bachelors

## Proby Says He's Not Vulgar; Just Doing What Elvis Did

(Continued from Page 11) wasn't obscene. I use the same style of stage presence that made Elvis so popular, but in a different vein, that's all.

Q: *Do You Mind All Of The Gossip And Talk About Your Act?*
A: Let them talk all they want, I still drive to the Bank of England in a white Rolls Royce.

Q: *Where Do You Live In England?*
A: In London, near Chelsea. I have a four-story home.

Q: *Do You Socialize A Lot?*
A: Sure. That's half the fun of being an entertainer. But I don't go out of my way to find fun. It just seems to find me.

Q: *What Other Entertainers Do You Mix With?*
A: None. Occasionally I'll run into The Beatles at The Ad Lib, and we'll sit around and talk, but as a rule I travel alone.

Q: *What Do You Think Of The Beatles?*
A: They're terrific, absolutely fantastic.

Q: *How Do You Think They Compare With The Rolling Stones?*
A: With WHO?

Q: *Who Is Your Favorite American Singer?*
A: No single favorite, I suppose. I like Roy Orbison, Gene Pitney and Ray Petersen. The Beach Boys, too, because they have a very good mechanical sound on their recordings.

Q: *How About Radio? Do The British Have The Ability To Match Ours?*
A: Oh, yes. I think that England's radio will be just like ours within ten years.

Q: *How About Your Hair?*
A: My hair? What hair? ... Oh, this. What about it?

Q: *Do YOU Like It That Long?*
A: Yes, and so does my bankbook.

Q: *About Your Torn Pants: How Did That Happen?*
A: I had bought eight outfits from the same tailor, all cut to exactly the same size. When one ripped, I knew that they all would.

Q: *What Has Been The Greatest To Your Career?*
A: Obviously it was Jack Good. That man has been greater to me than anyone I've ever met. He treated me wonderfully when I was nobody, and I'll do anything I can to repay him.

Q: *Your Promotion Campaign In England Closely Resembles That Of The Rolling Stones. Do You Know Why?*
A: First of all, let me tell you that there has never been a promotion "campaign" for me. The Rolling Stones used the idea "Would you let your daughter date a Rolling Stone?" The British press picked up the theme for me, only they said "Would you let your daughter see a P. J. Proby concert?"

Q: *Do You Think That You're Going To Be As Big In America As You Are In England?*
A: Maybe. I certainly hope so.

Q: *What Are Your Immediate Plans After You Leave The States?*
A: I'm to do a movie that's to be made into two versions; one for America and one for Europe.

Q: *Have You Ever Acted Before?*
A: Are you joking? My entire routine on stage is acting. Seriously though, I once did try and act, but it was a colossal joke. I used to go into Schwabbs Pharmacy, here in Hollywood, dressed just like James Dean. A red jacket, levi's, sloppy hair. One day I saw three other 'James Deans' and said to myself, "Forget it!"

Q: *Where Do You Eventually Hope To Go Later In Life?*
A: To the top if I can. Someday I suppose I'll move out of the teenage idiom, and into the adult world like Bobby Darin did.

## Stones Lead "Battle" Vote

The first round goes to the Rolling Stones!

Mick Jagger & Co. have taken an early lead over the Beatles in the BEAT'S first weekly "Battle of the Beat" poll. Fifty-eight per cent of those answering the questionnaire in last week's issue favored the Stones, with the remainder voting for John, Paul, George and Ringo.

With the possible exception of the Byrds, the Rolling Stones appear to be the hottest thing going at present. Their latest record, "Satisfaction", has been the fastest-climbing disc on the KRLA Tunedex.

But loyal Beatle fans insist that the Liverpool quartet is actually in a class by itself and that the Beatles' popularity will again skyrocket out of sight as the date approaches for the American tour and release of their second movie.

Beatlemaniacs also point out that response for tickets to the Beatles' Hollywood Bowl concert this year was just as fantastically heavy as it was last year, when every available seat was purchased within three hours.

We'll continue the poll for the next few weeks, so you still have time to help us prove which group is the most popular. Will the Beatles bounce back, or will the Rolling Stones continue to lead?

Whatever your choice, give your favorites a boost by voting for them on a postcard or filling out the form below.

Round two is coming up. Don't let them down.

**CASEY'S QUIZ ANSWER**
(Don't peek unless you've read the question elsewhere in the BEAT) GARY LEWIS.

# KRLA BEAT

Volume 1, No. 17    Los Angeles, California    Ten Cents    June 30, 1965

# PROBY FIRED!

"I WALKED OUT ON SHINDIG BECAUSE I'M DISGUSTED. THEY HAD PROMISED TO FEATURE ME AS THE TOP STAR."
— Proby

"LIES, LIES . . . HE DIDN'T WALK OUT. WE FIRED HIM BECAUSE HE WAS UNMANAGEABLE."
— Good

Did pants-splitting P. J. Proby really quit "Shindig" or did the television people become fed up with his arrogant demands and boot him out instead?

Roaring with mock indignation, Producer Jack Good charged that Proby didn't walk out but was fired because "he's unmanageable and wouldn't listen to reason".

Reading his one-time protege's remarks about the incident in last week's BEAT, Good appeared both amused and indignant.

"Lies, lies from beginning to end," he shouted. "Proby did not walk out on us—we fired him."

After taping the first of three scheduled shows on "Shindig", the American entertainer who has become England's number one single attraction abruptly left the studio during final rehearsals for the second program.

### Proby's Story

He later claimed that he walked out because Good broke an agreement and failed to feature him as the top star on the programs. Proby also stated that he and Good were not speaking to each other, even though the celebrated English producer had been a close friend since giving him the break which enabled him to become a success in England.

But Good tells a different story. He says P. J. demanded to do the opening and closing numbers of each "Shindig" show plus three numbers in the middle portion.

"That man must be out of his mind," Good told the Beat. "This isn't a spotlight show and not even the Beatles or Roll-

**TURN TO PAGE 3**

## INSIDE THE BEAT ▷

KING ELVIS REGAINING HIS CROWN
BEATLES BLASTED BY BRITISH HEROES
EDITORIAL — "PROBE MUST REFORM"
A NEW LOOK FOR PAUL — WOW!
BEATLES TRIM STONES' LEAD
CHAD and JEREMY RENT HOLLYWOOD LAIR

Peter and Gordon, Unit 4 and 2,
Dave Clark, Byrds,
Dick Clark, Derek Taylor,
Casey Kasem, Dave Hull,
Free Beatle Tickets, Picture Puzzle,
Beatle Quiz

# KRLA ARCHIVES

# P. J. PROBY INSPIRES HEATED EMOTIONS

## 'I Love Him' Sobs Teen - - - Others Want Him Banned

*By Louise Criscione*

Be aware that there is a sensation on the scene. His name is P. J. Proby, and the reason I call him a sensation is simple — he excites people. No one can be blase about Proby, they either love him or they hate him.

For his every good point, there seems to exist an equally bad point. He has been tabbed the greatest performer on the pop scene — he has been labeled obscene and lewd. He has drawn capacity houses — yet some of his tours have failed miserably. He has made hit records in England and he has had the dubious honor of being banned from British television as well as from British theaters.

Let's probe a little deeper into this man they call P. J. Let's find out what people really think about him. Let's hear the ringing compliments and the stinging criticisms.

### Teenage Reaction

In discussing Proby, the best place to start is with the teenagers themselves — the ones who actually pay money to see him perform — because it is they who, in the end, will either make him a star or doom him to obscurity.

Miss Mal Dale, a 15 year old Liverpool girl, had this to say after witnessing a Proby performance: "What can you say about him except I never cried so much in all my life and I don't know why. His suit was bright blue velvet and it was dead tight."

Another 15 year old, Janet Griffiths, was considerably more constrained after viewing Proby. "He was okay, but he kept dashing across the stage and sitting down on the stage which spoilt his act a bit, although the other girls didn't mind. They were too busy screaming and throwing shoes onto the stage."

### Shrine Show

Proby's antics at the Shrine Auditorium caused the curtain to ring down early. Sitting out front during the entire show, I caught some pretty choice comments concerning P. J. They ran the gamut from "Isn't he tough? I love him" to "He's repulsive. I hate him."

Also overheard:

"Those kind of bumps and grinds are not even found in strip joints."

"He's unbelievable — I just don't believe it."

"He's fantastic!"

"I don't dig him."

His controversial on-stage performance has cause P. J. a lot of trouble. On a tour of England, his pants split during an evening's show. The theater manager immediately stopped Proby's act. He was branded obscene, and he was banned from British television as well as from a certain chain of British theaters.

### Pants Splitting

Concerning the pants-splitting incident, P. J. says: "They just split. They were too tight. I would not be so darn crude as to stand on a stage and rip off my pants. I'm an act. I've an ego. Do people think I'm some kind of nut who does a striptease to pop music? Man, I tell you if I was, I'd want a lot more money than I was being paid!"

Dusty Springfield has not seen Proby in action but she feels that "what P. J. does, I believe, doesn't go beyond any reasonable bounds of decency, and he hasn't done anything disgusting. He's probably doing it tongue-in-cheek, anyway. It sounded very funny to me."

As a matter of principle, most performers felt the ban should never have been placed on Proby. John Lennon: "The Proby business is terrible. TV should not be able to rule a bloke like that — especially when he's popular. It's up to the public to decide if he should be banned and I don't believe the public wants him banned."

### Tom Jones

Tom Jones, a Proby rival, agrees with Lennon. "Nobody should be actually banned from TV. I can't understand the stupid TV attitude."

Others, however, felt the ban was certainly justified. Elkie Brooks was among that number. "As far as I'm concerned, keep Proby off TV. Why should we have such a diabolical act? I just can't stand P. J. Proby."

Petitions were signed, letters were written, and eventually the television ban on Proby was lifted. In his native America, Proby has had no such trouble. Of course, he has had no such success here either.

It is completely true that P. J. Proby is currently the biggest single act in England. He has a massive following of loyal fans. George Roberts is one of them.

"In my opinion," he says "P. J. Proby is a fantastic showman with a vocal range that comes second only to Lennon and McCartney in this country (Britain). P. J. Proby came to this county to collect antiques; if he must go he might as well take this island with him."

### Financial Failure

Yet despite this massive following, Proby does not always fill the house. Mervyn Conn, who arranged a Proby tour which ended in financial disaster, had this to say: "Attendances were terrible. I've lost a lot of money. I never want to hear the name Proby again."

During Proby's absence from the pop scene, necessitated by the ban and an attack of influenza and laryngitis, rumors flew fast and furious that Tom Jones was out to take Proby's place, along with Proby's fans.

Apparently Tom did give the subject some thought. "Could I take over from Proby? I would like to. In a few months? I wouldn't like to say. I think he has a great voice, but he overdoes things a bit!"

Proby shot back with an accusation that Tom Jones was merely copying him. But Jones is not a man to be put down easily — he answered back in an open letter to Proby:

"Dear Jim: (Proby's real name)

Thank you very much for the criticism. Although we have never met, I have always admired you as a performer.

As far as copying you goes, I have just heard that James Brown has begun to imitate your act. But I certainly don't go out to do so.

(signed) Tom Jones

P.S. I can also recommend a good tailor."

P. J. Proby is not the least bit concerned about his critics. "The people who came down on me about the striptease are going to need me in the end. I warned them. I'm the greatest."

To which Paul McCartney replied: "He's fantastic. He really believes he's the greatest. We must tell him sometime."

## UNIT-FOUR HAS ANOTHER COMER

Just as "Concrete and Clay" is falling off the charts the Unit Four Plus Two have come up with a brand new one, "You've Never Been In Love Like This Before".

Tommy Moulter, lead singer, had this to say about their new record: "We all think it's better than 'Concrete'. It's in the Unit Four Plus Two style—harmonies, etc.—but it's completely different from 'Concrete', with a powerful middle eight."

There is a definite reason for the change of sound. According to drummer, Hugh "Pigmy" Halliday: "We purposely made this record completely different so that nobody could say we were cashing in on 'Concrete'."

The cowbell, prominently featured in "Concrete" is still in evidence in their new one. Hugh gives us the reason why. "It fitted so well we just had to keep it."

Will the Unit Four Plus Two be paying Statesiders a visit in the near future? "We'd love to go to the U.S." say both Tommy and Hugh. For sure, they will play the Paramount Theatre in New York for two weeks in August, but as of now they have no plans to visit Los Angeles.

## A KRLA BEAT EDITORIAL
## RULE or RUIN

When it comes to trends, what happens in the Los Angeles area is usually a pretty good indication of what is going to happen throughout the country. And if P. J. Proby's wild reception at the recent KRLA "Freedom From Hunger" show is any indication, he may well follow up his boast to conquer America as he has already conquered England.

But in his immodest quest to become the "God of Pop Music", the British star from America appears on the road to "rule or ruin". At present the teenage world is no longer a real "problem" to parents. Adults might not see eye to eye with us, but they have at least loosened the reins and let us enjoy our activities. And rightly so. It's been a long time since there has been anything controversial enough to cause a parental revolt.

Teenagers have worked hard to make our music and stars acceptable in the eyes of our parents. So have our favorites. Elvis Presley is just one of many who have been wise enough to tone it down to a dull and pleasant roar.

But if the present Proby becomes the next national craze, look out. Such crude and vulgar stage antics as he has displayed in the past can quickly undo all of this. The teenage image of "kooky" but healthy fun will be shattered, and the reins will tighten again.

This doesn't have to happen. If P. J. does become popular in this country we're hoping he won't LET it happen. He's handsome and has a wonderful voice. He has all the qualifications necessary to become a star in America without making a public spectacle of himself and of us

There are only three choices: (1) Proby changes, (2) We change our own lives, lowering our standards to his, or (3) We ignore him, leaving P. J. to do his suggestive routines before a mirror with an audience of one.

Which will it be?

## Fan Clubs

(For information from any of the listed fan clubs enclose a self-addressed, stamped envelope.)

**PETER & GORDON**
c/o Patti & Cathi
22126 Linda Drive
Torrance, Calif. 90503

**HERMAN'S HERMITS**
c/o Sandi & Shar
21722 Anza Avenue
Torrance, Calif. 90503

**BEAU BRUMMELS**
c/o Linda Shibata
4420 Greentree Drive
Sacramento, Calif. 95823

**LESLIE GORE**
c/o John Beach
1925 E. Glenoaks
Glenoaks, Calif. 91206

**BEATLE LUVERS, LTD.**
c/o Barbie Hines
1045 W. Deodar
Oxnard, Calif. 93032

The above information is provided as a service to our readers. Accuracy of the information you receive is the responsibility of the officials of each club.

**Raise Money For Your Club**

Want to raise extra money for your club treasury? You could easily make several hundred dollars.

Write to: Fan Club Funds, KRLA, Sunset-Vine Tower, Suite 504, Hollywood, California — 90028.

# KRLA ARCHIVES

## ...And Then It Happened

BACKSTAGE AT "SHINDIG," P. J. Proby clowns around with Dick and DeeDee and Gerry Marsden. A short time later came the now-famous Proby-Good blowup. Dick, who had just signed himself and his partner for four more "Shindig" shows, wound up going to the hospital for a throat operation instead. Only DeeDee and Gerry seem to have escaped the jinx that struck that day.

## GOOD SAYS P. J. WAS FIRED

PETER and GORDON had the last laugh. Many in the music world predicted their popularity had ended, but their "True Love Ways" was an instant smash in both England and the U.S.

### CASEY'S QUIZ
#### By CASEY KASEM

Does a group comprised of a mortician, three college students and a shoe salesman have a chance at becoming a number one singing attraction? This group answered that question by doing just that!

They worked together in the New York area for six months before finally deciding that they were ready to go out and look for a recording contract. They found it, with United Artists records, in one single day! All members of the group, with the exception of one, are over six feet.

The group is noted for its flair in comedy as well as its great sound. (ANSWER ON PAGE 12)

(Continued from Page 1)
ing Stones did that much."

As for Proby's statement that the two were not speaking, Good declared, "Of course I'll speak to Proby — anytime he cares to talk to *me*."

### Still Likes Him

But while roasting Proby for his actions and statements concerning "Shindig", Good made it clear that he still likes the controversial entertainer and has great respect for his ability.

"Proby is still a great, great friend of a great talent," he said. "It's just that when it comes to a weekly television show, he is unmanageable.

But others on the "Shindig" staff voiced open dislike for the Texan, who was banned from British television after splitting his skin-tight velvet pants on a number of occasions while cavorting about the stage during a concert tour.

An American Broadcasting Company official told the BEAT, "I'm surprised that Proby gets along with himself — much less with other people."

He then quickly added, "On second thought, he obviously gets along very well with himself."

Proby, who was struggling as an unknown entertainer in this country before Good discovered him and scheduled him on a "Beatles" television show in England, predicts that he will soon be recognized as "The God of Pop Music".

This week Good had a final comment concerning the cocky entertainer's antics on stage.

"The man actually has talent," he declared. "He doesn't really have to do a strip-tease act on stage if he would just use his ability."

The Proby-Good blowup came during Good's final week as producer of Shindig. The highly-acclaimed trail-blazer has resigned from the program and is returning to England to develop other shows.

## Derek Taylor Reports
## BEATLES' AWARDS GOOD FOR ALL ENTERTAINERS

So, the only thing wrong with the Beatles' awards is that Brian Epstein should have been honored as well.

So far as I know, this is the first time in the history of show-business that a pop musician has been formally acknowledged by the British Establishment.

It's good for the whole entertainment industry. It doesn't matter that a couple of medals have been returned by people who still derive some macabre sense of vanity from their role in the war. I note with interest that one of the men who sent his medal back had received his honor for deciding who should, or should not be called up for active service.

Seems to me he had some good job during the war.

Enough of that. As I keep saying. The Beatles are now solidly established in the history books. Deservedly.

Great though the Rolling Stones are in show-business terms, I can't see how anyone could rationally equate them with the Beatles.

### Dick Has Operation

Dick St. John, brilliant male half of the enchanting Dick and DeeDee duo, is to be laid off for six weeks because of throat trouble. By the time you read this, he will have had a minor operation. Now follows three weeks of silence. It's a great shame because the attractive pair will miss two "Shindigs" and have had to postpone their European tour. They now cross the Atlantic in October instead of July.

The Standells are now busy rehearsing for their next single release. They deserve good material because they are an excellent group — pledged to solid rock 'n' roll. R & R remains the foundation-stone of commercial pop music.

Paul Revere and the Raiders enter the second month of filming their 65 Dick Clark's "Where the Action Is" — the network daily afternoon series due to be aired by ABC-TV later this month.

The group was a sensation once again in Portland — their home — at the Teen Fair. Their reputation should be consolidated coast to coast when "Where the Action Is" becomes established.

### Naylor Recording

Jerry Naylor — with 30-piece band and the talent of the brilliant and seasoned arranger, Ernie Freeman, behind him — is recording again soon.

Jerry is fortunate, not only in Freeman and the size of the musical line-up, but also in that he works for Tower Records, a powerful, pushing Capitol subsidiary.

The Byrds, by the way, made it to No. 1 in the U.S. Enough said. Except that . . . just let anyone try and stop them now.

Joe and Eddie are back in the West after their hard-driving promotional tour. They are due to record again very soon for Crescendo — another label which maintains a close and highly personal relationship with its artists.

I often wonder, by the way, whether it's better for an artist to have the massive resources and reputation of a big corporation behind him rather than the precise, single-minded endeavors of the small company.

Personally, I prefer the little man.

### Mersey Mate

"Townie" is the name an Englishman gives to a person born in the same area as himself. I met a young Birkenhead lad this week called Peter Sweeney, Age 20.

Peter — his stage name is Peter Flemying — came over here from Birkenhead (which is just across the Mersey from Liverpool) last year. He was a steel worker but when he saw the scene here, he decided to become a singer and composer.

He has hair all over the place and all the dry, out-going wit of the Merseysider. He has written a song for a New York friend of his called Jack Eden, 22 — now a singer in these parts.

He has appeared on "9th Street West" on TV, at the Palladium in Los Angeles, and the Teen Beat Club in Vegas. This last place is a swinging spot for young adults, highly organized and very attractive with its own TV show.

Jack's first recording — on the Corsair label — of a Peter Flemying song is "So In Love With You."

In the shadows behind the blinding lights, the neon, the chance successes and fame of those who have it made, are many stories of patience.

### Need A Name

There's a very good group playing at Los Angeles' "Prevue Club" in Inglewood. They're a foursome — Beatle line-up plus piano — currently called Sky Saxon and the Savages. But they're not happy with the name and are now toying with "Saxon and the Celts," having resisted the urge to call themselves "The Earls of England." The group has everything going for them — talent, drive and determination — except a name. They want a simple, straight-forward, hip new name. Any offers?

So, Presley's on top in England, and last week it was the Everly Brothers. The three of them are great pop artists — some say the greatest. But it seems to me there must be quite a slump in England when record buyers return to yesterday's idols.

Proby, the party's over.

# KRLA ARCHIVES

**CHARLIE WATTS and MICK JAGGER** of the Rolling Stones with George Sherlock, Tower Records' now-famous "Under Assistant West Coast Promotion Man."

INSPIRATION FOR A SONG

## Meet Stones' Promo Man

Songs have been written about every subject in the world, but the Rolling Stones probably set a precedent when they wrote and recorded a song about a record promotion man.

The song is "I Am The Under-Assistant West Coast Promotion Man," the flip side of their current number one smash, "Satisfaction."

The promotion man is George Sherlock, West Coast sales-promotion manager for Tower Records and former West Coast promotion for London Records.

Behind the unusual title lies an unusual story.

George became friends with the Stones when they made their first appearance in this country in Southern California during the spring of '64, where their initial hit, "Not Fade Away" first broke.

### Surfer Type

Seems that the Stones thought George epitomized what they had always pictured as the typical promotor of "West Coast Surfin' Sounds." They ribbed him constantly about "makin' it down to Malibu with your surfboard" —or "Where do you keep your promo records, George, in your woody wagon?" They even nicknamed him "Surfer Baby"—in their inimitable London accent.

George had a reunion with the Stones during a recent appearance in Fresno. At that time, he thought the Stones were "putting him on" about recording a song about him.

He didn't believe them until Tower's Ian Whitcomb sent him from England a copy of Andy Oldham's (The Stones' producer) column in the Music Echo, reporting the actual recording of the number.

## Learn To Talk Like A Bloody Englishman

Do you ever get tired of being the same old rational person? Don't you wish you could do something *irrational*? Like not being you any more? Like being English, maybe?

Of course you do! Of course you'd like to go round convincing everyone you're straight from the shores of Great (and how) Britain.

Well, here's how to do exactly that. Now don't go about saying we've never done you any favors!

1. Develope an English accent. Say claws instead of class and cawn't instead of can't. Also say bean instead of been, except when you're talking about the last time you were in London. People might suspect there's something phony about you if you sit around and reminisce about the last time you heard Big Bean striking the hour.

### Family Phrases

2. Always refer to football as rugby, baseball as cricket, and start calling your folks mum and daddy. They'll be very pleased by the change because they were secretly getting awful sick of you calling them Florence and Fatso.

3. Talk constantly about your important friends "back home". You know, Liz and Phil, Marg and Tony, the Queen Mum, Bonnie Prince Chuck, etc. Keep right on talking until the British Consulate sends over a guy with a net.

4. The next time you go to a restaurant with your friends, impress them by ordering kidney pie. Chances are they won't have it and you'll have to settle for something a little less nauseating . . . er . . . delicious. If they *do* have it, you've *had* it!

### Monicle

5. Buy yourself a monicle and learn to wear it. Follow these helpful instructions.

a. Go to your optometrists and say "I wish a monicle, please".

b. Allow your optometrist to lie there on the floor until he stops giggling. Then help him up.

c. Repeat your original demand and insist he provide you with the object of your affectations.

d. When the monicle is in hand, try it on and admire your new look.

e. When the monicle has crashed to the floor for the 13th or 14th time, secure aid from your optometrist. Ask him what you should do with the monicle.

f. After he tells you, never SPEAK to your optometrist AGAIN!

Seriously (folks), keep watching the BEAT for our forthcoming series on how to get to England for practically nothing and how to live there forever on even less!

---

# A RECORD MAKING ANNOUNCEMENT!

THE BYRDS Sing Their Smash Hit "Mr. Tambourine Man"

*Plus* It's No Use — The Bells of Rhymney — I Feel A Whole Lot Better — You Won't Have To Cry — Spanish Harlem Incident — We'll Meet Again — Chimes of Freedom — Don't Doubt Yourself, Baby — Here Without You — I Knew I'd Want You — All I Really Want To Do

PAUL REVERE AND THE RAIDERS Sing "Oo Poo Pah Doo"

*Plus* You Can't Sit Down — Money — Louie, Louie — Do You Love Me — Big Boy Pete — Sometimes — Gone — Bad Times — Fever — Time Is On My Side — A Kiss To Remember You By

CHAD AND JEREMY Sing "Before and After"

*Plus* Tell Me Baby — Why Should I Care — For Lovin' Me — I'm In Love Again — Little Does She Know — What Do You Want With Me — Say It Isn't True — Fare Thee Well — Can't Get Used To Losing You — Evil Hearted Me

## on COLUMBIA RECORDS

# KRLA ARCHIVES

## ON THE BEAT

*By Louise Criscione*

Ever wonder who *Nanker Phelge* is? Well I did, so I snooped around a little and came up with the answer. Are you ready for this? Nanker Phelge is really a pen name for *Mick Jagger* and *Keith Richard* and also for all five of the *Stones* together. You'll find the pen name on lots of their records, such as "Play With Fire" and "The Under Assistant West Coast Promo Man". Nanker Phelge? Only the stones could have thought that one up!

Looks like *Sonny* and *Cher* have come up with their third hit in a row with "I Got You Babe". These two are certainly among the most popular entertainers in L.A. They are breaking attendance records all over town, and no wonder—they're great!

### Byrd Popularity

Without a doubt, the other most popular group in L.A. is the *Byrds*. These guys are fantastic! Watch out for them to be as popular nationally as they are locally. What the heck, I might as well stick my neck all the way out and predict that they will be INTERNATIONALLY famous in the not too distant future! Not only have they come up with a fabulous album, but they have also taken two of the cuts and made them into a single for those of you who can't afford to buy the whole album. I love both sides of the record, "All I Really Want To Do" and "I'll Feel a Whole Lot Better", even more than I did "Mr. Tambourine Man". In simpler language, that means I like the Byrds' new one a whole lot!

As usual, I'm late with my birthday wishes, but a happy belated one to *Paul McCartney* anyway.

*Solomon Burke* is doing up his first tour of England in royal style. During his short visit, he will appear on five television shows, three radio shows, five major club dates and two festivals! And he is only going to be there one short week. How's this for a topper—*Princess Margaret* herself is expected to attend one of these performances.

### Beatles Honored

So they have actually done it — officially honored the *Beatles*. About two months ago, I reported that one of the British music papers, Melody Maker, had suggested that the Beatles be officially honored in some way. I also told you not to take it seriously; it was just someone's wishful thinking. Well, that just goes to show how much I know!

Why do some disc jockeys (and I'm naming no names) insist on saying "Mick Jagger and the Stones"? The *Rolling Stones* are a group, a five-man team. I don't think any one of them should be singled out for special honors. They all contribute to the Stone-sound and they should all be given equal mention. So there! I said it, and I'm glad.

Could it be that the *Lettermen* are going to make it back "in" again? They have certainly made a very nice attempt with that perennial favorite, "A Summer Place". Several years ago, the Lettermen were one of the most popular groups on the scene. Besides producing hit singles, they also manufactured some of the very best albums on the market. Hope their new one makes a terrific dent in the charts; with a sound like that, they deserve a hit!

### Quick Ones

*Roger Miller*, the old king of the road himself, is set for the Greek Theater from July 26 to August 1. . . . Don't miss *Bobby Fuller Four* now appearing at the Carolina Pines in Inglewood. Also watch for their record, "Let Her Dance", to go places . . . The *Disneyland* "Humdingers" began on June 22 and will continue throughout the summer each Tuesday night.

WATCH OUT FOR: Some great new records — "One More Time" by *Them*, "Heart Full of Soul" by the *Yardbirds*, "You Better Come Home" by *Petula Clark*, and "To Know You Is To Love You" by *Peter and Gordon*.

## They're 'Close' Friends

**DICK BIONDI AND GARY LEWIS** appear to be dancing cheek to cheek. They do make a lovely couple. Before starting any strange rumors, however, we'd better explain that there is a perfectly logical reason for them hugging. On stage at Shrine Auditorium, they suddenly got lonely.

## FORMER KING ELVIS RECLAIMING CROWN

Remember Elvis, the King of Rock 'n Roll? The good-looking ex-truck driver from Tennessee who sang and swivel-hipped his way to world stardom and became the number-one heartthrob of the universe?

Who could ever forget!

Now there is speculation that Elvis Presley, after a brief absence from the center ring, is on his way back to the top.

His latest record, "Crying in the Chapel," has skyrocketed to the top five on the national charts, both in the U.S. and England. Not long ago any Elvis record was a cinch for the magic number one spot.

### Back Seat

But King Elvis suddenly began to take a back seat about two years ago just as four mop-haired lads from Liverpool suddenly introduced a new sound and a new era to pop music. His records no longer topped the charts and many didn't even win a berth in the top thirty.

There were many other explanations offered for Elvis' obvious absence from the charts. Some placed the blame simply on the passage of time. After all, Elvis had been king for a long time. Most of those fans who had made him king were now married and had kids of their own. They had other things on their minds — they just weren't interested in Elvis anymore.

### Behind Times

Others pointed an accusing finger at the records Elvis was putting out. They were five years behind the times. They would have made great hits in 1960, but in 1965 the only thing they made were bombs. The real fans (and there are still plenty of

them left) scratched their heads in bewilderment. Elvis was one of the ones who had started rock 'n' roll in the first place. Yet now, ten years later, he couldn't even produce one really good rock record. Why? No one knew.

There was still another faction who declared that the reason Elvis was making bombs was because he was turning out rubbish. It was as pure and simple as that. Many thought "Do The Clam" was horrible, and it did horribly on the charts. Their advice to Elvis was direct: make a good record and you'll have a hit.

### Back Again

It's hard to say for sure which of these explanations was correct. Maybe none of them were. Maybe it doesn't matter because now Elvis is back in the groove again. All three of the national charts list "Cryin' In The Chapel" in their top five. And for the first time in about two years,

**(Turn to Page 12)**

## personals

To the KRLApes: I love you. You're the greatest! Please come to Redondo High next year. Our gym holds 2,100 people.
    One Of Many Fans

To Jim H. and Terry S.: I wish you the best of luck, but remember, Jim, I still like you.
    D. D.

To Diana Klass: Hi from the other Peter and Gordon fan in Canada, your pen pal!
    Sandy of Vancouver, B. C.

To Sandra Fernando of London, England: The Fourmost are fab!    Denice 5

To Dave Hull: Is the banner still in the back of your car? Have you looked at it? When can we get it?
    A Hullaballooer (and Chad & Jeremy) Fan

To Steven In Section 9-5-4: I'm sorry about the dance the other night. Give me another chance, please.
    A Friend In 9-5-2

To Joe: I'll keep remembering only the good times we had together. Always a friend. . . .
    Sandy of Medford

To Richie: Hi from that sweet, blue-eyed gal from Oregon.
    Jeanie H. of Medford

To Michael Jillip Jagger's bird in Manchester: Says WHO?
    His L.A. Bird

To June Krow (The Girl Who Jumped Off The Balcony At The Stones Show): Please write to me soon. My address is 323 N. Marguerita Ave., Alhambra. Stones rule! !
    Elaine Romero

To Jim McGuinn Of The Byrds: Yeh, it's me again. Those shades of your's are weird! Did you say you have a 14-year-old brother?
    Judi Weinberger

To U.N.C.L.E.: We have Ilya and Nappy. Come and get 'em, but don't forget to bring along the Beatles as ransom.
    The Thrushettes

To Duane: Miss you lots, Remember J. A. and tie pins!?
    Sue

To Susan Treadaway of Walthamstow, London, England: How does it feel to have your name in the gabulous KRLA Beat?
    Kathy of Anaheim

To Sydney, Merry, Katey & Martha: That party was swingin'! I felt like Donovan walking to and from it. I'll never listen to another Stones record in my life, even tho they're my fave group. Hee, hee.
    Tired Of Walking

To Derek: So where's my postcard?
    The Girl In The Phone Booth

To Roy: I'll save some cowboy movies for you!
    A Fellow TV Watcher

To G. H.: W. M. L.? I. W. Y. T. L. Y. C. D. I. A.!!
    C. C.

To B. B.: I think it's about your turn at bat.
    Umpire

To Jeremy: I can't find the right taxi driver. What do I do now.
    Blondie

To Joey Paige: We've missed you. Welcome back to L.A. Luv from all of us.
    Your Garden Grove Fan Club

To Dave Hull: I've stopped laughing about you getting the measles. Guess who has them NOW!
    Not Funny

# KRLA ARCHIVES

## Casey Goes Color On 'Shebang'

## Big Boost For Casey's Show

KRLA's Casey Kasem, who has a top-rated daily television show to go with his top-rated daily radio show, has come up with another major "first."

Casey's "Shebang"—produced by Dick Clark—is now being Telecast in living, georgeous color.

It's the first teenage show of its type to make the big switch to color.

Along with the addition of color, "Shebang" has added another improvement. It is now being broadcast live from Channel 5's Hollywood studios.

Anyone interested in appearing on "Shebang" can obtain full details by dropping a note to KTLA Television.

### BEST QUOTE

The *Best Quote of the Week* comes from Brian Jones:

"You see these albums all around the suite? We've picked them all up since we got here. You can't get a lot of this blues stuff back home. We spent years listening to records we ordered from America, just soaking up the R&B sound we love."

A short time later all the albums were stolen from their hotel suite.

---

**23 SKIDOO**

GIRLS AND GUYS 18 AND OVER
DANCING TO LIVE NAME BANDS
2116 Westwood Blvd., West L.A.

23 SKIDOO DANCERS are now seen on TV's Hollywood A Go Go
—CLOSED MONDAY & TUESDAY—

---

Back issues of the KRLA BEAT are still available, for a limited time. If you've missed an issue of particular interest to you, send 10 cents for each copy wanted, along with a self-addressed stamped envelope to:

KRLA BEAT
Suite 504
6290 Sunset Blvd.
Hollywood, California 90028

ISSUES AVAILABLE
4/14 — INTERVIEW WITH JOHN LENNON
4/21 — INTERVIEW WITH PAUL McCARTNEY
4/28 — CHIMP EXCITES TEEN FAIR
5/5 — HERMANIA SPREADS
5/12 — HERE COMES THE BEATLES
5/19 — VISIT WITH BEATLES
5/26 — FAB NEW BEATLE QUIZ
6/2 — L.A. ROCKS AS STONES ROLL
6/16 — BATTLE OF THE BEAT
6/25 — P. J. — HERO OR HEEL

---

## TIPS TO TEENS

Get set for this weeks Tips To Teens, and if you have a question you'd like answered or a hint you'd like printed, get them in the mail to TTT, KRLA BEAT, 6290 Sunset, Hollywood 28!

Q: *Is this column supposed to be just for girls, too? I hope not because I'm not! (Don't mean I'm not for girls . . . I mean I'm not one.) My problem is smoking. I started about three months ago and now I can't stop. Can you help me?*
(D. V., Reseda)

A: We can help you help yourself! There's a new cigarette on the market that contains no tobacco and no nicotine. It's made from herbs, called *Scarfe*, and imported from England at 45¢ a package. They don't taste bad at all, and will help you start stopping. Buy them at most health food stores.

Q: *Everyone always tells me how lucky I am to have dimples, but they're a big problem when I wear makeup. Powder sticks in them and it looks awful. Please help.* (K. J., La Canada)

A: Buy a makeup brush and whick all excess powder away *before* you smile. That way no powder will get caught in your dimples, you lucky soul!

Q: *I wear straight bangs and they seem to get dirty before the rest of my hair needs a shampoo. What causes this and what can I do about it?*
(T. R., Montrose)

A: Your bangs pick up your natural skin oils because they're in constant contact with your forehead. It sounds crazy to say wash your bangs, but do it anyway. Tuck the rest of your hair under a shower cap and shampoo away. This will also help keep your forehead from becoming excessively oily (it picks up the oils from your hair).

Q: *I have freckles in the summer, from being out in the sun and I HATE them. Please don't say what everyone else does and tell me they're cute. They're horrible!* (L. S., Pasadena)

A: Rumor has it that a large cosmetic company is working on a chemical process that will be put into a face cream for the purpose of creating *artificial* freckles. We didn't say they were *cute*, but need we say more?

Q: *When I smile, my nose crinkles and so do the corners of my eyes. I know the crinkles will turn into wrinkles someday. How can I prolong the time between now and then as long as possible?*

A: Keep your skin well lubricated with a good cream. When buying cosmetics, it's always wise to purchase a moderately expensive brand, because you get exactly what you pay for.

### HINT OF THE WEEK

I'm always discovering I don't have a pair of clean nylons at the last moment, and I've found a way to wash and dry them. Set the oven at 250 degrees for a moment or two, then turn it off. Wring the nylons out in a towel and then put them in the oven on a dry towel. They'll be ready to wear in seconds!
(W. K., Los Angeles)

## ? Guess Who??

Puzzle Piece #4

**WHO IS IT?** Here's your chance to win tickets to the KRLA Beatle Concert at the Hollywood Bowl. The strange object floating above is the fourth portion of the BEAT'S Puzzle Contest. Combine it with the pieces shown in the past three issues and see if you can guess who it is. There are ten parts to the puzzle and we will continue running one each week until someone guesses the name of our mystery star. The first contestant to guess who it is will win two tickets to see the Beatles at the Hollywood Bowl. The next two readers to come up with the right answer will each win one ticket to see the Beatles perform. The fourth place winner will win four record albums. Winners five through twelve will win a record album by a top favorite. You can enter as many times as you like. Just send your guesses to KRLA BEAT Puzzle Piece, 6290 Sunset Blvd., Suite 504, Hollwood, 90028. HINT: THE MYSTERY FACE DOES **NOT** BELONG TO ONE OF THE BEATLES.

# KRLA ARCHIVES

## 'WHERE THE ACTION IS'

**PAUL REVERE AND THE RAIDERS ENTERTAIN DURING BEACH BLAST ON NEW TV SHOW**

## Clark Begins Action-Packed New TV Show

Dick Clark, the man who originated the dance-party type television show with his long-running "American Bandstand", has come up with yet another first.

Clark will premiere a new show, "Where The Action Is", on ABC-TV on June 28. The show will showcase today's top talent in locales all over the country — literally whereever the action is.

A group you have read a lot about in the BEAT, Paul Revere and the Raiders, have been signed as regulars on the show. They will do a total of 65 shows which will carry them through the entire summer season.

The pilot film was taped at Leo Carillo Beach and starred the Supremes, Jan & Dean, Chad & Jeremy, Bobby Rydell, Frankie Avalon, Bobby Freeman, Dick & DeeDee, and the Four Seasons.

Other taping spots have included (or will include), Will Rogers Beach, Pacific Ocean Park, Pickwick, Griffith Park, the Hawaiian Islands, and Montreal, Canada.

**HOST DICK CLARK HAMS UP A SCENE WITH RAIDER PHILIP VOLK DURING FILMING**

# KRLA ARCHIVES

## DON'T PANIC IF YOU BUMP INTO A BEATLE

*By Maryann Marsh*

A couple of weeks ago, I had the misfortune of running into two of the Rolling Stones. I say misfortune because that's what it turned out to be.

My two girlfriends and I saw them in a restaurant and instead of using our heads, we went raving over to them and pretty soon everyone in the place was sitting on top of them.

And when they practically had to run for their lives, I hugged Brian and I thought he was going to faint or something. I later found out he had recently cracked two of his ribs.

The incident was exciting, but it could have been so much different. They tried to be so nice about it all, but we didn't give them a chance!

### Beatle Rule

The Beatles are coming to L.A. soon and will be here for several days, and there are always stars in town these days. That's why my friends and I have composed a set of rules we're going to put to good use if we ever have a second chance at meeting a star.

Here's the way we think every girl should act if she dumps into a Beatle or another favorite.

1. Keep quiet. Don't call everyones attention to the star you have spotted or he won't pay any attention to you. He'll just wish you'd go away and play with the other children.

2. Keep calm. Instead of screaming, go over and introduce yourself. This will catch the star off guard. He's so used to being mauled and shrieked over, you'll be a pleasant surprise, and if he has the time to spare, he'll probably give you a few moments. And remember, HANDS OFF!

### Be Yourself

3. Don't gush and don't "interview" him. He's flooded with questions and compliments all day long. Say something interesting and maybe he'll do the same. Stars don't get to know many of their fans (because of the way too many of us act) and you'd be surprised how many stars would welcome the opportunity to get to know us better.

4. If you're undoubtedly the *luckiest* girl in the world, and the star acts the least bit "interested", don't panic. A girl I know met Herman of the Hermits and she acted sensible until he asked for her phone number. Then she started crying! The worst part is, he might have called her. Stars spend so much time traveling and rarely get to meet girls away from home (except the same old groupies who always hang around, and if you don't give them every reason *not* to be interested, there is at least a chance they might become just that. Whatever you do, don't take the chance of ruining it.

5. If it's just a fleeting meeting and there's no time for anything but hello-goodbye, try to resist the natural urge to ask for an autograph. It makes you seem just like everyone else. If you can't resist, at least don't say it's "for your little sister" (or brother) or stand there and tell him what to write.

The final step of our rules for how to act if you bump into a Beatle (etc.) is to start praying that you WILL!

### Cliff Hangers

I just love your "Casey's Quiz", but I'm sure glad you stopped printing the name of the mystery star right under the quiz. I couldn't keep my eyes off the answer long enough to figure out the question!

L. S., Azusa

### Faithfull Fan

I would rather DIE than miss an issue of the KRLA BEAT. I ordered two subscriptions in case the mailman got interested in it and couldn't bear to part with my copy.

If you ever stop printing the KRLA BEAT, I KNOW I am going to go out of my mind or something. If my folks didn't bring me my copy every visiting day, I'd just go nuts!

G. B., Redondo Beach

### Beat Experiment

I bought my first issue of the BEAT today, and spent over two hours reading it. I did read a couple of things twice, but I still think that's a lot of enjoyment for only a dime.

Thanks for listening to my two cents worth.

K. K., Long Beach

### Out To Dry

Something hysterical happened that I just have to tell you about. The other day I was reading my BEAT on the lawn and left it there while I went into the house for something.

While I was gone, my dad turned on the sprinklers and my Beat got soaked! Instead of running away from home (I just couldn't, because we were having pizza for dinner that night) I stomped into the back yard and hung my Beat on the line to dry.

The neighbors now think I'm a hopeless case, but what do they know anyway? Anyone who doesn't like the Beat is all wet!

Y. B., Pasadena

### Fabulous Idea

Remember the letter you printed from the girl who said she was going to meet her English pen pal in front of Buckingham Palace on June 30, 1966? Well, it really gave me a fabulous idea.

I have a pen pal in England too, and now we're going to meet on July 4, 1967 in front of where George Harrison used to live in Liverpool.

I also got some fabulous ideas from your "How To Go To England If You Have The Nerve" article, and I hope I'll be able to control myself and wait for you to make some *rational* suggestions. Knowing me, I think you'd better hurry.

F. N., Malibu

## They're Still 'Supreme'

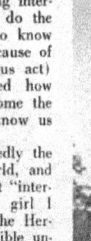

**THE SUPREMES STILL REIGN SURPREME,** sending still another fabulous record up the charts toward Number One. "Back in My Arms Again" is one of their best yet. With four consecutive number one songs, these young ladies from Detroit are reportedly grossing over $100,000 each this year. And they each recently purchased $35,000 homes. Their name was very chosen.

Here we go again with five more questions for the KRLA Beatle Quiz, America's most exciting and most rewarding contest.

Any of you Beatle Experts who missed the first five weeks of the Beatle Quiz can still catch up by ordering a June 23, June 16, June 9, June 2, and May 26 issue of the KRLA BEAT. Instructions for ordering these issues can be found elsewhere in the BEAT.

The winner of the Beatle Quiz will get to interview the Beatles for the Beat when they arrive in August and along with a friend will be invited to attend the Beatle Concert as guests of the KRLA Deejays.

Additional prizes will be provided for runner-ups. In case of a tie there will be additional questions or a drawing to decide the final winner. The contest will cover a ten-week period, with at least five new questions asked each week. KRLA's Derek Taylor, a close friend of the Beatles and their former press officer, will judge the entries for accuracy.

Beatle Quiz
KRLA BEAT
Suite 504
6290 Sunset Blvd.
Hollywood, Calif. 90028

**CONTEST EDITOR:**

Below are my answers to the fourth set of questions in the BEATLE QUIZ CONTEST.

My Name .................................................... Address ....................................................

City .................................................... State .................. Zip Code ..............

I (☐ am) (☐ am not) presently a subscriber to the KRLA BEAT.

### NEW QUESTIONS

26. Which Beatle visited with a relative in the Bahamas? ...............
27. Who is the Beatles' road manager? ...............
28. What kind of institution is next door to George's house? ...............
29. As of this date, what has been the Beatles' largest selling single record? ...............
30. How long was Ringo in the hospital during his first serious illness? ...............

## THE BEAT GOES TO THE MOVIES
## 'CAT BALLOU'

**By Jim Hamblin**

There is one very good reason to see "Cat", and his name is Lee Marvin. Mr. Marvin has been in movies and television for a while now, including the sucessful M SQUAD series, in which he reluctantly played a good guy, and a police officer at that. Rumor has it that Marvin is something of a maverick, and likes being a bad boy — on screen and off.

But whatever Lee Marvin may or may not be, he is *certainly* the chief attraction of "Cat Ballou".

This whimsical comedy, the saga of a good girl gone bad, has some great moments of comedy. And they all come from Marvin.

### No Nose

We see him as the desperado who has been hired to kill the old man who is holding out his cattle land from the townspeople. He wears a silver nose cap tied around his head. (The nose got bitten off in a fight.)

While his evil look frightens the ranch hands, the old man makes the logical observation that if they're going to be afraid of anyone, *"seems like it oughta be the guy who bit off his nose"!*

The heroine (Jane Fonda) sends away for the famous Kid Sheleen, Hero Of The West, and star of the dime novels she's been reading about the great gunman of the frontier. She figures that with such a fast gun on the ranch, such keen and alert terror on guard, the silver-nosed gunman will never get her father.

### Farce Begins

Sheleen, when he's dumped into the dust from the stagecoach, turns out to be the raunchiest, dirtiest, most disreputable skag and drunk in the state. He's shaking so bad from a week-long binge that he cannot even hold a gun, much less hit the side of the barn.

He also turns out to be Lee Marvin, in a dual role.

It is from here on in that you had better have a good grip on your popcorn, b e c a u s e the laughs come fast and heavy. No one with recent surgery should go — it's liable to kill you.

Much of the story is told by two wandering minstrels, who fill us in on the story behind the story. With music and narration, the minstrels keep us up with the developments.

### Sad Note

There's a note of nostalgia and perhaps even sadness here, for one of the minstrels is Nat King Cole, in his last appearance. Accompanied by Stubby Kaye, he sings the lament of Catherine Ballou.

Things get pretty involved near the end of the movie, and our gal Cat has done something bad. The townspeople decide to hang her. For the occasion she chooses a symbolic white gown.

All is in readiness. The gallows built, the day dawns, and our minstrels are bemoaning the loss of such a pretty girl.

But the boys have not failed Cat Ballou, and rescue is on the way. Everything is planned, except for the fact that Kid Sheleen has gone back off the wagon in a rather specacular way — along with his horse.

### Too Much

This scene is almost too much to bear, and I am sure I saw several people fall out of their seats, holding their sides in hysterical laughter. Sure hope they hadn't had any of that surgery lately.

Lee Marvin's adventures on horse back defy description.

As for the rest of the cast, they have given good performances, and — whether they intended this or not — have provided perfect support f r o m which Lee Marvin has launched his marvelous characterizations.

Story pacing is excellent, and so is the sound and the color. We mention those items because so many times what might have been a good film is sand-bagged by technical incompetence. This one's good in every department, and Columbia Pictures is to be congratulated. (Which is what the box office is for.) Here, at least, is one GREAT evening of comedy delight. That's "CAT BALLOU."

CAT (JANE FONDA) PREPARES TO BECOME A "SWINGER"

LEE MARVIN IN DUAL ROLE AS TWO MEAN HOMBRES

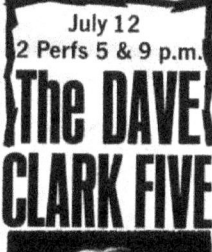

**July 12
2 Perfs 5 & 9 p.m.
The DAVE CLARK FIVE**

WITH
**The ASTRONAUTS
The PREMIERS
SONNY & CHER**

Prices: $2.50, $3.50, $4.50, $5.50
CHOICE SEATS NOW at box office, by Mail, and at all Southland Ticket Agencies

For Info.
call
Anaheim
(714)
776-7220

**Melodyland THEATRE**
Opposite Disneyland

"ATTRACTION FOR"
SHOWS-DANCES
FAN CLUB:
P.O. Box 12
Stanton, Calif.
Tel. (714) 539-5880

## A New Look For Paul - WOW!

### Paul McCartney

**PHOTOGRAPHED IN AUSTRIA** during filming of "Help," Paul's familiar cherub face appears to have hardened and matured, giving him a rugged, handsome, adventurous look. Wonder if he'll look that way at Hollywood Bowl?

---

### KRLA BEAT SUBSCRIPTION

As a special introductory offer—if you subscribe now you will save 40% of the regular price.

☐ 1 YEAR — 52 Issues — $3.00   ☐ 2 YEARS — $5.00

Enclosed is $..........

Send to:........................................................Age............

Address:........................................................................

City:..........................State:..................Zip:..............

MAIL YOUR ORDER TO: **KRLA BEAT**
1401 South Oak Knoll Avenue
Pasadena, California 91106

Outside U.S.: $9.00 — 52 Issues

---

### BATTLE OVER MEDALS
# Beatles Blasted!

Great Britain is involved in a major controversy, and the Beatles are right in the middle of it!

It began quite innocently when John, Paul, George and Ringo were recently accorded one of England's highest honors by Her Majesty, Queen Elizabeth II. She bestowed upon them the Order of the British Empire.

But no sooner had the prized honor been announced than a storm of protest was aroused.

A least four holders of the coveted M. B. E. have sent back their medals, claiming they were debased and cheapened because the Beatles were given the same honor.

#### "Nincompoops"

One of them announced he was sending his back because "English royalty wants to place me on the same level as those vulgar nincompoops." Another — a war hero — declared he did not want to be in the same order "that recognizes such stupidity and hysteria as that long-haired Mersey group exhibits." And another charged the Queen's recognition of the Beatles had made the award a "farce".

The BEAT has learned that Prime Minister Harold Wilson has received a number of other complaints — some from high sources — about the decorations given to the Beatles.

But John, Paul, George and Ringo have not been left speechless by the furor.

#### "Duffy-Duddies"

George promptly called them complaining "Duffy-Duddies" and said if they don't like their medals they should turn them over to the foursome so they can give one to their manager, Brian Epstein.

Declared Ringo: "People are being childish. They can eat their medals for all I care."

Ringo added, "We never asked for the award. For once young people get an award. What's wrong with that?"

---

**KRLA BEAT**
The KRLA BEAT is published weekly by Prestige Publishing Company; editorial and advertising offices at 6290 Sunset Boulevard, Suite 504, Hollywood, California 90028.
Single copy price, 10 cents.
Subscription price: U.S. and possessions, $3 per year or $5 for two years. Outside U.S., $9 per year.

---

**THE BYRDS**
Official National
**FAN CLUB**
Suite 504
6290 Sunset Blvd.
Hollywood

Send $1.00 plus two 5-cent stamps and receive photos, fact sheets, biographies. Fun contests each month.

Free Concerts Planned
For Members Only

Be a chapter president. Enlist ten (10) new members now!

The BYRDS Are Great

---

## THE CINNAMON CINDERS
### Southern California's Young Adult Night Club

★ Wednesday, July 7th ★
BOTH LOCATIONS ★

**THE RONETTES**

11345 VENTURA BOULEVARD
STUDIO CITY, CALIFORNIA
4401 PACIFIC COAST HIWAY
LONG BEACH, CALIFORNIA

AGES 18 - 25

Open Nightly Wed. thru Sunday

# KRLA ARCHIVES

## For Girls Only

By Sheila Davis

If you're a boy and you're reading this, why don't you go out and play or something?

If you're a girl, I hope you will bear with me today. I'm in kind of a serious mood. I watched a re-run of a "Mr. Novak" show the other night and it really made me think. You've probably seen it, too. It was the one about hazing and social clubs on campus.

I can see why social clubs are prohibited in most schools. A few groups got too carried away and now all of us have to share the consequences. But there's something I don't understand at all. I can't see why all the fuss about teenagers being clique-ish (I hope that's the right way to spell it).

Cliques sure aren't limited to teenagers only. My folks have a certain circle of friends, and so do yours. So does everyone. Once you find a few close companions, people you really enjoy being around, it's only natural to want to spend as much time together as you possibly can.

### Snobbery

Guess what. I just looked clique up in the dictionary. And I did spell it wrong back there a few paragraphs. Should have been *cliquish*. But anyway, Webster's definition of the word is: "A small, exclusive set or snobbish group of people." Now I am really in a serious mood.

Oh, brother. Several times. I think someone had better find a new word for circles of friends. I have four special girlfriends in addition to a lot of other acquaintances but we certainly aren't *snobbish*.

You probably know exactly what I'm trying to say. Why give a bad name to something that's good for everyone concerned? I don't think a person should devote every ounce of his spare time to one group, but kids who do have friends they can trust and have fun with are really very lucky. Snobbish my wooden leg!

### Boys Different

Thinking about all this has started me thinking about something else. I don't know this for a *fact*, but doesn't it seem like more boys have close long-time friends than girls? I mean, when boys get into a certain group of buddies (or whatever they call them), the friendship seems to last longer and remain more stable. I wonder why this is.

Maybe it's because boys don't have to compete with each other quite so madly. If a boy finds himself interested in his friend's girl, he can always rush to the phone and take his mind off his "secret pang" by going out with a different girl every night until he gets over it. That way, nothing happens to break up the friendship between the two guys.

But, if a girl finds herself interested in a close friend's ex-boyfriends, someone the friend still likes, she can't rush to the phone and take her mind off her troubles. And if the interest sort of blossoms into an irresistable urge, there goes the friendship right down the drain.

I wonder whoever dreamed up the old-fashioned customs we've been living with since practically the beginning of time. A man, I'm sure. And when I think that there was a time when we couldn't even *vote*, I want to EXPLODE!

Oh, brother again. Down off your soap box, old girl.

Enough of that. Let's talk about something a little less traumatic, whatever that means!

### Phone Decoration

If you have your own telephone in your room (some people have all the luck), here's a cute way to decorate it without getting into trouble with your folks or the phone company. (I knew a girl who painted polka dots on her phone with nail polish and the phone company almost had her shot at sunrise.) (Her folks were considering paying for the bullets.)

Take off the dial thing where your telephone number is and replace the number with a pic of your favorite star, or a pic of a flower, etc. Whatever happens to appeal to your tastes. It looks sharp. I have a photo of my favorite Beatle (George) in mine and it really adds something to the room. Course the "room" the phone is in is the hall (like I said, some people have all the luck) and my folks give me an icy stare every time they make a call, but I've learned to live with it.

I know this was a rather weird column, and I'm really sorry it wasn't a little more rollicking in content, but the things I talked about have been bothering me and probably have bothered you at one time or another. If you have any views on the subjects of my ravings this week I love to hear them.

And please keep your letters coming to me c/o the Beat.

## ALL-GIRL BAND CALLS FOR HELP

Out of all the wonderful letters the KRLA Beat has received, this is one of our favorites. Besides being a crack-up, it contains a really great idea.

Read it and then see what you think of our P.S. at the end!

"Dear Beat:

The Swingin' Angels have a problem (decidedly). We are an all-girl group in desperate need of members to support one drummer and one rhythm guitarist, which is all that is left since "The Row".

(Dear me. I forgot that our bass guitarist said she'd stick with us a while longer.)

"The Row", by definition, was a slight lecture which Geri, the drummer and my co-leader of the group, directed at the other two because they didn't make any effort to show up at rehearsals.

We hope you'll print this advertisement for replacements. We are looking for girls around 16-17 who play guitar or piano, preferably sing, and live near the San Gabriel-Temple City area.

Experience isn't necessary, but if they are not willing to work and don't like to make utter fools of themselves, they may as well not apply.

Perhaps you could also start a "Situations Vacant" column. I know it would go over big with your readers!

Hope our request went over big, too. Anyone interested in joining the Swingin' Angels, please write!

Janice Sutliff
5336 N. Noel Drive
Temple City, California

*Editor's Note:* We're all for Janice's idea about a "Situations Vacant" column, how about you? The column could work both ways as we'd be printing the names and qualifications of "unemployed" teenagers and news of possible jobs. If you'd like a job, or know where one is available, drop a line to HELP!, c/o the Beat, 6290 Sunset, Hollywood.

---

CONTEST DEADLINE EXTENDED TO JULY 30

# NEED A SUMMER JOB? BECOME A KRLA BEAT REPRESENTATIVE!

## You Can Earn Money, Prizes As A Beat Representative

HERE'S ALL YOU HAVE TO DO: Send your name, address, telephone number and the school you attend to KRLA BEAT, 1401 S. OAK KNOLL, PASADENA, Calif. But do it fast — first come, first served. We will send you all the necessary information to become a successful KRLA BEAT representative. You will earn handsome profits on each subscription. Earnings are unlimited, because EVERY TEENAGER SHOULD BE A SUBSCRIBER!

And There Are Special Prizes for Those Who Sell The Most Subscriptions Between Now and July 7th

---

I would like to be a KRLA BEAT REPRESENTATIVE in the city of:
Please send me additional information and forms for selling subscriptions.

Name_____ Age_____

Address_____ City_____

Phone_____ Zip Code_____

# KRLA ARCHIVES

## KRLA TUNEDEX

**#1 RED HOT**

| THIS WEEK | LAST WEEK | | |
|---|---|---|---|
| 1. | 1. | SATISFACTION | Rolling Stones |
| 2. | 2. | I CAN'T HELP MYSELF | The Four Tops |
| 3. | 3. | WHAT THE WORLD NEEDS NOW IS LOVE | Jackie De Shannon |
| 4. | 4. | WOOLY BULLY | Sam The Sham & The Pharaohs |
| 5. | 20. | ONCE UPON A TIME | Tom Jones |
| 6. | 5. | BACK IN MY ARMS AGAIN | The Supremes |
| 7. | 6. | SHAKIN ALL OVER | Guess Who? |
| 8. | 7. | HELP ME RHONDA | The Beach Boys |
| 9. | 16. | LAURIE | Dickie Lee |
| 10. | 9. | JUST YOU | Sonny & Cher |
| 11. | 10. | HERE COMES THE NIGHT | Them |
| 12. | 8. | MR. TAMBOURINE MAN | The Byrds |
| 13. | 13. | CRYING IN THE CHAPEL | Elvis Presley |
| 14. | | WHITTIER - BOULEVARD | The Midnighter |
| 15. | 11. | GOOD LOVIN' | The Olympics |
| 16. | 31. | YES, I'M READY | Barbara Mason |
| 17. | 21. | HUSH, HUSH SWEET CHARLOTTE | Patti Page |
| 18. | 29. | I'M A FOOL | Dino, Desi & Billy |
| 19. | 17. | WONDERFUL WORLD | Herman's Hermits |
| 20. | 12. | YOU TURN ME ON | Ian Whitcomb & Bluesville |
| 21. | | HOLD ME, THRILL ME, KISS ME | Mel Carter |
| 22. | 14. | FOR YOUR LOVE | The Yardbirds |
| 23. | 18. | THE LAST TIME/PLAY WITH FIRE | The Rolling Stones |
| 24. | 30. | SEVENTH SON | Johnny Rivers |
| 25. | | ALL I REALLY WANT TO DO | Cher |
| 26. | 22. | GOODBYE, SO LONG | Ike And Tina Turner |
| 27. | 23. | THIS LITTLE BIRD | Marianne Faithfull |
| 28. | 36. | THE DIP | The Whispers |
| 29. | 15. | OOO BABY BABY | The Miracles |
| 30. | | THE HALL OF THE MOUNTAIN KING | Sounds Incorporated |
| 31. | 34. | SUNSHINE, LOLLIPOPS, & ROSES | Lesley Gore |
| 32. | 32. | TRAINS AND BOATS AND PLANES | Billy J. Kramer |
| 33. | | I'VE GOT YOU | Sonny & Cher |
| 34. | | OOO WEE BABY I LOVE YOU | Fred Hughes |
| 35. | 40. | I LIKE IT LIKE THAT | The Dave Clark Five |
| 36. | | THEME FROM A SUMMER PLACE | The Lettermen |
| 37. | | ANYWAY, ANYHOW, ANYWHERE | The Who |
| 38. | | CARA MIA | Jay and the Americans |
| 39. | | MARIE | The Bachelors |
| 40. | | LET HER DANCE | Bobby Fuller |

SOUTHERN CALIFORNIA'S MOST ACCURATE RECORD SURVEY — BASED ON RETAIL SALES FIGURES

BULK RATE
U.S. Postage
PAID
Los Angeles, Calif.
Permit No. 25497

### BRITISH TOP TEN

1. CRYING IN THE CHAPEL — Elvis Presley
2. THE PRICE OF LOVE — The Everly Bros.
3. I'M ALIVE — The Hollies
4. LONG LIVE LOVE — Sandie Shaw
5. THE CLAPPING SONG — Shirley Ellis
6. TRAINS AND BOATS AND PLANES — Burt Bacharach
7. COLOURS — Donovan
8. POOR MAN'S SON — The Rockin' Berries
9. SET ME FREE — The Kinks
10. LOOKING THROUGH THE EYES OF LOVE — Gene Pitney

### SNEAKING VISIT HERE
## Chad, Jeremy Rent Secret Hideaway In Hollywood

Chad and Jeremy are secretly renting an apartment in Hollywood!

They have frequently visited here in the past without anyone knowing it except for their closest friends.

It all came to light last week when they spent six days here in their secret hideaway while making a number of television and nightclub appearances.

"We have a secret apartment in Hollywood, "Chad revealed to the BEAT. "No one knows, but we've been coming here often. We just slip in."

After a brief lull in which many claimed they were "washed up," Chad and Jeremy are back on top of the record charts with "True Love Waits."

### Big Crowds

Proof of their popularity came as they received enthusiastic receptions at various stops before arriving in Los Angeles.

Chad told the BEAT, "In San Francisco they were at us from all directions. One chap came flying toward me from a running jump of about 10 feet."

It would have been like that at Los Angeles, too, but for the fact they were tardy. The two missed an earlier flight from Sacramento, disappointing several hundred anxious fans gathered at the airport. When they finally arrived, only about 100 of the faithful were still around.

### CASEY'S QUIZ ANSWER

(Don't peek unless you've read the question elsewhere in the BEAT.

JAY and THE AMERICANS

Chad and Jeremy have now wound up their current stay here, flying on to New York.

But they'll be back—slipping in and out of their secret Hollywood hideaway unnoticed.

Unnoticed, that is, except for eager reporters from the BEAT. But that doesn't count.

### BEATLES NOSE STONE LEAD

As the Battle of the Beat slides into its third week, the Rolling Stones remain ahead by a scant 3 per cent in the Southland popularity poll.

The Beatles are gaining however. In the first round of the contest last week, Mike Jagger and Co. had a comfortable 58 per cent lead, according to the readers answering the questionnaire in the June 16 issues of the Beat.

This week thousands of new questionnaires have flooded the office with loyal Beatle fans insisting that the Beatles will never be topped by anyone.

"Beatlemania will reach a peak when the Beatles come to American in August which will never be touched by another pop group," predicted one Beatle fan.

Rolling Stone fans are equally confident.

"The Beatles better roll over. The Stones are coming!" declared one reader.

"Are the Beatles bouncing back or will the Stones continue their lead in the "Battle of the Beat?" We'll continue the poll for the next few weeks, so you still have time to help us prove which group is the most popular.

Whatever your choice, give your favorites a boost by voting for them on a postcard and sending it to The KRLA Beat, 6290 Sunset, Suite 504, Hollywood 90028.

Round three is coming up. Don't let them down.

### FORMER KING ELVIS . . .
(Continued from Page 5)

Elvis has made it into the top five in England.

Could it be that once again we will have to start addressing Elvis Presley as The King?

# KRLA ARCHIVES

**Beatle Tickets** — MORE PRIZE WINNERS IN THIS ISSUE

# KRLA BEAT

**Stones Falter** — NEW RESULTS IN WEEKLY POLL

Volume 1, No. 18 — Los Angeles, California — Ten Cents — July 7, 1965

"ALL I REALLY WANT TO DO" is...

TURN TO PAGE 2

# KRLA ARCHIVES

WAR OR PEACE?

# SONNY & CHER vs. THE BYRDS

By Derek Taylor

Nobody really wanted a fight. It just sort of started. Columbia said: "Come outside," and Imperial said "O.K." and took its coat off.

But outside, the scene changed. Columbia looked at Imperial and Imperial looked at Columbia. One or other—I don't know which—smiled sheepishly and suddenly they shook hands.

It was over.

This, in essence, was the story of "All I Really Want to Do," the Bob Dylan song recorded by the Byrds and by the lovely Cher Bono.

Cher was first on the market —on the Imperial label. The kids loved the song.

Then the Byrds' version was released. On Columbia. This too was adored by the kids.

But, reasoned the record companies, there aren't enough kids to love them both to Number One.

So the fight was on. And Cher, being first, looked like winning the battle in Los Angeles though there were those who thought she might not do so well further east.

The Byrds hated the situation because they liked Cher. And anyway, they argued, who wants a row over a Dylan song?

Cher wasn't happy because she dug the Byrds and she too didn't want a public argument over a beautiful number.

The shadowy men in the background were still spoiling for a fight. "All I Really Want to Do," looked like the Liston-Clay weigh-in.

Then, as I say, it was all over. Columbia decided, and the Byrds decided—and Sonny and Cher smiled benignly—to plug the other side of the Byrds version.

This is called: "I Feel a Whole Lot Better" and certainly the Byrds did and Cher did.

And not only this. Both groups agreed to sing "All I Really Want to Do" TOGETHER—at their next joint public concert.

Explained Jim McGuinn, amiable leader of the Byrds: "We loved the Cher version. We just love the song, period. We didn't want a hassle. So we just turned our record over."

And said Cher: "We don't know where the row started. We know the Byrds dig us and we certainly dig them. There's room at the top for everyone."

Yes. There is.

Show business is a lousy enough affair without *nice* people getting involved in the muddy undercurrents.

## BEST QUOTE OF THE WEEK

The *Best Quote of the Week* comes from Mick Jagger concerning American color television. "The standard's not very high, but the novelty of color television appealed to me. You can alter the picture so you've got purple men and red grass and can in actual fact obtain a completely different picture made by using different color separations!"

## Patty Duke's New Record Won't 'Just Stand There'

There seems to be nothing Patty Duke can't do, and do well!

She went directly from the cradle into acting, and at the age of eighteen can boast (not that she would) of many television and stage awards, an Oscar, her own television show and her first hit record.

Patty's very first recording hit the national charts at an enviable number 79 during its second week of release, and its chances of climbing right straight to the top are the best bet in town. It's called "Don't Just Stand There", and don't worry. It won't!

Nothing about Patty is just standing there! She's just completed her first movie since her award-winning "Miracle Worker". The film is a screen version of the play "Time Out For Ginger", re-titled "Billie". Patty plays the part of a gal athlete, and the fun races on for 90 hilarious minutes.

From now on, Patty's TV show will be filmed in Hollywood, making it twice as nice for her California fans.

If you aren't her fan already, don't just stand there! Join the fun and become one!

**KRLA BEAT**
The KRLA BEAT is published weekly by Prestige Publishing Company; editorial and advertising offices at 6290 Sunset Boulevard, Suite 504, Hollywood, California 90028.
Single copy price, 10 cents.
Subscription price: U.S. and possessions, $3 per year or $5 for two years. Outside U.S., $9 per year.

## Guess Who??

Puzzle Piece #5

**YOU STILL HAVE A CHANCE TO WIN.** A first place puzzle piece winner has shown up. However, there are still no runner-ups. And you can still win tickets to the Beatle Concert at the Hollywood Bowl. The strange object floating above is the fifth piece in the BEAT'S Puzzle Piece Contest. Combine it with the pieces shown in the past four week's issues and see if you can guess who it is. There are ten pieces in all and we'll continue running one each week until 11 more readers come up with the right answer. As soon as all prize winners are in, they will be notified by mail and their names will be published in the BEAT. The next two readers to come up with the right answer will each win a ticket to see the Beatles. The fourth place winner will receive four record albums, and winners five through twelve will win a record album by a top favorite. Enter as many times as you want. Send your guesses to KRLA BEAT Puzzle Piece, 6290 Sunset Blvd., Suite 504, Hollywood 90028. HINT: THE MYSTERY PIECE DOES NOT BELONG TO ONE OF THE BEATLES.

# KRLA ARCHIVES

## Herman Loses His 'Fang'

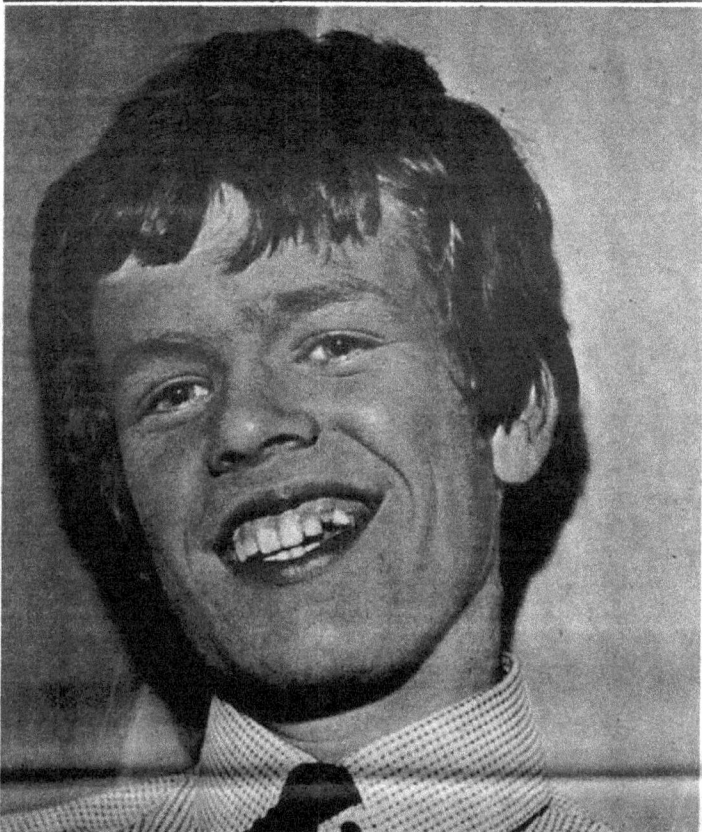

**HERMAN'S FAMED FANG** is no more. "It had been loose for sometime. Surprisingly, its been pushed out by a new one, so I won't have a gap for long," Herman explains. Fans will just have to sit and wait to see if he sprouts another one.

## Derek Taylor Reports
## ENTERTAINERS ARE HUMAN BUT OFTEN FANS ARE NOT

Maybe by the time you read this, Peter Herman Noone will have arrived in Hollywood and his countless fans will know where he's staying.

This will relieve pressure on the turbulent switchboard in my office where, for the last three months, minute by minute, the wires have throbbed with the breathless question: "Is Herman in town?"

If telephone calls are any guide to an artist's popularity, then Herman clearly leads the field. I hope by now that you have all tracked him down and that you are not giving him too hard a time.

While we're on the subject of pop stars and their fans, it might be helpful for me to say that while all artists are conscious of the importance of fans, they cannot reasonably be expected to meet each and every record-buyer.

Nor is it possible for them, at all times, to keep smiling and appear to be amiable and friendly.

Pop stars, like ordinary mortals, are human. What is different about them is that they are confronted with inhuman situations.

I have sat with John, Paul, George and Ringo inside an embattled limousine with forty impassioned Beatlemaniacs smashing on the windows, punching the fenders and the hood, snatching at the windshield wipers, and wrenching off the aerial.

### FANS LACK UNDERSTANDING

Somehow, for some of the time, the Beatles have managed to smile and wave. Yet, surprisingly, these same fans have been heard later to voice complaints like: "Ringo's real mean. We saw him in his car and he just turned away."

Remember this, because it's important and because it's true: no one in the entertainment industry owes anybody anything beyond an obedience to fulfill contracts. Simply because a fan buys a record and/or a ticket to a concert, the star is not obliged to do any more than perform on stage. If you are lucky and you win a smile or a brief wink or a handshake between the stage door and the limousine, then it's a bonus.

The Beatles are extraordinarily patient because they, more than any star in the history of show business, have endured unimaginable pressures and still remain normal and friendly.

I have seen unbelievable things happen in the Beatles' own suites on tour. They returned one night after a wild show in Holland to find that their sitting room had been converted into a television studio. Weary, harassed by police and torn up by fans, they plunged thankfully into what they believed to be the sanctuary of their suite. Only to be greeted by blinding arc lights and a microphone.

Do you wonder that their patience ran out and that their language became unprintable.

They, and hundreds of other groups besides, have now grown used to the painful bombardment of jelly beans—in their eyes, their ears, on their temples, and even in their mouths.

So, when you next spot a star, rememmber that it's not all gold and glory. Give him a chance to be a human being.

### BYRDS MEET FANS

The Byrds attended their first fan club group meeting a few days ago—at the pleasant little Stratford-on-Sunset teenage nightclub in Hollywood. By and large it was a success, with the more talkative fans on the front row and the shy ones huddling together a few rows back.

The Byrds are emerging as easy conversationalists with a nice, relaxed, off-stage manner. It takes time for new groups to learn how to confront rows and rows of eager teenage faces. But the Byrds are coping well.

Also winning new friends day by day is the Stratford Club on Sunset Strip. This is for 18-25 year-olds—no intoxicating drinks—and the Byrds' management were so impressed with the atmosphere of the club they agreed to put the group in for a last-minute 3-night stint for a nominal fee.

It's as well for the Byrds to take on these local engagements while they can. In a few months they will be so much in demand at such a high fee that their time will not be their own.

What else is happening?

Joe and Eddie have a new one—again on the enterprising Crescendo label. This time it's a fast, powerful number. Title: "Walkin' Down the Line."

### SATISFACTION IS SMASHING

"Satisfaction" is smashing its way up the charts and should be No. 1 on most national lists by the time this KRLA BEAT is blistering on the sun-baked newsstands.

Marianne Faithfull is in town—for "Shindig."

Dick St. John (of Dick and Deedee) is recovering from his throat operation. Deedee is filling in time during his convalescence by taking flying lessons.

Mr. Bobby Vinton, without fuss and bother is still lingering on the charts with "L-O-N-E-L-Y."

The patience of the Guilloteens—emigrants to this benevolent and lovely metropolis from Memphis—has been rewarded by a record contract with Hanna-Barbera. Their first single is on release now. It's good and so is the new Missing Link's "Heartbreak Hill."

George Harrison's song, "The Night Before," made a brief appearance on some opportunist's radio station before being ignom-

**TURN TO PAGE 11**

---

## THE CINNAMON CINDERS
### Southern California's Young Adult Night Club

★ Wednesday, July 7th ★
BOTH LOCATIONS
★

**THE RONETTES**

11345 VENTURA BOULEVARD
STUDIO CITY, CALIFORNIA
4401 PACIFIC COAST HIWAY
LONG BEACH, CALIFORNIA

AGES 18 - 25

Open Nightly Wed. thru Sunday

---

## GROWING BEAT MAY BE LATE

The KRLA BEAT continues to expand!

There has been an increasing demand for the BEAT throughout Southern California. In fact, subscriptions have been pouring in from practically every state in the Union, plus several foreign countries.

Due to this huge response, it will soon be bigger and more plentiful than ever.

Those who have encountered "sold out" signs in the past will soon find the BEAT available in several thousand additional outlets, including supermarkets, grocery stores, drug stores and other convenient locations, plus an even greater number of newsstands and record stores.

Because of this expansion your next issue may be a few days late in arriving.

But please bear with us through these "growing pains." In return, we'll do our best to provide you with even more of the exclusive information and pictures which have made the BEAT America's leading teenage newspaper.

---

"ATTRACTION FOR"

SHOWS-DANCES
FAN CLUB
P.O. Box 12
Stanton, Calif.
Tel. (714) 539-5880

# KRLA ARCHIVES

## A KRLA BEAT EDITORIAL
### BEATLES DESERVE IT

The loud protests against awarding the Beatles the Order of the British Empire is a lot of stuffy nonsense by narrow-minded men who have forgotten the true meaning of the awards.

For one thing, the honor is not limited to war heroes. It has traditionally been bestowed upon outstanding men in government, trade, cultural affairs, music and even athletics. In short, those who have contributed significantly to the welfare of Great Britain.

While all of us are indebted to war heroes for our very existence, there are also heroes during peacetime.

True, the Beatles have fought no military wars, but they have made a dramatic and significant contribution to their country. For decades the pop music industry in Britain fell weakly under the shadow of the American music industry, depending upon American songs and artists.

Today, thanks largely to the Beatles, a dramatic change has taken place. British songs and British artists are setting the popularity pace throughout the world. This has produced millions of dollars for the British treasury and has helped boost their economy. Equally important, it has instilled a new spirit and pride in English hearts.

The Beatles have improved what the war heroes protected.

And the fact that they did it with laughter and lyrics rather than picks or swords does not diminish their contribution. Those who are objecting have forgotten the joy of living.

For that is what the Beatles stand for.

### New 'Hell's Angels' Recruits

MOTORCYCLE DAREDEVILS DICK BIONDI, BOB EUBANKS, JOHNNY HAYES

 ## TIPS TO TEENS

*Q: I tried both the products you recommended for dry complexion problems, but my problem is still unsolved. Where do I go from here?*
(B. N., La Crescenta)

A: I still recommend the first two products mentioned (Noxzema and Phi-So-Hex) for similar problems, but I've discovered another that also works like a charm. It's transparent facial soap, imported from France, called Savon. It costs $1.50 a bar, but it is worth it! I bought mine in the Broadway Hollywood, so check the Broadway or drug stores in your area. If this soap doesn't help, you'd better see your family doctor. Something other than a complexion problem may be causing your dry skin. (Guess what. I think I have just given the world's longest answer.)

*Q: I'm invited to the wedding of a close friend next month, and I want to know if I have to wear a hat to the ceremony? My mother says I do, but I don't want to unless I'd be considered impolite if I didn't.*
(S. K., Compton)

A: If you aren't going to be in the wedding party or reception line, the rule about wearing a hat is a bit old hat. Well, the rule still exists, but at least half of the gals at most weddings don't observe it. However, some churches require the head to be covered, so check on that before you decide.

*Q: I forgot to take my boyfriend's sterling silver ring off my hand the other night and the medicated cream I use on my face turned the ring all black. What on earth am I going to do?*
(G. A., Los Angeles)

A: Clean it the same way you would sterling silverware, with a polishing cloth or silver polish. If that doesn't work (it probably will), try this old-time remedy. Pour out half a cup of vinegar and add a half teaspoon of baking soda. When the mixture fizzes, drop the ring in and let it soak for a few moments. This method works best on gold or brass, but just might work on silver too.

*Q: I was afraid you wouldn't deal with smoking, but you answered one on this topic recently, so here's mine. I smoked for about six months and then stopped. Ever since I gave it up, I'm afraid to breathe on anyone because I feel like I have you-know-what. I made my friends PROMISE they'd tell me if I needed a vat of Listerine and they say no, but I still taste funny or something. Help!*
(J. U., Burbank)

A: This happens to many people when they stop smoking. Cigarettes dull your taste buds to such a degree, you're unaware of the taste in your mouth. When you stop smoking, you become acutely aware because your taste buds are back in full action. Be calm. You're probably worrying about nothing. If

**TURN TO PAGE 7**

### Singer to Debut New Song On TV

Mike Clifford, a 21-year-old Los Angeles boy, will come to Shindig for the first time at the end of the month.

During the show he will be featured singing his new song taken from the movie "Village of Ants," in which he appears.

Clifford, a former student at Dorsey High and Audubon Junior High, has been working with the Dick Clark Caravan of Stars since his high school days.

SPEED DEMON CASEY KASEM, MINUS BLACK LEATHER JACKET

### START KNOCKING NOW
## 30 Free Motorcycle Prizes In KRLA's New Suzuki Contest

If people keep knocking on your door, don't be surprised. KRLA's Suzuki Hide and Seek Contest has eager participants knocking on doors throughout every neighborhood in Southern California.

And it's no wonder, for each day of this month one of those "knockers" will win a sleek new Suzuki motorcycle. A total of 30 will be given away.

Here's how it works: Each day a Suzuki is hidden in a particular home, perhaps somewhere right in your own neighborhood. The first person who knocks on the front door of that house or apartment and asks, "Is this the KRLA Suzuki House?" will win the motorcycle.

If no one knocks and asks the proper question between 7 a.m. and 8 p.m., the owner of the home where it is hidden will win the Suzuki. However, the owner must be interviewed over KRLA once per hour, giving clues to its location.

That may sound complicated, but it actually isn't. All you have to do is start knocking on doors and asking, "Is this the KRLA Suzuki House?"

This is one KRLA contest we don't mind "knocking." In fact, we hope you "knock" off one of those motorcycles for your very own.

# KRLA ARCHIVES

# MEET ENGLISH SINGER IAN WHITCOMB

## Beat Takes You For Chat At Tower Records Setting

**By Louise Criscione**

The BEAT has made it a policy to show you the entertainment business from the inside. We've already taken you to Petula Clark's meet-the-press party and brought you backstage for the Rolling Stones' Long Beach show. Now, we'd like to take you to Tower Records for an informal meeting with British singer Ian Whitcomb.

It's a set-up interview, which means it has been arranged beforehand. This kind of an interview is much easier on everyone involved. The reporter is not forced to grab the entertainer just as he steps inside the stagedoor, stick a microphone into his face, and shoot questions at him in rapid-fire succession. As for the entertainer — he does not feel as if he is talking merely to a microphone; people are not rushing around pulling him in about six different directions at once; and he can relax, he doesn't have to make a mad dash for the stage.

So you see, this kind of an interview is much better all the way around. And quite frankly, it's a lot of fun!

As I enter the reception room of Tower Records, I find Ian sitting inside one of the offices. He is wearing a black and white striped shirt, green corduroy pants, and black boots. He stands as I come into the room (surprise, surprise, there ARE a few gentlemen left in this business after all!).

"How do you do? Just a minute, I'll get you a chair," he smiles.

Chair secured and myself seated in it, the interview begins.

*What made you decide to become an entertainer?*

"I enjoy singing — that's why I'm doing it. It's not for the money really. I don't care much about 'laughing on the way to the bank'," he said refering to P. J. Proby's remark that he (Proby) "laughs on the way to the bank."

*How did you get started?*

"I came over on one of those Greyhound tours. In Seattle, I sang in this club — they didn't pay me anything, just my room and board. Later, I sold a tape of a song called 'Fizz' which was the flip of 'This Sporting Life'. I've been very lucky so far."

*You're pretty well-known for singing in that high voice, do you plan to continue using it?*

"I don't want to get stuck with a gimmick. I like to have a kind of different sound each time. The cuts on my album are all different. I might use the high voice again. My voice is rather high-pitched anyway."

*How was your airport reception here is L.A.?*

"It was fantastic! It was the first time something like that ever happened to me. There was only one thing which I was a bit disappointed about. As soon as I got off the plane, the cops grabbed me and rushed me out of there, so I didn't even get a chance to talk to the kids. And I really would've liked to."

*Have you ever been to a Southern California beach?*

"Yeah, once I went to a place called 'Portuguese Bend'. There were a bunch of surfers out there and I had this rubber blow-up thing." With a broad smile creasing his face, Ian laughs "they told me to get lost."

*What do you think about the Beatles receiving the coveted MBE?*

"I think they deserved it. They have brought a lot of money into England. They've done a lot for the country economically. They are a big part of the London Stock Exchange with their Northern Songs. The people who are complaining about it are looking at it culturally, and they just don't think the Beatles have contributed much culture."

*What about the work permit trouble and the attempted ban on English artists?*

"I didn't have any trouble getting a work permit. But I don't even think there should be such things as passports. After all, it's everybody's world, isn't it? Of course, that would never happen, but it's sort of an ideal.

"I think pop music has done the most to break down nationality barriers. It's great to see the Beatles number one in Japan.

"You know, Bluesville and I can be having a big fight just before we go on stage, but once we start playing everything's all right."

A little note ought to be injected right here so that you get the connection between Bluesville and nationality barriers. Bluesville is the band which backs Ian, and it consists of four Irishmen, one Englishman, and one American!

The name Bluesville brings something to Ian's mind.

"Would you do me a favor if you can? Mention Bluesville — they're really great, but nobody ever mentions them. I've gotten a lot of compliments on the backing of 'You Turn Me On', especially the drumming. I can give you their names."

Okay, I'm always willing to do a favor, especially if the credit is deserved. So, here they are — BLUESVILLE — featuring Ian McGarry, Gerry Ryan, Mick Molloy, Deke O'Brien, and Peter Adler!

*Did you think "You Turn Me On" would be such a big hit?*

"No I didn't. In fact, I like the other one, 'This Sporting Life', better. 'You Turn Me On' is falling off in L.A., but it's only just started all over the country. It still has one of those red bullets on it!"

For those of you not familiar with the national charts, a red "bullet" is a dot placed beside the name of the record which indicates a sharp move upward. In this case, it means "You Turn Me On" is destined to go even higher than number 19 in the nation.

*How did you come up with "that sound" you use in "You Turn Me On".*

"Well, the background for the song is kind of interesting. We used to do this song around the clubs in Dublin. It was called 'Roadrunner', and it had this funny sound in it. (At this point Ian demonstrated the "sound"— but I don't know how to explain it and even if I did I couldn't spell it, so you readers will just have to improvise!) One night when we were singing it, the guys started making that sound I use on 'You Turn Me On' and the girls seemed to like it. So I rewrote and rearranged the whole thing using that sound and just making it up as I went along."

*Once a hit record has been made, the mind naturally turns to the follow-up. Have you recorded a follow-up to "You Turn Me On" yet?*

"We've got about ten songs in the can, but I don't know

**TURN TO PAGE 10**

## Help Available for Launching British Trip At Travel Agencies, Information Services

The Beat thanks you for your many letters regarding our forthcoming series of articles on England.

Beginning with the next issue we'll be exploring all the possibilities of traveling the U.K. without going into debt for the next seventy years.

If you'd like to get a head start on planning your trip (even if it's still in the "dreaming" stages), why not drop a line to one or all of the following agencies?

A "Travellers Guide To Britain" and an additional information-packed booklet can be obtained by mail from the British Travel Association, 680 Fifth Avenue, New York, N.Y., 10019. The Association also has a Los Angeles office, located at 612 South Flower Street.

**Technical Facts**

If you're interested in technical facts about Britain (government, economy, industry, etc.) write for information to British Information Services, 845 Third Avenue, New York, N.Y. 10022.

Another service of the British Travel Association (listed two paragraphs back) comes in the form of two booklets; "Traveling Economically In Britain" and "Students Visiting Britain". When you write them, be sure and ask for these folders too.

If you're thinking of applying for a passport, the place to do so in this area is 500 South Figueroa Street, Los Angeles. A Passport is necessary to enter Britain. As an American citizen, you won't need a visa.

**Job Opportunity**

Anyone traveling to England in hopes of finding work should consult the nearest British Consulate. The Los Angeles British Consulate is located at 3324 Wilshire Blvd., and the telephone number is 385-7381. Finding a job in England is quite a complicated process which we'll be talking more about in future Beats.

Attending school in England is equally complicated. If you're interested in attending a British summer school or college (we'll be going into detail about that also), you can obtain information by writing to the Institute of International Education, 1 East 67th Street, New York, N.Y., 10021.

More about England next week!

**THE RISING SONS**
ASH GROVE   8162 Melrose Ave., Los Angeles   OL 3-2070
JUNE 29 - JULY 11 — (NO MINIMUM AGE LIMIT)

## CASEY'S QUIZ

**By CASEY KASEM**

This week's mystery stars take their music extremely seriously. Several members of the group have gone to college, although they certainly don't look like scholars. Most of their music is of the earthy rhythm-and-blues variety, inspired by the earlier works of American artists.

They adopted their name from a song by their idol, Chuck Berry. If I told you how many are in the group and where they are from, it would be almost a dead give-away. But here's a hint: their latest record appears to be their biggest hit yet. You find the answer on Page 12.

# KRLA ARCHIVES

## For Girls Only

Notice To All Boys Who Are Sneakily Reading This Column: Please send me your photographys quickly! I need them for something I'm making.

A dart board!

I'm kidding, I'm kidding, but not about the dart board. And I've already finished my masterpiece. My dart board fits right in with the English phase I'm going through, and also gives me a great way to take out my fits of temper. I change the photo in the center every week or so, and at the moment I'm throwing darts at a picture of my little brother.

Reason? He SAT on my "Beatles VI" album! And if I had my way about it, he would not be doing any more sitting for about a month!

Speaking of my English phase, I was browsing about in the stationery store the other day and saw the wildest note paper. On top of the box it said "Old Liverpool Air Mail" and the paper and envelopes were tissue thin and very English.

After I'd tripped triumphantly home with my imported purchase (only $1.25) and dashed off impressive-looking letters to everyone I could think of, I happened to notice the side of the box.

### Goofed Again

It said Lane Paper Company, Pasadena, California.

Do you ever have the feeling you can't do ANYTHING right?

Shiver, shiver. That just reminded me of something. Have you also ever had the feeling that you've done something before and know exactly what the person you're talking to is going to say next? Or walked into a strange room or building and had the strange sensation that you'd been there before when you knew very well that you hadn't?

That happens to me every once in awhile and it just has to be the creepiest feeling in the world. Any doctor will tell you this is caused by your being reminded of something similar that really did happen, or that you once dreamed about a similar building or situation.

### Poor Explanation

Personally, I don't think that's a very good explanation. I mean how do they know for sure? It certainly isn't very romantic. I like to think it happens because I'm reliving something that occurred when I used to be the Queen of England or someone equally British. (Think big, I always say.)

A friend of mine is having a problem, and a lot of you are probably going through the same trauma. Her boyfriend is going away on a month's trip and although he's promised not to date other girls, she's afraid he'll weaken and break his promise.

I don't know if the following information will help ease your minds any, but statistics prove that ninety-nine per cent of the couples (of high school and college age) who "fall in love" while either the guy or gal is on a holiday never end up together.

### Vacation Romances

Does that paragraph sound weird! Well, it's hard to explain. What I mean is, if you go out of town and meet a wonderful new boy and come down with a mad crush, chances are when you go back home the crush won't last long. When you do get back, you plunge headlong into a lot of activities to get over missing him, and all of a sudden you find yourself not missing him at all!

It makes a lot of sense, really. If you go with someone a long time and then have to be separated, then forgetting isn't nearly so simple. But during the summer you don't get to know enough about each other to keep the memory from fading once you're apart.

I'm not saying it always works that way. But it most often does.

If I were my girlfriend (who is going to read this and kill me) I'd tell my steady to go ahead and date anyone he wants to on his vacation, just as long as he comes back to me. That way dating others wouldn't be twice as irresistable (you know how boys just LOVE to do things everyone says they shouldn't), and after all, the important thing is that he *does* come back.

### Important Message

We now pause for an important message from another of my brothers (the one who is 16). He's been pressuring me ever since I started writing this column, so I have decided to devote no more than a few lines to his cryptic announcement.

"LISTEN, GIRLS: All the guys I know wish girls would stop wearing white lipstick. You all look like you're dead!"

See what I have to put up with? Well, maybe now he'll leave me alone for awhile. Say a second or two.

### New Idea

I'm running out of room, but before I go, I have to tell you about a great idea that was sent to me by a girl named Tami Martin (from L.A.).

Tami feels that since they have St. Christopher Medals for surfers and skiiers, one should be made especially for rock and roll stars.

They do so much traveling, especially the English groups, and have more than their share of dangerous scrapes. It would be a really wonderful gesture to have a special medal that you could send to your favorite.

**TURN TO PAGE 8**

---

**23 SKIDOO**
GIRLS AND GUYS 18 AND OVER
DANCING TO LIVE NAME BANDS
2116 Westwood Blvd., West L.A.
23 SKIDOO DANCERS are now seen on TV's Hollywood A Go Go
—CLOSED MONDAY & TUESDAY—

---

## 'The Winner - Ahhhhh!'

**DAVE HULL AND DICK MORELAND,** drawing the winning entry in the Rolling Stones' Shindig Script Contest, received quite a shock. Reaching deep into the box filled with entries, Dick grabbed hold of a frog which someone had hidden under the postcards. After calming down a bit, he was finally able to select a winner: Marilyn Stocker of Sylmar, Calif. Marilyn wins the script used by the Rolling Stones during their last appearance of "Shindig". It's a real souvenir, autographed by all the Stones, plus other stars who appeared on the show.

## ?Beatle Quiz?

Okay Class, come to order. It's KRLA Beatle Quiz Time and we have five more questions for the most educational and rewarding contest in Beatleland.

You Beatle Students who missed the first six weeks of the Beatle Quiz can still catch up by ordering the June 30, June 23, June 16, June 9, June 2 and May 26 issue of the KRLA BEAT.

The winner of the quiz will be rewarded with a personal interview with the Beatles for the Beat when the group arrives in August and along with a friend will be invited to attend the Beatle Concert as guests of the KRLA Deejays.

Additional prizes will be provided for runner-ups and in case of a tie there will be additional questions or a drawing to decide the final winner. The contest will cover a ten-week period, with at least five new questions asked each week. Beatle Expert Derek Taylor, a close friend of the Beatles and their former press officer, will judge the entries for accuracy.

Beatle Quiz
KRLA BEAT
Suite 504
6290 Sunset Blvd.
Hollywood, Calif. 90028
**CONTEST EDITOR:**

Below are my answers to the fourth set of questions in the BEATLE QUIZ CONTEST.

My Name ................................ Address ................................
City ................................ State ................ Zip Code ................
I (☐ am) (☐ am not) presently a subscriber to the KRLA BEAT.

### NEW QUESTIONS

31. How long was Ringo engaged to Maureen Cox before their marriage? ................
32. What kind of car does John drive? ................
33. Who filled in as Beatles' drummer when Ringo fell ill in 1964? ................
34. The Beatles once had a double name with "Beatles" as part of it. What did they call themselves at that time? ................
35. What was the first Beatles' song to become number 1 in England? ................

# KRLA ARCHIVES

## ON THE BEAT

*By Louise Criscione*

We American Beatle fans had better correct our grammar — the boys are having a hard time dissecting our fan letters. Says John: "You want to see the letters the Japanese write us. You wouldn't believe it. Better than the one we get from America. You wouldn't believe them either! A lot of the American fans are just plain illiterate. You can hardly make out what they're all about!

I hat to say it, but I don't like the Righteous Brothers' new one, "Hung On You". It has Phil Spector written all over it, which isn't bad except that it means that this is their third same-sounding record in a row! I can understand the reasoning behind it. They had a tremendous smash with "Lovin' Feeling", and they would like to do it again. So, they keep repeating the sound. I don't like the idea — it shows lack of originality. It's a sad situation because the Righteous Brothers are fantastic entertainers. Really, they are two of the best performers in the business; they don't need to lean on just one sound.

### Image Breaker

Sandie Shaw is always going around destroying her image. And here she is at it again. "You know those pictures of me where I look all dewy-eyed and sexy? Well, it's only 'cos they've taken away me specs. I can't see a thing without them!"

Did you know Brian Jones cracked a couple of ribs during the Stones stay in Jacksonville, Florida? Seems the boys were practicing a little karate, and Brian fell on the cement. He had to wear an elastic belt, which the other Stones affectionately tabbed "his corsets"!

I haven't been able to place my finger on just what it is, but Jeremy (the other half of Chad) sure looked good on his recent visit to L.A. Maybe it's his hair or maybe it's his livelier personality. Anyway whatever it is, I like it!

### Stone's Mobbed

Just heard Bill Wyman's account of the Stones getaway after the Long Beach show. I'm afraid it was a lot closer than most people suspected. In part, he said: "We Stones have been in some awful crushes and jams in our career, but this was the worst ever. I thought we would all be crushed and suffocated in that big limousine in Long Beach. There must have been a hundred teenagers on the roof of the car and more piling on to them like a rugby scrum. The car was surrounded and bodies were jammed against the side and windows. We in the car all stood up and pushed for our lives on the roof to keep it from coming in on us. We couldn't have got out of the car if it had. I really thought the roof would come in. My arms ached as we pushed for quite a few minutes to keep the roof up. The car was battered and dented." Enough said.

WATCH OUT FOR: Tom Jones to visit the West Coast around the end of July. He'll arrive Stateside in July, do a stint at the Brooklyn Paramount form July 14-21, and then move on to the Coast. On August 2, Tom will head out on a Dick Clark Caravan of Stars. Altogether, he will be in the U.S. for three months.

### Clanton Returns

Remember Jimmy Clanton? He's the guy who made big hits like "Just A Dream" and "Venus In Blue Jeans". He's been absent from the scene for awhile. "I haven't been singing for a couple of months. I had these little do-dads in my throat. You know it's funny — a person always takes his craft for granted. I found out about it one day when I was doing this show. Nothing would come out — my octaves just weren't making it! So, I went to a doctor and found out what was wrong. Anyway, I'm all right now. I'm back on the scene again." We're glad to hear that because Jimmy Clanton is one of our all-time favorites.

QUICK ONES: The Four Tops were the first to feel the British sting of retaliation regarding immigration difficulties despite the public announcement by the British Government that they would not retaliate . . . Chad & Jeremy do a great job on the Lennon-McCartney penned, Bill J. Kramer hit, "From A Window" . . . Bobby Vinton has broken all the attendance records at the famed Copacabana . . . Brenda Lee is doing a month-long tour of the Orient . . . Jewel Akins has topped the charts in Holland with this "The Birds And The Bees" . . . Glad to see that the Beach Boys have recorded a record which sings the praises of we West Coast girls — it's entitled oddly enough, "California Girl".

## U. S. Teens, Deejays, Hotels Bend Minds Of 'Wayne Fontana and The Mindbenders'

Wayne Fontana and the Mindbenders will be able to retest the opinions they formed on American teenagers, hotels and deejays when they visit here this summer.

The British group had a brief visit here a while ago which was preceded by a hassle with immigration authorities concern-those hard-to-come-by work permits. During this visit several aspects of American life stood out in their minds.

### Curious Teenagers

The curiosity of American teenagers was a source of some embarrassment for the group.

"We just couldn't get used to American teenagers," Wayne said. "They used to come up to us and say, 'say something', so we immediately clammed up. I'm sure a few thought we were very unsociable."

Wayne feels that American hotels outclass the ones he's visited in Britain.

"The service is excellent and that's the way it should be — as long as you pay the bill," Wayne said.

"In some British hotels we've stayed at it can be quite embarrassing. The hotel staff seem to have the impression that just because you don't earn your money through big business they are doing you a favor by serving you.

### Late Meals

In the States everybody went out of their way to help us. If we came into the hotel late one night we were always asked if we would like a meal. I can't quite see that happening in a British hotel at 3 a.m. in the morning!"

The patter of American deejays is quite different from that of the British jocks and the boys had quite a job figuring them out.

"Most of them we couldn't understand as they drawled in their localized dialect, but from what we gathered they were good. Instead of just introducing the records they made numerous cracks and interrupted all the adverts."

### Hullaballo Appearance

Thanks to the work permit tie-up, they were only able to do one television show, Hullabaloo, which the group was very enthusiastic about.

"Making Hullabaloo was the epic of our tour. It's a fantastic program. It's a chance to do something creative!"

We hope that during their next visit Wayne Fontana and the Mindbenders will stay longer, not have any work permit difficulties, be able to understand the deejays and talk to the teenagers, and will still get meals at 3 a.m.

## Tips to Teens Continued

(Continued from Page 4)

you can't get over the feeling, try that vat of Listerine you mentioned. It can't hurt anything.

Q: This is going to sound stupid, but whenever I cry my eyes are always swollen the next day. The lids swell up to about twice their size and I look incredible! Don't want to make it seem like I sit around and cry all the time, but this happens even if I shed two tears in a sad movie! What can I do?
(I. V., Pasadena)

A: Before you go to bed, put a cold wet cloth on your eyes and leave it there as long as possible. Then use a few drops of Murine. If that doesn't work, repeat the same process the next morning.

### HINT OF THE WEEK

I have several wool dresses that I just love, but all of them get little snagglies all over them. I was moaning about this at dinner one night and my dad told me to touch a burning match to the snags. It worked, believe it or not. Don't do it while you're wearing the problem dress or skirt, and BE CAREFULL. Do it by the sink so you will have a built-in extinguisher handy if things go wrong. And whatever you do, don't try this on sweaters or anything made out of yarn. (F. S., Glendora)

---

Back issues of the KRLA BEAT are still available, for a limited time. If you've missed an issue of particular interest to you, send 10 cents for each copy wanted, along with a self-addressed stamped envelope to:

KRLA BEAT
Suite 504
6290 Sunset Blvd.
Hollywood, California 90028

ISSUES AVAILABLE
4/14 — INTERVIEW WITH JOHN LENNON
4/21 — INTERVIEW WITH PAUL McCARTNEY
4/28 — CHIMP EXCITES TEEN FAIR
5/5 — HERMANIA SPREADS
5/12 — HERE COMES THE BEATLES
5/19 — VISIT WITH BEATLES
5/26 — FAB NEW BEATLE QUIZ
6/2 — L.A. ROCKS AS STONES ROLL
6/16 — BATTLE OF THE BEAT
6/23 — P. J. — HERO OR HEEL
6/30 — PROBY FIRED

# KRLA ARCHIVES

## Christy Minstrels Entertain Astronauts

Astronauts James McDivitt and Edward White were entertained by the New Christy Minstrels after returning from their fabulous space flight last month.

The performance took place during the National Aeronautics and Space Administration (NASA) dinner-dance held in Washington, D.C. to celebrate the successful flight and honor the two astronauts.

Over 600 people, including high-ranking NASA officials, attended the dinner-dance. The show was emceed by Frank Harden and Jackson Weaver of radio station WMAL in Washington.

In the past few years the New Christy Minstrels have entertained at the White House several times during the Kennedy Administration and were invited to perform at the first White House social event under President Johnson. Last summer the group opened the Democratic Convention in Atlantic City and have recently been invited by the State Department to tour the Soviet Union.

### FOR GIRLS ONLY . . . .
(Continued from Page 6)

Then you could buy another to wear yourself.

See, I told you it was a great idea! Hope someone reading this can put this plan into action.

Whoops. If I don't end this column like fast I'll be writing right on top of someone else's. Please keep your letters coming. I just luv them!

See you next week.

## Advice From A Star

**SINGING STAR NANCY WILSON**, performing at the Cocoanut Grove, offers a few words of backstage encouragement to a young lady who hope to follow in her footsteps. The visitor (right) is Mary Love, a personable Los Angeles songstress who recently recorded a popular number in the blues field, "You Turned My Bitter Into Sweet".

## From Birmingham to Berlin . . . The British Are Singing

Airline companies must be making most of their money from British singers who have been whisking around the world at a phenomenal pace for their various tours.

The six Britishers who form the Unit Four Plus Two are due for a 24-day visit to the United States beginning September 1.

Included in their schedule is a recording for Hullaballoo in New York on September 9. Before arriving here they will tour Scotland for six days.

Meanwhile Fats Domino may visit Britain for the first time. Attempts are being made by a British promoter to woo the singer to England for two weeks of concerts and TV in November.

The Searchers and the Zombies will tour America together beginning July 15 in Chicago. Following their stay in the "Windy City", they will play Milwaukee, Louisville, Indianapolis, St. Louis and Pittsburgh.

In September they will visit Atlanta, Birmingham, Montgomery, Rhode Island, Boston, New Haven and Hartford. Each group can also be seen on Shindig twice.

The Animals recently returned from a tour of Japan for a three week European tour with appearances in Barcelonia, Spain, and Munich and Berlin, Germany.

The Animals were to have played six days in the Southern States but the booking was postponed until September.

### Singing Doctor Revives Oldie

Vince Edwards, smiling Ben Casey himself, has revived an oldie, "No Not Much" which has recently been released by Colpix Records. The handsome doctor just might have a hit on his hands with this one.

It's a good sounding record, but unfortunately being good does not assure the record being a hit. However, this one is breaking out regionally and could go nationally as well.

This is not Vince's first attempt at singing. He has put together a highly successful night club act which has already been tried and proven in Las Vegas.

### Beat Extends Rep Contest

Due to the large number of late-comers, the KRLA BEAT Representatives' Contest deadline has been extended to July 30.

This means you still have time to earn one of the fabulous prizes for taking subscriptions, plus earning a summer income.

You'll find a run-down on the prizes in the special ad below. For information on the additional summer income available, simply fill out the form at the bottom and drop it in the mail.

But hurry, while there's still time!

# KRLA ARCHIVES

## BEAT Slates Cartoon Contest

When Woody Alexander of Altadena, Calif., sent this cartoon to the KRLA Beat last week, our editor had a brainstorm.

"Let's have a cartoon contest for our readers!" he shouted joyously.

"A cartoon contest?" we questioned him skeptically, "How would we run that."

"We'd offer two record albums to the person who sends in the best KRLA cartoon. If we get enough response, there will be a new winner every week," he explained patiently.

"What's in it for us?" we demanded.

### Original Contest

"An original cartoon for our paper every week. It'll be great," he gushed, caught up with enthusiasm over the ingenuity of his plan.

A wake-like hush fell over the room as we contemplated his idea.

"Well what do you think?" he demanded, breaking the silence.

The bravest member of our staff spoke up timidly, "Don't you think we have enough contests as it is? We're going broke."

Poor guy. I hope he can get his old job on the paper route back again. Meanwhile, I have been delegated to inform you readers that:

### Generous BEAT

"THE BEAT never has too many contests. The more we can give to you readers the happier we are. Therefore we are now holding a cartoon contest. Each week a winning cartoon will be selected and printed in the BEAT and the artist will receive two brand-new record albums.

If you are a talented young artist, this is your golden opportunity to win both prestiege among your friends as a BEAT cartoonist, and happiness as the proud owner of two brand new record albums. So do not waste another minute. Send your cartoon to: CARTOON CONTEST, KRLA BEAT, Suite 504, 6290 Sunset Blvd., Hollywood, Calif. 90028."

### JEREMY ON BROADWAY?

The singing duo of Chad and Jeremy are not splitting up, but Jeremy will go off on his own in an acting venture. He has landed the top male lead in a new British musical, "Passion Flower Hotel".

Rehearsals have begun, and the show is expected to premiere in London sometime in August. If the show goes well, it will eventually land on Broadway and conceivably Jeremy will land with it.

Meanwhile, the musical will not interrupt the boys' record-making activities. Ken Glancy of Columbia Records, says the boys "will even have more time to devote to recording sessions since they won't have to go through a series of one-niters."

## Dealer Lambasts Red Coats For Stealing Soul Sound

Are British singers lifting the "soul sound" of the American Negro artists?

Ray Dobard, the owner of a Music City outlet in Berkeley, says they are, and doing a poor job of it at that. He urges that we remedy the situation by tightening immigration work visas.

According to Dobard the laws should have more "teeth," so that they "keep the plagarizing British Red Coats in England."

Dobard charges that British acts lack originality and distinguished merit, therefore failing both tests needed to gain a work visa.

He points out that while a few giant record companies profit by the British invasion, independent labels and small publishers are certain to suffer.

The record store owner has one more axe to grind: "English disk jockeys play one American produced record compared to 30 of the English product."

This he feels, is indicative of the methods used to keep our records from English fans while cashing in on U.S. tax free money.

## Record By Billy Joe Royal Wins Optomistic Predictions

You have to watch out for these Southerners—they'll sneak up on you when you're not looking. Take Southerner Billy Joe Royal. He's a tall (six feet), handsome, 23 year-old native of Valdosta, Georgia, with a record which is going to be a big hit.

The name of the record is "Down In The Boondocks," and it's sure to be a hit because the Emperor has placed his royal stamp of approval on it. And when the "Emp" says it is going to be a hit—it had darn well better be a hit or face the royal consequences!

Getting back to Billy—he has been singing since he was in grade school and in high school he formed his own group which performed at school functions and parties. He picked up his professional style at a place called Bamboo Ranch in Savannah, Georgia.

Billy does not confine himself to merely singing; he plays the guitar, drums, and piano as well. He lists his two favorite recording artists as—Ray Charles and Gene Pitney. Billy spends his leisure time as any Southern gentlemen would, riding horses!

### Beats Make Book Covers

The KRLA BEAT is really busting its buttons off today!

We were driving past a high school in the Hollywood area, and happened to see several students eagerly (oh, sure) entering the building for summer school classes.

You'll never guess what they were carrying! Books with covers made out of the KRLA Beat! We really flipped!

What a great way to protect your books from damage (and tear stains during classes). And what a great way to send us back to the office feeling about ten feet tall!

Our thanks to the Beat reader who came up with this fabulous idea!

# KRLA ARCHIVES

## Dave Clark's Visit to L. A. Heralded By Hospitable Fan

*By Lenore Longpre*

*(This article was written by the Dave Clark Five Fan Club president to welcome the English group to our country, by telling them that "We are Glad All Over" that they are here.)*

Last November they shook up their audience at Long Beach Arena with their famous "Tottenham Sound".

Since then "Glad All Over" toppled the Beatles from their Number One position and Dave Clark said: "We've always been hoping for this sort of success. But we didn't expect it. We've had too many disappointments."

All the things of the past that helped the Dave Clark Five become what they are today, haven't changed them in in any way.

Yet it was hardly what you could call an over-night success story for these boys. It wasn't overnight that their exciting past history became like a fairy tale for five equally exciting boys on the way up. More or less, as Dave said, life was full of disappointments until the day they toppled the Beatles with "Glad All Over".

The enthusiasm with which their fans greet them at the airport arrivals proves to all bystanders what the "Five" means to us.

As Dave put it, "America is our second home, luv." And fans all over echo that statement a thousand times over as once again the Dave Clark Five return to "their second home".

## FAN CLUBS

*(For information from any of the listed fan clubs enclose a self-addressed, stamped envelope.)*

**P. J. PROBY**
c/o Jeanette Grittani
45 Vernon Street
Toronto 9, Ontario,
Canada

**ROLLING STONES**
c/o Terry Liblick
116 Via Colusa
Redondo Beach,
Calif. 90277

**JOEY PAIGE**
c/o Pat Smith
13452 Elmwood
Garden Grove, Calif.

**HERMAN'S HERMITS**
c/o Merrie Phillips
425 S. San Jose
Covina, Calif. 91722

**BEATLES**
c/o Joyce Keen
640 Gorsuch
Baltimore, Md. 21218

**PETER & GORDON**
c/o Norma J. Reill
9744 Mango Drive
Fontana, Calif. 92335

**SAXON AND THE CELTS**
c/o Geri Grace
6631 W. 83rd Street
Los Angeles, Calif. 90045

P. J. PROBY

**SONNY & CHER**
P.O. Box 84
Montrose, Calif.

**HERMAN'S HERMITS**
c/o Shelley Stephens
147 Rosemont Avenue
Los Angeles, Calif. 90026

**IAN WHITCOMB**
c/o Paula Stump
740 E. Palmyra Avenue
Orange, Calif. 92667

*(The above information is provided as a service to our readers. Accuracy of the information you receive is the responsibility of the officials of each club.)*

## Whitcomb Continued

*Continued from Page 5)*

which one will be released. There's one I especially like. It has a ukulele in it, and it's kind of a Herman-type song. But just because I like it doesn't mean it will sell or that it will even be released! 'You Turn Me On' will be a hard record to follow-up."

Ian has completed his studies at Trinity College — that is, as soon as he takes his exams in September. And then?

"Well, if I'm still heard of, I might come out here and go to UCLA or somewhere like that. I like Los Angeles."

Quite obviously, the British influence the American pop scene, but who influences the British?

"The Americans! You know, whenever an English group is asked to name their favorite entertainers, they always mention people like John Lee Hooker, Chuck Berry, and Muddy Waters. They're always American and primarily American Negroes. That's where the blues came from. It used to be confined to just the colored stations. Then the groups picked it up, and people thought it was new, but it isn't really.

"Now, it's getting away from real rock—more of a folk sound with everybody doing Dylan songs."

*Do you think there will be a big folk boom in the U.S. similar to the one in England?*

"Well, you had one here a few years ago, didn't you? But it was a crewcut college thing with all those hootenannies. Now with Dylan, it's more down-to-earth. That's why I like Dylan. That's why I like the Beatles — they're down-to-earth too."

A glance at my watch brought the interview to an end. But before I left I did remember to ask Ian for a list of the shows he would be doing while he is in town. Besides several personal appearances (including the Hollywood Bowl on July 3), Ian will hit practically every TV show originating from Hollywood. Among these will be Shindig, American Bandstand, Shivaree, Hollywood A' Go Go, Where The Action Is, and Lloyd Thaxton. Following his stay in Los Angeles, Ian will venture out on the one-nighter trail with Dick Clark Caravan of Stars.

Ian and I rode down in the elevator together. He was about to be taken out to lunch, and I was about to make a two-block run up Vine Street to explain to my editor why a 20 minute interview had lasted an hour and 20 minutes!

## BEATLES SURGE AHEAD OF STONES IN LATEST POLL

The Battle of the Beat has taken a turn in favor of the Beatles, giving them a meager half of a percent lead over the Rolling Stones.

At the start of the contest the Rolling Stones pulled out way ahead of the Beatles, but as the contest continued, the men from Liverpool pulled up steadily.

Some attribute the Beatle's rise in popularity to the medals

## Letters

Dear People:
The Beat is the best thing that ever happened to papers! The June 9 issue is darling.
Before I forget, James Bond does look a lot like Derek.
Keep up the good work.
Yours Truely,
Carol Marquette,
Santa Barbara, Calif.

Dear Editor:
We think the Beat is the greatest thing to come along since Paul McCartney. The contests are great. When are you going to have a contest and give away Dave Hull as the prize? Now that's worth entering.
Your Faithful Readers,
The United Scuzzies.

Dear Editor:
When I read in the June 16 issue of the Beat that someone had actually taken Brian Jones' record collection, I was so surprised. I just couldn't imagine how anyone could be so mean and heartless.
It's just like if you had a really great Rolling Stones, Beatle, or any kind of collection that you treasured, and someone had taken it from you! Well wouldn't you just want to die! To me this is how Brian Jones must have felt.
So whoever took it come on and give it back. You could probably bring it to the KRLA deejays or mail it to them if you don't want them to know who you are. And don't think people will think less of you because you took it. They'll think more of you for bringing it back!
Jorbie Presta.

Dear Editor:
I was wondering if you could tell me why the Beatles didn't let their fans line up and meet them after a performance like they do in England? Also, could you tell me if they are going to perform on any television shows?
If you can answer even one of my questions, I promise to buy two copies of the Beat every week.
Sincerely,
Lyn Dearkirs.

*Editor's Note:*
We took these questions to Derek Taylor, former press manager for the Beatles, and this is what he said:
"There were only two performances in England for the Beatle fans. One was in London, and the paid-up members of the Beatle fan club actually got to line up and meet the Beatles. The other performance was in Liverpool and while the Beatles

they received two weeks ago. Others have suggested all along that there popularity would zoom back as the date for their appearance at the Hollywood Bowl draws near.

The Battle of the Beat will continue for one more week, so do not let your favorite group down. Send your choice on a postcard to: BATTLE OF THE BEAT, 6290 Sunset, Suite 504, Hollywood, 90028.

did a special show for their fans they did not personally meet them.

In both cases the situation was manageable because the audiences were reasonably small. Where in America can the Beatles meet their fans after a show? The answer is no where, so they don't. Furthermore the Beatles are never in any one place long enough and no police force could guarantee them the needed protection. Therefore it would be impossible for them to meet their fans after a show."

As for your second question, the Beatles will appear on the Ed Sullivan Show and possibly Shindig.

Hope you enjoy your two copies of the BEAT every week.
THE BEAT.

Dear KRLA BEAT Guys:
I just wanna let you know that the KRLA BEAT is justly-grandly-flabbist and good too! WE ALL appreciate all the stuff you guys do to get the news to write (especially BEATLE things). Keep it going forever!
Your new subscriber and
Beatlemaniac,
Kim Brown,
Los Altos, Calif.
P.S. Los Altos is on the San Francisco Bay Peninsula. You are even going strong up here.

Dear KRLA Beat:
Many thanks for printing my pen pal advertisement in your June 2 BEAT. It had a wonderful effect. The postman here has been kept very busy indeed.
I have a few copies of your great paper. It makes interesting reading, keep it up.
Would you please do me one more favour? That of putting my Thank You note in your Personals column as a medium of communication to those readers who wrote me.
Sincerely,
John Issac,
Liverpool, England.
*Editor's Note: See Personals.*

## Open Letter To A Star ★

Dear One:
Maybe I shouldn't write this letter, but *I Can't Help Myself*. *This Little Bird* has written you many times before, and you have never answered. *I Can't Get No Satisfaction* unless I hear from you *Just Once In My Life*.
It would be *A Little Bit Of Heaven* for this *Little Lonely One* if you'd take *Just A Little* time to say *Mrs. Brown You've Got A Lovely Daughter*.
I'll *Keep Holding On* until you write back, but *Don't Just Stand There! I've Been Loving You Too Long* not to be *Shakin' All Over* from you *Keeping Me Waiting*.
Asking someone as busy as you for a personal note is like trying to *Catch The Wind*, but please try to *Remember Me, I'm The One Who Loves You*.
And remember, because I feel this way, *You'll Never Walk Alone*. If you'll drop a line, I won't either.
*Laurie Brown.*

July 7, 1965      KRLA BEAT      Page 11

# Famous Songwriter Bob Dylan Mystery Man to Most Americans

Who is Bob Dylan, the man who is causing such a sensation on today's pop scene.

Since he has been relatively ignored by the American press he is kind of a mystery man here, despite the records, concerts and dozens of hit songs he has written for other entertainers.

Most people are familiar with the name, but not with the man. Who is this eccentric-looking song writer? What does he possess? What does he believe in? Or does he believe in anything at all?

Because he is the hottest American artist in England, because his album "Bring It All Back Home" is riding high on American charts, and because he has made some rather interesting and controversial comments about today's world, we feel it is time for the BEAT to introduce you to the man Bob Dylan.

*Is there a Dylan cult?*

"The image — there's nothing to it. If someone wants to believe something about me, they can. It doesn't matter a little bit to me. At one time it did. That was some years ago when I was on the streets and trying to make some impression. Right now, I don't care what people think — the cult is something other people talk about. Not me."

*Do his songs contain some kind of a message?*

"The message isn't in the words. I don't do anything with a sort of message. I'm just transferring my thoughts into music. All I can hope to do is sing what I'm thinking, and maybe remind you of something. Don't put me down as a man with a message. My songs are just me talking to myself."

*John Lennon has sung Dylan's praises all over England, but what does Dylan think of Lennon?*

"I dig John. As a writer, a singer, and a Beatle. There are very few people I dig everytime I meet them, but him I dig. He doesn't take things seriously as so many guys do. I like that."

*What does Dylan think about money?*

"I don't depend on the money. I don't take any interest in it. It goes into some kinda bank. I buy anything I want to buy, but that's not much. I have to buy clothes all the time because I leave them around wherever I go. I have a little car — a Chevy, but it's a wreck. That's all I need y'know? I have the money thing clearly sorted out in my mind."

*What about politics?*

"No politics. Politics is just a commercial bandwagon."

*What about his clothes, how come he never wears a suit and tie?*

"I have nothing to say against suits, and nothing to say in their favor either. Why should I wear a suit? To go and eat supper? I have nothing against ties. It never struck me before people asked questions that I never wore a tie. Must I wear a tie? It's nice of people to show their concern in what I wear. I don't share it."

*How does Dylan feel about religion?*

"I don't think religion can show anybody how to live. I don't have any religion."

*What about death?*

"I used to be afraid of it, but no more. Great men die — Shakespeare died. Napoleon died. We all die.

*Well then, what does he think about life?*

"If anything influences my songs, life does. I could write songs called 'Where's My Baby Gone?' I'm not putting them down, but I want to say things different. I guess catastrophe and confusion are the basis of my songs. But basically my songs are really about love — love of life."

This is Bob Dylan, folksinger and poet, the most successful writer of folk songs in the world today. You may like him or dislike him, agree with him or disagree. He doesn't particularly care. Despite his outstanding commercial success, he seems to be looking for something else.

And perhaps he has found it.

## Man With A Message

# PERSONALS

Dear Sirs:

I have five English pen pals who enjoy reading my KRLA BEATS. They send me issues of their Pop magazines in return. That way we can be better informed on both American and English groups. I'd like to say "hi" to two of my pen pals, Keith Ely and Roger Hodgkin. Try sending your English friends a KRLA BEAT. You get an English magazine in return.

              Joanne Beroiz,
              Wilmington, Calif.

Dear BEAT Readers:

Thank you all very much for the response to my advertisement for a pen pal. My choice has been made very difficult as I have received stacks of letters and they are still coming in!

As you can well imagine it would be far too costly to reply to all who wrote from places like Long Beach, L.A., El Segundo, Oxnard, Palos Verdes, Pasadena, etc. Boy the list is too long to mention, and I have solved the problem by using the FAB KRLA BEAT.

I am trying to find other boys from school to write to those who wished it, but as pen friendship has been such a big craze in Liverpool lately, every boy I have asked already has at least one American pen friend. But I shall keep trying for you.

If I ever come to California, which is one of my ambitions, I shall look some of you up as I am keeping all these letters. Thank you all so much
                      again,
              John A. Issac,
                Liverpool.

P.S. Rockers now call themselves "Greasers".

Dear BEAT:

Here is the name of an English boy who would like a pen pal in the United States. He is 16 and likes pop and folk music especial Mariann Faithful. He also likes natural history and exchanging ideas and will come to America before he's 20.

    Oswald Julian Post
    Hulland Vicarage
    Near Derby
    Derbyshire, England.
            Thank You,
            A Reader.

## DEREK TAYLOR Continued
(Continued from Page 3)

iniously removed from the air. I believe it's worse to have been played and removed than never to have been played at all.

### ANTICIPATING HELP

The Beatles have seen "Help." And they liked it. This is important because they don't always like their own work. I can't wait to see their first color movie. Make it soon.

Anything else? Paul Revere and the Raiders have just returned from Hawaii after filming for "Where the Action Is" — the Dick Clark coast-to-coast TV show which received its first daily airing on Monday (June 28).

Jerry Naylor arrived in Hawaii this week to tape "Hollywood a Go Go" and a special "Aloha a Go Go."

I nearly forgot . . .

On Thursday of last week, unmourned, and unsung, James Marcus Smith, alias Jet Powers, otherwise known as P. J. Proby, self-styled god of popular music, slipped silently out of Los Angeles bound for London. The party was indeed over . . .

**THESE ARE THE SPATS**, and they're soon to be featured in a national magazine as an example of clean-cut American youths who have resisted the long-hair movement. They have appeared at Disneyland and on numerous television shows, and will be featured with Dave Clark Five at Pasadena Civic Auditorium July 10. The group from Garden Grove recently released a new record, "Billy the Blue Grasshopper."

# KRLA ARCHIVES

Page 12 — KRLA BEAT — July 7, 1965

## KRLA TUNEDEX

### #1 RED HOT

| This Week | Last Week | Title | Artist |
|---|---|---|---|
| 1. | 1. | SATISFACTION | The Rolling Stones |
| 2. | 2. | I CAN'T HELP MYSELF | The Four Tops |
| 3. | 5. | ONCE UPON A TIME | Tom Jones |
| 4. | 16. | YES, I'M READY | Barbara Mason |
| 5. | 21. | HOLD ME, THRILL ME, KISS ME | Mel Carter |
| 6. | 25. | ALL I REALLY WANT TO DO | Cher |
| 7. | 3. | WHAT THE WORLD NEEDS NOW | Jackie DeShannon |
| 8. | 14. | WHITTIER BOULEVARD | The Midnighters |
| 9. | 9. | LAURIE | Dickie Lee |
| 10. | 4. | WOOLY BULLY | Sam the Sham & The Pharaohs |
| 11. | 33. | I'VE GOT YOU | Sonny & Cher |
| 12. | 13. | CRYING IN THE CHAPEL | Elvis Presley |
| 13. | 18. | I'M A FOOL | Dino, Desi & Billy |
| 14. | 6. | BACK IN MY ARMS AGAIN | The Supremes |
| 15. | 8. | HELP ME RHONDA | The Beach Boys |
| 16. | 10. | JUST YOU | Sonny & Cher |
| 17. | 12. | MR TAMBOURINE MAN | The Byrds |
| 18. | 27. | THIS LITTLE BIRD | Marianne Faithfull |
| 19. | 11. | HERE COMES THE NIGHT | Them |
| 20. | 7. | SHAKIN ALL OVER | Guess Who? |
| 21. | 17. | HUSH, HUSH SWEET CHARLOTTE | Patti Page |
| 22. | 15. | GOOD LOVIN' | The Olympics |
| 23. | 24. | SEVENTH SON | Johnny Rivers |
| 24. | 19. | WONDERFUL WORLD | Herman's Hermits |
| 25. | 23. | THE LAST TIME/PLAY WITH FIRE | The Rolling Stones |
| 26. | 38. | CARA MIA | Jay and the Americans |
| 27. | 20. | YOU TURN ME ON | Ian Whitcomb & Bluesville |
| 28. | 46. | I'M HENRY THE VIII I AM | Herman's Mermits |
| 29. | 34. | OOO WEE BABY I LOVE YOU | Fred Hughes |
| 30. | 39. | MARIE | The Bachelors |
| 31. | 42. | ALL I REALLY WANT TO DO | The Byrds |
| 32. | | HUNG ON YOU | The Righteous Brothers |
| 33. | 44. | SAVE YOUR HEART FOR ME | Gary Lewis & The Playboys |
| 34. | 40. | LET HER DANCE | Bobby Fuller |
| 35. | 43. | YOU BETTER COME HOME | Petula Clark |
| 36. | 41. | AND I REALLY LOVE HIM | Esther Phillips |
| 37. | | PRETTY LITTLE BABY | Marvin Gaye |
| 38. | | WHATEVER HAPPENED TO THE GOOD TIMES | The Peddlers |
| 39. | | ONE MORE TIME | Them |
| 40. | | EASY QUESTION | Elvis Presley |

**SOUTHERN CALIFORNIA'S MOST ACCURATE RECORD SURVEY — BASED ON RETAIL SALES FIGURES**

KRLA BEAT
6290 Sunset, No. 504
Hollywood, Cal. 90028

BULK RATE
U.S. Postage
PAID
Los Angeles, Calif.
Permit No. 25497

If you were a KRLA BEAT subscriber your name and address would be printed here and you would receive your copy at home, saving 40%.

1. CRYING IN THE CHAPEL — Elvis Presley
2. I'M ALIVE — The Hollies
3. THE PRICE OF LOVE — The Everly Brothers
4. COLOURS — Donovan
5. LOOKING THROUGH THE EYES OF LOVE — Gene Pitney
6. LONG LIVE LOVE — Sandy Shaw
7. TRAINS AND BOATS AND PLANES — Burt Bacharach
8. THE CLAPPING SONG — Shirley Ellis
9. POOR MAN'S SON — Rockin' Berries
10. ANYWAY ANYHOW ANYWHERE — The Who

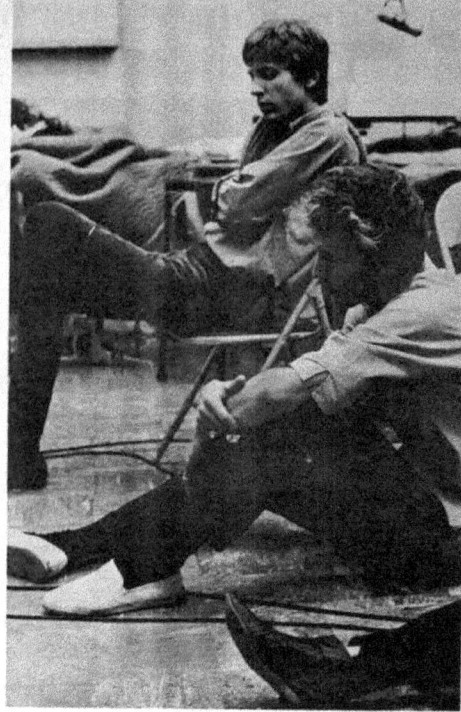

## Group Begins Climb to Top By Winning British Hearts

While Britain is way ahead of us in the field of exporting popular entertainers, a couple of our local boys have managed to win British hearts.

P. J. Proby, who was nothing here, simply torpedoed Britain. And in the same tradition, a three man group known as the Walker Brothers who were completely inconspicuous in Hollywood, has raised a storm in the British Isles.

While in Hollywood they did appear more or less regularly on Hollywood A' Go Go, they did do a couple of Shindig shows.

Gary explains how the Walker Brothers finally decided to make the trek to England. "Jack Good saw us playing in a club in Hollywood and invited us to England, to do a Shindig. We had no record, but after the show all the companies had offers ready. We cut 'Pretty Girls Everywhere', and Jack asked us to do another Shindig. It was about this time we met the Rolling Stones. They said we should go to England." And so they did.

### Smart Move

Apparently, it was a very smart move because the Walker Brothers now have a smash record, "Love Her", on the British charts, have been given an abundance of press in the British music papers and magazines, and are the first American male group to really make an impression in England.

Because they use a 38-piece band on "Love Her", the Walker Brothers have been accused of imitating the Righteous Brothers. Answering this charge Gary said, "There are two Righteous Brothers, three of us. They have short hair; we have long hair. We were around before they were too."

### Not Brothers

The Walker Brothers are not really brothers and come from opposite points of the U.S. 21-year-old Gary, who plays drums for the group, is a native Californian, born in Glendale. He is the one who accompanied P. J. Proby when Proby was still known as "Jet Powers".

John, the 22 year-old lead guitarist, was born in New York City and once thought of becoming a history teacher.

The last "brother" is 21-year-old Scott. He plays bass guitar and can also play the drums, piano, and harmonica.

Because of their success in Britain, the Walker Brothers have renewed their work permits and plan to become "permanent fixtures" on the English scene.

—Louise Criscione

### CASEY'S QUIZ ANSWER

(Don't peek unless you've read the question elsewhere in the BEAT.

**The Rolling Stones**

# KRLA BEAT

Volume 1, No. 19 — Los Angeles, California — 15 Cents — July 24, 1965

# KRLA BEAT

Page 2 — July 24, 1965

## NEW BEAT E-X-P-A-N-D-S TO 16 PAGES OF NEWS

We're proud to unveil the new 16-page edition of the KRLA BEAT.

It is another big step forward for America's first and foremost teen newspaper. The "News" in newspaper should be emphasized, because that's what the KRLA BEAT is in every sense. Not a magazine prepared months in advance. Not a throw-away sheet to promote KRLA's popularity, but a real, honest-to-goodness weekly newspaper with at least 16 pages filled with exclusive news and exciting pictures of your favorite entertainers and personalities.

While we have increased the single copy price to 15 cents to offset a portion of the increased cost, KRLA will still receive no financial profit from the BEAT.

As before, the KRLA BEAT is published exclusively for YOU. Instead of merely advertising KRLA, it is a newspaper designed to entertain and inform the teenagers and young adults of Southern California . . . the same function served by KRLA as a broadcaster.

It is your newspaper. And with your help we will continue to make it an even bigger and better newspaper.

. . . STILL IN THE DRIVERS SEAT

## BEATLES TOP STONES IN 'BATTLE OF BEAT'

*By Dave Hull*

Okay! Kings-X! Cool it! We surrender!

We've got mail piled up to the ceiling here in the BEAT offices and the phones are ringing off the wall. KRLA's "Battle of the BEAT" poll is now officially over and here is the result:

### THE BEATLES WON!

Beatle fans throughout California jumped up in arms during the final week of balloting. Beatle votes came pouring in like an avalanche and they wound up with a 2-1 lead over the Rolling Stones.

If you remember, the Stones had taken a lead during the first two weeks of the write-in poll. But John, Paul, George and Ringo caught them during the third week, and after the fourth week the Beatles wound up with 65.8 per cent of the total vote.

So, don't underestimate the Beatles, Or their fans.

But the final results are no reflection on the Rolling Stones. They're still burning up the record charts with "Satisfaction"—their greatest hit yet—and the

### Beatles Reveal Secret Desire

If you were one of the BEATLES, and you could do anything or have anything in the world, what would you like most of all on your next trip to the United States?

A spokesman for the BEATLES revealed that the first thing, the most important thing, the one BIG thing they want to do . . . is visit Disneyland!

It's not as easy as it sounds. Such a famous person as the former premier of Russia, Nikita Krushchev, was unable to attend because of security problems—and the same situation may face the BEATLES.

Getting to the Anaheim amusement park may be one thing, but what about the thousands of kids who will storm the place when the word spreads? One idea has been to have them get a quick look by helicopter, but so far no definite plans, or even approval, has been announced by Disney officials.

Beatles do not have a current hit.

### Surprise?

The outcome of the popularity poll will come as a surprise to many people. The Beatles have been drawing extremely poor crowds in some European cities. Even here in California they're running into some problems at the box office.

Their two performances at Hollywood Bowl were instant sell-outs, but they have had trouble selling tickets for the San Diego concert, sponsored by the House of Sight and Sound. This in spite of the fact it has been heavily promoted by other radio stations in Los Angeles and other cities who claim to be sponsoring the concert.

But the excitement of the Beatles receiving the cherished Order of the British Empire and the criticism which followed in many quarters must have aroused the Southern California Beatlemaniacs. I think that had a lot to do with the flood of mail we received during the final week of the BEAT poll.

### More Beatlemania

And when the Beatles release their next record I think it will be as big a smash as any of their previous hits. I think the combined impact of releasing their new movie plus the approach of their U.S. concert tour will start another mass wave of Beatlemania.

Getting back to the popularity contest, I think it also proved that most Californians like both groups. Many found it hard to choose between them because they have completely different styles and both are tremendously talented.

But that's the case in any popularity contest. It's like putting Elizabeth Taylor and Deborah Kerr in the same category and choosing between them for an Academy Award. That's not easy, either.

Many people, in fact, voted for BOTH the Beatles and the Rolling Stones.

I was one of them.

**ANYONE FOR SWIM?** These two KRLA lovelies are Linda Luback (left) of Burbank and Edy Nielsen of Costa Mesa, two of the entries in Bill Slater's "Girls on the Beach" contest. The contest was inspired by the hit movie of that title, now playing in the Los Angeles area. Bill spends most of his time at the beach these days.

# KRLA ARCHIVES

# KINKS PLAYFUL AS PORPOISES ON CALIFORNIA VISIT

## Spend Secret Night Prowling Los Angeles

By Jean Watson

Four Kinks from London pranced energetically around a Los Angeles hotel room, throwing ice cubes, cracking jokes, playing records, and interrupting each other.

Meanwhile a photographer and a reporter from the BEAT, confused and charmed, joined forces to capture their quick-silver personalities.

The mischeivous quartet had sneaked into L.A. on June 26, to the surprise of a Warner Brothers public relations man, who along with the BEAT photographer and a black limousine, waited patiently to greet them at the airport the following day.

"We had a lot to do, so we came early," they explained.

### Secret Night

During his secret night in Los Angeles, adventurer Ray Davies, the lead singer of The Kinks, investigated the city.

"I rode around Los Angeles and Hollywood and got insulted by a few people because I had long hair," he reported good naturedly.

What do The Kinks want to do while they are in California?

"I want to try some speed boats," Pete Quaife, the bass guitarist for the group, offered enthusiastically.

"I want to get some California sun, eat some California food and go swimming," Ray Davies said.

While in California, the good-looking lead singer, (too bad girls, he's been married for nearly a year), has two other ambitions.

"I want to go to Palm Springs and I want to see Jack Benny. He's my idol. I saw him on TV in England," he explained.

### Sun Worshippers

His desire to go to Palm Springs coincides with his hope to soak up a lot of California rays. "I love to sun bathe, but I move around too much to ever get enough sun," he said, critically examing his white skin.

And what about handsome, dark-haired Mick Avory, who was sitting quietly in the background. What plans did he make for his stay in Los Angeles?

"To go to Shelly's Manhole", he offered shyly.

"When do you think you'll get to go?" the BEAT reporter asked, eager for a scoop.

"I went . . . last night," he replied matter-of-factly. "I always try to catch great musicians whenever I can. Especially drummers."

### Camera Bug

Dave Davies, 18, and the youngest member of the group, will probably spend his free time like any other tourist, taking pictures. One of the first L.A. visits made by the camera bug was to the nearest photography shop.

As for their thoughts on American women, the four were full of information on the subject.

"American girls are cute, and they're with it," said Ray. "By with it, I mean they are very smart, as are the girls in England."

"In fact" he added, accents are the only difference between English and American girls. And lots of American girls try to talk with English accents."

### Amercian Clothes

Pete Quaife, nodding his approval of American females, interrupted to comment on the one thing he doesn't like about our women . . . their "sense of fashion."

"I hate to see them in bermuda shorts. If I had a date with a girl in America and she came up with Bermuda shorts—ugh," he said, waving away a mythical female clad in Bermuda shorts.

What other corrections should be made in the dressing habits of American girls?

"Well, I don't like white high-heeled shoes," Pete said, eyeing the white high-heeled shoes worn by the red-faced BEAT reporter."

"American girls put something on that looks good on one particular part of their body, with no concern over whether it goes with the rest of their outfit. They end up wearing orange blouses and green shoes and all kinds of wild colors together," he continued.

Noticing the lingering embar-
**TURN TO PAGE 4**

**RAY DAVIES**, lead singer of the Kinks and BEAT reporter Jean Watson discuss Ray's plans during his visit to Los Angeles. In addition to being lead singer, he also writes many of the songs for the group.

**THE FOUR KINKS** staring into the camera are (from left Ray Davies, Dave Davies, Mick Avory and Pete Quaife. The four took time out from their first afternoon in California to pose for the BEAT photographer.

# KRLA ARCHIVES

## Tell Likes, Dislikes On U. S. Women

*(Continued from Page 3)*

rassment of the white high-heels wearer, Ray interceded.

**Casual Dresser**

"I don't care much about clothes," he said kindly. "I wanted to get married in jeans and a sweatshirt. Because of my wife's religious convictions, I was forced to wear a suit."

"I rarely wear a shirt unless my girl friend tells me to," said Pete, who likes to dress as casually as possible.

"As for long hair, the Beatles didn't start that craze in England. It stemmed from the art schools," Pete said.

"I was a long-haired art student long before the Beatles ever came around," Ray agreed.

Ray, who writes the songs for the group, says that the name of the group comes from the word kinky, a saying that is going around England.

**Kinky People**

"Kinky means a couple of things," he said. "For one it means someone who is different. Like if a person went around in leather clothes when everyone else is wearing a suit, they would be kinky."

While in Los Angeles the group will do a show for Shindig, Shivaree and appear at Hollywood Bowl. Their appearances in California will include shows

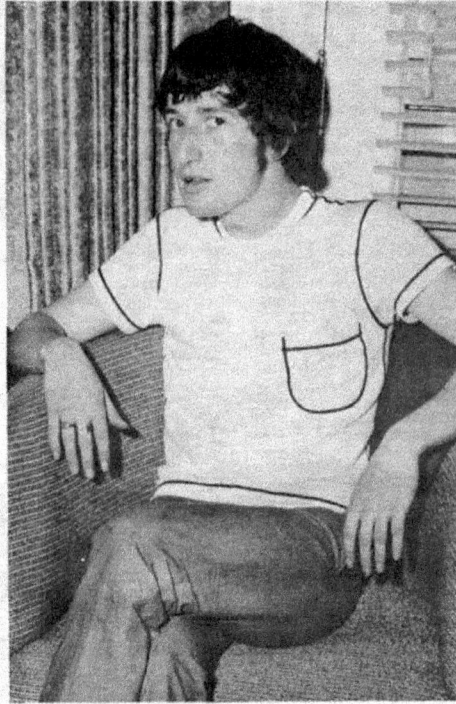

PETE QUAIFE gives the BEAT one of his famous "Kinky" looks. Pete, who plays the bass guitar, loves to go shooting. He is also fond of bow and arrows.

in San Diego, Honolulu and at the Cow Palace in San Francisco.

The four are very happy about the whole arrangement.

"We started playing for kicks and still do," said Ray.

"The stuff I've done isn't as good as what I'm going to do," Pete predicted firmly.

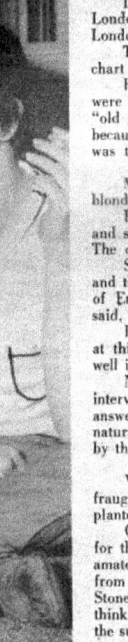

**READING THE BEAT** are (from left) Mick Avory, Ray Davies and Pete Quaife. They are in their Los Angeles hotel, where they will be staying when they are not running from show to show.

## Derek Taylor Reports

### MARIANNE FAITHFULL LIKE A BREATH OF FRESH AIR

Marianne Faithfull flew out of Los Angeles and somehow the city didn't seem quite as bright.

She has the poise and limitless charm. Like most English girls who have endured the rigors and disciplines of boarding school, she has developed a capacity to put up with almost anything.

Marianne was not exactly dragged into the entertainment industry — but her sudden emergence as a singer with a record in the charts was not the result of ambition, or drive, or a yearning for fame.

For, really, she had only a fringe-interest in show business. She and her then boyfriend, Cambridge under-graduate John Dunbar — now her husband and an honors graduate with an "urge to write" — were on the "party-scene" in London at the time when the new wave of pop music was at its most exciting.

That was in the misty past — in the days when Peter and Gordo had just recorded "World Without Love" which—though they didn't know it — was to bring them immense international fame and great wealth. It was in the days when Paul and John, Ringo and George were learning their way about London's sophisticated West End and drawing delighted gurgles from the "smart set" who had never heard a Liverpool accent.

**Money Was Scare**

The Beatles apart, none of the party-goers had very much money. Dunbar had still not left Cambridge, and Marianne was living on an allowance from her mother, who had a European title.

Dunbar, in Hollywood with Marianne last week, recalled: "I used to get my bread from Marianne." She smiled and said gently: "And paid most of it back."

Anyway.... one of the party-goers was a thin young man with a startling white face, a long knitted scarf which he wound round and round his neck, and brown-tinted spectacles.

He was fair-haired and his name was Andrew Loog Oldham. Oldham, by that time, was manager of the up-and-coming Rolling Stones, who were still becoming used to newspaper articles which asked: "Would you let your daughter marry a Rolling Stone?"

Dunbar and Oldham had been members of a Hampstead (London) socialist club and at one of the weekend parties in a London apartment, he asked Marianne to record for him.

The result was "As Tears Go By." A by-product was sufficient chart interest to make Marianne known to all the fans.

Remember that, at that time, the only girls who meant anything were Cilla Black and Dusty Springfield. Dusty represented the "old guard" of seasoned artists — not because she was old, but because she had been in the business for some years — and Cilla was the female symbol of the big breakthrough from Liverpool.

**New Way of Life**

Marianne came onto the scene as the cool, fragile, long-haired blonde who had nothing to lose by making a record.

But . . . . there are no half-measures in the record industry and she had to take her place on the hard, grinding, road shows. The one-night stands.

She was booked on a tour with Freddie and the Dreamers and the Hollies. Both of them rumbustious groups from the north of England. "It was a completely new way of life," Marianne said, "but it was a gorgeous experience."

Dunbar, who had induced her to toy with show business, was at this time in Spain, holidaying. Said Marianne: "It's just as well it worked out right because John landed me in it."

None of this appears to have altered her. Interviews are interviews. Nobody enjoys the first few moments of question and answer. Marianne's quality as an interviewee is that she has a natural flow of conversation which no amount of contamination by the entertainment industry can hinder or pervert.

**Refreshing Candor**

Very often interviews with artists can be hideous experiences fraught with mistrust, slogans, ready-made pre-digested quotations planted in the mind of the artists by press agents.

One of the most attractive features of the pop music scene for the past three years has been the freshness of the new, gifted, amateurs with something to say and no inhibitions to prevent them from saying it. The candor of the Beatles is now legendary. The Stones, too, have established a reputation for saying what they think. When they were in America recently they were asked about the success of Herman and his Hermits. Jagger felt obliged, finally, to say something like, "Herman's fine. A nice little chap. But he's not doing what we're doing. We don't think about him musically."

That sort of quote is what makes life worthwhile for the interview. It may not always be good for the image, but at least it's not an insult to the intelligence of the reader.

So far as I am concerned — and I'm quite sure that I'm speaking for you — the more Marianne Faithfulls, Mick Jaggers, John Lennons, and Jim McGuinns there are, the better. They bring to a humid scene a great gale of fresh air and honesty.

# KRLA ARCHIVES

# WEDDING BELLS FOR UNMARRIED BEATLES?

... PATTIE BOYD

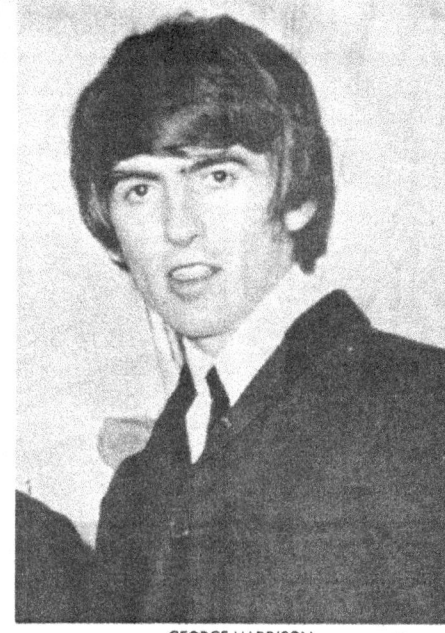

... GEORGE HARRISON

Beatle marriage rumors continue to grow and Beatles continue to fight these rumors by promising that when they DO get married, they will announce it themselves.

There are now only two unmarried Beatles left, and up until two weeks ago both denied that they were even considering marriage.

Paul is still holding to his story. Just recently, Jane Asher appeared on a British television show where she stated: "Paul and I are not married, engaged, or thinking about getting married. I'm just his girlfriend."

However, George Harrison admitted to a reporter in Paris two weeks ago that he and model Patti Boyd, "have definite plans to marry, but where and when is another question. We're not in a mad rush to do anything."

"We have time on our side, and can wait for the right day and the right moment to come along."

"There is no doubt that I will marry Patti. I'm the youngest in the group and Patti's career means a lot."

It's a welcome change to see a pop star (and such a popular one too) admit that he has a girlfriend and that they are thinking of marriage. Much too often such things are hidden from the fans. Why? Do they really think fans won't accept the fact that pop stars are human, that they fall in love, that they get married?

Apparently, George feels his fans deserve honesty from him. It's nice to see that somebody credits fans with having some intelligence and maturity, isn't it?

## FOLK MOVEMENT BOOM WON'T ROLL OVER ROCK

Will folk music replace rock in the U.S.?

A quick glance at the national charts will reassure you that rock is still very much king, but there ARE a few folk songs creeping in among the amplified guitars and throbbing drums.

The Seekers, folk singers from Austrialia, have made it back into the charts with their latest, "A World Of Our Own".

Donovan is still trying to "Catch The Wind" and Marianne Faithful is singing about a "Little Bird".

Although the Byrds cannot be classified merely as folk singers, their national chart-topper, "Mr. Tambourine Man", is a Bob Dylan composition and Bob Dylan cannot be classified as anything but a folk singer.

Still another Dylan composition, "All I Really Want To Do", is riding the charts in both the Byrds' version and Cher's rendition.

In the category of best selling albums, such names as Peter, Paul and Mary, the Kingston Trio, the New Christy Minstrels, Ian and Sylvia, Marianne Faithful, and of course, Bob Dylan, keep popping up.

So while folk does not seem to have replaced rock, it certainly has found a place for itself.

### KRLA BEAT

The KRLA BEAT is published weekly by Prestige Publishing Company; editorial and advertising offices at 6290 Sunset Boulevard, Suite 504, Hollywood, California 90028.

Single copy price: 15 cents.

Subscription price: U.S. and possessions, $3 per year or $5 for two years. Outside U.S., $9 per year.

---

Back issues of the KRLA BEAT are still available, for a limited time. If you've missed an issue of particular interest to you, send 15 cents for each copy wanted, along with a self-addressed stamped envelope to:

KRLA BEAT
Suite 504
6290 Sunset Blvd.
Hollywood, California 90028

ISSUES AVAILABLE
4/14 — INTERVIEW WITH JOHN LENNON
4/21 — INTERVIEW WITH PAUL McCARTNEY
4/28 — CHIMP EXCITES TEEN FAIR
5/5 — HERMANIA SPREADS
5/12 — HERE COMES THE BEATLES
5/19 — VISIT WITH BEATLES
5/26 — FAB NEW BEATLE QUIZ
6/2 — L.A. ROCKS AS STONES ROLL
6/16 — BATTLE OF THE BEAT
6/23 — P. J. — HERO OR HEEL
6/30 — PROBY FIRED
1/7 — SONNY & CHER vs. THE BYRDS

## ?Beatle Quiz?

Okay Class, come to order. It's KRLA Beatle Quiz Time and we have five more questions for the most educational and rewarding contest in Beatleland.

You Beatle Students who missed the first seven weeks of the Beatle Quiz can still catch up by ordering the July 7, June 30, June 23, June 16, June 9, June 2, and May 26 issues of the KRLA BEAT.

The winner of the quiz will be rewarded with a personal interview with the Beatles for the BEAT when the group arrives in August and along with a friend will be invited to attend the Beatle Concert as guests of the KRLA deejays.

Additional prizes will be provided for runner-ups and in case of a tie there will be additional questions or a drawing to decide the final winner. The contest will continue for two more weeks, with at least five new questions asked each week. Beatle Expert Derek Taylor, a close friend of the Beatles and their former press officer, will judge the entries for accuracy.

Beatle Quiz
KRLA BEAT
Suite 504
6290 Sunset Blvd.
Hollywood, Calif. 90028

CONTEST EDITOR:

Below are my answers to the fourth set of questions in the BEATLE QUIZ CONTEST.

My Name .................................................. Address ..................................................

City .................................................. State .................. Zip Code ..................

I (☐ am) (☐ am not) presently a subscriber to the KRLA BEAT.

### NEW QUESTIONS

1. The Beatles were once sculptured in 1800 pounds of butter. In what country was this artistic masterpiece displayed?........................

2. John Lennon spent most of his early life in the care of his aunt. What is her name?
........................

3. Which Beatle washes his hair most often? ........................

4. John Lennon once appeared with a group and was billed as "Barking John Lennon." What was the name of the group?........................

5. Who is Anne Collingham and what is her connection with the Beatles?........................

# KRLA ARCHIVES

## There's More Than One Way To Uncover a BEAT Subscriber

How does one go about selling enough BEAT Subscriptions to win the Beatle Ticket Contest and a chance to see the Beatles in person?

Here are some suggestions for our new circulation agents.

But don't stop here. There are about a million ingenious methods that an ambitious salesman can come up with.

The best way to begin is to make up a sample kit of two or three copies of the BEAT, so you can show your wares like a professional type salesman.

After you've exhausted your supply of friends, start peddling those wares elsewhere. To the members of any clubs you may belong to, your church youth group, etc. You will probably be able to sell individual subscriptions as well as get orders for the club headquarters.

Another good place to go peddling is the office of your family doctor. Doctors try to have a good selection of reading material on hand to take your mind off your troubles, and the BEAT would be an unBEATable distraction. Don't forget to include your optometrist and dentist in your pitch.

### Approach Doctors

If you're really energetic, and you're going to have to be to win this great contest, why not contact ALL the doctors in your area, whether you're a patient or not? (Tell them you plan to be sick a lot, real soon.)

Beauty salons are another good bet for subscription sales. They too like to provide a variety of things to do under the dryer.

Selling the BEAT can also be a wonderfully sneaky way of getting to meet someone you've always wanted to know a lot better. If there's a new boy in town, or even an old boy you've never had the nerve to say "hi" to, race to his doorstep and sell him a subscription while you're getting acquainted.

Your neighbors are good sales prospects, and so are any of the businesses in your area that deal with teenagers in any possible way. Teenagers have an important voice in what the family buys today, and most businessmen need and want to keep up with the latest teenage activities.

### Parent's Friends

Your parents can come in very handy, too. They probably have a long list of friends who are always selling them raffle tickets or collecting contributions. Ask your folks for a copy of that list. They will probably be delighted to give some of those friends a taste of their own medicine.

Also ask your father to check around at work. Some of his fellow employees may be wondering what a teenage son or daughter would like for a birthday present, and what could be better than a subscription to the BEAT?

One of the most fun ways to sell the BEAT is to pack a large lunch, grab your sample kit and go on a door-to-door hike. Threaten your best friend into going with you. It'll be twice as much fun if you have someone to share the experience with. And don't think it won't be an experience! A profitable one at that.

If you really want to go all out, you can always offer a bonus to anyone who orders a subscription through you. Extras are always a good sales booster.

### Courtesy Beats

You might take a small portion of the commissions you've made so far and invest in a few copies of the BEAT. Present the free copy, to buying customers only, of course. You'd be spending a bit of your own money, but you'd undoubtedly make more in the long run. You might also win those Beatle tickets!

Another possible extra would be (are you ready for this?) blue chip stamps! If you promise to wash the dishes every day for the rest of your life and then some, without griping, your mom might be coaxed into parting with a few of her stamps. You could then give away ten or so blue chips to each person who purchases the BEAT, as a way of showing your appreciation.

This may sound ridiculous, but if you and your friends are musically inclined, nag one or two of them into joining your campaign, complete with guitars. Give your customers a free song with every subscription!

We could go on forever, and almost have, but this is just a drop in the over-flowing bucket of possibilities. There are a million ways to sell the BEAT. And all of them are a ball!

What we would like to know is why we are sitting here thinking up fun things to do when we really want to be out doing them.

One of these days we should trade places. You come into the office and publish the BEAT and we'll go out and have fun selling it.

(We don't want to rush you or anything, but how about tomorrow?)

## PERSONALS

### To A Bird
To Marilyn, My One And Only Love:
And to a fab bird who I'll never ever forget. You're the only bird I've ever loved.
My Love To You Always,
Gordon.

### Thanks Stones
To Mick Jagger (and all you Stones):
Thanks so much for printing my letter in your monthly book! I don't know what to do with all those letters I'm getting from the United Kingdom. Help! It was groovy talking to you on May 15. I luv you!
Author of "Rolling Stones Come to Los Angeles",
M.A., L.A.

### Spinners
D.M. and M.H.
Please make sure Spinners goes on.
G.B.

### Holt Herman
To Herman:
Stop asking girls for their phone numbers! Unless its me.
Shrieking Mad,
Venice, Calif.

### Missed Beatles
Sallie Luv:
Pauly and Lennon were over last night. I called ya'—too bad you couldn't come — Twas Smashing Fun.
Tina,
Brea, Calif.

### We Touched Them!
To Sandy:
I can't believe that we touched Chad and Jeremy at their performance. Wasn't Jeremy neat in the yellow car!
Your Best Friend.

### Can't Help It
To Mike Haver:
Sorry if we're driving you nutty. We can't help it.
Us Again.

### Surfer Boy Wanted
Dear BEAT:
This is Linda writing to you. Guess where I'm from? Correct—Liverpool, home of "You know who." I am just dropping you a line (thud—I've dropped it too soon) to ask you if you could possibly please get me a penpal from America. Here's the requirements:

A boy who is aged 16-19, good-looking with long, long hair, preferably blond. A boy who surfs and one who likes mad Liverpool girls who like Donovan, Dylan and the Byrds. Also one who could possibly come over here this summer.

If anyone fits those requirements and wants to write, here's my address:
Linda Gerard: 9, Herondale Road, Mossley Hill, Liverpool 18, England.
Thanks Again,
Linda Gerard.

# KRLA ARCHIVES

**ROBIN KINGSLEY WHITCOMB**, younger brother of Ian Whitcomb, changed his name to Kingsley becuse "my name isn't that well known and Robin and Ian doesn't sound that much different." Robin, who has a new record called "In and Out," has also signed with Tower Records.

## Who's Robin Kingsley? .. Another Whitcomb

Who is Robin Kingsley? He is Robin Whitcomb, the brother of one of the fastest-rising and top-selling vocalists in America — Ian Whitcomb.

Robin, whose first single, "In and Out", was released last week by Tower Records, uses an alias because he prefers not to cash in on the fame of his brother.

"It would be easy to do," he says, "but what purpose would it serve? I'd never know whether people were buying Robin Kingsley or buying the brother of an established singing star."

Like his brother, Robin was born in Northern England. His first contact with music came at the age of eight when Ian bought him a set of drums.

"I pounded those things and before I realized what was happening, I was playing for my brother's Blues band which was one of the hottest groups in London," he recalled.

When Ian took off for the U.S., Robin was faced with a difficult decision. "Should I go to work for my grandfather's oil company or follow in my brother's footsteps — naturally I took the entertainment path."

The 6 foot-2 inch blonde-haired, blue-eyed singer arrived in the U.S. about four months ago and landed a job with a New Orleans band.

From there he worked his way to Seattle, Wash., where he met Jerry Dennon, manager of the Kingsmen, and the same man who introduced Ian to Tower.

After hearing the 21-year-old Robin sing a few tunes, Dennon decided that Tower might be interested in another potential hit-maker.

"We may differ in many ways," says Robin Kingsley Whitcomb, "but we both agree that we'd like to be hits."

## Sonny & Cher Profit From Shindig Error

A Shindig show which was aired by mistake turned out to be a real money-maker for Sonny and Cher.

Murry (The K) Kauffman, a famous deejay from New York, was in California to film a 90-minute spectacular for President Johnson's Job Opportunities Corp. and happened to catch the show.

The deejay was so impressed with Sonny and Cher that he spent half the night racing around to find the two.

He found them, and Sonny and Cher found their way into a 90-minute spectacular which will be aired on Channel 2 at 8:00 tonight.

Unfortunately the two will not be able to see their network show because they will be singing at the Valley Music Theater.

There will be other opportunities. They are scheduled for two more Shindig shows which will be aired July 14 and July 21 and taped on July 1 and 8. During the July 14 show they will sing their record, "I Got You Babe," which will be the "Shindig Pick of The Week."

## Group Excursions Can Be Cheaper If You're Traveling To England

This is the first in a series of articles on how to get to England on the least possible money, and how to stay there awhile for even less!

The best way to get there as cheaply as possible is to go with a group. Airlines and shipping companies (not all, but many) give up to a 25 per cent reduction in fares for groups of 25.

The leader of the "group" must be over the age of eighteen, but the other 24 members can be any age. Groups can be organized by clubs, schools organization, or private parties. And most airlines and shipping companies can provide you with information about groups already being formed.

If you want to form one yourself, get as many "members" as possible and then let the transportation company of your choice know you're looking for more travelers.

You might also try checking with travel agents in the area to see if they know of groups being formed.

### Return Together

When you travel with such a group, this does not mean you have to stay together when you get to England. But you will have to return together or the fare reduction rates will no longer be valid.

As far as prices are concerned, the most inexpensive trans-Atlantic rate by ship is approximately $203 one way. (When traveling in a group, that would be reduced to about $150.) There is also a 5 per cent reduction on your fare if you buy a round trip ticket, with a group or without.

The $203 figure (which was quoted us by the Holland-American Line, known for their low rates and good service) is the rate from New York to London, and tourist accommodations at this price are available only during the "Thrift Season", beginning sometime in August and ending the following April. The remainder of the year (the highly-traveled summer months), the price goes up.

The crossing would take approximately seven to nine days by boat.

### Round Trip

The average round trip fare by plane (economy class, New York to London varies between $300 and $500 dollars, depending upon which time of the year you choose to do your traveling. The $300 rate is available only if you are staying less than 14 days during one of the three airline "Thrift Seasons". Call the airline of your choice for information about these seasons, as they vary.

The above figures can also be reduced greatly if you're traveling with a group.

We checked into the possibility of crossing on freighters, etc. After all, we wouldn't mind riding with a herd of cows if it would get us to Jolly Olde, would you? But, it seems those days are gone forever. All freighters crossing between New York and London are now limited to first class rates for passengers, and first class is about twice as much as the amounts we've mentioned.

Stay tuned to the KRLA BEAT for more on this subject next week!

## CASEY'S QUIZ

**By CASEY KASEM**

In her own words, this week's mystery star is "skinny as a rake." She celebrated her first national number one disc in her native country) by knitting a patchwork blanket. She's not really the domesticated type. She just happened to be down with a severe case of bronchitis at the time! Still in her teens, she dislikes hair rollers, makeup and never bothers to carry a handbag. Her father is a welder and she is probably the only star around who stores her on-stage costumes in a wrought iron wardrobe. This ex-accounts machine operator is "Mod" all the way!

---

**KRLA BEAT SUBSCRIPTION**

you will SAVE 60% of the regular price!
AS A SPECIAL INTRODUCTORY . . . if you subscribe now . . .

☐ 1 YEAR — 52 Issues — $3.00      ☐ 2 YEARS — $5.00

Enclosed is $..........

Send to:.......................................................... Age:................

Address:..........................................................................

City:................................. State:................ Zip:............

MAIL YOUR ORDER TO: **KRLA BEAT**
1401 South Oak Knoll Avenue
Outside U.S.: $9.00 — 52 Issues      Pasadena, California 91106

# KRLA ARCHIVES

## THE BEAT GOES TO THE MOVIES

# I'll Take Sweden

*By Jim Hamblin*

QUESTION: Can a couple of adults get together and write a good rock and roll song for a movie about the teen set?

ANOTHER QUESTION: Does Bob Hope still make good movies?

The answer to both, we found out in fine fashion, is a resounding *Yes!*

The new United Artists release starring Bob Hope, Frankie Avalon, and Tuesday Weld, is one of the funniest pictures of the year, and has made this summer one of the best yet for enjoyable pictures. This is not a murky drama full of shadowy scenes of confusing symbolism and that kind of jazz.

"Sweden" starts funny, and stays that way. It is full of fast-paced comedy and some of the best music we've heard in a film. For the music part, we are indebted to several people, including Jimmie Haskell and By Dunham, as well as James Economides and Bob Beverly.

There's a feature number done by Frankie Avalon called, "Would You Like My Last Name?", that is really a gasser. Written by Diane Lampert and Ken Lauber, who also pen the title song, it's got a great beat and really swings.

### We Dig Frankie

Nice to see Frankie on the screen again. Handsome and obviously very talented, he's a credit to any film cast. And there is the unmistakable feeling he knew what the movie was trying to do and enjoyed every minute of it.

Tuesday Weld, who is getting to be a specialist in Problems Of The American Teen-Ager, plays Bob Hope's daughter, and falls in love with a guy named Klinger (Avalon), very much to the dissatisfaction of her father. So pop takes daughter to Sweden to make her "forget" . . . and that's where all the trouble, and the fun, starts.

There is really nothing we need to say about Bob Hope. He's a national institution, and with the help of wonderful writing, gags his way through the whole hilarious film.

### Girls Galore

Men, if your special is girl-watching this summer, the picture affords some excellent opportunities.

The film also stars Jeremy Slate who has been in many pictures, and whose face you will recognize immediately. What is new is his perfect Sweden accent. He's just right for the part.

NOTE TO SCRIPT SUPERVISOR DIXIE McCOY. The next time a scene shot supposedly in Sweden comes up, please be sure the *State of California* registration tags and numbers are not left on the sides of the boats! Scene taken at Lake Arrowhead, perhaps?

The American view of Sweden's morals provides much of the material for the funny lines in the story, but it is all done in excellent taste, and the kind of film that any family, and especially one with teen-agers, ought to go see. It's funny!

**FRANKIE AVALON ENTERTAINS** in a couple of scenes from the hilarious new movie, "I'll Take Sweden", co-starring Tuesday Weld and Bob Hope. At a party (above) he belts out one of the great new original songs introduced in the movie. Below, he prepares to do a watery finish to another number. In the film Frankie and Tuesday carry on an international love affair and discover some startling differences in the American and Swedish outlooks on marriage.

# KRLA ARCHIVES

**DOES THIS FACE LOOK FAMILIAR?** It should, because we've been running portions of it for several weeks in the BEAT's Puzzle Piece Contest. He should look even more familiar to fans of "Bonanza," who will recognize him instantly as Television and recording star Lorne Green — the Ponderosa's Ben Cartwright. Among the 7,800 entries in the contest, the first 10 who came up with the correct answer won a fabulous array of prizes.

## Twelve BEAT Followers Uncover Puzzle Personality

So now you know — our mystery star in the BEAT'S Puzzle Piece Contest was Lorne Greene.

And that information was worth plenty to the 12 contestants who came up with it first. Our eagle-eyed judges have announced the following results:

Jan McQuary of Pasadena was the first place winner. Jan wins two tickets to see the Beatles at Hollywood Bowl.

The second and third place winners are Kathleen Kietala of Hollywood and Kris Quade of Pacific Palisades. They each win one ticket to a Beatle performance here.

The fourth place winner was Debbie Brateng of Seal Beach. She wins four record albums.

Winners five through twelve will each receive one record album. They are Kathy Wescott of Sepulveda, Gigi Gail of La Canada, Chris Ardley of Temple City, Nancy La Perch of Tarzana, James M. Randall of Camarillo, Linda Fouzer of Pacoima, Kathy Doyle of Manhattan Beach, and Terrie Shasberger of Chatsworth.

Congratulations to all of you.

We'll have more big contests starting in the next issue of the BEAT, and we have some prizes that are really fabulous. Be watching for it.

## GEORGE'S SISTER RECORDS ALBUM

Another "Beatles" album is on the market.

But this one is not by John, Paul, George and Ringo. It's by George's talkative sister, Louise Harrison Caldwell, and she discusses her favorite subject.

Mrs. Caldwell, who reportedly incurred her brother's anger when she began making her living by talking about the Beatles and George's family life, has titled the album "All About the Beatles".

It contains excerpts from news conferences in five cities in which she answered questions posed by local school newspaper reporters and special contest winners.

## Trini Lopez Invited To Appear On Benefit

Trini Lopez has been invited by Princess Grace to be the star solo attraction at the annual Gala de la Croix Rouge de Monaco in Monte Carlo on August 6. Trini's appearance at the Monte Carlo Sporting Club last year is credited with his invitation to appear in the ninth annual Red Cross Benefit. Approximately 1500 guests, including leaders in international society and show business are invited to the Benefit. Each guest will pay $100 for the privilege of attending the Gala.

## For Girls Only
### By SHEILA DAVIS

Hi, everyone! (Including some boys who just can't seem to take a hint from certain titles of certain columns.)

I have another one of those "why can't I ever do anything right" feelings today. Last night my girlfriend and I were trying to practice a new dance step, and her father finally stalked in and ordered us to turn the radio down to a dull roar.

Then I had the most brilliant idea. We stuck our transistor radios in our pockets, attached the ear phones and danced on. It really looked funny, us high-stepping all over her room to a background of complete silence. We about died laughing looking at ourselves in the mirror, and I naturally felt I'd discovered a great new comedy routine.

However, when I went into the BEAT office this morning and started raving about my discovery, I found out that the very same scene can be seen in one of American-International's beachy-type movies. Boy, everytime I think of something really stupendous, someone's already thought of it.

But it was still a crack up. Try it if you want your friends and neighbors to think you're completely gone!

### Interesting Letter

I had the most fascinating letter from a BEAT reader. Remember when I was blowing off steam about boys and who made the rules we live by and all that? Well, part of her letter was that subject, but another portion concerned something that has never dawned on me before. Just listen to this excerpt and see if it doesn't make you think, too.

"One of my favorite subjects is the battle that adults wage against going steady. I never realized how much I'd missed until I found one boy I really liked and settled down to dating just him.

"Before I had a steady, every time my friends and I would go anywhere, we'd be looking for boys. I don't mean *looking* for them, that sounds band. I mean we'd be so *conscious* of boys and afraid we didn't look absolutely gorgeous and that no one would pay any attention to us.

"We paid so much attention to ourselves, in hopes of meeting some fabulous boy, we did not pay much attention to anything else.

### More Confident

"Now that I go steady, I don't feel like I have to look like a fashion plate any more. I used to actually stay home from things if my hair didn't turn out, etc. I'm so much more relaxed now, and my steady and I go places I never even thought of going before.

"We've gone around to all the museums and the Planetarium, and other places that are so much fun when you can concentrate on what they have to offer instead of worrying about who you might meet there.

"Going steady may have its
**TURN TO PAGE 15**

**EPIC RECORDS**

## Esther's Back

**ANOTHER COMEBACK FOR ESTHER PHILLIPS.** She had her first hit at 14 but didn't score again until she was 21, when she recorded an all-time class — "Release Me." Now, three years later, she has another national hit — "And I Really Love Him." Oops — sorry about those revealing numbers, but Esther's latest number figures to be a great one.

# KRLA ARCHIVES

"ITS NOT UNUSUAL" to see the name of Tom Jones, England's greatest single export, on the top of the charts. His latest hit is "What's New Pussy Cat" from the movie of the same tite.

(Q): I have a speech problem that I've almost completely conquered, but there are still about ten words that sound weird when I say them. My doctor says "practice more", but what can I do until I have these remaining words mastered? You know how embarrassing this sort of problem can be.
(Francine D)

(A): We're with your doctor about the practicing part, but we can also understand your hesitation to use your "unconquered" words. Keep working on them in private and find substitutes to use in public. If you aren't satisfied with the dictionary's supply of synonyms, buy a copy of Roget's Theasaurus. It's available in paperback, and will give you a host of words to use until practice makes perfect, and after!

(Q): My hair has completely collapsed. It's breaking right in the middle because I backcomb it every day, and wear the back of it in a rubber band. I've stopped doing both, and no longer use spray, but nothing seems to help. Please don't tell me to go to a beauty salon because my allowance would never stretch that far.
(Bonnie N.)

(A): This is a common problem with back-combers and pony tailers. Your hair needs a conditioner, and badly. Look in the yellow pages of the telephone book for the Beauty Supply House nearest you. This is where beauty operators buy their products, and the same items are for sale to outside customers. Ask the saleswoman's advice about what product would be the best solution to your problem.

(Q): I won't bore you with the long story about why I have to wear cotton in my ears for about a month, but I do and it looks so terrible! Is there any possible way I can make it a little less obvious? I've even though of cutting my hair (which I wear up), but I'm hoping you'll be able to think of something a little less drastic.
(Arline K.)

(A): You might try cutting just the sides of your hair and fashioning curls to sort of "hide" your ears, and here's another possibility! Glue a small pearl to the cotton before inserting. That way you'll have a pearl in your ear instead of just a wad of cotton. When people ask why the pearl, say it's the latest fad and sit back and watch pearls starting to appear in ears all over the place!

(Q): Can you recommend a good astringent, a medicated one I can use after washing my face? I've tried about everything, and am getting nowhere fast.
(Deanne G.)

(A): Try Shulton's Ice-O-Derm. It's soothing and a month's supply costs only a dollar. It's great for problem complexions and also a great way to keep from having one. And it's recommended for guys and gals.

(Q): Will you please settle two arguments? My girlfriend says you shouldn't wear earrings unless you're wearing high heels. She also says it's "uncool" to have your ears pierced. I feel just the opposite. Who is right?
(Jolene B.)

(A): Both are entirely a matter of taste. Earrings do rather signify a "dressed-up" look, and they go well (and perhaps better) with high heels than they do with flats. As for having your ears pierced, there are no "social" rules which govern this practice. However, it is kind of unnecessary now that the majority of earring styles are created in the clip-on variety.

(Q): You'll probably laugh at this question, but I'm serious. What is a girl supposed to do if she goes to a restaurant or drive-in with a boy and he orders a hamburger-with? I mean if it's a boy you really want to kiss goodnight?
(Irene C.)

(A): This question has been asked ever since onions were invented and there's really no answer to the dilemma. You'd think the boy would know better than to create the problem, but most of them get completely carried away at the mention of the word "food". What you should REALLY do in this case is order garlic toast and give him a dirty look. What you probably should do, if he really matters, is order likewise. Some boys do this just to see what the girl will do, thereby determining his reward before reaching the doorstep. If he's worth all the trouble, humor the sneaky so-and-so.

### HINT OF THE WEEK

This is probably going to sound like some dumb commercial, but here goes. I don't wear makeup, and when my face starts to shine like a harvest moon, I can't pull out a powder puff and calm things. I finally discovered a way to solve this problem. When I go out, I dip a cotton pad in Ten-O-Six and stash it away in one of those little plastic bags they're always yapping about on television (the kind you roll off a roll or something I can't say correctly). When I start "radiating", I just excuse myself and have a rubdown. The product is great (Ten-O-Six is medicated and great for every type of skin), and it's a lot better than having to wear a bunch of powder.

P.S.: If anyone makes a commercial out of this, please tell them to send me the money.
(Lois L.)

## Stones Making Movie Debut

When the Rolling Stones were here in May, Mick Jagger revealed to the BEAT that the Stones were definitely going to make a movie. But as to the location, plot, or shooting schedule, Mick just didn't know because nothing was "for sure".

Although still not definite, plans are beginning to take shape. The Stones' co-managers, Eric Easton and Andrew Oldham, have secured a script which Easton says the boys are "extremely pleased" with. However, no one will disclose the contents of that script.

If all goes according to schedule, the film will begin shooting in July and continue through August and part of September. Where will the film be shot? Again, no one is talking.

This is not the Stones first movie appearances. Well, not exactly. They were in a seventeen minute short subject film which was supposed to be issued by United Artists in April. But for some mysterious reason, the film was never released, at least, not here.

When their first full-length movie winds up filming, the Stones will embark on a four-week tour of Britain. And then in late October or early November, the Stones are coming Stateside again! However, no dates have yet been set for the tour.

Their last U.S. tour was such a smashing success that the Stones left a trail of screaming girls, exasperated policemen, and broken attendance records from one end of the U.S. to the other. No wonder they're anxious to come back!

MOVIE CAMERAS WILL ROLL for the Roliing Stones. In addition to being among the world's most popular recording stars, it looks like they will soon become movies stars. It should be a gasser.

# KRLA ARCHIVES

# MAIL BOX

### Pen Pals Information
Dear Editor:

Perhaps some of your readers are having as much trouble getting foreign pen pals as I did. I have finally found two clubs which have helped me immensely, the International Friendship League (I.F.L.) and Our World Neighbors.

To find out about the World Neighbors they should look in the Sunday Herald Examiner. To contact the I.F.L. write to: Doreen Smyth, I.F.L. North American Pen Friend Section, P.O. Box 42, Hove 3, Sussex, England.

Give your name address, age, sex, occupation and interest. It will save time if an international reply coupon is enclosed, but if it is impossible, it really isn't necessary.

I hope this helps someone, and I hope they are as lucky as I was with their correspondents.

Sincerely,
Diane Suelling,
El Monte, Calif.

### BEAT Fan
Dear Editor:

I think the BEAT is great! I buy it every week. I will subscribe sometime, but I can't seem to get the bread together right now. I support the BEAT editorials. I think it's time teenagers had a newspaper to represent them. Keep it up!

John Harvell,
Long Beach, Calif.

### More Fan Clubs
Dear Sir:

I find that my very favorites are not in the line up of fan clubs. I'm speaking of the "Righteous Brothers". Let's start a Righteous Brother's Fan Club. I am sure you would have a good response. To me they are the greatest. They are the two finest performers in the world. Another I would like to see is that one guy who has been a big smash recently. Of course I'm speaking of P. J. Proby. Well, how about this one?

Your Friend,
Gary L. Crawford.

### Proby Praised
Dear Editor:

I would like to say that the person who wrote the editorial "Rule or Ruin", in the June 25 issue of the BEAT must have been someone who thinks he knows how to run P. J. Proby's career as well as everyone's life.

I have only see Mr. Proby perform a few times. But what I have seen is not to be considered by any standards crude and vulgar stage stage antics. I think P. J. Proby is a dramatic talent with unlimited possibilities.

When ever a new talent that is as fabulous as his comes along there is always some one who thinks he knows more about the management of a pop star than his manager.

The reason I'm writing is I enjoy the BEAT immensely and hate to see something like this. I would like some type of reply, personal or through the BEAT.

W. L. Pritchard,
West Covina, Calif.

*Dear W. L. Pritchard:*
*The editorial to which you refer expresses the sincere opinion of the editor on P. J. Prody. We feel your ideas deserve our consideration and are grateful to you for taking the time to express yourself. Surely you do not deny us the same right to voice our opinions, however they may differ from your's or anyone else's.*

*THE BEAT.*

## Have Motorbike - Will Travel

Let's face it. There is only one way to be a big wheel these days, and that's to have your own motor bike.

Having your own motor bike has been known to present a number of problems. Riding it correctly requires many skills and much patience. This special feature is designed to solve many of those problems.

Here, at last, are ten ways to drive a motor bike properly, and everyone else around you crazy.

1. Riding a motor bike is similar to riding a bicycle (which always comes back to you). Ride your motor bike up and down the drive-way until your skills return.

2. Pick yourself up off the drive-way. Falling *off* a bicycle also comes back to you.

3. Promise never to use that kind of language again. The neighbors are pointing.

4. When you feel you are ready for the open road, affix a portable radio to your motor mike. If there is anything more fun than a motor bike it is a noisy motor bike.

### Parking Spot

5. Never park your motor bike without locking it. If you are worried that someone might come along and make off with it, why not ask the owner of a nearby parked car if you may rent his back seat for a small fee. Another possibility is to carry the motor bike with you at all times, in one of your smaller purses.

6. No matter what the television commercials may advise, do not attempt to re-load your Instamatic Camera while en route. This negative approach to safety is a sure-fire way to end up with your picture in the Post Office.

### Signal Correctly

7. Always remember to give the correct signals when you wish to make a turn. If other motorists seem to be paying no attention to you, rap gently on their car window as you whiz by.

8. Courteously apply first aid to any motorists who faint from shock during your attempts at establishing a rapport.

9. Regardless of what they may do in the movies, it is not advisable to ride your motor bike while clad in a bikini. If you choose to ignore our warning, please drive by our office a lot.

10. When transporting a passenger on your motor bike, always drive to the nearest gas station and have your friend fill the tank. If your friend protests, remind him that he *asked* you to take him for a ride!

## Red Rock Fans Get Beat From Voice of America

Rock has been seeping under the iron curtain to enthusiastic teens in Hungry who listen to their favorite artists on Radio Free Europe.

Broadcasting rock n' roll is a great way to win friends for the West, Hungarian-born Geza Ekecs, a Radio Free Europe deejay, reports.

The deejay, who has been with the station since 1951, gets 1,000 letters a month from Hungarian teenagers, praising his program and requesting certain songs.

Favorites include Elvis Presley, Brenda Lee, Pat Boone, Duane Eddy, the Beatles, the Beach Boys and the Rolling Stones.

The only records available to Hungarians in their own state-operated record stores are the classics. "These don't go over too well with the young people," the deejay commented.

Since they can't get rock at home, the Hungarians have found a way to smuggle it through the iron curtain.

The ingenious teens tape the records played over Radio Free Europe and with the help of friends who work in the state recording studios, spend the wee hours putting it on a disc cut from an old X-ray picture.

These bootlegged records, despite their poor quality, sell like hotcakes all over Hungry.

The major problem facing the Hungarian deejay, unfamiliar with American slang, is translating the titles of records like "Too Pooped to Pop", to his listeners.

Webster's dictionary wasn't much help, but fortunately Ekecs found an American teenager in Munich who could break the code for him.

## Quote Of The Week...

The *Best Quote of the Week* comes from Tom Jones concerning his visit to America:

"Funniest thing that happened to me over there was when we hired a zoo in New Jersey, and I sang 'It's Not Unusual' while feeding potato chips to the fans who were locked in the cages — after the animals had been removed, of course!"

## A BEAT EDITORIAL
## TEENS BEING 'KNOCKED'

There's a season for everything. Hunting, fishing, you name it.

At the moment, it is open season on teenagers. The name of the game is Grab A Pen (Because It's Mightier Than The Sword) And Go-Go.

The game is presently being played by several of America's leading adult magazines. There are no rules for this popular sport. There is also no sportsmanship.

If you haven't read the magazines in question, don't. The Let's Put Down Teenagers League has come up with enough misinformation to send every responsible teenager to the nearest analyst's couch, and every responsible parent out back to build a bigger and better woodshed.

We don't know why this is happening, other than the obvious reason of selling more magazines. But we do know what's happening because of it. Whatever headway teenagers have made in their battle for respect is slowly being destroyed.

If your parents haven't actually seen the page-by-page inadequate discriptions of the American teenager, they've heard about them.

We hope this editorial will assure them, and you, that we know better. Because we know something else these adult magazines don't.

You.

# ON THE BEAT

By Louise Criscione

Guess who's back? Bobby Rydell. Bobby's been in the Army for the last six months, but he's out now. He recently paid we Southlanders a visit and also gave us a few choice comments on Army life. My favorite: "Well, I drew KP the first week I was in. I don't know how many pans I washed, but somebody sure ate a lot of baked macaroni!"

Bobby has a new record out. The "A" side is a swinger called "Sideshow" and Bobby says "it's my most commercial record in a long time." Flip is an Anthony Newley composition, "The Joker". Both sides are great — Bobby has one of the best voices in the business.

By the way, you might not recognize Bobby — his hair is now short. Seems Uncle Sam doesn't care WHO you are; he cuts your hair anyway! But Bobby assures us that is IS growing back.

Going in the opposite extreme, the Bobby Fuller Four have let their hair grow long. Although I'm all in favor of long hair, I'm afraid I don't like the Four's new look. Doesn't do much for them. Especially Randy Fuller. Actually his hair is not that much longer. It's just combed forward into his face, and with a face like his I can't imagine why he would want to hide it!

QUICK ONES: George Harrison has come up with a novel idea. He suggests that the next Beatle movie be filmed in Liverpool using all the Beatle relatives and titling the movie, "Everything's Relative" . . . The Rolling Stones got a big giggle out of some enlightened journalist's labeling of their sound as "Mersey Beat" . . . George and John are the co-owners of a supermarket in England . . . Paul McCartney likes the Beatles next single, "Help", thinks it's good, and hopes he doesn't sound bigheaded . . . Herman reveals that every night that the group was appearing on the Caravan, they were presented with cakes and other goodies by their fans. But Dick Clark wouldn't let them eat any of them because one time a performer was poisoned that way . . . Freddie Garrity admits that he is influenced by Charlie Chaplin and Jerry Lewis . . . Herman think Kentucky moonshine tastes a lot like iodine! Really

Here's a tip for you London-bound people. Brian Jones, Eric Burdon and Hilton Valentine (both of the Animals), Chris Curtis (of the Searchers), and the Walker Brothers all live on page 76 of the London A-Z map! That ought to narrow your search down a little bit anyway.

Did you ever wonder what the Rolling Stones do on a long ride from one city to another? Well, I guess they read because Bill Wyman writes: "Everyone has suddenly started reading books like mad. Brian and I are reading science fiction by Ray Bradbury, while Mick and Keith are James Bond fans. Charlie found a magazine with Civil War or something in it, so he was happy."

WATCH OUT FOR. The Beatles — they're coming, you know.

# KRLA ARCHIVES

## The Pacemakers With The BEAT

**By MICHELLE STRAUBING and SUSAN WYLIE**

EDITOR'S NOTE: When Gerry and the Pacemakers where in Los Angeles last week, BEAT Reporters Michelle Straubing and Susan Wylie had an exclusive interview with Gerry, Fred and Les. Here are some excerpts from that interview

Q: *How would you compare American schools to English?*
Gerry—Well now, really, that is a very difficult question.
Les—They're the same because they don't teach. (This statement is greeted with applause by the other).
Q: *If you were not singing what would you be doing?*
Gerry—I'd be a boxer.
Fred—I'd be a miner.
Gerry—A miner Fred would be. What about you Les?
Les—I'd want to be a spaceman.
Q: *Have your fans ever gotten carried away . . .*
Gerry—Yes, the police carried them out.
Q: *It doesn't bother you if they tear your clothes?*
Gerry—No. Not at all, because after all . . .
Fred—They paid for it.
Gerry — They gave me the money to buy the clothes that I'm wearing and I think that they are wonderful.
Q: *Have you ever been mobbed by your fans?*
Gerry—Yes
Fred—Many's the day . . .
Q: *Can you tell us about one time?*
Gerry—In Sheffield in England. Sheffield is a place that makes knives, and forks and spoons. It's a very hard life type of place. We were playing there and I came up to the hotel disguised in a coat and hat. I was half way across the road and there were a few fans waiting outside the hotel. They saw me and ran after me. I ran and fell over them. They didn't fall over. They just ran over me and I didn't like it very much.
Q: *What do you think of the problem the English groups have coming over here?*
Gerry — I feel very deeply about this because American artists have been coming to England for years and we've never stopped them from earning money. But now we find that the American Government does not like us coming over because we're earning the money. It's all take and no give.
Q: *What is the quality in women you find most attractive?*
Gerry—I think I like femininity, being a female.
Les—I agree with him.
Fred—I like girls with short hair.
Q: *What do you think of the dancing that is done now?*
Gerry—I like the what-yo-tu-see and the happily-go-luckily.
Q: *What's that?*
Gerry—The dances they do in England. The American, rock-around-the-clockily, the schwin, the surfi-royalty-smoke. All good for me, yes.
Q: (To Gerry) *You just got engaged?*
Gerry—Yeah.
Q: *Did you set the date yet?*
Gerry—Yep, in 18 month's time.
Q: *How did you meet her?*
Gerry—I said, "Hello." She said, "We'll be married." I said, "Alright." I met her in the cavern, the romantic spot of Liverpool. In the midst of the fog and the smog and the soot . . . I met her in the cavern around five years ago and since then everything's been happening.
Q: *What is your opinion of the fan letters you receive?*
Gerry—We get some stupid, soft ones . . ignorant stuff . . We want to marry you, we hate you cause you look at girls, can I come to your house and live with you for three weeks?
Q: *What were your first impressions of Americans?*
Gerry—A lot better than what I imagined before I ever came here. They're a lot nicer.
Q: *What is your impression of teenage morality?*
Gerry—It's the same all over the world, boys are boys and girls are girls, and God bless them all.

. . . GERRY MARSDEN

## 'Kinks' Keep Popping Up In Life of British Quartet

They have been plagued with all sorts of mishaps and have had more than their share of trouble.

It all started last March on the Kinks' tour of Scotland. Ray Davies collapsed during one of their shows. He was brought back to the hotel, but he didn't improve, fans found the hotel and caused all kinds of trouble and then the doctors diagnosed Ray's illness as pneumonia. He was quickly moved to London by train, and the Kinks were forced to cancel the rest of their tour.

The rest of the Kinks also made their way back to London, but only to meet up with more trouble. This time Pete Quaife was the victim. He hadn't been feeling to well "that" day, but come night he decided he wasn't sick enough to stay home and went to the show. He really should have stayed home. He passed out at the theatre, hit his head on the stone floor, and received a cut on the back of his head which required three stitches to close.

During this same period, Dave Davies caught himself the bronchitis bug, which incapacitated him for a while. But for Dave the worse was yet to come.

Toward the end of May the Kinks were playing a date in Cardiff, Wales. Their road manager, Sam Curtis, had come up with what he considered a fabulous idea. He thought "You Really Got Me" should be presented dramatically. So he suggested that Dave dance around and swing his guitar in the air while Mick Avory swung his cymbals in all directions. Unfortunately, Dave stepped back into Mick's drums just as Mick was swinging his cymbals. The cymbals made contact with Dave's head. Result: sixteen stitches to close the wound!

The only Kink to escape "disaster" so far is drummer Mick Avory. He'd better knock on wood fast! Also, he'd better keep away from Dave Davies when Dave is swinging his guitar around.

It's been a month since the last Kink misfortune. Maybe the curse has vanished. Here's hoping it has the Kinks were doing just fine without it!

## Beatles Map Busy Summer

From now until September the Beatles will be one busy group. As a matter of fact, they are already pretty busy — but the hardest part is still to come.

The Beatles began their summer season and also a continental tour on June 20 when they appeared in Paris to an overflowing and over-enthusiastic crowd. The Paris fans got out of hand, stormed the stage, and literally tore up the auditorium! The Beatles, however, escaped uninjured.

The Beatles then moved on to Lyons, Milan, Genoa, Rome, Nice, Madrid, and Barcelona. The standout city in this package had to be Rome because a very strange incident occurred in the Eternal City. At least, it was unusual for the Beatles. When they arrived at the Roman airport, 150 policemen were there to insure the group's safety from the massive following which inevitably greets the Beatle's airport arrival.

But the Roman massive following consisted of nine fans, all of whom were English! Must have quite a let-down for the Liverpool four.

But then again, maybe they should have expected it because the day before in Genoa only 3,000 turned out to see the Beatles when the stadium could have held 20,000!

Early in July, the Beatles will go to Buckingham Palace to meet the Queen and have their M.B.E. awards presented to them. What higher honor than for an Englishman to meet his Queen.

The rest of July will be filled with radio and television dates, and on August 1 the Beatles will appear on "Blackpool Night Out", a British television show.

And then the Beatles' second American tour begins. In case you haven't memorized the dates yet, here they are. August 14 — Ed Sullivan Show; 15 — Shea Stadium; 16th — "Rain Date" in case Shea Stadium show is rained out; 17th — Toronto; 18th — Atlanta; 19th — Houston; 20th — Chicago; 21 — Minneapolis 22nd — Portland; 23rd to 26th — stay in Los Angels; 28th — San Diego; 29th and 20th — Hollywood Bowl; 31st — San Francisco; September 1 — return to London.

Although plans for the autumn are not definite yet, look for the Beatles to undertake a British tour and then start work on their third film.
—Louise Criscione.

**KEEP YOUR EYE ON RONNIE KING.** The Oklahoma-born artist, often compared to Elvis Presley, has a hot new record called "Is She Waiting For Me?" Ronnie, who is part Indian, worked his way from Oklahoma to Hollywood by singing with a travelling antique show. With his new group, the Knights, the wandering minstrel has already been booked for a number of top engagements on the West Coast.

# KRLA ARCHIVES

**THE DAVE CLARK FIVE, DAPPER AND DASHING, ARRIVE AT WIND-SWEPT LOS ANGELES INTERNATIONAL AIRPORT.** They're on a nationwide tour which includes several television shows, a performance at Melodyland Theatre (with Sonny & Cher) and other concert dates.

## FROM SUNNING TO SCRUBBING
# SUMMER MONEY-MAKING IDEAS

Summer is the world's greatest time of year. There's no school, there's plenty of sunshine, and there are about a million things to do.

There's only one thing wrong with this wonderful season. Allowances just don't stretch the way they do during the school year. And your dad keeps giving you those large glares when you ask for an advance.

Well, here's your chance to leave the ranks of the poverty-stricken and make your own extra money. And have fun in the bargain!

1. Get together with a few of your friends and start a nursery. This is completely different from just plain babysitting because the little monsters . . . er . . . tots would come to your house instead of vice versa. And the more "clients" you have, the better. They'll keep themselves occupied with a little help from you, and you can sit back and supervise!

### Record Sale
2. Have a record rummage sale. This should be a cooperative-type venture, undertaken by several people. Set a date for the sale, pass the news and then display all the old records you can find. Before the sale, scour the neighborhood for contributions. Many people have records they're tired of, or old hi-fi discs they can't play on their new stereo.

3. Have a rummage sale, period. Again, the more involved the better, and again scour the neighborhood for contributions. Articles on sale could range from clothes to back issues of magazines to anything that's been taking up space in the attic.

4. Sponsor a weekly car wash. The best way to announce any venture of this nature is to post notices in the markets around your area, and distribute hand bills if possible. Parents will contribute space (and water) for the wash if you change locations each week. Offer to pay part of the water bill if necessary.

### Beach Sitting
5. Post a notice that you are available for Beach Sitting. Many families don't go to the beach because the parents can't enjoy themselves and keep track of their children at the same time.

6. Set up your own traveling hairstyle salon. Pass the word that you will come directly to someone's home, wash and set the lady of the house's hair with her own curler and leave slightly richer. Many women can't take the time to go to a beauty salon, and this would be their chance not to have to!

7. Gather up a bunch of paintings and ceramics done by you and your friends and peddle them. If the prices are low enough, you should be able to sell the items even if they aren't the greatest ever.

8. Another idea would be to start a scrapbook service. Practically every person has a big lumpy bundle of things they're "going to put in a scrapbook someday", but someday never seems to come. Hasten it by offering to save them all the trouble. This idea may sound weird, but watch how many people will come unglued when they hear about it!

### Musical Cleaning
9. Musical instruments are another big problem in many families. Every so often they have have to be cleaned and all that (the instruments, not the families) and wouldn't it be great if they knew of someone who would do all the work and not charge the kind of prices they'd have to pay at a music store? Get the hint?

10. You may have to wheedle your mother into this one, but there's a lot of extra money to be had by starting a neighborhood lunch brigade. During the summer months, mothers would be all too happy to have their children fed and out of their hair for a couple of hours during the day.

11. Another great idea for busy moms is a neighborhood maid service. You'll be amazed how many housewives would be more than happy to have someone come in for an hour or two and do a few chores around the house. Doesn't sound like much fun, but it would be more so if you worked in pairs.

12. A Window Wash in another excellent possibility, because that's another of the things there never seems to be enough time to do. Again, it's work, but could be fun if several of you worked together.

### Folk Singing
13. Start a folk singing group and post a notice that you're available to play for private parties, etc. People are always looking for new and inexpensive ways to entertain a Bridge Club or liven up an evening with friends.

14. Speaking of singing, you'd again be amazed to discover how many parents would love to have their children learn songs and simple chords on the uke or guitar. This would be great fun for the kids, and for their "teachers".

15. Many families don't own washing machines and for a small fee would be overjoyed to have someone do their trotting to the laundromat for them. Just let them know you're available!

## Bobby Has Returned

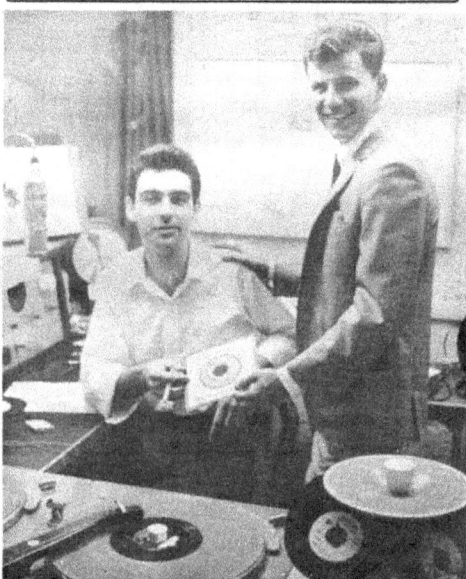

**BOBBY RYDELL visits the KRLA** broadcasting studios to hand Johnny Hayes a hot-off-the-press copy of his latest record, "Sideshow." Bobby recently completed a six-month Army hitch at Fort Dix, N.J., where he was selected as one of the outstanding trainees. You'll notice he still has an Army haircut.

# KRLA ARCHIVES

## A MILKMAN'S DREAM

The day Freddie and The Dreamers became a professional group began as Freddie reported for duty, as usual, at the depot of a large northern dairy where he was employed as a milk roundsman.

The time was 5:30 a.m. At 6:15 a.m. Freddie started delivering milk. At 8:35 a.m. his group manager Jim O'Farrell called to say that he was to audition for BBC-TV at 10 a.m.

At 8:36 a.m. Freddie stopped delivering milk, drove his electric milk float home, changed into his stage clothes and went on to the B.B.C. His milk float was left parked outside the studios.

At precisely 9:07 a.m. came the first of many telephone calls from angry housewives who wanted to "drinka their pinta milka thata day."

The Dairy located the milk float outside the B.B.C.'s Manchester studios at 10:45 a.m. and at 10:46 a.m. Freddie turned professional.

Freddie and the dreamers passed the audition. Since they had a full date-book at the time, their decision to turn professional was a unanimous one.

After appearing in ballrooms, clubs and on stage and television, they have built up an enviable following with a fresh comical approach to the 'beat' scene.

In February, 1963, they appeared at the Top Ten Club in Hamburg and the following month released their first record, "If You Gotta Make a Fool of Somebody".

Since then life for Freddie Garratty, has been a milkman's dream come true.

### Freddy and The Dreamers

Freddie Garratty, born in Manchester on Nov. 14, 1940, is 5 feet 6 inches tall and lists his main ambition as writing a hit record.

So far he has written the songs "This Feeling of Love", "You're the One" and "Feel So Blue", the flipside of his debut disc.

He likes food, fast cars, and playing the guitar. He dislikes humorless people.

The Dreamers include Derek Quinn, lead guitarist, Roy Crewdson, rhythm guitarist, Pete Birrell, bass guitarist and Bernie Dwyer, drummer.

The 23 year-old drummer (his birthday is on May 24) also plays harmonica. Quinn lists his likes as "girls," and his dislikes as "losing sleep."

Roy Crewdson, 24, also plays piano and drum. He likes girls and dislikes cold weather. The rhythm guitarists birthday is on May 29.

Pete Birrell, also 24, likes girls and dislikes traffic wardens. He also plays bass and accordion. His birthday is on May 9.

The drummer, the oldest member of the group, is 25. He plays the piano, likes girls, and dislikes Pete Birrell's driving. Dwyer's birthday is on September 11.

**IN ONE DAY** Freddie and the Dreamers saw their dream of becoming professional popular entertainers come true. The day began at 5:30 a.m. when Freddie began his milk route and ended with a successful audition for BBC-TV.

## They're 'Alive'

**THE HOLLIES HAVE A HIT.** The group from Manchester hit the top of the British charts last week with "I'm Alive." They're a clean-cut, talented fivesome, at home with both swinging ballads and rock.

## Fan Clubs

(For information from any of the listed fan clubs enclose a self-addressed, stamped envelope.)

**DICK BIONDI**
c/o Janis Livesay
5412 Hillmont Ave.,
Los Angeles, Calif.

**PETER & GORDON**
c/o Patti & Cathi
22126 Linda Drive
Torrance, Calif. 90503

**SONNY & CHER**
c/o Barbara Messer
2829 East Walnut
Orange, California

**ROBIN KINGSLEY**
c/o Mollie Curry
617 W. 107 Street
Los Angeles, Calif. 90044

**ROLLING STONES**
c/o Jeri Holloway
310 Ratcliff
Shreveport, La. 71104

**DAVID McCALLUM**
c/o Debby Paulsen
1302 Candlewood St.
Anaheim, Calif. 92805

**ELVIS PRESLEY**
c/o John Rich
5422½ Carlton Way
Hollywood, Calif.

**IAN WHITCOMB**
c/o Kathie Raisler
14720 Gandesa Road
La Mirada, Calif.

Dick Biondi

**CHAD & JEREMY**
c/o Madeline Jen Kin
1800 Orange Grove
Orange, Calif.

**DAVE CLARK FIVE**
c/o Dawn Lee
4809 Oliva Avenue
Lakewood, Calif. 90712

The above information is provided as a service to our readers. Accuracy of the information you receive is the responsibility of the officials of each club.

### Studio City Girl Wins Beatle Ticket Contest

Hard work has paid off in a big way for Jeanette Topalean of Studio City.

Jeanette is the winner of the KRLA Petition Contest. And that makes her the most popular girl in her neighborhood, because her prizes include ten tickets to the KRLA Beatle concerts at Hollywood Bowl.

Jeanette's other prizes include a gold record of "Hard Day's Night" which the Beatles presented to KRLA and an original autographed picture of —John, Paul, George and Ringo.

More than two million names were turned in to KRLA during the petition contest! Jeanette hit the jackpot by turning in almost 14,000 certified names with "KRLA" correctly printed after each one.

At that, she barely nosed out several other contestants.

. . . Ian

## English Penpals

These are the names of some Britishers who have written to the BEAT asking for American pen pals. If you are interested in corresponding with someone from England, here's your chance.

**Miss Janet Wilson**
16 Tennyson Road
Herringthorpe
Rotherham, Yorkshire
England

**Miss Janet Constantine**
49 Jeffery's Crescent
Roby
Liverpool, Lancs
England

**Miss Denise Conley**
21 Glovecester St.
Gorton
M/C 18
England

**Miss Anne Kleven**
132 Borough Road
Birkenhead
Cheshire
England

**Miss Margaret Rennison**
7, Buent Houses, Folly
Greenside, Ryton-on-Tyne
Co. Durham, England

**Miss Pat Reid**
7, Clarondon Road
Haughton
Darlington
Co. Durham, England

**Miss Lesley Salmon**
2 East Reach
Stevenage
Hertfordshire, England

**Miss Jennifer Hutton**
27, Rushams Rd.
Horsham
Sx., England

**Miss Jane Ward**
34 Hill Top
Bolsover
Chesterfield
Derbyshire, England

# KRLA ARCHIVES

### British Top 10

1. I'M ALIVE — The Hollies
2. CRYING IN THE CHAPEL — Elvis Presley
3. LOOKING THROUGH THE EYES OF LOVE — Gene Pitney
4. THE PRICE OF LOVE — The Everly Brothers
5. COLOURS — Donovan
6. MR. TAMBOURINE MAN — The Byrds
7. GOT LIVE IF YOU WANT IT E.P. — The Rolling Stones
8. ONE IN THE MIDDLE E.P. — Manfred Mann
9. HEART FULL OF SOUL — The Yardbirds
10. TO KNOW YOU IS TO LOVE YOU — Peter & Gordon

**Byrd Specs**

**BACKSTAGE WITH THE BYRDS.** KRLA's Charlie O'Donnell and Dave Hull examine the now-famous "Benjamin Franklin" eyeglasses worn by Jim McGuinn. That's Dave Crosby of the Byrds on the left. Casey Kasem has had a similar pair made and plans to wear them on "Shebang."

## Royalty to Attend Premiere of 'Help'

"Help", the Beatles second film, will receive its royal premiere on July 29 at the London Pavilion in Piccadilly Circus, the same theatre in which "A Hard Days's Night" was pre-premiered last year on July 6.

The premiere will be for charity, and royal attendance is expected although members of the royal family have not as yet confirmed their invitations.

Each year the Beatles present their annual Christmas show in London. Last Christmas, the boys did a total of forty shows at the Hammersmith Theatre,

## GIRLS ONLY CONTINUED
(Continued from Page 9)

bad points, but all I can say is that it has an awful lot of good ones."

See what I mean? That letter really made me think. Going steady is limiting in a way, but in other ways it opens a lot of doors between you and your real self.

Enough on that semi-serious subject. But do let me know your thoughts on the topic.

**Beatle Clock**

Have you ever seen a Beatle clock? Well, I have, and are they darling! You have to make them yourselves, by buying a clock with a large face and substituting a pic of your special Beatle for same. I'm going to make one as a present for a John Lennon fan, and then make a George (sigh) clock for little ole me. If you want to try it, just be careful you don't touch the hands of the clock too often when you're Beatle-ing it. And there's no need to print numbers over the Beatle face (or whichever star happens to make you tick). Just remember that three o'clock is his right ear, six o'clock is his chin, etc. Probably sounds rather nutty, as I can't quite explain it, but really looks sharp!

Oh, I just have to tell you this. I probably shouldn't because I don't like to go around complaining about things, but have you seen the TV commercial where some girl is trying to fix her hair and when her boyfriend or husband or whatever he is tells her to hurry, she wails "My hair won't comb!"

**Fairy Godmother**

Then, just as he says "Not again" and walks away in disgust, a fairy-godmother type pops up out of nowhere, holding a can of hair spray.

I have never been able to catch the name of the product, because the lady says "I'm Wanda the Witch" and I roll off the couch in hysterics. Wanda the Witch? Someone has GOT to be kidding! Who makes up these ridiculous commericals? And WHY? Don't they realize that everyone laughs themselves silly over that sort of thing? Guess not.

Speaking of laughing yourself silly, can you think back and remember the first time you raced for the Sunday funnies and found out they weren't funny any more? Awful feeling, huh? Like you've just closed another chap-

which afforded their London-based fans plenty of opportunity to view the four "live". But many of their fans scattered throughout England cannot make the trip to London and so miss the show.

Now Joe Collins, the man who promoted the Beatles' last two Christmas shows, has come up with a fabulous idea. The Beatles would still appear at just one London theatre, but the show would be broadcast to other theatres via closed-circuit television! In that way, fans all over the British Isles could catch the show.

Of course, it is still just a suggestion. Mr. Epstein has not as yet okayed the idea, but then he hasn't rejected it either!

Now here's another suggesion. Since we have the Early Bird Satellite floating around in space, why not utilize it to transmit the Beatles Christmas show to America? Then U.S. fans would have the chance to view one of those now-famous Yuletide Beatle shows without having to travel all the way to London.

## HELP!

*(Editor's note: We seem to feel a gentle tugging at a leg on the item below, but we'll run it as we received it and let you be the judge.)*

FOR HIRE: Boy who makes noise with guitar and harmonica, but can't play them. Has no musical training of any sort. Has horrible singing voice.

Perfect for any group wanting to sound like English singers.

Wire Paladin, San Francisco
or:
Dale Balok,
915 N. Frederic Street,
Burbank, California

Female drummers and guitarists in Arcadia area, HELP! We need you if you're 16 or up, willing to work, and want to be in a group, drop a line.

Sue Kovais
5608 Marshburn
Arcadia

*If you would like HELP from the BEAT readers, send the letter you would like printed in our Help Column to HELP, 6290 Sunset Blvd., Suite 504 Hollywood 90028.*

ter or something equally melodramatic.

Well, my faith in the funnies has been restored, thanks to a little Englishman name Andy Capp. Have you read this comic? If you have, and you're in luv with anything English like I am, I'll bet it flips you, too! I sure hope so. I wouldn't like to go round (I just luv to say that) thinking it was the rest of the world, not me!

Well, I've done it again. Raved on longer than I'm supposed to, that is. Please keep your letters coming and let me know what you'd like for me to rave about in the future!

**CASEY'S QUIZ ANSWER**
(Don't peek unless you've read the question elsewhere in the BEAT)

**SANDIE SHAW**

# KRLA ARCHIVES

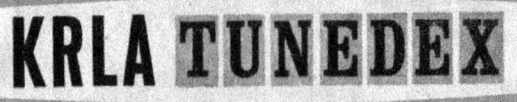

#1

| This Week | Last Week | Title | Artist |
|---|---|---|---|
| 1. | 1. | SATISFACTION | The Rolling Stones |
| 2. | 6. | ALL I REALLY WANT TO DO | Cher |
| 3. | 2. | I CAN'T HELP MYSELF | The Four Tops |
| 4. | 3. | ONCE UPON A TIME/WHAT'S NEW PUSSYCAT | Tom Jones |
| 5. | 5. | HOLD ME, THRILL ME, KISS ME | Mel Carter |
| 6. | 4. | YES, I'M READY | Barbara Mason |
| 7. | 11. | I'VE GOT YOU | Sonny & Cher |
| 8. | 7. | WHAT THE WORLD NEEDS NOW IS LOVE | Jackie De Shannon |
| 9. | 13. | I'M A FOOL | Dino, Desi & Billy |
| 10. | 9. | LAURIE | Dickie Lee |
| 11. | 8. | WHITTIER BOULEVARD | The Midnighters |
| 12. | 28. | I'M HENRY VIII, I AM | Herman's Hermits |
| 13. | 18. | THIS LITTLE BIRD | Marianne Faithfull |
| 14. | 12. | CRYING IN THE CHAPEL | Elvis Presley |
| 15. | 10. | WOOLY BULLY | Sam the Sham & Pharaohs |
| 16. | 26. | CARA MIA | Jay & the Americans |
| 17. | 15. | HELP RHONDA | The Beach Boys |
| 18. | 24. | WONDERFUL WORLD | Herman's Hermits |
| 19. | 16. | JUST YOU | Sonny & Cher |
| 20. | 23. | SEVENTH SON | Johnny Rivers |
| 21. | 21. | HUSH, HUSH SWEET CHARLOTTE | Patti Page |
| 22. | 17. | MR. TAMBOURINE MAN | The Byrds |
| 23. | 14. | BACK IN MY ARMS AGAIN | The Supremes |
| 24. | 19. | HERE COMES THE NIGHT | Them |
| 25. | 35. | YOU BETTER COME HOME | Petula Clark |
| 26. | 32. | HUNG ON YOU | The Righteous Brothers |
| 27. | 33. | SAVE YOUR HEART FOR ME | Gary Lewis & Playboys |
| 28. | 27. | YOU TURN ME ON | Ian Whitcomb & Bluesville |
| 29. | 31. | ALL I REALLY WANT TO DO | The Byrds |
| 30. | 34. | LET HER DANCE | Bobby Fuller |
| 31. |  | I'VE BEEN LOVING YOU TOO LONG | Otis Redding |
| 32. |  | TAKE ME BACK | Little Anthony |
| 33. | 38. | WHATEVER HAPPENED TO THE GOOD TIMES | The Peddlers |
| 34. | 37. | PRETTY LITTLE BABY | Marvin Gaye |
| 35. |  | TO KNOW YOU IS TO LOVE YOU | Peter & Gordon |
| 36. |  | PAPA'S GOT A BRAND NEW BAG | James Brown |
| 37. |  | BABY I'M YOURS | Barbara Lewis |
| 38. |  | GIRL COME RUNNING | The Four Seasons |
| 39. | 40. | EASY QUESTION | Elvis Presley |
| 40. |  | DOWN IN THE BOONDOCKS | Billy Joe Royal |

**SOUTHERN CALIFORNIA'S MOST ACCURATE RECORD SURVEY — BASED ON RETAIL SALES FIGURES**

BULK RATE
U.S. Postage
**PAID**
Los Angeles, Calif.
Permit No. 25497

If you were a KRLA BEAT subscriber your name and address would be printed here and you would receive your copy at home, saving 40%.

KRLA BEAT
6290 Sunset, No. 504
Hollywood, Cal. 90028

KRLA ARCHIVES

# KRLA BEAT

Volume 1, Number 20     Los Angeles, California     15 Cents     July 31, 1965

FROM SHOWER TO STARDOM

LOOK WHAT ELVIS STARTED — Page 3 • BRIAN JONES' PAST — Page 7
WHY JACK GOOD LEFT SHINDIG • WHY BOYFRIENDS HATE STARS — Page 7
also — BEATLES • HERMAN • ELVIS • MARIANNE FAITHFULL

www.ingramcontent.com/pod-product-compliance
Lightning Source LLC
Chambersburg PA
CBHW081128170426
43197CB00017B/2792